LEGAL RESEARCH AND CITATION

Fourth Edition

By

Larry L. Teply
Professor of Law
Creighton University

AMERICAN CASEBOOK SERIES®

St. Paul, Minn.
WEST PUBLISHING CO.
1992

Preface

This book is designed to introduce students to legal research and citation. A separate set of in-library exercises is available for use with this book. These optional library exercises provide "follow-up" to a student's initial exposure to the discussion in this text and give students practice in learning how to cite materials in proper form. The citations in this text are keyed to the fifteenth edition of *The Bluebook: A Uniform System of Citation* (1991).

This fourth edition reflects a continuing evolution in how to best organize and present materials on legal research and citation. The first two editions (1982 and 1986) followed a "traditional" format—with chapters on federal court decisions, state court decisions, digests, *Shepard's Citations*, federal statutes, state statutes, etc. The third edition (1989) began a shift toward an emphasis on how legal research is conducted— where to begin, how to develop initial research, what purpose each type of research source serves, the relative authority of research sources, and when and why a particular research source would be used. In the third edition, Chapter 7 (based on a spite fence problem) demonstrated how a single problem could be researched, how the various secondary and primary research sources are coordinated, how the facts interplay with the law as it is found during legal research, and how the common law and statutes relate to each other in the context of researching a specific problem. The fourth edition extends this approach throughout the text.

This edition stresses the following: (1) how primary sources of law are published (chronologically and by subject); (2) the natural steps in the progression of the legal research process, ordinarily moving from secondary sources to primary ones; (3) the factual context for finding, reading, applying, and updating the law; (4) the methods for developing legal research; (5) functional aspects of legal research, such as using scope notes, pocket parts, the index and topic methods of search, etc.; and (6) legal citation. Bibliographical information is provided as it is needed within this framework. New material and recent developments have been incorporated throughout the text.

Chapter 1 of this edition provides a broad introduction to legal research and citation. It gives the reader an overview of primary sources and their publication; it introduces the basic aspects of legal citation; and it discusses the uses of primary and secondary authority, the legal research process, and ethical aspects of legal research. This chapter gives the reader the necessary background to understand the material on secondary sources that immediately follows the introduction.

The materials in this edition are designed to be primarily self-teaching. They utilize the basic learning principles of direct reader involvement, self-testing, visual aids, immediate "feedback," and repetition. The materials also permit readers to work at their own pace. For convenience of the readers, this edition places the discussion of the problems in the text rather than in a separate appendix.

In the third edition, the discussion of computer-assisted legal research was integrated with the discussion of "manual" legal research. Although it may have been better from a learning perspective to integrate the discussion in this way, this approach caused practical problems for those instructors who, for one reason or another, covered computer-assisted legal research in a single, concentrated period. Based on requests from several teachers, most of the computer-assisted legal research material has now been placed in Chapter 7 ("WESTLAW Computer Legal Research Service") and Chapter 8 ("LEXIS Computer Legal Research Service").

I thank Creighton Law Library Director Kay Andrus for his most helpful comments and suggestions. I am indebted to Carolyn Sue DePriest Mouttet (Class of 1992) for her valuable and excellent assistance in reviewing these materials.

I acknowledge the support for this project provided by Dean Lawrence Raful and the Creighton Law School administration. I thank Associate Law Library Director Patricia Cervenka, Legal Reference Librarian Paul Hill, Reference/Computer Services Librarian Aris Woodham, and other members of the library staff for their support in preparing this work. I thank Lori Langholdt and Amy Korus of the Creighton Law School secretarial staff and Tim Brown of the Creighton Law School Copy Center for their assistance. I also acknowledge those publishers who permitted me to reprint copyrighted material in the figures used in the text.

I appreciate the encouragement and support of all my colleagues and friends at Creighton Law School. In particular, special thanks is owed to Associate Dean Barbara Gaskins and Professor Angela G. Smith. Finally, I appreciate the continuing support and encouragement of my family—my wife Frances Gayle and my two children Robert and Benjamin—during the preparation of this fourth edition.

L.L.T.

Omaha, Nebraska
March, 1992

Summary of Contents

*

Table of Contents

Table of Figures and Acknowledgements

Chapter 1: Introduction to Legal Research
and Citation

Chapter 2: Analyzing Facts and Legal Problems
And Finding Commentary and Summaries
of the Law in Secondary Sources

FIGURE 2-AA to 2-II   A.L.R. FEDERAL, Copyright 1971 by Lawyers Cooperative Publishing, a division of Thomson Legal Publishing Inc. and Bancroft-Whitney Co.   Reprinted with permission.

FIGURE 2-JJ   A.L.R. FEDERAL POCKET PART, Copyright 1991 by Lawyers Cooperative Publishing, a division of Thomson Legal Publishing Inc.   Reprinted with permission.

FIGURE 2-KK   INDEX TO ANNOTATIONS, VOLUME 5 POCKET PART, Copyright 1992 by Lawyers Cooperative Publishing, a division of Thomson Legal Publishing Inc.   Reprinted with permission.

Chapter 3: Coordinating Research in Secondary Sources and Focusing on the Law in Specific Jurisdictions

FIGURES 3-A to 3-C   AMERICAN JURISPRUDENCE SECOND, Copyright 1967 by Lawyers Cooperative Publishing, a division of Thomson Legal Publishing Inc. and Bancroft-Whitney Co. Reprinted with permission.

FIGURES 3-D to 3-F   AMERICAN JURISPRUDENCE SECOND, Copyright 1966 by Lawyers Cooperative Publishing, a division of Thomson Legal Publishing Inc. and Bancroft-Whitney Co. Reprinted with permission.

FIGURE 3-G and 3-H   CORPUS JURIS SECUNDUM, Copyright 1972 by West Publishing Co.

FIGURE 3-I AMERICAN JURISPRUDENCE SECOND POCKET PART, Copyright 1991 by Lawyers Cooperative Publishing, a division of Thomson Legal Publishing Inc. and Bancroft-Whitney Co. Reprinted with permission.

FIGURE 3-J   CORPUS JURIS SECUNDUM POCKET PART, Copyright 1991 by West Publishing Co.

FIGURE 3-K AMERICAN JURISPRUDENCE SECOND, Copyright 1966 by Lawyers Cooperative Publishing, a division of Thomson Legal Publishing Inc. and Bancroft-Whitney Co.   Reprinted with permission.

FIGURES 3-L to 3-P RESTATEMENT (SECOND) OF TORTS, Copyright 1979 by the American Law Institute.   Reprinted with the permission of the American Law Institute.

FIGURE 3-Q   A.L.R.3D, Copyright 1977 by Lawyers Cooperative Publishing, a division of Thomson Legal Publishing Inc. and Bancroft-Whitney Publishing Co.   Reprinted with permission.

FIGURE 3-R to 3-T A.L.R. (1ST SERIES), Copyright 1946 by Lawyers Cooperative Publishing, a division of Thomson Legal Publishing Inc.   Reprinted with permission.

Chapter 4: Reading, Citing, and Updating Cases

FIGURE 4-F   U.S. SUPREME COURT DIGEST TABLE OF CASES, Copyright 1986 by West Publishing Co.

FIGURE 4-G WEST'S SUPREME COURT REPORTER, Copyright 1978 by West Publishing Co.

FIGURE 4-H   SHEPARD'S UNITED STATES CITATIONS PAPER-COVERED PAMPHLET, Copyright 1991 by McGraw-Hill, Inc. Reproduced by permission of Shepard's/McGraw-Hill, Inc. Further reproduction is strictly prohibited.

FIGURE 4-I SHEPARD'S UNITED STATES CITATIONS (1984 CASE EDITION), Copyright 1984 by McGraw-Hill, Inc. Reproduced by permission of Shepard's/McGraw-Hill, Inc. Further reproduction is strictly prohibited.

FIGURE 4-J FEDERAL REPORTER SECOND, Copyright 1956 by West Publishing Co.

FIGURES 4-K to 4-M FEDERAL SUPPLEMENT, Copyright 1966 by West Publishing Co.

FIGURE 4-N MICHIGAN REPORTS.

FIGURE 4-O NATIONAL REPORTER BLUE BOOK, Copyright 1928 by West Publishing Co.

FIGURE 4-P NORTH EASTERN REPORTER SECOND, Copyright 1964 by West Publishing Co.

FIGURES 4-Q and 4-R SHEPARD'S NORTH EASTERN REPORTER CITATIONS, Copyright 1989 by McGraw-Hill, Inc. Reproduced by permission of Shepard's/McGraw-Hill, Inc. Further reproduction is strictly prohibited.

FIGURES 4-S and 4-T AMERICAN LAW REPORTS, Copyright 1977 by Lawyers Cooperative Publishing, a division of Thomson Legal Publishing Inc. and Bancroft-Whitney Co. Reprinted with permission.

FIGURE 4-U REPRINTED WITH SPECIAL PERMISSION FROM U.S. LAW WEEK, Copyright 1979 by the Bureau of National Affairs, Inc., Washington, D.C.

Chapter 5: Legislative Legal Research

FIGURES 5-A to 5-I AMERICAN JURISPRUDENCE SECOND, Copyright 1989 by Lawyers Cooperative Publishing, a division of Thomson Legal Publishing Inc.. Reprinted with permission.

FIGURES 5-J and 5-K CODE OF LAWS OF SOUTH CAROLINA (GENERAL INDEX), Copyright 1989 by the State of South Carolina, published by Lawyers Cooperative Publishing, a division of Thomson Legal Publishing Inc. Reprinted with permission of the State of South Carolina.

FIGURE 8-X   LEXIS PRINTOUT, Copyright 1983 by Northwestern School of Law of Lewis and Clark College.   Reprinted with the permission of Mead Data Central, Inc., provider of LEXIS[R]/ NEXIS[R] services.   Copyright 1992, Mead Data Central, Inc.

FIGURES 8-Y to 8-CC   LEXIS PRINTOUTS, Reprinted with the permission of Mead Data Central, Inc., provider of LEXIS[R]/ NEXIS[R] services and Lawyers Cooperative Publishing, a division of Thomson Legal Publishing Inc.   Copyright 1992, Mead Data Central, Inc. and Lawyers Cooperative Publishing, a division of Thomson Legal Publishing Inc.

FIGURES 8-DD to 8-FF   LEXIS PRINTOUTS, Reprinted by permission of Shepard's/McGraw-Hill, Inc. and Mead Data Central, Inc., provider of LEXIS[R]/NEXIS[R] services.   Copyright 1992, Mead Data Central, Inc. and McGraw-Hill, Inc.   Further reproduction is strictly prohibited.

FIGURES 8-FF to 8-II   LEXIS PRINTOUTS, Reprinted with the permission of Mead Data Central, Inc., provider of LEXIS[R]/ NEXIS[R] services.   Copyright 1992, Mead Data Central, Inc.

Tables in the Text

Chapter 5: Legislative Legal Research

Chapter 6: Administrative Legal Research and
Rules of Evidence, Practice,
Procedure, and Ethics

Chapter 7: WESTLAW Computer Legal
Research Service

Chapter 8: LEXIS Computer Legal
Research Service

LEGAL RESEARCH
AND CITATION

*

Chapter 1
INTRODUCTION TO LEGAL RESEARCH
AND CITATION

Section 1A. The Nature of Legal Research

Lawyers, legal assistants, and others use legal research skills to "find" the law to find answers to legal questions, advise clients about their rights and responsibilities, and help clients plan future activities. In other words, legal research is a skill-based, problem-solving activity. Like other legal skills, legal research techniques can be learned. The purpose of this text is to help you learn how to conduct legal research effectively and how to cite legal sources in proper form.

Imagine yourself in the middle of a law library surrounded by literally thousands of books, pamphlets, binders, and periodicals. You also have access to thousands of other sources via computer terminals. At this point, you are much like a worker who is standing in the middle of a warehouse surveying piles of building materials and stacks of tools.

Suppose that you are in the library for the purpose of solving a particular legal problem or answering a specific legal question. Assume that Midas, who had accumulated a large amount of gold during his lifetime, has recently died. Assume also that you are the attorney for his estate or a law clerk or legal assistant working for that attorney. Midas' will states that "all my property is to be divided share and share alike among my children." Midas' illegitimate daughter claims that she should receive a share of his estate. No doubt exists that she is Midas' illegitimate child. Is she legally entitled to receive a share of Midas' estate?

In considering the Midas problem, you should first realize that the "law" of some particular jurisdiction will apply to this situation. The

1

legal system in the United States allocates the final authority to determine law in a particular situation generally along political lines. For example, federal law regulates some matters and controls throughout the United States as the supreme law of the land on those matters. On other matters, the power to set and finally determine the law falls to the states. Thus, rules of law are derived from the federal or state governments.

Deciding which jurisdiction's law applies on particular issues is a matter of "conflict of laws"—the legal subject that addresses such concerns. Traditionally, most matters of wills and trusts are dealt with by state law. In deciding which particular state's law will apply, the basic conflicts rule focuses on where Midas' will was executed. Federal law, however, may also apply to some issues. For example, federal constitutional questions may arise if a state attempts to discriminate against illegitimate children.

Assuming that Midas' will was executed in Florida and that the law of Florida will control the interpretation of the language in the will, how would you determine what Florida law is on this issue? In this instance, the Florida Legislature may have enacted a law stating that illegitimate children are to be treated like legitimate children for purposes of inheritance unless the testator (the person who died leaving a will) clearly intended otherwise. This statute, as interpreted by the Florida state courts, would provide the definitive answer and would be "mandatory primary authority." Also useful in interpreting this statute would be the legislative history of the statute, which provides an explanation of the purpose, basis, and meaning of the legislation. Provisions in the Florida Constitution may likewise be relevant.

Even in the absence of a controlling statute, the Florida courts may have considered this issue before. The prior decisions of the Supreme Court of Florida will be mandatory or controlling "precedent" or "authority" for deciding future similar cases. When such primary authority exists, your main concern may be whether the present case is somehow appropriately distinguishable from the prior cases to justify a different result or whether those precedents should be overruled and a new rule established. Ideally, by examining and analyzing Florida statutes and court decisions, you could arrive at a firm conclusion as to whether Midas' illegitimate daughter should receive a share of the estate.

You may find that neither the Florida Legislature nor the Florida courts have considered this particular question. In that situation, the question is described as "one of first impression." Then your main sources for argument will be "persuasive" authorities, including (1) judicial decisions from other jurisdictions on the same question ("persuasive primary authority"), (2) judicial decisions of Florida courts and of other jurisdictions that do not directly apply but provide a useful analogy or

contain rules that may be extended to the current situation ("persuasive primary authority"), and (3) views of legal writers and commentators found in secondary sources ("persuasive secondary authority").

In researching this question, you are likely to consult commentary in secondary authorities to obtain background information, perspective, and research leads to primary authority. Indeed, secondary sources will ordinarily be the most efficient starting point. Secondary authority includes commentary in treatises, legal encyclopedias, and legal periodicals as well as other persuasive materials.

This chapter provides the basic framework for learning research skills. First, it introduces the basics of legal citation. Second, it provides an overview of how legal materials are organized in law libraries. Third, it introduces the law-creating institutions in the United States and shows how the law created by those institutions is published. Fourth, it illustrates how legal materials are used to solve legal problems. Fifth, it presents an overview of the legal research process. Sixth, it highlights the most important ethical components of legal research.

Section 1B. Legal Citation

A researcher seeking to solve a legal problem will try to find rules of law embodied in primary sources of law emanating from the various branches of the federal or state governments and supporting statements in secondary sources. Legal citation is the means of identifying where those primary and secondary sources are published.[1] It is also the means of identifying the support they lend for particular propositions. In this way, persons reviewing the research are able to assess relative significance of the cited rule of law or statement.[2]

All minimally acceptable legal citations provide sufficient information to find the cited source in a law library. However, law book publishers, legal periodicals, judges, and lawyers vary in the specific ways that they cite legal materials. The most widely accepted system of citation is *The Bluebook*.[3] *The Bluebook* is compiled by the editors of the *Harvard Law Review, Columbia Law Review, University of Pennsylvania Law Review,* and *Yale Law Journal.* A more flexible system of

---

[1]It has aptly been pointed out that this general "obligation to respect legal authorities explains the emphasis lawyers place on legal citation." Christina L. Kunz et al., The Process of Legal Research: Successful Strategies 3 (2d ed. 1989).

[2]Thus, "[p]roper and complete citation for each statement of law enables fellow lawyers, judges, legislators, and others to assess the weight and reliability of [each] statement" and allows the researcher to "prove to others that [the] research is sound." Id.

[3]Columbia Law Review et al., The Bluebook: A Uniform System of Citation (15th ed. 1991) [hereinafter The Bluebook].

citation is set out in *The University of Chicago Manual of Legal Citation* (*The Maroon Book*).[4] The citations in the text and footnotes follow the typeface conventions and rules established in *The Bluebook* for use in legal memoranda and court documents by practitioners.[5]

Citing legal research sources in accord with an accepted citation system is often viewed as one indication of quality legal work. Learning how to cite materials in accord with these systems is a technical skill that is best mastered by practice. Over time, citation of most material becomes routine. Initially learning the "rules," however, is often a frustrating experience. This book is designed, in part, to ease this process.

Section 1C. Organization of Legal Materials in Law Libraries

Imagine again that you are in the middle of a law library and that you are there to find the materials that will be of use to you in solving a particular problem or in answering a specific question. Fortunately, the materials in law libraries are not arranged like those in garbage dumps or junk yards—they are not heaped up randomly on top of each other in huge piles. Law libraries, like well-run warehouses, are highly organized places. Librarians have developed various systems of classifying materials in a logical way.

1. LIBRARY OF CONGRESS CLASSIFICATION

The most widely used system in organizing law libraries is the Library of Congress classification. This classification system is relatively easy to understand. It uses single capital letters to designate broad

[4] University of Chicago Law Review & University of Chicago Legal Forum, The University of Chicago Manual of Legal Citation (1989) [hereinafter The Maroon Book].

[5] You should consult the citation rules in The Maroon Book if you are learning that system of citation. The appearance of The Maroon Book sparked a lively interchange about the proper approach to a system of citation. See, e.g., Richard A. Posner, Goodbye to the Bluebook, 53 U. Chi. L. Rev. 1343, 1343-44 (1986) ("[a]nthropologists use the word 'hypertrophy' to describe the tendency of human beings to mindless elaboration of social practices. The pyramids in Egypt are the hypertrophy of burial. The hypertrophy of law is [The Bluebook]." Posner concludes that The Bluebook prescribes form for the sake of form, not function, in which the superficial dominates the substantive); Manual Labor, Chicago Style, 101 Harv. L. Rev. 1323, 1323-24 & n.7 (1988) (observing that if The Bluebook is analogous to the hypertrophy of burial, The Maroon Book, "in proposing legal citation as an art form, is analogous to the ritual of cremation in an embroidered shroud and a hand-carved coffin" and suggesting that The Maroon Book brings to "citation form an unstructured creativity that most would have thought impossible, or at least improbable"); Mary I. Coombs, Lowering One's Cites: A (Sort of) Review of the University of Chicago Manual of Legal Citation, 76 Va. L. Rev. 1099 (1990); Richard Saver, Singing the Blues Over Cite Rules, Legal Times, Oct. 28, 1991, at 46, 46 ("the [Chicago] rebellion appears to have failed, at least for now").

classes. The letter assigned to law is K. The principal subclass is KF, the law of the United States. Within this subclass, triple capital letters are used to identify the law of particular states. For example, California law—and that of all other states beginning with C—is classified under KFC; New York law is classified under KFN, and so on. On the shelves, you will find all KF material (federal law) together, followed by the law of particular states in alphabetical order (KFA, KFC, etc.).

Librarians assign each source a classification number (based upon the subject of the work) and a cutter number (based upon the principal entry—generally, the author's last name for monographs or the title for edited works).[6] The classification and cutter number become the exact "address" of the work in the library. For example, all KD works (the law of Great Britain) are shelved together first, followed by all KF works, then all KFA works, and so on. Within each subclass, the works are arranged from the smallest classification number to the largest (e.g., KF1 to, e.g., KF9827). Works with the same classification number (e.g., KF240) are shelved alphanumerically (.A1 to .Z9).

Some law libraries still utilize local systems (such as the one developed by the Los Angeles County Law Library) in varying degrees. Other libraries still use the Dewey Decimal system, under which classes 340-349 are assigned to American law-related publications.

2. UNCLASSIFIED MATERIALS

Many law libraries have significant sections of unclassified materials (materials not assigned a call number). Usually, they must be located by type of material and often are alphabetically or numerically arranged. For example, in many law libraries, legal periodicals are shelved alphabetically by title. Reporters are often grouped by jurisdiction or region and then are shelved in numerical volume order.

3. MECHANICAL AIDS FOR FINDING MATERIALS

Like the worker in the warehouse, you will have various tools to aid you in your search. These tools may be as simple as signs, charts, library guides, maps, or directories. For classified material, the card catalog will indicate the location of particular materials or types of materials. A card catalog is an alphabetical index of all classified materi-

---

[6] For example, this book is assigned to the KF subclass because it primarily deals with the law of the United States. Its classification number is 240 (classification numbers 240 to 246 cover legal research, citation, and legal bibliography in the Library of Congress scheme). The cutter number is .T46 (based on Teply—the author's last name). The date of this edition (1992) also is included: KF240/.T46/1992.

als in a particular library. It usually provides access by (1) author, (2) subject, and (3) title.[7] Many libraries have replaced their card catalogs with "online public catalogs."[8]

4. SPECIALIZED FINDING AIDS

Specialized legal research tools also exist to assist you in your task. Good illustrations are periodical indexes, digests (books containing brief statements of court holdings arranged by subject and subdivided by jurisdiction and courts), and *Shepard's Citations* (books containing references showing, *inter alia*, when and how another court has cited a judicial opinion).[9]

5. COMPUTER DATABASES

Computer-assisted legal research involves the retrieval of relevant material from the databases stored in a computer memory. The two principal computer-assisted legal research services available are WESTLAW (West Publishing Co.) and LEXIS (Mead Data Central). These services bring to a researcher a wide variety of legal and nonlegal sources and research tools that may not otherwise be readily available. The strength of computer-assisted legal research lies in its speed, accuracy, thoroughness, and flexibility. Its limitations include the lack of completeness of some databases compared to print sources and the researcher's own ability to develop useful search requests.

Section 1D. An Overview of Primary Sources of Law and Their Publication Patterns

This section presents a brief overview of primary sources of law in the United States and their publication. This baseline of information will help you understand the institutions that create law, the types of books in which the law is found, and the link between the law-creating

---

[7]Some libraries use "divided" card catalogs that separate author and title entries from subject entries. Other libraries use "dictionary" card catalogs that include author, title and subject entries in one alphabetical sequence.

[8]These online catalogs allow more access points than traditional card catalogs and permit multiple users to view a single entry. Users of online catalogs may search a library's records from multiple locations. Not all of these locations need to be physically located in the library. Online catalogs usually provide access by title, author, and subject. In most instances, they also allow key word and combined author-title access.

[9]These tools are not "authority" and are never cited. See infra § E of this chapter.

institutions and law books themselves.[10] This section also presents basic
information on how these primary sources of law are cited and how they
can be found in a library when a citation to them has been identified.

1. PUBLICATION PATTERN OF PRIMARY
SOURCES OF LAW

Primary legal authority can be divided into three (simplified)
principal classes: (1) statutory law (legislation, such as constitutions, statutes, municipal ordinances, and treaties); (2) common law (judicial opinions); and (3) administrative law (regulations and agency decisions). As
shown in the following chart, these primary sources of law are published
(with a few exceptions) in two basic ways: (a) *chronologically* (e.g., in
order of the date of enactment, promulgation, or decision); or (b) *topically* (e.g., statutes and regulations arranged by subject matter or points of
law in judicial opinions classified by topic).

PUBLICATION OF PRIMARY LEGAL SOURCES[11]

Kind of Law	Chronological Publication	Topical (Subject) Publication
Statutory law (legislation)	Session laws	Statutory codes
Common law (judicial opinions)	Case reports and case reporters	Case digests (summaries of points of law in judicial opinions)
Administrative law (regulations and agency decisions)	Administrative registers (for regulations) and reporters (for decisions)	Administrative codes (for regulations) Looseleaf services (for decisions)

---

[10] See Christopher G. Wren & Jill R. Wren, The Teaching of Legal Research, 80 Law
Libr. J. 7, 34 (1988) ("Legal System Orientation").

[11] See id. at 34-36.

2. LEGISLATIVE PRIMARY SOURCES

Legislation (in a broad sense) includes a wide variety of legal sources: constitutions, statutes, treaties, municipal ordinances, charters, and legislatively enacted rules of practice and procedure.

(a) Constitutions

(i) Constitutions as Sources of Law. In the United States, constitutions are the most basic written source of law. Constitutions establish the structure and powers of the government. The United States Constitution replaced the Articles of Confederation in 1789. The first ten amendments to the Constitution (Bill of Rights) were ratified in 1791. Likewise, each state has a constitution. As primary sources of law, constitutions establish fundamental rules and principles.

First, federal and state constitutions allocate power within a government. On both the state and federal levels, the underlying concept is a separation of powers between the legislative, executive, and judicial branches of government. Based on this concept, constitutions prohibit one branch from usurping the powers of another branch.

Second, federal and state constitutions guarantee personal liberties. Good examples of constitutional guarantees of personal liberty are the state and federal due process clauses. These clauses prohibit deprivations of life, liberty, or property without due process of law.[12]

Third, state and federal constitutions together establish our federal system of government. Under this system, the states are independent sovereigns, except to the extent that they ceded power to the federal government when they approved the United States Constitution and entered the Union. The Tenth Amendment emphasizes this relationship: "The powers not delegated to the United States by the Constitution, nor prohibited by it to the states, are reserved to the states respectively, or to the people."[13]

Fourth, constitutions establish a priority of law. Within a state, state laws, local ordinances, judicial rulings, and other governmental actions must conform to state constitutional standards. On the federal level, federal laws, administrative regulations, judicial rulings, and other governmental actions must conform to federal constitutional standards.

---

[12] See, e.g., U.S. Const. amends. V, XIV.

[13] Id. amend. X.

Fifth, as between the states and the federal government, standards set by the United States Constitution and federal law have priority. The Supremacy Clause establishes this relationship:

> This Constitution, and the laws of the United States which shall be made in pursuance thereof; and all treaties made, or which shall be made, under the authority of the United States, shall be the supreme law of the land; and the judges in every state shall be bound thereby, anything in the constitution or laws of any state to the contrary notwithstanding.[14]

Sixth, constitutions establish procedures that must be followed. Constitutions establish a wide variety of procedures, such as impeachment procedures, succession, extradition methods, and the availability of jury trials. Likewise, constitutions may prohibit the use of certain other procedures, such as bills of attainder (acts passed by a legislature to punish a person without a trial).[15]

(ii) Publication of Constitutions. The texts of federal and state constitutions are ordinarily included in statutory compilations (codes)—the same sets of books that contain the statutes of those jurisdictions (arranged by subject matter). These sources usually provide historical notes, annotations of judicial decisions, and other references related to the constitution of a jurisdiction. Constitutions are sometimes published in pamphlet form and are often included as appendices in casebooks and other sources.

(iii) Basic Citation Form. Citations of constitutions have four elements: (1) the abbreviated name of the constitution; (2) the article or amendment number; (3) the section (if any); and (4) the clause or other subsection (if any). A date is added only if the cited provision is no longer in force. The following are typical citations to constitutional provisions in *Bluebook* form (Rule 11):

U.S. Const. art. I, § 9.
U.S. Const. amend. V.

Fla. Const. art. VI, § 1.
(Current 1968 Florida Constitution is cited).

Fla. Const. art. X, § 2 (1885).
(Former 1885 Florida Constitution is cited).

---

[14] Id. art. VI, § 2.

[15] See, e.g., id. art. I, § 9, cl. 3 (ex post facto laws and bills of attainder prohibited).

PROBLEM 1.1 Assume that you want to locate section 11 of
the Maine Constitution. Because constitutions are ordinarily included in
the statutory compilations of each jurisdiction, you would need to locate
a compilation of the statutes of Maine. How can you determine what
statutory compilations exist for the state of Maine? One easy way is to
consult Table "T.1 United States Jurisdictions" in *The Bluebook* (located
on the blue pages near the end of that volume). Shown in Figure 1-A
is the relevant portion of that table. What is the name of the Maine
statutory compilation?

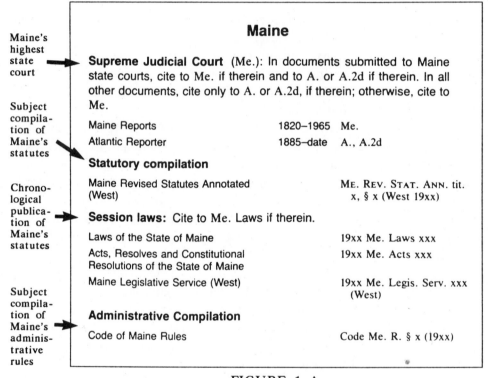

FIGURE 1-A
T.1 UNITED STATES JURISDICTIONS
BLUEBOOK: A UNIFORM SYSTEM OF CITATION
(15TH ED. 1991)

DISCUSSION OF PROBLEM 1.1 Table T.1 United States Jurisdictions provides a variety of useful information about the past and
present structure of the legal system in a jurisdiction, the publications
containing primary sources of law for a jurisdiction, the proper authority
to cite, and the appropriate abbreviations for those sources. As indicated
above, the statutory (subject) compilation is the *Maine Revised Statutes
Annotated*. Tables T.2 through T.4 provide similar information for
Foreign Jurisdictions (T.2), Intergovernmental Jurisdictions (such as the

United Nations) (T.3); and Treaty Sources (T.4). In addition, Tables T.5 through T.17 are general tables covering abbreviations for a variety of items, such as case names, court names, geographical terms, and the like.

PROBLEM 1.2 Assume that you decide to check the card catalog in the library that you are using. Because you know the title of the set (*Maine Revised Statutes Annotated*), you would find the title card for this set shown in Figure 1-B. Does that card indicate the location of this set in the library? How would you find this set?

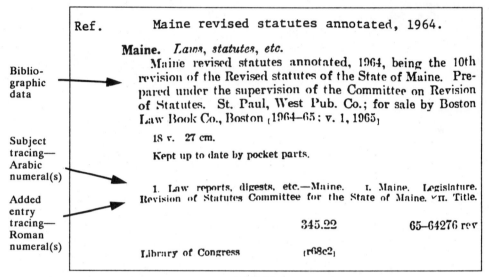

Ref.   Maine revised statutes annotated, 1964.

Maine. *Laws, statutes, etc.*
Maine revised statutes annotated, 1964, being the 10th revision of the Revised statutes of the State of Maine. Prepared under the supervision of the Committee on Revision of Statutes. St. Paul, West Pub. Co.; for sale by Boston Law Book Co., Boston [1964–65; v. 1, 1965]

18 v. 27 cm.

Kept up to date by pocket parts.

1. Law reports, digests, etc.—Maine.   I. Maine. Legislature. Revision of Statutes Committee for the State of Maine. VII. Title.

345.22   65–64276 rev

Library of Congress   [r68c2]

Bibliographic data

Subject tracing—Arabic numeral(s)

Added entry tracing—Roman numeral(s)

FIGURE 1-B
TITLE CARD FROM THE CARD CATALOG

DISCUSSION OF PROBLEM 1.2 Cards in a card catalog provide a variety of useful information. For example, the bibliographic data on the above card indicates that the *Maine Revised Statutes Annotated* are kept up to date by "pocket parts" inserted in the inside back cover of each volume. The subject tracing on a card lists all the subject headings under which a book was indexed—which, under appropriate circumstances, might also be checked for other useful sources. "Ref." at the top of the card indicates that this compilation is a reference work. In many law libraries, state statutory compilations are unclassified. In this instance, this set was not assigned a call number and is not shelved in a classified location—KFM materials in the Library of Congress system, for example.

To find the location of unclassified material in a law library, you must look for a sign, a library guide, a notation on a library map, or some other finding aid provided by the library. Typically, state statutory compilations are shelved together alphabetically by state.

After you have found the relevant state statutory compilation, you can usually locate the relevant volume or volumes by looking for "CONSTITUTION" on the outside binding. Figure 1-C shows the relevant part of the page showing § 11 of Article I of the Maine Constitution.

Section 11 of the Maine Constitution prohibits bills of attainder, ex post facto laws, and laws impairing the obligation of contract.

Maine's statutory compilation is "annotated." In annotated compilations published by West Publishing Co., the principal annotations are "Notes of Decisions" that list and briefly describe court decisions related to a particular provision.

Other editorial features include cross-references to related sources and "Library References."

Opinion of the Justices (1961) 157 Me. 187, 170 A.2d 660.

Since it is necessary that habeas corpus be at all times available to a patient hospitalized as mentally ill, a patient hospitalized pursuant to the provision for hospitalization upon court order corpus under proposed bill or 14 M.R. S.A. § 5501 et seq., even though the patient sought a writ of habeas corpus within 3 days of his hospitalization, or within 3 months of having been denied a reexamination of his order of hospitalization, solely on the grounds that he had completely recovered. Id.

§ 11. Attainder, ex post facto and contract-impairment laws prohibited

Section 11. The Legislature shall pass no bill of attainder, ex post facto law, nor law impairing the obligation of contracts, and no attainder shall work corruption of blood nor forfeiture of estate.

Library References

Constitutional Law ⊜82, 113, 186.
C.J.S. Constitutional Law §§ 199 et seq., 274, 414 et seq.

United States Code Annotated

Attainder, ex post facto and contract impairment, see U.S.C.A.Const. Art. I, §§ 9, 10; Art. III, § 3.

Notes of Decisions

In general 1
Attainder, generally 2
Contract impairment 5–18
Ex post facto laws, generally 3
Impairment of contracts 5–18
  In general 5
  Divorce 12
  Franchises 16
  Licenses 17
  Limitation of actions 9
  Marriage 11
  Police power 6
  Public and semi-public funds, property, and obligations 13
  Public or private charters 14
  Public utilities 15
  Relief from liability 10
  Remedies 8
  Retrospective laws, generally 7
  Standing 18
Taxation 4

1. In general

Legislature has full power to regulate and change form of remedies in actions if no vested rights are impaired or personal liabilities created. Thut v. Grant (1971) Me., 281 A.2d 1.

2. Attainder, generally

Bill of attainder is penal in nature. State v. Myrick (1981) Me., 436 A.2d 379.

To deny to murderer, because of his act, privilege of taking property which he is technically entitled to inherit would not be to inflict an additional punishment upon him but merely to prevent him from profiting by his own wrong, and he would not suffer a "forfeiture" of estate within purview of constitutional prohibition on attainder which works corruption of blood or forfeiture of estate, because he would not thereby be deprived of any property which he might have acquired rightfully. Dutill v. Dana (1955) 148 Me. 541, 113 A.2d 499.

3. Ex post facto laws, generally

Constitutional prohibition against ex post facto legislation is limited to statutes which are designed to impose further punishment. State v. Myrick (1981) Me., 436 A.2d 379.

The Legislature may pass laws altering or modifying, or even taking away, remedies for the recovery of debts, and of compensation in damages for torts, without incurring a violation of the provisions of the Constitution which forbid the passage of ex post facto laws. Lord v. Chadbourne (1856) 42 Me. 429, 66 Am.Rep. 290.

582

FIGURE 1-C
MAINE REVISED STATUTES ANNOTATED

(b) Statutes

(i) Statutes as Sources of Law. The legislative branch of government is responsible for enacting statutes that have the force of law. The United States Constitution, for example, authorizes Congress to enact federal statutes. Article I of the Constitution, however, limits the law-making power of Congress to specific areas.[16] The "Necessary and Proper Clause" reinforces this law-making authority. It provides that Congress shall have the power "[t]o make all Laws which shall be necessary and proper for carrying into Execution the foregoing Powers, and all other Powers vested by this Constitution in the Government of the United States, or in any Department or Officer thereof."[17]

In contrast to Congress, state legislative bodies derive their authority from the "police power" vested in the legislative branch of the state governments. Thus, each state legislature is empowered to regulate the relative rights and duties of persons and corporations within its jurisdiction for the "public convenience" and "public good." State statutes enacted pursuant to this police power are limited by the provisions of (1) the United States Constitution (particularly the Supremacy Clause and the amendments applying to the states) and (2) the relevant state constitution.

(ii) The Legislative Process. On the federal level and in all states (except Nebraska, which has a one-house legislature), the legislature consists of two houses. Most of the work of legislatures is conducted through committees rather than on the floors of the legislative chambers. Legislative proposals ("bills") are regularly referred to the committee that has the responsibility for the proposal's subject matter.

Ordinarily, hearings on proposed legislation are conducted, and reports will accompany a committee's recommendation. These hearings and reports are useful extrinsic sources for determining the "intent" of the legislature: (1) whether the legislature intended the statute to *apply* to a particular situation or person and (2) if the legislature did intend the statute to apply, what *effect* the legislature intended the statute to have.

To become law, a bill must be passed in the same form by both houses and approved by the appropriate chief executive—the President or

---

[16] These areas include the following: (1) coining and borrowing money; (2) imposing taxes and duties; (3) punishing the counterfeiting of federal currencies, coins, and securities; (4) regulating commerce with foreign nations, among the states, and with Indian tribes; (5) establishing post offices and postal roads; (6) fixing standard weights and measures; (7) promoting the progress of science and arts by granting patents and copyrights; (8) establishing uniform laws for bankruptcy and naturalization; (9) declaring war; (10) providing for military defense; (11) punishing piracies and felonies committed on the high seas and offenses against the law of nations; and (12) constituting tribunals inferior to the United States Supreme Court. Id. § 8.

[17] Id.

the governor. If the chief executive vetoes the bill, the legislature can override the veto, provided the required percentage is achieved (on the federal level, two-thirds of each house).

(iii) Public and Private Laws and Legislative Resolutions. Legislatures enact two basic types of laws. The most familiar type of legislation is a "public" law that affects the community at large. In contrast, "private" laws are confined to particular individuals or business entities and do not have general application.

In addition to enacting laws, each house of a legislature may adopt "resolutions." "Concurrent" resolutions adopted by Congress or by both houses in almost all state jurisdictions do not have the force of law because they are not approved by the chief executive. Such resolutions ordinarily bind only the members and officers of the legislative body. In contrast, properly adopted and approved "joint" resolutions have the same binding force as an act (law) on the federal level. In some states, however, joint resolutions have a lesser status than an act.

(iv) Chronological Publication of Federal Statutes. Laws enacted by Congress are published officially (by the federal government) in two basic forms: (1) slip laws and session laws; and (2) a statutory code. Initially, each recently enacted statute is published in a pamphlet form known as a slip law. After each session of Congress, all laws enacted during that session (along with Presidential proclamations, reorganization plans, interstate compacts approved by Congress, and concurrent resolutions) are published in chronological order (by date of their enactment) in the *United States Statutes at Large* (session laws).

(v) Finding the United States Statutes at Large in the Library and the Basic Citation Form for Provisions Therein. In many law libraries, the *United States Statutes at Large* set is not classified. Instead, it is often shelved with other federal statutory materials. The following are *United States Statutes at Large* citations in *Bluebook* form (Rule 12):

Employee Polygraph Protection Act of 1988, Pub. L. No. 100-347, § 7, 102 Stat. 646, 648-50.

(Section 7 of the Act is cited. The text of the Act begins on page 646 in volume 102 of the *United States Statutes at Large* (Stat.) set. Section 7 is located on pages 648, 649, and 650.)

Act of Aug. 12, 1958, Pub. L. No. 85-623, 72 Stat. 562.

(To find the last cited statute in the library, for example, you would (1) locate the *United States Statutes at Large* set by consulting the card catalog, a library map, or posted signs, (2) find volume 72, and (3) then turn to page 562—the page on which the statute begins. This session law is shown in Figure 1-D. Note particularly § 2 of the Act.)

The marginal notes are editorial aids and are not part of the law.

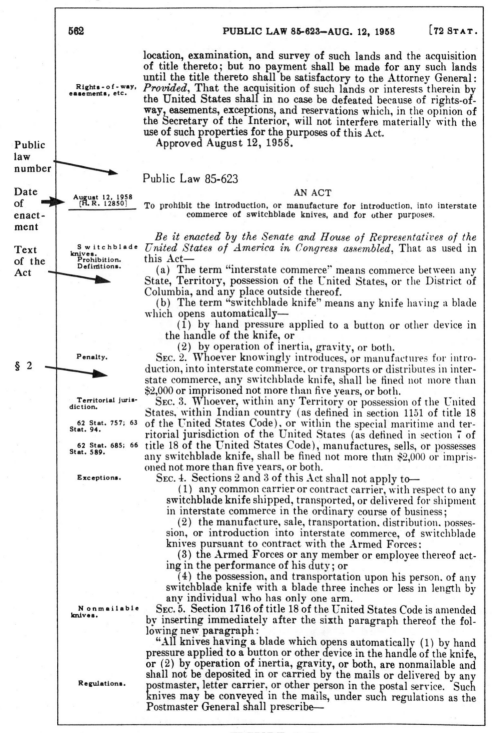

562   PUBLIC LAW 85-623—AUG. 12, 1958   [72 STAT.

location, examination, and survey of such lands and the acquisition of title thereto; but no payment shall be made for any such lands until the title thereto shall be satisfactory to the Attorney General: *Provided*, That the acquisition of such lands or interests therein by the United States shall in no case be defeated because of rights-of-way, easements, reservations, exceptions, and reservations which, in the opinion of the Secretary of the Interior, will not interfere materially with the use of such properties for the purposes of this Act.

Rights-of-way, easements, etc.

Approved August 12, 1958.

Public Law 85-623

August 12, 1958
[H.R. 12850]

AN ACT

To prohibit the introduction, or manufacture for introduction, into interstate commerce of switchblade knives, and for other purposes.

Be it enacted by the Senate and House of Representatives of the United States of America in Congress assembled, That as used in this Act—

Switchblade knives. Prohibition. Definitions.

(a) The term "interstate commerce" means commerce between any State, Territory, possession of the United States, or the District of Columbia, and any place outside thereof.

(b) The term "switchblade knife" means any knife having a blade which opens automatically—

(1) by hand pressure applied to a button or other device in the handle of the knife, or

(2) by operation of inertia, gravity, or both.

Penalty.

SEC. 2. Whoever knowingly introduces, or manufactures for introduction, into interstate commerce, or transports or distributes in interstate commerce, any switchblade knife, shall be fined not more than $2,000 or imprisoned not more than five years, or both.

Territorial jurisdiction.

SEC. 3. Whoever, within any Territory or possession of the United States, within Indian country (as defined in section 1151 of title 18 of the United States Code), or within the special maritime and territorial jurisdiction of the United States (as defined in section 7 of title 18 of the United States Code), manufactures, sells, or possesses any switchblade knife, shall be fined not more than $2,000 or imprisoned not more than five years, or both.

62 Stat. 757; 63 Stat. 94.

62 Stat. 685; 66 Stat. 589.

Exceptions.

SEC. 4. Sections 2 and 3 of this Act shall not apply to—

(1) any common carrier or contract carrier, with respect to any switchblade knife shipped, transported, or delivered for shipment in interstate commerce in the ordinary course of business;

(2) the manufacture, sale, transportation, distribution, possession, or introduction into interstate commerce, of switchblade knives pursuant to contract with the Armed Forces;

(3) the Armed Forces or any member or employee thereof acting in the performance of his duty; or

(4) the possession, and transportation upon his person, of any switchblade knife with a blade three inches or less in length by any individual who has only one arm.

Nonmailable knives.

SEC. 5. Section 1716 of title 18 of the United States Code is amended by inserting immediately after the sixth paragraph thereof the following new paragraph:

"All knives having a blade which opens automatically (1) by hand pressure applied to a button or other device in the handle of the knife, or (2) by operation of inertia, gravity, or both, are nonmailable and shall not be deposited in or carried by the mails or delivered by any postmaster, letter carrier, or other person in the postal service. Such knives may be conveyed in the mails, under such regulations as the Postmaster General shall prescribe—

Regulations.

Marginal labels (left side): Public law number / Date of enactment / Text of the Act / § 2

FIGURE 1-D

UNITED STATES STATUTES AT LARGE

(vi) Codification of Federal Statutes (Subject Arrangement). The first codification of federal statutes took place in the *United States Revised Statutes of 1875*. The first edition of the current *United States Code* was published in 1926. The 1926 edition of the *Code* compiled all sections of the *Revised Statutes* that had not been repealed and all public laws from the *United States Statutes at Large* enacted after 1873 that were still in force. Those laws were arranged by subject under fifty titles. Each title is divided in sections. Title 15 contains all laws in force relating to commerce and trade. Title 28 contains all laws in force relating to the judiciary and judicial procedure. The *Code* is supplemented by annual cumulative supplement volumes and is reissued by the U.S. Government Printing Office every six years.

(vii) Finding the United States Code in the Library and the Basic Citation Form for Provisions Therein. Like the *United States Statutes at Large*, the *United States Code* is often not classified in many law libraries. Typically, the *Code* is shelved with other federal statutory materials.

Because of (1) the slow initial distribution of the *United States Statutes at Large* and the *United States Code* by the U.S. Government Printing Office and (2) their lack of convenient updating and other editorial services, most lawyers consult one of the two commercial editions of the *Code*, either West's *United States Code Annotated* or Lawyers Cooperative/Bancroft Whitney's *United States Code Service*.

The official *United States Code*, however, is the preferred source to cite for federal statutes *currently in force*. The following are typical citations to the *United States Code* and its unofficial annotated versions in *Bluebook* form (Rule 12):

Lanham Act § 14(c), 15 U.S.C. § 1064(c) (1988).
(Section 1064(c) is cited. This section is contained in Title 15 of the 1988 edition of the *United States Code*.)

33 U.S.C.A. § 1507 (West 1986).
28 U.S.C.S. § 961 (Law. Co-op. 1988).
(The above citations are to the two unofficial versions of the *United States Code*: West's *United States Code Annotated* and Lawyers Cooperative/Bancroft Whitney's *United States Code Service*.)

Section 2 of the Act shown in Figure 1-D has been codified as § 1242 in Title 15 of the *United States Code*. This section (as published in West's *United States Code Annotated*) is shown in Figure 1-E.

The text of the statute in West's <u>United States Code Annotated</u> is the same as you would find if you consulted the official version of the <u>United States Code</u>.

---

§ = section

Section 1242

Citations to original (and any amending) act(s) of Congress in the <u>United States Statutes at Large</u>.

Reference to the legislative history for this section

The editorial features in the other annotated version (<u>United States Code Service</u>) are similar but not identical to the ones shown here.

Ch. 29   SWITCHBLADE KNIVES   **15 § 1242**
Note 4

§ 1242. Introduction, manufacture for introduction, transportation or distribution in interstate commerce; penalty

Whoever knowingly introduces, or manufactures for introduction, into interstate commerce, or transports or distributes in interstate commerce, any switchblade knife, shall be fined not more than $2,000 or imprisoned not more than five years, or both.

(Pub.L. 85–623, § 2, Aug. 12, 1958, 72 Stat. 562.)

Historical Note

Legislative History. For legislative history and purpose of Pub.L. 85–623, see 1958 U.S. Code Cong. and Adm.News, p. 3435.

Cross References

Exceptions from application of section, see section 1244 of this title.

West's Federal Forms

Sentence and fine, see § 7531 et seq.

Library References

Commerce ☞82.5.   C.J.S. Commerce § 125 et seq.

Notes of Decisions

Construction 1
Jurisdiction 3
Liability under entry bonds 2
Production of evidence 4

---

1. Construction

Congressional purpose of aiding the enforcement of state laws against switchblade knives and in barring them from interstate commerce would easily be frustrated if knives which could be quickly and easily made into switchblade knives, and one of whose primary uses is as weapons, could be freely shipped in interstate commerce and converted into switchblade knives upon arrival at the state of destination, and this chapter should not be so construed as to permit such facile evasion. Precise Imports Corp. v. Kelly, C.A.N.Y. 1967, 378 F.2d 1014, certiorari denied 88 S. Ct. 472, 389 U.S. 973, 19 L.Ed.2d 465.

2. Liability under entry bonds

While language of entry bonds was not wholly free of ambiguity, judgment for United States on its counterclaim for liquidated damages under entry bonds was proper, whether or not imported knives were barred by this chapter, since clear purpose of entry bonds under section 1499 of Title 19, was to place Bureau of Customs, if it demands return of goods released under the bonds, in as good a position as if it had not released them,

which purpose would be frustrated if importers were held to be liable under the bonds for failure to redeliver the knives only if such knives were finally held to violate this chapter. Precise Imports Corp. v. Kelly, C.A.N. Y.1967, 378 F.2d 1014, certiorari denied 88 S. Ct. 472, 389 U.S. 973, 19 L.Ed.2d 465.

3. Jurisdiction

Court of appeals had jurisdiction of action seeking a declaratory judgment that shipments of knives imported into United States were not barred from entry by this chapter, since this chapter was a criminal statute of general application rather than a provision of the customs laws. Precise Imports Corp. v. Kelly, C.A.N.Y.1967, 378 F.2d 1014, certiorari denied 88 S.Ct. 472, 389 U.S. 973, 19 L. Ed.2d 465.

4. Production of evidence

Plaintiffs seeking a declaratory judgment and an injunction against enforcement of this chapter should have been directed to produce the imported knives, or to stipulate that the knives in evidence were representative, and should not be allowed to profit by defendants' inability to produce the knives which had been released to plaintiffs and which plaintiffs bound themselves to redeliver, but which in fact were never redelivered. Precise Imports Corp. v. Kelly, C.A.N.Y.1967, 378 F.2d

501

FIGURE 1-E

UNITED STATES CODE ANNOTATED

(viii) Uniform Laws and Model Acts. Some state laws are based on recommended uniform laws and model acts. The Uniform Commercial Code, which has been adopted by every state, is a prime example. The National Conference of Commissioners on Uniform State Laws drafts and proposes these uniform laws and acts. The American Law Institute likewise drafts and proposes model acts, such as the Model Penal Code. States are free to adopt, modify, or reject these proposals.

(ix) Publication and Citation of State Statutes. State statutes are published in the same pattern as federal laws—in (1) slip form and session laws (chronologically) and (2) statutory (subject) compilations. Most law libraries have a subject compilation for each state but ordinarily have slip and session laws for only the state in which they are located. Academic law libraries often hold state session laws in microfiche formats.

The following are typical citations of state statutory compilations in *Bluebook* form (Rule 12):

Del. Code Ann. tit. 16, § 5006 (1983).
Minn. Stat. Ann. § 69.26 (West 1986).
Cal. Bus. & Prof. Code § 4980 (West 1990). (When a code contains separate parts or sections identified by distinct subject-matter titles, that subject-matter title is included in the name of the code, such as the Cal. Bus. & Prof. Code.)

PROBLEM 1.3 Re-examine Figure 1-A on page 10, showing the statutory compilation and session laws for the state of Maine. (1) What is the proper format for citing the *Maine Revised Statutes Annotated*? (2) Of the sources listed in the table, which do you think is the best source to find the latest laws enacted by the Maine Legislature?

DISCUSSION OF PROBLEM 1.3 The table indicates that Maine's statutes are organized by titles and sections. The proper citation form is Me. Rev. Stat. Ann. tit. x, § x (West 19xx). The date used in the citation is (in order of preference): (1) the year that appears on the spine of the volume; (2) the year that appears on the title page; or (3) the latest copyright year. (*Bluebook* Rule 12.3.2) The best source for recent legislation enacted in Maine is West's *Maine Legislative Service*. Advance legislative services such as this one provide monthly or bimonthly pamphlets containing the latest laws enacted by state legislatures.

(x) Finding State Statutes in Law Libraries. State statutory compilations are often unclassified and shelved alphabetically by state. Figure 1-F shows a page in a state statutory collection.

The California and Texas statutes are organized into sections within various subject codes (here the Business and Professions Code). Most states organize their statutes by titles and sections, by chapters and sections, or by sections alone.

---

§ 4980   **HEALING ARTS**
                                                                    Div. 2

§ 4980. Necessity of license

(Text of the section →)

(a) Many California families and many individual Californians are experiencing difficulty and distress, and are in need of wise, competent, caring, compassionate, and effective counseling in order to enable them to improve and maintain healthy family relationships.

Healthy individuals and healthy families and healthy relationships are inherently beneficial and crucial to a healthy society, and are our most precious and valuable natural resource. Marriage, family, and child counselors provide a crucial support for the well-being of the people and the State of California.

(b) No person may for remuneration engage in the practice of marriage, family, and child counseling as defined by Section 4980.02, unless he or she holds a valid license as a marriage, family, and child counselor, or unless he or she is specifically exempted from that requirement, nor may any person advertise himself or herself as performing the services of a marriage, family, child, domestic, or marital consultant, or in any way use these or any similar titles to imply that he or she performs these services without a license as provided by this chapter. Persons licensed under Article 4 (commencing with Section 4996) of Chapter 14 of Division 2, or under Chapter 6.6 (commencing with Section 2900) may engage in such practice or advertise that they practice marriage, family, and child counseling but may not advertise that they hold the marriage, family, and child counselor's license.

(Added by Stats.1986, c. 1365, § 4.)

Historical and Statutory Notes

Former § 4980, added by Stats.1983, c. 928, § 5, relating to similar subject matter, was repealed by Stats.1986, c. 1365, § 3.

Derivation: Former § 4980, added by Stats. 1983, c. 928, § 5.

Former § 17800, added by Stats.1963, c. 1823, p. 3759, § 1, amended by Stats.1965, c.

1506, p. 3539, § 1; Stats.1969, c. 298, p. 666, § 5; Stats.1970, c. 1310, p. 2436, § 1; Stats. 1975, c. 198, p. 572, § 1; Stats.1977, c. 1244, p. 4215, § 1.

Cross References

Privileged communications, see Evidence Code § 1010.

WESTLAW Electronic Research

See WESTLAW Electronic Research Guide following the Preface.

Notes of Decisions

Grandfather clause   1

---

1. Grandfather clause

"Grandfather clause" would not be implied in statutory plan of marriage counseling licensure, so as to permit psychologist who practiced marriage, family, and child counseling before 1970 to obtain counseling license without meeting subsequently stiffened legislative requirements. Packer v. Board of Behavioral Science Examiners (1975) 125 Cal.Rptr. 96, 52 C.A.3d 190.

694

FIGURE 1-F

WEST'S ANNOTATED CALIFORNIA CODES

(c) Treaties and Other International Agreements

(i) Treaties as Sources of Law. Treaties and other international agreements are, in effect, written contracts between nations based on the consent of the contracting parties. The United States Constitution provides that the President has the authority to make treaties with the advice and consent of Congress and two-thirds approval by the Senate.[18] Under Article VI of the Constitution, treaties made under the authority of the United States are declared the supreme law of the land, and state laws inconsistent with such treaties are invalid.[19] In contrast to treaties, "international agreements" or "executive agreements" are entered into by the President under the President's own constitutional power or under authority granted by an act of Congress.

(ii) Chronological Publication of Treaties. Treaties and other international agreements can be found in a variety of sources. The current, official (government-sponsored) sources for the texts of treaties to which the United States is a party are: (1) *U.S. Treaties and Other International Agreements* (since 1950) (referred to as U.S.T.); and (2) the U.S. State Department's *Treaties and Other International Acts Series* (since 1945) (referred to as T.I.A.S.). Before 1950, United States treaties were printed in the *United States Statutes at Large*. Multilateral agreements to which the United States is a party also appear in other treaty sources, such as the *United Nations Treaty Series* (U.N.T.S.). There is no official, subject-organized publication (equivalent to the *United States Code*) of the various provisions of treaties and other international agreements. However, a one-volume publication (*Treaties in Force*) serves as an index to all treaties currently in force into which the United States has entered.

(iii) Basic Citation Form. The following is a typical citation of treaties and other international agreements in *Bluebook* form (Rule 20.4):

Extradition Treaty, May 29, 1970, U.S.-Spain, 22 U.S.T. 737.
This treaty was signed on May 29, 1970. It was published in volume 22 of *United States Treaties and Other International Agreements* (U.S.T.), beginning at page 737.

To find this treaty, you would locate the *U.S.T.* title card catalog to find its call number (JX231.A34). (The Library of Congress classification for public international law materials is JX, a subclass of political science (J).) Figure 1-G shows the beginning page of this treaty.

---

[18] Id. art. II, § 2, cl. 2.

[19] Id. art. VI, § 2.

Ratification information   Treaty with   Subject of the treaty

SPAIN

Extradition

Treaty signed at Madrid May 29, 1970;
Ratification advised by the Senate of the United States of America
February 17, 1971;
Ratified by the President of the United States of America March 1,
1971;
Ratified by Spain May 8, 1971;
Ratifications exchanged at Washington June 16, 1971;
Proclaimed by the President of the United States of America July 2,
1971;
Entered into force June 16, 1971.

BY THE PRESIDENT OF THE UNITED STATES OF AMERICA

A PROCLAMATION

CONSIDERING THAT:

The Treaty on Extradition between the United States of America and Spain was signed on May 29, 1970, the original of which Treaty is annexed hereto;

The Senate of the United States of America by its resolution of February 17, 1971, two-thirds of the Senators present concurring therein, gave its advice and consent to ratification of the Treaty;

The Treaty was ratified by the President of the United States of America on March 1, 1971, in pursuance of the advice and consent of the Senate, and has been duly ratified on the part of the Government of Spain;

The respective instruments of ratification were exchanged at Washington on June 16, 1971;

It is provided in Article XVIII of the Treaty that the Treaty shall enter into force upon the exchange of ratifications;

Now, THEREFORE, I, Richard Nixon, President of the United States of America, proclaim and make public the Treaty, to the end that it shall be observed and fulfilled with good faith on and after June 16, 1971 by the United States of America and by the citizens of the United States of America and all other persons subject to the jurisdiction thereof.

(737)   **TIAS 7136**

FIGURE 1-G

U.S. TREATIES AND OTHER INTERNATIONAL AGREEMENTS

(d) Municipal Ordinances and Charters

On the local level, charters regulate the city councils, county boards, and other subordinate political subdivisions. In addition, these entities enact ordinances governing local matters. The publication, citation, and use of these primary authorities are discussed in later chapters.

(e) Legislatively Enacted Rules
of Practice and Procedure

Sometimes legislatures enact statutes establishing court practice and procedure. Sometimes that power is delegated to the courts. These matters will be discussed in later chapters.

3. PRIMARY JUDICIAL SOURCES

One result of many appellate (and some trial court) cases is the writing of judicial opinions. These opinions ordinarily indicate the matters presented to the court for decision, how those matters were resolved, and the reasons for that resolution. Like statutes, constitutions, and treaties, judicial opinions are primary sources of (common) law.

(a) The Federal Court System

The federal court system can be visualized as a pyramid. At the base are the federal trial courts. In the middle of the pyramid above the trial courts are the federal appellate courts, which review decisions of the trial courts. At the apex is the United States Supreme Court, which, *inter alia*, reviews decisions made by the federal appellate courts.

Article III of the United States Constitution vests the judicial power of the United States "in one supreme Court, and in such inferior Courts as the Congress may from time to time ordain and establish."[20] The first Congress carried out this provision by creating a federal court system. Its specific organization, however, has varied over time.

Currently, the principal trial courts in the federal system are the United States District Courts.[21] The federal district courts handle (1) all federal crimes, (2) civil actions (a) "arising under the Constitution,

---

[20] *Id.* art. III, § 1.

[21] Several specialized trial courts also exist in the federal system. These courts include the United States Claims Court (claims against the United States government), United States Tax Court (tax deficiency cases), Court of International Trade (customs and trade matters, such as litigation under the Tariff Act), and bankruptcy courts (bankruptcies and reorganizations).

laws, or treaties of the United States" or (b) involving parties with diverse citizenship when more than $50,000 is in controversy (e.g., when a citizen of Texas is suing a citizen of New York for $75,000 for injuries occurring in an automobile accident), and (3) miscellaneous matters.

Above the federal trial courts are various federal appellate courts. In general, these federal appellate courts review decisions of the federal trial courts. The number and composition of these judicial circuits are set by Congress in section 41 of Title 28 of the *United States Code*. There are currently eleven numbered circuits, a District of Columbia Circuit, and a Federal Circuit. Figure 1-H shows the geographic boundaries of the United States Courts of Appeals.

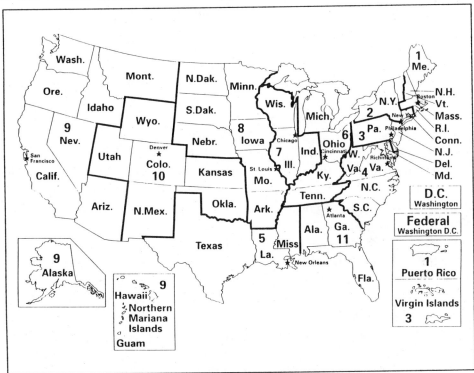

FIGURE 1-H

WINNING RESEARCH SKILLS (WEST PUBLISHING CO.)

In addition to the United States Courts of Appeals, several other specialized federal appellate courts exist.[22]

---

[22]For example, Congress created the Temporary Emergency Court of Appeals as a part of the Emergency Price Control Act of 1942. Although this Act expired in 1947, the Emergency Court of Appeals has continued to function for various periods. This court has handled appeals involving the Housing and Rent Act of 1948, the Defense Production Act of 1950, the Economic Stabilization Act of 1970, and the Emergency Natural Gas Act of 1977. The United States Court of Appeals for the Federal Circuit and the United States

(continued...)

The highest federal court is the United States Supreme Court. It currently consists of a Chief Justice and eight Associate Justices. The United States Supreme Court has both original and appellate jurisdiction. Within the Supreme Court's original jurisdiction, for example, are controversies between states.

More importantly, the Supreme Court reviews decisions of the federal courts of appeals and, in limited circumstances, decisions of other lower federal courts. The United States Supreme Court also reviews decisions of the highest state courts when federal questions are involved. In this way, supremacy of federal law and consistency in interpretation are assured. Today, all appellate review in the United States Supreme Court is essentially discretionary review (pursuant to a writ of certiorari) rather than appeal as a matter of right.[23]

(b) State Courts

In addition to a federal court system in the United States, each state has its own court system. The organization of these state judicial systems varies. All states have trial courts and a court of final resort. Some states have intermediate appellate courts.

The names of these various state courts differ. The most common name for the highest state court is the "supreme court" (e.g., Minnesota Supreme Court). New York designates its highest state court as the "New York Court of Appeals." The name of the highest state court in Massachusetts is the "Supreme Judicial Court." The most common names for the principal state trial courts are "district courts" (e.g., Nebraska District Court), "superior courts" (e.g., California Superior Court), or "circuit courts" (e.g., Florida Circuit Court). Some courts have changed names over time (e.g., the Delaware Supreme Court was previously called the Delaware Court of Errors and Appeals).

(c) Reporting of Judicial Opinions

(i) Authoritative Functions and Importance. Judicial opinions provide evidence of the authoritative functions that courts perform in our

---

[22](...continued)
Court of Military Appeals are other examples of specialized federal appellate courts. The United States Court of Appeals for the Federal Circuit has appellate jurisdiction principally over patent law issues. See 28 U.S.C.A. § 1295 (West Supp. 1991) (detailing the jurisdiction of the Federal Circuit). The United States Court of Military Appeals was created in 1950 to review various military cases that arise under the Uniform Code of Military Justice.

[23]See Act of June 27, 1988, Pub. L. No. 100-352, 102 Stat. 662 (eliminating appeals as a matter of right).

legal system. First, in absence of controlling legislation, courts have the authority to develop and enforce the common law through their decisions. Common-law development of the legal rules proceeds on a case-by-case basis. Properly enacted statutes, however, take precedence over conflicting common-law rules previously developed by the courts. Second, courts review the validity of legislative enactments and determine their meaning and application. Third, courts review the validity of executive and administrative actions.

The reporting of judicial opinions is important because courts rely on past decisions as a guide to deciding current cases. This approach to decision making rests on the basic premise that like cases ought to be decided in the same way. Perhaps courts have adopted this approach simply as a matter of fairness or as a means of encouraging more disciplined decision making and judicial economy. In any event, private parties rely upon prior decisions (precedents) to organize and plan their behavior and to determine their rights and obligations in courts of law.

(ii) Brief History. In England, judges traditionally delivered their opinions orally in court. Their opinions were transcribed and published by "reporters." If they were signed or initialed by any barrister who was present in court that day, these opinions could be cited as a precedent. As a result, prior to the mid-eighteenth century, systematic, successive case reporting in England did not exist. Many of the volumes of these published opinions were duplicative, and the text of the same opinions varied in content.

In contrast, written opinions of American courts traditionally have been issued by the court. Published reports of these opinions take two forms: official and unofficial. "Official" reporters have been responsible for publishing court opinions based upon official texts supplied by the courts. In addition, privately published unofficial reports of opinions containing the same text as the official reports have been published. The difference between the two has been the more elaborate editorial features and the more rapid publication of the unofficial reporters. The principal source for unofficial reports is West Publishing Company. West's philosophy has emphasized comprehensive case reporting and "completeness."[24] On the other hand, Lawyers Cooperative Publishing Company's philosophy has emphasized selective case reporting and "condensation."[25]

---

[24]See Nancy P. Johnson et al., <u>Winning Research Skills</u> 5 (1991) (John West, the founder of West Publishing Co. stated in 1890: "The profession has now the immense advantage of being able to turn to a single set of reports and digests, and [of] be[ing] sure of finding everything which the courts have said on any given subject") (emphasis deleted).

[25]See <u>id.</u> (quoting James Briggs, the first president of Lawyers Cooperative Publishing Co., as stating: "Much is said by certain contemporaries about 'completeness,' referring simply

(continued...)

(iii) Designation of Reporters and the Relationship Between Official and Unofficial Reporters. Although use of unofficial reporters is widespread, the official reporter is technically the authoritative text. In recent years, however, some states have ceased publishing their official reports; thus, unofficial reporters are the only published sources for judicial opinions in those states.

Today, most reporters are designated by: (1) the court (e.g., *California Appellate Reports*); (2) the geographic jurisdiction (e.g., *Nebraska Reports*); or (3) the geographic region (e.g., *Pacific Reporter*). Up to the late 1800's, however, reporters ordinarily were designated by the last name of the individual who prepared the volume. These nominative reports for the most part have been incorporated into the court-named or jurisdiction-named reporter series.

In spite of their subsequent inclusion in these series, the nominative reports nonetheless must be referenced in certain case citations (using *Bluebook* form). For example, the original volume and last name of the first seven nominative reporters of United States Supreme Court decisions must still be indicated in *Bluebook* citations—even though those ninety volumes eventually were numbered consecutively and incorporated into the official jurisdiction-named Supreme Court reporter, *United States Reports*. Thus, in *Bluebook* citations, the nominative reporter's name and the original volume number must be included in the citation of cases like *Marbury v. Madison* (Rule 10.3.2 and Table T.1):

Marbury v. Madison, 5 U.S. (1 Cranch) 137 (1803).

(iv) Modern Reporting of Federal Court Opinions. In general, case reporting follows the basic organization of the judicial system. For example, the following (simplified) list shows the principal modern reporters for each level of the federal system. More detailed information will be provided in later chapters.

UNITED STATES SUPREME COURT
Official Reporter: *United States Reports* (U.S.)
Unofficial Reporters: West's *Supreme Court Reporter* (S. Ct.); Lawyers Co-operative's *U.S. Supreme Court Reports, Lawyers' Edition* (L. Ed. and L. Ed. 2d); and *United States Law Week* (U.S.L.W.).

---

[25](...continued)
to the agglomeration of all the opinions of the various jurisdictions of the United States into masses of what are, in fact, largely made up of useless repetitions. . . . [The] work undertaken by my Company . . . is to give that most valuable in the most elaborate form, and that least valuable in the most condensed").

UNITED STATES COURTS OF APPEAL
West's *Federal Reporter* (F. and F.2d)

UNITED STATES DISTRICT COURTS
West's *Federal Supplement* (F. Supp.) and West's *Federal Rules Decisions* (F.R.D.)

(v) Modern Reporting of State Court Opinions. The reporting of state court decisions emphasizes appellate court opinions which review alleged errors committed by lower state courts. Decisions of the highest appellate court of each state are reported. In addition, some states have reporter series covering decisions of their intermediate appellate courts as well as those of their trial courts.

The two principal sources for state court opinions are (1) official reporters (for example, *Maine Reports*) and (2) West's unofficial regional reporters (for example, *Atlantic Reporter*). West's regional reporters divide the fifty states into seven geographic regions which are part of West's "National Reporter System" (discussed below).

The traditional rule has been that when state court decisions appear in both types of reporters, a reference to the official and preferred unofficial reporter (parallel citations) had to be included in the citation of the case. The fifteenth edition of the *Bluebook* continues this requirement of parallel citation of state court reporters in only one situation. In documents submitted to a state court, all citations to cases decided by the courts of that state (but not other states) must include a citation to the official state reporter, if available, and West reporters. In all other situations, only the relevant regional reporter should be cited (assuming the case is reported therein) (Rule 10.3.1 and Practitioners' Note P.3). Consider the following examples illustrating this *Bluebook* rule:

Hincks Coal Co. v. Milan, 134 Me. 208, 183 A. 756 (1936).
(*Bluebook* form for citation of this case in documents submitted to Maine state courts)

Hincks Coal Co. v. Milan, 183 A. 756 (Me. 1936).
(*Bluebook* form for all other situations)
(The *Hincks* opinion has been published in volume 134 of *Maine Reports* (Me.), beginning on page 208 and also in volume 183 of West's *Atlantic Reporter* (A.), beginning on page 756.)

PROBLEM 1.4 One easy way to determine (1) the basic structure and (2) the names of the courts in a particular jurisdiction is to consult T.1 "United States Jurisdictions" in the *Bluebook*. This table also indi-

cates if and when a state has ceased publishing its official reporter. For example, re-examine the listing for Maine shown in Figure 1–A and answer the following questions based on the information in this table:

(a)   What is the name of the highest court in Maine (listed first in the table)?

(b)   Does Maine have an intermediate appellate court?

(c)   Has Maine ceased publishing its official reporter? The official reporter is listed first (*Maine Reports*), followed by the preferred unofficial reporter (West's *Atlantic Reporter*).

(d)   Is there any period of time when only the official reporter will be cited?

DISCUSSION OF PROBLEM 1.4   The table indicates that (a) the official name of the highest court is the Maine Supreme Judicial Court. No other appellate courts are listed. Thus, (b) Maine does not have an intermediate appellate court. The table indicates that (c) Maine ceased publishing its official reporter (*Maine Reports*) in 1965. Thus, decisions of the Maine Supreme Judicial Court (Maine's highest appellate court) decided after 1965 are published only in West's *Atlantic Reporter*. The table indicates that (d) West's *Atlantic Reporter* began reporting the opinions of the Maine Supreme Judicial Court in 1885. Thus, only *Maine Reports* can be cited for decisions from 1820 (the beginning of *Maine Reports*) to 1885.

(vi) West's National Reporter System.   Beginning in 1879, West Publishing Company began to unofficially report opinions. This reporting soon was expanded to cover all court systems in the United States and is now known as West's "National Reporter System." This system has the advantage of common editorial features and of publishing opinions much more rapidly than official reporters. In *Bluebook* citations, the preferred unofficial (commercial) reporters for state appellate court opinions are West's seven regional reporters:

ATLANTIC REPORTER (A. or A.2d)—Connecticut, Delaware, Maine, Maryland, New Hampshire, New Jersey, Pennsylvania, Rhode Island, Vermont, and the District of Columbia Municipal Court of Appeals.

NORTH EASTERN REPORTER (N.E. or N.E.2d)—Illinois, Indiana, Massachusetts, New York, and Ohio.

NORTH WESTERN REPORTER (N.W. or N.W.2d)—Iowa, Michigan, Minnesota, Nebraska, North Dakota, South Dakota, and Wisconsin.

       PACIFIC REPORTER (P. or P.2d)—Alaska, Arizona, California, Colorado, Hawaii, Idaho, Kansas, Montana, Nevada, New Mexico, Oklahoma, Oregon, Utah, Washington, and Wyoming.

       SOUTH EASTERN REPORTER (S.E. or S.E.2d)—Georgia, North Carolina, South Carolina, Virginia, and West Virginia.

       SOUTH WESTERN REPORTER (S.W. or S.W.2d)—Arkansas, Kentucky, Missouri, Indian Territories, Tennessee, and Texas.

       SOUTHERN REPORTER (So. or So. 2d)—Alabama, Florida, Louisiana, and Mississippi.

       Other West reporters that are part of its National Reporter system include the following:

       (1) some of the reporters of federal court cases previously mentioned (West's *Supreme Court Reporter*, *Federal Reporter*, *Federal Supplement*, and *Federal Rules Decisions*); and

       (2) localized reporters for New York and California (West's *New York Supplement* and West's *California Reporter*, which cover respectively many New York and California lower and intermediate court decisions as well as decisions of the highest courts of those states).

       Later chapters will discuss case reporting in (1) specialized reporters collecting decisions on specific topics, (2) selective annotated reports containing extensive notes and analyses, and (3) in looseleaf services.

(d) Elements of a Case Citation

       Generally speaking, a citation to a reported case should contain six basic elements (*Bluebook* Rule 10):

       (1) the case name;

       (2) the volume number of the reporter;

       (3) the abbreviated name of the reporter;

       (4) the page number on which the opinion begins;

       (5) the full abbreviated name of the court, including its geographic jurisdiction; and

       (6) the year or date of decision.

       PROBLEM 1.5 Figure 1-I presents a page of a reported case in volume 579 of West's *South Western Reporter, Second Series*, which is part of West's National Reporter System. This volume was published in 1979. (a) Examine carefully the editorial features noted. All opinions reported in West's National Reporter system will have these editorial features (although slight variations may occur). (b) Locate each of the six elements (listed above) that you would use to cite this case.

Jurisdiction

(2) Volume Number   (3) Reporter

Text of the opinion

Writer of
the opinion

(1) Case Name

(4) Page
Number

Docket
Number

(5) Court

(6) Date of
the decision

Case
synopsis
prepared
by West's
editors

Topics and
key numbers

Headnote
number
indexed
to the
discussion
of the
point in
the text
of the
opinion

Statutes
construed

Headnote
prepared by
the editors
that
summarizes
the legal
points or
facts of
the case

Attorneys

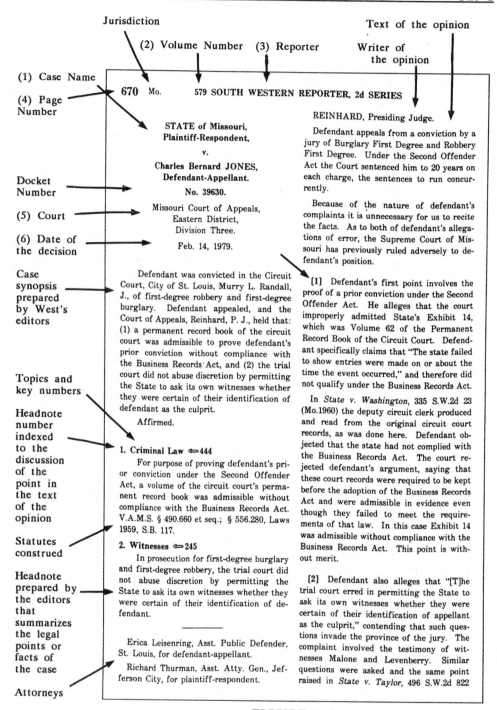

670 Mo.   579 **SOUTH WESTERN REPORTER, 2d SERIES**

STATE of Missouri,
Plaintiff-Respondent,

v.

Charles Bernard JONES,
Defendant-Appellant.

No. 39630.

Missouri Court of Appeals,
Eastern District,
Division Three.

Feb. 14, 1979.

Defendant was convicted in the Circuit Court, City of St. Louis, Murry L. Randall, J., of first-degree robbery and first-degree burglary. Defendant appealed, and the Court of Appeals, Reinhard, P. J., held that: (1) a permanent record book of the circuit court was admissible to prove defendant's prior conviction without compliance with the Business Records Act, and (2) the trial court did not abuse discretion by permitting the State to ask its own witnesses whether they were certain of their identification of defendant as the culprit.

Affirmed.

1. Criminal Law ⊶444
    For purpose of proving defendant's prior conviction under the Second Offender Act, a volume of the circuit court's permanent record book was admissible without compliance with the Business Records Act. V.A.M.S. § 490.660 et seq.; § 556.280, Laws 1959, S.B. 117.

2. Witnesses ⊶245
    In prosecution for first-degree burglary and first-degree robbery, the trial court did not abuse discretion by permitting the State to ask its own witnesses whether they were certain of their identification of defendant.

Erica Leisenring, Asst. Public Defender, St. Louis, for defendant-appellant.
    Richard Thurman, Asst. Atty. Gen., Jefferson City, for plaintiff-respondent.

REINHARD, Presiding Judge.

Defendant appeals from a conviction by a jury of Burglary First Degree and Robbery First Degree. Under the Second Offender Act the Court sentenced him to 20 years on each charge, the sentences to run concurrently.

Because of the nature of defendant's complaints it is unnecessary for us to recite the facts. As to both of defendant's allegations of error, the Supreme Court of Missouri has previously ruled adversely to defendant's position.

[1] Defendant's first point involves the proof of a prior conviction under the Second Offender Act. He alleges that the court improperly admitted State's Exhibit 14, which was Volume 62 of the Permanent Record Book of the Circuit Court. Defendant specifically claims that "The state failed to show entries were made on or about the time the event occurred," and therefore did not qualify under the Business Records Act.

In *State v. Washington*, 335 S.W.2d 23 (Mo.1960) the deputy circuit clerk produced and read from the original circuit court records, as was done here. Defendant objected that the state had not complied with the Business Records Act. The court rejected defendant's argument, saying that these court records were required to be kept before the adoption of the Business Records Act and were admissible in evidence even though they failed to meet the requirements of that law. In this case Exhibit 14 was admissible without compliance with the Business Records Act. This point is without merit.

[2] Defendant also alleges that "[T]he trial court erred in permitting the State to ask its own witnesses whether they were certain of their identification of appellant as the culprit," contending that such questions invade the province of the jury. The complaint involved the testimony of witnesses Malone and Levenberry. Similar questions were asked and the same point raised in *State v. Taylor*, 496 S.W.2d 822

FIGURE 1-I
SOUTH WESTERN REPORTER, SECOND SERIES

DISCUSSION OF PROBLEM 1.5   Depending on the particular action, the case name used in a citation will be one of the following:

(a) the names of the opposing parties;

(b) the subject of the action when the proceeding is "in rem" technically against a "res" (a thing such as a piece of real property, a ship, etc.); or

(c) the popular name of a case (on rare occasions).

The opinion reproduced in Figure 1-I involves a criminal prosecution by the State of Missouri against Charles Bernard Jones. This case would be cited by the names of the opposing parties: State v. Jones (*Bluebook* form). Detailed rules governing what part of the listed names should be included in the citation are discussed in later chapters.

The opinion shown in Figure 1-I has been reproduced from Volume 579 of the *South Western Reporter Second*. This reporter is published by West Publishing Co. and covers state appellate court decisions in Missouri, Texas, Arkansas, Kentucky, and Tennessee.

The *South Western Reporter* is currently in a second series. When a publisher begins a second series, the volume numbering of the second series begins again with one. In order to prevent confusion with the first series, a "2d" must be added to the citation of the reporter. Because the case begins on page 670 of Volume 579 and the accepted abbreviation of the reporter is "S.W.2d," the proper reporter designation for the case reproduced in Figure 1-I would be 579 S.W.2d 670 (*Bluebook* form).

When state court decisions appear in both an official and a West regional reporter, a reference to both reporters (parallel citations) must be included in the citation of the case if you were going to cite this case to a Missouri state court. In this instance, however, the State of Missouri ceased publishing its official reporter (*Missouri Appeal Reports*) for its Court of Appeals in 1952. Because the case reproduced in Figure 1-I was decided in 1979, only the unofficial West reporter can be cited in any event.

The last two elements in the citation of the case shown in Figure 1-I are references to the court, including its geographic jurisdiction, and the year of decision. In *Bluebook* citations, the abbreviated name of the court is "Mo. Ct. App." The year of decision is 1979. Both of these items are given together in a parenthetical: (Mo. Ct. App. 1979) (*Bluebook* form).

Detailed rules covering these matters are discussed at a later point in this book. The full citation of the case shown in Figure 1-I in *Bluebook* form would be:

State v. Jones, 579 S.W.2d 670 (Mo. Ct. App. 1979).

(e) West's Topics and Key Numbers

Several editorial features accompany opinions published in West's National Reporter System. One of the most useful features is the classification of points of law by topic and key number. This feature is an important means of finding relevant discussion of particular points of law through West's digests (collections of headnotes organized by topic and key numbers). You will find references to topics and key numbers in other West publications. Digests allow you to access points of law made in cases by subject.

West Publishing Company publishes digests collecting headnotes arising in a single state (e.g., *Florida Digest*), a group of states (e.g., *South Eastern Digest*, particular courts (e.g., *United States Supreme Court Digest*), and the entire nation covering all reported American cases (*American Digest*). The following is a list of available West digests:

STATE DIGESTS
Every state except Delaware, Nevada, and Utah.

REGIONAL DIGESTS (currently published)
Atlantic, *North Western*, *Pacific*, and *South Eastern*.

FEDERAL DIGESTS
Headnotes from lower federal court opinions and the U.S. Supreme Court: *Federal Digest* (all cases prior to 1939), *Modern Federal Practice Digest* (1939-1960), *Federal Practice Digest 2d* (1961-1975), *Federal Practice Digest 3d* (1976-1989), *Federal Practice Digest 4th* (1989 to date).

Headnotes from the U.S. Supreme Court only:
United States Supreme Court Digest (1970 to date).

AMERICAN DIGEST SYSTEM
All cases—federal and state:
Century Digest (1658-1896), *Decennial Digests* (First through Tenth, Part 1, 1897-1991), and the *General Digest 8th* (1991 to date).

In *Jones* case in Figure 1-I, two points of law discussed in the opinion were classified by West's editors: Criminal Law 444 and Witness 245. These headnotes would appear in the relevant state digest (*Missouri Digest*) and in the *Ninth Decennial (Part 1, 1976-1981)*. The following figure shows where the headnote covering Criminal Law appears in West's *Missouri Digest 2d*. The use of digests in legal research will be discussed in detail at a later point in these materials.

Headnote from the State v. Jones case classified under Criminal Law 444

☞444 | CRIMINAL LAW   12 Mo D 2d—370

▼ **For later cases see same Topic and Key Number in Pocket Part**

Mo.App. 1979. For purpose of proving defendant's prior conviction under the Second Offender Act, a volume of the circuit court's permanent record book was admissible without compliance with the Business Records Act. V.A.M.S. § 490.660 et seq.; § 556.280, Laws 1959, S.B. 117.

State v. Jones, 579 S.W.2d 670.

Mo.App. 1979. Trial court is vested with substantial discretion in determining whether a witness is qualified to testify under Uniform Business Records as Evidence Act. V.A.M.S. §§ 490.660, 560.045.

State v. Rogers, 578 S.W.2d 362.

Refusing to allow State's fingerprint expert to testify as to police report prepared by another officer covering investigation was not an abuse of discretion in absence of evidence that expert could testify from personal knowledge as to current practices of keeping police reports or their mode of preparation. V.A.M.S. §§ 490.660, 560.045.

State v. Rogers, 578 S.W.2d 362.

Mo.App. 1978. Two eyewitnesses to robbery, who both testified in robbery prosecution that they identified defendant from his photograph in lineup with five other persons, as identifying witnesses, could both properly testify to their extrajudicial identification of defendant from photograph, and since defendant's photograph itself then became relevant and material on issue of identification by witnesses, admission of that photograph into evidence was not error on theory that it was done without proper foundation.

State v. Sykes, 571 S.W.2d 456.

Mo.App. 1978. Certification, under seal of Secretary of State, that annexed pages contained a full, true and complete copy of lists of controlled substances and amendments thereto was sufficient to make the document admissible for purpose of establishing that phenmetrazine is a Schedule II, rather than a Schedule III, controlled substance. V.A.M.S. § 490.180.

State v. Harris, 564 S.W.2d 561.

Mo.App. 1977. In view of testimony that photographs of stolen items discovered in automobile were fair and accurate representations of the objects depicted and testimony by arresting officer tracing the objects from the automobile in which defendant was riding to their removal, identification and photographing in his presence at police headquarters, there was sufficient identification and proper foundation for admission.

State v. Savu, 560 S.W.2d 244.

Mo.App. 1977. In prosecution for murder, State proved elements required to show admissibility of tape recorded confession, including that changes, additions or deletions were not made, and that recording was authen-

tic and correct, by testimony of police officer that no changes, additions or deletions had been made and taped and that tape as played in court was authentic and correct even though there was discrepancy between the noted playing time and actual playing time.

Williams v. State, 558 S.W.2d 671.

Mo.App. 1977. A police officer who overhears or is a participant to a conversation may verify transcript of the conversation.

State v. King, 557 S.W.2d 51.

Mo.App. 1977. In homicide prosecution, testimony of custodian hospital records identifying victim's hospital records and explaining the admissions procedure and record keeping constituted sufficient foundation for admission of copy of victim's hospital records under business records exception to hearsay rule. Section 490.680 RSMo 1969, V.A.M.S.

State v. Stephens, 556 S.W.2d 722.

Mo.App. 1977. Where State sought to introduce in evidence, in prosecution for first-degree robbery and assault with intent to do great bodily harm, a letter which defendant had written to a state's witness and where the State was required to resort to the "reply letter doctrine" in order to obtain admission of defendant's letter, proof of the genuineness and authenticity of the prosecution witness' letter to defendant was required before defendant's alleged reply would be admissible.

State v. Holman, 556 S.W.2d 499.

Mo.App. 1976. In order to qualify for admission in evidence under Uniform Business Records as Evidence Act, record of an act, condition or event must not only be made in the regular course of business, but it must also be shown, to the satisfaction of the court, that the sources of information, method and time of preparation were such as to justify its admission; thus, for an item contained in a report to be admissible, it must be based on the entrant's own observation or on information of others whose business duty it was to transmit it to the entrant. Section 490.680 RSMo 1969, V.A.M.S.

State v. Boyington, 544 S.W.2d 300.

If content of record could not have been testified to by reporter had he been offered as a witness present in court, then that content will not be admitted into evidence as a part of a business record. Section 490.680 RSMo 1969, V.A.M.S.

State v. Boyington, 544 S.W.2d 300.

Mo.App. 1976. Where manager of store, who was custodian of the stolen record albums, identified invoices for the records which were sent by store to record distributor, accounted for invoices' origin and transmission from record distributor to manager in normal and ordinary course of business, near in time

For legislative history of cited statutes see Vernon's Annotated Missouri Statutes

---

FIGURE 1-J

WEST'S MISSOURI DIGEST, SECOND SERIES

(f) Finding Cited Reporters in the Library

Most law libraries treat reporters as reference materials. Usually, the best way to locate particular types of reporters is to look for an appropriate sign or to consult a library map or guide. Once the reporter series is found, look for the appropriate volume (listed on the outside binding) and then consult the cited page. Be careful to note whether you are looking for the second series of a reporter because the numbered volumes otherwise look the same.

(g) Judicially Promulgated Court Rules

Rules promulgated by the courts that govern practice, procedure, and evidence are another type of judicial primary source of law. These rules have the force of law. They are based either on a court's inherent authority to issue them or a statute authorizing a court to promulgate them. These rules are discussed in later chapters of this text.

4. PRIMARY ADMINISTRATIVE SOURCES

In addition to legislative (statutory) and judicial (common-law) sources, administrative primary sources constitute another broad category of primary source of law. Sometimes, for a variety of reasons, it is inefficient for a legislative body to enact statutory provisions containing all the details necessary to carry out a law or regulatory scheme. Thus, a legislative body may authorize an administrative body to establish those details and enforce the rules that are established. Administrative regulations properly promulgated for that purpose have the same force as statutory provisions.

(a) Federal Administrative Regulations

(i) Chronological Publication of Federal Regulations. On the federal level, administrative regulations and a variety of other matters are published daily (except Saturday, Sunday, and days following legal holidays) in the *Federal Register* (established in 1936). Because of the large number of pages and the relatively poor paper quality, many law libraries maintain their noncurrent holdings of the *Federal Register* on microfilm or microfiche. Figure 1-K shows a page from the January 10, 1990, *Federal Register*, in which the United States Parole Commission amended its standard conditions of parole. The amendment requires, as a condition of release, that a parolee must submit to a drug test whenever the parolee is ordered to take one by his or her Probation Officer (§ 2.40(a)(14)).

New paragraph (14) added to § 2.40(a)

862 Federal Register / VoL 55, No. 7 / Wednesday, January 10, 1990 / Rules and Regulations

referred to herein upon request to the Piper Aircraft Corporation, 2926 Piper Drive, Vero Beach, Florida 32960, or may examine these documents at the FAA, Central Region, Office of the Assistant Chief Counsel, Room 1558, 601 East 12th Street, Kansas City, Missouri 64106.

Issued in Kansas City, Missouri, on December 21, 1989.

J. Robert Ball,

Acting Manager, Small Airplane Directorate, Aircraft Certification Service.

[FR Doc. 90–600 Filed 1–9–90; 8:45 am]

BILLING CODE 4910-13-M

DEPARTMENT OF JUSTICE

Parole Commission

28 CFR Part 2

Paroling, Recommitting and Supervising Federal Prisoners; Drug Testing of Federal Parolees

AGENCY: United States Parole Commission, Justice.

ACTION: Final rule.

SUMMARY: The Parole Commission is adopting a proposed amendment to the standard conditions of parole at 28 CFR 2.40, to provide that all parolees and releasees shall be subject to drug testing whenever ordered by their U.S. Probation Officer. Currently, persons on parole supervision are subject to drug testing if the Commission has imposed a special drug aftercare condition, or if the probation officer suspects drug use, or there is an established pattern of random testing in the parolees or releasees district of supervision. The Commission believes that drug abuse is so pervasive that all released prisoners under supervision should be subject to an immediate drug test whenever ordered by their U.S. Probation Officer.

EFFECTIVE DATE: February 9, 1990.

FOR FURTHER INFORMATION CONTACT: Richard K. Preston, Attorney, Office of General Counsel, U.S. Parole Commission, Telephone: (301) 492–5959.

SUPPLEMENTARY INFORMATION: Drug abuse among released criminal offenders is not limited to those with prior drug histories whose need for drug treatment and testing is clear. The Commission believes that a parolee who is subject to being tested for illicit drug use will more likely be deterred from illicit drug use than would be the case if he were not so subject. The potential for being drug tested will have a positive effect on the parolee's readjustment to the community, as well as diminishing the demand for illicit drugs. Intervention for sanction and treatment purposes is

more possible if the probation officer has the authority to order an immediate drug test and the parolees and releasees will modify their behavior once on notice that they may be tested.

The Commission published a proposed rule at 54 FR 27844 (June 30, 1989). The Commission received public comment from two Federal inmates, the Chief U.S. Probation Officer for the Central District of California, and one public interest law foundation. The three comments can be summarized as follows: First, comments from the Washington Legal Foundation, a non-profit public interest law and policy center, strongly supported the proposed regulation and, in fact, would like the Commission to expand it to include random alcohol testing. Second, Chief U.S. Probation Officer for the Central District of California, Robert Latta, stated that his staff is "very much in favor of the proposed rule." Third, comments from one inmate opposed the condition generally on grounds that there are inadequate resources (administrative time and prison space) to handle the implementation of the new condition. The comment also noted that there were insufficient guidelines on how to protect parolees from possible abuse by probation officers. Finally, another inmate criticized the proposed rule on the grounds that he had never engaged in or had any history of drug involvement and believed that drug testing for individuals such as himself would be inappropriate and contrary to the intent of Congress. Additionally, this inmate believed that those released on mandatory release cannot have special drug aftercare conditions because the government had no choice in releasing them. After considering the comments, the Commission decided to let the proposed rule be published without change.

List of Subjects in 28 CFR Part 2

Administrative practice and procedure, Prisoners, Probation and parole.

The Amendment

Accordingly, the Parole Commission proposes to amend part 2 of CFR as follows:

PART 28—[AMENDED]

1. The authority citation for 28 CFR part 2 continues to read:

Authority: 18 U.S.C. 4203(a)(1) and 4204(a)(6).

2. Section 2.40 is amended to add a new paragraph (a)(14) to read as follows:

§ 2.40 Conditions of release.

(a) * * *

(14) The parolee shall submit to a drug test whenever ordered by his Probation Officer.

* * * * *

Dated: December 14, 1989.

Benjamin F. Baer,

Chairman, U.S. Parole Commission.

[FR Doc. 90–557– Filed 1–9–90; 8:45 am]

BILLING CODE 4410-01-M

DEPARTMENT OF THE INTERIOR

Bureau of Land Management

43 CFR Public Land Order 6761

[CO–930–00–4214–10, C–34653]

Withdrawal of Public Lands for Windy Gap Archaeological Site, CO

AGENCY: Bureau of Land Management, Interior.

ACTION: Public land order.

SUMMARY: This order withdraws 397.8 acres of public lands from surface entry and mining for a period of 20 years for the Bureau of Land Management to protect the Windy Gap Archaeological Site. The lands have been and remain open to mineral leasing.

EFFECTIVE DATE: January 10, 1990.

FOR FURTHER INFORMATION CONTACT: Doris Chelius, BLM Colorado State Office, 2850 Youngfield Street, Lakewood, Colorado 80215–7076, 303–236–1752.

By virtue of the authority vested in the Secretary of the Interior by Section 204 of the Federal Land Policy and Management Act of 1976, 90 Stat. 2751; 43 U.S.C. 1714, it is ordered as follows:

1. Subject to valid existing rights, the following described public lands are hereby withdrawn from settlement, sale, location, or entry under the general land laws, including the United States mining laws (30 U.S.C. Ch. 2), but not from leasing under the mineral leasing laws, to protect a Bureau of Land Management Archaeological site:

Sixth Principal Meridian

T. 2 N., R. 76 W.,

Sec. 17, S½SE¼,

Sec. 20, N½NE¼, SW¼NE¼.

T. 2 N., R. 77 W.,

Sec. 23, Lot 8;

Sec. 24, Lot 4;

Sec. 25, Lots 1 and 2;

Sec. 26, Lot 1.

The areas described aggregate approximately 397.8 acres of public land.

2. The withdrawal made by this order

FIGURE 1-K

FEDERAL REGISTER (JANUARY 10, 1990)

(ii) Subject-Organized Publication of Federal Regulations. The *Code of Federal Regulations* (C.F.R.) organizes federal regulations currently in force into fifty subject titles and is issued in pamphlet form (subject publication). Figure 1-L shows where the amendment shown in the preceding figure was added to the *Code of Federal Regulations.*

The titles of the Code are revised and reissued quarterly on a rotational basis so that the Code is revised completely once each year. The page shown here is from Title 28 (Judicial Administration). This title is revised every July 1st.

Section 2.40(a)(14) appears in the Code here. →

Department of Justice   **§ 2.40**

are illegally sold, dispensed, used, or given away.

(10) The parolee shall not associate with persons who have a criminal record unless he has permission of his probation officer.

(11) The parolee shall not possess a firearm or other dangerous weapon.

NOTE: Such permission may not be considered in cases in which the parolee is prohibited from such possession by any federal, state, or local law.

(12) The parolee shall permit confiscation by his Probation Officer of any materials which the Probation Officer believes may constitute contraband in the parolee's possession and which he observes in plain view in the parolee's residence, place of business or occupation, vehicle(s), or on his person.

(13) The parolee shall make a diligent effort to satisfy any fine, restitution order, court costs or assessment, and/or court ordered child support or alimony payment that has been, or may be, imposed, and shall provide such financial information as may be requested, by his Probation Officer, relevant to the payment of the obligation. If unable to pay the obligation in one sum, the parolee will cooperate with his Probation Officer in establishing an installment payment schedule.

(14) The parolee shall submit to a drug test whenever ordered by his Probation Officer.

(b) The Commission or a member thereof may at any time modify or add to the conditions of release pursuant to this section, on its own motion or on the request of the United States Probation Officer supervising the parolee. The parolee shall receive notice of the proposed modification and unless waived shall have ten days following receipt of such notice to express his views thereon. Following such ten day period, the Commission shall have 21 days, exclusive of holidays, to order such modification of or addition to the conditions of release.

(c) The Commission may require a parolee to reside in or participate in the program of a residential treatment center, or both, for all or part of the period of parole.

(d) The Commission may require a parolee, who is an addict, within the

meaning of section 4251(a), or a drug dependent person within the meaning of section 2(8) of the Public Health Service Act, as amended, to participate in the community supervision program authorized by section 4255 for all or part of the period of parole.

(e) The Commission may require that a parolee remain at his place of residence during nonworking hours and, if the Commission so directs, to have compliance with this condition monitored by telephone or electronic signaling devices. A condition under this section may be imposed only as an alternative to incarceration.

(f) A parolee may petition the Commission on his own behalf for a modification of conditions pursuant to this section.

(g) The notice provisions of paragraph (b) of this section shall not apply to modification of parole or mandatory release conditions pursuant to a revocation proceeding or pursuant to paragraph (f) of this section.

(h) A parolee may appeal an order to impose or modify parole conditions under § 2.26 not later than thirty days after the effective date of such conditions.

(i) A prisoner who, having been granted a parole date, subsequently refuses to sign the parole certificate, or any other consent form necessary to fulfill the conditions of parole, shall be deemed to have withdrawn the application for parole as of the date of refusal to sign. To be again considered for parole, the prisoner must reapply for parole consideration. With respect to prisoners who are required to be released to supervision through good time reductions (pursuant to 18 U.S.C 4161 and 4164), the conditions of parole set forth in this rule, and any other special conditions ordered by the Commission, shall be in full force and effect upon the established release date regardless of any refusal by the releasee to sign the parole certificate.

(j) Any parolee who absconds from supervision has effectively prevented his sentence from expiring. Therefore, the parolee remains bound by the conditions of his release and violations committed at any time prior to execution of the warrant, whether before or

125

FIGURE 1-L
CODE OF FEDERAL REGULATIONS (1991)

(iii) Finding Federal Regulations in the Law Library. In many law libraries, the *Federal Register* and the *Code of Federal Regulations* are shelved near the federal statutes.

(iv) Basic Citation Form. The following are typical *Bluebook* citations (Rule 14.2) to administrative rules in the *Federal Register* and *Code of Federal Regulations*:

56 Fed. Reg. 50,235 (1991).
27 C.F.R. § 20.235 (1991).
(This regulation is located in section 235 of Part 20 in Title 27.)
EPA Fuels and Fuel Additives Regulations, 40 C.F.R. §§ 80.1-.7 (1991).

(b) Federal Executive Orders and Proclamations

As head of the executive branch, commander-in-chief of the armed forces, and officer in charge of foreign relations, the President of the United States issues a variety of executive orders and proclamations. These documents announce policy and direct action by federal agencies and officials. They are based on the President's inherent powers or statutory authority and have the force of law. Most executive orders and proclamations are published in the *Federal Register* and are included in Title 3 of the *Code of Federal Regulations*. As discussed in later chapters, other sources also publish these orders and proclamations.

(c) State Administrative Regulations

State legislatures authorize state agencies to issue regulations. Such regulations deal with administrative matters within a state and likewise have the force of law. Some states (e.g., California, New York, and Michigan) publish codifications or compilations of their administrative regulations. Other states publish regulations periodically in pamphlets or separate publications, usually covering the regulations of only one department, commission, board, or agency. State administrative regulations generally are not widely available beyond the state of their applicability.

(d) Administrative Decisions

In enforcing the law, state and federal administrative agencies may be authorized to adjudicate disputes or take action against violators in various administrative proceedings. Good examples are the decisions of the Federal Trade Commission and the Securities and Exchange Commission.

Decisions of administrative agencies are published chronologically in sets of administrative reports. Subject access to points of law in administrative decisions is most often available through looseleaf services.

Section 1E. Using Authority

An essential part of legal research is the ability to evaluate how the legal rules and arguments contained in various authorities apply to a particular research problem.[26] To enhance this ability, this section discusses basic legal reasoning, precedent, and the differences between mandatory and persuasive authority.[27]

1. BASIC LEGAL REASONING

In legal arguments, lawyers assert various propositions of law. These legal propositions are often derived from a constitutional provision, statute, administrative regulation, municipal ordinance, or court rule. For example, a lawyer trying to convince a court in a legal argument may begin with a proposition with which the judge will readily agree:

Section 1461 of Title 18 of the *United States Code* prohibits the mailing of obscene or crime-inciting matter in the United States mails.

A legal proposition asserted by a lawyer in a legal argument may also be derived from the holding of a judicial decision. The proposition may be set out explicitly in the opinion or it may be formulated by inductive reasoning and analogy based on earlier decisions. For example, a lawyer may begin with the following proposition:

The United States Supreme Court has held that in order to establish a violation of section 1461 of Title 28, the prosecution must show the defendant had knowledge of the contents of the materials that were mailed.

In the lawyer's argument, these legal propositions would form the major premise of a syllogism. The minor premise would be the facts of the present case. For example, a lawyer may attempt to show that the facts establish one of the following propositions:

The material that was mailed was not obscene.

---

[26] See Christopher G. Wren & Jill R. Wren, The Teaching of Legal Research, 80 Law Libr. J. 7, 42 (1988).

[27] See Larry L. Teply, Legal Writing, Analysis, and Oral Argument 155-205, 227-30 (1990) for a more detailed discussion of the doctrine of stare decisis, authority, legal reasoning, and application of legislation.

The defendant did not know what the packages contained when the defendant mailed them.

If the lawyer's major and minor premises are accepted, the court will conclude in favor of the defendant—in this instance, that the statute was not violated. The real debate in most litigation will often center on the minor premise—the proof of the facts and their classification (for example, whether the material mailed was "obscene").[28]

2. PRECEDENT (STARE DECISIS)

Courts in the Anglo-American legal system follow the doctrine of precedent (stare decisis). Under this doctrine, past judicial decisions by the highest court within a jurisdiction control future decisions by courts in that jurisdiction. Once a court has determined a point of law, that point will be followed in similar, subsequent cases involving different parties—unless, for example, that point of law is changed by a subsequent statute or is overruled in a subsequent judicial decision.

3. MANDATORY AND PERSUASIVE AUTHORITY

(a) Mandatory Primary Authority

As discussed previously, primary authority states the law and emanates from one of the branches of government. Constitutional provisions, statutes, administrative regulations and decisions, municipal ordinances, and court rules from a particular jurisdiction are "mandatory primary authority" within that jurisdiction. Consider these examples:

(1) A municipal ordinance is the controlling law within the territorial limits of the municipality that enacted it.

(2) The criminal and civil statutes enacted by the legislature of the state of Texas regulate activity within and affecting the state of Texas. These Texas statutes do not apply to activity that solely occurs in and affects, for example, the state of New York.

(3) The federal statutes regulating the mailing of obscene matter apply only to the territory of the United States and not to a French citizen mailing obscene materials to another French citizen in France.

Judicial decisions follow the same principles. For example, a Texas Supreme Court decision that establishes a common-law rule is mandatory primary authority within Texas but not within Oklahoma. Likewise, a Texas Supreme Court decision interpreting the constitution or statutes of Texas is mandatory primary authority in Texas.

---

[28] See David P. Derham et al., An Introduction to Law 167-69 (2d ed. 1971).

(b) Persuasive Primary Authority

In contrast, persuasive primary authority, by definition, is not "binding." It does, however, furnish persuasive arguments about how this situation should be handled. For example, assume that a driver negligently causes an accident. The driver's insurer refuses to pay for the damage that the driver caused. The insurer claims that the driver cannot be held legally responsible because the driver was afflicted with an insane delusion. Assume further that the accident occurred in the state of New Mexico and the New Mexico legislature has not enacted a statute dealing with the situation nor has the New Mexico Supreme Court decided a case directly on point. In other words, assume that no mandatory primary authority is applicable. In this situation, the New Mexico courts will consider "persuasive primary authority" in deciding whether to recognize this purported defense.

There are two basic types of persuasive primary authority:

(1) judicial decisions from other jurisdictions which are directly on point and would be mandatory if they had been decided by the New Mexico Supreme Court;

(2) judicial decisions of the New Mexico courts and from other jurisdictions that do not directly apply but provide a useful analogy or that contain rules that could be extended to the present situation (for example, a decision recognizing a sudden and unanticipated heart attack as a defense to a negligence action).

(c) Persuasive Secondary Authority

In absence of mandatory authority, courts will also consider "persuasive secondary authority." Secondary authority includes legal treatises, legal encyclopedias, articles in legal periodicals, textual annotations, dictionaries, and other materials that do not have the force of law but which might provide a persuasive basis for deciding the question.

One type of secondary source deserves special mention: Restatements of the Law. Restatements are drafted by committees or leading legal authorities under the auspices of the American Law Institute. This type of authority is unique to the law. Restatements cover basic (mostly common-law) areas of the law. A position taken by a Restatement can be particularly persuasive.

Although secondary authority does not have the force of law, secondary authority is important for several reasons. First, in absence of controlling primary authority on point, courts may be persuaded by *a suggested resolution of the issue* in a secondary source. For example, the New Mexico courts will consider persuasive secondary authority such

as the position taken in a leading torts treatise or in an article published in a legal periodical in deciding whether to recognize the sudden mental illness defense. Similarly, the position taken in a Restatement (discussed below) has been very influential on the courts in absence of controlling primary authority dealing with a particular issue.

Second, secondary authority can be used to *clarify ambiguities in primary authority*. For example, courts may be strongly influenced by a law review article that demonstrates how apparently conflicting judicial opinions can be harmonized.

Third, secondary authority can be cited to a court in an attempt to *convince the court that a prior decision ought to be limited or overruled*. A court may have considered and decided a legal issue. That decision ordinarily is a mandatory precedent and like cases will be decided in the same way. Over time, such a decision may become inconsistent with another line of cases or modern social policy. Usually under these circumstances, commentators in legal periodicals and other secondary sources will provide persuasive arguments for reform. Similarly, the position taken in a Restatement may provide good reason for reevaluating prior precedent.

Fourth, secondary authority is especially useful for *finding citations to primary authority*. For example, texts, treatises, and legal encyclopedias cite primary authority as a means of supporting their textual discussion. Likewise, annotated sources, such as *A.L.R.* annotations (discussed in the next chapter), provide a wealth of citations to judicial opinions relating to the topic discussed. These secondary sources thus enable researchers to identify (1) leading authorities that have been influential in the development of the law and (2) statutes, cases, and other relevant primary authority from a particular jurisdiction.

Fifth, secondary authority is the best source for *acquiring background information and perspective*. If a researcher is unfamiliar with an area of law, the most efficient way to gain perspective on the subject is to read a discussion of the topic in a text, treatise, legal encyclopedia, or legal periodical. In this way, a researcher can identify critical terminology and can often clarify the issues to be researched.

Section 1F. The Process of Legal Research

Webster's Dictionary defines a "process" as "a series of actions or operations conducing to an end."[29] This definition implies what successful legal researchers have long known. In addition to knowledge about the various sources of law, their publication, and their relative usefulness

---

[29]Webster's Ninth New Collegiate Dictionary 937 (1990).

in solving legal problems, an essential component of successful research is knowledge about the beginning points, the steps, and the methods that are involved in completing a research project.

The specific steps in the legal research process can be described in various ways. For example, one way to look at the process is to divide the process into four basic steps: (1) analyzing the facts and identifying the legal problems that are relevant to the client's situation; (2) planning the research and choosing a logical starting point; (3) developing the research, reevaluating the issues, and updating the law; and (4) refining the research and final updating.

Another way of describing the legal research process is to divide the process into a prelibrary phase and a library phase. The prelibrary phase focuses on fact-related steps that precede research—(1) gathering the facts; (2) analyzing the facts; (3) identifying legal issues raised by the facts; and (4) arranging the legal issues in a logical order for research. The library phase involves three basic steps: (1) finding the law; (2) reading the law, and (3) updating the law.[30]

Still another way of describing the legal research process is to focus closely on the functional steps that researchers take: (1) analyzing the facts; (2) generating research vocabulary; (3) using commentary sources to obtain background information (when the researcher is unfamiliar with the relevant areas of the law); (4) formulating and ordering the issues and sub-issues; (5) searching for authority; (6) reevaluating the issues; and (7) deciding to call it "quits."[31]

These descriptions illustrate that general agreement exists about several aspects of the legal research process: the importance of factual considerations; the need to develop a research approach or plan prior to beginning the use of books or other sources in the library or legal databases; the need to analyze the substance of what is found during the course of the research and to reevaluate the issues in light of those findings; and the importance of updating to assure that the latest law on the subject has been found. Commentators, however, are quick to point out that a researcher's approach to the legal research process must be flexible.[32] Just as the descriptions of that process differ, so will the specific approaches necessarily have to differ in light of the context for

---

[30] See Christopher G. Wren & Jill R. Wren, The Teaching of Legal Research, 80 Law Libr. J. 7, 36-48 (1988).

[31] See Christina L. Kunz et al., The Process of Legal Research: Successful Strategies 7-14 (2d ed. 1989).

[32] See, e.g., id. at 6-7 ("[Y]our research strategy should incorporate flexibility. Successful researchers continually reevaluate their research methodology and consider alternative research approaches as they find that various sources or research approaches are helpful or fruitless").

completing the research project and the initial success or failure of the starting point chosen. Furthermore, legal research results will often stimulate additional factual inquiries.

1. INVESTIGATING AND ANALYZING THE FACTS AND IDENTIFYING THE LEGAL PROBLEMS

The common starting point in describing the legal research process is factual investigation and analysis.[33] Ordinarily, the facts may be developed by you in the course of interviews with your client and witnesses, an analysis of documents and reports, and other sources of factual information.[34] Generally speaking, the basic problem can be identified by focusing on what the client wants.

Do these facts give rise to a cause of action for our client?

What remedies are available in this situation?

Is the sudden mental illness of the client a valid defense to a negligence claim?

When you have been assigned a research project by another lawyer, the facts and legal issue may be specifically stated for you:

What is the measure of damages for a buyer's breach of a land sales contract in Ohio?

Are bottle rockets or cherry bombs illegal in South Carolina?

Similarly, the legal problem may be identified by an opposing party's motion or appellate brief:

Is a foreign government a "person" entitled to sue for treble damages under section 4 of the Clayton Act?

At other times, the basic research problem will be tied specifically to legal documents or actions. In that context, the problem often centers on procedural concerns or on the practicalities of litigation. Again, in this situation a researcher should carefully identify the basic problem to be researched:

Is the defendant's motion to strike proper?

Are there any viable defenses to the complaint or should liability be conceded?

---

[33] See, e.g., id. at 7 ("The Starting Point: Factual Analysis"); Christopher G. Wren & Jill R. Wren, The Teaching of Legal Research, 80 Law Libr. J. 7, 36-42 (1988) (gathering and analyzing facts as the first steps in assessing the research problem prior to the library phase of legal research); Larry L. Teply, Legal Writing, Analysis, and Oral Argument 59-67 (1990) ("Factual Investigation, Analysis, and Preliminary Identification of Legal Issues").

[34] See Christopher G. Wren & Jill R. Wren, The Teaching of Legal Research, 80 Law Libr. J. 7, 36-42 (1988) ("[S]tudents need to realize that lawyers do not acquire facts in neat packages ready-made for legal research. Rather, facts come to light through activities like interviewing clients and witnesses, reviewing documents such as police or medical reports, consulting experts, and inspecting tangible evidence such as murder weapons").

When you are researching issues like the ones just stated, be especially careful to take into account the procedural context in which a substantive issue arises. Failure to consider the effect of the procedural context can result in inaccurate research and misleading conclusions on substantive issues. For example, sometimes the evidence relating to a substantive issue must be viewed in the most favorable light for one party or allegations of fact must be taken as true for purposes of legal research and argument. At other times, resolution of the substantive issue may not be procedurally ripe.

To be successful, the research must address the legal issues arising out of the facts at hand. Obviously, it does little good to research the *wrong* question in light of the facts—no matter how thorough and accurate that research may be. To help prevent this fundamental error, you first should analyze the facts and your research problem in a systematic way before beginning research.

Several different ways of categorizing the facts have been recommended for this purpose. West Publishing Company suggests that the facts be analyzed by listing "the five elements common to every case." These elements are (1) the parties involved in the case; (2) the places where the facts arose and things involved; (3) the basis of the action or issue involved; (4) the defense(s) to the action or issue involved; and (5) the relief sought.[35] Lawyers Cooperative Publishing Company suggests that the "TAPP Rule" be used to analyze the facts. This rule focuses on the words that describe the *T*hing(s), *A*ct(s), *P*erson(s), and *P*lace(s) involved in the case.[36]

Another approach is to focus on the following: (1) the legal subjects involved; (2) the specific terms that describe the parties, place, and things involved; (3) the specific legal issues involved—the theories of recovery, defenses, relief, or other problems (to the extent that they are known); and (4) the research leads, if any. By focusing on the legal subject (e.g., property law, antitrust), legal terms that describe the parties, places, and things (e.g., vendor, aliens, dram shop), and specific legal issues (e.g., negligence, temporary restraining orders, parol evidence), you will be much better prepared to search for and recognize relevant legal materials.[37] Your analysis of the facts and legal issues will be limited,

---

[35]West Publishing Co., West's Law Finder: A Legal Research Manual 18 (1991).

[36]Lawyers Cooperative Publishing Co., A Student's Guide to Am Jur 2d, ALR and USCS 11 (1990).

[37]It has been aptly pointed out that an analysis using categories such as the ones described above to "filter" the facts serves two essential purposes for legal researchers: (1) "the categories guide researchers in developing fact (or 'descriptive') words for gaining access to law books by, for example, looking up the words in the index to a case digest, statutory

(continued...)

of course, by your general knowledge of the law, which in turn, as discussed below, will affect your selection of the initial source in which you will begin your research.

You should carefully consider whether the problem, as presented, identifies any research leads. Sometimes, research requests will identify relevant *primary* sources that constitute significant research leads. These leads may be in the form of full citations or names of cases or statutes. Similarly, an opposing party's memorandum or brief may provide the same sort of leads: the *Tea Rose* case;[38] the Clayton Act;[39] State v. Jones, 579 S.W.2d 670 (Mo. Ct. App. 1979).[40]

Another type of significant research lead is a possible indication of the *scope* of the research. Is the law of a particular state, federal law, or general law the focus of the research? Are there any specific limiting instructions?

Experienced researchers engage in the type of analysis described above almost intuitively. If you are not an experienced researcher, you should record your analysis on paper before beginning your research.

2. PLANNING THE RESEARCH AND CHOOSING A LOGICAL STARTING POINT

Before beginning your research, you should develop a research plan. The most important part of that plan is choosing an initial starting point. For a given factual situation or research problem, you will be faced with choosing between a large variety of primary, secondary, and purely search sources. This choice deserves careful consideration and should be a logical one.

Generally speaking, the choice of an initial research source should be guided by five basic factors: (1) the particular type of substantive area involved in the legal problem; (2) the clarity of the issue to be researched; (3) the general familiarity with the relevant substantive or procedural law; (4) the purpose of the research; and (5) the practical availability of the research sources.

---

[37](...continued)
or administrative code, or other resource"; and (2) "the categories enable researchers to identify the legal issues raised by the facts." Christopher G. Wren & Jill R. Wren, The Teaching of Legal Research, 80 Law Libr. J. 7, 39 (1988).

[38]For instance, the Tea Rose case may be mentioned in your instructions from a supervising lawyer assigning a research project.

[39]For instance, a reference to the Clayton Act may be made in statement of the issue in the opposing party's brief.

[40]For instance, this case may be cited in the opposing party's memorandum in support of the opposing party's position.

As noted earlier, in absence of research leads to specific primary sources, the best initial source ordinarily is a secondary one, particularly a text, treatise, legal encyclopedia, or looseleaf service. Consulting one or more of these secondary sources first has several advantages. These sources will orient you to the basic law on the subject and possibly allow you to formulate a tentative answer to your research problem or to reformulate a broad research question into a more specific one. At the same time, secondary sources often direct you to relevant primary or other secondary sources. Ordinarily, secondary sources are also the most useful sources when a limited amount of time is available for researching a problem. They are essential sources when you are unfamiliar with the substantive area of law.

In some situations, a primary source is the logical first choice. Specific statutes, cases, or other primary sources ordinarily are cited in opposing parties' briefs or memoranda. They also may be mentioned in a request for research. When such sources are known, they are often the best starting point for research. On the other hand, when the research question involves a broad area of statutory law, such as federal antitrust law, labor law, or worker's compensation, a leading treatise or looseleaf service covering the field usually is a better starting point. This approach also works better when the statutory scheme is complicated, such as the federal tax laws.

3. DEVELOPING THE RESEARCH, REEVALUATING THE ISSUES, AND UPDATING THE LAW

The next step in the legal research process is to develop your initial research. This step involves consulting, reading, and applying to your research problem relevant primary authorities, legislative history, and secondary sources. Cross-references and specialized finding tools will aid you in this process. As you read and apply the material that you find, you will reevaluate the issues in light of your continuing research. During this process, you will also bring your research up to date. Otherwise, you may find yourself relying on a case that has been overruled or on a statute that has been repealed or amended.

4. FINAL UPDATING AND REFINEMENTS

Before you finally complete your research, you must make certain that the authorities on which you are relying for your answer to the research problem are up to date. You may also want to add refinements to your research in light of your particular purpose. For example, if

your research is for an appellate brief, you may want to find quotations or illustrations for the brief.

   PROBLEM 1.6   Assume that you work for a law firm representing Rip Van Winkle.   Rip is a defendant in a negligence action for damages arising from an automobile accident.   The plaintiff was a passenger in Rip's automobile and was injured when Rip fell asleep at the wheel and hit a tree.   Assume that the accident occurred in Maine and that all tort law issues are controlled by Maine state law.   Assume that you have been asked to research whether the doctrine of implied assumption of risk will bar the plaintiff's recovery—if it can be shown that the plaintiff knew of Rip's propensity to fall asleep and yet proceeded in the face of that danger.
   Which of the following do you think would provide the best starting point for research?

   (a) *Maine Reports* or West's *Atlantic Reporter*
   (b) the Maine statutory compilation
   (c) a treatise on tort law or a legal encyclopedia
   (d) the *United States Code*

   DISCUSSION OF PROBLEM 1.6   Generally speaking, in absence of a direct reference to a specific case or an indication that the problem is controlled by a specific Maine statute, most researchers would suggest that you begin research with a secondary source.   Thus, most researchers would begin by consulting a treatise on tort law or a legal encyclopedia to gain perspective and background information as well as to find citations to Maine primary sources.   Thus, answer (c) is probably the best starting point.

   PROBLEM 1.7   Assume that you have encountered all of the following sources during your research on the question whether implied assumption of risk is a viable defense in a negligence action controlled by Maine law.   Which of the following would be the "best" authority on which to base your answer to this legal question?

   (a) a 1984 Maine statute stating that implied assumption of risk is an available defense;
   (b) a treatise or legal encyclopedia stating that the prevailing legal rule in the United States is that implied assumption of risk is not a defense;

(c) a 1980 decision of the Maine Supreme Judicial Court specifically stating that implied assumption of risk is not a viable defense—overruling a contrary 1923 decision of the Maine Supreme Judicial Court;

(d) a recent article written by a law professor in the *Harvard Law Review* (a leading legal periodical) that convincingly presents the position that implied assumption of risk should not be a defense and that the matter should be handled through the comparative negligence doctrine.

DISCUSSION OF PROBLEM 1.7   This problem focuses on the relative value of primary and secondary authority.   For the purpose of finding an answer to the research question, secondary authority should be used only when primary authority is unavailable or unclear.   Thus, when both case and statutory law exist in the relevant jurisdiction, it would be improper to base your answer on general statements in a treatise or legal encyclopedia (answer (b)).   Likewise, the law review article (answer (d)) should not be used for the same reason.

The final authority to establish Maine state tort law is with the Maine Legislature and the Maine Supreme Judicial Court.   Because the Maine statute (1984) was enacted after the Maine judicial decision (1980), the statute controls the law on the issue and thus would be the best source on which to base your answer (answer (a)).

PROBLEM 1.8   Assume that the accident occurred in the State of Utopia, a newly admitted state, rather than in Maine.   Assume further the negligence action was commenced in a Utopia state court and that the question is one of first impression in Utopia.   Which of the source(s) listed in *Problem 1.7* would not be useful to you?   Which do you think would initially be the most useful in researching the problem?

DISCUSSION OF PROBLEM 1.8   Under modern conflict of laws rules, the Maine statute would not apply to accidents occurring outside that state.   (You should note, however, that the Maine statute might be applied by the Utopia courts in unusual circumstances—for example, if the facts stated that both the plaintiff and defendant were citizens of Maine, the trip originated in Maine, and would have ended in Maine but for the accident in Utopia en route.)   Thus, in absence of further facts, the Maine statute would not be useful to you (answer (a)).

On the other hand, the other three sources are persuasive precedents and would be helpful to you in presenting arguments or predicting what the courts in Utopia are likely to do in this situation.   The particular approach that will be taken by the courts in Utopia depends on the persuasiveness of the underlying rationales for the various possible rules

or approaches. Many researchers would regard the discussion in a leading treatise as the most useful initial source—with the law review article a close second.

5. COMPUTER-ASSISTED LEGAL RESEARCH (CALR) IN THE LEGAL RESEARCH PROCESS

The preceding discussion focused on the traditional research process. As noted earlier, however, computer databases are now available for legal research. Although the basic research process (including the primary goal of finding controlling primary authority) remains basically the same when computer-assisted legal research (CALR) is utilized, there are important differences in approaches. Furthermore, researchers should be constantly aware of both the strengths and limitations of computer-assisted legal research during the research process.

The heart of computer-assisted legal research is the search query or search request. You can ask the computer to retrieve documents—for example, cases or statutes—involving certain fact patterns or particular terms that cannot be readily found by using traditional legal research tools. In effect, by using personally tailored search queries, researchers can create their own search index. For example, the computer can easily retrieve all cases involving picketing at shopping centers or products liability cases involving dead mice in soft drink bottles. It can also easily retrieve all cases involving particular names or terms, such as "Miller," "light beer," or "drunk driving."

The content of a search query consists of words or terms that you think are likely to appear in the relevant sources in the database you are searching. WESTLAW and LEXIS search queries follow a similar, but not identical format.[41] For example, the following simple LEXIS search request would find all cases in the database searched in which the word indispensable and the word party occur within fifteen words of each other (in the same segment of the case):

indispensable w/15 party

The following WESTLAW search query would retrieve all cases in the database searched in which the word automobile, auto, vehicle, bus, truck, or car appears in the same paragraph as the word cliff:

automobile auto vehicle bus truck car /p cliff

---

[41]The mechanics and suggested methods of formulating search queries are discussed in Chapters 7 (WESTLAW) and 8 (LEXIS).

One limitation of computer-assisted research relates to the difficulty of formulating search queries. If a search query is too broad or too narrow, either a large number of irrelevant documents will be retrieved or relevant documents will be missed. Furthermore, computer-assisted legal research is literal. Effective use of an automated legal research system requires, for example, knowledge of how a court is likely to phrase its opinion and what legal terms it is likely to use.

Relevant documents may be missed when a court has used terms or phrases different from those used in the search query to address the issue (unless the West key-number indexing of the WESTLAW service is used as part of the search query). For example, in a search for cases involving defects in "thermos bottles," you would miss cases in which the courts had called the product a "vacuum bottle." In contrast, asking for cases involving "accidents" and "negligence" would result in a large number of irrelevant cases.

Remember that you cannot expect the computer to retrieve material that you have not asked it to retrieve. Remember also that the computer will retrieve everything that meets the conditions of your request—which means that you must be careful to design your request in such a way that the computer does not retrieve too much material.

Another limitation on computer-assisted legal research relates to the databases or files stored in the computer. Currently available databases or files include cases, statutes, administrative regulations, attorney general opinions, and law review articles. The coverage of these items, however, is not always complete. For example, the databases in the WESTLAW service and the files in the LEXIS service do not cover all reported cases. Cases reported prior to certain years (not included in the database or file) cannot be searched by either service. Thus, a search may not find an early case directly on point.

On the other hand, because of the cost of legal materials and infrequent demand for some resources, libraries at law firms and even some law schools cannot, as a practical matter, maintain all of the possible sources legal researchers might want to use. One advantage of computer-assisted legal research services is that they provide easy access to a vast number of legal and nonlegal research sources that otherwise may not be available.

WESTLAW and LEXIS services also provide other convenient research functions. Most prominent among them is on-line use of *Shepard's Citations*. WESTLAW and LEXIS also have citation verification services that provide the direct history of a case and parallel citations. On WESTLAW, this function is called Insta-Cite. On LEXIS, this function is called Auto-Cite. The use of these functions is discussed in later

chapters. Other legal and nonlegal databases can also be accessed through the computer.[42]

CD-ROM (Compact Discs with Read-Only Memory) provides additional research possibilities. CD-ROM discs can hold 300,000 typed pages on a small disc. By attaching a CD-ROM disc player to a personal computer, you can retrieve CD-ROM information using computer search techniques or traditional table of contents/index methods of search. For example, West Publishing Company has available CD-ROM discs with comprehensive collections of research materials (reporters, treatises, etc.) available in several fields, such as tax, bankruptcy, and federal civil practice. The discs themselves are periodically updated. For the latest material, you can access online update databases, which act as "electronic pocket parts" for the discs.

Section 1G.   Ethical Components of Legal Research

1. PROFESSIONAL ETHICS

The two principal sources for rules governing the professional conduct of lawyers are (1) the American Bar Association's *Model Rules of Professional Conduct* (1983) (the current ethical standards of the American Bar Association which have been adopted in a majority of jurisdictions) and (2) the American Bar Association's *Model Code of Professional Responsibility* (1980) (still used for professional discipline in some jurisdictions).

The first rule of the Model Rules of Professional Conduct states that "[a] lawyer shall provide competent representation to a client. Competence requires the legal knowledge, skill, thoroughness and preparation reasonably necessary for the representation."[43] The notes to the final draft of this rule make clear that the requisite "legal knowledge" consists of the well-settled principles of law applicable to a client's problem and the law that can be found through a "reasonable search."[44]

Failure to meet this standard may result in a professional disciplinary proceeding. For example, the Colorado Supreme Court held that a lawyer incompetently represented his clients in the purchase of a busi-

---

[42] These databases include a large variety of legal and nonlegal sources, such as foreign legal materials, the Index to Legal Periodicals, restatements of the law, Dunn and Bradstreet, and newspapers.

[43] Model Rules of Professional Conduct Rule 1.1 (1983).

[44] Id. Rule 1.1 notes (Proposed Final Draft 1981).

ness because he was ignorant of the law and failed to make any meaningful inquiry about the problems that might arise. Based upon this violation and others, the court disbarred the attorney.[45]

Similarly, the Nebraska Supreme Court censured an attorney for failing to determine "what the law was or how it had been changed by [a recent] amendment [or] how it might affect him personally."[46] The Nebraska Supreme Court emphasized:

> It is inexcusable for an attorney to attempt any legal procedure without ascertaining the law governing that procedure. Of all classes and professions the lawyer is most sacredly bound to understand and uphold the law. [This attorney] was guilty of extreme negligence in his failure to familiarize himself with [the relevant] section [of the Nebraska statutes], as amended. The fact that he was extremely busy . . . does not absolve him of responsibility. It would have taken comparatively little time to have read the statute, as amended.[47]

2. LEGAL MALPRACTICE

The failure to do adequate research also may be a basis for legal malpractice. For example, the California Supreme Court held that an attorney could be liable for advising a client on an uncertain point without conducting research.[48] In that case, the court upheld a client's recovery of $100,000 based on her attorney's failure to assert her community property interest in her husband's future retirement benefits. The court explained:

> [A]n attorney does not ordinarily guarantee the soundness of his opinions and, accordingly, is not liable for every mistake he may make in his practice. He is expected, however, to possess knowledge of those plain and elementary principles of law which are commonly known by well-informed attorneys, and to discover those additional rules of law which, although not commonly known, may be found by standard research techniques. . . . [W]ith respect to an unsettled area of the law, we believe an attorney

---

[45] People v. Yoakum, 552 P.2d 291, 293-94 (Colo. 1976).

[46] State ex rel. Nebraska State Bar Ass'n v. Holscher, 230 N.W.2d 75, 79 (Neb. 1975).

[47] Id. at 80.

[48] Smith v. Lewis, 530 P.2d 589 (Cal. 1975).

assumes an obligation to his client to undertake reasonable research in an effort to ascertain relevant legal principles and to make an informed decision as to a course of conduct based upon an intelligent assessment of the problem. In the instant case, ample evidence was introduced to support a jury finding that [the attorney] failed to perform such adequate research into the [unsettled] question of the community character of retirement benefits and thus was unable to exercise informed judgment to which his client was entitled.[49]

These and many other cases demonstrate the importance of legal research in the competent representation of clients. The dire consequences that can result from inadequate research should be sufficient to stimulate prospective attorneys to learn effective research techniques and to encourage practicing attorneys to hone their research skills. Clients cannot reasonably expect attorneys to know the law on all subjects, and they should understand that the law can change rapidly. That is why lawyers are justified in charging for legal research conducted for a client's benefit.

3. LIBRARY RULES

Library rules protect library resources, make those resources reasonably available to all library patrons, and help ensure a pleasant working environment. Following those rules is an integral part of the professional ethical responsibility of a lawyer, law student, or legal assistant.

---

[49]Id. at 595. Accord Copeland Lumber Yards v. Kincaid, 684 P.2d 13, 14-15 (Or. Ct. App. 1984) (attorney's reliance on "vague recollection of an 1899 case" improper); Horne v. Peckham, 158 Cal. Rptr. 714, 717-20 (Ct. App. 1979) (attorney's negligent failure to research before drafting a trust improper).

Chapter 2

ANALYZING FACTS AND LEGAL PROBLEMS AND FINDING COMMENTARY AND SUMMARIES OF THE LAW IN SECONDARY SOURCES

Section 2A. Preliminary Factual Analysis and Problem Identification

Legal research is a problem-solving activity that ordinarily takes place in a factual context.[1] Before you begin legal research, you first should conduct a preliminary analysis of the facts and the legal research problem. One way in which you can perform this analysis is to consider four basic areas: (1) the legal subjects involved; (2) the specific legal terms used to describe the parties, places, and things involved; (3) the specific legal issues involved—the theories of recovery, defenses, relief, or other problems; and (4) any research leads based on the material or information that you have received.[2]

By focusing on these items, you will be better prepared to choose a logical starting point for your research, to find background information, and to recognize relevant legal materials.

---

[1] See Christopher G. Wren & Jill R. Wren, The Teaching of Legal Research, 80 Law Libr. J. 7, 38-41 (1988) (emphasizing fact gathering and analysis as an essential part of the legal research process).

[2] See supra § 1F ("The Process of Legal Research") in Chapter 1.

The following three problems give you practice in preparing a preliminary analysis of a research problem. They also show some of the various contexts in which research problems can arise—ranging from "pure facts" obtained in a client interview to a formal research assignment that a senior partner might give an associate or legal assistant.

PROBLEM 2.1   Assume that the following interview has been conducted:

LAWYER: Hello, Mr. Stone, it is nice to meet you. . . . In our telephone conversation, you said that you have been having a problem with your neighbor concerning use of a road. Why don't you tell me some more about the problem?

CLIENT: The trouble started with the new owner of the property Jason Carston about six months ago. We haven't gotten along well ever since my son Andrew started dating his daughter.

LAWYER: And this is when the trouble started?

CLIENT: That's right. I've been using the road up to my house ever since I bought my place. I have an acreage located outside town. The road up to my house cuts across my neighbor's land. Carston has now put a gate with a lock on it, so I'm now forced to use a back road, which adds about fifteen minutes to the trip into town each way. I want to know if there is some way I can force him to open up the road. Does he have the right to block off the road just because he's mad at my son?

   . . . .

LAWYER: How long have you been using the road?

CLIENT: Ever since I moved here to New York and bought my place—let's see—about twenty-five years. The former owner built the road a few years before I bought my place.

LAWYER: You said that this is a new neighbor. Did you or the person you bought the land from have an agreement with the prior owner about using the road?

CLIENT: The former owner was Elmyra Smith. I always thought she was a peculiar bird—sort of a hermit. We never talked about the road. I just kept using the road. I figured that she would have objected if she didn't want me using the road.

LAWYER: Then you didn't ever get permission from her?

CLIENT: No, I suppose that I should have gotten something in writing . . . like a deed or something . . . giving me permission, but I never expected to have this problem.

   . . . .

LAWYER: Is Elmyra Smith, your former neighbor, still alive?

CLIENT: No, that's why the property was sold.

LAWYER: So we don't have any proof—other than your own subjective impressions—how your former neighbor personally viewed your use of the road. In other words, we don't really know for sure whether she was just being nice or whether she really objected to your use?

CLIENT: Well, she certainly knew that I was using the road. I once heard from one of my friends in town that she had told one of her relatives that she didn't like me using the road because it disturbed her peace and quiet. For a while, there was a lot of traffic on the road when I was putting an addition on my house. She stopped some of the construction people and told them she was ticked off about all the noise and told them to stay off.

LAWYER: Is there anyone else who uses the road?

CLIENT: About the only people who use the road are my family and occasional visitors.

. . . .

LAWYER: My initial reaction is that you may be able to claim that you have a right to continue to use the road as a result of your use of the road for such a long period of time. Have you tried to negotiate with your neighbor for a right to use the road? That would be a lot simpler than trying to force your use of the road on your neighbor.

CLIENT: I've tried to talk with him, but he won't listen. I think you had better proceed on the assumption that he will fight this.

. . . .

LAWYER: I think the key factor here is that you have used the road without permission for a long period. In some cases, the law will recognize your right to continue to use the road. Are there any other related concerns that I should know about?

CLIENT: Well, in addition to the gate on the road, my neighbor is also building a very high fence close to the property line near my house. Is there some way to have the fence removed or reduced in height?

LAWYER: I'm not sure if anything can be done about the fence. Tell me some about the situation.

CLIENT: . . . I measured the fence, and it is 12-feet high. What really disturbs me is that the fence looks so tacky and it blocks my view.

LAWYER: I will check into the law and get back to you in a few days. As I research this problem, I may need to get some additional information from you. . . .

Complete the following preliminary analysis of the problem(s) raised by the information provided in this interview.

(a) What legal subject(s) are involved in this research problem?

(b) What words could be used to describe the parties, places, and things involved in this research problem?

(c) What words could be used to describe the legal issues (theories, defenses, relief, and other issues) involved in this research problem?

(d) What research leads are there (if any)?

DISCUSSION OF PROBLEM 2.1 For this situation, the following preliminary problem analysis could be recorded (which, of course, would be dependent on the extent of your knowledge about this area of law). There may be other items that could be properly listed.

Preliminary Problem Analysis (Stone v. Carston)

Legal Subject(s):
Property or tort law

Legal Description of the Parties, Places, and Things:
Landowner, neighbor, adjoining landowners, user, property, land, gate, obstruction, acreage, access, right of way, road, lane, and fence

Legal Issues (Theories, Defenses, Relief, and Other Problems):
Adverse possession, prescription, easement, license, trespass, proof of adverse possession or hostile use, nuisance, spite fence, damages, injunction, and declaratory judgment

Research Leads:
No applicable cases or statutes are known. The jurisdiction is the State of New York, and state law appears to be involved.

PROBLEM 2.2 Assume that Jack T. Simpson has been convicted of the crimes of rape and murder and that Simpson is presently serving a life sentence in the State of Texas. Simpson drafted and filed a habeas corpus petition in a state court to test the legality of his imprisonment.

Simpson's pro se petition alleges that he is in the custody of Warden John Albertson and is imprisoned in a Texas state prison. Simpson's petition alleges that his imprisonment is illegal because three of the twelve jurors in his case were illegal aliens. Simpson's petition further alleges that these jurors were not legally qualified to be jurors and, therefore, the jury in his case was improperly selected and impaneled. Finally, Simpson alleges that he did not become aware that aliens had served on the jury until recently.

Assume that you are a judicial clerk working for the judge who is considering whether to grant a hearing on the petition. The judge has asked you to research whether the circumstances alleged by Simpson constitute a proper ground for issuing a writ of habeas corpus. Complete the following preliminary analysis of the problem.

(a) What legal subject(s) are involved in this research problem?

(b) What words could be used to describe the parties, places, and things involved in this research problem?

(c) What words could be used to describe the legal issues (theories, defenses, relief, and other issues) involved in this research problem?

(d) What research leads are there (if any)?

DISCUSSION OF PROBLEM 2.2 For this research project, the following preliminary problem analysis could be recorded (which, of

course, would be dependent on the extent of your knowledge about this area of law). There may be other items that could be properly listed.

Preliminary Problem Analysis (Simpson v. Albertson, Warden)

Legal Subject(s):

Criminal law, criminal procedure, and habeas corpus

Legal Description of the Parties, Places, and Things:

Jurors, aliens, warden, prison, penitentiary, custody, writ of habeas corpus, pro se petition, and illegal imprisonment

Legal Issues (Theories, Defenses, Relief, and Other Problems):

Propriety of habeas corpus petition, grounds for issuing a writ of habeas corpus, errors in selecting and impaneling the jury, and aliens prohibited from jury service by state law

Research Leads:

No cases or statutes are cited in the problem. The jurisdiction is the State of Texas, and apparently state law is involved.

PROBLEM 2.3 Assume that you have been asked to research for a senior partner whether a "John Doe" complaint can be filed in a diversity action in federal court. The firm has a client, Lisa Wilder, who was injured in an automobile accident while she was visiting in the State of Virginia. The client was passenger in the rear seat of an automobile that was sideswiped in Virginia by a hit-and-run Cadillac occupied by four males. The Cadillac stopped, but immediately drove away, and escaped pursuit. The Cadillac bore Virginia license plates, but the numbers could not be determined.

The firm wants to bring suit in federal court under the Virginia uninsured motorist statute. That statute provides that if an owner or operator of any vehicle causing injury or damages is unknown, an action may be instituted against the unknown defendant as "John Doe." Wilder is a citizen of the District of Columbia. As you know, to bring an action in federal court, there must be diversity of citizenship between the parties and more than $50,000 in controversy. Do we have a problem in meeting this jurisdictional requirement if we simply name "John Doe" as a defendant?

(a) What legal subject(s) are involved in this research problem?

(b) What words could be used to describe the parties, places, and things involved in this research problem?

(c) What words could be used to describe the legal issues (theories, defenses, relief, and other issues) involved in this research problem?

(d) What research leads are there (if any)?

DISCUSSION OF PROBLEM 2.3 For this research project, the following preliminary problem analysis could be recorded (which, of course, would be dependent on the extent of your knowledge about this area of law). There may be other items that could be properly listed.

Preliminary Problem Analysis (Wilder v. Doe)

Legal Subject(s):
Civil procedure, torts, and federal practice

Legal Description of the Parties, Places, and Things:
John Doe, fictitious persons, parties to the action, automobile, hit-and-run accident, uninsured motorists, uninsured motorist coverage, and personal injuries

Legal Issues (Theories, Defenses, Relief, and Other Problems):
Negligence, diversity of citizenship requirement, "John Doe" defendants, subject-matter jurisdiction, proof of citizenship, status of residents of the District of Columbia for diversity purposes, and damages

Research Leads:
A reference is made to the Virginia Uninsured Motorist statute, but no specific citation has been given. The jurisdiction is the State of Virginia. State tort law is involved, but federal law applies to the jurisdictional requirement of diversity.

Section 2B. The Principal Methods of Search and Access to Secondary Sources

In absence of research leads to specific primary sources, the best research source for you to consult in researching legal problems is ordinarily a secondary one, particularly a text, treatise, legal encyclopedia, law review article, or looseleaf service. As noted in Chapter 1, consulting one or more of these secondary sources first has several advantages. These sources will orient you to the basic law on the subject and possibly will enable you to formulate a tentative answer to your research problem or to reformulate a broad research question into a more specific one.

Secondary sources often direct you to relevant primary or other secondary sources. Likewise, secondary sources are the most useful sources when time is limited. They are essential sources when you are unfamiliar with the substantive law of the area being researched.

When you use a secondary legal research source and you do not have a specific reference to relevant discussion in that source, there are four basic search methods that you can use. These methods are summarized in the following table:

METHODS OF SEARCH IN SECONDARY SOURCES

Search Method	Description
Index Method	Checking pertinent words and legal terms in an index to find references to relevant entries
Topic Method	Consulting the table of contents or topic outline for entries that might contain relevant discussion
Word or Phrase Method	Consulting directly the relevant word or phrase in sources organized in this manner (e.g., a law dictionary, legal thesaurus, or legal glossary)
Table of Cases Method	Consulting a table of cases to find where a known case is discussed, cited, or contained in the source

The following table summarizes the publication of and principal access to secondary legal sources:

PUBLICATION OF AND ACCESS TO SECONDARY LEGAL SOURCES

Kind of Secondary Source	Publication	Principal Access (Other than a Direct Citation or Computer-Assisted Legal Research)
Commentary	Treatises or texts	Card catalog/index or table of contents
	Legal encyclopedias	Topic or index method of search and cross-references
	Legal periodicals	Legal periodical indexes
	Looseleaf services	Topic or index method of search
	Textual annotations	Annotation indexes and cross-references
Dictionaries	Legal and other dictionaries	Card catalog/word or phrase method of search
Restatements of the Law	Restatements	Index or topic method of search

Section 2C. Using Law Dictionaries to Clarify Legal Terminology and the Word or Phrase Method of Search

Before consulting a secondary source in researching the legal issues in *Problems 2.1, 2.2,* or *2.3,* you can use a law dictionary to clarify your understanding of any unfamiliar legal terms and to develop alternative search terms. The following sources are helpful for this purpose:

TRADITIONAL LAW DICTIONARIES—*Black's Law Dictionary* (6th ed. 1990); *Ballentine's Law Dictionary* (3d ed. 1969).

STUDENT-PARALEGAL-NON-LAWYER LAW DICTIONARIES— Stephen H. Gifis, *Law Dictionary* (2d ed. 1984); Daniel Oran, *Oran's Dictionary of the Law* (1983); Valera Grapp, *Paralegal's Encyclopedic Dictionary* (1979); *The Law Dictionary* (Wesley Gilmer, Jr. 6th ed. 1986) (previously titled *Cochran's Law Lexicon*); *The Plain-Language Law Dictionary* (Robert E. Rothenberg ed. 1981).

LEGAL THESAURI—William C. Burton, *Legal Thesaurus* (1980); William P. Statsky, *Legal Thesaurus/Dictionary: A Resource for the Writer and Computer Researcher* (1985).

LEGAL GLOSSARIES—Kenneth R. Redden & Enid L. Veron, *Modern Legal Glossary* (1980).

SPECIALTY AND OTHER DICTIONARIES—Max Radin, *Radin's Law Dictionary* (2d ed. 1970); Jacob E. Schmidt, *Attorneys' Dictionary of Medicine and Word Finder* (16th ed. 1962-date) (4 vols.; frequently updated); Robert L. Bledsoe & Boleslaw A. Bockek, *The International Law Dictionary* (1987); Ralph C. Chandler et al., *The Constitutional Law Dictionary* (1987); Bryan A. Garner, *A Dictionary of Modern Legal Usage* (1987); Robert S. Smith, *West's Tax Law Dictionary* (1992).

In many law libraries, dictionaries are treated as reference sources. They are often shelved in a special location or placed on appropriate stands in the library. To find a desired term, the word or phrase method of search can be used. To use this method, you simply look up the desired term. Assume, for instance, in the context of *Problem 2.3*, you want to look up "John Doe." Shown in Figure 2-A are entries for "John Doe" and related terms in *Ballentine's Law Dictionary*.

Lawyers Cooperative/Bancroft-Whitney's Ballentine's Law Dictionary was first published in 1930 and is now in its third edition (1969).

Note the useful cross-reference to a section in the American Jurisprudence Second legal encyclopedia.

At the end of both Black's Law Dictionary and Ballentine's Law Dictionary, there is a table of abbreviations that can be used to identify unfamiliar abbreviations of law reports and other legal materials.

John Doe. A fictitious name of a person which is often substituted in an action or proceeding for a party's real name until the latter can be ascertained.

John Doe action. An action brought against "John Doe" as an unknown uninsured motorist. 7 Am J2d Auto Ins § 137. Any action in which the defendant is designated as "John Doe," his real name being unknown to the plaintiff.

John Doe summons. A summons in which the name of the defendant being unknown to the plaintiff at time of issuance, the defendant is designated as John Doe, his true name to be added after service. 42 Am J1st Proc § 16.

John Doe warrant. A warrant for the arrest of a person designated as John Doe or by some other fictitious name because his real name is unknown. 5 Am J2d Arr § 9.

FIGURE 2-A

BALLENTINE'S LAW DICTIONARY

Similarly, in the context of *Problem 2.1*, you might vaguely remember that "prescription" might be relevant to establishing Mr. Stone's right to use the road. The following figures show the relevant entries for this and related terms in several sources. Compare the nature of the entries in these sources.

---

prescription (Usucapio, Rom.), the transfer of rights in, or title to, real property by enjoying it peaceably without interruption, openly, and as if it were of right, over a long period of time, *e.g.*, 15 years or 21 years. The period of time required for prescription was originally time out of mind, but is now the time after which a person is prevented by the statutes of limitation from recovering real property or an interest therein.

FIGURE 2–B
THE LAW DICTIONARY (GILMER 6TH ED. 1986)

PRESCRIPTION a means of acquiring an **easement** in or on the land of another by continued regular use over a statutory period. See 81 A. 2d 137. Requisite elements are similar to those of **adverse possession**, except that acquisition by prescription does not require **hostile possession** or use and therefore, an easement can be acquired through permissive use (i.e., without an assertion of right). Adverse possession may eventually give one absolute title, but prescription only provides one with an easement.

PRESCRIPTIVE EASEMENT see **easement**.

Cross-reference from the entry for "PRESCRIPTIVE EASEMENT" to "EASEMENT" (shown in the adjoining column)

PRESCRIPTIVE EASEMENT [EASEMENT BY PRESCRIPTION] an easement acquired through the uninterrupted use of another's land for the same statutory period of time necessary to satisfy **adverse possession** requirements. At common law, prescriptive easements were based on the fictitious "lost grant doctrine" which conclusively presumed [see **presumption**] that there had been a grant of the right which had been lost. This fiction has generally been discarded and prescriptive easements now operate by analogy to adverse possession, under the application of the **Statute of Limitations**. 16 F. 2d 395, 169 N.E. 428. The use must be adverse to the rights of the **owner**, open and notorious, continuous and uninterrupted, and with knowledge and acquiescence of the owner. 201 N.W. 880. There can be no prescriptive rights acquired where the use is with the permission of the record owner or his **agent**. The easement only permits a certain **use**, and has no effect on the underlying **title**.

FIGURE 2–C
STEPHEN H. GIFIS, LAW DICTIONARY (2D ED. 1984)

istry of Gladstone. At present, the royal prerogative .is a matter primarily of historical interest. W. R. Anson, Law and Custom of the Constitution.

2. A right to enjoy certain privileges as an incident to holding office. In the United States, these privileges are likely to be ceremonial rather than substantial. Sometimes applied to usages which have no legal warrant, such as the privilege claimed by Senators and Congressmen of the same party as the President, of being consulted in the distribution of patronage within their states or Congressional districts.

PREROGATIVE COURT. 1. In England, formerly applied to courts of the Archbishops of Canterbury and York and the Anglican Archbishop of Armagh over the administration of estates by decedents, when property was left located in more than one diocese. The jurisdiction was transferred in 1857 to the Court of Probate.

2. The Probate Court of the State of New Jersey up to the reorganization of the courts in that state.

PREROGATIVE WRITS. Writs that were formerly issued by the king in the exercise of the royal prerogative, and later issued by the Royal Courts. They are nearly always matters of discretion. In the United States they are in some cases a matter of right, and improper issuance or refusal may be appealable error. The prerogative writs include **procedendo** (obsolete), **mandamus, prohibition, quo warranto, habeas corpus, certorari.** Seaside Mem. Hosp. v. Cal. Emp. Comm., 143 P. (2) (Cal.) 503.

PRESCRIBE. 1. To assert a claim based on possession or use for a definite period, or from immemorial times. 2. To outlaw or extinguish a right by usage which contradicts it. See **Prescription.**

PRESCRIPTION. 1. At common law, the acquisition of title to land, or to an **easement** or an interest in land, by long user or enjoyment against the will of the former owner, or in disregard of any other claim of title. Formerly it was necessary to show that this user had continued from time immemorial, that is to say, that no one could be found who remembered any other owner, a time so long that "the memory of man runneth not to the contrary." But a fixed period was established in England, i. e., twenty years, by statute of 32 Hen. VIII (1541). This period was adopted in the American colonies and is

still the rule in most of the Eastern states. In the Middle West and West, a much shorter period is required, generally five years. In many states, to establish such a title, the claimant must have paid the taxes during that period.

The term was taken over from the Roman law, and since the history of the word was not known, the fiction of the "lost grant" was invented to account for the etymology, "prae" being taken in its literal sense of "before" and "scriptio" in its literal sense of "writing." See **Adverse Possession; Immemorial; Lost grant.**

2. At Roman law, prescription (Lat. "Praescriptio") was purely a matter of procedure. It was a plea like the **Statute of Limitations,** but in Roman formulary procedure it was placed first, to indicate that no claim would be considered that had not accrued within a certain time. The use of this praescriptio, which was merely a matter of defense and did not create a title, was especially common in suits to recover land so that the term was commonest in this sense. The establishment of such a period of limitations for this type of action took place in imperial times (199 A.D.), and the time was fixed at ten years if both litigants were residents in the same city and twenty, if they were not. Justinian, in 531 A. D. (Cod. Just. 7, 31, 1) assimilated "praescriptio" to "usucapion" which was the older term and which did establish title.

PRESENTATION. 1. In English ecclesiastical law, the nomination by the owner of an **advowson,** to the bishop, of a benefived clergyman to be the rector or vicar of a parish.

2. Equivalent to presentment in the law of commercial paper.

PRESENTMENT. 1. In the law of commercial paper, the producing and offering of a **negotiable instrument** to the maker, drawee or acceptor at the proper time and place. Presentment is one of the conditions necessary to fix the liability of an indorser or anyone secondarily liable. See **Protest.**

2. The formal statement made by a **Grand Jury** of some condition of affairs which has been brought to their notice and which in their opinion requires amendatory action. It is sometimes used of an inquest of office.

3. Before the Copyhold Act of 1894 in England, the official notice taken in court of the surrender of a copyhold.

4. In Victoria, Australia, the formal

263

FIGURE 2-D

MAX RADIN, RADIN'S LAW DICTIONARY (2D ED. 1970)

Burton's <u>Legal Thesaurus</u> (shown below) is divided into two parts: (1) "Main Entries" (front part of the book) and (2) "Index Entries" (back part of the book).

"INDEX ENTRY"   ↓

prescription assignment *(designation)*, brevet, bylaw, canon, citation *(charge)*, cloud *(incumbrance)*, code, codification, condition *(contingent provision)*, constitution, dictate, direction *(order)*, directive, drug, fiat, guidance, law, mandate, measure, order *(judicial directive)*, practice *(custom)*, recommendation, regulation *(rule)*, requirement, rubric *(authoritative rule)*, rule *(legal dictate)*, title *(right)*, usage
prescriptive compulsory, decretal, formal, legislative, orthodox, rightful, traditional, unalienable
prescriptive right droit

"MAIN ENTRY"   ↓

PRESCRIPTION *(Claim of title)*, **noun**
authority, claim, inalienable right, interest, license, prerogative, right, vested interest, vested right
ASSOCIATED CONCEPTS: adverse possession, easement by prescription, right by prescription, title by prescription
FOREIGN PHRASES: *Praescriptio et executio non pertinent ad valorem contractus, set ad tempus et modum actionis instituendae.* Prescription and execution do not affect the validity of the contract, but the time and manner of instituting an action. *Usucapio constituta est ut aliquis litium finis esset.* Prescription was established so that there be an end to lawsuits. *Nihil praescribitur nisi quod possidetur.* There is no prescription for that which is not possessed. *Interruptio multiplex non tollit praescriptionem semel obtentam.* Frequent interruptions do not defeat a prescription once obtained. *Praescriptio est titulus ex usu et tempore substantiam capiens ab auctoritate legis.* Prescription is a title by authority of law, deriving its force from use and time.

PRESCRIPTION *(Custom)*, **noun**
convention, conventional usage, fashion, habit, institution, observance, practice, precedent, tradition, usage, use

PRESCRIPTION *(Directive)*, **noun**
act, authority, axiom, canon, charge, command, decree, dictate, direction, doctrine, edict, enactment, formula, formulary, injunction, instruction, law, maxim, measure, order, ordinance, precept, prescript, principle, proposal, regulation, rubric, rule, ruling, statute, theorem

PRESCRIPTIVE, *adjective*
accepted, acknowledge, acknowledge through possession, acknowledge through use, admitted, binding, commanded by long use, commanding, compulsory, customary, decretal, determined, dictated, established, fixed, legalized, long-established, longstanding, obligatory, ordained by custom, popular, preceptive, prescribed, recognized, recognized because of continued possession, recognized through use, required by custom, rooted, set, settled, timehonored, traditional, traditive, understood, unwritten, usual, vested, wonted
ASSOCIATED CONCEPTS: prescriptive rights

In the "Main Entry" section, whenever a main heading (e.g., prescription) has more than one usage, it is divided into separate subheadings (e.g., claim of title, custom, and directive).

The "Main Entry" section also provides an alphabetical listing of "associated concepts." This listing allows a researcher to find complete legal concepts when only a single, central word comes to mind.

"Foreign phrases" are included under each main heading. This listing is useful because most reference books list foreign phrases alphabetically under the first letter of the foreign word rather than the pivotal English concept.

Using these sources and others, you should be able to develop working definitions that will make you more efficient in using indexes in secondary sources. These sources will also provide synonyms and related concepts that will be useful in using indexes or computer search requests.

FIGURE 2-E
WILLIAM C. BURTON, LEGAL THESAURUS (1980)

pres. See cy pres.

Pres. Abbreviation of "president." 1 Am J2d Abbr § 5.

presbyter (pres'bi-ter). An elder in the church; a delegate representing a local church in presbytery. A priest or minister.

Presbyterian Church. A protestant church. The United Presbyterian Church in the United States of America.

    See **General Assembly; presbytery; synod.**

Presbyterianism. See Calvinism.

presbytery (pres'bi-ter-i). The governing body of the United Presbyterian Church in the United States of America in a district of the church. The district itself.

prescribable (prē-skrī'ba-bl). Capable of, or subject to, being acquired by prescription.

prescribe. To lay down beforehand as a rule of action; to ordain, appoint, define authoritatively. To impose as a peremptory order; to dictate, appoint, direct, ordain. Sevier v Riley, 198 Cal 170, 175, 244 P 323. To give law. State v Seattle Nat. Bank, 130 Wash 69, 226 P 259, 33 ALR 1206, 1209. To give a prescription.

prescribed by law. Made law by actual legislation. Exline v Smith & McFarland, 5 Cal 112. Broadly, made law by any authorized body.

prescribing in a que estate. Prescription in a man and all those persons whose estate he has. 25 Am J2d Ease § 58.

prescription. The acquisition of an easement by adverse user under claim of right for the prescriptive period. The acquisition of incorporeal hereditaments by adverse user. Plaza v Flak, 7 NJ 215, 81 A2d 137, 27 ALR2d 324. A presumption of grant from long possession and exercise of right. 25 Am J2d Ease § 39. In the broad sense of modern times, the gaining of a title by adverse possession. 3 Am J2d Adv P § 4. A direction in writing prepared by a physician, to be presented by the patient to a druggist, setting forth the drug or medicine to be furnished the patient by the druggist and the manner in which it shall be prepared, and directions for its use by the patient. 25 Am J2d Drugs § 5. Any direction to a patient for the use or application by him of any drug for the cure of any bodily disease; even an oral direction for the use of a drug. State v Baker, 229 NC 73, 48 SE2d 61.

    While it has been contended that the term refers only to medical provision for human beings, there seems to be no reason why a recipe or formula for the treatment of animals may not be called a "prescription," from whatever source it may proceed. Ray v Burbank, 61 Ga 505.

    See **municipal corporation by prescription; negative prescription; positive prescription; presumed grant.**

prescription acts. Statutes establishing the respective periods of time within which various rights or titles may be acquired by prescription.

prescriptive easement. An easement arising, created, or acquired by prescription.

    See **prescription.**

prescriptive license. A license in real property acquired by prescription. 33 Am J1st Lic § 97. An anomalous concept, since use under a license, being permissive, cannot ripen into a prescriptive right.

Los Angeles Brick & Clay Products Co. v Los Angeles, 60 Cal App 2d 478, 141 P2d 46.

prescriptive period. The period of time necessary to acquire an easement by prescription. 25 Am J2d Ease § 50.

prescriptive title. See title by prescription.

prescriptive way. See way by prescription.

presence. The bearing or personality of a person. The fact of being at a place at a particular time.

    The meaning of the word depends upon the circumstances. No one can accurately define it. It implies an area which has no metes and bounds. Anything done within the four walls of a room which is free from outside interference is usually done in the presence of all who are in the room whether it is seen or not. But proximity and consciousness may create presence. Nock v Nock's Exrs. 51 Va (10 Gratt) 106, 117.

    See **constructive presence.**

presence of accused. The fundamental principle of criminal procedure that after indictment found, nothing shall be done in the absence of the prisoner and the correlative right of the accused to be present at his own trial. 21 Am J2d Crim L § 271. The right of the accused to be present at all stages of his trial, applicable in all capital cases, in fact, in all felonies; also applicable in prosecutions for misdemeanors to the extent that the accused undoubtedly has the right to be present, although in some jurisdictions authority to proceed in his absence is recognized where only a misdemeanor is involved. 21 Am J2d Crim L § 272.

presence of officer. When an offense is committed so as to justify an arrest without a warrant:—being in such a position that the commission of the offense is on view or that knowledge of the commission of the offense may be acquired by him through any of his senses, including the sense of hearing or smell. 5 Am J2d Arr § 31.

    Under the usual statutory provision authorizing a peace officer to arrest without warrant where an offense is committed in his "presence," the words do not necessarily mean within his sight, but it is held sufficient if the officer arrives on the scene immediately after the encounter, attracted by the noise of it. Porter v State, 124 Ga 297, 52 SE 283.

presence of the court. A phrase to be given a liberal interpretation as it appears in a statute defining contempt of court.

    The court consists not of the judge, the courtroom, the jury, or the jury room individually, but all of these combined, so that the court is present wherever any of these constituent parts is engaged in the prosecution of the business of the court according to law. Anno: 42 ALR2d 970; 17 Am J2d Contpt § 7.

    A court in session is considered present where its officers. jurors, and witnesses are required to be in the performance of their several duties, so that an assault. threat, or act of intimidation against such a person while attendant upon the court is a direct contempt. State v Goff, 28 SC 17, 88 SE2d 788, 52 ALR2d 1292.

    Since the grand jury is an arm of the United States District Court, proceedings before the grand jury are to be regarded as being proceedings in the court. Hence, contempts occurring in the presence of the grand jury are to be treated as taking place in the presence of the court and are therefore subject to be punished summarily by the court, without

FIGURE 2-F

BALLENTINE'S LAW DICTIONARY

Prescribe. To assert a right or title to the enjoyment of a thing, on the ground of having hitherto had the uninterrupted and immemorial enjoyment of it.

To lay down authoritatively as a guide, direction, or rule; to impose as a peremptory order; to dictate; to point, to direct; to give as a guide, direction, or rule of action; to give law. To direct; define; mark out.

In a medical sense "prescribe" means to direct, designate, or order use of a particular remedy, therapy, medicine, or drug.

Prescription. A direction of remedy or remedies for a disease, illness, or injury and the manner of using them. Also, a formula for the preparation of a drug or medicine.

Prescription is a peremptory and perpetual bar to every species of action, real or personal, when creditor has been silent for a certain time without urging his claim. Jones v. Butler, La.App., 346 So.2d 790, 791.

Acquisition of a personal right to use a way, water, light and air by reason of continuous usage. *See also* Prescriptive easement.

International law. Acquisition of sovereignty over a territory through continuous and undisputed exercise of sovereignty over it during such a period as is necessary to create under the influence of historical development the general conviction that the present condition of things is in conformity with international order. State of Arkansas v. State of Tennessee, 310 U.S. 563, 60 S.Ct. 1026, 1030, 84 L.Ed. 1362.

Prescription in a que estate. A claim of prescription based on the immemorial enjoyment of the right claimed, by the claimant and those former owners "whose estate" he has succeeded to and holds.

Real property law. The name given to a mode of acquiring title to incorporeal hereditaments by immemorial or long-continued enjoyment. Hester v. Sawyers, 41 N.M. 497, 71 P.2d 646, 649. Prescription is the term usually applied to incorporeal hereditaments, while "adverse possession" is applied to lands. *See* Hereditaments.

In Louisiana, prescription is defined as a manner of acquiring the ownership of property, or discharging debts, by the effect of time, and under the conditions regulated by law. Each of these prescriptions has its special and particular definition. The prescription by which the ownership of property is acquired, is a right by which a mere possessor acquires the ownership of a thing which he possesses by the continuance of his possession during the time fixed by law. The prescription by which debts are released, is a peremptory and perpetual bar to every species of action, real or personal, when the creditor has been silent for a certain time without urging his claim. In this sense of the term it is very nearly equivalent to what is elsewhere expressed by "limitation of actions," or rather, the "bar of the statute of limitations."

See also Adverse possession; Prescriptive easement.

Prescriptive easement. A right to use another's property which is not inconsistent with the owner's rights and which is acquired by a use, open and notorious, adverse and continuous for the statutory period (*e.g.* twenty years). To a certain extent, it resembles title by adverse possession but differs to the extent that the adverse user acquires only an easement and not title. To create an easement by "prescription," the use must have been open, continuous, exclusive, and under claim of right for statutorily prescribed period with knowledge or imputed knowledge of the owner. Matsu v. Chavez, 96 N.M. 775, 635 P.2d 584, 587. *See also* Adverse possession.

Presence. Act, fact, or state of being in a certain place and not elsewhere, or within sight or call, at hand, or in some place that is being thought of. The existence of a person in a particular place at a given time particularly with reference to some act done there and then. Besides actual presence, the law recognizes *constructive* presence, which latter may be predicated of a person who, though not on the very spot, was near enough to be accounted present by the law, or who was actively co-operating with another who was actually present.

Presence of an officer. An offense is committed in "presence" or "view" of officer, within rule authorizing arrest without warrant, when officer sees act constituting it, though at distance, or when circumstances within his observation give probable cause for belief that defendant has committed offense, or when he hears disturbance created by offense and proceeds at once to scene, or if offense is continuing, or has not been fully consummated when arrest is made.

Presence of defendant. In the trial of all felonies, the defendant or accused has the right to be present at every stage of the criminal proceeding unless he wilfully and without justification absents himself or by his conduct renders it impossible to conduct the trial. In many states, this rule does not obtain as to misdemeanors. Fed.R.Crim.P. 43 specifies when the presence of the defendant is required and not required.

Presence of the court. A contempt is in the "presence of the court," if it is committed in the ocular view of the court, or where the court has direct knowledge of the contempt.

Presence of the testator. Will is attested in presence of testator if witnesses are within range of any of testator's senses. In re Demaris' Estate, 166 Or. 36, 110 P.2d 571, 585, 586. *See* Attestation.

Present, *n.* A gift; a gratuity; anything presented or given.

Present, *adj.* Now existing; at hand; relating to the present time; considered with reference to the present time. *See also* Presentment.

Present ability. As used in describing an element of the crime of assault, it means immediate or a point near immediate as regards the defendant's capacity to inflict harm. People v. Ranson, 40 Cal.App.3d 317, 114 Cal. Rptr. 874, 877.

Present conveyance. A conveyance made with the intention that it take effect at once and not at a future time.

FIGURE 2–G
BLACK'S LAW DICTIONARY

The first edition of <u>Black's Law Dictionary</u> was published in 1891. It is now in its sixth edition (1990). Note that cases or statutes are sometimes cited. Pronunciation of legal terms is also included, when appropriate. A general guide to the pronunciation of Latin terms is provided on pages vii-x in <u>Black's</u>.

Prescription, *n.* **1.** A method of acquiring the right to use a way, water, light, or air by reason of continuous usage (easement by prescription). Claim, interest, right, license, authorization, liberty, warrant, franchise, permit, privilege, title, entitlement, sufferance, clearance, leave, power. **2.** A bar to bringing an action or using a remedy as to claims that have been unasserted for an extended period of time. **3.** A direction or a formula for the preparation and use of a medicine. See prescribe, treatment, medicine, drug, doctor. **4.** A direction or order. See direction (1), command (1), law.

Prescriptive, *adj.* Arising or sanctioned by continuous usage (prescriptive easement). Long-standing, settled, rooted, long-established, fixed. See also customary, immemorial.

Prescriptive easement A right to use another's property, which is acquired by usage that is open, notorious, exclusive, adverse, under claim of right, and continuous for the statutory period of time. See easement, adverse (1), notorious.

FIGURE 2-H
WILLIAM P. STATSKY, LEGAL THESAURUS/DICTIONARY:
A RESOURCE FOR THE WRITER AND COMPUTER RESEARCHER

The above entries would alert a researcher that prescription is closely associated with the term "prescriptive easement." Thus, in checking the index in a secondary source, you would want to check for entries under the terms "prescription" and "prescriptive easement" as well as under the more general term "easement."

Dictionaries, thesauri, and glossaries are also sometimes cited in support of legal arguments. Thus, if the meaning of a word is in dispute, a law dictionary or a general dictionary such as *Webster's* are sometimes relied upon as secondary authority. Law dictionaries are often cited using a special form. For example, the *Bluebook* form for *Black's* is Black's Law Dictionary 210 (6th ed. 1990).

The word or phrase method of search is the principal method of search in some sources other than dictionaries and thesauri, such as West's *Words and Phrases* set. This set is an encyclopedia of definitions and interpretations of legally significant words and phrases in judicial opinions. The permanent edition of this set consists of forty-six principal volumes and is supplemented by annual pocket parts inserted in the back of each volume. To use West's *Words and Phrases* set, you simply look up the word or phrase.

West's *Word and Phrases* set is particularly useful for categorization problems. For example, if your research problem is to determine whether a crane is a "vehicle" for insurance purposes, West's *Words and Phrases* can direct you to cases in which a crane has or has not been characterized as a vehicle in various situations (e.g., when the crane was moving, when it was immobile, when its outriggers were extended, etc.).

Section 2D. Using the Subject Card Catalog to Find Secondary Sources

The subject card catalog can be used to identify texts and treatises dealing with a particular subject. Assume, for example, that you decide to consult the subject card catalog to find secondary sources relevant to the habeas corpus research problem stated in *Problem 2.2*.[3] Several relevant sources could be found by examining cards under the subject heading "HABEAS CORPUS—UNITED STATES" and the subject heading "CRIMINAL PROCEDURE—UNITED STATES." An example of such a source is shown in the following figure.

Library of Congress Call Number   Imprint (place of publication, publisher, and copyright date)

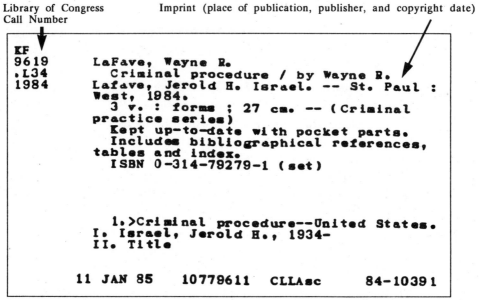

```
KF
9619      LaFave, Wayne R.
.L34          Criminal procedure / by Wayne R.
1984      Lafave, Jerold H. Israel. -- St. Paul :
          West, 1984.
              3 v. : forms ; 27 cm. -- (Criminal
          practice series)
              Kept up-to-date with pocket parts.
              Includes bibliographical references,
          tables and index.
              ISBN 0-314-79279-1 (set)




              1.>Criminal procedure--United States.
          I. Israel, Jerold H., 1934-
          II. Title

          11 JAN 85    10779611  CLLAsc     84-10391
```

FIGURE 2-I

TITLE CARD FROM THE CARD CATALOG

A legal text or treatise can be a good source for persuasive arguments as well as citations to cases, law review articles, and other relevant

---

[3]In addition to using the card catalog, several other methods of finding treatises are possible. For example, because the Library of Congress classification is by subject, you can "browse the shelves" (or the reserve stacks) using the call number for the general subject. Other methods that have been suggested include the following: looking in a casebook for citations to treatises or for a list of treatises published by the same publisher; asking the library staff for assistance; and checking for treatises and texts at a bookstore that carries law books. See Christina L. Kunz et al., The Process of Legal Research: Successful Strategies 29 (2d ed. 1989). See also id. at 31 (noting that "[e]xperienced researchers regularly use this [browsing-the-shelves] method" to find texts and treatises). Researchers may encounter electronic card catalogs rather than traditional card catalogs in many libraries. These online catalogs often provide keyword and subject-heading access.

legal materials. Treatises are works that systematically examine a subject. In law, they generally follow traditional topics and categories. They are often multi-volume works. For instance, there are treatises on search and seizure (e.g., LaFave's *Search and Seizure*), insurance law (e.g., Appleman's *Insurance Law and Practice*), and federal practice (e.g., Wright, Miller, and Cooper's *Federal Practice and Procedure*).

Texts differ from treatises in that they generally are shorter and are oriented to formal study of a subject. In law, one-volume texts devoted to a single legal subject are called "hornbooks." They are designed primarily for student use and quick reference by lawyers. Hornbooks present a textual treatment of the fundamentals of a subject (e.g., Teply and Whitten's *Civil Procedure*; *Prosser and Keeton on the Law of Torts*). They generally address the traditional topics as they are taught in law schools.

In recent years, other types of materials that perform hornbook-like functions have proliferated, such as West's Nutshell series (e.g., Teply's *Legal Negotiation in a Nutshell*), Matthew Bender's Legal Text series (e.g., Sheve and Raven-Hansen's *Understanding Civil Procedure*), and West's Black Letter series (e.g., *Property* or *Family Law*).

Teaching materials designed for classroom use are another kind of specialized text. Today, such materials often mix cases with text, problems, notes, and references. Casebooks are not ordinarily used for legal research, but in extraordinary instances they may be cited by courts.[4]

Section 2E. Index Method of Search

In absence of a known citation to relevant discussion in a text, treatise, or legal encyclopedia, the principal method of finding relevant materials is using the index that accompanies the secondary source that you are consulting. For example, both *American Jurisprudence Second* and *Corpus Juris Secundum* have "General Indexes" and more detailed indexes accompanying each volume of the legal encyclopedia. The index method of search involves checking all pertinent words and legal terms in the index to find references to a specific discussion.

PROBLEM 2.4　Assume that you are researching the "John Doe" problem posed in *Problem 2.3* above. Shown in Figure 2-J are entries in the Index accompanying the "Federal Practice and Procedure" topic in *American Jurisprudence Second*. Find the entry for "Fictitious persons

---

[4]An example of an influential casebook cited by courts is Hart and Wechsler's The Federal Courts and the Federal System. It has been cited even by the United States Supreme Court.

as parties" under "Diversity and alienage jurisdiction."   To which sections are you directed?

Index for the topic "Federal Practice and Procedure"

The citations are to sections of the topic, which appear in three different volumes (32, 32A, and 32B).

INDEX

§§ 1–530 are in Vol. 32; §§ 531–2162 are in Vol. 32A; §§ 2163–2609 are in Vol. 32B

FIGURE 2-J
AMERICAN JURISPRUDENCE SECOND

DISCUSSION OF PROBLEM 2.4 The entry refers to §§ 1443, 1487, and 1494. The following two figures show § 1443 and § 1487.

Volume number →

Section number →

Text of the section →

Supporting citations →

Cross-references to related sources →

32A Am Jur 2d FEDERAL PRACTICE AND PROCEDURE § 1445

§ 1443. Fictitious persons.

State practice often permits the naming of fictitious parties, or "Doe" defendants. It has been held that where there is a cause of action against defendants designated by fictitious names, and substantial relief is sought against them, they are real parties in interest.[18] The naming of such parties does not necessarily divest the court of diversity jurisdiction,[19] but the party invoking the court's jurisdiction has the burden of demononstrating that complete diversity exists. In a removed case, the named defendant must show that none of the Doe defendants are citizens of the plaintiff's state, if the Doe defendants are sufficiently identified in the complaint.[20] But where defendants are designated by fictitious names because their real names are unknown to the plaintiff, it has been held that such parties are merely formal parties.[21]

§ 1444. Garnishees.

A garnishee is merely a nominal party whose citizenship need not be considered.[22]

§ 1445. Guardians.

The citizenship of a general guardian is determinative of federal diversity jurisdiction where under the law of the forum state he has the right to sue in his own name without joining the ward.[23] However, a number of lower federal courts have held that it is the citizenship of the ward, rather than that of the guardian, which is controlling, where, under the law of the forum state, the title to property is in the ward and not in the guardian.[24] Where the conservator has nothing to gain or lose in the action, the injury having been suffered by the ward and recovery belonging to him alone, the citizenship of the ward is determinative of diversity jurisdiction.[25]

The citizenship of an infant or incompetent, rather than that of his guardian ad litem or next friend, is controlling for the purpose of determining whether there is federal diversity jurisdiction.[26] However, it has been held that where

18. Grosso v Butte Electric R. Co. (DC Mont) 217 F 422.

19. Ward v Connor (ED Va) 495 F Supp 434.

As to the possibility that the naming of a fictitious party may constitute collusive joinder, see § 1487, infra.

20. Littlefield v Continental Casualty Co. (CD Cal) 475 F Supp 887.

As to the joinder of fictitious defendants to defeat removal jurisdiction, see § 1494, infra.

21. Loop v Winters' Estate (CC Nev) 115 F 362; Parkinson v Barr (CC Nev) 105 F 81.

Annotation: 8 ALR Fed 675, 687 § 5[b].

22. Bacon v Rives, 106 US 99, 27 L Ed 69, 1 S Ct 3.

US L Ed Digest, Courts § 394.

23. Mexican C. R. Co. v Eckman, 187 US 429, 47 L Ed 245, 23 S Ct 211.

Practice Aids.—Allegation of jurisdiction in diversity case with personal representative as plaintiff and individual as defendant. 1 FED PROC FORMS L Ed § 1:48.

24. Toledo Traction Co. v Cameron (CA6 Ohio) 137 F 48; Ansaldi v Kennedy (DC Mass) 41 F2d 858.

25. Vallentine v Taylor Invest. Co. (DC Colo) 305 F Supp 1104, 8 ALR Fed 546.

26. Mecom v Fitzsimmons Drilling Co., 284 US 183, 76 L Ed 233, 52 S Ct 84 (not followed Miller v Perry (CA4 NC) 456 F2d 63) as stated in Betar v De Havilland Aircraft, Ltd. (CA7 Ill) 603 F2d 30, cert den 444 US 1098, 62 L Ed 2d 785, 100 S Ct 1064, reh den 445 US 947, 63 L Ed 2d 782, 100 S Ct 1347.

Annotation: 68 ALR2d 752; 8 ALR Fed 550.

Practice Aids:—Motion and notice, affidavits, and orders for appointment of guardian ad litem. 1 FED PROC FORMS L Ed §§ 1:224 et seq.

615

FIGURE 2-K
AMERICAN JURISPRUDENCE SECOND

Section number →

Textual discussion →

Section 1494 (the third cited section in the Index) has not been reproduced because it deals with removal jurisdiction.

Supporting footnotes and cross-references →

Molnar case cited →

Page number →

---

§ 1486　　　FEDERAL PRACTICE AND PROCEDURE　　32A Am Jur 2d

decree against a defendant with common citizenship as the plaintiff[81] or where the party making the disclaimer is not dismissed from the action.[82]

§ 1487. Use of fictitious names.

Generally, federal jurisdiction cannot be invoked on the basis of diversity of citizenship by joining a defendant by a fictitious name unless such fictitiously designated defendant actually exists and his citizenship can be truthfully alleged and proved.[83] However, federal jurisdiction may be invoked where the fictitiously named parties are not indispensable, have not been served, and have never been alleged to exist, despite the fact that the complaint could have been dismissed for a failure to show diversity among the parties on its face, where the use of such fictitiously designated parties serves solely to permit the plaintiffs to amend the complaint by the inclusion of other parties if they are discovered.[84]

A plaintiff whose action might be subject to dismissal because of want of diversity of citizenship as a result of having joined, in addition to specifically named defendants, other defendants designated with fictitious names, and who feels, notwithstanding the defective complaint as regards diversity of citizenship, that the action can still be litigated in a federal court, might, prior to appealing the dismissal, offer to amend the complaint by striking the fictitiously designated defendants from the title, and may also employ liberal discovery procedures to turn up other persons who might have the citizenship and connection with the alleged occurrence requisite to joinder as defendants.[85] Appealing solely on the ground of the dismissal as it pertains to the joinder of defendants designated with fictitious names could result in the cost of the appeal being taxed to the party.[86] However, a plaintiff is not guilty of collusion if he sues fewer than all possible defendants, if the absent defendants are not indispensable parties.[87]

---

81. American Fomon Co. v United Dyewood Corp. (DC NY) 1 FRD 171.

82. Wetherby v Stinson (CA7 Wis) 62 F 173.

Annotation: 31 ALR2d 918.

Practice Aids.—Motion for permission to amend complaint to drop party defendant. 1 FED PROC FORMS, L Ed § 1:254.

Order dropping party plaintiff. 1 FED PROC FORMS, L Ed § 1:256.

Order dropping one of several defendants on motion of plaintiff. 1 FED PROC FORMS, L Ed § 1:257.

Defense of lack of diversity. 1 FED PROC FORMS, L Ed § 1:542.

Notice of dismissal without prejudice by plaintiff against defendant improperly sued with reservation of rights against codefendant. 1 FED PROC FORMS, L Ed § 1:935.

Motion and notice, affidavit, and order to dismiss action for lack of diversity. 1 FED PROC FORMS, L Ed §§ 1:1035 et seq.

83. Molnar v National Broadcasting Co. (CA9 Cal) 231 F2d 684; Johnson v General Motors Corp. (ED Va) 242 F Supp 778.

Annotation: 75 ALR2d 717; 8 ALR Fed 675.

634

Practice Aids.—Defense of lack of diversity. 1 FED PROC FORMS, L Ed § 1:542.

Motion to dismiss on jurisdictional grounds. 1 FED PROC FORMS, L Ed § 1:1024.

Motion and notice, affidavit, and order to dismiss action for lack of diversity. 1 FED PROC FORMS, L Ed § 1:1035 et seq.

84. Roth v Davis (CA9 Cal) 231 F2d 681; Hannah v Majors (DC Mo) 35 FRD 179.

As to the citizenship of fictitious parties, see § 1443, supra.

85. Molnar v National Broadcasting Co. (CA9 Cal) 231 F2d 684.

86. Roth v Davis (CA9 Cal) 231 F2d 681.

Practice Aids.—Motion and notice for leave to file amended pleading. 1 FED PROC FORMS, L Ed § 1:681.

Amendment of pleading as a matter of course. 1 FED PROC FORMS, L Ed § 1:682.

Stipulation for amendment of pleading by attorneys. 1 FED PROC FORMS, L Ed § 1:685.

87. Kaplan Co. v Industrial Risk Insurers (ED

FIGURE 2-L

AMERICAN JURISPRUDENCE SECOND

American Jurisprudence Second shown in the foregoing figures and other legal encyclopedias discuss broad legal topics, and the text is supported by citations to cases and other research sources. Like texts and treatises, legal encyclopedias are particularly useful for finding background information on legal subjects and citations to primary sources. Lawyers and courts sometimes cite these encyclopedias for basic legal rules and propositions.

Two legal encyclopedias are national in scope: (1) West's *Corpus Juris Secundum* and (2) Lawyers Cooperative's *American Jurisprudence Second*. These multi-volume sets comprehensively treat all aspects of the law. They are arranged alphabetically by topic, and their text is completely footnoted. They are written and kept up to date by the staff of the publishing companies. Virtually all law libraries have these two sets. Although they may be assigned classification numbers, legal encyclopedias are often treated as reference material. The card catalog and library guide are the best sources for determining which legal encyclopedias the library has and their location in the collection.

Locally oriented legal encyclopedias are available for some jurisdictions. They generally use a format similar to that of the national encyclopedias. Examples include *Florida Jurisprudence Second*, *California Jurisprudence Third*, *Illinois Law and Practice*, *New York Jurisprudence Second*, *Ohio Jurisprudence Third*, *Texas Jurisprudence Third*, *Pennsylvania Law Encyclopedia*, and *Maryland Law and Practice*.

CITING LEGAL ENCYCLOPEDIAS

According to *Bluebook* Rule 15.7(a), legal encyclopedias such as *American Jurisprudence Second* (Am. Jur. 2d) and *Corpus Juris Secundum* (C.J.S.) are cited using a special form:

(1) volume number;

(2) abbreviated title of the encyclopedia;

(3) topic or title in the encyclopedia (in italics or underlined);

(4) section number;

(5) page number(s) ("only if the specific matter cited could not otherwise be readily located within the section") (Rule 3.4); and

(6) copyright date of the volume.

PROBLEM *2.5* Assume that you want to cite discussion in section 1443 shown in Figure 2-K in a memorandum. Based on the above *Bluebook* rules, which one of the following citations would be correct? You may assume that the copyright date of the volume is 1982.

(a) 32A Am Jur 2d <u>Federal Practice & Procedure</u> 615 (1982).

(b) 32A Am. Jur. 2d <u>Federal Practice & Procedure</u> § 1443 (1982).

(c) 32A Am. Jur. 2d 615 (1982).

(d) 32A Am Jur 2d <u>Federal Practice & Procedure</u> § 1443 (1982).

(e) 32A Am. Jur. 2d § 1443 (1982).

DISCUSSION OF PROBLEM 2.5 According to *The Bluebook*, the volume number (32A), the abbreviated name of the encyclopedia (Am. Jur. 2d) (with periods), the title of the section (<u>Federal Practice & Procedure</u>) (underlined or in italics), the section number (§ 1443), and the copyright date of the publication of the volume (1982) should be used to cite the relevant discussion in this encyclopedia. In this instance, because section 1443 is contained on one page, citation of the section is all that is needed. The correct answer is thus answer (b). Had it been necessary to add a reference to the page to identify specific material within the section, the citation would appear as follows: 32A Am. Jur. 2d <u>Federal Practice & Procedure</u> § 1443, at 615 (1982) (assuming, for example, that the specific point cited appeared on page 615 and the section covered several pages—making the location of the relevant material difficult).

In addition to consulting the sections of *American Jurisprudence Second* reproduced in Figures 2-K and 2-L in researching the "John Doe" problem, assume that you consulted the card catalog and found Wright, Miller, and Cooper's treatise on federal practice and procedure. Assume that you consulted the index. Under the main index entry "Diversity of Citizenship," assume that you are directed to § 3642 by the following subentry, "John Doe defendants, defeating jurisdiction, § 3642." Assume that you have located § 3642 of the treatise.

Examine the following figures showing the beginning pages of § 3642 of Wright, Miller, and Cooper's treatise on federal practice and procedure.

Wright, Miller,
and Cooper's
multi-volume
treatise on
federal practice
and procedure
provides
detailed
background
information on
various topics
and commen-
tary on them.
It also provides
supporting
citations that
can lead you to
primary and
other secondary
sources.

Beginning of
§ 3642   ➤

Ch. 3   UTILIZATION OF JOHN DOE DEFENDANTS § 3642

Courts also are beginning to be more realistic in determining diversity on the basis of the citizenship of fiduciaries appointed for special purposes. The Fourth Circuit, in an important decision, has held that when state law requires the appointment of a resident ancillary administrator with limited duties to represent the interests of a nonresident beneficiary in a wrongful death action, the beneficiary's citizenship controls for diversity purposes.[39]

The foregoing discussion has focused on attempts by one party to prevent a dispute from reaching the federal courts on the basis of diversity of citizenship jurisdiction. It has not dealt with bilateral agreements not to resort to the federal courts. Absent the violation of some substantive right, there appears to be no reason why the parties should not be able to negotiate with regard to limiting suit to the state courts. At least one court has so held.[40]

§ 3642.   —— Utilization of John Doe Defendants

The naming of John Doe defendants in the complaint when the identities of the actual defendants are unknown at the time the action is instituted is a device sanctioned by the laws of several states. Basically, it serves two functions.[1] The first is that when a John Doe is named in a complaint, the statute of limitations for the cause of action involved in the litigation is tolled. Consequently, the substitution of a real person for the fictitious defendant can take place well after the statute of limitations has

plaintiff in obvious violation of the legislative purposes underlying diversity jurisdiction." Recent Case, 1969, 83 Harv.L.Rev. 465, 469.

See also

Picquet v. Amoco Production Co., D.C. La.1981, 513 F.Supp. 938.

39. Important decision

Miller v. Perry, C.A.4th, 1972, 456 F.2d 63. The case is discussed at vol. 13B, § 3606.

See also

In Vaughan v. Southern Ry. Co., C.A. 4th, 1976, 542 F.2d 641, Chief Judge Haynsworth reviews the development of this doctrine in the Fourth Circuit.

But compare

Herrick v. Pioneer Gas Prods. Co., D.C.Okl.1976, 429 F.Supp. 80.

40. One court held

Spatz v. Nascone, D.C.Pa.1973, 368 F.Supp. 352.

Compare

M/S Bremen v. Zapata Off-Shore Co., 1972, 92 S.Ct. 1907, 407 U.S. 1, 32 L.Ed.2d 513.

1. Functions of John Doe

Note, Designation of Defendants by Fictitious Names—Use of John Doe Complaints, 1961, 46 Iowa L.Rev. 773.

Comment, Unknown Parties: The John Doe Defendant, 1970 Law & Social Order 256.

143

FIGURE 2-M
WRIGHT, MILLER, & COOPER'S FEDERAL PRACTICE
AND PROCEDURE (2D ED. 1985)

Section →

§ 3642   DIVERSITY OF CITIZENSHIP   Ch. 3

Textual discussion →

run, which means that the action would have been barred but for the naming of a Doe defendant.[2] The second is that personal jurisdiction can be obtained by the service of a John Doe complaint in accordance with the provisions of state law without serving the real person whose identity and whereabouts in the state are unknown. Indeed, if John Doe service is accomplished and the real defendant subsequently leaves the state, that service usually is sufficient to confer personal jurisdiction over him.

The practice of naming John Doe defendants, which appears to be particularly popular in California, has created some subject matter jurisdiction problems for the federal courts. The general rule is that the diverse citizenship of the fictitious defendants must be proven in a federal court action.[3] Thus, for example, in

2. Limitations tolled

Amendments substituting actual for fictitious defendants are treated as amendments to add new parties and will not relate back unless the requirements of Rule 15(c) are satisfied. See, e.g., Craig v. U.S., C.A. 9th, 1969, 413 F.2d 854, certiorari denied 90 S.Ct. 483, 396 U.S. 987, 24 L.Ed.2d 451; Bufalino v. Michigan Bell Tel. Co., C.A.6th, 1968, 404 F.2d 1023, certiorari denied 89 S.Ct. 1468, 394 U.S. 987, 22 L.Ed.2d 763; Hoffman v. Halden, C.A.9th, 1959, 268 F.2d 280, 304; and Phillip v. Sam Finley, Inc., D.C.Va.1967, 270 F.Supp. 292.

Supporting citations and references →

See generally vol. 6, §§ 1498–1503 for a discussion of the relation back of amendments changing parties.

Note, Doe Defendants and Other State Relation Back Doctrines in Federal Diversity Cases, 1983, 35 Stan.L.Rev. 297.

3. Must be proven

Fifty Associates v. Prudential Ins. Co. of America, C.A.9th, 1970, 446 F.2d 1187.

Molnar v. National Broadcasting Co., C.A.9th, 1956, 231 F.2d 684.

Goldberg v. CPC International, Inc., D.C.Cal.1980, 495 F.Supp. 233.

When plaintiff who sought recovery under the Virginia Uninsured Motorist Law in a diversity action in

the federal district court in Virginia named an unknown motorist in the accident as a John Doe defendant and plaintiff could not offer any proof as to the citizenship of that defendant, he failed to sustain his burden of establishing diversity and motions to dismiss would be sustained. Johnson v. General Motors Corp., D.C.Va.1965, 242 F.Supp. 778, 779.

Aetna Ins. Co. of Hartford, Connecticut v. Southern, Waldrip & Harvick, D.C.Cal.1961, 198 F.Supp. 505.

In Stenhouse v. Jacobson, D.C.Cal. 1961, 193 F.Supp. 694, 696–697, the court, in dictum, stated: "[I]f plaintiff desires to join fictitious parties in any further amended complaint * * * he must not only plead, *affirmatively*, but he must prove, *affirmatively*, the citizenship of such defendants * * *. The indiscriminate inclusion of fictitious defendants can serve no purpose except to cloud the jurisdiction of this Court * * *. As the guardian of its own jurisdiction, this Court will look beyond the pleadings, and require factual proof of the citizenship of any fictitious parties in a diversity of citizenship suit." (per Halbert, J.)

The court in Miller & Lux, Inc. v. Nickel, D.C.Cal.1956, 141 F.Supp. 41, ordered the case dismissed un-

Page number →

144

FIGURE 2–N
WRIGHT, MILLER, & COOPER'S FEDERAL PRACTICE
AND PROCEDURE (2D ED. 1985)

Reference to
the leading
case
(Molnar)

Ch. 3   UTILIZATION OF JOHN DOE DEFENDANTS § 3642

Molnar v. National Broadcasting Company,[4] the leading case on
this matter, plaintiff, a citizen of California, brought an action in
federal court against a corporate citizen of Delaware and ten
John Does, who also were alleged to be Delaware citizens, for
injuries allegedly received when she fell on a stairway in the corporation's building. The district court dismissed the complaint
without prejudice because it failed to establish complete diversity. In affirming, the Ninth Circuit stated:

Basic facts of
the case

Quotation from
the court's
decision

> If the identity of defendants were known so that the pleader
> could state they were citizens of Delaware, she could also state
> their names and allege what part each had in the management
> and control of the stairway. But, if the allegation that they are
> citizens of Delaware be, as on the face of the complaint it is,
> unfounded guesswork, the jurisdiction of the court is not estab-
> lished. * * *

less plaintiff dropped some 2,000
John Doe defendants or identified
them with sufficient clarity so that
the court could determine if diversity actually existed.

See also

Claim involving several Doe defendants was properly dismissed because it destroyed federal diversity
jurisdiction. Plaintiffs' leave to
amend might be affected by their
admission in an answer to an inter-
rogatory that they were willing to
dismiss the Doe defendants. Gar-
ter-Bare Co. v. Munsingwear, Inc.,
C.A.9th, 1980, 622 F.2d 416, rere-
ported C.A.9th, 1980, 650 F.2d 975.

See also

Tolefree v. Ritz, C.A.9th, 1967, 382
F.2d 566.

Congress of Racial Equality v. Clem-
mons, C.A.5th, 1963, 323 F.2d 54,
certiorari denied 84 S.Ct. 632, 375
U.S. 992, 11 L.Ed.2d 478.

Littlefield v. Continental Cas. Co.,
D.C.Cal.1979, 475 F.Supp. 887.

But see

The appellate court held that evidence
of Virginia license plates on the car
driven by a Doe defendant involved
in a hit-and-run accident was sufficient to support a finding that the
driver was a Virginian, especially in
the absence of contradictory proof,
and thus to support a finding of diversity, even though it was not established that the driver owned the
car. Sligh v. Doe, C.A.4th, 1979,
596 F.2d 1169 (but compare dissent,
id. at 1172).

Although plaintiff could not prove at
the outset that John Doe defendants were of diverse citizenship,
the court allowed plaintiff to proceed with his suit pending developments that might destroy diversity
jurisdiction. Ward v. Connor, D.C.
Va.1980, 495 F.Supp. 434, reversed
on other grounds C.A.4th, 1981, 657
F.2d 45, certiorari denied 102 S.Ct.
1253, 455 U.S. 907, 71 L.Ed.2d 445.

Until an amendment making someone
that really exists a defendant in
place of a Doe defendant was permitted, Doe defendant allegations
were surplusage and an action
brought by the residents of one
state against the residents of another was not subject to dismissal for
lack of diversity for failure to state
the residence of the Doe defendants. Hannah v. Majors, D.C.Mo.
1964, 35 F.R.D. 179.

4. **Molnar case**

C.A.9th, 1956, 231 F.2d 684.

145

FIGURE 2-O
WRIGHT, MILLER, & COOPER'S FEDERAL PRACTICE
AND PROCEDURE (2D ED. 1985)

§ 3642   DIVERSITY OF CITIZENSHIP   Ch. 3

Continuing
textual
discussion

It is clear, in the absence of this identification or connection or name, that the allegation of citizenship in Delaware is illusory.[5]

Even though the John Doe device is disfavored by many federal courts,[6] and some courts have stated that it is not permitted in federal practice,[7] there is no express statutory or rule prohibition against its use.[8] Since the practice plays an important part in some states in the tolling of the statute of limitations and in the procedure for acquiring personal jurisdiction, an absolute rule against its use in federal court actions seems unwise. On the other hand, as stated above, Doe defendants can be utilized only when plaintiff can prove that their presence does not destroy diversity.[9] Of course, if it is shown that the John Does are not parties whose citizenship typically would be considered in determining diversity,[10] or that the claim being asserted against them is sham or frivolous,[11] their citizenship should be ignored and jurisdiction upheld.

Like many texts
and treatises,
this treatise is
kept up to date
by annual
pocket parts.
You should
always check
the pocket part
for the latest
cases and
developments.

5. Unfounded guesswork

231 F.2d at 686–687 (per Fee, J.).

6. Disfavored device

Fifty Associates v. Prudential Ins. Co. of America, C.A.9th, 1970, 446 F.2d 1187.

Craig v. U.S., C.A.9th, 1969, 413 F.2d 854, certiorari denied 90 S.Ct. 483, 396 U.S. 987, 24 L.Ed.2d 451.

Supporting
footnotes

"These John Doe complaints are dangerous at any time. It is inviting disaster to allow them to be filed and to allow fictitious persons to remain defendants if the complaint is still of record." Sigurdson v. Del Guercio, C.A.9th, 1956, 241 F.2d 480, 482.

7. Not permitted

Applegate v. Top Associates, Inc., D.C.N.Y.1969, 300 F.Supp. 51, affirmed on other grounds C.A.2d, 1970, 424 F.2d 92.

Hall v. Pacific Maritime Ass'n, D.C. Cal.1968, 281 F.Supp. 54, 61.

8. No express prohibition

Craig v. U.S., C.A.9th, 1969, 413 F.2d 854, certiorari denied 90 S.Ct. 483, 396 U.S. 987, 24 L.Ed.2d 451.

"[T]here is no prohibition in judicial or administrative practice to openly and frankly use a fictitious [name] * * * until the true one is made known so long as due process is accomplished." Johnson v. Udall, D.C.Cal.1968, 292 F.Supp. 738, 751.

The inclusion of John Doe defendants in a complaint was held to be mere surplusage unless an amendment actually naming the parties were permitted so that jurisdiction was upheld. Hannah v. Majors, D.C.Mo. 1964, 35 F.R.D. 179.

9. Not destroy diversity

John Hancock Mut. Life Ins. Co. v. Central Nat. Bank in Chicago, D.C. Ill.1983, 555 F.Supp. 1026.

10. Not considered

The citizenship of merely formal or nominal parties to an action is not considered in determining the existence of diversity jurisdiction. See vol. 13B, § 3606.

11. No claim asserted

Plaintiff, a citizen of Ohio, commenced an action in federal court against citizens of California and ten John Doe defendants. After losing on the merits in the district court, plaintiff appealed on the ground that the existence of the Does in the complaint meant that there was no

146

FIGURE 2-P

WRIGHT, MILLER, & COOPER'S FEDERAL PRACTICE
AND PROCEDURE (2D ED. 1985)

PROBLEM 2.6 As noted previously, legal texts and treatises (and other secondary sources) are excellent starting points for gaining perspective and background on unfamiliar areas of the law. They will often provide citations to relevant primary authority and will allow you to formulate a tentative answer to research questions. Based on the text and footnotes shown in the Figures 2-M to 2-P, answer the following questions:

(a) What principal functions does a John Doe complaint serve?

(b) Is there any express statutory authority or rule prohibiting the use of John Doe complaints in federal court?

(c) What is the general rule concerning proof of diverse citizenship of fictitious defendants?

(d) What is the name of the leading case dealing with diversity of citizenship problems in Joe Doe complaints?

DISCUSSION OF PROBLEM 2.6 (a) The text of the treatise (on pages 143-44) explains that John Doe complaints perform two functions. They allow plaintiffs to file actions before the statute of limitations expires (the legal time period during which a plaintiff is allowed to file a claim) and to effect service of process without actually serving the real person whose identity and whereabouts in the state are unknown.

(b) The text (on page 146) indicates that no federal statute or rule expressly prohibits the practice (even though the device is disfavored by many courts and even prohibited by some).

(c) The text (on page 144) states that the general rule is that the diverse citizenship of fictitious defendants must be proven in federal court actions.

(d) The text (on pages 145-46) discusses the leading case on this issue: Molnar v. National Broadcasting Co., 231 F.2d 684 (9th Cir. 1956).

PROBLEM 2.7 Reconsider the discussion of "John Doe" defendants in Figures 2-K and 2-L reproduced from *American Jurisprudence Second* and compare that discussion with the discussion of the subject in Wright, Miller, and Cooper's treatise (Figures 2-M to 2-P). Then, answer the following questions:

(a) Do these sources explain the subject in a different way?

(b) Do they reach the same conclusions as the treatise in the preceding section did?

(c) Do they cite different sources?

(d) In what other ways do legal encyclopedias and treatises differ?

DISCUSSION OF PROBLEM 2.7 Because of the differences in organization and orientation of treatises and encyclopedias, you will find different perspectives and approaches. These differences are due, in part, to the authorship of these sources. Encyclopedias are written by attorneys on the staffs of publishing companies. Treatises are usually written by professors and practicing lawyers. For this reason, in a memorandum or brief, treatises are generally regarded as more respected authority.

In terms of approach, legal encyclopedias fit the treatment into a topic outline (discussed and illustrated in the next section) and tend to present broad, general statements. The discussion in the treatise is more specific and focuses on the particular problem. National legal encyclopedias (*C.J.S.* and *Am. Jur. 2d*) describe the law as it exists in most U.S. states. The law of any one jurisdiction or state is not emphasized and sometimes the distinctions or differences between the laws in various states are not thoroughly explored. While majority and minority positions are described, more specific information on the law of a particular state must be gained from state legal encyclopedias, if available.

Both sources cited the leading case—Molnar v. National Broadcasting Co., 231 F.2d 684 (9th Cir. 1956).[5] The encyclopedia provided references to other works of the publisher, including references to *A.L.R.* annotations, related forms, and other practice aids. Because they take different approaches and cite different sources, both the encyclopedia and treatise provide useful information to a researcher.

In more general terms, legal encyclopedias differ from treatises in the following ways:

(1) legal encyclopedias cover all legal topics in alphabetical order, not just one discrete area of the law (e.g., federal practice and procedure);

(2) legal encyclopedias are written by the editorial staffs of the publishing companies; in contrast, treatises are usually written by law professors or practicing attorneys; and

(3) legal encyclopedias are usually descriptive in nature; in contrast, treatises usually provide critical commentary in addition to description of the state of the law.

The title page of the volume containing the pages reproduced in Figures 2-M through 2-P is shown in Figure 2-Q.

---

[5]The beginning page of the Molnar case is shown in Figure 4-J in Chapter 4 on page 202.

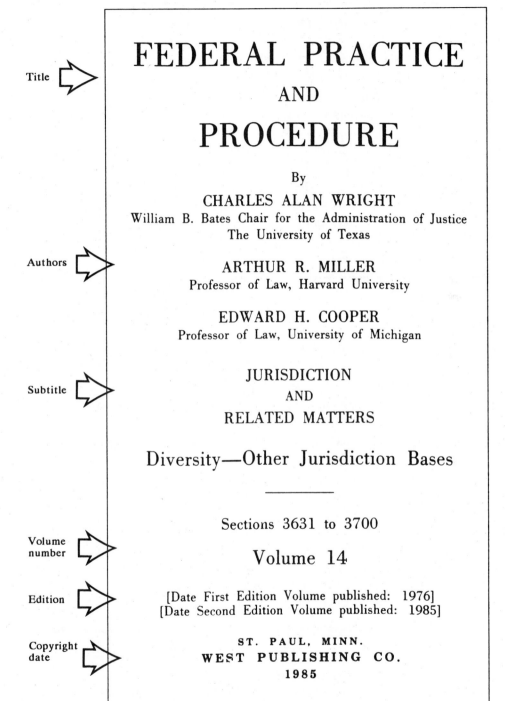

Title ⟹

FEDERAL PRACTICE

AND

PROCEDURE

By

CHARLES ALAN WRIGHT
William B. Bates Chair for the Administration of Justice
The University of Texas

Authors ⟹

ARTHUR R. MILLER
Professor of Law, Harvard University

EDWARD H. COOPER
Professor of Law, University of Michigan

Subtitle ⟹

JURISDICTION
AND
RELATED MATTERS

Diversity—Other Jurisdiction Bases

Sections 3631 to 3700

Volume number ⟹

Volume 14

Edition ⟹

[Date First Edition Volume published: 1976]
[Date Second Edition Volume published: 1985]

Copyright date ⟹

ST. PAUL, MINN.
WEST PUBLISHING CO.
1985

FIGURE 2-Q
WRIGHT, MILLER, & COOPER'S FEDERAL PRACTICE
AND PROCEDURE (2D ED. 1985)

CITING TEXTS AND TREATISES

According to *Bluebook* Rule 15, texts and treatises are generally cited by:

(1) volume number (if more than one);

(2) author's full name as it appears on the publication, with the following modifications:

(a) any middle name(s) should be shortened "to a middle initial unless the author uses an initial in place of his or her name"; in the latter situation the first initial and the full middle name should be retained;

(b) any designation such as "Jr." or "III" should be included; a comma should be inserted "before the designation only if the author does";

(c) a book with two authors should be cited "in the order in which they appear in the publication" (connected with an ampersand (e.g., Larry L. Teply & Ralph U. Whitten);

(d) a book with three or more authors should be cited to the first, followed by "et al.";

(e) when a single volume of a multi-volume work is cited, only the author(s) of the volume cited should be given;

(3) main full title as given on the title page (including a serial number, if any, but omitting a subtitle unless it is particularly relevant);

(4) section, page, or paragraph (if a specific part of the volume is cited)—if the book is organized by sections or paragraphs, the page number(s) should be given "only if the specific matter cited could not otherwise be readily located within the section or paragraph" (Rule 3.4);

(5) edition (if other than the first); and

(6) year of publication.

PROBLEM 2.8 Assume that the section numbers are sequential throughout the treatise and that you want to cite the following quotation from the above treatise in a brief or memorandum: "The general rule is that the diverse citizenship of the fictitious defendants must be proven in a federal court action." Based on *The Bluebook* rules, which one of the following citations would be correct?

(a) 14 Charles A. Wright et al., <u>Federal Practice and Procedure</u> § 3642, at 144 (2d ed. 1985).

(b) Charles Alan Wright, Arthur A. Miller, & Edward H. Cooper, 14 <u>Federal Practice and Procedure</u> § 3642, at 144 (West, 2d ed 1985).

(c) Charles Alan Wright, Arthur A. Miller, & Edward H. Cooper, 14 <u>Federal Practice and Procedure</u> 144 (West, 2d ed 1985).

(d) Charles A. Wright et al., <u>Federal Practice and Procedure</u> § 3642 (2d ed. 1985).

(e) 14 Charles Alan Wright et al., <u>Federal Practice and Procedure</u> 144 (1985).

DISCUSSION OF PROBLEM 2.8   According to *The Bluebook*, treatises, texts, and other books are ordinarily cited by the following: (1) volume number (if more than one) (14); (2) the author's full name but shortening the middle name to a middle initial and et al. when there are three or more authors (Charles A. Wright et al.); (3) title (including a serial number, if any) (<u>Federal Practice and Procedure</u>) (underlined or in italics); (4) section, page, or paragraph (if a specific part of the volume is cited) (§ 3642); (5) edition (if other than the first) (2d ed.); and (6) year of publication (1985).

Because the material quoted appears in the fourteenth volume (see title page reproduced in Figure 2-L), the volume number must precede the authors' names. Thus, answers (b), (c), and (d) are incorrect.

One of the differences between several of the answers is the citation of the section or page (or both). As previously noted, when a book is organized by sections or paragraphs, the section or paragraph number is cited and the page number is added only when "the specific matter could not otherwise be readily located within the section." In this instance, the section number (§ 3642) alone does not easily identify the location of the quoted sentence. Therefore, it is insufficient to cite this treatise by page number or section number alone, and answer (a) (§ 3642, at 144) is correct. Answer (e) is also incorrect because it fails to indicate that the second edition is being cited.

Answers (b) and (c) are incorrect because they include the full names for each author; a book with three or more authors should be cited to the first, followed by "et al." Answers (b), (c), and (e) fail to abbreviate the author's middle name to the initial "A." Answers (b) and (c) are also incorrect because they include the name of the publisher.

Note that you could add the subtitle ("Jurisdiction and Related Matters") of this volume (see Figure 2-Q) if you thought it to be particularly relevant:

14 Charles A. Wright et al., <u>Federal Practice and Procedure: Jurisdiction and Related Matters</u> § 3642, at 144 (2d ed. 1985).

Section 2F. Topic Method of Search

Another method of search is the topic method. Assume that you want to use this method of search in a legal encyclopedia. Each title or topic in a legal encyclopedia commences with a topic outline detailing the organization of the topic. By carefully examining this outline, you can usually find relevant discussion. In using this approach, however, you must recognize how the discussion is likely to be classified, and thus the index approach is often preferred, particularly if the area of law treated in the topic is new to you.

PROBLEM 2.9 Assume that you are interested in locating a discussion of relevant cases concerning the availability of the writ of habeas corpus to remedy an error in impaneling the jury in *Corpus Juris Secundum*. To use the topic method, you would first need to select the proper title. *C.J.S.* has a list of titles that can be consulted. The "General Index" can also be used to find the proper title.

Assume that you have decided that "Habeas Corpus" is the topic that is most likely to contain the relevant discussion and citations. Examine the "Analysis" of this topic shown in Figure 2-R. Which part of the title appears to be the most relevant?

Analysis   Topic   References are to sections

HABEAS CORPUS

Analysis

Sub-Analysis

See also descriptive word index in volume containing end of this Title

452

FIGURE 2-R

CORPUS JURIS SECUNDUM

DISCUSSION OF PROBLEM 2.9   The part of the title that appears to be most relevant is "[Part] III.   GROUNDS FOR RELIEF; ILLEGALITY OF RESTRAINT, §§ 35-135."   Within this part, "[Subdivision] B. PARTICULAR DEFECTS OR ERRORS FOR WHICH RELIEF GRANTED, §§ 41-103" appears to focus on the issue of whether habeas corpus will lie for an error in impaneling the jury.   Within Subdivision B, entry "1. *Defects in Proceedings and Authority for Detention Generally*, §§ 41-68" appears to be on point.

PROBLEM 2.10   Assume that you have decided to turn to the "*Sub-Analysis*" of the title covering §§ 41-68 shown in Figure 2-S. which section appears to be the most relevant?

HABEAS CORPUS   39 C. J. S.

III.   GROUNDS FOR RELIEF; ILLEGALITY OF RESTRAINT—Continued

   B.   PARTICULAR DEFECTS OR ERRORS FOR WHICH RELIEF GRANTED — p 586

      1.   *Defects in Proceedings and Authority for Detention Generally* — p 586

         § 41.   Existence of offense — p 586
         42.   Statutory authority for detention — p 587
         43.   —— Unconstitutional or invalid statute or ordinance — p 588
         44.   Courts, judges, and officers — p 593
         45.   Executive restraints and administrative action generally — p 595
         46.   Acquisition of jurisdiction of person — p 596
         47.   Priority of right to custody — p 596
         48.   Process, warrant, and commitment generally — p 598
         49.   —— Detainer warrant — p 605
         50.   Matters preliminary to criminal charges — p 607
         51.   —— Preliminary detention generally — p 608
         52.   —— Arrest — p 611
         53.   —— Search and seizure — p 614
         54.   —— Preliminary hearing or examination — p 617
         55.   Indictment, information, affidavit, or complaint — p 619
         56.   —— Grand jury proceedings and return of indictment — p 629
         57.   —— Absence of accusatory pleading or use of wrong form — p 633
         58.   Trial generally — p 633
         59.   Delay in proceedings — p 644
         60.   Representation by counsel — p 650
         61.   —— Inadequacy of representation — p 659
         62.   —— Waiver of right to counsel — p 669
         63.   Plea of guilty—Continued
         64.   —— Effect of prior errors or deprivation of rights — p 680
         65.   Defenses — p 683
         66.   —— Former jeopardy — p 687
         67.   Jury — p 690
         68.   Instructions and verdict — p 695

      2.   *Error as to Evidence and Witnesses* — p 698

         § 69.   General considerations — p 698
         70.   Federal habeas corpus to review evidence in state trials generally — p 699
         71.   —— Exhaustion of state remedies — p 701
         72.   Nondisclosure or suppression by prosecution of material evidence — p 708
         73.   Admissibility of evidence generally — p 711
         74.   Confessions and inculpatory statements — p 717
         75.   —— Federal habeas corpus to review state trials — p 719

FIGURE 2-S

CORPUS JURIS SECUNDUM

DISCUSSION OF PROBLEM 2.10 The "Sub-Analysis" leads you to "§ 67. Jury." The beginning of this section is shown below.

---

§§ 66–67 HABEAS CORPUS   39 C.J.S.

ed, by a federal court,[31] where a state's detention of a person violates the constitutional prohibition against double jeopardy,[32] provided petitioner has exhausted his state remedies,[33] in accordance with the rules discussed supra § 24 et seq. In testing a state prisoner's claim of double jeopardy a federal court will apply federal standards.[34] When double jeopardy does not factually exist, the federal courts will not release a person detained under state authority on the ground that his detention is in violation of the Fourteeth Amendment to the federal Constitution.[35]

§ 67. Jury

    a. In general
    b. Exclusion of members of group

a. In General

Habeas corpus ordinarily will not lie because of error or irregularities in drawing, summoning, impaneling, or discharging the jury, or because of a wrongful denial of a jury trial, or disqualification of a juror.

Research Note

    Errors with respect to grand jury proceedings as grounds for habeas corpus are discussed supra § 56. Jury panels and the selection of trial juries are considered generally in C.J.S. Juries §§ 164 et seq., and 192 et seq., respectively.

Library References

    Habeas Corpus ⊕=25.1(3, 4), 45.3.

Generally, habeas corpus will not lie because of error or irregularities in drawing, summoning, or impaneling the jury,[36] or in discharging the jury,[37] although such discharge may be ground

---

31. U.S.—U. S. ex rel. Hetenyi v. Wilkins, C.A.N.Y., 348 F.2d 844, certiorari denied Mancusi v. Hetenyi, 86 S.Ct. 896, 383 U.S. 913, 15 L.Ed.2d 667—U. S. ex rel. Jones v. Nash, C.A.Mo., 264 F.2d 610, certiorari denied 79 S.Ct. 1459, 369 U.S. 936, 3 L.Ed.2d 1548—Hunter v. Wade, C.A.Kan., 169 F.2d 973, affirmed 69 S.Ct. 834, 336 U.S. 684, 93 L.Ed. 974, rehearing denied 69 S.Ct. 1152, 337 U.S. 921, 93 L.Ed. 1730.

Contention rejected by state court
Where prisoner if tried on charge of murder in first degree would be subjected to double jeopardy, but his double jeopardy contention had been rejected by state court, case was not one for abstention by federal district court, and federal district court would grant relief in habeas corpus on charge of murder in the first degree.
U.S.—Grizzle v. Turner, D.C.Okl., 387 F. Supp. 1.

Failure to apply to Supreme Court
Failure of state prisoner to apply to the United States Supreme Court for writ of certiorari to state supreme court's affirmance of his murder conviction with respect to contention of double jeopardy was not bar to federal habeas relief.
U.S.—Smith v. State of Mississippi, C.A. Miss., 478 F.2d 88, certiorari denied 94 S.Ct. 844, 414 U.S. 1113, 38 L.Ed.2d 740.

32. U.S.—Fain v. Duff, C.A.Fla., 488 F. 2d 218—U. S. ex rel. Russo v. Superior Court of New Jersey, Law Division, Passaic County, C.A.N.J, 483 F.2d 7, certiorari denied 94 S.Ct. 447, 414 U.S. 1023, 38 L.Ed.2d 315—Barnett v. Gladden, C.A.Or., 375 F.2d 235.

Special circumstances
Where habeas corpus petitioner was confined in county jail awaiting retrial on charge of murder after his first trial had been declared a mistrial by judge following a finding that jury could not reach a verdict and petitioner contended that retrial would violate his constitutional

right not to be placed twice in jeopardy, special circumstances existed enabling federal court to entertain application for writ of habeas corpus notwithstanding fact that petitioner had not yet gone through the trial.
U.S.—McGuire v. Blubaum, D.C.Ariz. 376 F.Supp. 284.

33. U.S.—U. S. ex rel. Rogers v. La-Vallee, C.A.N.Y., 463 F.2d 185, appeal after remand, 517 F.2d 1330—Lindsay v. U. S., C.A.Pa., 453 F.2d 867, certiorari denied 92 S.Ct. 1796, 406 U.S. 925, 32 L.Ed.2d 127—Johnson v. Beto, C.A.Tex., 436 F.2d 1063—Smart v. Balkcom, C.A. Ga., 352 F.2d 502—Phillips v. McCauley, C.C.A.Wash., 92 F.2d 790.

Aguilar v. Swenson, D.C.Mo., 351 F. Supp. 907—Johnson v. Woods, D.C.Cal., 323 F.Supp. 1393—Lawson v. Neil, D.C. Tenn., 319 F.Supp. 550.
Jurisdiction of federal courts to release persons in state custody see infra §§ 147–156.

Remedies held exhausted
U.S.—Thomas v. Beasley, C.A.Tenn., 491 F.2d 507, certiorari denied 94 S.Ct. 3083, 417 U.S. 955, 41 L.Ed.2d 674—Fain v. Duff, C.A.Fla., 488 F.2d 218.

Thames v. Justices of Superior Court, D.C.Mass., 383 F.Supp. 41—McGuire v. Blubaum, D.C.Ariz., 376 F.Supp. 284.

34. U.S.—U. S. ex rel. Somerville v. State of Illinois, C.A.Ill., 429 F.2d 1335, vacated on other grounds Somerville v. Illinois, 91 S.Ct. 1250, 401 U.S. 1007, 28 L.Ed.2d 543, on remand, C.A., 447 F.2d 733, reversed, State of Illinois v. Somerville, 93 S.Ct. 1066, 410 U.S. 458, 35 L.Ed.2d 425—Amrine v. Tines, C.C.A. Kan., 131 F.2d 827.

35. U.S.—Smith v. Cox, C.A.Va., 435 F. 2d 453, vacated on other grounds Slayton v. Smith, 92 S.Ct. 174, 404 U.S. 53, 30 L.Ed.2d 209—Tipton v. Baker, C.A. N.M., 432 F.2d 245—Povich v. Sanford, C.C.A.Ga., 157 F.2d 873, certiorari de-

nied 67 S.Ct. 977, 330 U.S. 840, 91 L.Ed. 1286—U. S. ex rel. Herndon v. Nierstheimer, C.C.A.Ill., 152 F.2d 453—Amrine v. Tines, C.C.A.Kan., 131 F.2d 827.

People of State of New York v. Baker, D.C.N.Y., 354 F.Supp. 162—U.S. ex rel. Mayberry v. Yeager, D.C.N.J., 321 F.Supp. 199—U.S. ex rel. Bland v. Nenna, D.C.N.Y., 282 F.Supp. 754, affirmed 393 F.2d 416, certiorari denied 88 S.Ct. 2323, 392 U.S. 941, 20 L.Ed.2d 1403.
Double jeopardy for same offense as denying due process of law see C.J.S. Constitutional Law § 582.

36. U.S.—U. S. v. Oates, C.C.A.Alaska, 61 F.2d 536.
Harrison v. Skeen, D.C.W.Va., 125 F. Supp. 547, appeal dismissed 226 F.2d 217.
Idaho.—In re Blades, 86 P.2d 737, 59 Idaho 682.
Iowa.—Sieren v. Hildreth, 118 N.W.2d 575, 254 Iowa 1010.
Ky.—Sexton v. Buchanan, 168 S.W.2d 19, 292 Ky. 716.
N.J.—In re Davis, 152 A. 188, 107 N.J.Eq. 160.
Okl.—Corpus Juris Secundum quoted in In re Hackett, 225 P.2d 184, 186, 93 Okl.Cr. 82.
Wash.—In re Miller, 225 P. 429, 129 Wash. 538.
29 C.J. p 48 note 77.

37. Ala.—Parham v. State, 231 So.2d 899, 285 Ala. 334.
Md.—Brigmon v. Warden of Md. Penitentiary, 131 A.2d 245, 213 Md. 628, certiorari denied 77 S.Ct. 1390, 354 U.S. 927, 1 L.Ed.2d 1440.
Neb.—In re Salistean, 235 N.W. 330, 120 Neb. 757.
Nev.—Adams v. State, 469 P.2d 65, 86 Nev. 358.
N.J.—In re Davis, 152 A. 188, 107 N.J.Eq. 160.
N.Y.—People ex rel. Totalis v. Craver, 20

690

FIGURE 2-T
CORPUS JURIS SECUNDUM

The topic method of search described on the preceding pages could have been used to find the relevant discussion in *American Jurisprudence Second*. *American Jurisprudence Second* titles are listed in the "Desk Book" accompanying the set as well as on the outside bindings. It also has an initial "Skeleton Outline," followed by an expanded outline of the topic.

PROBLEM 2.11 Shown in Figure 2-U is a portion of the detailed organization of the "Habeas Corpus" topic covering trial in *American Jurisprudence Second*. Under which section would you look to find the discussion of defects in impaneling the jury?

§ 40. Generally
§ 41. Excessive bail
§ 42. Capital cases
§ 43. Pending appeal

3. ACCUSATORY PLEADING AND RELATED MATTERS

§ 44. Generally; lack of indictment or failure to indict
§ 45. Irregularity in finding or return of indictment
§ 46. Defects and irregularities in indictment
§ 47. Defects in allegations
§ 48. — Failure to charge criminal offense
§ 49. Organization of grand jury

4. TRIAL

§ 50. Generally
§ 51. Denial of speedy trial
§ 52. Holding trial at improper time or place; venue
§ 53. Denial of right to counsel
§ 54. Use of involuntary confession
§ 55. Denial of or interference with right to appeal
§ 56. Denial of jury trial
§ 57. Exclusion of members of petitioner's race from jury
§ 58. Defects in organization of trial jury
§ 59. Failure to present matters of defense
§ 60. — Insanity or mental incompetence
§ 61. — Former jeopardy
§ 62. Admission or exclusion of evidence
§ 63. Erroneous or irregular verdict

5. JUDGMENT, SENTENCE, AND COMMITMENT THEREUNDER

§ 64. Generally
§ 65. Effect of foreign judgment
§ 66. Duration and extent of sentence and punishment
§ 67. — Excessive sentence
§ 68. — Fine and imprisonment
§ 69. Deficient sentence
§ 70. Place of imprisonment
§ 71. Errors and irregularities in commitment to and detention in prison
§ 72. Delay in executing sentence of death
§ 73. Cruel and unusual punishment

6. PARDON, PAROLE, AND PROBATION

§ 74. Generally; continued detention after grant of pardon
§ 75. Recommitment of prisoner

175

Outline of the topic ➤

FIGURE 2-U
AMERICAN JURISPRUDENCE SECOND

DISCUSSION OF PROBLEM 2.11 The relevant discussion appears to be located in "§ 58 Defects in organization of trial jury" listed under the general heading "Trial." The beginning part of § 58 is shown below.

tion of a judgment of conviction on a plea of guilty of murder, and the fixing of the punishment without the intervention of a jury, are not jurisdictional errors and, hence, not open to attack on habeas corpus.[10] It seems equally clear that in a jurisdiction which adheres to the view that the denial of the right to a jury trial is ground for relief in habeas corpus against imprisonment under a judgment of conviction, the competency of the accused to waive such right may be tested in a habeas corpus proceeding.[11] There is authority that denial of the right to a jury trial may not be raised on habeas corpus but must be raised by appeal.[12]

§ 57. Exclusion of members of petitioner's race from jury.

Where the petitioner has been convicted by a jury from which members of his race have been systematically excluded because of their race, he is entitled to be discharged from confinement on habeas corpus,[13] regardless of whether the exclusion was accomplished through the legislature, through the courts, or through executive or administrative officers.[14]

Relevant Section (§ 58) →

§ 58. Defects in organization of trial jury.

Textual discussion →

Mere errors or irregularities in the selection or formation of petit juries cannot be inquired into in habeas corpus proceedings.[15] Thus, disqualification of a juror is not available as a ground for release on habeas corpus, being a mere error or irregularity.[16] Nor, although there is authority to the contrary,[17] does the writ lie for error in discharging a jury.[18] The contention that a conviction of a misdemeanor was based on the verdict of a jury not sworn cannot be raised in habeas corpus proceedings.[19] And the facts that, in a capital case, the accused exhausted his peremptory challenges and the court erroneously overruled his challenges for cause cannot be raised in a habeas corpus proceeding brought with the purpose of attacking a conviction, notwithstanding that such rulings operated to deprive the accused, partially at least, of opportunity to obtain an impartial jury.[20]

Footnotes →

hill v Smyth, 185 **Va** 986, 41 SE2d 11; Re Staff, 63 **Wis** 285, 23 NW 587.

10. Lowery v Howard, 103 **Ind** 440, 3 NE 124.

As to plea of guilty as waiver of jury trial, see 21 Am Jur 2d, CRIMINAL LAW §§ 484 et seq.

11. Re Staff, 63 **Wis** 285, 23 NW 587.

12. Canter v Warden of Maryland House of Correction, 211 **Md** 643, 127 A2d 139, cert den 353 US 913, 1 L Ed 2d 667, 77 S Ct 671.

13. Brown v Allen, 344 US 443, 97 L Ed 469, 73 S Ct 397, reh den 345 US 946, 97 L Ed 1370, 73 S Ct 827, ovrld on other grounds Townsend v Sain, 372 US 293, 9 L Ed 2d 770, 83 S Ct 745; United States ex rel. Seals v Wiman (CA5 Ala) 304 F2d 53, cert den 372 US 915, 9 L Ed 2d 722, 83 S Ct 717, cert den 372 US 924, 9 L Ed 2d 729, 83 S Ct 741; United States ex rel. Goldsby v Harpole (CA5 Miss) 263 F2d 71, cert den 361 US 838, 4 L Ed 2d 78, 80 S Ct 58.

14. United States ex rel. Goldsby v Harpole, supra.

15. Sieren v Hildreth, 254 **Iowa** 1010, 118 NW2d 575; Ex parte Benefield, 31 **Okla** Crim 1, 236 P 625; Younger v Hehn, 12 **Wyo** 289, 75 P 443.

16. Ex parte Sullivan (CA9 Ariz) 83 F2d 796; Ex parte Blades, 59 **Idaho** 682, 86 P2d 737.

Annotation: 124 ALR 1084.

17. Ex parte Tice, 32 Or 179, 49 P 1038 (discharge of jury on Sunday).

18. Ex parte McLaughlin, 41 **Cal** 211.

The discharge of a jury in a criminal case on Sunday, if unlawful, and thereby equivalent to an acquittal, will not entitle the defendant, afterward committed on a judicial day for further trial, to a discharge on habeas corpus, since the unlawful discharge does not divest the trial court, where the question of former jeopardy must be determined, of jurisdiction. Hovey v Sheffner, 16 **Wyo** 254, 93 P 305.

19. Ex parte English (**Tex** Crim) 53 SW 106.

20. Re Schneider, 148 US 157, 162, 37 L Ed 404, 406, 13 S Ct 572.

220

FIGURE 2-V

AMERICAN JURISPRUDENCE SECOND

PROBLEM 2.12 Compare the discussion in section 58 of *American Jurisprudence Second* shown in Figure 2-V with the Black Letter summary and the initial text of section 67 in *Corpus Juris Secundum* shown in Figure 2-T.

(a) Do these sections reach similar conclusions?

(b) Are the same cases cited in footnote 36 of *Corpus Juris Secundum* and in the footnotes shown in section 58?

DISCUSSION OF PROBLEM 2.12 Both encyclopedias state that habeas corpus generally will not lie to inquire into errors or irregularities in impaneling the jury. Both encyclopedias cite the same Idaho case (the *Blades* case). Several other cases are cited in footnote 36 in *Corpus Juris Secundum*. Footnotes 15 and 16 in *American Jurisprudence Second* list fewer cases. In footnote 16, however, a reference to an *A.L.R. Annotation* on point is given, which could be consulted to find additional cases.

Section 2G. Finding and Citing Legal Periodicals

Recall from Chapter 1 that articles in legal periodicals, like treatises and legal encyclopedias, are persuasive secondary authorities sometimes cited by courts. Articles in legal periodicals usually provide thorough analysis of legal topics supported by extensive case and statutory citations. These citations provide a wealth of information for a researcher. Articles in legal periodicals are also particularly useful for identifying trends in the law and for finding criticism of decisions and legal rules.

Legal periodicals are published by law schools, bar associations, and commercial sources. Some focus on specialized areas of law. Most law libraries have a wide array of legal periodicals. Small law libraries generally will have legal periodicals published in the local area or region and perhaps some of the leading national reviews, such as the *Harvard Law Review*, *Yale Law Journal*, and others. Many periodicals are now also available through legal databases.

The following table summarizes the types of legal periodicals available and their general characteristics:

LEGAL PERIODICALS, NEWSLETTERS, AND NEWSPAPERS

Type of Publication	General Characteristics
Traditional Academic Law Reviews (e.g., *University of Florida Law Review*)	Intellectual discussion and critique of the legal theories, recent developments, and trends in the law; ordinarily edited by students at American law schools; typical issue divided into three basic sections—(1) "lead" articles written by professors or practitioners; (2) "notes," "comments," "case notes," "case comments" written by students; and (3) book reviews; some issues ("symposium") focus entirely on particular topic; some issues ("annual survey") focus on legal developments in a state or judicial circuit.
Special Interest Periodicals (e.g., *Georgetown Immigration Law Journal*)	Focus on a specialty area of the law; published by law schools, organizations, or commercial publishers; some are interdisciplinary.
Bar Association Journals (e.g., *Florida Bar Journal*)	Articles on legal subjects and matters of interest to the members of the bar; published by national, state, and local bar associations; also published by sections of the American Bar Association (e.g., Section of Antitrust Law publishes the *Antitrust Law Journal*).
Legal Newsletters (e.g., *Resource Law Notes*)	*Legal Newsletters in Print* lists over 1000 newsletters on legal topics; newsletters generally focus on recent developments in specialty areas.
Legal Newspapers (e.g., *New York Law Journal* and *Legal Times*)	Coverage of legal issues, legal developments, and the legal profession in the national legal newspapers; legal notices and matters of local interest in local daily legal newspapers.

One way to find a legal periodical is through a direct reference in some source (e.g., in footnote 1 in Figure 2-M: "Note, Designation of

Defendants by Fictitious Names—Use of John Doe Complaints, 1961, 46 Iowa L. Rev. 773" and "Comment, Unknown Parties: The John Doe Defendant, 1970 Law & Social Order 256." Figure 2-W shows the beginning page of the cited *Iowa Law Review* article.

Once a citation to a legal periodical is known, a particular source can ordinarily be located by first finding the periodical in the library—legal periodicals are not classified in many law libraries but instead are shelved alphabetically by title.

After the particular review has been located, the relevant volume and page can be located (the volume numbers and dates are printed on the bindings).

IOWA LAW REVIEW

Published four times a year by students of the College of Law of the State University of Iowa. Issued Fall, Winter, Spring, and Summer.

$4.50 Per Year   **$1.75 This Issue**

If the subscriber wishes his subscription to the Review discontinued at its expiration, he should send notice to that effect; otherwise it will be assumed that a continuation is desired.

BOARD OF EDITORS

RICHARD R. ALBRECHT
Editor-in-Chief

DONALD R. HARRIS
CHARLES R. WOLLE
Notes Editors

JOHN A. BRADY
WALTER P. DOYLE
JAMES L. KELLEY
Comments Editors

L. MINOR BARNES, CRAIG A. BECK, ROBERT E. BOUMA, ALLEN E. BRENNECKE, PHILLIP L. BUSH, WILLIAM H. CARMICHAEL, JOHN C. CORTESIO, ALAN D. CULLISON, CHARLES F. FAIRALL, RICHARD W. FARWELL, DAVID J. FISHER, G. LARRY GRIFFITH, RICHARD L. HARRING, DON A. JENSEN, DAVID E. KINTON, PHILIP C. MILLS, THOMAS J. SCHEUERMAN, LARRY L. VICKREY, LYNN K. VORBRICH, THOMAS L. WINE

Other Student Contributors to the Summer Issue
GARY L. ANDERSON, DONNIE R. BENNETT, DAVID E. BYERS, FRANKLIN S. FORBES, BRIAN R. HEANEY, ROGER L. LANDE

NOTES

DESIGNATION OF DEFENDANTS BY FICTITIOUS NAMES—
USE OF JOHN DOE COMPLAINTS

In a mobile and impersonal society, situations occasionally arise in which a person finds it necessary to sue another whose name is unknown.[1] The value of a procedure which allows an action to be brought against an unknown defendant by the use of a fictitious name, such as John Doe, is apparent in several instances. The most obvious situation is when the plaintiff does not know the name of the person whom he wishes to sue and the running of the statute of limitations threatens to bar his cause of action.[2] A procedure allowing the designation of such a party by a fictitious name will avoid this difficulty because the defendant, when actually served, is deemed to have been a party

---

[1] It is not within the scope of this Note to consider John Doe indictments in criminal cases. For statutes allowing this procedure, see, *e.g.*, CAL. PEN. CODE § 953; IOWA CODE § 773.7 (1958); OKLA. STAT. tit. 22, § 409.3 (1951); S.D. CODE § 34.3010 (3) (Supp. 1960); TENN. CODE ANN. § 40-1803 (1955).

[2] See, *e.g.*, Hoffman v. Keeton, 132 Cal. 195, 64 Pac. 264 (1901); Irving v. Carpentier, 70 Cal. 23, 26, 11 Pac. 391, 392 (1886); Farris v. Merritt, 63 Cal. 118, 119 (1883); Larson v. Barnett, 101 Cal. App. 2d 282, 288-90, 225 P.2d 297, 301-02 (3d Dist. 1950).

773

FIGURE 2-W
IOWA LAW REVIEW

In absence of a direct citation of an article in a legal periodical, access to legal periodicals can be gained by using various periodical indexes, many of which are now available in databases. The following table summarizes the principal indexes and their general characteristics:

PRINCIPAL LAW AND LAW-RELATED PERIODICAL INDEXES

Index	Coverage	Sources Indexed
"Jones-Chipman" Index to Periodical Literature	1770-1933	Provides access to articles prior to 1908 (when the traditional *Index to Legal Periodicals* began)
Index to Legal Periodicals (also "Wilsonline" and on LEXIS and WESTLAW)	1908 to present (online since 1981)	Uses same basic format as the traditional *Readers' Guide to Periodical Literature*; indexes 500+ legal periodicals
Current Law Index	1980 to present	Indexes 700+ legal and law-related periodicals
Legal Resource Index (also "Legal-Trac" and on LEXIS)	1980 to present	Same as *Current Law Index* but also legal newspapers and several general newspapers and magazines
Current Index to Legal Periodicals	Current	300+ very recent legal periodicals
Legal Contents	Current	Tables of contents from about 175 newly issued legal periodicals
Index to Foreign Legal Periodicals	1960 to present	400+ periodicals, primarily from non-common-law countries; emphasis on international law
Index to Periodical Articles Related to Law	1958 to present	Wide range of non-legal periodicals not indexed in the principal American legal indexes

Figure 2-X below shows where the *Iowa Law Review* article reproduced in Figure 2-W was indexed in the *Index to Legal Periodicals.*

The <u>Index to Legal Periodicals</u> currently has a combined "Subject and Author Index," "Table of Cases Commented Upon," "Book Review Index," and "Table of Statutes Commented Upon."

Until 1983, the entry under an author's name referred to the main topic under which the author's article was indexed; the first letter of the title of the article was given in parentheses to facilitate finding the article under the listed topic (because the articles are listed alphabetically by title).

INDEX TO LEGAL PERIODICALS, 1958-1961   SUBJECTS   473

Parol evidence admissible to establish fraud in inducement of contract containing merger clause [Dallas Farm Mach. Co. v. Reaves (Tex) 307 S W 2d 233] S T L J 3:271 Spring '58
Parol evidence for the construction of deeds and wills in Alabama. J. E. Thornton. Ala L Rev 12:1 Fall '59
Parol evidence of agency capacity admitted to defeat indorsee [Norman v. Beling (NJ) 163 A 2d 129] Stan L Rev 13:407 Mr '61
Parol evidence shows release limited to original tortfeasor [Couillard v. Charles T. Miller Hosp. Inc (Minn) 92 N W 2d 96] Ohio S L J 20:375 Spring '59
Parol evidence to explain intention underlying a writing. N Y U Intra L Rev 14:52 N '58
Parol evidence to explain written contract [Henry Boot & Sons v. London County Council [1959] 1 W L R 133] L Q Rev 75:149 Ap '59
Property—transfer of immovable community property—estoppel and the parol evidence rule. [Cato v. Bynum (La) 98 S 2d 257] La L Rev 18:746 Je '58
Relaxation of the parol evidence rule. J. L. Buchanan. S A L J 76:271 Ag '59
Sales—admission of parol evidence to annul an authentic act [Smith v. Smith (La) 119 S 2d 827] La L Rev 21:680 Ap '61
Sales—effect of ambiguity in description of land excepted from sale—admissibility of parol evidence [Blevins v. Manufacturer's Record Publ. Co (La) 105 S 2d 392] La L Rev 20:178 D '59

PAROLE
Adult probation, parole, and pardon in California. H. R. MacGregor. Tex L Rev 38:887 O '60
Concepts of treatment in probation and parole supervision. C. L. Newman. Fed Prob 25:11 Mr '61
Criminal law—appearance bond held improper as a condition for parole in Colorado [Logan v. People (Colo) 332 P 2d 897] How L J 5:242 Je '59
Criminal law: the effect of a felony committed by a prisoner who is on parole: a comparison of the New York and California rules [People ex rel Watkins v. Murphy (NY) 143 N E 2d 910] Hastings L J 10:105 Ag '58
Day-parole of misdemeanants. S. B. Powers. Fed Prob 22:42 D '58
Effect of parole on public assistance grants. P. J. Gernert. NPPA J 5:273 Jl '59
Federal convict on conditional release held to have no right to counsel at parole board revocation hearing [Lopez v. Madigan, 174 F Supp 919] U Pa L Rev 108:423 Ja '60
Federal parole and the indeterminate sentence. G. J. Reed. Fed Prob 23:12 D '59
Interstate cooperation in probation and parole. E. A. Burkhart. Fed Prob 24:24 Je '60
Law of parole. Wayne L Rev 5:237 Spring '59
National parole board. T. G. Street. Crim L Q 2:415 F '60
Pardon, probation and parole in Kansas. D. A. Spiegel. Kan L Rev 6:421 My '58
Parole supervisor in the role of stranger. E. H. Johnson. J Crim L 50:38 My-Je '59
Parolees in the Army during World War II. H. W. Mattick. Fed Prob 24:49 S '60
Policies of the parole board. G. J. Reed. F R D 27:324 Je '61
Problems, policies and objectives of the Oklahoma pardon and parole board. C. C. Chesnut. Okla B A J 32:795 Ap 29 '61
Rules and regulations of the board of pardons of the State of Utah. Utah B Bull 29:85 My-Ag '59
Speaking as a citizen. E. S. Gardner. Fed Prob 23:3 Mr '59
Strong man bends steel and straightens men. E. C. DiCerbo. Fed Prob 24:26 S '60
Supervision of paroled drug addicts. W. C. Bailey. NPPA J 5:53 Ja '59
Use of section 4208(a), eligibility for parole. G. H. Boldt. F R D 27:303 Je '61
  See also
Pardon

PARTIES TO ACTION
Compulsory joinder of unwilling plaintiffs in civil actions. Mo L Rev 25:63 Ja '60
Designation of defendants by fictitious names —use of John Doe complaints. Ia L Rev 46:773 Summer '61

Entire properly laid cause of action erroneously transferred when plea of privilege of one joint obligor was not controverted [Steadman v. International Harvester Co (Tex) 319 S W 2d 791] Tex L Rev 38:345 F '60
Equitable assignment and joinder of parties. Vict U C L Rev 2:52 N '56
Federal court interpretations of the real party in interest rule in cases of subrogation. T. L. Kessner. Neb L Rev 39:452 My '60
Federal rule 21—federal jurisdiction preserved and perfected. Ia L Rev 44:193 Fall '58
Federal rules of civil procedure: substitution of public officers: the 1961 amendment to rule 25(d). C. A. Wright. F R D 27:221 My '61
In personam jurisdiction in multiple-party suits. U Chi L Rev 26:643 Summer '59
Incompetency—right of unadjudicated incompetent to sue or to hire attorneys in his own behalf [Sengstack v. Sengstack (NY) 151 N E 2d 887] Fordham L Rev 27:629 Winter '58-'59
Joinder of controlling non-parties: eliminating hide-and-seek in patent litigation [Schnell v. Peter Eckrich & Sons, 81 Sup Ct 557] Yale L J 70:1166 Je '61
Joinder of parties in civil actions in California. So Calif L Rev 33:428 Summer '60
Joinder of parties in Louisiana. H. G. McMahon. La L Rev 19:1 D '58
Joinder of parties when litigating water rights. Baylor L Rev 11:181 Spring '59
Joinder of state in quiet title and foreclosure proceedings. J. W. Reynolds. Wis B Bull 33:27 D '60
Misnomer and mistaken choice [In re Nos. 55 & 57 Holmes Road [1958] 2 W L R 975] L Q Rev 74:346 Jl '58
Mutuality and conclusiveness of judgments. J. W. Moore. T. S. Currier. Tul L Rev 35:301 F '61
Parties to dram shop actions. W. J. Voelker, Jr. U Ill L F 1958:207 Summer '58
Physicians and surgeons—concurrent negligence—joint liability [Cassity v. Brady (Kan) 321 P 2d 171] J B A Kan 27:301 F '59
Practice and procedure—parties to action—federal employees' liability act—refusal to grant motion to implead third party defendant not an abuse of trial court's discretion [Missouri Kan. Tex. R.R. v. Wright (Tex) 311 S W 2d 440] Tex L Rev 37:111 N '58
Problem of capacity in union suits—a potpourri of Erie, diversity and the federal rules of civil procedure [Underwood v. Maloney, 256 F 2d 334] Yale L J 68:1182 Mv '59
Procedure—joinder—royalty owners as necessary or indispensable parties [Royal Petroleum Corp. v. Dennis (Tex) 332 S W 2d 313] Sw L J 15:172 '61
Property—land suits—necessity of the wife's joinder as a party defendant [Wilson v. Mitchell (Tex) 299 S W 2d 406] Baylor L Rev 10:79 Winter '58
Representative action: the modern position. S. J. Stoljar. U Western Aust Ann L Rev 4:58 D '57
Revival. L T 228:34 Ag 21 '59
Sovereign consent to suit: third-party practice and the right to jury trial. Geo L J 48:737 Summer '60

PARTITION
Mineral interests in Oklahoma [Harper v. Ford (Okla) 317 P 2d 210] Okla L Rev 11:345 Ag '58
Partition of land by grantee of easement [Baltimore G. & E. Co. v. Bowers (Md) 157 A 2d 610] Md L Rev 21:146 Spring '61
Partition of mineral interests. C. B. Wallace. Inst Oil & Gas L & Taxation 9:211 '58
Power of equity to bind unborn persons to a sale for partition [Hardy v. Leager (Md) 130 A 2d 737] Md L Rev 18:254 Summer '58

PARTNERSHIPS
Action in Indiana on Kintner-type organizations. E. E. Lyon. Taxes 39:266 Mr '61
Agency and partnership. C. R. Morris, Jr. Rutgers L Rev 14:375 Winter '60
Association problem in joint ventures and limited partnerships. J. P. Driscoll. N Y U Inst Fed Taxation 17:1067 '59
—Oil & Gas Tax Q 9:64 Ja '60

FIGURE 2-X

INDEX TO LEGAL PERIODICALS, 1958-1961

Figure 2-Y shows additional citations to articles under the subject entry "Diversity" in the excerpts reproduced from the 1989 *Current Law Index* volume.

Relevant article ➡️

> Forum-selection clauses: should state or federal law determine validity in diversity actions? (case note) Stewart Organization v. Ricoh Corp. 108 S. Ct. 2239 (1988) by Eric Fahlman
>   *64 Washington Law Review 439-458 April '89*
> Doe pleading to be disregarded in diversity jurisdiction: congressional response. (Ninth Circuit Survey) (case note) Bryant v. Ford Motor Co. 844 F.2d 602 (9th Cir. 1987) by Susan E. Foe
>   *19 Golden Gate University Law Review 127-176 Spring '89*
> Limited partners and diversity jurisdiction. (Annual Eighth Circuit Survey) (case note) Stouffer Corp. v. Breckenridge 859 F.2d 75 (8th Cir. 1988) by Chad M. Neuens
>   *22 Creighton Law Review 1055-1080 Spring '89*
> Diversity jurisdiction in Indian country: what if no forum exists? (case note) Iowa Mutual Insurance Co. v. Laplante 107 S. Ct. 971 (1987) by Jean Pendleton
>   *33 South Dakota Law Review 528-545 Fall '88*
> The return of Section 905(b) vessel negligence claims to the realm of traditional maritime torts. (case note) Richendollar v. Diamond M Drilling Co. 819 F.2d 124 (5th Cir. 1987) by Roy A. Perrin III
> *12 Tulane Maritime Law Journal 405-416 Spring '88*

> Changes in federal diversity and removal jurisdiction. by Richard Bisio and Cynthia M. York   *68 Michigan Bar Journal 649(1) July '89*
> Streamlining federal procedure - recent practice changes. by Dale T. Miller
>   *3 CBA Record 31(3) July-August '89*
> Judicial tort reform: federal common law inroads into state tort damages. by Patricia T. Morgan
> *21 Arizona State Law Journal 349-401 Summer '89*
> Recent changes to federal practice and procedure: the Judicial Improvements and Access to Justice Act. by Elizabeth Vranicar Tanis
>   *25 Georgia State Bar Journal 198(9) May '89*
> Federal court abstention in diversity of citizenship cases. by Kelly D. Hickman
> *62 Southern California Law Review 1237-1262 March-May '89*
>
> **-litigation**
> Foreign state - Republic of the Marshall Islands - treaties - sovereignty - Trust Territory of the Pacific Islands. by Mark A. Chinen
>   *83 American Journal of International Law 583-586 July '89*
> Recognition of governments - standing of foreign states to sue in U.S. courts - diversity jurisdiction. by Jerome M. Marcus
>   *83 American Journal of International Law 368-371 April '89*
> Erie Railroad v. Tompkins - after fifty years. by Joseph L. Lenihan
>   *53 Kentucky Bench and Bar 22(4) Spring '89*
> Forum selection clauses designating foreign courts: does federal or state law govern enforceability in diversity cases? A question left open by Stewart Organization, Inc. v. Ricoh Corp. by Matthew W. Lampe
> *22 Cornell International Law Journal 307-334 Spring '89*
> Ascertaining state law: the continuing Erie dilemma. by Geri J. Yonover
>   *38 De Paul Law Review 1-42 Fall '88*

Relevant article ➡️

> John Doe strikes out in the Ninth: the Ninth Circuit's rule on Doe defendants raises more questions than it answers. by William R. Slomanson   *8 California Lawyer 51(4) May '88*
> The preclusive effect of foreign-country judgments in the United States and federal choice of law: the role of the Erie doctrine reassessed. by John D. Brummett Jr.
> *33 New York Law School Law Review 83-109 Spring '88*

FIGURE 2-Y
CURRENT LAW INDEX

The *Current Law Index* is published by Information Access Corporation. The *Current Law Index* is divided into four parts: a "Subject Index," "Author/Title Index," a "Table of Cases," and a "Table of Statutes." The Subject Index uses the index headings developed by the Library of Congress. Most topics have subheadings.

The *Legal Resource Index* connects with the printed *Current Law Index*. It is available on an automated microfilm reader, CD-ROM (called LegalTrac), and online on LEXIS. It includes the titles listed in the *Current Law Index* and other titles, such as newspapers and newsletters. One important difference between the *Current Law Index* and the *Legal Resource Index* is that the *Legal Resource Index* is cumulative. Thus, once the proper topic has been found, all articles indexed under that topic since 1980 are listed. When using the *Current Law Index* (and other printed indexes), all of the volumes covering the relevant time frame must be individually examined.

CITING LEGAL PERIODICALS

According to *Bluebook* Rule 16, most articles in legal periodicals are generally cited by:

(1) the author's full name as it appears in the publication—with the following modifications:

(a) any middle name(s) should be shortened "to a middle initial unless the author uses an initial in place of his or her name"; in the latter situation the first initial and the full middle name should be retained;

(b) any designation such as "Jr." or "III" should be included; a comma should be inserted "before the designation only if the author does";

(c) an article with two authors should be cited "in the order in which they appear in the publication"; and

(d) an article with three or more authors should be cited to the first, followed by "et al.";

(2) title of the article (in italics or underlined);

(3) volume number;

(4) abbreviated title of the periodical (abbreviations are listed in Tables T.13 (periodicals) and T.10 (geographic terms));

(5) beginning page number of the article and any cited page(s) (see *Bluebook* Rule 3.3); and

(6) date.

The following are some examples of periodical citations complying with these rules:

Larry L. Teply, <u>Antitrust Immunity of State and Local Governmental Action</u>, 48 Tul. L. Rev. 272 (1974). (This article appeared in Volume 48 of the *Tulane Law Review*; it begins on page 272.)

Ralph H. Folsom & Larry L. Teply, <u>Trademarked Generic Words</u>, 89 Yale L.J. 1323, 1350-51 (1980). (This article begins on page 1323 and specific material on pages 1350 and 1351 is cited.)

Nancy W. Perry & Larry L. Teply, <u>Interviewing, Counseling, and In-Court Examination of Children: Practical Approaches for Attorneys</u>, 18 Creighton L. Rev. 1369, 1369 & nn.2-6 (1985). (This article begins on page 1369. Specific material on the first page of the article is cited. Footnotes 2 through 6 on page 1369 are also cited. *Bluebook* Rule 3.3(b) and (c) cover citation of footnotes.)

Slightly varying forms are used for student works and book reviews. According to *Bluebook* Rule 16.5.1(a), signed and titled student works are cited in the same manner, except that the designation of the work (e.g., Note, Comment, Special Project, etc.) should be given before the title of the work to indicate that it has been written by a student. A work is considered signed "if a student or students is/are credited with writing or contributing to the piece anywhere within the issue in which the work appears."

Martin Kessler & Larry Teply, Comment, <u>Jetport: Planning and Politics in the Big Cypress Swamp</u>, 25 U. Miami L. Rev. 713 (1971).

Larry L. Teply & Richard L. Williams, Commentary, <u>Interruption of Use: A Prescription for Prescription</u>, 25 U. Fla. L. Rev. 204 (1972).

According to *Bluebook* Rule 16.5.1(b), unsigned student works should be cited by the designation given in the periodical, following by the title. A student work signed only with initials is considered to be an unsigned work. *Bluebook* Rule 16.5.1(a).

Note, <u>Designation of Defendants by Fictitious Names—Use of John Doe Complaints</u>, 46 Iowa L. Rev. 773 (1961).

Note that certain periodicals do not have volume numbers. If the volume is paginated consecutively throughout the *entire* volume, you should use the year of publication as the volume number and omit the year designation at the end of the citation. *Bluebook* Rules 3.2(a) and 16.2.

Comment, <u>Unknown Parties: The John Doe Defendant</u>, 1970 Law & Soc. Ord. 256.

Several periodicals paginate each *issue* separately. In this situation, you should cite the periodical by the date or period of publication and omit the year designation at the end of the citation. Note also how the page is cited in the example below. *Bluebook* Rule 16.3 ("Nonconsecutively Paginated Journals and Magazines").

Gene H. Wood, <u>The Child as Witness</u>, 6 Fam. Advoc., Spring 1984, at 14.

Section 2H. Finding, Citing, and Updating Annotations

Textual annotations are critical commentaries with explanatory notes that accompany judicial opinions. Because they contain judicial opinions, annotated volumes frequently are shelved with other case reporters in the library, but their primary usefulness is the commentary and citations that accompany the opinions.[6]

The leading publisher of several series of legal annotations is Lawyers Cooperative/Bancroft-Whitney. Their *A.L.R.* annotations contain (1) selected cases and (2) annotations that discuss points of law or fact situation involved in those cases. The annotations usually include historical background, current law, and probable future developments. In most instances, the annotations will cite all prior court decisions on the topic. Indeed, *A.L.R.* annotations are known for their thoroughness. The more recent *A.L.R.* volumes include practice pointers and cross-references. Currently, lawyers consult the six basic series of *American Law Reports* shown in the table on the following page.[7]

---

[6] In fact, <u>American Law Reports</u> "is the nation's most cited lawbook today." Lawyers Cooperative Publishing Co./Bancroft-Whitney Co., <u>The Living Law 1989/1990</u>, at 17 (1989) (emphasis deleted).

[7] The current <u>American Law Reports</u> series replaced the <u>Lawyers Reports Annotated</u> (<u>L.R.A.</u>) (First Series, 1888-1906, New Series, 1906-1914, Dated Series, 1915-1918). Other annotated <u>A.L.R.</u> predecessors include the following: <u>American and English Annotated Cases</u> (<u>Ann. Cas.</u>) (1906-1918) and the "Trinity Series," consisting of <u>American Decisions</u> (1760-1869); <u>American Reports</u> (1869-1887); and <u>American State Reports</u> (1887-1911). These early series normally are not consulted for current research problems.

MODERN A.L.R. SERIES AND SUPREME COURT ANNOTATIONS

Series	Scope of Coverage
A.L.R. (1st Series)	1918-1947—State and federal topics
A.L.R.2d	1947-1965—State and federal topics
A.L.R.3d	1965-1980—State and federal topics to 1969; state topics only from 1969
A.L.R.4th	1980 to 1991—State topics only
A.L.R.5th	1992 to date—State topics only
A.L.R. Federal	1969 to date—Federal topics only
U.S. Supreme Court, Lawyers' Edition	Points of law covered in the decisions of the U.S. Supreme Court; in the first series of the *Lawyers' Edition*, the annotations directly follow the reported case; in the second series, the annotations (and summaries of the briefs of counsel) appear at the end of each volume.

The principal access to annotations in the *A.L.R.* series (other than a direct citation) is through the *Index to Annotations* (replacing the "Quick Indexes"). The five-volume *Index to Annotations* covers *A.L.R.2d* and later series as well as annotations in the *Lawyers' Edition of U.S. Supreme Court Reports Second* (L. Ed. 2d). The first series of *A.L.R.* is indexed in its *Word Index* and *Quick Index*. Figure 2-Z shows the *Index* reference to an annotation dealing with the "John Doe" problem.

There were also several cross-references to this annotation in American Jurisprudence Second (e.g., footnote 83 shown in Figure 2-L above).

ASSUMED OR FICTITIOUS NAMES —Cont'd

Federal District Court: propriety and effect of use of fictitious name of party in complaint in Federal District Court, 8 ALR Fed 675

FIGURE 2-Z
INDEX TO ANNOTATIONS

CITING ANNOTATIONS

The Bluebook in Rule 16.5.5 states that discussions in annotations such as *American Law Reports* should be cited by:

     (1) the author's full name (see Rule 15.1.1);

     (2) "Annotation";

     (3) title of the annotation in italics or underlined;

     (4) volume number;

     (5) volume designation (e.g., A.L.R.5th);

     (6) the page on which the annotation begins (not the page on which the accompanying case begins); and

     (7) the copyright date of the volume.

PROBLEM 2.13 Examine the following figures showing various features of the annotation in *A.L.R. Federal* dealing with "John Doe" parties in federal court. The first figure shows the beginning page of the annotation. Answer the following questions about this annotation:

(a) Based on the outline at the beginning of the annotation (on page 675) or entries in the internal Index (on pages 676-77), which section(s) or subsection(s) of the annotation discusses the effect of designating defendants by fictitious names in actions originally brought in federal district courts for purposes of invoking diversity jurisdiction?

(b) What advice does the "practice pointers" section (on pages 680-81) give to lawyers who have joined specifically named defendants with fictitious defendants who might cause the complaint to be dismissed on the ground that there is a lack of complete diversity between the parties?

(c) Find the discussion of the *Johnson* case (on pages 687-88), which involved diversity-of-citizenship problems arising under the Virginia uninsured motorist law. Compared to the facts of the *Johnson* case, do the facts of *Problem 2.3* present a stronger case for concluding that a diversity action should be permitted?

(d) How does the discussion of the *Molnar v. National Broadcasting Co.* case (on pages 688-89) differ from the discussion of that case in Wright, Miller, and Cooper's treatise?

(e) Assuming that the copyright date of the volume containing the annotation is 1971, is the following citation of the annotation correct? Annotation, <u>Propriety and Effect of Use of Fictitious Name of Party in Complaint in Federal District Court</u>, 8 A.L.R. Fed. 675 (1971).

Title of the annotation →

Author →

Outline of the coverage of the annotation →

Cross-references to other related works within the "Total Client-Service Library" →

Method of updating the annotation →

Page number →

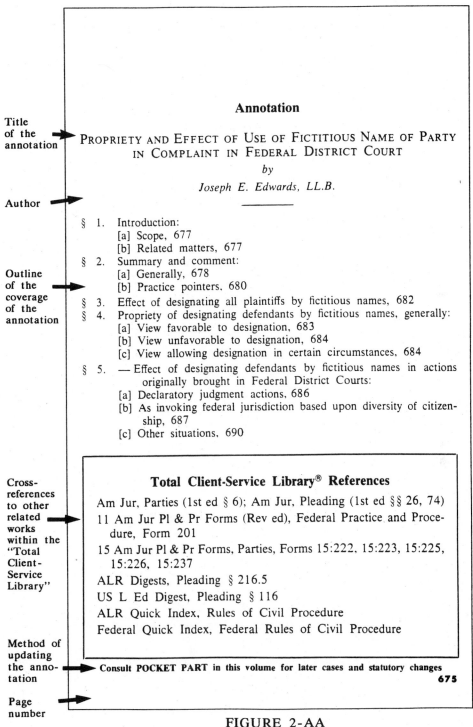

Annotation

PROPRIETY AND EFFECT OF USE OF FICTITIOUS NAME OF PARTY IN COMPLAINT IN FEDERAL DISTRICT COURT

by

Joseph E. Edwards, LL.B.

§ 1. Introduction:
  [a] Scope, 677
  [b] Related matters, 677
§ 2. Summary and comment:
  [a] Generally, 678
  [b] Practice pointers. 680
§ 3. Effect of designating all plaintiffs by fictitious names, 682
§ 4. Propriety of designating defendants by fictitious names, generally:
  [a] View favorable to designation, 683
  [b] View unfavorable to designation, 684
  [c] View allowing designation in certain circumstances, 684
§ 5. — Effect of designating defendants by fictitious names in actions originally brought in Federal District Courts:
  [a] Declaratory judgment actions, 686
  [b] As invoking federal jurisdiction based upon diversity of citizenship, 687
  [c] Other situations. 690

Total Client-Service Library® References

Am Jur, Parties (1st ed § 6); Am Jur, Pleading (1st ed §§ 26, 74)

11 Am Jur Pl & Pr Forms (Rev ed), Federal Practice and Procedure, Form 201

15 Am Jur Pl & Pr Forms, Parties, Forms 15:222, 15:223, 15:225, 15:226, 15:237

ALR Digests, Pleading § 216.5

US L Ed Digest, Pleading § 116

ALR Quick Index, Rules of Civil Procedure

Federal Quick Index, Federal Rules of Civil Procedure

Consult POCKET PART in this volume for later cases and statutory changes

675

FIGURE 2-AA

A.L.R. FEDERAL

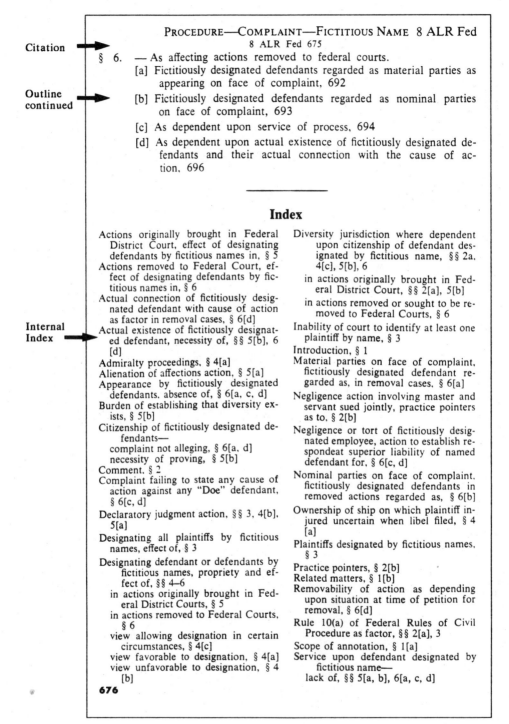

Citation

Outline
continued

Internal
Index

Index

FIGURE 2-BB
A.L.R. FEDERAL

Internal
Index
continued

This table
allows you
to find
cases from
a specific
circuit
efficiently.
A similar
table
refers
to specific
states in
annota-
tions
based on
state law.
The
table in
A.L.R.5th
provides
complete
citations.

This brief
scope note
delineates
the exact
coverage
of the
annotation
and points
out what
topics
have been
excluded.

"Related
matters"
alert you
to other
annota-
tions that
treat
related
questions.

8 ALR Fed Procedure—Complaint—Fictitious Name   § 1[b]

8 ALR Fed 675

Service upon defendant designated by
fictitious name—Cont'd
made only after named defendant's
petition for removal filed, § 6[c]
service as invalid because of fictitious
name designation, § 5[c]
State practice authorizing designation
of defendants by fictitious names as
factor, § 4[c]

Statute of limitations, use of fictitious
names in complaint as affecting running of, § 5[c]
Subsequent disclosure of true names of
plaintiffs, § 3
Summary, § 2
True names of defendants unknown to
plaintiff when action commenced, §§
4[a, c], 5 [b]

Table of Courts and Circuits

Consult POCKET PART in this volume for later cases and statutory changes

Sup Ct: § 6[d]
Second Circuit: §§ 2[b], 3, 5[a]
Third Circuit: § 5[a]
Fourth Circuit: §§ 4[c], 5[b], 6[b]
Fifth Circuit: § 6[c]

Sixth Circuit: §§ 2[b], 6[c]
Seventh Circuit: § 5[c]
Eighth Circuit: §§ 4[a], 5[b], 6[c]
Ninth Circuit: §§ 2[a, b], 4–6

§ 1. Introduction

[a] Scope

The purpose of this annotation is
to collect the cases discussing the propriety and effect of designating parties
by fictitious names[1] in complaints in
Federal District Courts.[2]

[b] Related matters

Status, in federal court, of judgment or order rendered by state court
before removal of case. 2 ALR Fed
760.

What constitutes, under 28 USC
§ 1359, improper or collusive making
or joinder of parties to invoke Federal District Court's jurisdiction. 75
ALR2d 717.

Removal of causes as affected by
right to join master and servant as
defendants in court action based on
respondeat superior. 59 ALR2d
1066.

Federal court's jurisdiction as affected by common citizenship of
third-party defendant with either or
both of original parties. 37 ALR2d
1411.

Federal diversity of citizenship
jurisdiction where one of the states
in which multistate corporation party
litigant is alleged to be incorporated
is also state of citizenship of oppo-
nent. 27 ALR2d 745.

Effect upon jurisdiction of state
court of 28 USC § 1446, relating to
removal of cause to federal court. 25
ALR2d 1045.

Use of abbreviations of name of
municipal body or private corporation in designating party to judicial
proceedings. 167 ALR 1217.

Realigning of parties as regards
question of diversity of citizenship as

---

1. The annotation does not include
cases concerned only with instances of
misnomer or an alleged fraudulent joinder of parties.
2. The annotation is not concerned

with complaints or petitions filed in administrative agencies, but it does include
cases where the complaints were originally filed in a state court and removed
to a Federal District Court.

677

FIGURE 2-CC
A.L.R. FEDERAL

Beginning of the summary relating to "Doe" defendants

§ 2[a]   PROCEDURE—COMPLAINT—FICTITIOUS NAME   8 ALR Fed
8 ALR Fed 675

ground of federal jurisdiction.   132 ALR 193.

Construction and effect of statute as to doing business under an assumed or fictitious name or designation not showing the names of the persons interested.   45 ALR 198, 42 ALR2d 516.

The article in the Iowa Law Review is cited.

Note, Designation of Defendants by Fictitious Names—Use of John Doe Complaints.   46 Iowa L Rev 773.

§ 2. Summary and comment

[a] Generally

Although some state statutes and rules of procedure provide for the designation of parties' fictitious names, there is no federal counterpart allowing such a practice in the Federal District Courts.[3]   Notwithstanding the absence of federal statutes or rules expressly providing for use of fictitious names of parties in a complaint filed in the Federal District Courts, both plaintiffs and defendants have been so designated with varying results.

This section briefly reviews the legal principles involved in the annotation.

With respect to the use of fictitious names of plaintiffs, it has been held, pursuant to Rule 10(a) of the Federal Rules of Civil Procedure, which requires a complaint to contain the names of all the parties, that a complaint filed by several plaintiffs all using fictitious names would not be sufficient to commence an action in the Federal District Court.[4]

The greater number of cases involving a party being designated by a fictitious name in a complaint filed in a Federal District Court are those concerned with defendants fictitiously described as "Does."

Where the general propriety of joining "Doe" defendants has been squarely presented to the courts and has been the subject of express comment by the court, conflicting conclusions have resulted.   For instance, it has been held that there is no prohibition in judicial or administrative practice to openly and frankly use a fictitious name for unknown parties until the true one is made known so long as due process is accomplished.[5]   On the other hand, it has been held in the same circuit that "Doe" defendants are not permitted in federal practice.[6]   But it has also been held, and it appears to be the generally accepted view, that a defendant may be designated by a fictitious name if such a person actually exists but his true name is unknown by the plaintiff and the plaintiff intends to substitute the real name of the defendant for the fictitious one when the true name is ascertained by the plaintiff.[7]   Moreover, the designation of a defendant by a fictitious name has apparently been permitted where the practice was permitted by state law,[8] but it does not appear that such a rationale is the prevalent view.[9]

The use of fictitious names for defendants in complaints in federal

---

3. See the discussion in 46 Iowa L Rev 773.
4. § 3, infra.
5. See Johnson v Udall (1968, **DC Cal**) 292 F Supp 738, infra § 4[a].
6. See Hall v Pacific Maritime Asso. (1968, **DC Cal**) 281 F Supp 54, infra § 4[b].
7. § 4[c], infra.

8. § 4[c], infra.
9. See the discussion in 46 Iowa L Rev 773, where it was suggested that the use of fictitious names for defendants might be urged on the basis that state statutes allowing fictitious names for unknown defendants are substantive provisions within the purview of the "Erie doctrine."

FIGURE 2-DD
A.L.R. FEDERAL

§ 2[b]   PROCEDURE—COMPLAINT—FICTITIOUS NAME 8 ALR Fed
8 ALR Fed 675

their character or existence beyond the face of the pleadings, and as such, if said fictitiously designated defendants' citizenship was alleged to be in the same state as that of the plaintiff's, removal of the action to the Federal District Court on the ground of diversity of citizenship would be precluded.[1]

Conversely, there is authority supporting a view that, for the purposes of removal, a fictitiously designated defendant would be considered a mere nominal party, and as such, disregarded in the petition for removal.[2]

On the other hand, on the principle that the situation existing at the time the petition for removal is filed determines whether a cause may properly be removed to the Federal District Court, it has been held that defendants designated by fictitious names would not prevent removal for lack of diversity of citizenship where no service of process was had on such fictitiously designated defendants and the only parties to the action at the time the petition for removal was filed were citizens of different states.[3]

Finally, in what appears to be the prevalent view, many courts, in considering whether a defendant designated by a fictitious name and alleged to be a citizen of the state where the plaintiff resides will prevent removal of the cause to the Federal District Courts, will look beyond the pleadings to ascertain the actual existence of the fictitiously designated defendants and whether they have an actual connection with the cause of action.[4] It has been suggested that this is the proper approach to the problem.[5]

[b] Practice pointers

Counsel for plaintiffs desirous of shielding their true identity from the public because of the sensitive nature of the action, to avoid unnecessary delay, should give consideration to the following three methods: (1) filing a complaint using the true names of the plaintiffs but requesting amendments or protective orders, on a proper showing, which could shield the identity of the plaintiffs; (2) employing fictitious names in the complaint but setting forth in a letter annexed to the complaint the true name and address of the plaintiff; or (3) employing fictitious names in the complaint but verifying the complaint by the signature of the plaintiff under his true name.[6]

Counsel for a plaintiff whose action might be subject to dismissal because of want of diversity of citizenship as a result of having joined, in addition to specifically named defendants, other defendants designated with fictitious names, and who feels, notwithstanding the defective complaint as regards diversity of citizenship, that the action can still be litigated in a Federal District Court, should, prior to appealing the dismissal, offer to amend the complaint by striking the

"Practice pointers" provide useful ideas relating to pleading, proof, evidentiary matters, and trial tactics.

Specific comments concerning diversity actions involving "Doe" defendants

---

1. § 6[a], infra.
2. § 6[b], infra.
3. § 6[c], infra.
4. § 6[d], infra.
5. See the article in 46 Iowa L Rev 773, where it was stated: "If a court fails to look behind the pleadings, the joinder of a Doe defendant will prevent removal to a federal court even though the fictitiously named defendant does

680

not exist. On the other hand, a plaintiff who in good faith joins an unknown defendant in an action brought in a state court would be prejudiced if the federal court allowed the case to be removed and ignored or summarily dismissed the Doe party."

6. See Roe v New York (1970, DC NY) 49 FRD 279, 8 ALR Fed 670, infra § 3.

FIGURE 2-EE
A.L.R. FEDERAL

Continuing discussion concerning diversity actions involving "Doe" defendants

fictitiously designated defendants from the title, and to also consider employing liberal discovery procedures to turn up other persons who might have the citizenship and connection with the alleged occurrence requisite to joinder as defendants.[7] In this respect, appealing solely on the ground of the dismissal as it pertains to the joinder of defendants designated with fictitious names could result in the cost of the appeal being taxed to the attorney.[8]

Counsel representing specifically named defendants in an action instituted in a state court who may desire to have the cause removed to a Federal District Court but who are also confronted with the possibility that removal will be prevented as a result of the plaintiff's having joined other defendants designated by fictitious names and alleged to reside in the same state as that of the plaintiff should attempt to determine if such defendants actually exist or have any real connection with the plaintiff's cause of action. At least one commentator has suggested criteria for making such a determination. Lack of intention to serve a defendant designated with a fictitious name and lack of any attempt to recover judgment against him may cast some doubt upon that defendant's real existence or connection with the plaintiff's cause of action.[9] Similarly, plaintiff's expressed willingness to proceed to trial without service of process having been made on the fictitiously designated parties has been suggested to be indicative that the naming of a fictitious party should not preclude the named defendants' petition for removal.[10] The absence in the pleading of allegations actually charging participation in the alleged wrong by the fictitious defendant and stating a cause of action against him may be a factor.[11]

It has been held that the normal time limitations provided for removal after an action has been commenced in the state court may be extended in the event of the discovery of a purely fictitious defendant.[12]

The _Molnar_ case is cited, which is discussed in § 5[b].

7. See Molnar v National Broadcasting Co. (1956, **CA9 Cal**) 231 F2d 684, infra § 5[b], where an attorney's failure to consider the above-described methods was condemned as "bitter insistence upon shallow technicality" and as the "imposition of frivolous appeals."

8. See Roth v Davis (1956, **CA9 Cal**) 231 F2d 681.

9. See the discussion in 46 Iowa L Rev 773 of Herzig v Twentieth Century-Fox Film Corp. (1955, **DC Cal**) 129 F Supp 845.

10. See the discussion in 46 Iowa L Rev 773 of Southern P. Co. v Haight (1942, **CA9 Cal**) 126 F2d 900.

11. In this respect see the discussion in 46 Iowa L Rev 773 of Grigg v Southern Pacific Co. (1957, **CA9 Cal**) 246 F 2d 613, reh den 248 F2d 949, and Scurlock v American President Lines, Ltd.

(1958, **DC Cal**) 162 F Supp 78, and Herzig v Twentieth Century-Fox Film Corp. (1955, **DC Cal**) 129 F Supp 845.

12. Where a defendant filed his petition for removal in the Federal District Court more than 20 days after a copy of the complaint, and a summons had been served upon him but within 20 days after the dismissal in the state court of the fictitious defendants, it was held in Fred Olsen & Co. v Moore (1958, **DC Cal**) 162 F Supp 82, that the petition for removal was timely where the plaintiff named fictitious defendants. The court said that the defendant may wait until the fictitious defendants are dismissed and it appears affirmatively that there is a diversity of citizenship. Moreover, continued the court, a plaintiff who chooses to name "Doe" defendants in an action where actually

FIGURE 2-FF

A.L.R. FEDERAL

8 ALR Fed PROCEDURE—COMPLAINT—FICTITIOUS NAME § 5[b]
8 ALR Fed 675

any court in the commonwealth seeking to recover upon the cause of action abolished by the Act and another section provided that to do so shall be a criminal offense. The court said that it appeared that of the two vitally interested parties whose legal relations the court had been asked to declare, only one was before the court, the other one apparently having had no notice or knowledge of the proceeding. Moreover, the court said that although it had been held that it is not necessary under the Federal Declaratory Judgment Act that all interested parties be joined, a petition for a declaratory judgment is usually, in fact if not in form, adversary process, and the principle "audi alteram partem" is vital to the proper administration of justice under such procedure.

☆ COMMENT: The petitioner later brought an action in the same Federal District Court as a citizen of Illinois against the attorney general of the Commonwealth of Pennsylvania and the district attorney of Philadelphia County to enjoin the defendants from enforcing against plaintiff and his attorney the provisions of the Pennsylvania statute which abolished causes of action for alienation of affections of husband or wife, in Wilder v Reno (1941, **DC Pa**) 39 F Supp 404. The court, inter alia, rejected the defendants' contention that the whole matter was merely a counterpart of the above declaratory judgment action, the court remarking that the situation was entirely differ-

ent in the instant case in that here there was a plaintiff who sought to enjoin state law enforcement officers from performing their duties under an allegedly unconstitutional statute, and that those law enforcement officers were here defendants arguing in support of the constitutionality of the Act in question; there were adversary parties, and the proper adversary parties were before the court.

See also Sigurdson v De Guercio (1956, **CA9 Cal**) 241 F2d 480, supra § 4[b], also an action for declaratory judgment, where the court said that "John Doe" complaints are dangerous and that it is inviting disaster to allow them to be filed and to allow fictitious persons to remain defendants if the complaint is still of record.

[b] As invoking federal jurisdiction based upon diversity of citizenship

In the following cases it was held, either expressly or by necessary implication, that federal jurisdiction cannot be invoked on the basis of diversity of citizenship by the method of joining a defendant by a fictitious name unless said fictitiously designated defendant actually exists and his citizenship can be truthfully alleged and proved.[16]

The practice of attempting to invoke diversity jurisdiction in the Federal District Courts through joining fictitious persons as defendants, such as "John Doe," was regarded as "unwarranted" except "under unusual circumstances," in Johnson v General Motors Corp. (1965, **DC Va**) 242 F Supp 778, where the court sustained

Beginning of § 5[b]

Discussion of the <u>Johnson</u> case, which involved a "John Doe" defendant and arose under the Virginia uninsured motorist law

---

16. See also the cases in § 6, infra, involving the question of diversity of citizenship with respect to defendants

designated by fictitious names in actions originally brought in state courts.

FIGURE 2-GG
A.L.R. FEDERAL

§ 5[b]   PROCEDURE—COMPLAINT—FICTITIOUS NAME 8 ALR Fed
8 ALR Fed 675

§ 5[b]
(continued
discussion
of the
Johnson
case) ↘

the motion of two corporate defendants to dismiss on the ground that there was a failure of diversity jurisdiction between the plaintiff and "John Doe." The plaintiff, a citizen of Virginia relying on the Virginia uninsured motorist law, sued two corporations organized and existing under the laws of the state of Michigan and Delaware, in addition to a party designated as "John Doe," as to whose citizenship the plaintiff conceded that he could not offer any proof—indeed, according to the court, since the accident giving rise to the cause of action took place in Norfolk, it was more probable than not that the unknown driver of the motor vehicle, which allegedly forced the vehicle occupied by plaintiff's decedent off the highway, was a citizen of Virginia. The court said that it is fundamental that where diversity is challenged, the plaintiff has the burden of establishing that diversity exists, and "the unusual circumstances" with respect to joining fictitious defendants in order to invoke diversity jurisdiction covers the situation where the plaintiff has a definite person in mind but does not know his true name, although plaintiff can truthfully aver that the "John Doe" defendant is a citizen of an alleged state. The court additionally pointed out that defendants, as well as plaintiffs, are prevented from removing "John Doe" actions from state to federal courts on the basis of diversity of citizenship, although if a cause of action is not stated in the complaint filed against a "John Doe" defendant, such unidentified person need not be joined in the removal petition.

Key facts
summa-
rized ↘

Beginning
of the
discussion
of the
Molnar
case →

▶ A trial court's order dismissing a plaintiff's complaint because it did not disclose complete diversity of citizen-

688

ship between the parties was affirmed in Molnar v National Broadcasting Co. (1956, CA9 Cal) 231 F2d 684, where the defendants were described in the original title as the National Broadcasting Company, Inc., a corporation, and Doe 1-X, and were also alleged to be citizens and residents of the state of Delaware, and, although plaintiff alleged that there were actual persons thus joined as defendants under fictitious designations, she did not describe them or make any allegations about the respective function of each or the connection of each with the alleged action in question. The court said that it was clear, in the absence of identification or connection or name, that the allegation of citizenship in Delaware was illusory and it was impossible for the court to say that the defendants thus joined were not indispensable from the face of the complaint. The court said that the attempt to join fictitious defendants, notwithstanding its justification in California practice, is not warranted in any of the Rules of Civil Procedure under which federal courts operate, that while the Federal Rules of Civil Procedure are **not** universally inclusive of all possible colorings of practice, no justification can be found therein for violation of jurisdictional principles, that the methods used by the common law to extend jurisdiction of particular courts cannot be tolerated under the Federal Constitution, that the national trial courts are a special jurisdiction, and that at the outset of every proceeding there, jurisdiction should be established by allegations of essential facts. Unquestionably, the court said, if the plaintiff had offered to amend, even after the order of dismissal was entered, by striking "Doe 1-X" from the title and striking the allegations relat-

FIGURE 2-HH
A.L.R. FEDERAL

§ 5[b]
(continued discussion of the *Molnar* case) ▼

ing to these from the complaint, the court would have permitted the order to be set aside and the cause to proceed, since a complaint defective in allegation of diversity of citizenship can be amended to show the true state of facts even in the United States Supreme Court, and moreover, there would have been plenty of time, had the cause been allowed to remain or be reinstated against National Broadcasting Company, Inc., alone, to pursue the liberal procedures as to discovery and to turn up other postulated persons who might eventually have been found to have the citizenship and connection with the alleged occurrence requisite to joinder as defendants. Even a new complaint naming the broadcasting company only as defendant could have been filed with like opportunities, the court added. However, the order of dismissal was modified to permit the filing of an amended complaint against the National Broadcasting Company, Inc., alone, as defendant, if the other defendants who were joined but not identified could be dispensed with.

The section continues to discuss other cases. ▼

Where the trial court, at the end of the trial, and of its own motion, dismissed certain fictitious defendants designated in the complaint as "Doe 1-X," it was held that the diversity jurisdiction of the court was not defeated, in Roth v Davis (1956, **CA9 Cal**) 231 F2d 681, although the complaint, according to the court, might have been dismissed because it did not show on its face complete diversity of citizenship between plaintiffs and all designated defendants. It appeared that no fictitious defendants named as "Doe 1-X" were ever served, and by the end of the trial it appeared that the fictitious defendants were "obviously sham." The

sole point of the appeal, as stated by attorneys for plaintiff, was whether the United States District Court has jurisdiction over a case on the basis of diversity of citizenship where the complaint names unknown defendants and alleges that they are citizens and residents of the same state as the known named defendants, which state of citizenship and residence is diverse from that of the plaintiff. Affirming a jury verdict for the known named defendant, the court said that jurisdiction cannot be defeated by joining formal or unnecessary parties, but the trial judge removed even this "simulacrum" of a technicality by dismissing the fictitious defendants. Such extreme care in protecting the record, the court said, was highly commendable and it left the plaintiff without a place to stand for appeal. Yet, continued the court, counsel for plaintiff filed an appeal, printed a record and brief, and thereby forced defendant to print a supplemental record and brief, and the cause was argued orally, and "an extremely busy appellate court" was required to give consideration thereto."

Where the plaintiff corporation brought suit against several of its former officers and directors and also sued numerous defendants by fictitious names, invoking the jurisdiction of the federal court on a diversity of citizenship between the plaintiff, a Nevada corporation, and all of the defendants, who were alleged to be citizens of states other than Nevada, it was held, inter alia, in Miller & Lux, Inc. v Nickel (1956, **DC Cal**) 141 F Supp 41, that the plaintiff must drop the fictitious parties or identify them with sufficient clarity so that the court could find that actual persons

FIGURE 2-II
A.L.R. FEDERAL

DISCUSSION OF PROBLEM 2.13 (a) The outline at the beginning of the annotation (on page 675) directs you to "§ 5. —Effect of designating defendants by fictitious names in actions originally brought in Federal District Courts . . . [b] As invoking federal jurisdiction based upon diversity of citizenship, [page] 687." The most relevant entry in the internal Index (on pages 676-77) also directs you to § 5[b] as well as § 2[a], the "Summary and comment" section. The entry ("in actions originally brought in Federal District Court, §§ 2[a], 5[b]") appears under the general index heading "Diversity jurisdiction where dependent upon citizenship of defendant designated by fictitious name . . . ."

(b) The "practice pointers" section (on pages 680-81) advises lawyers, prior to appealing a dismissal, (1) to offer to amend the complaint by striking the fictitious defendants from the title and (2) consider employing discovery procedures to identify unknown defendants. The "practice pointers" section also warns that costs of the appeal may be taxed to the lawyer who appeals solely on the ground that the fictitious defendants were improperly dismissed.

(c) The *Johnson* case (discussed on pages 687-88) involved diversity-of-citizenship problems arising under the Virginia uninsured motorist law. The facts of *Problem 2.3* present a stronger case for concluding that a diversity action should be allowed. In the *Johnson* case, the plaintiff failed to carry the burden of establishing diversity existed. The plaintiff in the *Johnson* case was a citizen of Virginia. "[S]ince the accident giving rise to the cause of action took place in Norfolk [Virginia], it was more probable than not that the unknown driver of the motor vehicle, which allegedly forced the vehicle occupied by plaintiff's decedent off the highway, was a citizen of Virginia." Thus, with the absence of any showing of "unusual circumstances," it appeared that the plaintiff and the unknown motorist were both citizens of Virginia.

In contrast, *Problem 2.3* indicated that the hit-and-run vehicle bore Virginia license plates, but the numbers could not be determined. The plaintiff is a citizen of the District of Columbia. Thus, these additional circumstances make a stronger case for believing that diversity of citizenship between the plaintiff and the unknown motorist exists.

(d) The discussion of the *Molnar* case (on pages 688-89) in the annotation focuses closely on the holding and reasoning of the court. In contrast, Wright, Miller, and Cooper provide a brief summary of the factual situation (the plaintiff in *Molnar*, a citizen of California, was suing a corporate citizen of Delaware and ten John Does, who were also alleged to be Delaware citizens, for injuries received when the plaintiff fell on a stairway in the corporation's building). Wright, Miller, and Cooper also quote specific language from the court's decision rather than summarizing the court's discussion and holding.

(e) The citation of the annotation should have included the author's full name (*Bluebook* Rule 16.5.5); otherwise, the citation is correct: Joseph E. Edwards, Annotation, <u>Propriety and Effect of Use of Fictitious Name of Party in Complaint in Federal District Court</u>, 8 A.L.R. Fed. 675 (1971).

Although the formats of other *A.L.R.* series are similar to that of *A.L.R. Federal* shown in the preceding figures, there are important differences. For example, *A.L.R.5th* provides the full citations of all cited statutes and cases by jurisdiction at the beginning of the annotation in a "Jurisdictional Table of Cited Statutes and Cases." *A.L.R.5th* also provides cross-references to West's Key Numbers, suggested electronic search queries, and secondary sources of other publishers.

SUPPLEMENTATION OF A.L.R. ANNOTATIONS	
Series	**How the Annotations Are Supplemented**
A.L.R. (1st Series)	Chronological *A.L.R. Blue Book of Supplemental Decisions* (e.g., vol. 1 covers 1919-46, vol. 2, 1946-52, etc.)
A.L.R.2d	Cumulative *A.L.R.2d Later Case Service* with pocket supplements in the back of each volume of the *Later Case Service* set
A.L.R.3d, A.L.R.4th, A.L.R.5th, and *A.L.R. Federal*	Cumulative pocket supplements in the back of each volume
U.S. Supreme Court, Lawyers' Edition	Annotations in Volumes 1-31 of L. Ed. 2d are supplemented by a two-volume *Later Case Service*, updated by annual, cumulative pocket parts; beginning with Volume 32 of L. Ed. 2d, the volumes have cumulative pocket supplements.

Reproduced in Figure 2-JJ is a page from the pocket part in the *A.L.R. Federal* volume updating this annotation.

Reference to the annotation being updated

LATER CASE SERVICE   **8 ALR Fed 675–700**

For latest cases, call the toll-free number appearing on the cover of this supplement.

customary and constitutionally embedded presumption of openness in judicial proceedings. In action challenging prayer and bible readings in school, plaintiffs were entitled to proceed anonymously where case generated threat of violence, where evidence on record indicated that plaintiffs could expect extensive harassment if their identities were disclosed, and where some of plaintiffs were children. Doe v Stegall (1981, **CA5 Miss**) 653 F2d 180, 32 FR Serv 2d, reh den (CA5 Miss) 659 F2d 1075.

In civil rights suit by parents and child alleging that defendants deprived plaintiff of constitutional rights and privileges by removing plaintiff minor from custody of her parents for seven weeks, court granted plaintiffs' request to use fictitious names where case involved allegedly false charges of sexual abuse of small child, which constituted important privacy interest and which was highly sensitive issue. Roe v Borup (1980, **ED Wis**) 500 F Supp 127, 31 FR Serv 2d 1045.

In breach of contract action removed to federal court, trial court properly dismissed action for improper venue, notwithstanding plaintiff's argument that action should have been remanded due to fact that presence of Doe defendants defeated diversity jurisdiction, since trial court properly found that Doe defendants were shams and that named parties were diverse; subsequent controlling precedent provides that Does defeat diversity jurisdiction unless "all Doe defendants are either named, unequivocally abandoned by the plaintiff, or dismissed by the state court." Bogan v Keene Corp. (1988, **CA9 Cal**) 852 F2d 1238, 11 FR Serv 3d 1376.

§ 2.5 Propriety of designating defendants by fictitious names, generally

Superseded by 97 ALR Fed 369.

§ 3. Effect of designating all plaintiffs by fictitious names

Superseded by 97 ALR Fed 369.

§ 4. Propriety of designating defendants by fictitious names, generally

[c] View allowing designation in certain circumstances

Notwithstanding that fictitious defendants are not provided for in Federal Rules of Civil Procedure, fictitious parties are proper under certain limited circumstances, at least until reasonable discovery permits actual defendants to assume their places. Klingler v Yamaha Motor Corp. (1990, **ED Pa**) 738 F Supp 898.

In action under Civil Rights Act, 42 USCS § 1983, court would deny what amounted to motion for judgment on pleadings plaintiffs were not prejudiced by court permitting Doe defendants to remain in action, pending reasonable

discovery or showing of prejudice. Scheetz v Morning Call, Inc. (1990, **ED Pa**) 130 FRD 34.

§ 5. —Effect of designating defendants by fictitious names in actions originally brought in Federal District Courts

[a] Declaratory judgment actions

John Doe or fictitious party pleading device is not sanctioned or permitted by federal law in civil cases filed directly in federal court when jurisdiction is based upon diversity of citizenship under 28 USCS § 1332, and use of that pleading device in those cases generally destroys federal jurisdiction. McAllister v Henderson (1988, **ND Ala**) 698 F Supp 865.

[b] As invoking federal jurisdiction based upon diversity of citizenship

New material relevant to § 5[b]

Under applicable law of New Jersey, statute of limitations began to run in cause of action against manufacturer of defective surgical sutures at time of discovery of defect, notwithstanding plaintiff's ignorance of manufacturer's name and consequent use of "John Doe" in complaint; since New Jersey case law permitting relation back of amendment to complaint replacing fictitious name with true name was merely procedural, federal law construing Rule 15(c) of Federal Rules of Civil Procedure and prohibiting relation back under circumstances would bar action under applicable statute of limitations. Britt v Arvanitis (CA3 NJ) 590 F2d 57.

Court was not divested of diversity jurisdiction by presence of unnamed parties to suit, where complaint had alleged complete diversity of citizenship of parties by contending that, while plaintiff was citizen of New York, each of defendants was citizen of state other than New York. Plaintiff was allowed opportunity to proceed with claim in federal court, pending further developments. Final decision on diversity jurisdiction was withheld until time for serving defendants had come to end. At end of allotted period, if plaintiff had identified and served "Doe" defendant with process, and it appeared that defendant, like plaintiff, was citizen of New York, suit would be dismissed altogether for want of subject matter jurisdiction. Ward v Connor (1980, **ED Va**) 495 F Supp 434, revd on other gnds (CA4 Va) 657 F2d 45, cert den 455 US 907, 71 L Ed 2d 445, 102 S Ct 1253.

Note that another Virginia case has been summarized.

Note also that sometimes sections are superseded by later annotations.

Failure of plaintiff in foreclosure action where jurisdiction was based upon diversity of citizenship, to properly allege citizenship of each member of defendant unincorporated association, could not be corrected by use of fictitious "John Doe" defendants, since if identity of Doe defendants was known so that New Jersey plaintiff could state that none of them were citizens of New Jersey or had their principal places of

85

The latest cases can be found by calling a toll-free number.

FIGURE 2-JJ
A.L.R. FEDERAL

Note that the pocket part in Figure 2-JJ indicates that certain sections of the annotation have been superseded by a later annotation. This information is also given in the "Annotation History Table" found in Volume 5 of the *Index to Annotations*. This table lists annotations in all series of *American Law Reports* and *United States Supreme Court Reports, Lawyers Edition* that have been superseded or supplemented by later annotations. This table is kept up to date by entries in the pocket supplement of Volume 5. Figure 2-KK shows the relevant portion of the pocket part providing the entry for "8 ALR Fed 675."

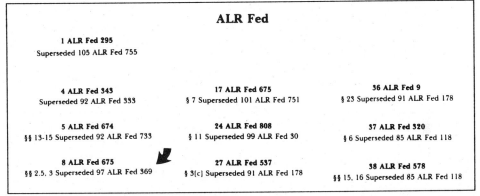

FIGURE 2-KK
INDEX TO ANNOTATIONS, VOLUME 5 POCKET PART

Section 2I. Commentary in Looseleaf Services

Looseleaf services are another important secondary source. These services are topically oriented (e.g., federal excise tax, bankruptcy, equal employment opportunity, and trade regulation) and are updated frequently (often weekly). They generally contain the text or summaries of cases, recently enacted statutes, or administrative materials as well as descriptive and explanatory text.

Sometimes looseleaf services publish the text of related cases that often are not readily available from other sources. At the end of a year, these cases may be removed and placed in transfer binders or published in bound volumes.

Looseleaf services are often treated as reference materials. Sometimes, they are treated as treatises or reporters and are shelved accordingly. The card catalog or electronic equivalent, a library guide, or library map are the best means of finding these services.

The following citation is a typical *Bluebook* citation to looseleaf services (*Bluebook* Rule 18.1):

428 Pat. Trademark & Copyright J. (BNA) A-15 (May 10, 1979).

Chapter 3
COORDINATING RESEARCH IN SECONDARY
AUTHORITIES AND FOCUSING ON THE
LAW IN SPECIFIC JURISDICTIONS

Section 3A. Research Aids in Secondary Sources

Recall or review *Problem 2-1* in Chapter 2, in which the client complained that a neighbor had built a 12-foot high fence. The client was upset because the fence looked tacky and blocked the view. In seeking a lawyer's help, the client wanted to know whether there was some way to have the fence removed or reduced in height.

During the course of an interview, the lawyer will elicit specific facts about the situation in light of the general legal framework that the lawyer learned in law school. For example, the lawyer may remember something about "spite fences" from the Property course, "nuisances" from the Torts course, or the lawyer may know that the location and height of fences within municipalities is typically governed by municipal ordinances or possibly by state statutes. This general knowledge is likely to lead to specific questions, such as the exact location of the fence in relation to the property line, the intent of the neighbor, and the nature of the view that is blocked.

1. SCOPE NOTES

Assume that the lawyer working on the fence problem described in *Problem 2.1* decides to select a legal encyclopedia as a starting point. A secondary source such as a treatise, legal encyclopedia, or law review article allows the lawyer to get the "big picture" and to develop research leads to other sources—both primary and secondary ones. Assume that the lawyer examines *American Jurisprudence Second* and selects volume

35 containing the topic "Fences" as a starting point. The beginning page of that topic is shown in Figure 3-A.

PROBLEM 3.1   Examine the "Scope of Topic," "Treated elsewhere" information, and the portion of the outline shown. What sources or sections, if any, appear to be relevant to this problem?

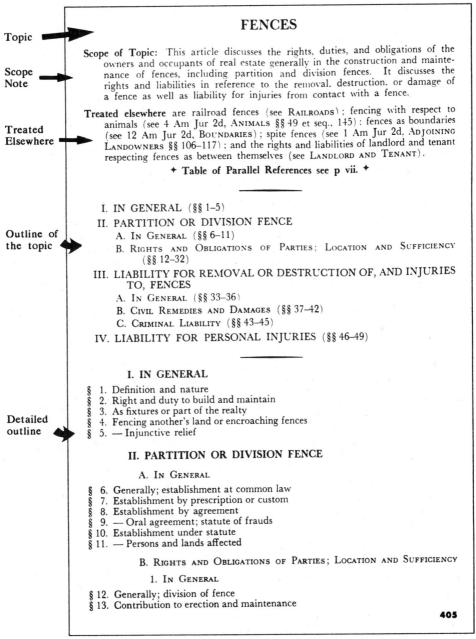

Topic

Scope Note

Treated Elsewhere

Outline of the topic

Detailed outline

FENCES

Scope of Topic: This article discusses the rights, duties, and obligations of the owners and occupants of real estate generally in the construction and maintenance of fences, including partition and division fences. It discusses the rights and liabilities in reference to the removal, destruction, or damage of a fence as well as liability for injuries from contact with a fence.

Treated elsewhere are railroad fences (see RAILROADS); fencing with respect to animals (see 4 Am Jur 2d, ANIMALS §§ 49 et seq., 145); fences as boundaries (see 12 Am Jur 2d, BOUNDARIES); spite fences (see 1 Am Jur 2d, ADJOINING LANDOWNERS §§ 106–117); and the rights and liabilities of landlord and tenant respecting fences as between themselves (see LANDLORD AND TENANT).

✦ Table of Parallel References see p vii. ✦

I. IN GENERAL (§§ 1–5)

II. PARTITION OR DIVISION FENCE
  A. IN GENERAL (§§ 6–11)
  B. RIGHTS AND OBLIGATIONS OF PARTIES: LOCATION AND SUFFICIENCY (§§ 12–32)

III. LIABILITY FOR REMOVAL OR DESTRUCTION OF, AND INJURIES TO, FENCES
  A. IN GENERAL (§§ 33–36)
  B. CIVIL REMEDIES AND DAMAGES (§§ 37–42)
  C. CRIMINAL LIABILITY (§§ 43–45)

IV. LIABILITY FOR PERSONAL INJURIES (§§ 46–49)

I. IN GENERAL

§ 1. Definition and nature
§ 2. Right and duty to build and maintain
§ 3. As fixtures or part of the realty
§ 4. Fencing another's land or encroaching fences
§ 5. — Injunctive relief

II. PARTITION OR DIVISION FENCE

A. IN GENERAL

§ 6. Generally; establishment at common law
§ 7. Establishment by prescription or custom
§ 8. Establishment by agreement
§ 9. — Oral agreement; statute of frauds
§ 10. Establishment under statute
§ 11. — Persons and lands affected

B. RIGHTS AND OBLIGATIONS OF PARTIES; LOCATION AND SUFFICIENCY

1. IN GENERAL

§ 12. Generally; division of fence
§ 13. Contribution to erection and maintenance

405

FIGURE 3-A
AMERICAN JURISPRUDENCE SECOND

DISCUSSION OF PROBLEM 3.1 The "Scope of Topic" indicates that the "Fences" topic discusses the basic rights (and duties) of landowners concerning fences. The outline indicates that definitions and the nature of fences are discussed in § 1. Rights and duties are discussed in § 2. Partition or division fences are given extended treatment in §§ 6-32. Inapplicable to this situation is the discussion of liability for removal or destruction of fences in §§ 33-45. Nor is the discussion of liability for personal injuries resulting from contact with fences in §§ 46-49 relevant. The "Treated elsewhere" note indicates that spite fences are discussed in "1 Am Jur 2d, Adjoining Landowners §§ 106-117").

2. INTERPLAY BETWEEN LEGAL RESEARCH AND CONTINUING FACTUAL INQUIRIES

Before consulting the discussion in the topic "Adjoining Landowners" dealing with spite fences, assume that you have decided to read the general discussion of fences in §§ 1 and 2 in the Fences topic. In particular, § 2 of the "Fences" topic in *American Jurisprudence Second* covers the right and duty to build and maintain fences. If you are uncertain of those basic rights and duties, reading these general sections will provide you with important background information and basic legal principles.

PROBLEM 3.2 An important aspect of legal research is the interplay between what a researcher finds and new questions that need to be asked. In other words, as legal research progresses, a researcher sees that additional facts are needed based on the legal rules and principles that the researcher has found. Sections 1 and 2 of the Fences topic are reproduced in Figures 3-B and 3-C. Read these sections, including the footnotes. Do they stimulate any factual questions that you might want to ask the client about the fence? What basic principles do these sections suggest?

I. IN GENERAL

§ 1. Definition and nature.

Generally, a fence is an inclosing structure or barrier about a field or other space, or about any object, intended to prevent intrusion from without or straying from within.[1] With respect to real property, it is a visible or tangible obstruction interposed between two portions of land so as to part off and shut in the land and set it off as private property.[2] It may be constructed of wood, iron, stone, or wire,[3] or it may be a natural obstacle, such as a steep bank, a watercourse, a ditch, a trench, or a hedge,[4] if it is an effective barrier in its natural state or has been made such by artificial means.[5] It has been held that a fence is a building, in the sense that the term "building" embraces all useful structures erected by man on land.[6]

What constitutes a good, lawful, or sufficient fence for various purposes is often particularly defined by statutes.[7] Frequently, a lawful fence is prescribed by statute as one such as good husbandmen generally keep.[8]

§ 2. Right and duty to build and maintain.

A landowner has the inherent right to fence his land[9] or leave it unfenced,[10] in the absence of a valid statute or contractual restriction to the

---

1. Parrish v Hainlen, 124 **Colo** 229, 236 P2d 115; Polizzi v Lotz, 240 **La** 734, 125 So 2d 146.

Tennis court backstops and sidestops erected by a homeowner near the borders of his land to keep the tennis balls within the playing area are not "fences" within the meaning of an ordinance prohibiting the building of fences of certain height. Shamberg v Lincoln, 174 **Neb** 146, 116 NW2d 18.

Posts merely set around a piece of land on which wire has not yet been strung do not constitute a fence within contemplation of law. Burch v State (**Tex** Crim) 67 SW 500.

2. Kimball v Carter, 95 **Va** 77, 27 SE 823.

A fence is a structure erected upon or near the dividing line between adjoining owners, for the purpose of separating the occupancy of their lands. Lovell v Noyes, 69 **NH** 263, 46 A 25.

A fence is a structure used to protect man in the use of land and premises. Mutual Lumber Co. v Sheppard (**Tex** Civ App) 173 SW2d 494.

3. Wolf v Schwill, 289 **Ill** 190, 124 NE 389; Brown v Johnson (**Tex** Civ App) 73 SW 49, error dismd.

4. Wideman v Faivre, 100 **Kan** 102, 163 P 619.

5. Jones v Witherspoon, 52 **NC** (7 Jones L) 555 (wherein the stream involved appears to have been insufficient as a barrier); Kimball v Carter, 95 **Va** 77, 27 SE 823.

6. Parrish v Hainlen, 124 **Colo** 229, 236 P2d 115; Mutual Lumber Co. v Sheppard (**Tex** Civ App) 173 SW2d 494.

Fences as fixtures or part of the realty, see § 3, infra.

7. Polizzi v Lotz, 240 **La** 734, 125 So 2d 146.

As to what constitutes a sufficient or lawful division or partition fence, see § 6, infra.

As to what constitutes a sufficient or lawful fence to keep animals in or out, see 4 Am Jur 2d, ANIMALS § 54.

8. Meyer v Perkins, 89 **Neb** 59, 130 NW 986.

9. Dyba v Borowitz, 136 **Pa** Super 532, 7 A2d 500.

A landowner has the inherent right, in the absence of any valid statute, or contractual restriction to the contrary, to erect a boundary fence along the division line of his property. Green v Mutual Steel Co. 268 **Ala** 648, 108 So 2d 837.

A landowner cannot be enjoined from erecting a fence along one side of his land for the purpose of preventing his neighbor's cattle from crossing it to reach uninclosed public land on which they have been in the habit of grazing. Anthony Wilkinson Live Stock Co. v McIlquam, 14 **Wyo** 209, 83 P 364.

As to injunction to restrain removal or destruction of fences, see § 38, infra.

10. Villani v Wilmington Housing Authority, 48 **Del** 450, 106 A2d 211; Van Gorder v Eastchester Estates, Inc. 207 Misc 335, 137 NYS2d 789.

As to injunction to restrain erection of a fence on land of another, see § 5, infra.

As to the duty of a railroad to fence its tracks or right of way, see RAILROADS (1st ed §§ 151 et seq.).

407

FIGURE 3-B
AMERICAN JURISPRUDENCE SECOND

§ 3   FENCES   35 Am Jur 2d

contrary.[11] He may build his fences on his own property as he sees fit,[12] and he is free to choose the kind of fence reasonably suited to his purpose.[13] However, a landowner may not plant the corner post of his front fence so that half of it is on his neighbor's land, and if he does so, it is considered a trespass.[14]

Since the title to the bed of a nonnavigable freshwater stream to the center of the stream is in the adjacent riparian proprietors, one who owns both banks bordering on such a stream has title to the land in its bed and may lawfully maintain a fence across it[15] or across a lake formed on his premises by damming such a stream.[16]

In many jurisdictions, there are statutes regulating the construction and maintenance of fences.[17] Frequently, the whole scheme of fence legislation in a particular jurisdiction applies only to rural districts, urban districts being excluded.[18] The construction placed upon a state fencing statute by the courts of the state will be followed by the federal court.[19]

§ 3. As fixtures or part of the realty.

A fence permanently affixed to the land is generally considered in law as part of the realty, belongs to the person owning the land,[20] and passes with the conveyance of the land.[1] This has been held to be the case notwithstanding that the fence was built on adjoining land as a result of mistake,[2] unless there is a statute to the contrary,[3] or the fence was built with the consent, knowledge, inducement, or participation of the adjoining

---

11. Green v Mutual Steel Co. 268 **Ala** 648, 108 So 2d 837.

A municipal ordinance directing and compelling the removal of a fence erected on private property not subject to an easement is void as an attempt to take private property without compensation. Riley v Greenwood, 72 **SC** 90, 51 SE 532.

Easement as affecting the right to build fences, see 25 Am Jur 2d, EASEMENTS AND LICENSES §§ 89–91.

Practice Aids.—Restriction against building fence for specified term. 5 AM JUR LEGAL FORMS 5:1291.

12. Thomas Cusack Co. v Cincinnati, 9 **Ohio** NP NS 466, 20 Ohio Dec 219.

13. Slaughter v Collup, 22 **Tex** Civ App 578, 55 SW 182.

14. Hubbell v Peck, 15 **Conn** 133.

15. Griffith v Holman, 23 **Wash** 347, 63 P 239.

16. Greisinger v Klinhart (**Mo** App) 282 SW 473, reh quashed (**Mo**) 292 SW 75. 75.

17. As to statutes regulating partition or division fences, see § 10, infra.

18. Zarbaugh v Ellinger, 99 **Ohio** St 133, 124 NE 68, 6 ALR 208.

Lot fronts in a city need not be fenced unless there is an ordinance requiring it. Detroit v Beecher, 75 **Mich** 454, 42 NW 986.

408

19. New York C. & H. R. R. Co. v Price (CA1) 159 F 330, wherein the statutory duty of a railroad company to fence its tracks was held not for the benefit of other than adjoining landowners.

20. Bagley v Columbus S. R. Co. 98 **Ga** 626, 25 SE 638; Climer v Wallace, 28 **Mo** 556; Schmuck v Beck, 72 **Mont** 606, 234 P 477; Wentz v Fincher, 34 **NC** (12 Ired L) 297.

As to ownership of a partition or division fence, see § 16, infra.

1. Foulke v McIntosh (**Mo** App) 214 SW2d 735.

Annotation: 130 ALR 1049 et seq.

A fence, whether permanently annexed to the soil or constructed of rails so arranged as to constitute an inclosure, is a fixture, a part of the land, and passes with the freehold. Wheeler v State, 109 **Ala** 56, 19 So 993.

A fence built by one upon the land of another, under a parol agreement that the builder may remove it at will, passes with a grant of the land to a purchaser in good faith without notice of the agreement. Rowand v Anderson, 33 **Kan** 264, 6 P 255.

2. Seymour v Watson, 5 Blackf (**Ind**) 555; Kimball v Adams, 52 **Wis** 554, 9 NW 170.

Annotation: 130 ALR 1035 et seq.

3. Garrett v Sewell, 95 **Ala** 456, 10 So 226; Scholl v Kinitzer, 83 **Wis** 307, 53 NW 450.

Annotation: 130 ALR 1044 et seq.

FIGURE 3-C
AMERICAN JURISPRUDENCE SECOND

    DISCUSSION OF PROBLEM 3.2   The initial sentence of the section defines a "fence" to be "an inclosing structure or barrier about a field or other space, or about any object, intended to prevent intrusion from without or straying from within."   Footnote 1 indicates that in "Shamberg v Lincoln, 174 **Neb** 146, 116 NW2d 18," tennis court back-stops were not considered to be a "fence" within the meaning of an ordinance prohibiting the building of fences of a certain height.

    The lawyer thus would want to ask the client what was on the other side of the fence (e.g., a tennis court, baseball field, golf course). This footnote would also reinforce any earlier general notion that the height of the fence might be regulated by a local ordinance.   If the lawyer had not already determined the location of the land involved, the lawyer would want to ask the client if the property is within the city limits of a municipality.

    The first sentence in § 2 indicates that "[a] landowner has the inherent right to fence his [or her] land . . . in the absence of a valid statute or contractual restriction to the contrary."   This basic principle again directs the lawyer to consider whether legislation might restrict the neighbor's otherwise "inherent right to fence his [or her] land."   The reference to the contractual restriction should stimulate another line of inquiry.   Are there any oral or written agreements between the parties?

    In the context of land, the relevant contract is the deed by which a landowner holds title.   The lawyer would want to determine if there are any restrictive covenants concerning fences in the neighbor's deed. This possibility should stimulate a factual inquiry (checking for restrictive covenants in the register of deeds) and possibly additional legal research based upon the results of that inquiry—for example, may the covenant be enforced by the adjoining landowner and, if so, how?

    The first sentence of this section is supported by footnote 11, which, in part, refers to "[e]asement[s] as affecting the right to build fences."   Thus, another factual inquiry that this reference might stimulate is whether the adjoining landowner (or the landowner's predecessor) has ever granted an easement (which, like a restrictive covenant, would appear in the chain of title).   If there is not a contractual easement, can one be implied or acquired by usage?   Does such an easement extend to the right to receive light?   To pursue this line of inquiry, you would consult the cross-reference to "25 Am Jur 2d, Easements and Licenses §§ 89-91" provided in footnote 11.

    The discussion in this section of the "Fences" topic in *American Jurisprudence Second* emphasizes the right of the landowner to "build his [or her] fences on his [or her] own property as he [or she] sees fit, and he [or she] is free to choose the kind of fence reasonably suited to his [or her] purpose."   This proposition should raise questions in the

researcher's mind. Although the landowner is free to build fences, is the fence that this landowner built "reasonably suited to his [or her] purpose"? What was the landowner's purpose or intent? Is this "reasonably suited" restriction enforceable by an adjoining landowner?

As noted above, the "Treated elsewhere" note in Figure 3-A suggests a related line of inquiry concerning the landowner's intent or purpose. "Spite fences" are discussed in "1 Am Jur 2d, Adjoining Landowners §§ 106-117." Why did the landowner build such a high fence? What was the landowner's intent?

The next sentence in § 2 states that "a landowner may not plant the corner post of his [or her] front fence so that half of it is on his [or her] neighbor's land." This encroachment would be considered a trespass. This discussion should stimulate yet another line of inquiry. Where exactly in relation to the property line is the fence located? Was the property surveyed before the fence was built?

The outline in Figure 3-A indicates that § 4 discusses "Fencing another's land or encroaching fences." The availability of injunctive relief is discussed in § 5. Depending on the results of further factual inquiries (e.g., after a survey), research in these areas could be continued.

The last paragraph in § 2 indicates that statutes regulating the construction and maintenance of fences have been enacted in many jurisdictions. It also indicates, however, that many of these statutes apply only to rural districts.

The scope of topic and the outline in Figure 3-A indicate that it may make some difference if the fence erected by the landowner is a "Partition or Division Fence" (§§ 6-32). Where in relation to the boundary line is the fence located? Is this relevant to the client's problem? What is the fence made of? Is there, for example, barbed wire across the top of the fence?

3. CROSS-REFERENCES

PROBLEM 3.3 Assume that the lawyer decides to pursue the reference to 1 Am. Jur. 2d, *Adjoining Landowners* §§ 106-117, which discusses "spite fences." Sections 106 and 107 have been reproduced in Figures 3-D, 3-E, and 3-F. The relevant sections (§§ 71-73) from *Corpus Juris Secundum* on the same topic have been reproduced in Figures 3-G and 3-H. Not only will these sections stimulate additional factual inquiries and provide initial summaries of the law, but they will also provide you with cross-references for developing your legal research. Based on the above figures, determine (1) which *A.L.R.* annotation(s) directly relate(s) to this research question and (2) which West topic(s) and key number(s) cover points of law relating to spite fences.

1 Am Jur 2d   ADJOINING LANDOWNERS   § 106

§ 104. Change in dominant estate; destruction or alteration of building.

It has been stated broadly in cases involving express easements that a substantial change in the dominant estate may result in the extinguishment of an easement of light and air, as where the building to which such an easement is appurtenant has ceased to exist.[8] An easement of light and air attaching to a building as the dominant tenement is extinguished where the building is destroyed or so altered that the easement is no longer possible.[9] One who has an easement of light, air, and view over another's land will generally lose such right by the destruction of the building to which it appertained and the erection of a new building without windows situated similarly to those in the old building.[10] Usually, however, the easement is not lost by a mere nonuser resulting from the destruction of the old building if a later new building is erected with similar windows.[11] An easement of light and air is not lost by a change of use of the dominant tenement where there was nothing in the deed creating the easement limiting it to a particular use and the windows in the building thereon were not changed.[12]

§ 105. Foreclosure of mortgage.

The view is generally taken that an easement is lost by the foreclosure of a mortgage on the servient tenement, where the mortgage was executed prior to the creation of the easement.[13] Where a servient state which was subject to a mortgage executed prior to the creation of an easement of light and air was conveyed to one who did not assume payment thereof, and he permitted foreclosure of the mortgage and bid the property in at the foreclosure sale to rid it of the easement, it has been held that the easement was extinguished by the foreclosure.[14]

V. SPITE FENCES OR STRUCTURES

§ 106. Generally; at common law.

A spite fence or structure is defined as one which is of no beneficial use or pleasure to the owner but was erected and is maintained by him for the purpose of annoying his neighbor[15] or with the malicious motive of injuring him by shutting out his light, air, and view.[16] Whether the common law permits an owner to

---

8. Hopkins the Florist, Inc. v Fleming, 112 Vt 389, 26 A2d 96, 142 ALR 463.
Annotation: 142 ALR 481.

9. Hopkins the Florist, Inc. v Fleming, supra.

Where an easement of view was appurtenant to a building on a corner lot when facing on a certain street, the moving of such building so that it faced another street extinguished the easement, where such change was intended to be permanent. Hopkins the Florist, Inc. v Fleming, 112 Vt 389, 26 A2d 96, 142 ALR 463.

10. Dyer v Sanford, 50 Mass (9 Met) 395.
Annotation: 142 ALR 481; 25 ALR2d 1321, § 22.

11. City Nat. Bank v Van Meter, 59 NJ Eq 32, 45 A 280, affd 61 NJ Eq 674, 47 A 1131.
Annotation: 25 ALR2d 1321, § 22.

12. Hennen v Deveny, 71 W Va 629, 77 SE 142 (church converted into a business building without changing windows).

13. See EASEMENTS AND LICENSES (1st ed § 168).

14. Christ P. E. Church v Mack, 93 NY 488, the court adding, however, that if the owner of the easement had desired to save it he should have sought to modify the foreclosure decree upon showing the peril to the easement and offering to bid the full amount of the mortgage and costs upon the sale subject to the servitude and should have asked that the sale be so made; that the mortgagee could not have objected thereto, since his debt would have been paid in full, and the owner of the property subject to the mortgage could have asserted no equity to have the sale made to him free of the easement.

15. Burris v Creech, 220 NC 302, 17 SE 2d 123.
Annotation: 133 ALR 691.

16. Racich v Mastrovich, 65 SD 321, 273 NW 660.

761

FIGURE 3-D

AMERICAN JURISPRUDENCE SECOND

§ 107   ADJOINING LANDOWNERS   1 Am Jur 2d

erect such a fence or structure is a question upon which there has been much divergence of opinion.[17] The early cases and some of the more recent ones at common law hold that a man can build a fence or like structure upon his own land as high as he pleases, even though he erects it solely out of spite and for the purpose of annoying his neighbor.[18] Such a rule precludes the maintenance of an action to recover damages on account of the erection of a spite fence or structure,[19] and an injunction cannot be maintained under it to restrain the erection of such a fence or structure as a private nuisance.[20] In some more recent cases, however, there has been a decided tendency to abandon the rule laid down by the earlier decisions and to adopt what is deemed to be a more just and common-sense view of the question. Accordingly, it is now widely held that an adjoining landowner may sue for damages caused by, or may enjoin the erection or maintenance of, a spite fence or like structure erected for the sole purpose of injuring him in the lawful and beneficial use of his property.[1] Thus, it is held that if an owner builds a fence without any benefit or pleasure to himself, but solely with the malicious motive of injuring the adjoining owner by shutting out his light, air, or view, he thereby violates the rights of the adjoining owner.[2] In justification of this view, it is said that the malicious use of property resulting in injury to another is never a lawful use, that the right to use one's property is qualified rather than absolute, and that the right of landowner to the free passage of light and air from adjoining premises is subject only to a superior right of the adjoining owner to make use of his property in good faith for the purpose of increasing his enjoyment of it.[3] It has also been said that the grounds upon which various courts have upheld spite fence statutes are those upon which spite fences should be held to constitute nuisances at common law, on the theory that if the structures were not nuisances at common law any statute restricting the right to erect such structures would be unconstitutional.[4]

§ 107. Prohibitions and regulations by statute or ordinance.

Statutes have been enacted in many jurisdictions prohibiting the erection and maintenance of spite fences or structures.[5] Some provide in effect that if

---

17. *Annotation:* 133 ALR 691.

18. Camfield v United States, 167 US 518, 42 L ed 260, 17 S Ct 864; Falloon v Schilling, 29 **Kan** 292; Rideout v Knox, 148 **Mass** 368, 19 NE 390 (recognizing rule); Bordeaux v Greene. 22 **Mont** 254, 56 P 218; Mahan v Brown (NY) 13 Wend 261; Letts v Kessler, 54 **Ohio St** 73, 42 NE 765; Cohen v Perrino, 355 **Pa** 455, 50 A2d 348; Karasek v Peier, 22 **Wash** 419, 61 P 33 (dictum); Koblegard v Hale, 60 **W Va** 37, 53 SE 793; Metzger v Hochrein, 107 **Wis** 267, 83 NW 308.
Annotation: 133 ALR 697.

19. Guest v Reynolds, 68 Ill 478; Mahan v Brown (NY) 13 Wend 261; Metzger v Hochrein, 107 **Wis** 267, 83 NW 308.
Annotation: 133 ALR 698 et seq.

20. Letts v Kessler, 54 **Ohio St** 73, 42 NE 765; Koblegard v Hale, 60 **W Va** 37, 53 SE 793.
Annotation: 133 ALR 698 et seq.

1. Norton v Randolph, 176 **Ala** 381, 58 So 283; Hornsby v Smith, 191 **Ga** 491, 13 SE2d 20, 133 ALR 684; Flaherty v Moran, 81

Mich 52, 45 NW 381; Burke v Smith, 69 Mich 380, 37 NW 838; Dunbar v O'Brien. 117 **Neb** 245, 220 NW 278, 58 ALR 1033 (pile of old lumber obstructing light and air at cellar windows); Bush v Mockett, 95 Neb 552, 145 NW 1001; Barger v Barringer, 151 NC 433, 66 SE 439; Hibbard v Halliday, 58 Okla 244, 158 P 1158; Erickson v Hudson, 70 Wyo 317, 249 P2d 523.
Annotation: 133 ALR 692.

Practice Aids.—Complaint for removal of spite fence. 15 Am Jur Pl & Pr Forms 15:4.
Complaint to enjoin malicious construction of fence closing windows. 9 Am Jur Pl & Pr Forms 9:161.

2. Racich v Mastrovich, 65 SD 321, 273 NW 660.

3. Hornsby v Smith, 191 Ga 491, 13 SE 2d 20, 133 ALR 684.

4. Barger v Barringer, 151 NC 433, 66 SE 439. To like effect, see Burke v Smith, 69 Mich 380, 37 NW 838.

5. Rapuano v Ames, 21 **Conn** Supp 110, 145

FIGURE 3-E

AMERICAN JURISPRUDENCE SECOND

a landowner maliciously and with an intent to injure an adjoining landowner in the use or disposition of his lands erects or maintains any structure which impairs the value of the lands, he shall be liable to pay the damage caused, and that the commission of such an act may be restrained by injunction.[6] Others have provided that a landowner shall not erect any structure on his land, however lawful it would be otherwise, if he does it maliciously and with the intent to injure his neighbor.[7] Some statutes prohibit any fence, or other structure in the nature of a fence, unnecessarily exceeding a certain height, maliciously erected or maintained for the purpose of annoying the adjoining owners.[8] Some statutes prohibiting or regulating spite fences or structures declare such a fence or structure to be a private nuisance.[9]

§ 108. — Constitutionality.

Statutes prohibiting the erection of spite structures maliciously and for no useful purpose have generally been upheld as against the contention that they constitute a taking of property without due process of law.[10] Some courts have said that the right to erect a spite fence, though a legal right, is not one of the immediate rights of property, and that the loss of such right is so inconsequential that the state may deprive one thereof in the exercise of the police power without making compensation therefor. Another view is that such statutes are valid on the theory that there is no legal or property right to use one's land solely to injure another, and that consequently the statute does not constitute a taking.[11] Thus, statutes preventing the unreasonable maintenance of a structure that shuts out the light and air from the adjoining premises with a bad motive for its sole purpose are within the limits of the constitutional exercise of police power.[12]

A statute making it unlawful to build structures on one's own land, which are primarily or solely intended to injure and annoy an adjoining owner and which serve no really useful or reasonable purpose, is not unconstitutional, although, if it prohibited the erection of useful and valuable structures, it would deprive the owner of property without due process of law and compensation.[13]

A2d 384; Humphrey v Mansbach, 265 Ky 675, 97 SW2d 573; Rideout v Knox, 148 Mass 368, 19 NE 390; Horan v Byrnes, 72 NH 93, 54 A 945; Karasek v Peier, 22 Wash 419, 61 P 33.

Annotation: 133 ALR 704.

6. *Annotation:* 133 ALR 704.

In those jurisdictions wherein statutes have been enacted which prohibit the erection of any structure on one's own land impairing the value of the adjacent land, the owner of the structure must answer for the damage caused by the erection of a structure maliciously and with an intent thereby to injure the adjacent owner in the use or disposition of his lands, or the commission of the wrongful act may be restrained by injunction. Hasselbring v Koepke, 263 Mich 466, 248 NW 869, 93 ALR 1170; Karasek v Peier, 22 Wash 419, 61 P 33; Metzger v Hochrein, 107 Wis 267, 83 NW 308.

Annotation: 133 ALR 704 et seq.

An unusually high fence is a structure within the meaning of such a statute. Karasek v Peier, 22 Wash 419, 61 P 33.

7. Whitlock v Uhle, 75 Conn 423, 53 A 891; Gallagher v Dodge, 48 Conn 387.

A fence is a structure within such a statute. Rapuano v Ames, 21 Conn Supp 110, 145 A2d 384.

8. Taliaferro v Salyer, 162 Cal App 2d 685, 328 P2d 799 (10 feet).

Annotation: 133 ALR 704.

9. Rideout v Knox, 148 Mass 368, 19 NE 390.

Annotation: 133 ALR 704.

10. Rideout v Knox, 148 Mass 368, 19 NE 390; Horan v Byrnes, 72 NH 93, 54 A 945; Karasek v Peier, 22 Wash 419, 61 P 33.

Annotation: 133 ALR 704.

11. *Annotation:* 133 ALR 704 et seq.

12. Horan v Byrnes, 72 NH 93, 54 A 945; Metzger v Hochrein, 107 Wis 267, 83 NW 308.

Annotation: 133 ALR 704 et seq.

13. Karasek v Peier, 22 Wash 419, 61 P 33.

763

FIGURE 3-F
AMERICAN JURISPRUDENCE SECOND

§§ 69-71 ADJOINING LANDOWNERS 2 C. J. S.

this may contribute to the enjoyment of his estate.[69]

§ 70. Right to Privacy from Overlooking Windows

A landowner cannot assert by action, a right of privacy from overlooking doors or windows in the absence of a statute, contract, or grant protecting him.

Library References

Adjoining Landowners ⊕10(2).

In the absence of statute, or of a contract or grant otherwise, a landowner has a right to place doors, windows, or openings overlooking adjoining land, and the adjoining owner has no action for an interference with his privacy, his only remedy being to build on his own land so as to obstruct the view.[70]

B. OBSTRUCTION

§ 71. In General

Generally, in the absence of statute or a contract to the contrary, a landowner may, by building on his own land, deprive the adjoining owner of the light, air, and view of which he was the recipient before the structure was erected without inflicting a legal injury by such obstruction.

Library References

Adjoining Landowners ⊕10.

In the absence of statute it may be said generally that a landowner may, by building on his own land, deprive the adjoining owner of the light, air, and view of which he was the recipient before the structure was erected without inflicting a legal injury by such obstruction,[71] at least in the absence of a malevolent purpose,[72] unless it is in violation of a contract;[73] and the adjoining landowner has no cause for complaint, and cannot recover damages or obtain equitable relief, where his neighbor constructs a house or fence, or otherwise interferes with the light and air previously coming over the property.[74]

The fact that the landowner was granted a permit by the municipality, acting under a valid ordinance, for the installation of an electric sign, does not grant the sign owner complete immunity from damages inflicted on the adjoining property owner;[75] nor does the existence of an authorizing ordinance preclude the granting of an injunction against the

69. D.C.—Ash v. Tate, 73 F.2d 518, 64 App.D.C. 9.
Ind.—Giller v. West, 69 N.E. 548, 162 Ind. 17.
Mo.—Stroup v. Rauschelbach, 261 S. W. 346, 217 Mo.App. 236.
Okl.—City of McAlester v. King, 317 P.2d 265.
Tex.—Vissering v. Granberry, Civ. App., 344 S.W.2d 898, error refused no reversible error.
1 C.J. p 1228 note 89.

Acquired by agreement
S.C.—Marshall v. Columbia, etc., Electric St. R. Co., 53 S.E. 417, 73 S.C. 241.

70. Mass.—Christ Church v. Lavezzolo, 30 N.E. 471, 156 Mass. 89.
N.Y.—Corpus Juris Secundum cited in Pica v. Cross County Const. Corp., 18 N.Y.S.2d 470, 473, 259 App.Div. 128.
Pa.—Cohen v. Perrino, 50 A.2d 348, 355 Pa. 455.
1 C.J. p 1229 note 91.

71. Ark.—De Mers v. Graupner, 53 S.W.2d 8, 186 Ark. 214.
D.C.—Ash v. Tate, 73 F.2d 518, 64 App.D.C. 9.
Ga.—S. A. Lynch Corp. v. Stone, 87 S.E.2d 57, 211 Ga. 516.
Mich.—Krulikowski v. Tide Water Oil Sales Corp., 232 N.W. 223, 251 Mich. 684.

Mo.—Stroup v. Rauschelbach, 261 S. W. 346, 217 Mo.App. 236.
N.J.—Blumberg v. Weiss, 17 A.2d 823, 129 N.J.Eq. 34.
N.M.—Metz v. Tierney, 83 P. 788, 13 N.M. 363.
N.Y.—D'Inzillo v. Basile, 40 N.Y.S.2d 293, 180 Misc. 237, affirmed 43 N. Y.S.2d 638, 266 App.Div. 875—De Muro v. Havranek, 275 N.Y.S. 186, 153 Misc. 787.
Myers v. Gemmel, 10 Barb. 537.
Okl.—City of McAlester v. King, 317 P.2d 265—Bixby v. Cravens, 156 P. 1184, 57 Okl. 119, L.R.A.1916E 871.
Pa.—Maiorello v. Arlotta, 73 A.2d 374, 364 Pa. 557—Corpus Juris Secundum cited in Cohen v. Perrino, 50 A.2d 348, 349, 355 Pa. 455.
Tenn.—Corpus Juris Secundum cited in Southern Advertising Co. v. Sherman, 308 S.W.2d 491, 494, 43 Tenn. App. 323.
Tex.—Scharlack v. Gulf Oil Corp., Civ. App., 368 S.W.2d 705—Harrison v. Langlinais, Civ.App., 312 S.W.2d 286—Dallas Land & Loan Co. v. Garrett, Civ.App., 276 S.W. 471.
1 C.J. p 1229 note 92.

Fence eighteen or twenty feet high
Where there is no servitude of view existing in favor of a lot owned by plaintiff, defendant has a right to build a fence on his lot to the height of eighteen or twenty feet.
La.—Parle v. D'Arcy, 28 La.Ann. 424.

72. Ga.—S. A. Lynch Corp. v. Stone, 87 S.E.2d 57, 211 Ga. 516.
Motive of obstruction see infra § 72.
73. Or.—Silverfield v. Frank, 73 P. 1032, 43 Or. 502.
74. Cal.—Taliaferro v. Salyer, 328 P. 2d 799, 162 C.A.2d 685.
Ga.—S. A. Lynch Corp. v. Stone, 87 S.E.2d 57, 211 Ga. 516.
Ind.—Wolf v. Forcum, 161 N.E.2d 175, 130 Ind.App. 10.
Okl.—City of McAlester v. King, 317 P.2d 265.
Tex.—Boys Town, Inc., v. Garrett, Civ.App., 283 S.W.2d 416, error refused no reversible error.

Shrubbery
A deprivation of air and light by reason of height of shrubbery on land of adjoining landowner would not entitle plaintiff to an order to cause removal of shrubbery or to limit its height.
Tenn.—Granberry v. Jones, 216 S.W. 2d 721, 188 Tenn. 51.

Fence to keep out trespassers
A landowner may not enjoin the construction or maintenance of an eight-foot high solid board fence, which an adjoining owner has built to keep out trespassers.
Ark.—De Mers v. Graupner, 53 S.W.2d 8, 186 Ark. 214.
75. Tex.—Rogers v. Scaling, Civ. App., 298 S.W.2d 877, error refused no reversible error.

66

FIGURE 3-G
CORPUS JURIS SECUNDUM

2 C.J.S.   **ADJOINING LANDOWNERS §§ 71–73**

erection of the sign.[76]

The obstruction of light, air, and view in the aspect of a nuisance is treated in C.J.S. Nuisances § 25.

§ 72. Motive of Obstruction

Motive is immaterial where the landowner erects a structure which, although it incidentally obstructs the light, air, and view of adjoining owners, is of substantial benefit to him; but if the structure serves no useful purpose and is erected solely to injure or annoy the adjoining owner, in the absence of statute, in a number of jurisdictions legal or equitable relief may be had by the adjoining owner, although this is not the rule in all jurisdictions.

Library References

Adjoining Landowners ⬅10(3).

The motives which actuate a landowner to make improvements for the substantial betterment of his property are immaterial although the light, air, and view of his neighbor are incidentally obstructed.[77]

Where a structure is erected solely to injure or annoy the adjoining owner and serves no useful purpose, in the absence of a governing statute, the rule in some jurisdictions is that here, too, motive is immaterial;[78] but in other jurisdictions the malevolence furnishes a ground for legal or equi-

table relief from the injury.[79] However, even under the latter view, a high fence or structure constructed for spite is not actionable if it also serves a useful purpose.[80]

§ 73. —— Under Statutes

Statutes providing for relief against fences and like structures erected and maintained to spite or annoy the owners of adjoining lands are not unconstitutional, and, when in derogation of the common law of the jurisdiction, are to be strictly construed.

Library References

Adjoining Landowners ⬅10(3).

By statute in some jurisdictions remedies are provided for the malicious erection of any structure intended to annoy and injure any owner or lessee of adjacent land in respect to his use or disposition of the property.[81] Under a statute making the construction and maintenance of such a fence an offense punishable by a daily fine, it has been held that the adjoining landowner can recover damages caused by the fence.[82]

Under other statutes, fences or like structures exceeding a prescribed height and maliciously erected and maintained to spite or annoy the owners or occupants of adjoining land are declared a private nuisance, and a remedy is prescribed therefor.[83]

---

76. Ark.—Smith v. Rose Courts, Inc., 246 S.W.2d 554, 220 Ark. 179.

77. Pa.—**Corpus Juris Secundum cited in** Cohen v. Perrino, 50 A.2d 348, 349, 355 Pa. 455.
Tex.—Harrison v. Langlinais, Civ. App., 312 S.W.2d 286—Dallas Land & Loan Co. v. Garrett, Civ.App., 276 S.W. 471.

Erection partly for spite
Where a structure serves a useful and beneficial purpose, it does not give rise to a cause of action, either for damages or for an injunction under the maxim sic utere tuo ut alienum non laedas, even though it causes injury to another by cutting off the light and air and interfering with the view that would otherwise be available over adjoining land in its natural state, regardless of the fact that the structure may have been erected partly for spite.
Fla.—Fontainebleau Hotel Corp. v. Forty-Five Twenty-Five, Inc., Civ. App., 114 So.2d 357.

Construction tainted with spirit of retaliation
The erection of a fence to exclude obnoxious odors and disturbing noises from an automobile carburetor plant will not be enjoined, although its construction may be tainted with a spirit of retaliation.

Ala.—Daniel v. Birmingham Dental Mfg. Co., 93 So. 652, 207 Ala. 659.

78. Ky.—Saddler v. Alexander, 56 S. W. 518, 21 Ky.Law 1835.
Pa.—Maioriello v. Arlotta, 73 A.2d 374, 364 Pa. 557.
1 C.J. p 1229 note 94.

79. Mich.—Krulikowski v. Tide Water Oil Sales Corp., 232 N.W. 223, 251 Mich. 684.
Neb.—Dunbar v. O'Brien, 220 N.W. 278, 117 Neb. 245, 58 A.L.R. 1033—Bush v. Mockett, 145 N.W. 1001, 95 Neb. 552, 52 L.R.A.,N.S., 736.
Okl.—Hibbard v. Halliday, 158 P. 1158, 58 Okl. 244, L.R.A. 1916F 903.
S.D.—Racich v. Mastrovich, 273 N.W. 660, 65 S.D. 321.
1 C.J. p 1230 note 95.

Common law rule held inapplicable
Ga.—Hornsby v. Smith, 13 S.E.2d 20, 191 Ga. 491, 133 A.L.R. 684.

No useful purpose
Failure of a proposed fence to serve any useful purpose to promote the convenience or welfare of party proposing to erect is a factor to be considered by court of equity whose assistance is sought in the erection thereof.
Neb.—State, Dept. of Roads v. Merritt Bros. Sand & Gravel Co., 144 N.W. 2d 180, 180 Neb. 660.

Pile of lumber
Old lumber maliciously piled on a

lot to shut out light and air from neighbor's windows is a nuisance and may be abated.
Neb.—Dunbar v. O'Brien, 220 N.W. 278, 117 Neb. 245, 58 A.L.R. 1033.

Responsibility of joint owners
Both of two joint owners may be held responsible for the maintenance of a fence where, although only one lives on the property, both are opposed to the removal of the fence.
Mich.—Peek v. Roe, 67 N.W. 1080, 110 Mich. 52.

80. Okl.—Green v. Schick, 153 P.2d 821, 194 Okl. 491.

81. Conn.—United Petroleum Corp. v. Atlantic Refining Co., 212 A.2d 589, 3 Conn.Cir. 255.

Determination of motive
Question whether structure was maliciously erected within statute authorizing action against adjacent landowner who maliciously erects any structure thereon with intent to injure owner of adjacent land, is to be determined rather by its character, location and use than by inquiry into actual motive in mind of person erecting it.
Conn.—Rapuano v. Ames, 145 A.2d 384, 21 Conn.Sup. 110.

82. Ky.—Humphrey v. Mansbach, 97 S.W.2d 573, 265 Ky. 675.

83. Cal.—Bar Due v. Cox, 190 P. 1056, 47 C.A. 713.

FIGURE 3-H
CORPUS JURIS SECUNDUM

DISCUSSION OF PROBLEM 3.3   Several footnotes in these sections of *American Jurisprudence Second* indicate that an early annotation ("133 ALR 691") covers many of the points of law discussed in this section. The Library References in *Corpus Juris Secundum* indicate that the relevant points of law are digested under Adjoining Landowners 10 and, more particularly, Adjoining Landowners 10(3).

4. POCKET PARTS

Like many legal publications, *American Jurisprudence Second* and *Corpus Juris Secundum* are kept current by annual pocket parts.

PROBLEM 3.4   Examine the portion of the pocket part covering the relevant sections (beginning with section 106) of the topic "Adjoining Landowners" in *American Jurisprudence Second* in Figure 3-I. What additional information is provided, if any?

(Rev), Easements and Licenses, Form 34.1.

Additional case authorities for section:
In action to prevent neighbor from building house in violation of covenant in deed requiring setback of 25 feet from street in order to protect plaintiff's view of ocean, mandatory injunctive relief was appropriate where plaintiff might not have been readily compensated by damages and defendants had been informed of violation in time to minimize expense of removing structure. Roehrs v Lees (1981) 178 **NJ** Super 399, 429 A2d 388.

§ 102. Generally

p 760—*Add following note 3:* The fact that windows were not used as a source of light has been held not to show an abandonment of the easement.[3.5]

n 3.5—First Nat. Trust & Sav. Bank v Raphael, 201 **Va** 718, 113 SE2d 683.

§ 106. Generally; at common law

Practice Aids: Malicious design and construction of fence. 22 Am Jur Proof of Facts 2d 683.

p 762, n 1—Brittingham v Robertson (Del Ch) 280 A2d 741.
Sundowner, Inc. v King, 95 **Idaho** 367, 509 P2d 785.

§ 110. As nuisances

Practice Aids: Fence as nuisance, 80 ALR3d 962.

p 764, n 3—Sundowner, Inc. v King, 95 **Idaho** 367, 509 P2d 785.

220

agement, Ltd. (1979, **Fla** App D4) 373 So 2d 411.
In an action to establish the boundary lines between the parties' respective properties and to recover damages resulting from being deprived of a use of a portion of property encroached upon by a building, the trial court submitted an improper measure of damages to the jury where it submitted a special issue containing elements of both temporary and permanent measures of damages but apparently considered the injury temporary in nature, and there was nothing to indicate the parties, whose pleadings prayed for judgment for title and possession of the property, considered the injury to be permanent. Lone Star Development Corp. v Reilly (1983, **Tex** App 5th Dist) 656 SW2d 521.

§ 124. Limitations

p 774, n 14—Cox v Berry, 233 **Ark** 910, 349 SW2d 661 (three years).

Annotation: When does cause of action accrue, for purposes of statute of limitations against action based upon encroachment of building or other structure upon land of another. 12 ALR3d 1265.

p 774, n 17—
See 509 Sixth Ave. Corp. v New York City Transit Authority, 15 **NY2d** 48, 255 NYS2d 89, 203 NE2d 486, 12 ALR3d 1258, holding that though cause of action for trespass through encroachment by underground structure (subway) accrued when invasion of plaintiff's property occurred 21 years before institution of action, and though action would be barred by 3-year statute governing injuries to real property if encroachment were considered to be a

[1 Am Jur 2d Supp]

FIGURE 3-I
AMERICAN JURISPRUDENCE SECOND POCKET PART

DISCUSSION OF PROBLEM 3.4 The pocket part covering the relevant sections (beginning with section 106) of the topic "Adjoining Landowners" in *American Jurisprudence Second* in Figure 3-I cites (in § 110) another *A.L.R.* annotation ("80 ALR3d 962") ("Fence as nuisance"). Also cited (in § 106 and § 110) is an Idaho case, "Sundowner, Inc. v King, 95 **Idaho** 367, 509 P2d 785."

5. TABLES OF PARALLEL REFERENCES

American Jurisprudence Second and *Corpus Juris Secundum* volumes are periodically replaced with updated volumes. Sometimes, you will have a citation (from an older case, for example) to the earlier version of the encyclopedia. These volumes have "Tables of Parallel References" (*Am. Jur. 2d*) and "Tables of Corresponding Sections" (*C.J.S.*), which are used to find where a known citation to a prior version is treated in a later edition.

PROBLEM 3.5 Assume that you are reading a source that has the following citation: 2 C.J.S. Adjoining Landowner § 52 (1936). Assume that you have located *C.J.S.* volume 2 and have turned to § 52 and that you immediately notice § 52 does not deal with erecting structures that interfere with a neighbor's enjoyment of his or her land. By consulting the title page, you could determine that the current version of volume 2 was published in 1972. Use the "Table of Corresponding Sections" shown in Figure 3-J to find where material in § 52 is discussed in the current version of *Corpus Juris Secundum*.

ADJOINING LANDOWNERS

TABLE OF CORRESPONDING SECTIONS

The following table lists the former sections of the C.J.S. title Adjoining Landowners corresponding to the sections of the revised title in this volume.

Former §§	New §§	Former §§	New §§	Former §§	New §§
1	2	17	26–28	34	42
2	7	18	29	35	43
3	8	19	30	36	44–49
4	9	20	31	37	50
5	9, 11	21	32	38	52–54
6	12	22	35, 36	39	55
7	14	23	33	40	56, 57
8	3, 15	24	34	41	58
9	16	25	37	42	60
10	17	26	38	43	61
11	18	27	39	44	62
12	19	28	9, 11, 12, 14–39, 68–74	45	63–66
13	20	29	9, 11, 12, 14–38	46	67
14	21–23	30	40, 41	47	68
15	24	31	39, 43–49	48	69
16	25	32	30–37, 44–49, 74	49	70
		33	40, 41	50	71
				52	72, 73
				52	74

FIGURE 3-J
CORPUS JURIS SECUNDUM POCKET PART

DISCUSSION OF PROBLEM 3.5 The corresponding sections for § 52 in the current version of *C.J.S.* are §§ 72-74.

PROBLEM 3.6 Examine the Table of Parallel References from the volume of *American Jurisprudence Second* containing the "Fences" topic. Assume that you have found a citation to § 35 of *American Jurisprudence* (1st ed.). Using the Table in Figure 3-K below, determine in which sections of the second edition you could find corresponding discussions.

TABLE OF PARALLEL REFERENCES

This table shows where the subject matter of the various sections of articles in the first edition of American Jurisprudence is treated in American Jurisprudence 2d. It enables one to translate references in the Am Jur General Index, in the AM JUR FORMS books and in AM JUR PROOF OF FACTS as well as the many references to "Am Jur" in the reported cases in other legal publications, into references to Am Jur 2d.

When a particular subject matter is treated in another topic the title of the other topic is indicated.

The reader should always consult the volume index for detail and for matter not appearing in the first edition.

FENCES

AM JUR §§	AM JUR 2d §§	AM JUR §§	AM JUR 2d §§	AM JUR §§	AM JUR 2d §§
1	Scope note	20	10, 13	33	34
2	1	21	11, 19	34	35, 41
3	2	22	14, 15, 23, 35	35	20, 35, 38
4–9	ANIMALS	23	1, 17	36	39
10	3, 16	24	18	37	LANDLORD AND TENANT
11	6, 16	25	18	38	41, 42
12	13	26	13, 17, 19, 23	39	43, 44
13	ANIMALS	27	24, 27	40	46, 48, 49
14	8, 21	28	22, 23	41	47
15	8	29	23	42	48, 49
16	9	30	18, 25, 27, 30	43–46	ADJOINING LANDOWNERS
17	19	31	28, 29		
18	7, 19	32	33, 36, 37		
19	7				

FERRIES

AM JUR §§	AM JUR 2d §§	AM JUR §§	AM JUR 2d §§	AM JUR §§	AM JUR 2d §§
1	Scope note	21	28	41	50, 56, 63–65, 69, 74, 76
2	1, 2	22	31–35, 37	42	57, 76
3	4	23	29, 30	43	58, 76
4	3, 4, 11	24	29	44	63, 69
5	4, 26	25	44, 46	45	63, 65, 69
6	11, 17–19	26	30, 46, 47	46	59
7	15	27	45	47	60, 70, 76
8	16, 18	28	46, 49, 50	48	NEGLIGENCE
9	11	29	13	49	67
10	12	30	EXECUTIONS	50	38, 41, 42
11	12, 25	31	34–36, 41	51	39, 40
12	13, 14, 23, 53	32	35	52	48
13	33	33	36		

FIGURE 3-K
AMERICAN JURISPRUDENCE SECOND

DISCUSSION OF PROBLEM 3.6   The Table of Parallel References from the volume of *American Jurisprudence Second* indicates that §§ 20, 35, and 38 are the corresponding sections in the second edition.

6. RESTATEMENT PROVISIONS, COMMENTS, ILLUSTRATIONS, AND REPORTER'S NOTES

As noted in Chapter 1, restatements are drafted by committees or leading legal authorities under the auspices of the American Law Institute. This type of secondary authority is unique to the law.   Restatements cover basic (mostly common-law) areas of law. The primary organization of the restatements is by section.   Each section begins with a statement of the principle of law, followed by comments, illustrations, and, if appropriate, caveats.

The Restatement of Contracts, the first Restatement, was published in 1932.   Subsequently, the Restatements of Restitution, Property, Torts, Security, Judgments, Agency, Trusts, and Conflicts of Law were published.   Some of the original Restatements have been revised by the American Law Institute and have been published as "Restatement Seconds."   There is now a "Restatement Third" of the Foreign Relations Law of the United States.

Restatements can be located through the card or online catalog. They are often shelved in a reserve section.

PROBLEM 3.7   Assume that during the course of your research you have identified § 829 of the Second Restatement of Torts. Read this section, noting particularly clause (a),   "Comment on Clause (a)," and the accompanying "Illustration" in Figures 3-L and 3-M. What is the Restatement's position on structures that are built for the sole purpose of annoying an adjoining landowner?

---

§ 829.   Gravity vs. Utility—Conduct Malicious or Indecent

An intentional invasion of another's interest in the use and enjoyment of land is unreasonable if the harm is significant and the actor's conduct is

   (a) for the sole purpose of causing harm to the other; or

   (b) contrary to common standards of decency.

Comment:

   a. Public nuisance. The rule stated in this Section applies to conduct that results in a private nuisance, as defined in § 821D.

See Appendix for Reporter's Notes, Court Citations, and Cross References

133

FIGURE 3-L

RESTATEMENT (SECOND) OF TORTS

---

§ 829   TORTS SECOND   **Ch. 40**

A similar rule may also be, and commonly is, applied to conduct that results in a public nuisance, as defined in § 821B. Thus, in determining whether the gravity of the interference with the public right outweighs the utility of the actor's conduct (see § 826, Comment *a*), the fact that the conduct is inspired solely by hostility to the public right and a desire to interfere with it or that it is contrary to common standards of decency, will normally be sufficient to make any significant interference unreasonable. Particular statutes may, however, provide or be construed to mean that the interference with the public right is criminal without regard to the character of the actor's conduct; and in this case the rule stated here may have no application.

b. Private nuisance. The rule stated in this Section is a specific application of the general rule stated in § 826 to certain types of intentional invasion that are so uniformly regarded as unreasonable that they can be said to be so as a matter of law.

The rule here stated applies only when the harm is significant and the facts of a case clearly bring it within the requirements stated in Clauses (a) or (b). When it is doubtful whether the facts of a case bring it within the rule here stated, the unreasonableness of the invasion is determined by the trier of fact under the general rule stated in § 826.

Comment on Clause (a):

c. Malicious conduct. If one's sole purpose in what he is doing is to annoy and harm his neighbor, his conduct has no utility that the law will recognize. Even the owner of land in fee simple is not privileged to use the land solely for the purpose of harming his neighbors, and if he causes them significant harm, he is responsible if his conduct was for a nonbeneficial use and solely for the purpose of causing the harm.

Illustration:

> 1. A and B own adjoining residences. A quarrel between them results in hard feelings, and A builds a fence 25 feet high along the boundary between his lot and B's lot. A's sole purpose in building this fence is to annoy B by shutting out the light and view from his windows. A's conduct is malicious and he is subject to liability to B.

Comment on Clause (b):

d. Indecent conduct. Certain types of indecent conduct are illegal and clearly have no social value or utility. There are,

FIGURE 3-M

RESTATEMENT (SECOND) OF TORTS

DISCUSSION OF PROBLEM 3.7 The comment and illustration accompanying clause (a) of § 829 of the Second Restatement of Torts indicate building a structure such as a fence for the sole purpose of annoying an adjoining landowner will subject the builder to liability on a nuisance theory.

The appendices that accompany the second restatements of law provide another excellent source for case citations and cross-references.

PROBLEM 3.8 Examine the Reporter's Note accompanying § 829 and the Cross References shown in Figures 3-N and 3-O. (a) What digest topic and key numbers are relevant to this section? (b) What sections of *Corpus Juris Secundum* are relevant to this section?

Public dances or dance halls as nuisance. 44 A.L.R.2d 1381.
Sewage disposal plant as nuisance. 40 A.L.R.2d 1177.
Undertaking establishment as nuisance. 39 A.L.R.2d 1000.
Private school as nuisance. 27 A.L.R.2d 1249.
Tourist or trailer camp, motor court or motel, as nuisance. 24 A.L.R. 2d 571.
Use of phonograph, loud-speaker, or other mechanical or electrical device for broadcasting music, advertising, or sales talk from business premises, as nuisance. 23 A.L.R.2d 1289.
Stockyard as a nuisance. 18 A.L.R.2d 1033.
Animal rendering or bone-boiling plant or business as a nuisance. 17 A.L.R.2d 1269.
Coalyard as a nuisance. 8 A.L.R.2d 419.

§ 829. Gravity vs. Utility—Conduct Malicious or Indecent.

REPORTER'S NOTE

Clause (a): Spite fences: Norton v. Randolph, 176 Ala. 381, 58 So. 283 (1912); Hutcherson v. Alexander, 264 Cal.App.2d 126, 70 Cal.Rptr. 366 (1968); Hornsby v. Smith, 191 Ga. 491, 13 S.E.2d 20 (1941); Sundowner, Inc. v. King, 95 Idaho 367, 509 P.2d 785 (1973); Flaherty v. Moran, 81 Mich. 52, 45 N.W. 381 (1890); Barger v. Barringer, 151 N.C. 433, 66 S.E. 439 (1909); Burris v. Creech, 220 N.C. 302, 17 S.E.2d 123 (1941); Hibbard v. Halliday, 58 Okl. 244, 158 P. 1158 (1916); Racich v. Mastrovich, 65 S.D. 321, 273 N.W. 660 (1937); Erickson v. Hudson, 70 Wyo. 317, 249 P.2d 523 (1952).

Malicious interference with subterranean waters: Katz v. Walkinshaw, 141 Cal. 116, 70 P. 663 (1903); Gagnon v. French Lick Springs Hotel Co., 163 Ind. 687, 72 N.E. 849 (1904); Barclay v. Abraham, 121 Iowa 619, 96 N.

Cit.—cited; fol.—followed; quot.—quoted; sup.—support.
A complete list of abbreviations faces page 1.

Restate.Torts 2nd.App. §§ 708–840E—18   **529**

FIGURE 3-N
RESTATEMENT (SECOND) OF TORTS (APPENDIX)

§ **829**   TORTS, SECOND   Ch. 40

W. 1080 (1903); Chesley v. King, 74 Me. 164, 43 Am.Rep. 569 (1882); Stillwater Water Co. v. Farmer, 89 Minn. 58, 93 N.W. 907 (1903).

See also Medford v. Levy, 31 W.Va. 649, 8 S.E. 302 (1888) (door left open to give plaintiff aroma of cooking onions); Hollywood Silver Fox Farm v. Emmett, [1936] 2 K.B. 468 (firing gun to interfere with fox breeding); Burnett v. Rushton, 52 So. 2d 645 (Fla.1951) (spiteful noise, barking dog, obscene gestures).

Clause (b): Illustration 2 is taken from Hayden v. Tucker, 37 Mo. 214 (1866). In accord upon similar facts is Farrell v. Cook, 16 Neb. 483, 20 N.W. 720 (1884).

See also Magel v. Gruetli Benevolent Society, 203 Mo.App. 335, 218 S.W. 704 (1920) (obscene language and indecent exposure); Burnett v. Rushton, 52 So.2d 645 (Fla.1951) (noise and obscene gestures); cf. Barnett v. Tedescki, 154 Ala. 474, 45 So. 904 (1908) (bawdy house).

Cross References to

1. Digest System Key Numbers

C.J.S. Nuisances §§ 2 et seq., 10.
West's Key No. Digests, Nuisance ☞2, 59.

2. A.L.R. Annotations

Massage parlor as nuisance. 80 A.L.R.3d 1020.
Pornoshops or similar places disseminating obscene materials as nuisance. 58 A.L.R.3d 1134.
Exhibition of obscene motion pictures as nuisance. 50 A.L.R.3d 969.
Modern status of rules as to balance of convenience or social utility as affecting relief from nuisance. 40 A.L.R.3d 601.
Saloons or taverns as nuisance. 5 A.L.R.3d 989.
Water sports, amusements, or exhibitions as nuisance. 80 A.L.R.2d 1124.

FIGURE 3-O
RESTATEMENT (SECOND) OF TORTS (APPENDIX)

DISCUSSION OF PROBLEM 3.8 (a) The cross-references to "Digest System Key Numbers" indicates that Nuisance 2 and Nuisance 59 are the relevant digest topic and key numbers. These references can be used to find other cases that involve the same point of law.

(b) The cross-references also indicate that sections 2 et seq. and 10 of the "Nuisances" topic in *Corpus Juris Secundum* are relevant. Never assume that *C.J.S.* section numbers and West's key numbers are interchangeable. There is not a one-to-one correspondence.

The title page of the Restatement volume containing § 829 is shown in Figure 3-P.

RESTATEMENT OF THE LAW
SECOND

TORTS 2d

Volume 4
§§ 708–End

As Adopted and Promulgated

BY

THE AMERICAN LAW INSTITUTE
AT WASHINGTON, D. C.

May 19, 1977

ST. PAUL, MINN.
AMERICAN LAW INSTITUTE PUBLISHERS
1979

FIGURE 3-P
RESTATEMENT (SECOND) OF TORTS

CITING RESTATEMENTS OF THE LAW

According to *The Bluebook* Rule 12.8.5, restatements are cited by section or other relevant subdivision, not by page number. The date used in the citation is the date that the restatement was *adopted*. When you are citing a comment or illustration in a restatement, do not capitalize those terms in the citation (Rule 3.5). Note that there is no comma after the section number and that comment, illustration, and appendix should be abbreviated "cmt.," "illus.," and "app."

The following are examples of citations to a restatement:

Restatement of Restitution § 12 (1937).
Restatement (Second) of Property § 2.1 (1977).
Restatement of Contracts § 372(1) cmt. a (1932).
Restatement (Second) of Conflicts § 253 illus. 2 (1969).

PROBLEM 3.9 Assume that you want to cite section 829 shown in Figure 3-L in a memorandum of law. Based on the appropriate *Bluebook* rules, which one of the following citations would be correct?

(a) Restatement (Second) of Torts § 829 (1977).
(b) 4 American Law Institute, <u>Restatement of the Law, Second, Torts 2d</u> § 829, at 133 (1979).
(c) A.L.I., <u>Restatement (Second) of Torts</u> § 829 (1979).
(d) Restatement (Second) of Torts § 829 (1979).

DISCUSSION OF PROBLEM 3.9 Restatements of the Law are cited in a special form. Restatements should be cited by section or other relevant subdivision, not by a page number. The American Law Institute (A.L.I.) is not cited. The date that should be cited is the year that the restatement was adopted (1977), not the copyright date (1979) (see Figure 3-P). The correct answer is thus answer (a).

As previously noted, the appendices to the restatements provide cross-references. Another source of cross-references is Lawyers Coopera-tive/Bancroft-Whitney's "Total Client-Service Library References." Exam-ine the box showing these references on the first page of the following *A.L.R.3d* annotation on "Fence as Nuisance" in Figure 3-Q.

ANNOTATION

FENCE AS NUISANCE

by

Deborah Tussey, J.D.

_____

I. PRELIMINARY MATTERS

§ 1. Introduction:
  [a] Scope
  [b] Related matters
§ 2. Summary and comment:
  [a] Generally
  [b] Practice pointers

II. SIGNIFICANCE OF MOTIVE FOR ERECTION OF FENCE

§ 3. View that motive irrelevant:
  [a] Generally
  [b] Absence of legal injury
§ 4. View that malicious motive may justify remedy
§ 5. Effect of useful purpose:
  [a] As precluding relief
  [b] Dominant purpose
  [c] Balance of utility against harm

TOTAL CLIENT-SERVICE LIBRARY® REFERENCES

1 Am Jur 2d, Adjoining Landowners §§ 106–112; 58 Am Jur 2d, Nuisances § 71

18 Am Jur Pl & Pr Forms (Rev Ed), Nuisances, Form 132

13 Am Jur Legal Forms 2d, Nuisances §§ 188:12–188:15

8 Am Jur Proof of Facts 527, Nuisances

4 Am Jur Trials 441, Solving Statutes of Limitation Problems § 9

US L Ed Digest, Fences § 1; Nuisances § 8

ALR Digests, Adjoining Landowners § 5; Nuisances § 57

L Ed Index to Annos, Fences; Nuisance

ALR Quick Index, Fences; Nuisance

Federal Quick Index, Fences; Nuisance; Spite Structures

Consult POCKET PART in this volume for later cases

962

FIGURE 3-Q
A.L.R.3D

The following table summarizes the basic functions of the various research aid discussed in this section:

RESEARCH AIDS IN SECONDARY SOURCES

Research Aid	Function
Scope Notes	Describe what is covered in a topic and what is covered elsewhere; especially helpful when using a topic method of search
Tables of Parallel References	List where sections or topics covered in an earlier version are now covered in a later version
West's Library References	Cross-references to related sources and material published by the West Publishing Co. (including digest topics and key numbers and *C.J.S.* references)
Lawyers Cooperative/ Bancroft-Whitney's Total Client-Library References	Cross-references to related sources and material published by Lawyers Cooperative/ Bancroft-Whitney (including *A.L.R.* annotations and *Am. Jur. 2d* references)
Restatement Reporter's Notes and Appendices	Support for particular Restatement sections and useful cross-references
Pocket Parts	Supplement inserted in a "pocket" in the back of a volume to keep the volume up to date

Section 3B. Focusing on the Law in Specific Jurisdictions

1. USING FOOTNOTES IN SECONDARY SOURCES TO FOCUS ON THE LAW IN SPECIFIC JURISDICTIONS

In examining the secondary sources shown in the preceding section, a lawyer would naturally focus upon finding legal authorities in the specific jurisdiction in which the fence was located. The researcher should note the basic principles supported by cases and other sources from that jurisdiction.

PROBLEM 3.10 Based on the discussion and the cases cited in the preceding figures (beginning with Figure 3-D), determine whether it appears that spite fences are legal in (a) Pennsylvania, (b) Nebraska, and (c) California.

DISCUSSION OF PROBLEM 3.10 The discussion in both *American Jurisprudence Second* and *Corpus Juris Secundum* indicates that there is a split of authority under the common law. The encyclopedias also indicate that statutes have been enacted in many jurisdictions prohibiting the erection and maintenance of spite fences.

(a) A Pennsylvania case ("Cohen v Perrino, 355 **Pa** 455, 50 A2d 348") is cited in footnote 18 in § 106 of *American Jurisprudence Second* in support of the following proposition: "The early cases and some of the more recent ones at common law hold that a [person] can build a fence or like structure upon his [or her] own land as high as he [or she] pleases, even though he [or she] erects it solely out of spite and for the purpose of annoying his [or her] neighbor."

The same case (*Cohen v. Perrino*) is cited in footnote 77 in § 72 of *Corpus Juris Secundum* in support of the following proposition: "The motives which actuate a landowner to make improvements for the substantial betterment of his [or her] property are immaterial although the light, air, and view of his [or her] neighbor are incidentally obstructed."

In footnote 78, another Pennsylvania case ("Maioriello v. Arlotta, 73 A.2d 374, 364 Pa. 557") is cited for the following proposition: "Where a structure is erected solely to injure or annoy the adjoining owner and serves no useful purpose, in the absence of a governing statute, the rule in some jurisdictions is that here, too, motive is immaterial . . . ."

Note that a reference in footnote 78 to *Corpus Juris* ("1 C.J. p 1229 note 94") indicates where early cases (in the first edition, *Corpus Juris*) on point could be found.

(b) Nebraska cases are cited in footnote 1 in § 106 of *American Jurisprudence Second* and footnote 79 in § 72 of *Corpus Juris Secundum*. The text indicates that Nebraska follows the opposite common-law rule and thus prohibits spite fences.

(c) The discussion in § 107 of *American Jurisprudence Second* indicates that "[s]ome statutes prohibit any fence, or other structure in the nature of a fence, unnecessarily exceeding a certain height, maliciously erected or maintained for the purpose of annoying the adjoining owners." Footnote 8 cites a California case ("Taliaferro v Salyer, 162 **Cal** App 2d 685, 328 P2d 799") in support of this statement. In footnote 83 in § 73, *Corpus Juris Secundum* cites a California case ("Bar Due v. Cox, 190 P. 1056, 47 C.A. 713") in support of a similar proposition.

The Reporter's Note to § 829, clause (a) of the Second Restatement of Torts also cites a California case, "Hutcherson v. Alexander, 264 Cal.App.2d 126, 70 Cal.Rptr. 366 (1968)," in support of the Restatement's position that spite fences are actionable.

2. USING A.L.R. ANNOTATIONS TO FOCUS ON THE LAW IN SPECIFIC JURISDICTIONS

Even if cases from the jurisdiction in which you are interested are not cited in these secondary sources, you can easily follow up your initial research by consulting the *A.L.R.* annotations (133 A.L.R. 691 and 80 A.L.R.3d 962) cited in *American Jurisprudence Second*. There will not always be an *A.L.R.* annotation on your topic. However, these annotations can be very helpful, if available. Shown in Figures 3-R, 3-S, and 3-T are the pages from the *A.L.R.* annotation appearing at 133 A.L.R. 691.

PROBLEM 3.11 Examine the organization of section II and the listing of cases in support of the view that useless spite structures are unlawful. Read sections I and II to the extent that they are shown in the following figures. What is the name of the leading case on point?

---

sion of the right to light and air, and will authorize a court to grant relief. The right of the plaintiff in this case to the free passage of light and air is subject only to a superior right of the defendant to make use of her property in good faith for the purpose of increasing her joy of ownership; and until the defendant makes such lawful use the plaintiff is entitled to prevent by legal process an interference with her right to light and air done solely for the

Burford, 173 Ga 821, 162 SE 120.

The question at this stage is, not what petitioner may be able to prove or what may be a reasonable interpretation of the defendant's act, but whether the petition shows a ground for relief if the allegations are upon the trial supported by evidence. We think that in such a case the evidence should be clear and convincing, before the plaintiff would be entitled to a verdict.

Judgment affirmed. All the Justices concur.

ANNOTATION.

Spite fences and other spite structures.

[Adjoining Landowners, § 5; Nuisances, § 3.]

I. Introduction and scope, 692.
II. In general:
    a. View that useless spite structures are unlawful, 692.
    b. View that useless spite structures are lawful, 697.
    c. Spite structures serving useful purpose, 701.
III. Statutes and ordinances affecting the right to erect or maintain spite structures:

FIGURE 3-R

A.L.R. (1ST SERIES)

692   AMERICAN LAW REPORTS, ANNOTATED.   [133 ALR

III.—continued.

I. Introduction and scope.

This annotation supersedes that in 43 ALR 27.

This annotation discusses the cases relating to spite fences and other spite structures which injure an adjoining landowner by cutting off his light, air, or view. Questions relating to actions and remedies involving spite structures are also discussed herein. However, since a structure which was not erected for any conscious purpose to annoy or injure could hardly be termed a spite structure, cases in which no such mental attitude is evident are not within the scope of this annotation. Under this heading cases dealing with obstructions to easements of light and air which are decided on grounds not involving any element of ill will or desire to injure are excluded herefrom.

As a general rule, where a structure serves a useful and beneficial purpose, it does not give rise to a cause of action although it may be that it causes injury to another by cutting off the light and air and interfering with the view which would otherwise be available over adjoining land in its natural state. In such cases it is damnum absque injuria, and the motive with which the structure may have been erected is immaterial. (See infra, II c.)

But where such structure serves no useful purpose or where its usefulness is accidental and the dominant reason for erecting the same is to annoy the adjoining landowner or injure him in his enjoyment of the premises, there is a sharp conflict of authority as to whether the structure may be abated or constitutes an actionable nuisance. In the cases decided prior to the decision in Burke v. Smith (1888) 69 Mich 380, 37 NW 838, 8 LRA 184, infra, II a, it was generally held that the motive with which a landowner erected a fence or other structure causing injury to an adjoining landowner could not be in-

quired into. However, since the decision in the Burke Case there has been a marked trend of authority towards the view that even in the absence of a statute a spite structure serving no useful purpose constitutes a private nuisance. (See infra, II a.) Indeed, regardless of the fact that prior to the decision in the Burke Case it was undoubtedly the majority rule, and perhaps an almost universal rule, that the motive with which a structure was erected could not be inquired into, though it injured an adjoining landowner, it seems that there is now about an even division of authority on this question, and, if jurisdictions in which there are mere dicta on this question are disregarded, it might be said that a majority of the courts which have passed upon the question are now of opinion that spite structures serving no useful purpose constitute private nuisances where they injure the owner or occupant of adjoining premises.

It is to be noted also that a large number of jurisdictions in which it had formerly been decided that a spite structure was not a private nuisance have adopted statutes declaring spite fences and other spite structures to be private nuisances. On this point see cases infra; III.

II. In general.

a. View that useless spite structures are unlawful.

It has been held that a spite fence or other spite structure which serves no useful purpose is unlawful and is actionable or may be abated.

Alabama. — Norton v. Randolph (1912) 176 Ala 381, 58 So 283, 40 LRA (NS) 129, Ann Cas 1915A 714.

Georgia. — HORNSBY v. SMITH (reported herewith) ante, 684.

Louisiana. — Parker v. Harvey (1935; La App) 164 So 507, infra, this subdivision.

Michigan.—Burke v. Smith (1888) 69 Mich 380, 37 NW 838, 8 LRA 184;

FIGURE 3-S

A.L.R. (1ST SERIES)

ANNO.—SPITE FENCES. 693

Flaherty v. Moran (1890) 81 Mich 52, 45 NW 381, 8 LRA 183, 21 Am St Rep 510; Kirkwood v. Finegan (1893) 95 Mich 543, 55 NW 457; Peek v. Roe (1896) 110 Mich 52, 67 NW 1080; Krulikowski v. Tide Water Oil Sales Corp. (1930) 251 Mich 684, 232 NW 223 (dictum).

Nebraska.—Bush v. Mockett (1914) 95 Neb 552, 145 NW 1001, 52 LRA (NS) 736; Dunbar v. O'Brien (1928) 117 Neb 245, 220 NW 278, 58 ALR 1033 (pile of old lumber obstructing light and air at cellar windows).

New Hampshire. — See Horan v. Byrnes (1903) 72 NH 93, 54 A 945, 62 LRA 602, 101 Am St Rep 670, infra, III a.

North Carolina.—Barger v. Barringer (1909) 151 NC 433, 66 SE 439, 25 LRA (NS) 831, 19 Ann Cas 472.

Oklahoma. — Hibbard v. Halliday (1916) 58 Okla 244, 158 P 1158, LRA 1916F 903.

South Dakota.—Racich v. Mastrovich (1937) 65 SD 321, 273 NW 660.

In the leading case of Burke v. Smith (1888) 69 Mich 380, 37 NW 838, 8 LRA 184, the court, in holding that a screen erected to shut out the light and view from a neighbor's windows was an abatable nuisance, said: "But his[counsel for plaintiff's] contention is that these screens being a damage to the houses of complainant, and being erected for no good or useful purpose, but with the malicious motive of doing injury, they become and are such a nuisance to the property of complainant that equity will cause their removal, and enjoin their future erection or continuance. He invokes the legal maxim that 'every man in the use of his own property must avoid injury to his neighbor's property as much as possible;' and argues that while it is true that when one pursues a strictly legal right his motives are immaterial, yet no man has a right to build and maintain an entirely useless structure for the sole purpose of injuring his neighbor. The argument has force, and appears irresistible, in the light of the moral law that ought to govern all human action. And the civil law, coming close to the moral law, declares that 'he who, in making a new work upon his own estate, uses his right without trespassing either against any law, custom, title, or possession, which may subject him to any service towards his neighbors, is not answerable for the damages which they may chance to sustain thereby, unless it be that he made that change merely with a view to hurt others without advantage to himself.' Thus the civil law recognizes the moral law, and does not permit the owner of land to do an act upon his own premises for the express purpose of injuring his neighbor, where the act brings no profit or advantage to himself. . . . If a man has no right to dig a hole upon his premises, not for any benefit to himself or his premises, but for the express purpose of destroying his neighbor's spring, why can he be permitted to shut out air and light from his neighbor's windows, maliciously, and without profit or benefit to himself? By analogy, it seems to me that the same principle applies in both cases, and that the law will interpose and prevent the wanton injury in each instance. . . . It must be remembered that no man has a legal right to make a malicious use of his property, not for any benefit or advantage to himself, but for the avowed purpose of damaging his neighbor. To hold otherwise would make the law a convenient engine, in cases like the present, to injure and destroy the peace and comfort, and to damage the property, of one's neighbor for no other than a wicked purpose, which in itself is, or ought to be, unlawful. The right to do this cannot, in an enlightened country, exist, either in the use of property, or in any way or manner. There is no doubt in my mind that these uncouth screens or 'obscurers,' as they are named in the record, are a nuisance, and were erected without right, and for a malicious purpose. What right has the defendant, in the light of the just and beneficent principles of equity, to shut out God's free air and sunlight from the windows of his neighbor, not for any benefit or advantage to himself, or profit to his land, but simply to gratify

FIGURE 3-T

A.L.R. (1ST SERIES)

DISCUSSION OF PROBLEM 3.11   The annotation identifies "Burke v. Smith (1888) 69 Mich 380, 37 NW 838, 8 LRA 184" as the leading case.[1]

In conducting research on this problem, you would want to find cases appearing after the publication of the above annotation, particularly because it is a relatively old annotation and it may have been subsequently supplemented or superseded.   As noted in Chapter 2, first series annotations such as the one shown in the preceding figures can be updated by using the *A.L.R. Blue Book of Supplemental Decisions*.[2]

PROBLEM 3.12   Figure 3-U shows the entry for the annotation shown in the preceding figures (133 ALR 691-720) in the *A.L.R. Blue Book of Supplemental Decisions* volume covering decisions from 1959-67. Remember that you would check each volume and pamphlet of the *A.L.R. Blue Book of Supplemental Decisions* to update the annotation.   According to Figure 3-U, from which jurisdictions have cases relevant to this annotation been decided during the period covered by this volume?

133 ALR	SUPPLEMENTAL DECISIONS	532
133 ALR 279–304 **Conn.**—Farnum v C. B. & T. C. (Super) 168 A2d 168 (citing anno) **Mass.**—Hurley v N. 196 NE2d 905 (citing anno)	**133 ALR 476–515** **Cal.**—O'Reilly v O. 208 Cal App 2d 203, 25 Cal Rptr 62 **Colo.**—Twin Lakes Reservoir & Canal Co. v B. 401 P2d 586 (citing anno) **Md.**—Cooper v D. 174 A2d 144 (citing anno) **Minn.**—Lowe v P. 120 NW2d 313 **Mo.**—Rose v M. 377 SW2d 372 **Ohio**—Dean v D. — Ohio App —, 78 Ohio L Abs 344, 152 NE2d 296	**N. Y.**—Re Chandler & Co. — Misc 2d —, 230 NYS2d 1012 **Wis.**—Fuller v K. 113 NW2d 25 **133 ALR 676–684** **U. S.**—Fidelity & Deposit Co. v B. (CA Tex) 291 F2d 34 O'Rieley v E. J Corp. (CA Iowa) 297 F2d 1 Re Lomax (DC NC) 233 F Supp 889 **La.**—C H F Finance Co. v J. 127 So 2d 534
133 ALR 319–360 **La.**—Murphy v D. E. C. 140 So 2d 249 **Mass.**—Murtagh v R. V. P. 166 NE2d 702 (citing anno) **Nev.**—Ingersoll v L. 333 P2d 982 (citing anno) **N. J.**—McCarthy v R. (Super) 142 A2d 914 Haack v R. 200 A2d 522 (citing anno) **N. Y.**—Buechel v B. 9 App Div 2d 916, 194 NYS2d 965 Foley v M. 42 Misc 2d 460, 248 NYS2d 354 (citing anno)	**133 ALR 524–549** **Conn.**—Empire Estates, Inc. v S. 159 A2d 812 **Pa.**—Re Tax Sale of Bolen's Real Estate 143 A2d 339	**133 ALR 691–720** **Conn.**—Rapuano v A. (Super) 145 A2d 384 **Fla.**—Fontainebleau Hotel Corp v F. (App) 114 So 2d 357 (citing anno) **La.**—Williams v B. (App) 160 So 2d 291 **N. C.**—Welsh v T. 133 SE2d 171 (citing anno) **Tex.**—Scharlack v G. O. Corp. (Civ App) 368 SW2d 705
133 ALR 365–376 Supplemented 152 ALR 239✦	**133 ALR 556–558** **Fla.**—Batteiger v B. (App) 109 So 2d 602 **Iowa**—Arnold v A. 133 NW2d 53 (citing anno) **Okla.**—Rakestraw v R. 345 P2d 888	
133 ALR 384–394 **U. S.**—Lundquist v C. B., Inc. (DC Wis) 202 F Supp 19 Radio Position Finding Corp. v B. Corp. (DC Md) 205 F Supp 850	**133 ALR 565–566** Superseded 67 ALR2d 936✦ **133 ALR 570–586**	**133 ALR 726–728** Superseded 93 ALR2d 287✦

FIGURE 3-U
A.L.R. BLUE BOOK OF SUPPLEMENTAL DECISIONS

[1] The citation to "LRA" is an early annotated report, <u>Lawyers Reports Annotated</u>, published between 1888 and 1906. <u>See supra</u> note 7 in § 2H ("Finding, Citing, and Updating Annotations") in Chapter 2.

[2] Other series of <u>A.L.R.</u> annotations are updated differently. <u>See supra</u> § 2H ("Finding, Citing, and Updating Annotations") in Chapter 2.

DISCUSSION OF PROBLEM 3.12   Decisions from Connecticut, Florida, Louisiana, North Carolina, and Texas are cited.

Recall from Chapter 2 that supplemental and superseding annotations are published. If an annotation has been supplemented, you will have to read both the original and the supplementing annotation. On the other hand, if it has been superseded, only the superseding annotation need be consulted. Note that sometimes only a portion of a prior annotation will be superseded.

To check for supplementing or superseding annotations for the first series of *A.L.R.*, you would first check the relevant "Supplemental Decisions" section of the *A.L.R. 1st Blue Book of Supplemental Decisions* for other annotations in *A.L.R.* first series and then the "Annotation History Table" in the *A.L.R. Index to Annotations.*

The full text of *A.L.R.3d*, *A.L.R.4th*, *A.L.R.5th*, and *A.L.R. Federal* also are now available as databases for computer retrieval through the LEXIS service. Annotations can also be updated using this service.

3. USING DIGESTS TO DEVELOP YOUR RESEARCH AND TO FIND CASES IN SPECIFIC JURISDICTIONS

The West topic and key number scheme divides case law into seven main divisions: (1) Persons; (2) Property; (3) Contracts; (4) Torts; (5) Crimes; (6) Remedies; and (7) Government. These main divisions are divided into thirty-two subheadings and into over 400 digest topics.

As discussed in Chapter 1, West Publishing Company publishes digests that collect headnotes from cases arising in a single state (e.g., *Nebraska Digest*), a group of states (e.g., *South Eastern Digest*), particular courts (e.g., *U.S. Supreme Court Digest*), and the entire nation covering all reported American cases (*American Digest*, consisting of the *Century Digest*, the *Decennial Digests*, and the *General Digest*).[3] These digests are

---

[3]West's <u>U.S. Supreme Court Digest</u> provides a complete index to Supreme Court decisions. West's <u>Federal Practice Digest</u> (prior to 1939), <u>Modern Federal Practice Digest</u> (from 1939-1961), <u>Federal Practice Digest Second</u> (1961-1975), <u>Federal Practice Digest Third</u> (1975-1989), and <u>Federal Practice Digest Fourth</u> (1989 to date) collectively cover the decisions of all federal courts, including the Supreme Court. West also has digests covering its <u>Bankruptcy Reporter</u>, <u>Military Justice Reporter</u>, and <u>U.S. Claims Court Reporter</u>. All of these digests are supplemented in the same manner as West's state digests (pocket parts, pamphlets, digest sections in current reporter volumes and advance sheets).

   The <u>American Digest</u> is the master index of all reported American cases. It currently consists of the <u>Century Digest</u> (1658-1896), <u>First Decennial</u> (1897-1906), <u>Second Decennial</u> (1906-1916), <u>Third Decennial</u> (1916-1926), <u>Fourth Decennial</u> (1926-1936), <u>Fifth Decennial</u> (1936-1946), <u>Sixth Decennial</u> (1946-1956), <u>Seventh Decennial</u> (1956-1966), <u>Eighth</u>

(continued...)

kept up to date by cumulative annual pocket parts, intervening pamphlets, and the digest sections in the current West reporter volumes, and advance sheets of the West reporter covering the jurisdiction.[4]

West's digests permit a researcher to find references to *all* cases discussing a particular point of law.[5] In general, you should choose the smallest digest in terms of coverage. For example, if your research problem involves the law of a particular state, you should choose the relevant *state* key number digest. This selection would allow you to find all relevant cases for that state. West has published digests for all states except Delaware, Nevada, and Utah. For Delaware, a researcher would instead use the *Atlantic Digest*. For Nevada and Utah, a researcher would instead use the *Pacific Digest*.

If you find that no cases have headnotes assigned to the topic and key number covering the relevant point of law in the state digest and fully update your search, then you will know that the courts of that state have not passed on the point.[6]

PROBLEM 3.13 Assume that the fence is located in Ohio and that you are interested in finding Ohio cases dealing with the legality of building such a fence. Recall that several relevant topics and key numbers were identified in the preceding sources. To find Ohio cases, you would (1) consult a digest containing headnotes from Ohio cases and (2) find the volumes containing the relevant topics and key numbers. Exam-

---

[3](...continued)
Decennial (1966-1976), Ninth Decennial (Part 1, 1976-1981 and Part 2, 1981-1986), Tenth Decennial (Part 1, 1986-1991), and the General Digest Eighth (covering the period after the last Decennial Digest).

[4]Each volume of the General Digest must be checked because the General Digest is noncumulative. This task, however, may be lessened by using the "Table of Key Numbers" accompanying the General Digest. This table lists the General Digest volumes in which cases under a specific key number are digested. If the table indicates that no cases are digested in a particular volume for that key number, of course that volume need not be checked. The General Digest is supplemented by the digest sections in the current volumes and the advance sheets of West's reporters issued after the last unit of the General Digest.

[5]The key number classification system was developed by West Publishing Company during the decade of the First Decennial (1897-1906). The Century Digest unit of the American Digest System (1658-1896) did not use the key number system of the First Decennial. To convert a Decennial key number into a Century Digest section number, cross-references are provided in the First Decennial and Second Decennial. The cross-references in the Second Decennial are easier to use because they are more specific than those given in the First Decennial. Conversely, to convert a Century Digest section number into the current key number classification system, cross-references are provided in a pink table in volume 21 of the First Decennial.

[6]In that situation, you may want to extend your search by examining the same topic and key number in other digests, such as a regional digest covering adjoining states, one covering the federal courts, or the American Digest to find cases that have dealt with the point of law from all other jurisdictions.

ine Figure 3-V showing the title page of the *Ohio Digest* containing the topic "Adjoining Landowners." What is the coverage of this volume?

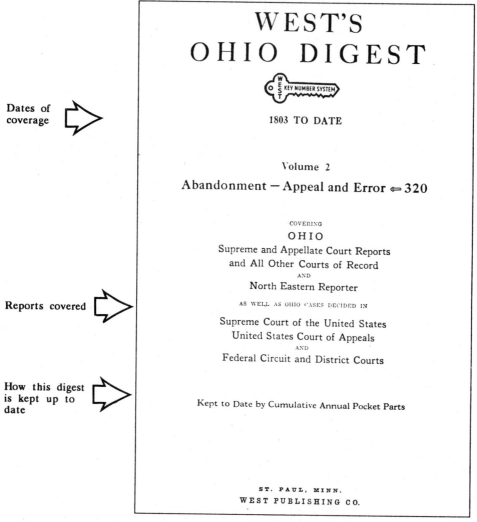

Dates of coverage

Reports covered

How this digest is kept up to date

WEST'S
OHIO DIGEST

1803 TO DATE

Volume 2

Abandonment — Appeal and Error ⟲ 320

COVERING
OHIO
Supreme and Appellate Court Reports
and All Other Courts of Record
AND
North Eastern Reporter
AS WELL AS OHIO CASES DECIDED IN

Supreme Court of the United States
United States Court of Appeals
AND
Federal Circuit and District Courts

Kept to Date by Cumulative Annual Pocket Parts

ST. PAUL, MINN.
WEST PUBLISHING CO.

FIGURE 3-V
WEST'S OHIO DIGEST

DISCUSSION OF PROBLEM 3.13 The *Ohio Digest* covers cases from 1803 up to the date this volume was published [1949]. Included in the digest are headnotes from Ohio courts of record and Ohio cases decided by the federal courts.

PROBLEM 3.14 Examine the entries in the digest under Adjoining Landowners 10(3) in Figure 3-W. This topic and key number is the one that was listed in the *C.J.S.* "Library Reference" in Figure 3-H. Based on these entries, what is the law in Ohio on spite fences?

```
2 Ohio D—213            ADJOINING LANDOWNERS            ⟨≈10(3)
```

v. Bowman, 10 Dec.Repr. 567, 22 Wkly.Law Bull. 111.

⟨≈10(2). Right to construct windows.

Super. Owner of a building may construct as many windows as he chooses overlooking the adjoining premises and the owner thereof cannot prevent it except by some obstructions on his own land, but the party to whom such license is given must act upon it strictly and not exceed it.—Stutzman v. Ach, Dayton, 395.

⟨≈10(3). Motive in erecting obstruction.

Ohio 1896. A lot owner has a legal right to erect and maintain a board fence on his lot, reaching to the roof of a house built on the adjoining lot, and standing on the division line, for the sole purpose of shutting light and air from the windows thereof, to the injury of the adjoining owner.—Letts v. Kessler, 42 N.E. 765, 54 Ohio St. 73, 40 L.R.A. 177, 35 Wkly.Law Bull. 62.

Clr. 1892. Where a lot owner, for no useful or ornamental purpose, but from pure malice, erects on his own land a high fence, which excludes the light and air from the windows of the house on the adjoining lot, such fence constitutes a nuisance, which will be restrained by injunction.—Kessler v. Letts, 3 O.C.D. 687, 7 Cir.Ct.R. 108, reversed

Letts v. Kessler, 42 N.E. 765, 54 Ohio St. 73, 40 L.R.A. 177, 35 Wkly.Law Bull. 62.

Com.Pl. 1894. Where plaintiff and defendant owned adjoining lots and each owned half of brick wall on boundary between the lots, act of defendant in nailing boards over apertures made by plaintiff in the wall, thereby completely covering the apertures and shutting off all light and air from plaintiff's house, was not enjoinable, even assuming that defendant's motives were malicious and that defendant, by such act, intended to annoy and injure plaintiff.—Dawson v. Kemper, 1 Ohio Dec. 556, 32 Wkly.Law Bull. 15, petition dismissed 5 O.C.D. 130, 11 Cir.Ct.R. 180.

An act done on one's own land, though lawful in itself, becomes unlawful and a nuisance when actuated by malice.—Dawson v. Kemper, 1 Ohio Dec. 556, 32 Wkly.Law Bull. 15, petition dismissed 5 O.C.D. 130, 11 Cir.Ct.R. 180.

Com.Pl. 1889. The erection of a high board fence near the lot line of the defendant, but entirely on his premises, near the windows of a neighboring house, to shut out the view therefrom, not from necessity, but from malice alone, is a nuisance which will be enjoined.—Peck v. Bowman, 10 Dec.Repr. 567, 22 Wkly.Law Bull. 111.

For Cross-References or Descriptive Words
see
DESCRIPTIVE–WORD INDEX

FIGURE 3-W
WEST'S OHIO DIGEST

DISCUSSION OF PROBLEM 3.14 In this problem, you were asked to examine the entries in the digest under Topic: Adjoining Landowners, Key Number: 10(3). Based on these entries, you were to determine the law in Ohio on spite fences. The case on which you should have focused is "Letts v. Kessler, 42 N.E. 765, 54 Ohio St. 73, 40 L.R.A. 177, 35 Wkly.Law. Bull. 62," decided by the Ohio Supreme Court in 1896. To the extent other earlier decisions by lower Ohio courts (e.g., *Peck v. Bowman*) are inconsistent with the *Letts* decision, they are no longer the law on the subject.

The *Letts* decision supports the view that the erection and maintenance of a spite fence is not an actionable wrong.

To find later cases, you would consult the pocket part in this digest volume. In the pocket part, you would check for entries under the relevant topic and key number.

PROBLEM 3.15 The "Closing Table" from the pocket insert in this volume of the *Ohio Digest* is reproduced in Figure 3-X. Why do you need to examine this table as part of the updating process? In other words, what is the purpose of this "Closing Table"?

Closing with Cases Reported in

Ohio State Reports, Third Series .... 59 Ohio St.3d (part)
Ohio Appellate Reports,
　　Third Series .... 59 Ohio App.3d (part)
Ohio Miscellaneous Reports .... 59 Ohio Misc.2d (part)
North Eastern Reporter, Second Series 568 N.E.2d
Supreme Court Reporter .... 111 S.Ct. 1434
Federal Reporter, Second Series 928 F.2d 1147
Federal Supplement .... 758 F.Supp. 1521
Federal Rules Decisions .... 134 F.R.D. 311
Bankruptcy Reporter .... 125 B.R. 326
Ohio Northern University
　　Law Review .... 17 Ohio North Univ.L.Rev. 227
University of Cincinnati Law Review ..... 58 U.Cin.L.Rev. 317

FIGURE 3-X
POCKET PART IN WEST'S OHIO DIGEST

DISCUSSION OF PROBLEM 3.15 The "Closing Table" tells you the last reporter volumes from which headnotes were included in the pocket supplement. To bring the research up-to-date, you would check the bound volumes or advance sheets issued *after* the closing date. Each reporter volume has a digest section that indexes the headnotes of cases in that volume. For example, in this instance you would examine the "Key Number Digest" section for each *North Eastern Second* volume and Advance Sheet issued after 568 N.E.2d (see closing table above).

Unless a researcher already knows the relevant topic and key number from another source, the name of a case on point, or the topic under which the point of law is digested, the "Descriptive Word Index" accompanying each digest is probably the best means of finding relevant topics and key numbers.

To use a "Descriptive Word Index," a researcher first prepares a list of words derived from an analysis of his research problem. Then the

researcher cross-checks these words against each other in the Index. The entries in the Index will refer the researcher to the topic and key number under which cases involving similar facts or legal issues have been classified.

USING THE DESCRIPTIVE WORD INDEX

In preparing your list of words to be checked in the Descriptive Word Index accompanying a digest, West Publishing Company suggests that you should draw your descriptive words from the following areas:

(1) the **classes** (e.g., defendant, motorist, tenant, child, witness), **occupations** (e.g., lawyer, pharmacist, sheriff, teacher, clerk), or **relationships** (e.g., heir, fiancee, guest, employer, neighbor, insurer) of the parties or persons involved;

(2) the **places** (e.g., bar, bank, intersection, motel) and **things** (e.g., gas, bullet, automobile, gorilla, martini, crossbar, acrylic resin, killer whale, piano, trademark) involved;

(3) the **basis of the action** (e.g., negligence, breach of contract, antitrust, trespass, Webb-Pomerene Act, fraud) or **legal issue** (e.g., last clear chance, negligence per se, privileged communication);

(4) **possible defenses** (e.g., accord and satisfaction, duress, estoppel, res judicata, statute of frauds, release); and

(5) the **relief sought** (e.g., damages, injunction, accounting for profits, ejectment, annulment, mandamus).

One benefit of using the descriptive word approach is that it does not depend on the researcher knowing under which digest topic the relevant points of law have been classified. The factual words on the list, even if you have not identified the correct legal topic or issue, ordinarily will lead a researcher to the appropriate topic or topics.

To illustrate, recall that in addition to the fence matter described by the client in *Problem 2.1* in Chapter 2, the client was concerned about the right to continue to use the road across his neighbor's land.

Assume that (1) you are generally aware that long use may create rights, but you are unsure of the legal theory; (2) the land is located in the state of New York and New York law controls the situation; and (3) you decide to check the descriptive word index accompany the *New York Digest*. (You should select the smallest digest available covering your jurisdiction—in this instance, the *New York Digest* because it contains only headnotes of decisions from New York.)[7]

    PROBLEM 3.16 The *New York Digest* is now in a fourth series. The coverage of each series is stated in the "Preface" to the latest series, shown in Figure 3-Y. Examine the beginning portion of the "Preface" to this digest. What is the coverage of this series? Where would you look to find earlier headnotes from New York cases? What information is given about new and revised topics and key numbers?

West's New York Digest 4th covers New York state and federal case law from 1978. It supplements earlier editions of the New York Digest which remain permanent reference works for their periods of coverage.

Additional case history to cases in earlier editions of the New York Digest may be found in the main volumes and pocket parts of this digest.

New York Digest 3d covers volumes 211–408 New York Supplement, Second Series, and federal cases from 1961–1978.

New York Digest 2d covers volumes 231 New York Supplement— 210 New York Supplement, Second Series, 1930 to 1961.

New York Digest (Consolidated Edition) covers volumes 1–230 New York Supplement and the pre-Reporter decisions, 1794 to 1929.

This Digest is compiled and arranged under the West Key Number plan. All Topics of the American Digest System are represented and each Topic carries a complete analysis of the scope of all of its Key Numbers.

New and revised topics and greatly expanded key numbers have been provided for many areas including attorneys' fees, bankruptcy, civil rights, civil service, class actions, double jeopardy, ERISA, federal preemption, habeas corpus, pardon and parole, RICO, searches and seizures, securities regulation, syndromes of battered women or children and teacher terminations or nonrenewals.

FIGURE 3-Y

WEST'S NEW YORK DIGEST FOURTH

---

[7]Use of a regional digest in this instance is foreclosed because no current key number digest is published covering opinions in the North Eastern Reporter. See supra § 1D(3)(e) ("West's Topics and Key Numbers") in Chapter 1 (table showing available digests).

DISCUSSION OF PROBLEM 3.16 As indicated in the portion of the Preface reproduced in Figure 3-Y, West's *New York Digest 4th* contains headnotes from New York state and federal cases from 1978 to date. To find earlier headnotes from New York cases, you would consult the three earlier series: *New York Digest 3d* (1961-1978); *New York Digest 2d* (1930-1961); and *New York Digest* (Consolidated Edition) (1794-1929).

The Preface indicates that several new and revised topics and key numbers have been added (e.g., attorney's fees, bankruptcy, civil rights, etc.). When a new topic was formerly part of one or more other topics, West provides a table showing where the prior topics and key numbers appear in the new topic or revised key numbers. A second table is provided to translate the key numbers in the new topic to the prior classifications. These tables, which accompany the new topic, permit a researcher to continue a search in another series of the digest or in a different digest.

Recall that the analysis of *Problem 2.1* in Chapter 2 produced several words that could be cross-checked against each other in the *Descriptive Word Index*. The words listed in conjunction with this problem included property, tort law, landowner, neighbor, adjoining landowners, user, property, land, gate, obstruction, acreage, access, right of way, road, lane, adverse possession, prescription, easement, license, trespass, proof of adverse possession or hostile use, damages, injunction, and declaratory judgment.[8]

PROBLEM 3.17 One of the obvious words that describes this situation is "road." Examine the entry for "Roads" in the *Descriptive Word Index* accompanying West's *New York Digest 4th* shown in Figure 3-Z. This entry refers you to the index entry "Private Roads," also shown in Figure 3-Z. What entries appear to be relevant to this problem?

---

[8]Another means of locating relevant topics and key numbers is the topic method of search. The topic method initially requires that the researcher select the correct topic. Considerable caution should be exercised in using the topic method of search unless you are familiar with the legal topic and its treatment in West's digests. If you have difficulty finding the relevant topic or key number, you should resort to the "Descriptive Word Index."

```
┌─────────────────────────┐   ┌──────────────────────────────────────────────┐
│ ROADS                   │   │ PRIVATE ROADS                                  │
│   See this index—       │   │ ABANDONMENT.  Priv Roads 4                     │
│     Highways            │   │ ALTERATION.  Priv Roads 3                      │
│     Private Roads       │   │ ASSESSMENTS.  Priv Roads 6                     │
│     Streets             │   │ AUTOMOBILES, contributory negligence of person crossing │
│     Turnpikes and Toll Roads │ │      private driveway.  Autos 217(8)       │
│                         │   │ CONSTRUCTION.  Priv Roads 5                    │
│                         │   │ EASEMENTS, see this index Easements            │
│                         │   │ ESTABLISHMENT.  Priv Roads 2                   │
│                         │   │   Bond.  Priv Roads 2(3)                       │
│                         │   │   Commissioners, viewers, jurors, surveyors and other like │
│                         │   │      officers.  Priv Roads 2(4)                │
│                         │   │   Costs and expenses of proceedings.  Priv Roads 2(6) │
│                         │   │   Judgment, order or decree.  Priv Roads 2(5)  │
│                         │   │   Jurisdiction and powers.  Priv Roads 2(2)    │
│                         │   │   Operation and effect of proceedings.  Priv Roads 2(7) │
│                         │   │   Petition.  Priv Roads 2(2)                   │
│                         │   │   Review.  Priv Roads 2(5)                     │
│                         │   │ INJURIES from defect or obstruction.  Priv Roads 12 │
│                         │   │ NATURE and essentials.  Priv Roads 1           │
│                         │   │ OBSTRUCTIONS and encroachments.  Priv Roads 7–10 │
│                         │   │   Civil liability.  Priv Roads 9               │
│                         │   │   Creation and removal.  Priv Roads 8          │
│                         │   │   Criminal responsibility.  Priv Roads 10      │
│                         │   │   Injuries from obstructions.  Priv Roads 12   │
│                         │   │     Care as to licensee.  Neglig 32(1)         │
│                         │   │   Removal.  Priv Roads 8                       │
│                         │   │ PARKING lot serving patrons of restaurant and bank— │
│                         │   │   Driving while intoxicated—                   │
│                         │   │     Criminal offense.  Autos 322               │
│                         │   │ RAILROAD crossings.  R R 247                   │
│                         │   │ REPAIR.  Priv Roads 5                          │
│                         │   │ TAXES.  Priv Roads 6                           │
│                         │   │ USE.  Priv Roads 11                            │
│                         │   │ VACATION.  Priv Roads 4                        │
└─────────────────────────┘   └──────────────────────────────────────────────┘
```

FIGURE 3-Z
WEST'S NEW YORK DIGEST FOURTH
DESCRIPTIVE WORD INDEX

DISCUSSION OF PROBLEM 3.17 The Descriptive Word Index is used by cross-checking the words on your list. For example, "use" is covered in "Priv Roads 11"; "establishment" is covered in "Priv Roads 2"; and "Obstructions and encroachments" are covered under "Priv Roads 7-10." Note that a cross-reference is given for "EASEMENTS, see this index Easements."

PROBLEM 3.18 How can you tell if the relevant points of law are contained in these key numbers in the topic "Private Roads"? A good means of determining the answer to this question is to examine the Scope Note—"Subjects Included" and the "Subjects Excluded and Covered by Other Topics" at the beginning of this digest topic. Figure 3-AA shows this information for the digest topic "Private Roads." Is "Private Roads" the relevant topic?

PRIVATE ROADS

SUBJECTS INCLUDED

Roads established by public authority for accommodation of private persons, but open for free passage to the public

Nature and scope of power to establish and maintain such roads in general

Constitutional and statutory provisions relating thereto

Establishment of such roads, construction, repair, and improvement thereof, and alteration, vacation and abandonment

Local assessments therefor

Title to and rights in the land occupied, and removal of and liabilities for obstructions, encroachments, etc.

Use of such roads, and liabilities for injuries from defects, obstructions, etc., therein

SUBJECTS EXCLUDED AND COVERED BY OTHER TOPICS

Eminent domain, see EMINENT DOMAIN

Rights of way over lands of others, see EASEMENTS

Roads established for public benefit, see HIGHWAYS

For detailed references to other topics, see Descriptive-Word Index

FIGURE 3-AA
WEST'S NEW YORK DIGEST FOURTH

DISCUSSION OF PROBLEM 3.18 The "Subjects Included" entries indicate that the main focus of the "Private Roads" topic is on "[r]oads established by public authority for accommodation of private persons, but open for free passage to the public" and related matters. Thus, this topic does not appear to deal with establishing a right to use a road based on long use. On the other hand, the "Subjects Excluded and Covered by Other Topics" entries indicate that "Rights of way over lands of others" is covered in the topic "Easements." As noted earlier, the index entries for "Private Roads" provides a cross-reference to Easements ("EASEMENTS, see this index Easements"). Likewise, entries under another fact word on the list, "Rights of Way," would have also referred you to the "Easement" topic in the *Descriptive Word Index*.

PROBLEM 3.19 When using the *Descriptive Word Index*, you would ordinarily cross-check all words on your list. Figures 3-BB and 3-CC illustrate this process. What key numbers appear to be relevant to the client's problem?

EASEMENTS

46 N Y D 4TH—516

References are to Digest Topics and Key Numbers

EASEMENTS—Cont'd

APPARENT easements affecting right of purchaser of servient tenement. Ease 22

APPEAL and error—
  Findings of court—
    Conflicting evidence. App & E 1011.1(9)
    Sufficiency of evidence in support. App & E 1010.1(9)

APPELLATE jurisdiction of suits relating to. Courts 219.12(11–13), 231(37)

APPROPRIATION to public use. Ease 33
  Amount of compensation. Em Dom 149(5)
  Compensable interest in property. Em Dom 85
  Extent of appropriation. Em Dom 58
  Measure of compensation for taking. Em Dom 147
  Necessity for appropriation. Em Dom 56
  Property subject to appropriation. Em Dom 50

APPURTENANT or in gross. Ease 3

AVIGATION, measure of consequential damages in cases involving. Em Dom 147

BREACH of covenant. Covenants, post

BURDEN of proof—
  Creation, existence or termination. Ease 36(1)

CEMETERIES, see this index Cemeteries

CERTAINTY of grant creating. Ease 12(3)

CHANGE of location. Ease 48(6)

COLOR of right affecting creation by prescription. Ease 9

COMMENCEMENT. Ease 25

COMPENSATION instead of injunction in actions to establish or protect. Ease 61(11)

CONDEMNATION, see Appropriation to public use, ante

CONDITIONS precedent to actions for establishment and protection of easements. Ease 61(3)

CONTINUITY of use affecting creation by prescription. Ease 7

CONTINUOUS easements affecting right of purchaser of servient tenement. Ease 22

CONVEYANCES—
  Creating easements. Ease 12, 13
  Of easements. Ease 24

COTENANT—
  Acquiring easement. Ten in C 17
  Creating easement in favor of third person. Ten in C 41

COVENANTS—
  Breach of covenant—
    Against incumbrances. Covenants 96(7)
  Construction and operation of covenants against incumbrances. Covenants 42(3)
  Operating as grant of easement. Ease 13

DAMAGES—
  For injuries. Ease 70
  Instead of injunction in actions to protect. Ease 61(11)

DECLARATORY judgment. Decl Judgm 185

DEDICATION, see this index Dedication

DEFENSES in actions for damages for injuries. Ease 64

DESTRUCTION of servient estate as terminating easement. Ease 26(4)

DEVIATION from way. Ease 49

DISTURBANCE. Ease 56–59

DOMINANT tenements—
  Alterations in as terminating. Ease 26(2)
  Relation between owners of dominant and servient tenements in general. Ease 38
  Severance of ownership of dominant and servient tenements. Ease 16
  Transfer of dominant tenement. Ease 24

DRAINS, see this index Drains

DURATION. Ease 25
  Of use affecting creation by prescription. Ease 7, 9(2)

EJECTMENT, title to support. Eject 9(5)

ELECTRIC utility, see also, this index Electricity

ELEMENTS of easement. Ease 1

EMINENT domain—
  Appropriation to public use, generally, ante

ESTABLISHMENT. Ease 61

EASEMENTS—Cont'd

EVIDENCE—
  Existence of easement. Ease 36
  In actions—
    For damages for injuries. Ease 69
    To establish or protect. Ease 61(9)

EXCLUSIVENESS of use, adverse character. Ease 8(4)

EXPRESS grant creating easement. Ease 12, 42

EXTENT of—
  Right. Ease 39–45
  Use affecting creation by prescription. Ease 6

EXTINGUISHMENT by agreement or license. Ease 29

FENCES obstructing. Ease 58(3)

FIXTURES as between owner of easement and owner of land subject thereto. Fixt 23

FORFEITURE for misuser. Ease 31

GATES obstructing. Ease 58(3)

HIGHWAYS, see this index Highways

IMPLIED easement, see this index Implied Easement

INJUNCTION—
  For protection—
    Ease 61(2, 6)
    Inj 34
  Maintenance and repair. Ease 53

INJURIES to. Ease 62–73

INTERFERENCE with use affecting creation by prescription. Ease 7(6)

IRRIGATION, see this index Irrigation

JUDGMENT—
  In actions—
    For damages for injuries. Ease 72
    To establish or protect easements. Ease 61(12)

JURISDICTION, see this index Jurisdiction

JURY—
  Questions for, see Questions for jury, post

LACHES in actions for establishment and protection. Ease 61(5)

LICENSE—
  Distinguished from easement. Licens 44(3)
  Extinguishing easement. Ease 29

LIGHT, see this index Light

LIMITATION of actions for—
  Damages for injuries. Ease 66
  Establishment and protection of easements. Ease 61(5)
  Statutory period, creation by prescription. Ease 7(4)

LOCATION. Ease 46–49

MAINTENANCE. Ease 53

MARKETABLE title as affected by. Ven & Pur 130(9)

MERGER. Ease 27

MISUSER. Ease 55
  Forfeiture. Ease 31

MODE of use. Ease 50
  Affecting creation by prescription. Ease 6

NATURE of easement. Ease 1
  License distinguished. Licens 44(3)

NECESSITY, ways of, see also, this index Ways of Necessity

NONUSER. Ease 30

NOTICE of easement to purchaser of servient tenement. Ease 22

OBSTRUCTION. Ease 56–60

PARTIES to—
  Actions for—
    Damages. Ease 67
    Establishment and protection. Ease 61(7)
  Creation of easements. Ease 2, 14(1, 3)

PARTY walls, see this index Party Walls

PERMISSIVE use affecting creation by prescription. Ease 8(2)

PERSONS entitled to—
  Locate way. Ease 48(2)
  Use. Ease 52

PLATTED lands, implied easement of way on sale. Ease 17(4)

PLEADING—
  As defense. Ease 35

FIGURE 3-BB
WEST'S NEW YORK DIGEST FOURTH DESCRIPTIVE WORD INDEX

46 N Y D 4TH—517   **EDUCATION**

References are to Digest Topics and Key Numbers

EASEMENTS—Cont'd
PLEADING—Cont'd
  In actions—
    For damages. Ease 68
    To establish or protect. Ease 61(8)
PRACTICAL location. Ease 48(5)
PRESCRIPTION, see this index Adverse Possession
PRESUMPTIONS—
  Creation, existence, or termination. Ease 36(1)
PRINCIPAL and agent, implied authority. Princ & A
  100(5)
PRIVITY of title, ways of necessity. Ease 18(4)
PROTECTION of easements, actions for. Ease 61
PURPOSES of use. Ease 51
QUESTIONS for jury—
  Damages for injuries to, or by use of, easements. Ease
    71
  Existence of easement. Ease 37
  Protection of easements. Ease 61(9½)
RELEASE. Ease 28
REMOVAL of obstruction. Ease 60
REPAIR. Ease 53
RESERVATION creating. Ease 14, 42
  Abandonment or nonuser of easement created by reserva-
    tion. Ease 30(2)
  Implied reservation. Ease 17(5)
REVIVAL of lost right. Ease 34
RIGHTS-OF-WAY, see this index Right–of–Way
SALE of land as creating implied easement. Ease 17(2–4)
SERVIENT tenement—
  Partial destruction of servient estate as terminating ease-
    ment. Ease 26(4)
  Relation between owners of dominant and servient tene-
    ments. Ease 38
  Right as against purchaser of. Ease 20–22
  Severance of ownership of dominant and servient tene-
    ments. Ease 16
SEVERANCE of—
  Ownership of dominant and servient tenements. Ease 16
  Right. Ease 23
STATUTE of frauds—
  Assignment, grant or surrender of interest created. Frds
    St of 63(3)
  Creation of easement. Frds St of 60
"STRANGER to deed" rule. Ease 14(3)
STREETS, see this index Streets
STRUCTURES in or over ways. Ease 58(2)
SUBJECT matter. Ease 2
TAX valuation. Tax 348(6)
TEMPORARY injunction in actions to establish and protect.
  Ease 61(6)
TERMINATION. Ease 26
TRANSFER of right. Ease 24
TRESPASS. Tresp 11
TRIAL in actions—
  For damages for injuries. Ease 71
  To establish or protect easements. Ease 61(9½)
USE. Ease 50–52
  Actions for damages for injuries to, or by use of ease-
    ments. Ease 62–73
VENDOR and purchaser, see this index Vendor and Purchas-
  er
VENUE of action for damages. Ease 65
VIEW, see this index View
WATERS—
  Generally, see this index Waters and Water Courses
  Riparian and littoral rights, see generally, this index Ri-
    parian and Littoral Rights
WAYS, appurtenant or in gross. Ease 3(2)
WAYS of necessity. Ease 18
  See also, this index Ways of Necessity
WIDTH—
  Right-of-way, see also, this index Width

EAVES
DRIPPING, right as to. Waters 121

EAVESDROPPING
INTERCEPTION or disclosure of telecommunications, generally, see this index Telecommunications

EBB AND FLOW
TEST of navigability. Nav Wat 1(4)

ECCENTRICITY
TESTAMENTARY capacity. Wills 41, 55(4)

ECCLESIASTICAL CORPORATIONS
See this index—
  Charities
  Religious Societies

ECCLESIASTICAL LAW
PART of common law. Com Law 5
  Relating to divorce. Divorce 3

ECCLESIASTICAL TRIBUNALS
  Generally. Relig Soc 12

ECOLOGY
ZONING, ecological considerations. Zoning 36.5

ECONOMIC BENEFITS
LABOR relations, unfair labor practices. Labor 393
LABOR relations boards, evidence. Labor 576

ECONOMIC CONDITIONS
JUDICIAL notice. Evid 11
WORKERS' compensation affected by, see this index Work-
  ers' Compensation

ECONOMIC LOSS
ELECTRIC utility, recovery of—
  From nuclear power plant contractor—
    Under strict products liability claim. Prod Liab 42
PURCHASERS—
  Suing sellers of defective goods. Prod Liab 17

ECONOMIC WASTE
MINES and minerals, see this index Mines and Minerals

ECONOMY
REMOVAL of civil service officer or employee on ground of.
  Offic 69.10

EDUCATION
  See also, this index—
    Colleges and Universities
    Schools and School Districts
ALIENS' education affecting naturalization. Aliens 62(4)
BOARD of Education, see this index Schools and School
  Districts
CHARITABLE gifts for. Char 12
  Certainty as to—
    Beneficiaries. Char 21(4)
    Purpose of gifts. Char 22(4)
  Designation of institution. Wills 516
CHILDREN. Parent & C 3
  Actions to compel support or payment for necessaries.
    Parent & C 3.3
  Adult children. Parent & C 3.1(4)
  Amount of award. Parent & C 3.3(7)
  Charges on child's separate estate. Parent & C 3.2
  Circumstances affecting duty. Parent & C 3.1(5)
  Contracts—
    Infants 53
    Parent & C 3.1(8)
  Decree. Parent & C 3.3(8)
  Defenses. Parent & C 3.3(4)

FIGURE 3-CC

WEST'S NEW YORK DIGEST FOURTH DESCRIPTIVE WORD INDEX

DISCUSSION OF PROBLEM 3.19 The *Descriptive Word Index* entries refer you to several key numbers under the Easement topic, especially those from Key Number 4 through 11. On the remedy issue (injunction), you are referred to Easement Key Number 61. On the question of proof (evidence and presumptions), you are referred to Easement Key Number 36.

PROBLEM 3.20 Assume that you want to focus on the problem of proving the existence of an easement, particularly proving a hostile or adverse use. Examine the entries under Key Number 36(1) in West's *New York Digest Fourth* shown in Figures 3-DD, 3-EE, and 3-FF. Based on those entries, decide what the best argument for the client would be in light of the circumstances described in the client interview set out in *Problem 2.1.*

---

but no occasion has arisen for its use, owner of servient tenement may obstruct easement, and such use will not be deemed adverse to existence of easement until such time as need for right-of-way arises, demand is made by easement owner that way be opened, and servient tenant refuses.

> Filby v. Brooks, 481 N.Y.S.2d 865, 105 A.D.2d 826, affirmed 495 N.Y.S.2d 362, 66 N.Y.2d 640, 485 N.E.2d 1027.

Plaintiff's easement had not been extinguished because of adverse possession where no need had ever arisen to use easement.

> Filby v. Brooks, 481 N.Y.S.2d 865, 105 A.D.2d 826, affirmed 495 N.Y.S.2d 362, 66 N.Y.2d 640, 485 N.E.2d 1027.

N.Y.A.D. 3 Dept. 1989. Right-of-way was not lost by adverse possession; prescribed ten-year period of alleged adverse use was not shown in that dominant owner had not attempted to use his easement until 1987.

> Carnemella v. Sadowy, 538 N.Y.S.2d 96, 147 A.D.2d 874.

N.Y.A.D. 3 Dept. 1986. Obstructions placed upon a right-of-way which never effectively interfered with easement owners' use and enjoyment thereof did not constitute assertion of rights in conflict with that of easement owners so as to support claim for adverse possession.

> Del Fuoco v. Mikalunas, 500 N.Y.S.2d 84, 118 A.D.2d 980.

N.Y.A.D. 1981. The right to the use of an easement may be lost by adverse possession.

> Rahabi v. Morrison, 440 N.Y.S.2d 941, 81 A.D.2d 434.

If plaintiff obtained an injunction prohibiting defendants from barring his entry over or around fence, its mere existence would then constitute an interference and inconvenience, but not a complete obstruction to plaintiff's use

☞33–34. *For other cases see earlier editions of this digest, the Decennial Digests, and WESTLAW.*

Library references

C.J.S. Easements.

☞35. Pleading as defense.

Library references

C.J.S. Easements § 67.

N.Y.A.D. 4 Dept. 1988. Trial court did not err in refusing to consider doctrine of merger since plaintiff, who alleged that defendant abandoned easement, failed to advance theory in complaint.

> Koshian v. Kirchner, 527 N.Y.S.2d 921, 139 A.D.2d 942.

☞36. Evidence.

Library references

C.J.S. Easements §§ 68, 69.

☞36(1). Presumptions and burden of proof.

N.Y.A.D. 2 Dept. 1988. Fact that adjoining landowner's predecessor also used driveway over which landowner claimed easement did not negate presumption of adverse or hostile use by landowner for purposes of establishing easement by prescription.

> Cannon v. Sikora, 531 N.Y.S.2d 99, 142 A.D.2d 662, appeal denied 549 N.Y.S.2d 960, 74 N.Y.2d 615, 549 N.E.2d 151.

Evidence that landowner shared cost of maintaining driveway established that his use of driveway was not merely neighborly accommodation on part of adjoining landowner's predecessor in title, so that presumption of adverse use of driveway remained for purposes of establishing easement by prescription over driveway.

> Cannon v. Sikora, 531 N.Y.S.2d 99, 142 A.D.2d 662, appeal denied 549 N.Y.S.2d 960, 74 N.Y.2d 615, 549 N.E.2d 151.

For legislative history of cited statutes see McKinney's Consolidated Laws of New York

FIGURE 3-DD
WEST'S NEW YORK DIGEST FOURTH

For references to other topics, see Descriptive-Word Index

N.Y.A.D. 2 Dept. 1988. Open, notorious, uninterrupted, and undisputed use of right-of-way is presumed to be adverse or hostile and casts burden on owner of servient tenement to show that use was by license, in connection with claim that easement was acquired by prescription.

 Boumis v. Caetano, 528 N.Y.S.2d 104, 140 A.D.2d 401.

Relationship of cooperation and neighborly accommodation gives rise to inference of permission in use of right-of-way, for purposes of claim of easement by prescription.

 Boumis v. Caetano, 528 N.Y.S.2d 104, 140 A.D.2d 401.

N.Y.A.D. 2 Dept. 1987. Under ordinary circumstances an open, notorious, uninterrupted and undisputed use of right-of-way, necessary for finding of easement by prescription, is presumed to be adverse or hostile, under claim of right, and casts burden upon owner of servient tenement to show that use was by license.

 Borruso v. Morreale, 514 N.Y.S.2d 99, 129 A.D.2d 604.

While neighborly relationship between parties and/or their respective predecessors in title may have created implication that use of disputed property was permissive and not adverse or hostile, fact that adjacent owners' predecessors also used driveway did not negate presumption of adverse or hostile use by property owners, to whom access to their garage was denied without driving over portion of adjacent owners' property.

 Borruso v. Morreale, 514 N.Y.S.2d 99, 129 A.D.2d 604.

N.Y.A.D. 2 Dept. 1986. Use of driveway over period of approximately 32 years was open, notorious, uninterrupted and undisputed, so that, since owners of servient estate could not demonstrate that use of driveway was by license, use was presumed to be adverse, and easement by prescription existed.

 Morrow v. Manes, 501 N.Y.S.2d 703, 120 A.D.2d 501.

N.Y.A.D. 2 Dept. 1985. Generally, open, notorious and continuous use of right-of-way is presumed to be adverse and casts burden on owner of servient tenement to show that use was by license.

 Susquehanna Realty Corp. v. Barth, 485 N.Y.S.2d 795, 108 A.D.2d 909.

Presumption of adversity is inapplicable when established use by claimant is not exclusive; use of particular strip of land in common with general public will not ripen into an easement by prescription.

 Susquehanna Realty Corp. v. Barth, 485 N.Y.S.2d 795, 108 A.D.2d 909.

N.Y.A.D. 3 Dept. 1990. Evidence established that property owner acquired right to prescriptive easement rather than title through adverse possession over parking area on neighbors' property; although exclusive possession or use was not adequately established, actual, open, notorious, and continuous use for period of ten years were established, and presumption of hostile use was not rebutted by neighbors' bald assertion that use was permissive.

 McLean v. Ryan, 550 N.Y.S.2d 184.

N.Y.A.D. 3 Dept. 1988. When plaintiffs have established existence of prescriptive easement by proof of open, notorious and continuous use for over 25 years, such showing gives rise to presumption that use was hostile and shifts burden to owner of servient land to show that use was by permission.

 Colpitts v. Cascade Valley Land Corp., 535 N.Y.S.2d 483, 145 A.D.2d 750.

N.Y.A.D. 3 Dept. 1988. Failure of current landowners and their predecessors in title to demonstrate existence of alleged easement in nearby access way did not preclude current landowners from using predecessor's use in establishing adverse use for statutory period where there was unbroken chain of privity between current and former landowners; past landowners were considered to have turned over the use of the access way to their successors.

 Brocco v. Mileo, 535 N.Y.S.2d 125, 144 A.D.2d 200.

N.Y.A.D. 3 Dept. 1988. Prescriptive easement arises by adverse, open, notorious and continuous use of another's land for prescriptive period; once it has been shown that use is open, notorious, uninterrupted and undisputed, presumption arises that it is adverse and under claim of right, and burden is on owner of servient tenement to show that use was by license.

 Kusmierz v. Baan, 534 N.Y.S.2d 786, 144 A.D.2d 829.

N.Y.A.D. 3 Dept. 1988. Entitlement to prescriptive easement requires proof of hostile use under claim of right, actual, open, notorious and continuous for a period of ten years; when all elements are proven except hostile use, latter will be inferred.

 Solimini v. Pytlovany, 534 N.Y.S.2d 769, 144 A.D.2d 801.

Landowners were entitled to prescriptive easement over strip of land lying between their property and that of adjoining landowners after adjoining landowners failed to prove use by permission sufficient to overcome presumption of hostility; defendant's assertions that they warned plaintiffs to keep their child away from under the eaves of their house, requested plaintiffs not to heap snow at their basement

For legislative history of cited statutes see McKinney's Consolidated Laws of New York

---

FIGURE 3-EE
WEST'S NEW YORK DIGEST FOURTH

☛36(1) **EASEMENTS**   20 N Y D 4th—24

For later cases see same Topic and Key Number in Pocket Part

windows and that plaintiffs offered to pay them for a written grant of easement were insufficient to rebut hostile possession or establish permissive use.

> Solimini v. Pytlovany, 534 N.Y.S.2d 769, 144 A.D.2d 801.

N.Y.A.D. 4 Dept. 1989. Owners established open and notorious, continuous and uninterrupted use of dirt road connecting public highway and property used as shooting preserve for prescriptive period, and neighbors failed to rebut presumption that use was adverse, so that owners were entitled to easement by prescription over lands owned by neighbors.

> Reiss v. Maynard, 539 N.Y.S.2d 228, 148 A.D.2d 996.

N.Y.A.D. 1983. Landowners' evidence that during 1956 to 1961 period of use of driveway by county's predecessors, sought to be tacked by county in establishing term statutorily required for prescriptive right, landowners' property was owned by predecessors' grandson did no more than rebut presumption favoring county's position that where use has been shown to be open, continuous and uninterrupted, hostility will be presumed. McKinney's RPAPL § 311.

> Slater v. Ward, 460 N.Y.S.2d 150, 92 A.D.2d 667.

N.Y.A.D. 1982. Open, notorious, and continuous use of right-of-way gives rise to presumption that use was adverse, and shifts burden onto owner of servient tenement to show that use was by permission.

> Miller v. Bettucci, 453 N.Y.S.2d 828, 89 A.D.2d 706.

Where adjoining landowner who, prior to purchase, saw map showing driveway curving onto his parcel, had not shown that neighbors' use of driveway was permissive, he had failed to rebut presumption of adverse use arising from neighbors' open, notorious, and continuous use of driveway for more than prescriptive period, and thus neighbors had established evidence of prescriptive easement and were entitled to injunction against adjoining landowner's use of part of driveway on neighbors' property.

> Miller v. Bettucci, 453 N.Y.S.2d 828, 89 A.D.2d 706.

N.Y.A.D. 1982. With respect to claim of adverse possession or easement by prescription, where all other elements are established by one claiming title or easement, element of hostile possession or user will be presumed and burden shifts to record owner to produce

evidence rebutting presumption of adversity. McKinney's RPAPL § 521.

> City of Tonawanda v. Ellicott Creek Homeowners Ass'n, Inc., 449 N.Y.S.2d 116, 86 A.D.2d 118.

N.Y.A.D. 1981. Showing that use of easement was open and notorious, continuous and uninterrupted for the required time to establish prescriptive easement gives rise to presumption that the use was adverse, and the burden is on the servient landowner to prove that the use was by permission.

> Beutler v. Maynard, 437 N.Y.S.2d 463, 80 A.D.2d 982, affirmed 449 N.Y.S.2d 966, 56 N.Y.2d 538, 434 N.E.2d 1344.

Servient landowners having offered no proof that use of right-of-way leading to summer cabins was permissive, and owners of cabins having demonstrated that the use was open and notorious, it followed that if the use was continuous and uninterrupted for the prescriptive period, owners of servient estate failed to rebut presumption of adverse use.

> Beutler v. Maynard, 437 N.Y.S.2d 463, 80 A.D.2d 982, affirmed 449 N.Y.S.2d 966, 56 N.Y.2d 538, 434 N.E.2d 1344.

N.Y.A.D. 1980. Where property owners and predecessors had used footpath on neighbors' property for approximately 40 years, footpath was so incorporated with property owners' lot that it appeared to be part of such lot, and there was no way it could be determined through physical examination whether footpath was part of one lot or the other, presumption of adverse user of footpath was created, and, since such presumption was not rebutted, property owners established that their use of footpath was not permissive, but, rather, was adverse to interest of neighbors giving rise to prescriptive easement.

> Kaufman v. Eidelberg, 432 N.Y.S.2d 401, 78 A.D.2d 674.

N.Y.A.D. 1980. Presumption that use of land by claimants and its predecessors in title was adverse was plainly not dispelled merely because others in addition to claimant and its predecessors may have made some use of the roadway.

> Denniston's Crossing, Inc. v. State, 429 N.Y.S.2d 304, 76 A.D.2d 988.

N.Y.A.D. 1979. As regards establishing existence of easement by prescription, where use has been shown to be open, continuous, and uninterrupted, hostility will be presumed; this presumption will be rebutted where user and landowner are related by blood, or user is small select group of friends.

> Weinberg v. Shafler, 414 N.Y.S.2d 61, 68 A.D.2d 944, affirmed 430 N.Y.S.2d 55, 50 N.Y.2d 876, 407 N.E.2d 1351.

For legislative history of cited statutes see McKinney's Consolidated Laws of New York

FIGURE 3-FF
WEST'S NEW YORK DIGEST FOURTH

DISCUSSION OF PROBLEM 3.20   Several digest entries under Easements Key Number 36(1) indicate that a party claiming an easement by prescription may be assisted by a presumption in his or her favor. For example, one of the headnote summaries in the *Boumis* case (see Figure 3-EE) states that "[o]pen, notorious, uninterrupted, and undisputed use of right-of-way is presumed to be adverse or hostile and casts [the] burden on owner of servient tenement to show that use was by license, in connection with claim that easement was acquired by prescription." Remember that headnotes are not authority and should not be cited. The full text of the cases would need to be read in the relevant reporter before any final conclusions are reached.

To find earlier cases on the same point, you would examine the same key number in the earlier series of the *New York Digest*. The following table summarizes the steps to find later cases.

UPDATING RESEARCH IN WEST'S DIGESTS

To find later cases, you should use the following four-step process:

(1) First consult the annual pocket part in the back of the digest volume you are using and check for entries under the relevant topic and key number;

(2) Then examine the *latest* supplement to the digest for entries under the relevant topic and key number; paper-bound supplements accompanying the entire digest cover cases decided after the pocket part was prepared; note, however, that sometimes the pocket parts will be the latest supplement (depending on the timing of their issuance);

(3) Then examine the "Closing Table" in the *latest* supplement accompanying the digest—either the pocket part or the paper-bound supplement; the "Closing Table" tells you the last reporter volumes from which headnotes were included in the supplement; and

(4) Then check the bound volumes and advance sheets issued *after* the closing date. Each West reporter volume has a digest section that indexes the headnotes of cases in that volume.

The following table summarizes the basic approaches to finding relevant points of law in West's digests.

SUMMARY OF HOW TO ACCESS WEST'S DIGESTS

Means of Access	Description of Use
"Library References" in West or other publications	Consult the relevant topic and key number in the appropriate digest.
Descriptive Word Index of the smallest digest covering the relevant jurisdiction	Cross-check words descriptive of (1) the classes, the occupations, or the relationship of the parties or persons involved, (2) the places and things involved, (3) the basis of the action or legal issue, (4) the possible defenses, and (5) the relief sought.
Known topic and key number on point	Consult the relevant topic and key number in the appropriate digest.
West's Digest Table of Cases	Check the name of a known case in the table; the key numbers involved in the cases (as well as its citation) are listed— this approach is illustrated in Chapter 4 in a different context.
Topic method of search	Consult the "Analysis" at the beginning of the Topic in the digest; this method is not recommended unless you are thoroughly familiar with the organization of the key number classification involved.

West's key number digest system provides the most comprehensive approach to case law in the United States. If that digest system is to be used effectively, however, its principal shortcomings must be recognized. First, the digest volumes do not conveniently indicate subsequent changes in the law. Second, the digest paragraphs tend to "overabstract" the cases so that a researcher must examine a large number of digest paragraphs reflecting dictum. Third, the digest paragraphs sometimes do not

accurately state the points of law that they purport to contain. Nevertheless, West's Digests remain an extremely useful research tool.

In light of these shortcomings, care should be taken to avoid the following common errors in using West's Digests:

COMMON ERRORS IN USING WEST'S DIGESTS

(1) Failure to analyze the factual situation fully in order to generate sufficient words for cross-checking when the descriptive word method is used;

(2) Failure to check the pocket parts (or more recent volumes) under the relevant topic and key numbers;

(3) Failure to check for subsequent *statutory* provisions that override cases found in the digest;

(4) Failure to use *Shepard's Case Citations* (discussed in the next subsection) to determine if cases found in West's digests have been modified, overruled, etc.; and

(5) Failure to select the proper topic and key numbers when the topic method is used.

Lawyers Cooperative Publishing Co. also publishes, *inter alia*, *A.L.R. Digests*, and a digest covering U.S. Supreme Court decisions, the *U.S. Supreme Court Digest, Lawyers' Edition*. These digests are based upon Lawyers Cooperative's headnotes in *A.L.R.* and Supreme Court *Lawyers' Edition* cases.

4. USING SHEPARD'S CITATIONS TO DEVELOP YOUR RESEARCH AND TO FIND CASES IN SPECIFIC JURISDICTIONS

Lawyers use *Shepard's Case Citations* to (1) find parallel citations, (2) trace the judicial history of a case, (3) verify the current status of a case, (4) find later cases that have cited a case, and (5) develop research leads to *A.L.R.* annotations, attorney general opinions, and legal periodicals.

There are separate sets of *Shepard's Case Citations* for each state (e.g., *Shepard's Michigan Citations*), the District of Columbia, and Puerto Rico as well as each of West's regional reporters (e.g., *Shepard's South Western Reporter Citations*), the *Federal Reporter*, and the *Federal Supplement*. *Shepard's United States Citations (Case Edition)* covers all three Supreme Court reporters.

To "shepardize" a case, you would find the appropriate entry in the *first Shepard's Citations* volume covering the decision. Under the entry for the case, the parallel citation (if there is one) is given in parentheses.

Immediately following the parallel citation is the history of the case, noted by the following symbols:

HISTORY OF A CASE IN SHEPARD'S

Shepard's Symbol	Meaning of the Symbol
a	Cited case was **affirmed** on appeal
r	Cited case was **reversed** on appeal
m	Cited case was **modified** on appeal
s	**Same case** as the cited case (such a case should always be examined if one is noted)
D	An appeal from the cited case was **dismissed**
US cert den	A writ of **certiorari** was **denied** by the United States Supreme Court
US cert dis	A writ of **certiorari** was **dismissed** by the United States Supreme Court
v	Cited case was **vacated** on appeal
s	The opinion was **superseded** (there has been a substitution for a former opinion)
cc	A **connected case** (a different case from the cited case that arises out of the same subject matter or otherwise related to the cited case)
US reh den	A **rehearing** was **denied** by the United States Supreme Court
US reh dis	A **rehearing** was **dismissed** by the United States Supreme Court

---

After the history of the case, the next items which follow are citations of cases that have cited the case that you are "shepardizing." If they have "treated" the case in a special way, that fact is noted by the symbols shown in the following table:

SUBSEQUENT TREATMENT OF A CASE IN SHEPARD'S

Shepard's Symbol	Meaning of the Symbol
c	Citing case **criticized** the soundness or reasoning of the case you are "shepardizing"
d	Citing case **distinguished** (on the law or facts) the case you are "shepardizing"
e	Citing case **explained** the case you are "shepardizing"
f	Citing case **followed** the case you are "shepardizing" as controlling
h	Citing case **harmonized** an apparent inconsistency in the case you are "shepardizing" by showing that the inconsistency does not exist
o	Citing case expressly **overruled** the case you are "shepardizing"
j	Citing case cited the case you are "shepardizing" in a **dissenting opinion**
L	Citing case **limited** the case you are "shepardizing" by refusing to extend it beyond the precise issues involved in the case
q	Citing case **questioned** the soundness of the case you are "shepardizing"
P	Citing case is **parallel** to the case you are "shepardizing" (the cases are viewed as "substantially alike or on all fours on the law or the facts")

When the case being "shepardized" has been cited with particular reference to a part of the opinion covered by one of its headnotes, the headnote number (e.g., 1, 4, etc.) is shown immediately after the reporter reference. At the end of an entry in *Shepard's Case Citations* are references to *A.L.R.* annotations ("n" refers to an annotation proper and "s" refers to a supplement to an annotation), attorney general opinions, and selected law reviews that have cited the decision.

In an earlier subsection, the *Burke* case was identified as the leading case for the proposition that a spite fence or other spite structure which serves no useful purpose is actionable and may be abated. Find the entry for the *Burke* case (37 N.W. 838) in Figure 3-GG. The volume number is listed in the top corner (Vol. 37) and the beginning page number of each case is listed in bold print (- **838** -).

NORTHWESTERN REPORTER **Vol. 37**

208NW[1]323
e44F[1]658
Mich
76NW[1]133
Nebr
106NW[1]1017
Fla
80So320
Ind
42NE1011
48NE797
Kan
139P1173
Miss
76So547
13So2d826
Nev
133P938
NC
97SE24
11ALR123n
54ALR2d1431n

– 804 –
(72Wis42)
s31NW268
49NW[1]808
65NW[4]375
j83NW[1]774
109NW[2]651
111NW[4]518
270NW[2]427
Nebr
114NW[4]572
Calif
46P2d784
Ill
82IlA466
La
21So164
Mo
161SW639
NM
91P734
NC
130SE639
28ALR1036n
32ALR1212n
107ALR17n
163ALR28n
50ALR3d720n

– 809 –
(71Wis502)
43NW[2]554
e8NW[2]389
d58NW[2]540
85NW[2]839
Iowa
95NW[2]526
Mo
28SW590
57SW285
Tenn
189SW872

– 811 –
(71Wis524)
84NW[1]438
281NW[2]914
120NW[1]118
Minn
83NW[1]471
SD
58NW[1]6
73ALR288n
82ALR650n
119ALR469n

– 813 –
(71Wis463)
58NW[2]396
86NW[2]162
110NW[1]821
132NW[2]1112
132NW[3]1113
j132NW[2]1117
Iowa
41NW[2]3
Ark
138SW467
Mo
51SW1017
RI
104At80
Tex
35SW693

– 815 –
(71Wis591)
47NW1126
129ALR1366n

– 817 –
(71Wis547)
f44NW[1]113
70NW[1]820
102NW[1]1103
184NW[1]383
194F[1]850
Mich
42NW[1]1096
Ky
58SW531
20ALR962n
31ALR763n

– 819 –
(71Wis454)
42NW[2]210
44NW[2]638
65NW[2]742
68NW[2]1010
69NW[2]367
85NW[1]362
93NW[1]22
106NW[2]683
150NW[2]182
204NW[2]332
248NW[1]781
d99NW[1]202
41F[2]512
183FS[1]186
q183FS[1]187
Nebr
52NW[2]399
62NW[2]887
75NW[1]541
82NW[1]313
SD
127NW[1]620
Fla
47So954
91So365
Ind
56NE261
Ky
67SW25
La
201So2d692
Md
38At31
Mass
54NE548
Miss
27So757
33So506
Mo
27SW721
31SW123
NC
13SE237
Ohio
24NE1076
Okla
87P872
122P196
130P275
160P63
Tenn
32SW7
Tex
37SW632
Vt
88At534
Wash
92P781
W Va
47SE100
82SE42
199SE367
36ALR2d620n

– 820 –
(71Wis538)
52NW[1]94
62NW[3]526
82NW[1]568
105NW[2]563
119NW[2]344
139NW[1]423
140NW[2]1097
203NW[3]928

– 822 –
(71Wis576)
e82NW[1]533
91NW[2]971
105NW[2]47
Iowa
82NW[2]1027
158ALR1103n

– 823 –
(71Wis553)
s45NW807
57NW[1]1111
85NW[1]644
130NW[1]509
141NW[1]1018
182NW[1]844
234NW[1]508
d31NW[1]570
e114F[1]719
121F2d[1]179
e139F2d[2]563
Iowa
102NW[1]833
121NW[2]49
150NW[1]731
165NW[2]420
Minn
d52NW648
96NW[2]913
99NW[2]630
Nebr
116NW[1]283
ND
j43NW[1]409
SD
84NW[2]563
Ala
102So909
Fla
42So524
Ill
82IlA676
139IlA261
Ky
104SW387
Miss
77So318
Okla
124P322
228P976
RI
52At898
73At628
So C
39SE719
Tex
82SW813
226SW496
Utah
52P627
Wash
115P834
76ALR965n
36ALR2d18n
36ALR2d121n

– 825 –
(71Wis529)
47NW[4]1126
69NW[4]164
74NW[6]115
94NW[6]35
95NW[4]394
116F[6]269
11F2d[1]244
Iowa
188NW[1]976
Nebr
72NW[4]489
ND
115NW[1]848
Ark
15SW836
Ore
66P915
Pa
35A2d307
Va
44SE764
23ALR473n

– 830 –
(71Wis490)
43NW[1]319
Ind
95NE602

– 832 –
(71Wis469)

– 834 –
(71Wis472)
s22NW519
48NW[1]599
j72NW397
74NW94
78NW772
79NW223
80NW919
81NW675
91NW983
j97NW271
119NW[2]315
121NW[1]641
161NW[1]753
70FS649
Mich
155NW[2]594
Nev
150P2d1018

– 836 –
(71Wis542)
s47NW936
45NW[1]323
71NW[1]598
90NW[1]187
143NW[1]180
90NW[1]153
d107NW[1]471
d180NW[1]560
202NW[1]276
275NW[1]640
Idaho
105P1070
Ore
68P425
69ALR1495n

– 838 –
(69Mch380)
f45NW[1]381
77NW25
248NW[1]872
Nebr
f145NW[1]1002
SD
f273NW[1]661
Wis
321NW[1]188
Ala
58So285
Ga
13SE22
65SE912
Idaho
509P2d786
Ill
136IlA494
La
164So512
Mo
261SW347
Mont
56P219
NH
54At947
NY
70S256
195S2
NC
66SE439
66SE443
Ohio
42NE767
Okla
158P1159
153P2d822
Pa
50A2d350
RI
75A2d127
75A2d177
Utah
656P2d419
Wash
521P2d748
Wyo
249P2d531
287P2d469
133ALR692n
133ALR693n
80ALR3d974n
80ALR3d990n

– 845 –
(69Mch488)
50NW[1]666
67NW[1]1088
f72NW[1]139
f86NW[1]991
d87NW[1]121
100NW[1]562
117NW[1]657
163NW[1]995
j163NW[1]996
173NW[1]488
f179NW[1]228
188NW[1]549
207NW[1]917
211NW[1]123
j211NW[1]125
217NW[1]4
227NW[1]742
227NW[1]747
233NW[1]163
233NW[2]163
23NW[1]119
e57NW[1]464
j194NW349
214NW858
f298NW685
j298NW686
327NW[1]843
j327NW860
270F[1]717
d81F2d[1]72
7FS[1]886
114FS[1]104
Minn
100NW696
Wis
76NW[1]278
145NW[1]819
Ark
83SW959
Ill
75NE786
Ind
191NE332
Mont
241P332
NY
137NE326
166S2d736
Ore
223P925
Pa
36PaS435
Tex
21SW571
Vt
55At660
Wash
63P243
296P2d1019
5ALR1060n
23ALR759n

– 872 –
(69Mch572)
cc38NW294
f62NW1011
f64NW[1]472
77NW812
94NW[1]1067
100NW[1]897
102NW369
112NW[1]744
121F[1]282
Mont
55P1049
Wash
115P102
8ALR417n

– 876 –
(70Mch44)
51NW[1]1118
118NW[1]474
35F677
Nebr
70NW[1]252
SD
54NW[1]928
35ALR2d67n

– 879 –
(70Mch49)
84NW[2]1085
90NW[3]334
129NW[3]27
Iowa
j159NW[3]1024
Nebr
57NW[3]165
NM
70P573

– 880 –
(70Mch76)
s28NW757
cc42NW853
cc42NW980
44NW[2]274
44NW[2]957
48NW[2]175
62NW[2]719
125NW[2]383
162NW[2]116
d198NW[2]937
q136NW18
e195NW339
345NW923
NY
150S878
Ore
120P4
Va
156SE755
Wash
287P2d132
76ALR2d536n

– 882 –
(70Mch80)
43NW600
59NW[1]443
160NW590
270NW242
270NW251
58NW[1]147
134NW[1]228
167NW[1]472
e135US[1]496
e34LE[1]261
e10SC[1]1012
Nebr
89NW[1]281
Calif
146P2d932
Ga
45SE460
Ind
35NE401
86NE978
41ALR212n
88ALR2d341n

– 886 –
(70Mch89)
138NW[1]260
33F2d[3]894
Nebr
135NW[1]232
Ky
294SW152
58SW586
Okla
131P925
Wash
162P42
6ALR1012n
6ALR1026n
6ALR1079n

– 888 –
(70Mch6)
44NW[3]615
f49NW[1]265
54NW[4]767
54NW[2]910
63NW[1]429
80NW991
f86NW[1]397
f90NW[1]1059
f94NW[5]601
98NW19
98NW988
100NW270
109NW855
151NW[2]626
151NW[3]626
151NW[1]627
158NW168
158NW[1]200
162NW[7]944
167NW[3]999
178NW[3]56
d205NW[3]161
262NW[2]900
264NW[1]862
269NW[1]197
35NW[1]357
272US[1]429
71LE[1]335
47SC[1]123
22F2d[1]580
Iowa
84NW[5]533
101NW[6]431
215NW[1]643
Nebr
54NW[3]514
SD
132NW[3]688
Continued

397

FIGURE 3-GG
SHEPARD'S NORTHWESTERN REPORTER CITATIONS

PROBLEM 3.21   Assume that you want to find Idaho cases dealing with spite fences. Examine Figure 3-GG, and determine the citation to an Idaho case that has cited the *Burke* case. Has the Idaho case cited a point of law contained in a particular headnote of the *Burke* case?

DISCUSSION OF PROBLEM 3.21   The citation of the Idaho case that has cited the *Burke* case is 509 P.2d at 786. The Idaho case did not cite a point of law contained in a particular headnote of the *Burke* case. If the Idaho case had cited a particular point of law, the headnote number would have been noted immediately after the reporter abbreviation (P2d). The *Shepard's* volume lists (after the parallel citation) the citing cases in the following order: first, Michigan state and federal cases; then, cases from states in the same regional reporter, arranged alphabetically by state (in this instance, Nebraska, South Dakota, and Wisconsin—see Figure 3-GG); and finally, cases from states covered in the other regional reporters, arranged alphabetically by state (in this instance, beginning with an Alabama case and ending with a Wyoming case—again see Figure 3-GG).

Note that *Shepard's Northwestern Reporter Citations* was used to find the Idaho case. Shepard's also has a state citator series that could be used to "shepardize" the *Burke* case—*Shepard's Michigan Citations*. In that volume, you could look up the official citation of the *Burke* case (69 Mich. 380). However, *Shepard's Michigan Citations* was not used because it only provides a listing of subsequent Michigan state and federal cases that have cited the *Burke* case; it does not provide citations to the *Burke* case from other jurisdictions. To find those cases, you must use *Shepard's Northwestern Reporter Citations*.

As part of "shepardizing" a case, the researcher must then check the appropriate *subsequent* volumes of *Shepard's Citations* for additional entries. The latest paper-bound *Shepard's* supplement has a table entitled "WHAT YOUR LIBRARY SHOULD CONTAIN" on its cover which serves as a guide to the available *Shepard's* volumes. You should *always* check this table to be sure that you have consulted all available *Shepard's* volumes. An example of such a table in a *Shepard's* paper-bound supplement is given in the next chapter.

PROBLEM 3.22   The Idaho case that has cited the *Burke* case is shown in the following figures. Find where the *Burke* case has been cited and discussed in the Idaho case. Determine what is the law on spite fences in Idaho based upon the discussion in this case.

SUNDOWNER, INC. v. KING   Idaho   **785**

Cite as 509 P.2d 785

95 Idaho 367

SUNDOWNER, INC., an Idaho corporation,
Plaintiff-Respondent,

v.

James C. KING and Agnes C. King,
husband and wife, Defendants-
Appellants.

No. 11043.

Supreme Court of Idaho.

May 10, 1973.

The District Court, Canyon County, Robert B. Dunlap, J., ordered partially abated a sign which the court found to be a spite fence and owner appealed. The Supreme Court, Shepard, J., held that evidence sustained trial court's finding that sign which was 85 feet in length and 18 feet in height, obscured approximately 80% of adjacent building and restricted passage of light and air to adjacent building was "spite fence" erected for sole purpose of annoying neighbor.

Affirmed.

1. Nuisance ⊂⇒33

Evidence sustained trial court's finding that sign which was 85 feet in length and 18 feet in height, obscured approximately 80% of adjacent building and restricted passage of light and air to adjacent building was "spite fence" erected for sole purpose of annoying neighbor.

2. Appeal and Error ⊂⇒1071.6

Absence of findings of fact may be disregarded by appellate court if record is so clear that they are not necessary for complete understanding of issues.

3. Adjoining Landowners ⊂⇒10(3)

No property owner has right to erect and maintain an otherwise useless structure for sole purpose of injuring his neighbor.

4. Nuisance ⊂⇒35

Trial court did not err in partially abating and enjoining sign which was erected as spite fence. White v. Bernhart,

509 P.2d—50

41 Idaho 665, 241 P. 367, disapproved of to extent it is inconsistent.

———◆———

Donald E. Downen, Gigray, Downen & Morgan, Caldwell, for defendants-appellants.

Robert P. Tunnicliff of Miller, Weston & Tunnicliff, Caldwell, for plaintiff-respondent.

SHEPARD, Justice.

This is an appeal from a judgment ordering partial abatement of a spite fence erected between two adjoining motels in Caldwell, Idaho. This action is evidently an outgrowth of a continuing dispute between the parties resulting from the 1966 sale of a motel. *See*: King v. H. J. McNeel, Inc., 94 Idaho 444, 489 P.2d 1324 (1971).

In 1966 Robert Bushnell sold a motel to defendants-appellants King. Bushnell then built another motel, the Desert Inn, on property immediately adjoining that sold to the Kings.

The Kings thereafter brought an action against Bushnell (H. J. McNeel, Inc.) based on alleged misrepresentations by Bushnell in the 1966 sale of the motel property. *See*: King v. H. J. McNeel, Inc., *supra*. In 1968 the Kings built a large structure, variously described as a fence or sign, some 16 inches from the boundary line between the King and Bushnell properties. The structure is 85 ft. in length and 18 ft. in height. It is raised 2 ft. off the ground and is 2 ft. from the Desert Inn building. It parallels the entire northwest side of the Desert Inn building, obscures approximately 80% of the Desert Inn building and restricts the passage of light and air to its rooms.

Bushnell brought the instant action seeking damages and injunctive relief compelling the removal of the structure. Following trial to the court, the district court found that the structure was erected out of spite and that it was erected in violation of a municipal ordinance. The trial court

FIGURE 3-HH
PACIFIC REPORTER SECOND

786　Idaho　　　**509 PACIFIC REPORTER, 2d SERIES**

ordered the structure reduced to a maximum height of 6 ft.

The Kings appeal from the judgment entered against them and claim that the trial court erred in many of its findings of fact and its applications of law. The Kings assert the trial court erred in finding that the "sign" was in fact a fence; that the structure had little or no value for advertising purposes; that the structure cuts out light and air from the rooms of the Desert Inn Motel; that the structure has caused damage by way of diminution of the value of the Desert Inn Motel property; that the erection of the structure was motivated by ill-feeling and spite; that the structure was erected to establish a dividing line; and that the trial court erred in failing to find the structure was necessary to distinguish between the two adjoining motels.

[1] We have examined the record at length and conclude that the findings of the trial court are supported by substantial although conflicting evidence. The trial court had before it both still and moving pictures of the various buildings. The record contains testimony that the structure is the largest "sign" then existing in Oregon, Northern Nevada and Idaho. An advertising expert testified that the structure, because of its location and type, had no value for advertising and that its cost, i. e., $6,300, would not be justified for advertising purposes. Findings of fact will not be set aside on appeal unless they are clearly erroneous, and when they are supported by substantial though conflicting evidence they will not be disturbed on appeal. Hisaw v. Bishop, 95 Idaho 145, 504 P.2d 818 (1972); I.R.C.P. 52(a).

[2] The absence of findings of fact may be disregarded by an appellate court if the record is so clear that they are not necessary for a complete understanding of the issues. Call v. Marler, 89 Idaho 120, 403 P.2d 588 (1965).

The pivotal and dispositive issue in this matter is whether the trial court erred in requiring partial abatement of the struc-

ture on the ground that it was a spite fence. Under the so-called English rule, followed by most 19th century American courts, the erection and maintenance of a spite fence was not an actionable wrong. These older cases were founded on the premise that a property owner has an absolute right to use his property in any manner he desires. *See*: 5 Powell on Real Property, ¶696, p. 276 (1949 ed. rev'd 1968); Letts v. Kessler, 54 Ohio St. 73, 42 N.E. 765 (1896).

Under the modern American rule, however, one may not erect a structure for the sole purpose of annoying his neighbor. Many courts hold that a spite fence which serves no useful purpose may give rise to an action for both injunctive relief and damages. *See*: 5 Powell, *supra*. ¶696, p. 277; IA Thompson on Real Property, § 239 (1964 ed.). Many courts following the above rule further characterize a spite fence as a nuisance. *See*: Hornsby v. Smith, 191 Ga. 491, 13 S.E.2d 20 (1941); Barger v. Barringer, 151 N.C. 433, 66 S.E. 439 (1909); Annotation 133 A.L.R. 691.

One of the first cases rejecting the older English view and announcing the new American rule on spite fences is Burke v. Smith, 69 Mich. 380, 37 N.W. 838 (1888). Subsequently, many American jurisdictions have adopted and followed *Burke* so that it is clearly the prevailing modern view. *See*: Powell, *supra*, ¶696 at p. 279; Flaherty v. Moran, 81 Mich. 52, 45 N.W. 381 (1890); Barger v. Barringer, *supra*; Norton v. Randolph, 176 Ala. 381, 58 So. 283 (1912); Bush v. Mockett, 95 Neb. 552, 145 N.W. 1001 (1914); Hibbard v. Halliday, 58 Okla. 244, 158 P. 1158 (1916); Parker v. Harvey, 164 So. 507 (La.App.1935); Hornsby v. Smith, *supra;* Brittingham v. Robertson, 280 A.2d 741 (Del.Ch.1971). Also see the opinion of Mr. Justice Holmes in Rideout v. Knox, 148 Mass. 368, 19 N.E. 390 (1889).

In *Burke* a property owner built two 11 ft. fences blocking the light and air to his neighbors' windows. The fences served no useful purpose to their owner and were erected solely because of his malice

FIGURE 3-II
PACIFIC REPORTER SECOND

SUNDOWNER, INC. v. KING   Idaho   **787**
Cite as 509 P.2d 785

toward his neighbor. Justice Morse applied the maxim *sic utere tuo ut alienum non laedas*, and concluded:

"But it must be remembered that no man has a legal right to make a malicious use of his property, not for any benefit or advantage to himself, but for the avowed purpose of damaging his neighbor. To hold otherwise would make the law a convenient engine, in cases like the present, to injure and destroy the peace and comfort, and to damage the property, of one's neighbor for no other than a wicked purpose, which in itself is, or ought to be, unlawful. The right to do this cannot, in an enlightened country, exist, either in the use of property, or in any way or manner. There is no doubt in my mind that these uncouth screens or 'obscurers' as they are named in the record, are a nuisance, and were erected without right, and for a malicious purpose. What right has the defendant, in the light of the just and beneficent principles of equity, to shut out God's free air and sunlight from the windows of his neighbor, not for any benefit or advantage to himself, or profit to his land, but simply to gratify his own wicked malice against his neighbor? None whatever. The wanton infliction of damage can never be a right. It is a wrong, and a violation of right, and is not without remedy. The right to breath the air, and to enjoy the sunshine, is a natural one; and no man can pollute the atmosphere, or shut out the light of heaven, for no better reason than that the situation of his property is such that he is given the opportunity of so doing, and wishes to gratify his spite and malice towards his neighbor." 37 N.W. at 842.

[3, 4] We agree both with the philosophy expressed in the *Burke* opinion and

with that of other jurisdictions following what we feel is the better-reasoned approach. We hold that no property owner has the right to erect and maintain an otherwise useless structure for the sole purpose of injuring his neighbor. The trial court found on the basis of substantial evidence that the structure served no useful purpose to its owners and was erected because of the Kings' ill-will and emnity toward their neighboring competitor. We therefore hold that the trial court did not err in partially abating and enjoining the "sign" structure as a spite fence.

Our decision today is not entirely in harmony with White v. Bernhart, 41 Idaho 665, 241 P. 367 (1925). *White* held that an owner could not be enjoined from maintaining a dilapidated house as a nuisance, even though the house diminished the value of neighboring property. *White* is clearly distinguishable from the case at bar. Rather than a fence, it involved a dwelling house which was not maliciously erected. The rule announced herein is applicable only to structures which serve no useful purpose and are erected for the sole purpose of injuring adjoining property owners. There is dictum in *White* which suggests that a structure may only be enjoined when it is a nuisance per se. Such language is inconsistent with our decision today and it is hereby disapproved.

Appellants King assign error to findings and conclusions of the trial court relating to the applicability and interpretation of Caldwell Zoning Ordinance No. 1085. Our disposition of this appeal makes it unnecessary to consider those issues.

The judgment of the trial court is affirmed. Costs to respondent.

DONALDSON, C. J., McQUADE and McFADDEN, JJ., and HAGAN, District Judge, concur.

FIGURE 3-JJ
PACIFIC REPORTER SECOND

DISCUSSION OF PROBLEM 3.22 *Shepard's Citations* indicated that the *Burke* case had been cited on page 786. Note that this page was in the middle of the case. The case begins on page 785. The Idaho Supreme Court held on page 787 of the opinion that "no property owner

has the right to erect and maintain an otherwise useless structure for the sole purpose of injuring his neighbor." Note that the Idaho Supreme Court on page 787 distinguished and disapproved dicta in an earlier Idaho case, White v. Bernhart, 241 P. 367 (Idaho 1925).

PROBLEM 3.23 *Shepard's Citations* is also useful for finding *A.L.R.* annotations. Re-examine the entry for the *Burke* case (37 N.W. 838) in Figure 3-GG, and find the references to *A.L.R.* annotations that have cited the *Burke* case.

DISCUSSION OF PROBLEM 3.23 *Shepard's Citations* indicates when a case has been cited in an *A.L.R.* annotation. At the end of the listing for the *Burke* case, two annotations are cited: 133 A.L.R. at 692 and 693 and 80 A.L.R.3d at 974 and 990.

PROBLEM 3.24 *Shepard's Citations* covers a wide range of publications, including the restatements. Assume that you want to find cases that have cited a specific provision of one of the restatements—in this instance, § 829 of the Restatement (Second) of Torts. The relevant part of *Shepard's* page covering this section is shown in Figure 3-KK. From what jurisdictions have courts cited this section?

Iowa			Ariz	1983WLR108		599P2d671	
347NW182	§ 828	§ 837	700P2d503	Illustra-	§ 850		
NJ	96Nev502	145Az210	Calif	tion 1	197Ct139		§ 869
449A2d477	108Wis2d241	111NYM347	170CaR704	1983WLR108	385Mas45	§ 858	141CA3d897
NM	Iowa	Ariz	178CaR786	Comment c	96Nev502	65H555	103Ida572
685P2d968	347NW182	700P2d908	636P2d1124	544FS1119	Conn	116McA714	Calif
Pa	Nev	NM	Mich	RI	496A2d185	150S384	190CaR653
444A2d1268	611P2d1075	701P2d386	316NW261	493A2d828	Mass	172NJS505	Idaho
450A2d5	NM	NY	Mo	1983WLR108	429NE1149	Haw	651P2d13
Utah	685P2d968	443NYS2d	689SW119		Mo	656P2d73	Mont
704P2d577	Tenn	[970	NY		589SW335	Ind	683P2d918
Wis	635SW119		426NYS2d	§ 840E	Nev	440NE500	359NW863
321NW190	Wis	§§ 838	[629	Comment b	611P2d1075	452NE962	Comment d
65ABA368	321NW192	to 840	Comment a	170GaA332		Mich	103Ida572
Comment b	64Cor782	138Az112	131CA3d	Ga	§ 850A	323NW527	108Ida261
NM	Comment f	Ariz	[1056	317SE234	197Ct139	NJ	386Mas563
685P2d968	NM	673P2d310	112McA573	Comment c	245Ga411	412A2d1072	Idaho
64Cor782	635SW120		Calif	170GaA332	385Mas47	Ohio	651P2d13
32StnL1087	Comment h	§ 838	182CaR730	Ga	96Nev502	474NE325	698P2d323
Comment e	105Ida336	DC	Mich	317SE234	Conn	Comments	Mass
105Ida329	Idaho	497A2d461	316NW261		496A2d185	a to f	437NE184
Idaho	669P2d659	NH	Mo	§ 841	Ga	Ind	Comment e
669P2d652		489A2d598	689SW119	et seq.	265SE589	440NE501	141CA3d897
Comment f	§ 829		NM	172NJS495	Mass	Comment d	Calif
32DC3d89	108Wis2d235	§ 839	703P2d180	NJ	429NE1150	Ind	190CaR653
105Ida329	Pa	601FS932	Illustra-	412A2d1067	Mo	452NE967	Comment f
108Ida609	444A2d1268	114CA3d419	tion 4		589SW335	Comment f	Mich
Idaho	Wis	153CA3d620	145Az116	§§ 841	496A2d185	172NJS512	311NW271
669P2d652	321NW189	143McA200	30C3d365	to 864	Nev	NJ	
701P2d229		331PaS256	Calif	Mo	611P2d1075	412A2d1076	§ 870
65ABA368	§ 829A	191NJS297	178CaR786	589SW335	65ABA368		769F2d1155
	303PaS434	Calif	636P2d1124	65ABA368	Comment j	§§ 865	142Az268
	Pa	200CaR584	NY		85CR980	to 886B	28DC3d412
	444A2d1270	220CaR783	426NYS2d			65ABA370	1HA387
	450A2d5	DC	[630				
	65ABA368		Illustra-				*Continued*
			tion 4				443
			132Ila834				

FIGURE 3-KK

SHEPARD'S RESTATEMENT OF THE LAW CITATIONS

DISCUSSION OF PROBLEM 3.24　*Shepard's Citations* indicates that courts from Wisconsin ("108 Wis2d 235" and its parallel citation "321 NW2d 189") and Pennsylvania ("444 A2d 1268") have cited this section during the period covered by this *Shepard's* volume. To find later cases, you would consult *Shepard's* paper-covered pamphlets.

5. USING PERIODICAL INDEXES TO DEVELOP CASE-RELATED RESEARCH

Chapter 2 discussed the various periodical indexes available to help researchers find articles that might provide useful commentary and citations to other authority. In particular, the subject index portion of the *Index to Legal Periodicals* and the *Current Law Index* will lead you to relevant articles.

These articles will often give you, *inter alia*, additional case citations. More importantly, they may provide you with a basis for criticizing a particular rule—especially with regard to the spite fence problem discussed earlier because there are two competing rules. For example, by consulting the periodical indexes, you could find the following article: Stewart E. Sterk, Neighbors in American Land Law, 87 Colum. L. Rev. 55 (1987) (discussing spite fence rules from an economic point of view).

The Table of Cases in the periodical indexes will also lead you to relevant articles about particular cases. For example, assume that you are interested in the Wisconsin case that cited § 829 of the Restatement (Second) of Torts (see Figure 3-KK). This case is Prah v. Maretti, 321 N.W.2d 182 (Wis. 1982). To find articles dealing with this case, you would examine the Table of Cases in the volume(s) of the periodical index covering the date of decision and a few years thereafter. Figures 3-LL and 3-MM show the Table of Cases entries for the *Prah* case from Volume 23 of the *Index to Legal Periodicals* (covering Sept. 1983-Aug. 1984) and Volume 4 of the *Current Law Index* (covering the calendar year 1983).

> **Prah** v. Maretti, 321 N.W.2d 182 (Wis.)
> 　34 *Case W. Res. L. Rev.* 367-400 '83/'84
> 　68 *Cornell L. Rev.* 941-78 Ag '83
> 　1984 *Det. C.L. Rev.* 101-16 Spr '84
> 　21 *Duq. L. Rev.* 1159-83 Summ '83
> 　11 *Ecology L.Q.* 47-72 '83
> 　14 *Envtl. L.* 223-39 Fall '83
> 　48 *Mo. L. Rev.* 769-82 Summ '83
> 　3 *N. Ill. U.L. Rev.* 187-215 Wint '82
> 　78 *Nw. U.L. Rev.* 861-92 N '83
> 　7 *Suffolk Transnat'l L.J.* 235-53 Spr '83
> 　29 *Wayne L. Rev.* 1449-70 Summ '83
> 　1983 *Wis. L. Rev.* 1263-304 '83

FIGURE 3-LL
INDEX TO LEGAL PERIODICALS

PRAH v. Maretti,
321 N.W.2d 182 (Wis. 1982) Wisconsin Supreme Court sees the light: nuisance remedy granted for obstruction of solar access.
11 Ecology L.Q. 47-72 Wint '83
Prah v. Maretti, 108 Wis. 2d 223, 321 N.W.2d 182 (1982). (nuisance suit for obstruction of solar collectors) (case note)
14 Envt'l L. 223-239 Fall '83

Casting a shadow on a solar collector - a cause of action recognized; an alternative resolution framework suggested. (case note)
68 Cornell L. Rev. 941-978 Aug '83
A private nuisance remedy for obstruction of solar access. (case note)
48 Mo. L. Rev. 769-782 Summ '83
Property law - obstruction of sunlight as a private nuisance. (case note)
29 Wayne L. Rev. 1449-1470 Summ '83
Tort law - private nuisance - access to sunlight - residential solar energy systems - the Wisconsin Supreme Court has held that an owner of a solar-heated residence, who alleged that an adjoining neighbor's proposed construction of a residence would interfere with his access to unobstructed sunlight, stated a claim upon which relief could be granted under a theory of private nuisance. (case note)
21 Duq. L. Rev. 1159-1183 Summ '83
Environmental law - solar energy - private nuisance as a remedy for solar access obstructions. (case note)
7 Suffolk Transnat'l L.J. 235-253 Spr '83
Solar rights and private nuisance law. (case note)
16 J. Mar. L. R. 435-455 Spr '83
Real property - nuisance - zoning - an owner of a solar-heated residence has a cause of action under Wisconsin Private Nuisance Law for an unreasonable obstruction of his access to sunlight by an adjoining landowner's home. (case note)
52 U. Cin. L. Rev. 208-224 Wntr '83
Private nuisance doctrine is applicable to interference with property owner's solar access. (case note)
6 Am. J. Trial Advocacy 360-361 Fall '82
Here comes the sun. (case note)
4 U. Bridgeport L. Rev. 153-176 Wntr '82
A new place under the sun: Prah v. Maretti and common law solar access remedies.
3 N. Ill. U. L. Rev. 187-215 Wntr '82

FIGURE 3-MM
CURRENT LAW INDEX

Section 3C. Relationship of Case-Oriented Research to Statutes

It was noted earlier that West's digests will not alert you to statutory changes affecting the common law. You would need to be especially careful in your research of spite fences because both legal encyclopedias indicated that statutes have now been enacted in many jurisdictions. Local ordinances may also apply to this kind of situation.

Generally speaking, to determine if a statute has been enacted on spite fences (or regulating the height of a fence), you would check the index to the statutory compilation covering the jurisdiction in which the fence is located. For example, if you checked the General Index to West's *Annotated California Code*, you would find the entry for "Spite Fences" shown in Figure 3-NN.

<table>
<tr><td>

SPEEDY TRIAL
  Generally, **Const. Art. 1, § 15; Pen 1381**
    et seq.
Trial, this index

SPEEDY TRIAL ACT
Generally, **Gov 68600 et seq.**

</td><td>

SPIRITUAL HEALING
Faith Healing, generally, this index

SPITE FENCES
Malicious erection or maintenance, CC 841.4

SPITTING
Expectoration, generally, this index

</td></tr>
</table>

FIGURE 3-NN
WEST'S ANNOTATED CALIFORNIA CODE

PROBLEM 3.25 The text of § 841.4 of the California Civil Code is shown in Figure 3-OO. How high does it appear that the fence can be?

---

§ 841.4.   Spite fences

Any fence or other structure in the nature of a fence unnecessarily exceeding 10 feet in height maliciously erected or maintained for the purpose of annoying the owner or occupant of adjoining property is a private nuisance. Any owner or occupant of adjoining property injured either in his comfort or the enjoyment of his estate by such nuisance may enforce the remedies against its continuance prescribed in Title 3, Part 3, Division 4 of this code.[1]

(Added by Stats.1953, c. 37, p. 674, § 2.)

  [1] Section 3501 et seq.

Forms

See West's California Code Forms, Civil.

Law Review Commentaries

Validity of Act of 1913 restricting power of landowner to erect spite fences. (1921) 9 C.L.R. 447, 459.

Library References

Nuisance ⇐3(12).   C.J.S. Nuisances § 39.

FIGURE 3-OO
WEST'S ANNOTATED CALIFORNIA CIVIL CODE

DISCUSSION OF PROBLEM 3.25 The text of the statute indicates that a fence "unnecessarily exceeding 10 feet in height maliciously erected or maintained . . . is a private nuisance." Thus, it appears that a fence that is less than 10 feet in height does not violate the statute.

Before you reach this conclusion, however, you should check the "Notes of Decisions" accompanying this provision. In particular, exam-

ine note 2, shown in Figure 3-PP. This case suggests that the common law has not been replaced by this statute with respect to fences less than 10 feet in height.

Notes of Decisions

Construction and application 2
Damages 3
Validity 1

---

1. Validity

Stats.1913, p. 342, providing that any fence or other structure in the nature of a fence unnecessarily exceeding 10 feet in height, maliciously erected or maintained for the purpose of annoying owner of adjoining property should be deemed a private nuisance which could be abated, was not unconstitutional. Bar Due v. Cox (1920) 190 P. 1056, 47 C.A. 713.

2. Construction and application

Even though board fence erected on adjoining property had not been ten feet in height so as to violate the spite fence law, still it would be a nuisance if it was constructed with malice and interfered with neighbor's full enjoyment of their home, and if its usefulness to persons erecting it was subordinate. Griffin v. Northridge (1945) 153 P.2d 800, 67 C.A.2d 69.

Six and one-half foot fence built within three inches of boundary line was not nuisance per se, under Stats.1913, p. 342, § 1. Haehlen v. Wilson (1936) 54 P.2d 62, 11 C.A.2d 437.

In an action under Stats.1913, p. 342, to have a fence erected on defendant's premises declared a private nuisance, evidence warranted a finding that the fence was maliciously erected for the purpose of annoying plaintiff. Bar Due v. Cox (1920) 190 P. 1056, 47 C.A. 713.

A structure standing wholly on the lot of the owner thereof was not within the inhibition of Stats.1885, p. 45, regulating the height of "division fences" and "partition walls" in cities and towns. Ingwersen v. Barry (1897) 50 P. 536, 118 C. 342.

Act March 9, 1885, Stats.1885, p. 45, regulating the height of division fences and partition walls in cities and towns, is a general law. Western Granite & Marble Co. v. Knickerbocker (1894) 37 P. 192, 103 C. 111.

3. Damages

$1,000 as damages for nuisance as result of acts of defendants who were plaintiff's neighbors in destroying flower beds, interfering with sale of premises, erecting board fence and other similar acts interfering with plaintiffs' comfortable enjoyment of life and of their home was not excessive. Griffin v. Northridge (1945) 153 P.2d 800, 67 C.A.2d 69.

FIGURE 3-PP
WEST'S ANNOTATED CALIFORNIA CIVIL CODE

In checking the statutes, you may find that there are no statutes on point (e.g., in Kansas). It should be remembered that sometimes the value of research is finding the absence of relevant provisions. Remember, too, that you would have to check local municipal ordinances for relevant provisions.

Section 3D. Practice Aids

In developing your research, you may want to consult various "practice aids"—specialized books providing forms, suggested methods of proof, and detailed discussion of particular types of causes of action. One way of finding relevant forms and other practice aids is through the frequent cross-references from other publications within a publisher's system. Another way to find practice aids is to use the card catalog and the indexes accompanying these sources.

PROBLEM 3.26 For example, re-examine Figure 3-I showing the pocket part from *American Jurisprudence Second*. What source could you consult to find suggestions on how to prove that a fence had been maliciously designed or constructed?

DISCUSSION OF PROBLEM 3.26 The note to § 106 refers you to "Malicious design and construction of fence. 22 Am Jur Proof of Facts 2d 683." The following figures illustrate the coverage of this practice aid.

MALICIOUS DESIGN AND CONSTRUCTION OF FENCE

JONATHAN M. PURVER, LL.B. *

Fact in Issue: Whether an adjoining landowner was motivated by malice in designing and constructing a fence that interferes with the use and enjoyment of plaintiff's property.

This fact question may arise where a landowner seeks to prevent an adjoining landowner from continuing to maintain a fence which was allegedly constructed solely for purposes of malice and spite.

Related Proofs: Damages [for injury to real property], 3 POF 491, 497; Nuisances, 8 POF 527

I. BACKGROUND
§ 1. In general; scope
§ 2. Spite fence as actionable—Generally
§ 3. —Usefulness of fence
§ 4. Statutory provisions
§ 5. Evidence of malicious nature of fence
§ 6. Remedies
§ 7. Practice
§ 8. Elements of damages: guide and checklist

II. PROOF OF MALICIOUS DESIGN AND CONSTRUCTION OF FENCE

   A. Elements of Proof
§ 9. Guide and checklist

   B. Testimony of Complainant
§ 10. Location and ownership of property

---

* Senior Editor, Bancroft-Whitney Company.

22 POF 2d   **683**

FIGURE 3-QQ
AMERICAN JURISPRUDENCE PROOF OF FACTS SECOND

22-683   SPITE FENCE

§ 11. Defendant's construction of fence
§ 12. Fence as obstructing preexisting view
§ 13. Fence as obstructing light
§ 14. Unsightly character of fence
§ 15. Fence as impairing value of complainant's property

C. Testimony of Defendant Landowner (Adverse Witness)

§ 16. Introduction
§ 17. Construction and character of fence
§ 18. Absence of beneficial uses of fence
§ 19. Fence as dissimilar to other fences in the area
§ 20. Animosity to complainant's malicious motive

COLLATERAL REFERENCES

Text References:

Spite fences, generally, 3 H. Tiffany, THE LAW OF REAL PROPERTY § 716 (1939, 1978 Supp); 5 R. Powell, THE LAW OF REAL PROPERTY § 696 (1977); 1 AM JUR 2d, Adjoining Landowners §§ 106–117

Legal Periodicals:

Comment, Constitutionality of the Pennsylvania Spite Fence Statute, 75 Dick L Rev 281 (1971)

Comment, Obstruction of Sunlight as a Private Nuisance, 65 Calif L Rev 94 (1977)

Note, A General Survey of the Rights and Duties of Adjoining Landowners in New England, 39 BU L Rev 228 (Spring 1959)

Legal Forms:

Agreement to let lands lie open—No construction of fence, 8 AM JUR LEGAL FORMS 2d (Supp), Fences § 114:17

Checklist of matters to be considered in drafting agreement affecting fences, 8 AM JUR LEGAL FORMS 2d, Fences § 114:4

Checklist of matters to be considered in drafting instrument creating or reserving easement for light, air, and view, 1 AM JUR LEGAL FORMS 2d, Adjoining Landowners § 8:43

Comprehensive multiparty fencing agreement, 8 AM JUR LEGAL FORMS 2d, Fences §§ 114:11-114:12

Grant of easement for light and air, 1 AM JUR LEGAL FORMS 2d, Adjoining Landowners § 8:44

Reservation in deed—easement for light, air, and unobstructed view, 1 AM JUR LEGAL FORMS 2d, Adjoining Landowners § 8:46

684   **22 POF 2d**

FIGURE 3-RR
AMERICAN JURISPRUDENCE PROOF OF FACTS SECOND

SPITE FENCE   22-683

Pleading Forms:

Complaint for malicious deprivation of light and air by wall—injunction and damages, 1 AM JUR PL & PR FORMS (rev ed), Adjoining Landowners Form 51

Complaints to enjoin construction or maintenance of spite fence, 1 AM JUR PL & PR FORMS (rev ed), Adjoining Landowners Forms 52–54

Complaint for wrongful erection of barbed wire fence adjoining school yard and for injury to child running into fence, 12 AM JUR PL & PR FORMS (rev ed), Fences Form 51

Complaint to enjoin defendant from adding to height of party wall, 19 AM JUR PL & PR FORMS (rev ed), Party Walls Form 3

Temporary restraining order—Order to show cause why preliminary injunction should not issue enjoining fence construction, 12 AM JUR PL & PR FORMS (rev ed), Fences Form 8

Trial Techniques:

Locating Public Records, 2 AM JUR TRIALS 409

Preparing and Using Diagrams, 3 AM JUR TRIALS 507

Preparing and Using Maps, 2 AM JUR TRIALS 669

Preparing and Using Photographs in Civil Cases, 3 AM JUR TRIALS 1

Annotations:

Fence as nuisance. 80 ALR3d 962.

Right to maintain gate or fence across right of way. 52 ALR3d 9.

"Coming to nuisance" as a defense or estoppel. 42 ALR3d 344.

Modern status of rules as to balance of convenience or social utility as affecting relief from nuisance. 40 ALR3d 601.

Rights and liabilities of adjoining landowners as to trees, shrubbery, or similar plants growing on boundary line. 26 ALR3d 1372.

Zoning regulations prohibiting or limiting fences, hedges, or the like. 66 ALR2d 1294.

INDEX

FIGURE 3-SS

AMERICAN JURISPRUDENCE PROOF OF FACTS SECOND

22-683   SPITE FENCE
§ 9

II. PROOF OF MALICIOUS DESIGN AND CONSTRUCTION OF FENCE

A. Elements of Proof

§ 9. Guide and checklist

The following facts and circumstances, among others, tend to establish grounds for injunctive relief against the continued existence of a fence, as a "spite fence," which has been constructed by an adjoining landowner on the adjoining landowner's own property:

☐ Location and ownership of property [§§ 10, 16]

☐ Defendant's construction of fence [§§ 11, 17]

☐ Fence as obstructing preexisting view [§ 12]

☐ Fence as obstructing light [§ 13]

☐ Unsightly character of fence [§ 14]

☐ Fence as impairing value of complainant's property [§ 15]

☐ Absence of beneficial uses of fence [§ 18]

☐ Fence as dissimilar to other fences in the area [§ 19]

☐ Animosity of defendant landowner toward complainant; malicious motive [§ 20]

[It is assumed in the following proof that a landowner has brought a suit for injunctive relief against the continued existence of a fence erected by an adjoining landowner on his own property.][78]

B. Testimony of Complainant

§ 10. Location and ownership of property

[After introduction and identification of witness]

Q. Are you the plaintiff in this action?

A. Yes.

Q. Please state your residence address.

A. I live at _____.

Q. Is that here in _____ County?

A. Yes.

---

78. ☐ **Note:** Portions of this proof are adapted from the trial transcript in De Cecco v Beach, 174 **Conn** 29, 381 A2d 543, in which the court entered a judgment ordering a portion of the defendant's spite fence removed.

FIGURE 3-TT

AMERICAN JURISPRUDENCE PROOF OF FACTS SECOND

SPITE FENCE   **22-683**
§ 10

Q. Who owns the property located at your residence address, the address which you have just stated?

A. I am the owner.

Q. The sole owner?

A. Yes.

Q. How long have you lived at this location?

A. _____ years.

Q. What is the size of your lot?

A. _____ square feet.

[At this point, counsel may have the court clerk mark a diagram of the complainant's lot and the surrounding area for identification.]

Q. I show you now a diagram of your lot and the surrounding area and ask whether you have previously seen this diagram.

A. Yes.

Q. What does this diagram represent?

A. The location, in scale, of my lot as well as the adjoining lots of other landowners.

Q. Was this diagram prepared by you?

A. I retained the services of a land surveyor here in _____ County who prepared it for me for this trial.

Q. Does this diagram, based on your personal knowledge of your lot and your knowledge of the surrounding lots, accurately portray your lot and the surrounding lots and the geographic terrain features in the area?

A. Yes, it does.

Counsel: I offer this diagram, marked for identification as plaintiff's Exhibit _____, in evidence as plaintiff's Exhibit _____.

The Court: It may be admitted.

> ☐ **Practice Note: Admissibility of map or diagram of area in question.** A diagram or a drawing illustrating the property in question may be important evidence to aid the trier of fact in understanding the location and nature of both parties' property, and the nature and character of the defendant's offending fence. When the representation of the property, as herein, is made out of the courtroom, there must be evidence to authenticate that the diagram accurately represents that which it purports to depict. See 29 AM JUR 2d, Evidence §§ 802, 803.

22 POF 2d   **703**

FIGURE 3-UU

AMERICAN JURISPRUDENCE PROOF OF FACTS SECOND

Assume that your client has decided to sue on the theory that the neighbor's fence is a spite fence. Where can you find a sample complaint? A substantial number of books contain forms for use in the preparation of legal documents. Some are oriented to a particular jurisdiction or a particular legal subject. Others have a more general orientation. Perhaps the most elaborate collection of forms (with annotations) is *American Jurisprudence Pleading and Practice Forms (Revised Edition)*. This form book, for example, is cited in Figure 3-SS ("Complaints to enjoin construction or maintenance of spite fence, 1 Am Jur Pl & Pr Forms (rev ed), Adjoining Landowners Forms 52-54." Cross-references are also given in "Total Client-Service Library References" at the beginning of *A.L.R.* annotations and in *American Jurisprudence Second*. Re-examine Figure 3-SS, and find the references to the various pleading forms. Shown below in Figure 3-VV is a portion of Form 52.

Form 52 Complaint, petition, or declaration—Malicious deprivation of light and air—To enjoin reconstruction of spite structure— Apartment premises rendered commercially uninhabitable

[*Caption, Introduction, see* CAPTIONS, PRAYERS, ETC.]

I

Plaintiff is now, and at all times referred to was, the owner of that certain lot in the City of ....1........., ...2......... County, State of ....3........., and of ....4......... [an apartment building] situated thereon, more particularly described as follows: ....5......... [*legal description*].

II

Defendant is now, and at all times referred to was, the owner of that certain lot in the mentioned city, and the dwelling house situated thereon, more particularly described as follows: ....6........., which lot adjoins plaintiff's lot on the ....7......... [*direction*] side.

III

On ....8......... [*date*], defendant unlawfully, wrongfully, and maliciously caused a high fence to be erected on ....9......... [the division line between the lots or on defendant's lot in close proximity to the line] for the express purpose of harassing and annoying plaintiff by shutting off light and air from the apartments located in the ....10......... [*direction*] portion of plaintiff's building, and further unlawfully, wrongfully, and maliciously caused the construction of the fence in order to make plaintiff's apartments unfit for occupancy, and thereby cause plaintiff's tenants to move out of the building. The fence constructed by defendant was ....11......... [*specify dimensions and type of construction*], and a photograph of the fence, marked Exhibit "....12....," is attached to and made a part of this complaint.

IV

The effect of defendant's fence is to shut off, almost completely, the air and light in the apartments located along the ....13......... [*direction*] side of plaintiff's building, with the further result that the apartments are now dark, necessitating the use of electricity, and are also stuffy from lack of ventilation. The distance between the ....14......... [*direction*] wall of plaintiff's building and the fence varied from ....15.... inches on the ....16......... corner of plaintiff's building to ....17.... inches on the ....18......... corner thereof.

FIGURE 3-VV

AMERICAN JURISPRUDENCE PLEADING AND PRACTICE FORMS

Another useful form book is West's *Modern Legal Forms* and its successor, *West's Legal Forms 2d*. The latter set is functionally planned around major legal topics (business organizations, domestic relations, commercial transactions, real estate transactions, employee benefit plans, retirement plans, debtor-creditor relations, employment agencies and service agreements, patents, copyrights, and trademarks, and general forms) rather than organized in the traditional alphabetical arrangement of forms. Other useful form books include *Nichol's Cyclopedia of Legal Forms*, Raskin and Johnson's *Current Legal Forms with Tax Analysis*, *Bender's Federal Practice Forms*, *West's Federal Forms*, *Bender's Forms of Discovery*, and *Federal Procedural Forms, Lawyers Edition*.

Assume that your client and his neighbor have decided to settle their dispute concerning the use of the road. Your client has agreed to pay $500 for the right to use the road and end the dispute. To prepare the agreement, assume that you have decided to consult *West's Legal Forms 2d*. Shown in the following figures is a page showing a portion of the table of sections for the forms dealing with easements, followed by the form for granting a right of way for all purposes and one granting a right of way in connection with a dwelling house. You could adapt this form to effectuate the settlement of this dispute.

Table of Sections

Sec.
34.1   In General.
34.2   Grant of Right of Way for All Purposes.
34.3   Grant of Right of Way in Connection With Dwelling House.
34.4   Agreement to Grant Right of Way Across Reserved Tract of Land.
34.5   Grant of Right of Way to Governmental Subdivision.
34.6   Granting Clause—Right of Way to Mortgagee.
34.7   ____ Right to Use in Common a Shore Line Strip.
34.8   ____ Covenant to Pay Damages.
34.9   ____ Right of Way for Electric Power Transmission Line.
34.10   ____ Right of Way for Construction of Slopes of Cuts and Fills.
34.11   ____ Right of Way for Aircraft.
34.12   Aviation Easement.
34.13   Aviation and Hazard Easement.
34.14   Consent of Tenant to Grant of Right of Way.
34.15   Highway Access Provisions.
34.16   Grant of New Right of Way in Substitution for Existing Right of Way.
34.17   Agreement Quieting Dispute as to Use of a Private Road.
34.18   Acknowledgment That Private Road Is Used by Permission.
34.19   Disclaimer of Interest in Land Made to Purchaser.
34.20   Grant of Right of Way to Railway Company.
34.21   ____ Another Form.
34.22   Clause Releasing Railway Company From Liability.

FIGURE 3-WW

WEST'S LEGAL FORMS 2D

Ch. 34   EASEMENTS   § 34.2

transfer; and the burden of an easement runs with the servient tenement binding all grantees except good faith purchasers without notice.[3]

The formal requisites for the creation of an easement by conveyance inter vivos are, in general, the same as those required in a conveyance of an estate in land of like duration.[4] The modes of creation, other than by implication or prescription, include the following: (1) formal grant; (2) reservation or exception in a conveyance of land; (3) convenant; (4) unsealed agreement based on valuable consideration; (5) conveyance by reference to a plat which depicts easements; (6) conveyance referring to a recorded declaration of easements; (7) deed of conveyance otherwise sufficient to convey fee title but which includes language construed to reduce the estate granted to a mere easement; (8) mortgage containing grant or reservation of easement, where such mortgage is subsequently foreclosed; and (9) informal documents of various kinds bearing little resemblance to formal tenement grants, but which are construed as easement grants in the interest of justice, usually to prevent revocation by the grantor.[5]

§ 34.2 Grant of Right of Way for All Purposes

Indenture, made the _____ day of _____, 19__, between _____, Grantor, and _____, Grantee.

Whereas, the Grantor is seised of an estate in fee simple of a parcel of land described as [*description*], and marked on the plan annexed hereto, across which there runs a private road shown on the plan by the dotted lines between point A, where the road opens into _____ street, and point B, where it opens into _____ lane;

Whereas, the Grantee is seised in fee simple of another parcel of land near the Grantor's land, described as [*description*]; and

Whereas, the Grantor has agreed, in consideration of the sum of $_____, to grant to the Grantee an easement or right of way over the said private road:

Witnesseth, that in pursuance of the said agreement and in consideration of the sum of $_____ paid by the Grantee to the Grantor, the receipt whereof is hereby acknowledged, the Grantor hereby grants to the Grantee, his heirs and assigns:

Full and free right and liberty for him and them, his and their tenants, servants, visitors, and licensees, in common with all others having the like right, at all times hereafter, with or without vehicles

---

3. C.J.S. Easements § 47.

4. 5 Restatement, Property § 467 (1944).

5. Kratovil, Easement Draftsmanship and Conveyancing, 38 California L.Rev.

426 (1950); Conard, Words Which will Create an Easement, 6 Missouri L.Rev. 245 (1941).

See generally, C.J.S. Easements §§ 23–29.

3

FIGURE 3-XX
WEST'S LEGAL FORMS 2D

§ 34.2   EASEMENTS   Pt. 3

of any description, for all purposes connected with the use and enjoyment of the said land of the Grantee, to pass and repass along the said private road for the purpose of going from the said _____ street to the said _____ lane, or vice versa.

To have and to hold the easement or right of way hereby granted unto the Grantee, his heirs and assigns, as appurtenant to the said land of the Grantee.

In Witness Whereof, the Grantor has hereunto set his hand and seal the day and year first above written.

[*Signature, Seal, and Acknowledgment*]

§ 34.3   Grant of Right of Way in Connection With Dwelling House

[*Begin as in preceding form, including first recital*]

Whereas, the Grantee is seised in fee simple of another parcel of land described as [*description*], upon which is erected a private dwelling house; and

Whereas, for the consideration hereinafter mentioned, the Grantor has agreed to grant to the Grantee such right of way over the said private road as hereinafter expressed:

Witnesseth [*grant as in preceding form*]:

Full and free right and liberty for him and them, his and their tenants, servants, visitors, and licensees, in common with all other persons having the like right, at all times hereafter, on foot or on horseback or in vehicles (but not with sheep, cattle, pigs, or other animals) to pass and repass along the said private road from the said _____ street to the said _____ lane for all lawful purposes connected with the use and enjoyment of the said premises of the Grantee as a single private dwelling house, but for no other purposes.

To hold the said right of way hereby granted to the Grantee, his heirs and assigns, as appurtenant to his said premises.

In Witness Whereof, *etc.*

§ 34.4   Agreement to Grant Right of Way Across Reserved Tract of Land

The Grantor agrees to include an easement for use as a roadway across the tract first above reserved and excepted from the _____ parcel above described; and that said driveway or easement is set forth for the purpose of making ingress and egress to and from the lands above conveyed, located along the _____ railroad tracks to the public highway; and said easement is to run along a strip of land described as follows: _____, said driveway to run from the public highway to the lands above conveyed.

4

FIGURE 3-YY
WEST'S LEGAL FORMS 2D

Chapter 4
READING, CITING, AND UPDATING CASES

Section 4A. Reading Cases

The preceding two chapters demonstrated how treatises, legal encyclopedias, annotations, digests, *Shepard's Citations*, and other sources can be used to find citations to published judicial opinions. Furthermore, secondary authorities can be cited as persuasive authority. For example, in absence of controlling primary authority, courts may be persuaded by a suggested resolution of an issue in a secondary source. Remember, however, that secondary authority does not have the force of law. A researcher's central focus is on controlling primary authority—constitutional provisions, statutes, treaties, administrative regulations, procedural rules, and judicial opinions.

One of the essential aspects of reading judicial opinions is understanding the procedural aspects of the case.[1] An overview of civil, criminal, and appellate procedure in the United States is provided in Appendix A. Other important aspects of reading judicial opinions are covered in detail elsewhere.[2] Case analysis, case "briefing," and note-taking are likewise covered in detail elsewhere.[3] Reference to these materials will help you to analyze and apply what you find in judicial opinions.

---

[1] See Larry L. Teply, <u>Legal Writing, Analysis, and Oral Argument</u> 116-26 (1990) ("Understanding the Procedural Aspects of Appellate Decisions"; and "Types of Errors Reviewed" and "Standards of Review" in "Reading Judicial Opinions for Substance").

[2] See <u>id.</u> at 105-15 ("Mastering the Facts, Transactions, and Occurrences Reported in Judicial Opinions") and 122-46 ("Reading Judicial Opinions for Substance").

[3] See <u>id.</u> at 146-54 ("Briefing Judicial Opinions for Legal Research and Writing Purposes") and 155-205 ("Authority of Judicial Decisions, Basic Legal Reasoning, and Case Synthesis").

Section 4B. Working With and Citing Cases

Recall from Chapter 1 that legal citation is the means of identifying where sources are published and how much support those sources lend for particular propositions. Furthermore, citing sources in accord with an accepted citation system is often viewed as one indication of the quality of the legal work. The most complex *Bluebook* rules are the ones that apply to citation of cases. This section and Appendix B ("Citing Case Names in *Bluebook* Form") illustrate those rules. This section also provides additional information about case-related legal research.

1. THE BASICS OF CITING CASES

Common to all systems of citation are several underlying principles. First, the case name used in a citation should be sufficiently descriptive of the case name so that it can be found through a table of cases reported, case name citator, or digest in the event the case is miscited.[4]

Second, the source cited must be identified in such a way that it can be found. For example, you must identify that the second series of a reporter (e.g., N.W.2d) is cited to avoid confusion with the first series (e.g., N.W.). The abbreviation of the source must be one that is readily identifiable or can be readily determined from an accepted listing of abbreviations.[5]

Third, a "pinpoint citation" or "jump cite" is required whenever you refer to specific material within a case. The standard practice is to cite the page on which the case begins and the page(s) on which the specific material appears (separated by commas).[6]

Fourth, the reader must be able to tell what court has decided the case. The general rule is that the name of the court, including its geographic jurisdiction (e.g., Missouri Court of Appeals; Mississippi Supreme Court; New York Supreme Court, Appellate Division; etc.) should

---

[4] Cf. The Maroon Book Rule 4.2(a)(i) (allowing the use of the running head "if it is sufficiently descriptive of the case name that the reader will be able to locate the case through the Table of Cases Reported, a case name citator, or a law digest in the event of miscitation"); The Bluebook Rule 10.2.1 ("[t]o facilitate index location, always retain in full the first word in each party's name . . . .").

[5] See, e.g., abbreviations listed in Black's Law Dictionary, Ballentine's Law Dictionary, Bieber's Dictionary of Legal Abbreviations Used in American Law Books, The Legal Citation Directory, Raistrick's Index to Legal Citations and Abbreviations, or The Bluebook.

[6] See, e.g., The Bluebook Rule 3.3(a) ("When referring to specific material within [a case, article, or other source that is not separately paginated], include both the page on which the source begins and the page on which the specific material appears, separated by commas"); The Maroon Book Rule 4.2(a)(iii) ("Indicate the particular pages of the case that support the proposition in [the] text").

be specifically noted in the citation *unless* the name of the reporter clearly identifies the court (including its geographic jurisdiction).[7]   A corollary of this general rule is that it will be assumed that the court deciding the case is the highest court in the jurisdiction *when* the name of the reporter is the same as the name of a jurisdiction and no other court is indicated.[8]

Fifth, "signals" (e.g., see, contra, accord, etc.) are used in legal citations to indicate (1) the purpose for which a case (or other types of authority) is cited or (2) the degree of support the cited case (or other types of authority) gives to a proposition.   In general, when a case is cited without a signal, it means that the authority directly supports a statement.   Citations without signals also are used to identify the source of a quotation or to identify a case referred to by name.[9]

Sixth, citations of authorities, including cases, often provide additional information (1) explaining the force or meaning of the authority, (2) noting that the authority makes a point different from that in the text, or (3) indicating alterations of quoted material.   This information is often provided parenthetically at the end of the citation.[10]

2. CITING U.S. SUPREME COURT DECISIONS

(a) The Official Reporter of U.S. Supreme Court Decisions

Recall from Chapter 1 that written opinions of American courts traditionally have been issued by the court and that published reports of these opinions take two forms: official and unofficial.   Official reporters acting under statutory authority have been responsible for publishing court opinions based upon official texts supplied by the courts.   United States Supreme Court decisions are published officially in *United States Reports*. A page from Volume 440 of this reporter is reproduced in Figure 4-A.

---

[7] See, e.g., The Bluebook Rule 10.4 ("Every case citation must indicate which court decided the case"); The Maroon Book Rule. 4.2(a)(iv) (Indicate the name of the court that decided the case, unless the court's identity is clearly indicated by the name of the reporter").

[8] See, e.g., The Bluebook Rule 10.4(b) ("[D]o not include the name of the court if the court of decision is the highest court of the state. . . . Omit the jurisdiction if it is unambiguously conveyed by the reporter title . . . . Thus, when the name of the reporter is the same as the name of a jurisdiction and no court is indicated, it is assumed that the decision is that of the highest court in the jurisdiction . . . .").

[9] See, e.g., id. Rule 1.2 ("Introductory Signals"); The Maroon Book Rule 3.1 ("Introducing Authorities").

[10] See, e.g., Bluebook Rule 1.5 ("Parenthetical Information") and 10.6 ("Parenthetical Information Regarding Cases"); The Maroon Book Rule 3.4 ("Explanatory Information").

PROBLEM 4.1 Examine the beginning page of the United States Supreme Court's opinion in this case and the items noted. Also read the syllabus and determine what was generally involved in this case.

Running head →

How the case got to the U.S. Supreme Court (Appeal, Writ of Certiorari, or Original Jurisdiction) and from which court below

Syllabus prepared by the reporter of decisions

In the past, a formal "Statement of the Case" often preceded the opinion. A separate statement is now seldom given; a few official reports, however, still do so.

MONTANA *v.* UNITED STATES 147

Syllabus

MONTANA ET AL. *v.* UNITED STATES

APPEAL FROM THE UNITED STATES DISTRICT COURT FOR THE DISTRICT OF MONTANA

No. 77–1134. Argued December 4, 1978—Decided February 22, 1979

Montana levies a 1% gross receipts tax upon contractors of public, but not private, construction projects. A public contractor may credit against the gross receipts tax its payments of personal property, corporate income, and individual income taxes. Any remaining gross receipts tax liability is customarily passed on in the form of increased construction costs to the governmental unit financing the project. In 1971, the contractor on a federal project in Montana brought a suit in state court contending that the gross receipts tax unconstitutionally discriminated against the Government and the companies with which it dealt. The litigation was directed and financed by the United States. Less than a month later, the Government brought this action in the Federal District Court challenging the constitutionality of the tax. By stipulation, the case was continued pending resolution of the state-court litigation, which concluded in a decision by the Montana Supreme Court upholding the tax. *Kiewit I.* The court found the distinction between public and private contractors consistent with the mandates of the Supremacy and Equal Protection Clauses. At the Solicitor General's direction, the contractor abandoned its request for review by this Court. The contractor then instituted a second state-court action regarding certain tax payments different from those in *Kiewit I.* The Montana Supreme Court, finding the second claim essentially no different from the first, invoked the doctrines of collateral estoppel and res judicata to affirm the dismissal of the complaint. *Kiewit II.* Thereafter the District Court heard the instant case on the merits, and concluded that the United States was not bound by *Kiewit I* and that the tax violated the Supremacy Clause. *Held:* The United States is collaterally estopped from challenging the prior judgment of the Montana Supreme Court. Pp. 153–164.

(a) The interests underlying the related doctrines of collateral estoppel and res judicata—that a "right, question or fact distinctly put in issue and directly determined by a court of competent jurisdiction . . . cannot be disputed in a subsequent suit between the same parties or their privies . . . ," *Southern Pacific R. Co.* v. *United States,* 168 U. S. 1, 48–49—are similarly implicated when nonparties assume control over litigation in which they have a direct financial or proprietary interest

FIGURE 4-A
UNITED STATES REPORTS

DISCUSSION OF PROBLEM 4.1 The case shown in Figure 4-A involved a challenge to the State of Montana's one percent gross receipts tax on contractors of public construction contracts. This tax was not levied on private contractors. At the direction of the federal government, a public contractor filed suit in a Montana state court. The contractor asserted that the tax unconstitutionally discriminated against the federal government and the companies which dealt with it. After the tax was upheld on appeal by the Montana Supreme Court, the public contractor abandoned its request for review by the U.S. Supreme Court at the Solicitor General's direction.

Subsequently, in another suit financed and directed by the federal government, the U.S. District Court for the District of Montana held that the tax violated the supremacy clause and that the federal government was not bound by the Montana Supreme Court's earlier decision upholding the tax. The State of Montana then appealed to the U.S. Supreme Court. The issue before the U.S. Supreme Court was whether the federal government was precluded from contesting the constitutionality of the tax because it had financed and directed the prior litigation.

(b) Star Paging

Prior to 1875, Supreme Court decisions were reported by individuals (e.g., A.J. Dallas, William Cranch, Henry Wheaton, Richard Peters, etc.). Their "nominative" reports were later numbered consecutively and reprinted as the first ninety volumes of *United States Reports*. "Star paging" is used in these first ninety volumes when the pagination in these volumes differs from the pagination in the original nominative report.

For example, assume the text of an early Supreme Court decision reprinted in *United States Reports* reads as follows:

> Provision was also made for gold coinage, consisting of eagles, half eagles, and quarter eagles, containing, respectively, two hundred and ninety, one hundred and thirty-five, and sixty-seven and a half grains of standard gold, and being * 248 of the value, respectively of ten dollars, five dollars, and two and a half dollars.

The last word on page 247 of the original nominative report is "being" and the first word on page 248 of the original report is "of."

Star paging is a common technique used to indicate the original paging in any reprinted or unofficial report. Stars, brackets, or indented page numbers are used—for example, in the two unofficial Supreme Court reporters (*Supreme Court Reporter* and *Lawyers' Edition*)—to indicate the pagination in *United States Reports* so that lawyers and other researchers can cite *United States Reports* without actually consulting it.

(c) Unofficial Supreme Court Reporters

As noted previously, in addition to *United States Reports*, United States Supreme Court decisions are reported in two privately published editions: West Publishing Company's *Supreme Court Reporter* (S. Ct.) and Lawyers Cooperative Publishing Company's *United States Supreme Court Reports, Lawyers' Edition* (L. Ed. and L. Ed. 2d). The *Lawyers' Edition* reports all the decisions that have been reported in the *United States Reports* to date. The *Supreme Court Reporter*, however, begins with Supreme Court cases decided in 1882 (Vol. 106 of *United States Reports*).

The two unofficial reporters contain the same text as the official *United States Reports* and additional editorial features, such as summaries of counsel's arguments in the *Lawyers' Edition*. Furthermore, the two unofficial editions report a few minor motion and memorandum decisions of the Supreme Court that were not reported officially.[11]

(d) Finding Supreme Court Decisions Using the Table of Cases Reported

PROBLEM 4.2   Assume that you know the name of a Supreme Court decision (*Montana v. United States*) and the approximate year it was decided by the Court (1979). Assume that one of the unofficial reporters (West's *Supreme Court Reporter*) is available and that you want to find the case in that reporter. How would you find the case?

A simple way of doing so is to find the case directly in West's *Supreme Court Reporter*. The dates of the Terms are printed on the outside binding of the reporter. The Supreme Court customarily has only one Term of court each year. It starts in October and lasts until June or July. If you thought the case was decided in 1979, you would most likely choose the volume that covered the "October Term 1978." If the case was not in this volume, you would have to consult the immediately preceding or following volumes.

After you have located a particular volume, you would next need to ascertain whether the opinion appears in that volume and, if so, on what page the opinion was published. Every reporter contains a Table of Cases Reported in the volume. Examine the relevant portion of the Table of Cases Reported in the volume covering the 1978 Term repro-

---

[11]The two unofficial reporters also report the "Chamber Opinions" of individual Supreme Court Justices, which prior to 1970 did not appear in United States Reports. Each Justice supervises one or more of the federal judicial circuits and handles petitions from that circuit when the Court is not in session. The chamber opinions are written in response to these petitions.

duced in Figure 4-B. Is the *Montana* case reported in that volume? If so, on what page is it reported in West's *Supreme Court Reporter*?

CASES REPORTED

	Page		Page
U. S.; McKee v. (Mem.)—U.S.	1283	U. S.; Medical Therapy Sciences, Inc. v. (Mem.)—U.S.	1049
U. S.; McKenna v. (Mem.)—U.S.	1498	U. S.; Meier v. (Mem.)—U.S.	570
U. S.; McKenzie v. (Mem.)—U.S.	165	U. S.; Mendel v. (Mem.)—U.S.	450
U. S.; McKethan v. (Mem.)—U.S.	333	U. S.; Mendoza v. (Mem.)—U.S.	584
U. S.; McKinney v. (Mem.)—U.S.	137	U. S.; Mendoza-Cardenas v. (Mem.)—U.S.	1431
U. S.; McKinney v. (Mem.)—U.S.	843	U. S.; Mercuri v. (Mem.)—U.S.	2168
U. S.; Macklin v. (Mem.)—U.S.	160	U. S.; Meyers Towing Service, Inc. v. (Mem.)—U.S.	1215
U. S.; McLaughlin v. (Mem.)—U.S.	111	U. S.; Michele v. (Mem.)—U.S.	163
U. S.; McLennan v. (Mem.)—U.S.	1018	U. S.; Midtaune v. (Mem.)—U.S.	2837
U. S.; McMahon v. (Mem.)—U.S.	2847	U. S.; Miebach v. (Mem.)—U.S.	186
U. S.; McMiller v. (Mem.)—U.S.	288	U. S.; Migely v. (Mem.)—U.S.	2887
U. S.; McMillian v. (Mem.)—U.S.	727	U. S.; Mignogna v. (Mem.)—U.S.	457
U. S.; McNair v. (Mem.)—U.S.	361	U. S.; Mikka v. (Mem.)—U.S.	1247
U. S.; Madonna v. (Mem.)—U.S.	838	U. S.; Miller v. (Mem.)—U.S.	85
U. S.; Maestas v. (Mem.)—U.S.	1546	U. S.; Miller v. (Mem.)—U.S.	599
U. S.; Magann v. (Mem.)—U.S.	855	U. S.; Miller v. (Mem.)—U.S.	1242
U. S.; Magee v. (Mem.)—U.S.	1517	U. S.; Miller v. (Mem.)—U.S.	1283
U. S.; Maggy v. (Mem.)—U.S.	86	U. S.; Miller v. (Mem.)—U.S.	1426
U. S.; Magouirk v. (Mem.)—U.S.	288	U. S.; Miller v. (Mem.)—U.S.	1499
U. S.; Maher v. (Mem.)—U.S.	1019	U. S.; Miller v. (Mem.)—U.S.	1792
U. S.; Mahler v. (Mem.)—U.S.	592	U. S.; Minnich v. (Mem.)—U.S.	3105
U. S.; Mahler v. (Mem.)—U.S.	885	U. S.; Minnifield v. (Mem.)—U.S.	131
U. S.; Mains v. (Mem.)—U.S.	569	U. S.; Miranda v. (Mem.)—U.S.	619
U. S.; Maldonado-Perez v. (Mem.)—U.S.	1242	U. S.; Mireles v. (Mem.)—U.S.	332
U. S.; Mancillas v. (Mem.)—U.S.	361	U. S.; Miroyan v.—U.S.Cal.	18
U. S.; Mangan v. (Mem.)—U.S.	320	U. S.; Miroyan v. (Mem.)—U.S.	258
U. S.; Mann v. (Mem.)—U.S.	1055	U. S.; Mitchell v. (Mem.)—U.S.	163
U. S.; Manning v. (Mem.)—U.S.	178	U. S.; Mitchell v. (Mem.)—U.S.	263
U. S.; Mansueto v. (Mem.)—U.S.	1516	U. S.; Mitchell v. (Mem.)—U.S.	326
U. S.; Mapes v. (Mem.)—U.S.	722	U. S.; Mitchell v. (Mem.)—U.S.	835
U. S.; Maravilla v. (Mem.)—U.S.	186	U. S. v. Mitchell (Mem.)—Ct.Cl.	2880
U. S.; Marcantoni v. (Mem.)—U.S.	2063	U. S.; Mitchell v. (Mem.)—U.S.	2881
U. S.; Marconi v. (Mem.)—U.S.	861	U. S.; Moenckmeier v. (Mem.)—U.S.	1995
U. S.; Markert v. (Mem.)—U.S.	83	U. S.; Monger v. (Mem.)—U.S.	1239
U. S.; Marks v. (Mem.)—U.S.	837	U. S.; Monroe v. (Mem.)—U.S.D.C.	621
U. S.; Marsili v. (Mem.)—U.S.	1244	U. S.; Montana v.—U.S.Mont.	970
U. S.; Martin v. (Mem.)—U.S.	456	U. S.; Montez v. (Mem.)—U.S.	2413
U. S.; Martin v. (Mem.)—U.S.	1222	U. S.; Montgomery v. (Mem.)—U.S.	850
U. S.; Martin v. (Mem.)—U.S.	2012		
U. S.; Martin v. (Mem.)—U.S.	2408		

FIGURE 4-B
WEST'S SUPREME COURT REPORTER

DISCUSSION OF PROBLEM 4.2 The Table of Cases Reported directs you to page 970 of the *Supreme Court Reporter*.

(e) Editorial Features of the Unofficial Supreme Court Reporters

Examine Figure 4-C showing page 970 of the *Supreme Court Reporter*. Parallel citations are given at the beginning of the report (if available). The footnote indicates the effect of the official syllabus.

970   99 SUPREME COURT REPORTER   440 U.S. 147

440 U.S. 147, 59 L.Ed.2d 210

State of MONTANA et al., Appellants,

v.

UNITED STATES.

No. 77–1134.

Argued Dec. 4, 1978.

Decided Feb. 22, 1979.

A government contractor, at the direction of the United States, filed suit in Montana courts attacking the constitutionality of Montana's imposition of a one percent gross receipts tax upon contractors of public, but not private, construction projects. After the Montana Supreme Court upheld the tax, and at the Solicitor General's direction, the contractor abandoned its request for review by the United States Supreme Court. Thereafter, in another suit challenging the constitutionality of the tax, also financed and directed by the Government, a three-judge panel in the United States District Court for the District of Montana, 437 F.Supp. 354, ruled that the United States was not bound by the Montana Supreme Court's decision and that the tax violated the supremacy clause. On appeal by the State of Montana, the United States Supreme Court, Mr. Justice Marshall, held that the prior judgment by the Montana Supreme Court upholding the tax precluded the United States from contesting its constitutionality.

Reversed.

Mr. Justice Rehnquist concurred and filed statement.

Mr. Justice White dissented and filed opinion.

1. Judgment ⚖828(3.32)

Where federal government required that federal construction contractor file suit in state court attacking constitutionality of Montana gross receipts tax on contractors of public construction projects, reviewed and approved complaint in such suit, paid attorney fees and costs, directed appeal in state courts, appeared and submitted brief

as amicus in state Supreme Court, directed filing of notice of appeal to United States Supreme Court, and effected contractor's abandonment of appeal on advice of solicitor general, United States had sufficient "laboring oar" in conduct of state court litigation to actuate principles of estoppel when suit raising same issues was later instituted by contractor in federal district court at Government's direction.

2. Judgment ⚖828(3.49)

United States, as party which had sponsored prior suit in state court by government construction contractor attacking constitutionality of Montana gross receipts tax on public contractors, was collaterally estopped, in separate action brought by contractor at its behest in federal district court, from relitigating constitutionality of such gross receipts tax where issues presented in federal court litigation were in substance the same as those resolved against government in state Supreme Court decision, where controlling facts and legal principles had not changed significantly since state court's judgment, and where no other special circumstances warranted exception to normal rules of preclusion. R.C. M.1947, §§ 84–3501, 84–3501(3), 84–3505(5), 84–3513, 84–3514; U.S.C.A.Const. art. 6, cl. 2; Amend. 14.

Syllabus *

Montana levies a 1% gross receipts tax upon contractors of public, but not private, construction projects. A public contractor may credit against the gross receipts tax its payments of personal property, corporate income, and individual income taxes. Any remaining gross receipts tax liability is customarily passed on in the form of increased construction costs to the governmental unit financing the project. In 1971, the contractor on a federal project in Montana brought a suit in state court contending that the gross receipts tax unconstitutionally discriminated against the Government and the companies with which it dealt. The litigation was directed and financed by the Unit-

---

* The syllabus constitutes no part of the opinion of the Court but has been prepared by the Reporter of Decisions for the convenience of

the reader. See *United States v. Detroit Timber & Lumber Co.*, 200 U.S. 321, 337, 26 S.Ct. 282, 287, 50 L.Ed. 499.

FIGURE 4–C

WEST'S SUPREME COURT REPORTER

The *Lawyers' Edition* also contains the same text as *United States Reports*. Like West's *Supreme Court Reporter*, it contains several additional editorial features.

U.S. SUPREME COURT REPORTS   59 L Ed 2d

Cross-reference to United States Reports →

[440 US 147]

STATE OF MONTANA et al., Appellants,

v

UNITED STATES

Parallel citations →

440 US 147, 59 L Ed 2d 210, 99 S Ct 970

[No. 77–1134]

Argued December 4, 1978. Decided February 22, 1979.

Principal holding of the decision →

Decision: United States held collaterally estopped from federal court challenge to constitutionality of Montana tax on public contractors by decision in prior state litigation which government directed and financed.

Editorial summary of the decision →

SUMMARY

A contractor on a federal project in Montana instituted an action in a Montana state court, alleging that Montana's one percent gross receipts tax upon contractors of public, but not private, construction projects violated the Federal Constitution because it discriminated against the federal government and the companies with which it dealt. Ultimately, the Supreme Court of Montana sustained the tax, finding that the distinction between public and private contractors was consistent with the supremacy clause (Art VI, cl 2) and the equal protection clause of the Fourteenth Amendment (161 Mont 140, 505 P2d 102). Subsequently, the contractor instituted a second state court action regarding certain tax payments different from those involved in its initial action, but the Montana Supreme Court, finding the second claim to be no different from the first, affirmed dismissal of the complaint on the grounds of collateral estoppel and res judicata (166 Mont 260, 531 P2d 1327). Thereafter, the United States District Court for the District of Montana resumed consideration of an action which the United States had brought approximately one month after the public contractor had initiated its first suit, the District Court having continued the case brought by the government to challenge the constitutionality of the gross receipts tax pending resolution of the state-court litigation. Concluding that the United States—which, had (1) required the contractor to file the action, (2) reviewed and approved the complaint, (3) paid the attorneys' fees and costs, (4) directed the appeal in such case to the Montana Supreme Court, (5) appeared and submitted a brief as amicus curiae in the Montana Supreme

This summary provides an overview of the points decided by the Court. It also gives a complete history of the case. In addition, the concurring and dissenting opinions are summarized.

Page on which a summary of the briefs can be found. →

Briefs of Counsel, p 847, infra.

210

FIGURE 4-D

U.S. SUPREME COURT REPORTS, LAWYERS' EDITION 2D

The *Lawyers' Edition* has headnotes summarizing the points of law in the opinion; the *Lawyers' Edition* also creates headnotes for dissenting opinions.

The headnotes are classified by subject in the U.S. Supreme Court Digest, Lawyers' Edition. The classification system differs from West's topic and key number system.

U.S. SUPREME COURT REPORTS   59 L Ed 2d

HEADNOTES

Classified to U. S. Supreme Court Digest, Lawyers' Edition

Judgment §§ 187, 205 — collateral estoppel — constitutionality of state tax — government controlling prior action

1a, 1b, 1c. Under the doctrine of collateral estoppel, the United States is precluded from challenging, in a federal court action, the constitutionality of a state law imposing a gross receipts tax upon contractors of public, but not private, construction projects, since (1) the United States, although not a party to litigation in a state court in which the state law's constitutionality had been upheld, had exercised control over the litigation by directing and financing it, (2) the constitutional question expressly and definitely presented in the federal court action is the same as that definitely and actually litigated and adjudged adversely to the government in the state court action, (3) the controlling facts in the state court litigation have not changed in the federal action, notwithstanding that the contract at issue in the state litigation contains a provision which the contracts involved in the federal litigation do not, (4) there have been no changes in controlling legal principles governing intergovernmental tax immunity since the state court judgment, and (5) there are no special circumstances justifying an exception to general principles of estoppel, the exception for unmixed questions of law in successive actions involving substantially unrelated claims being inapplicable in view of the close alignment in time and subject matter of the legal demands of the federal litigation to those involved in the state litigation, the federal action not implicating the right of a litigant who properly invokes the jurisdiction of a federal court to consider federal constitutional claims and who is compelled, without his consent, to accept a state court's determination of those claims, and the government not having alleged unfairness or inadequacy in the state procedures to which it voluntarily submitted. (White, J., dissented from this holding.)

Judgment §§ 79, 81, 82, 89 — res judicata — collateral estoppel

2. Under the doctrines of collateral estoppel and res judicata a right, question, or fact distinctly put in issue and directly determined by a court of competent jurisdiction cannot be disputed in a subsequent suit between the same parties or their privies; under res judicata, a final judgment on the merits bars further claims by parties or their privies based on the same cause of action, and under collateral estoppel, once an issue is actually and necessarily determined by a court of competent jurisdiction, that

The Total Client-Service Library References

TOTAL CLIENT-SERVICE LIBRARY® REFERENCES

47 Am Jur 2d, Judgments §§ 535 et seq.
US L Ed Digest, Judgment §§ 187, 205
L Ed Index to Annos, Collateral Estoppel Doctrine; Judgment
ALR Quick Index, Collateral Estoppel Doctrine
Federal Quick Index, Collateral Estoppel

ANNOTATION REFERENCE

Supreme Court's definition and application of doctrine of "abstention" where questions of state law are controlling in federal civil case. 20 L Ed 2d 1623.

212

FIGURE 4-E

U.S. SUPREME COURT REPORTS, LAWYERS' EDITION 2D

(f) Citing U.S. Supreme Court Decisions
in Bluebook Form

CITING U.S. SUPREME COURT DECISIONS

According to *The Bluebook*, published[12] U.S. Supreme Court decisions are cited as follows:

(1) Case Name. Appendix B sets out in detail how to cite case names using *Bluebook* rules;

(2) Reporter. Cite U.S. Supreme Court opinions only to *United States Reports* (U.S.) if the case has been reported therein. Parallel citations to West's *Supreme Court Reporter* and the *Lawyers' Edition* are improper. Citations to the first ninety volumes of *United States Reports* must include an appropriate indication of the original reporter. *See Bluebook* Rule 10.3.2 and Table T.1. If the year of decision is unavailable, use the year of the term of the court in the citation. The exact year of decision can often be determined by finding the case in the *Lawyers' Edition*. *Bluebook* Rule 10.5(a). The original reporters' names and usual abbreviations, if any, are Dallas (Dall.), Cranch, Wheaton (Wheat.), Peters (Pet.), Howard (How.), Black, and Wallace (Wall.); and

(3) Court, Geographic Jurisdiction, and Date. In citing U.S. Supreme Court decisions to *United States Reports*, omit the abbreviated name of the court, including the geographic jurisdiction, from the parenthetical containing the year of decision.

In citations conforming to *Bluebook* form, two conventions permit deletion of certain information from a citation that would otherwise be required. First, when the highest court of a jurisdiction is cited, the abbreviated name of the court may be omitted. Second, when the abbreviated name of the reporter in the citation unambiguously indicates the geographic jurisdiction, the geographic jurisdiction may also be omitted.

Thus, because the Supreme Court is the highest federal court in the United States and the abbreviation for *United States Reports* is the same as the Court's geographic jurisdiction (U.S.), neither the name of

---

[12]The citation of decisions not yet appearing in <u>United States Reports</u> is discussed in § 4C of this chapter.

the court nor its geographic jurisdiction is included in citations to this reporter; thus, only the year of decision should be given in the parenthetical:

Montana v. United States, 440 U.S. 147 (1979).

3. FINDING PARALLEL CITATIONS FOR U.S. SUPREME COURT DECISIONS

Because the unofficial Supreme Court reporters are much more popular than the official reporter and are much more widely available, many attorneys and courts provide parallel citations even when they are otherwise following *Bluebook* form (abbreviated S. Ct. and L. Ed. or L. Ed. 2d and traditionally given in this order following the U.S. citation). When an instruction has been given to follow *Bluebook* form without qualification, however, parallel citations should not be given.

Assume that you want to provide parallel citations to the two unofficial Supreme Court reporters in your citation of the *Montana* case reproduced in the preceding figures. How can you determine what the parallel citations are if you do not know both of them?

(a) Directly Consulting One of the Unofficial Reporters

One way to find parallel citations for Supreme Court decisions is to consult one of the unofficial reporters if a citation to one of them is known. As shown in Figures 4-C and 4-D above, each of the unofficial reporters lists the parallel citations. If only the case name (but not the year of decision) or the *United States Reports* citation is known, however, this approach will not work.

(b) Using a Digest Table of Cases

Another means is to locate the relevant entry in the "Table of Cases" volume of a digest, e.g., West's *U.S. Supreme Court Digest*.[13] The case names are arranged alphabetically in the volume and the pocket supplement; thus, when the case name is known, the parallel citations (listed immediately after the case name) can be determined.

---

[13] Lawyers Cooperative's U.S. Supreme Court Digest, Lawyers' Edition also has a "Table of Cases" which can be used to find parallel Supreme Court citations. A number of other digests have tables of cases listing parallel Supreme Court citations, including West's Federal Digest (for decisions prior to 1939), Modern Federal Practice Digest (for decisions from 1939-1960), Federal Practice Digest 2d (for decisions from 1961-1975), Federal Practice Digest 3d (for decisions from 1976-1989), Federal Practice Digest 4th (for decisions from 1989 to date).

PROBLEM 4.3 Examine the entries in the "Table of Cases" in West's *U.S. Supreme Court Digest* shown in Figure 4-F. Which one of the five marked entries corresponds to the *Montana* case reproduced in Figure 4-A?

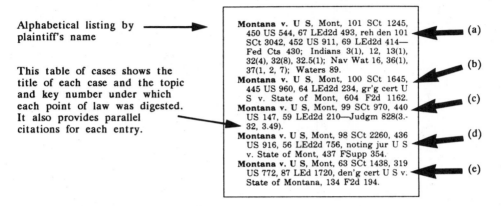

Alphabetical listing by plaintiff's name

This table of cases shows the title of each case and the topic and key number under which each point of law was digested. It also provides parallel citations for each entry.

Montana v. U S, Mont, 101 SCt 1245, 450 US 544, 67 LEd2d 493, reh den 101 SCt 3042, 452 US 911, 69 LEd2d 414—Fed Cts 430; Indians 3(1), 12, 13(1), 32(4), 32(8), 32.5(1); Nav Wat 16, 36(1), 37(1, 2, 7); Waters 89. **(a)**
Montana v. U S, Mont, 100 SCt 1645, 445 US 960, 64 LEd2d 234, gr'g cert U S v. State of Mont, 604 F2d 1162. **(b)**
Montana v. U S, Mont, 99 SCt 970, 440 US 147, 59 LEd2d 210—Judgm 828(3.-32, 3.49). **(c)**
Montana v. U S, Mont, 98 SCt 2260, 436 US 916, 56 LEd2d 756, noting jur U S v. State of Mont, 437 FSupp 354. **(d)**
Montana v. U S, Mont, 63 SCt 1438, 319 US 772, 87 LEd 1720, den'g cert U S v. State of Montana, 134 F2d 194. **(e)**

FIGURE 4-F
U.S. SUPREME COURT DIGEST TABLE OF CASES

DISCUSSION OF PROBLEM 4.3 When the Table of Cases contains several entries with the same names of the parties, you must be careful to find the correct one.

The entry that shows the parallel citations to the case in question, <u>Montana v. United States</u>, 440 U.S. 147 (1979), is the third one (c): "Montana v. U S, Mont, 99 SCt 970, 440 US 147, 59 LEd2d 210—Judgm 828(3.32, 3.49)." In addition to the citations, the other references in this entry are to the jurisdiction from which the case arose (Montana) and to the West's digest topics and key numbers (e.g., Judgment 828(3.32, 3.49)) involved in the case. As noted earlier, the latter are references to points of law and are editorial features of West Publishing Company. They are discussed in detail later in these materials.

Entry (d), "Montana v. U S, Mont, 98 SCt 2260, 436 US 916, 56 LEd2d 756, noting jur U S v. State of Mont, 437 FSupp 354," indicates the citation of when the Supreme Court noted probable jurisdiction over the case. The citation to "437 FSupp 354" (Volume 437 of the *Federal Supplement Reporter* at page 354) is a reference to the federal district court decision that prompted the State of Montana to appeal.

The decision identified in entry (d) is shown in the following excerpt from the *Supreme Court Reporter* (Volume 98 at page 2260):

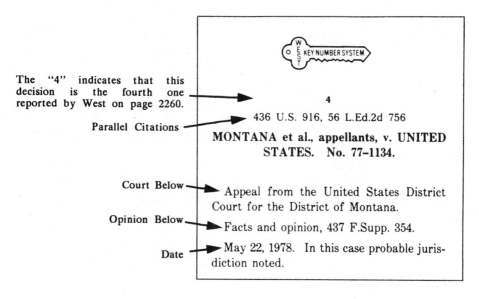

The "4" indicates that this decision is the fourth one reported by West on page 2260.

Parallel Citations

4

436 U.S. 916, 56 L.Ed.2d 756

MONTANA et al., appellants, v. UNITED STATES. No. 77–1134.

Court Below

Appeal from the United States District Court for the District of Montana.

Opinion Below

Facts and opinion, 437 F.Supp. 354.

Date

May 22, 1978. In this case probable jurisdiction noted.

FIGURE 4-G
WEST'S SUPREME COURT REPORTER

Decisions such as the one shown in Figure 4-G (noting probable jurisdiction, granting or denying petitions for certiorari, granting or denying motions for rehearing, etc.) are called memorandum decisions. Such a decision gives the brief ruling or holding of the Court, often without an opinion.

Re-examine the first (a), second (b), and fifth entries (e) marked in Figure 4-F. They refer to completely different cases with the same case name. How can you tell that those entries refer to a different case?

Entry (b) shows that certiorari was granted (100 SCt 1645) in a case appearing at "604 F2d 1162" (Volume 604 of the *Federal Reporter Second*, which primarily reports cases from the U.S. Courts of Appeals).

Entry (a) indicates the citation to the opinion in that case when it was heard on its merits ("101 SCt 1245"). The headnote references indicate that this case apparently involved a dispute by Indians in which navigability of waters was at issue ("Indians 3(1), 12, 13(1), 32(4), 32(8), 32.5(1); Nav Wat 16, 36(1), 37(1, 2, 7); Waters 89"). If you would consult these citations, you would see that they involved an action by the Crow Indians and the United States to quiet title to the bed and banks of the Big Horn River. These headnotes are obviously unrelated to collateral estoppel issues involved in the case we are considering.

Entry (e) shows that certiorari was denied in a case with an opinion published at 134 F2d 194. A denial of certiorari means that the Supreme Court refused to review the case. Certiorari means "to be certified" and refers to a writ from a superior court to an inferior court

directing a certified record of the case be sent up for review. Review by writ of certiorari is in the Court's discretion (as opposed to an appeal as a matter of right that the Court would be required to accept).

(c) Shepard's Citations

Another way to find parallel Supreme Court citations is to use *Shepard's Citations*. *Shepard's United States Citations (Case Edition)* provides parallel references in parentheses directly under the page number of the known official or unofficial citation. Parallel references are provided only in the first bound *Shepard's* volume following the publication of the report cited. They are not repeated in later bound volumes or supplements even though an entry for the case is given in later *Shepard's* volumes.

To facilitate location of parallel citations for Supreme Court cases, the following table is provided:

USING SHEPARD'S CITATIONS TO FIND PARALLEL CITATIONS FOR U.S. SUPREME COURT DECISIONS

If you need a parallel citation for:	The parallel citation appears ONLY in:
1 U.S. - 101 U.S. 1 L. Ed. - 25 L. Ed.	Case Edition 1988 (Vol. 1A)
102 U.S. - 154 U.S. 26 L. Ed. - 38 L. Ed. 1 S. Ct. - 14 S. Ct.	Case Edition 1988 (Vol. 1B)
155 U.S. - 214 U.S. 39 L. Ed. - 53 L. Ed. 15 S. Ct. - 29 S. Ct.	Case Edition 1988 (Vol. 1C)
215 U.S. - 259 U.S. 54 L. Ed. - 66 L. Ed. 30 S. Ct. - 42 S. Ct.	Case Edition 1988 (Vol. 2A)
260 U.S. - 289 U.S. 67 L. Ed. - 77 L. Ed. 43 S. Ct. - 53 S. Ct.	Case Edition 1988 (Vol. 2B)

**USING SHEPARD'S CITATIONS TO FIND PARALLEL CITATIONS
FOR U.S. SUPREME COURT DECISIONS (CONTINUED)**

If you need a parallel citation for:	The parallel citation appears ONLY in:
290 U.S. - 313 U.S. 78 L. Ed. - 85 L. Ed. 54 S. Ct. - 61 S. Ct.	Case Edition 1988 (Vol. 2C)
314 U.S. - 347 U.S. 86 L. Ed. - 98 L. Ed. 62 S. Ct. - 74 S. Ct.	Case Edition 1984 (Vol. 3)
348 U.S. - 381 U.S. 99 L. Ed. - 14 L. Ed. 2d 75 S. Ct. - 85 S. Ct.	Case Edition 1984 (Vol. 4)
382 U.S. - 408 U.S. 15 L. Ed. 2d - 33 L. Ed. 2d 86 S. Ct. - 92 S. Ct.	Case Edition 1984 (Vol. 5)
409 U.S. - 458 U.S. 34 L. Ed. 2d - 78 L. Ed. 2d 93 S. Ct. - 103 S. Ct.	Case Edition 1984 (Vol. 6)
Subsequent Volumes	Bound and paper supplements

To determine what bound and paper-covered supplements are available and to determine if any new permanent volumes have been issued, you would examine the front cover of the latest paper covered pamphlet. Figure 4-H shows the relevant portion of a typical cover of such a pamphlet.

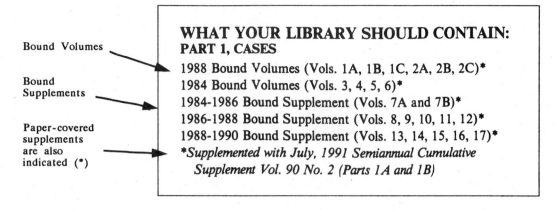

Bound Volumes

Bound Supplements

Paper-covered supplements are also indicated (*)

WHAT YOUR LIBRARY SHOULD CONTAIN:
PART 1, CASES
1988 Bound Volumes (Vols. 1A, 1B, 1C, 2A, 2B, 2C)*
1984 Bound Volumes (Vols. 3, 4, 5, 6)*
1984-1986 Bound Supplement (Vols. 7A and 7B)*
1986-1988 Bound Supplement (Vols. 8, 9, 10, 11, 12)*
1988-1990 Bound Supplement (Vols. 13, 14, 15, 16, 17)*
Supplemented with July, 1991 Semiannual Cumulative Supplement Vol. 90 No. 2 (Parts 1A and 1B)

FIGURE 4-H
SHEPARD'S UNITED STATES CITATIONS
PAPER-COVERED PAMPHLET

PROBLEM 4.4 Assume that you know only the official citation of the *Montana* case (440 U.S. 147). Using the above table, determine which one of the *Shepard's United States Citations (Case Edition)* volumes would be used to find the parallel citations for the *Montana* case reproduced in the preceding figures.

DISCUSSION OF PROBLEM 4.4 As the table indicates, volume 6 of the 1984 *Case Edition* covers opinions reported in volumes 409-458 of *United States Reports*. That volume thus should be selected.

To use *Shepard's Citations* to find the unofficial citations of a decision when its official citation is known (440 U.S. 147), you would turn to the part of the appropriate *Shepard's* volume which has at the top of the page "United States Supreme Court Reports." The volume numbers of *United States Reports* are given in the upper corner of each page, and the first page numbers of the cases, set in bold-face print, are listed in the columns. The parallel citations are directly below the page number in parentheses. If the *Supreme Court Reporter* or *Lawyers' Edition* citation is known, the official citation can be determined by consulting the "Supreme Court Reporter" or "Lawyers' Edition" sections of *Shepard's*.

PROBLEM 4.5 Using the page of *Shepard's Citations* reproduced below, which has the initial entry for the *Montana* case, determine what are the parallel citations for this case.

Vol. 440   UNITED STATES SUPREME COURT REPORTS

NY	534FS'80	684F2d'1190	672F2d'1325	Fla	644F2d'169	699F2d'496	Cir. 3
73Ap2d249	536FS'643	686F2d'413	674F2d1249	395So2d1162	644F2d180	f497FS2651	510FS900
89Ap2d535	545FS'974	687F2d840	681F2d1201	402So2d56	653F2d2846	498FS902	533FS21245
112Msc2d192	546FS'849	687F2d'841	694F2d'607	Haw	653F2d862	498FS2904	568FS2953
112Msc2d464	552FS596	700F2d'1070	703F2d'1092	63H459	655F2d'499	Cir. 11	Cir. 5
426S2d513	556FS'1392	j708F2d247	713F2d'543	629P2d1140	670F2d'1323	e710F2d2795	498FS2576
446S2d899	558FS'275	712F2d'1015	714F2d'939	Kan	681F2d2902	d485FS2910	520FS'506
446S2d988	562FS'570	713F2d1232	718F2d'1458	8KA2d286	691F2d31130	500FS21203	Cir. 6
452S2d614	567FS'540	723F2d'18	e723F2d726	655P2d475	501FS2781	Alk	499FS2573
Ore	571FS'1068	495FS'741	e521FS'831	Mass	542FS2882	619P2d432	558FS33
64OrA360	573FS'1299	514FS'786	529FS'1310	7MaA476	Cir. 4	649P2d246	Cir. 7
668P2d445	6BRW'359	535FS'895	529FS960	388NE709	636F2d257	Calif	470FS1274
Wis	6BRW'812	541FS'1325	547FS'641	Mo	651F2d'981	162CaR387	522FS'95
101Wis2d321	12BRW'563	567FS'1347	547FS'993	659SW264	478FS2472	166CaR696	522FS297
304NW725	14BRW'901	f570FS'1360	556FS'536	659P2d275	500FS21099	170CaR30	f552FS'1153
-147-	15BRW'787	4BRW'754	562FS880	NH	508FS80	620P2d616	556FS'648
(59LE210)	15BRW'876	16BRW'824	33BRW'284	120NH111	508FS81	Idaho	Cir. 10
(99SC970)	17BRW'364	17BRW'159	34BRW'776	411A2d1121	515FS2934	104Ida54	j612F2d479
s437FS354	28BRW'444	32BRW26	Cir. 7	NY	520FS547	656P2d115	643F2d21387
cc161Mt140	31BRW'448	Cir. 7	605F2d'1176	115Msc2d180	538FS2866	Ill	658F2d'780
cc166Mt260	Cir. 3	605F2d'300	608F2d'1355	453S2d1009	Cir. 5	81Il2149	Colo
Mont	470FS'420	649F2d'533	661F2d881	Ohio	616F2d157	94Il21118	622P2d533
cc505P2d102	d503FS'367	687F2d'1009	673F2d'1168	40S170	616F2d'819	83Il2d252	98Il2810
cc531P2d	510FS'986	700F2d'360	684F2d'696	447NE1296	d623F2d2346	401NE1272	424NE891
[1327	512FS'664	500FS'706	711F2d'932	Okla	e638F2d31310	415NE378	Okla
442US131	519FS1255	504FS272	713F2d'1486	645P2d516	d717F2d	419NE633	611P2d240
e449US'94	522FS'548	f504FS'1274	722F2d602	Va	[21498	Ind	661P2d894
j449US113	547FS'867	506FS1071	515FS'847	221Va641	717F2d'1501	422NE723	Pa
456US'467	f548FS'13	515FS'701	552FS'544	222Va814	553FS'1137	Ky	463A2d1072
51USLW	548FS'1362	529FS'414	565FS'77	272SE219	92FRD11	586SW713	-202-
[4329	551FS'168	536FS800	Cir. 11	284SE832	Cir. 6	Mass	(59LE257)
51USLW	552FS'1700	538FS'567	689F2d1383	W Va	621F2d811	388Mas196	(99SC1066)
[4979	562FS'1279	548FS'68	693F2d'1076	301SE219	j660F2d170	446NE49	Md
75TCt252	570FS'559	553FS'966	695F2d543	-173-	e664F2d558	Md	s574F2d238
76TCt133	576FS'1184	574FS'909	723F2d'844	(59LE230)	714F2d613	285Md403	s594F2d169
76TCt803	95FRD'177	90FRD'14	d471FS'757	(99SC983)	720F2d449	Mich	Cir. 5
76TCt856	5BRW'689	90FRD'1333	558FS98	s566F2d586	490FS2849	412Mch585	666F2d'285
99FRD458	8BRW'562	Cir. 8	570FS'1327	s433FS11	f498FS115	412Mch604	678F2d'22
Cir. D.C.	17BRW642	595F2d'449	2BRW'568	j441US585	f499FS2125	317NW5	679F2d266
658F2d'851	18BRW601	595F2d'450	4BRW'819	j444US907	f499FS'131	317NW14	696F2d353
j676F2d747	19BRW'960	599F2d278	26BRW753	j446US117	f499FS3131	Minn	e704F2d'804
f677F2d'120	Cir. 4	f599F2d'281	Cir. Fed.	j447US600	510FS31325	313NW383	f507FS'598
683F2d'484	640F2d'486	602F2d'1298	723F2d'1571	453US'500	551FS3426	313NW386	Cir. 8
711F2d'273	647F2d'455	604F2d'567	CtCl	454US279	Cir. 7	NJ	542FS'484
712F2d1424	669F2d'935	611F2d'707	225CCL61	455US3482	d614F2d	84NJ165	Cir. 9
530FS'899	519FS'413	d612F2d	229CCL134	j457US662	[21150	84NJ284	716F2d'717
549FS'1343	526FS'149	[1085	229CCL274		620F2d2147	417A2d1018	f92FRD'776
	526FS'246	669F2d'566			d657F2d2127		

FIGURE 4-I

SHEPARD'S UNITED STATES CITATIONS (1984 CASE EDITION)

DISCUSSION OF PROBLEM 4.5   The parallel citations are shown in parentheses immediately after the page number: (59 LE2d 210) and (99 SC 970).

(d) Insta-Cite and Auto-Cite

The Insta-Cite and Auto-Cite computer services available through WESTLAW and LEXIS respectively can also be used to find parallel citations.[14]

PROBLEM 4.6   Assume that you are going to cite the *Montana* case to all three Supreme Court Reporters. Based on the appropriate

---

[14] See Chapters 7 and 8 for illustrations of how these services can be used for this purpose.

Bluebook rules (but contrary to the *Bluebook* rule stating that only *United States Reports* should be cited), which of the following citations of the *Montana* case properly shows the parallel citations for this case?

    (a) <u>Montana v. United States</u>, 440 U.S. 147, 59 L.E.2d 210, 99 S.C. 970 (1979).

    (b) <u>Montana v United States</u>, 440 US 147, 59 LE2d 210, 99 SC 970 (1979).

    (c) <u>Montana v. United States</u>, 440 U.S. 147, 99 S. Ct. 970, 59 L. Ed. 2d 210 (1979).

    (d) <u>Montana v United States</u>, 440 US 147, 99 S Ct 970, 59 L Ed 2d 210 (1979).

    DISCUSSION OF PROBLEM 4.6   The abbreviations used in *Shepard's Citations* and the various reporters often differ in minor detail from those recommended by *The Bluebook* for use in citations. In this instance, the *Supreme Court Reporter* should be abbreviated "S. Ct." and the *Lawyers' Edition* "L. Ed. 2d" Because answers (a), (b), and (d) do not abbreviate these reporters properly, they are incorrect.

    The generally accepted order in which the parallel citations appear in a Supreme Court citation is to place the reference to *United States Reports* first, the reference to *Supreme Court Reporter* second, and the reference to *Lawyers' Edition* last—even though, for example, *Shepard's Citations* lists the *Lawyers' Edition* reference before the *Supreme Court Reporter* reference. The correct order and abbreviations are given in answer (c).

4. CITING LOWER FEDERAL APPELLATE COURT DECISIONS

    Under normal circumstances, decisions of the federal district courts are initially reviewed by intermediate federal appellate courts rather than the United States Supreme Court.[15] Examine the beginning portion of the case in Figure 4-J from volume 231 of the *Federal Reporter Second*. This figure shows a federal appellate court decision.[16]

---

[15]The relationship of the federal trial courts, the intermediate federal appellate courts, and the U.S. Supreme Court is detailed in § 1D(3)(a) ("The Federal Court System") in Chapter 1.

[16]There are no official reporters for the decisions of the U.S. District Courts or the U.S. Courts of Appeals, with the exception of the D.C. Circuit. Ordinarily, citations to the official reporter of the U.S. Court of Appeals for the D.C. Circuit are not included in lawyer's citations unless they are appearing in U.S. Court of Appeals for the D.C. Circuit. <u>The Bluebook</u> indicates that the official reporter for the D.C. Circuit should not be cited. <u>Bluebook</u> Table T.1 (in "United States Jurisdictions, Federal" part of that table).

Case Name ➤

Court deciding the case ➤

The U.S. Courts of Appeals replaced the Circuit Courts of Appeals in 1912.

The format of this report is the same as others in West's National Reporter System.

The early format of the Federal Reporter differs slightly from this current format.

---

684   231 FEDERAL REPORTER, 2d SERIES

Ellen MOLNAR, Appellant,

v.

NATIONAL BROADCASTING COM-
PANY, Inc., a corporation,
Appellee.

No. 14712.

United States Court of Appeals
Ninth Circuit.

Jan. 4, 1956.

Action by California plaintiff against corporate defendant with domicile in Delaware, and other unknown defendants allegedly residents of Delaware for injuries received by plaintiff when she fell on a stairway in corporation's building. The United States District Court for the Southern District of California, Central Division, William C. Mathes, J., dismissed the complaint without prejudice for lack of jurisdiction, and plaintiff appealed. The Court of Appeals, James Alger Fee, Circuit Judge, held that where California plaintiff in her complaint made a fictitious designation of certain unknown defendants allegedly residents of Delaware and did not describe them or make any allegations about the function of each or their connection with the accident, the allegations of such defendants' citizenship in Delaware were illusory, and trial court's dismissal of the action without prejudice was proper.

Remanded.

1. Courts ⊶322(5)

A complaint defective in allegation of diversity of citizenship can be amended to show the true state of facts even in the United States Supreme Court. Fed.Rules Civ.Proc. rules 1, 15, 61, 28 U.S.C.A.; 28 U.S.C.A. § 1653.

2. Courts ⊶322(2)

Where allegation of California plaintiff's complaint that certain defendants were citizens of Delaware was unfounded guesswork, jurisdiction of United States District Court was not established.

3. Courts ⊶322(2)
   Federal Civil Procedure ⊶1827

Where California plaintiff in her complaint made a fictitious designation of certain unknown defendants allegedly residents of Delaware and did not describe them or make any allegations about the function of each or their connection with the accident in which she was injured, the allegations of defendants' citizenship in Delaware were illusory, and trial court's dismissal of the action without prejudice was proper.

4. Courts ⊶279

Allegations founding jurisdiction of a federal court must be precise.

5. Federal Civil Procedure ⊶101

None of the Rules of Civil Procedure under which federal courts operate gives warrant for the use of the device of joining fictitious defendants.

6. Courts ⊶260

While the Federal Rules of Civil Procedure are not universally inclusive of all possible colorings of practice, no justification can be found therein for a violation of jurisdictional principles.

7. Courts ⊶261

Methods used by the common law to extend jurisdiction of particular courts cannot be tolerated under the federal Constitution.

8. Courts ⊶255, 279

The national trial courts are of special jurisdiction, and at the outset of every proceeding therein, jurisdiction should be established by allegation of essential facts.

9. Courts ⊶322(5)

In action by California plaintiff against corporate defendant with domicile in Delaware and other unknown defendants allegedly residents of Delaware for injuries received by plaintiff when she fell on stairway in corporation's building, where District Court dismissed the complaint without prejudice for lack of jurisdiction, on appeal, order would be modified to permit filing of an amended complaint against corporation alone, as defendant, if other defendants joined but not identified could be dispensed with.

FIGURE 4-J

FEDERAL REPORTER SECOND

CITING LOWER FEDERAL APPELLATE COURT OPINIONS

According to *The Bluebook*, published lower federal appellate court decisions should be cited as follows:

(1) Case Name. Appendix B sets out in detail how to cite case names using *Bluebook* rules;

(2) Reporter. Cite lower federal appellate opinions to the *Federal Reporter* (F. or F.2d). Cite early Circuit Court of Appeals opinions to the *Federal Reporter* or the *Federal Cases* set (discussed in § B(6) below). Decisions of the various specialized courts should be cited to the *Federal Reporter* if they have been published therein. Otherwise, they should be cited to the appropriate official reporter (e.g., *Court of Customs and Patents Appeals Reports* (C.C.P.A.) or *Court of International Trade Reports* (Ct. Int'l Trade));

(3) Court, Geographic Jurisdiction, and Date. According to Rule 10.4(a), citations of decisions of the U.S. Courts of Appeals and the former Circuit Courts of Appeals must include a parenthetical indication of the circuit and date of decision. The proper designations of the circuits are: 1st Cir., 2d Cir., 3d Cir., 4th Cir., 5th Cir., 6th Cir., 7th Cir., 8th Cir., 9th Cir., 10th Cir., 11th Cir., D.C. Cir., and Fed. Cir. Note particularly that the U.S. Court of Appeals for the District of Columbia Circuit and all its predecessors are abbreviated "D.C. Cir."

The following are examples of lower federal appellate court citations in *Bluebook* form:

Western Marine Elecs. v. Furuno Elec. Co., 764 F.2d 840 (Fed. Cir. 1985).

Reynolds Metals Co. v. FTC, 309 F.2d 223 (D.C. Cir. 1962).

United States v. Aluminum Co. of Am., 148 F.2d 416 (2d Cir. 1945).

In re Watanabe, 315 F.2d 924 (C.C.P.A. 1963).

PROBLEM 4.7 Based on the appropriate *Bluebook* rules, which one of the following citations of the case reproduced above in Figure 4-J is correct?

(a) <u>Molnar v. National Broadcasting Co.</u>, 231 F.2d 684 (C.C.A. 9th 1956).

(b) <u>Molnar v. National Broadcasting Co.</u>, 231 Fed. 2d 684 (9th C.A. 1956).

(c) <u>Molnar v. National Broadcasting Co.</u>, 231 Fed 2d 684 (9th CA 1956).

(d) <u>Molnar v. National Broadcasting Co.</u>, 231 F.2d 684 (9th Cir. 1956).

(e) <u>Molnar v. National Broadcasting Co.</u>, 231 F2d 684 (9th Cir 1956).

(f) <u>Molnar v. National Broadcasting Co.</u>, 231 Fed. 2d 684 (9th Cir. 1956).

DISCUSSION OF PROBLEM 4.7   This case was decided by the United States Court of Appeals for the Ninth Circuit. Courts of appeals for numbered circuits are designated by their number, followed by "Cir.," not "C.A. 9th," "9th C.A.," or other similar designations. Be careful to identify the number of the circuit properly (e.g., 3d Cir., not 3rd Cir.). The proper abbreviation of the *Federal Reporter* is "F.," not "Fed." The correct citation of the case is given in the fourth answer (d).

5. CITING FEDERAL TRIAL COURT DECISIONS

Examine the editorial features of the federal district court case[17] reproduced from West's *Federal Supplement* in Figures 4-K and 4-L. The decisions published in the *Federal Supplement*[18] represent only a small portion of the cases heard by the federal trial courts. The courts, not West Publishing Company, are responsible for selecting the opinions to be published.

---

[17]Opinions of the federal district courts originally were published in West's <u>Federal Reporter</u>. Beginning in 1932, their opinions no longer appear in the <u>Federal Reporter</u> but are published on a selective basis in West's <u>Federal Supplement</u> (F. Supp.), West's <u>Federal Rules Decisions</u> (F.R.D.) (beginning in 1938 covering opinions involving the Federal Rules of Civil and Criminal Procedure), and West's <u>Bankruptcy Reporter</u> (Bankr.) (beginning in 1980). Early federal district court opinions (1789-1880) are published in West's <u>Federal Cases</u> (F. Cas.) set (discussed in detail later in this section).

[18]The <u>Federal Supplement</u> has included selected decisions from the U.S. Court of Claims (1932-1960), the U.S. Customs Court (from 1949), and the Judicial Panel on Multi-District Litigation (J.P.M.D.L.). Decisions of the Claims Court (created in October, 1982) and the appellate tribunals reviewing the decisions of the Claims Court now appear in West's <u>U.S. Claims Court Reporter</u>. All of the above reporters are part of West's National Reporter System.

Page Number Volume Number

378 U.S. 368, 84 S.Ct. 1774, 12 L.Ed.2d 908 (1964).

State remedies have been exhausted. Commonwealth ex rel. Hargrove v. Maroney, 420 Pa. 120, 215 A.2d 635 (1966).

We issued a rule to show cause and directed the District Attorney of Allegheny County to submit the records required by Rule 16(g), Rules of Court, W.D.Pa. The District Attorney has complied.

The relator was indicted for murder and manslaughter in connection with the death of one Cleopatra Glass who was shot and killed in the evening of July 16, 1962. After the shooting the relator voluntarily surrendered himself to the police stating that he had just killed a woman. The next morning he gave a statement concerning the events surrounding the incident. Prior to giving the statement, the relator was warned of his right to remain silent and that anything he said could be used against him. The Commonwealth admits that he was not advised of his right to counsel.

On February 4, 1963, the relator, with the advice of counsel pleaded guilty to murder generally. That same day a hearing was held to determine the degree of guilt and to fix punishment. The statement which the relator gave on July 17, 1962 was admitted into evidence without objection and was read into the record.[1]

In our opinion the petition should be denied.

[1, 2] A voluntary and intentional plea of guilty on the advice of counsel constitutes a waiver to any objection of prior proceedings which may also include violation of a defendant's rights. United States ex rel. Maisenhelder v. Rundle, 349 F.2d 592 (3d Cir. 1965); see also, Commonwealth ex rel. Blackshear v. Myers, 419 Pa. 151, 213 A.2d 378 (1965). The relator does not attack the voluntariness of his plea and the record shows that it was voluntarily entered with knowledge of all the facts

and with the advice of counsel. In these circumstances, the relator is not entitled to relief on the grounds presented.

Moreover, the United States Supreme Court, in Johnson v. State of New Jersey, 384 U.S. 719, 86 S.Ct. 1772, 16 L.Ed.2d 882 (June 20, 1966), has held that its decisions in Escobedo v. State of Illinois, supra, and Miranda v. State of Arizona, 384 U.S. 436, 86 S.Ct. 1602, 16 L.Ed.2d 694 (June 13, 1966) were not to be applied to trials beginning before the respective dates of those decisions.

In the case at bar the relator's hearing occurred on February 4, 1963, long before the decision in *Escobedo*, which was handed down on June 22, 1964, and, of course, before the decision in *Miranda*. For this additional reason, the relator's claim under *Escobedo* must fail.

An appropriate order will be entered.

Lee McKINNEY and Lois Irene McKinney, husband and wife, Libelants,

v.

The UNITED STATES of America, Respondent,

and

Puget Sound Bridge and Dry Dock Company, Respondent-Impleaded.

No. 17065.

United States District Court
W. D. Washington, N. D.

Dec. 13, 1965.

Action to recover for injuries sustained while welding surfaces of public vessel of United States. The District Court, Beeks, J., held that United States owed no duty to provide, or to ensure that independent contractor provided,

The docket number (indicated below) is the serial number that was assigned to the action when it was initially filed in the clerk's office. It is useful for locating the court file at the courthouse.

Docket number

Court

1. Transcript of testimony of February 4, 1963, pp. 139–155.

FIGURE 4-K
FEDERAL SUPPLEMENT

Running head ➤

Publisher's suggested citation form (not Bluebook form) ➤

Headnotes ➤

West's headnotes are not authority but only indexes to authority.

Language of West's headnotes should not be cited in legal writing.

McKINNEY v. UNITED STATES   **715**
Cite as 255 F.Supp. 714 (1965)

ventilation equipment to libelant welder, employee of independent contractor, who felt sick to his stomach after approximately five hours of welding on surfaces of tank for United States Navy fleet oiler coated with an inorganic zinc silicate, and hence United States was not negligent in failing to take such precautions.

Decree accordingly.

1. Shipping ⊂⇁84(3¼)

United States owed no warranty of seaworthiness to libelant welder, employee of independent contractor, who felt sick to his stomach after approximately five hours of welding on surfaces of tank for U. S. Navy fleet oiler coated with an inorganic zinc silicate. Longshoremen's and Harbor Workers' Compensation Act, § 41 as amended 33 U.S.C.A. § 941; Public Vessels Act, § 1, 46 U.S.C.A. § 688.

2. Shipping ⊂⇁84(3¼)

United States owed no duty to provide, or to ensure that independent contractor provided, ventilation equipment to libelant welder, employee of independent contractor, who felt sick to his stomach after approximately five hours of welding on surfaces of tank for United States Navy fleet oiler coated with an inorganic zinc silicate, and hence United States was not negligent in failing to take such precautions.

3. Shipping ⊂⇁84(3¼)

United States was not negligent in authorizing or permitting the use of "Zinkote", an inorganic zinc silicate, coating in confined spaces of tank for U. S. Navy fleet oiler allegedly resulting in an injury to libelant welder who felt sick to his stomach after approximately five hours of welding on surfaces of tank. Longshoremen's and Harbor Workers' Compensation Act, § 41 as amended 33 U.S.C.A. § 941; Public Vessels Act, § 1, 46 U.S.C.A. § 688.

William N. Goodwin, U. S. Atty., John F. Meadows, Atty. in Charge, Admiralty & Shipping Section, by Henry Haugen, Sp. Atty., Admiralty & Shipping Section, and Michael Hoff, Asst. U. S. Atty., Seattle, Wash., for respondent United States.

Harry Margolis, of Walsh & Margolis, Seattle, Wash., for Lockheed Shipbuilding & Construction Co.

Charles Law, of Greive & Law, Seattle, Wash., for libelants.

FINDINGS OF FACT AND CONCLUSIONS OF LAW

BEEKS, District Judge.

This matter having come on for trial before the above-entitled Court, the Honorable William T. Beeks, presiding, on December 8, 1965; and the Libelants having appeared by and through Charles J. Law of Greive and Law, their proctors; and the respondent, United States of America, having appeared through William N. Goodwin, United States Attorney, John F. Meadows, Attorney in Charge, West Coast Office, Admiralty & Shipping Section, by Henry Haugen, Special Attorney, Admiralty & Shipping Section, Department of Justice, San Francisco, California and Michael Hoff, Assistant United States Attorney, Seattle, Washington; and Respondent-Impleaded, Lockheed Shipbuilding and Construction Company, having appeared by and through Harry Margolis of Walsh and Margolis, its proctors; and the Court sitting in admiralty having heard the testimony of witnesses appearing in behalf of the Libelant and having considered the pleadings on file herein, and being fully advised in the premises, now makes the following

FINDINGS OF FACT

1. Puget Sound Bridge and Dry Dock Company, now Lockheed Shipbuilding and Construction Company, hereinafter referred to as Lockheed, is and was at all times material hereto a shipbuilding and repair facility located in Seattle, Washington.

2. The USS WACCAMAW (AO–109) is, now and was at all times material hereto a public vessel of the United States

---

FIGURE 4-L
FEDERAL SUPPLEMENT

CITING FEDERAL TRIAL COURT DECISIONS

According to *The Bluebook*, published federal trial court decisions should be cited as follows:

(1) Case Name. Appendix B sets out in detail how to cite case names using *Bluebook* rules;

(2) Reporter. Cite federal trial court opinions to the *Federal Supplement* (F. Supp), and *Federal Rules Decisions* (F.R.D.), if therein. Cite earlier federal trial court opinions to the *Federal Reporter* (F.) or the *Federal Cases* set (F. Cas.) (discussed in § B(6) below). Otherwise, cite to a specialized reporter or looseleaf service, if therein (see *Bluebook* Table T.1, which details the rules, including those for specialized federal trial courts, such as United States Claims Court); and

(3) Court, Geographic Jurisdiction, and Date. In citations of federal district court cases, the district (but not the division within the district) and the state should be indicated parenthetically. In states having only one district, the district is indicated by "D." If there is more than one district in the state, the district must be specifically indicated (N.D. Cal. for the Northern District of California, not D. Cal.). In the parenthetical, states are identified as follows: Ala., Alaska, Ariz., Ark., Cal., Colo., Conn., Del., Fla., Ga., Haw., Idaho, Ill., Ind., Iowa, Kan., Ky., La., Me., Md., Mass., Mich., Minn., Miss., Mo., Mont., Neb., Nev., N.H., N.J., N.M., N.Y., N.C., N.D., Ohio, Okla., Or., Pa., R.I., S.C., S.D., Tenn., Tex., Utah, Vt., Va., Wash., W. Va., Wis., and Wyo. The District of Columbia is abbreviated "D.C." and Puerto Rico is abbreviated "P.R." The name of a specialized trial court should be appropriately indicated (see *Bluebook* Table T.1).

The following are examples of lower federal appellate court citations in *Bluebook* form:

<u>Sunrise Toyota, Ltd. v. Toyota Motor Co.</u>, 55 F.R.D. 519 (S.D.N.Y. 1972). (No space should be left between the adjoining single capitals.)

<u>Gott v. Simpson</u>, 745 F. Supp. 765 (D. Me. 1990). (A space should be left between "D." and "Me." because the "M" is part of a longer abbreviation—"Me.").

Power Replacements Corp. v. Air Preheater Co., 356 F. Supp. 872 (E.D. Pa. 1973). ("E.D." should be closed up; a space should be left between them and "Pa." because the "P" is part of a longer abbreviation.)

Lundy v. Interfirst Corp., 105 F.R.D. 499 (D.D.C. 1985). ("D.D.C." identifies the U.S. District Court for the District of Columbia.)

Miller v. Sullivan, 769 F. Supp. 1073 (E.D. Mo. 1991).

PROBLEM 4.8   Based on the appropriate *Bluebook* rules, which one of the following citations of the *McKinney* case (shown in Figure 4-K and 4-L) is correct?

(a) McKinney v United States, 255 F Supp 714 (1965).

(b) McKinney v. United States, 255 F. Supp. 714 (W.D. Wash. 1965).

(c) McKinney v. United States, 255 F. Supp. 714 (N.D. Wash. 1965).

(d) McKinney v United States, 255 F Supp 714 (W D Wash 1965).

(e) McKinney v. United States, 255 F Supp 714 (N D Wash 1965).

DISCUSSION OF PROBLEM 4.8   A correct citation of a federal district court decision must include a parenthetical indicating the district and state in which the case was decided. *Bluebook* Rule 10.4(a). Because it omits the district and state from the parenthetical, answer (a) is incorrect. Do not rely on the publisher's suggested form—"Cite as 255 F.Supp. 714 (1965)"—that appears at the top of page 715 (reproduced in Figure 4-L).

Sometimes it is difficult to identify the district in which the case was decided when the division is also listed in the opinion. The first page of the opinion, page 714, reproduced in Figure 4-K, lists the following: "W.D. Washington, N.D." Is it the Western Division of the Northern District or the Northern Division of the Western District?

One means of determining which abbreviation represents the district is to consult the beginning pages of the reporter volume that list the judges of the courts. The entries usually note the districts within the state. Figure 4-M reproduces the entries for the district judges in the State of Washington. Examine the relevant entry for the Honorable William T. Beeks.

JUDGES OF THE COURTS

NINTH CIRCUIT—Continued

DISTRICT JUDGES

CHARLES L. POWELL, Chief Judge ------------E. D. Wash. --------Spokane, Wash.
WILLIAM J. LINDBERG, Chief Judge -----------W. D. Wash. ---------Seattle, Wash.
GEORGE H. BOLDT -------------------------W. D. Wash. --------Tacoma, Wash.
→WILLIAM T. BEEKS ------------------------W. D. Wash. ---------Seattle, Wash.
WILLIAM N. GOODWIN ----------------------E. & W. D. Wash. ----Yakima, Wash.

FIGURE 4-M
FEDERAL SUPPLEMENT

As indicated on page 715 of the opinion (reproduced in Figure 4-L), the case was decided by District Judge Beeks. As Figure 4-M shows, the Honorable William T. Beeks presided in the Western District of Washington. Note that the State of Washington has an Eastern and Western District. Because answer (c) incorrectly lists the district as the Northern District, answer (b) is correct.

All reporters in West's "National Reporter System"[19] contain several special features to aid a researcher, such as the listing of all judges sitting on the courts covered by the particular reporter. The most significant feature, of course, is West's headnotes classifying the points of law involved in the case. Another extremely useful feature is the case synopsis prepared by West's editors. Other features include a "Key Number Digest" in each reporter volume and advance sheet, an alphabetical "Table of Cases Reported," a "Table of Cases," arranged by jurisdiction, a "Table of Statutes Construed," and a "Words and Phrases" table.

All units of the National Reporter System (except West's *Military Justice Reporter*) have tables listing cases in the reporter or advance sheet that interpret any Federal Rule of Evidence, Federal Rule of Civil Procedure, Federal Rule of Criminal Procedure, or Federal Rule of Appellate Procedure. All reporters in the System (except West's *Bankruptcy Reporter*) also have a table listing cases in the reporter volume citing the ABA's Standards for Criminal Justice, first and second editions. These features provide a useful index to the researcher and serve as a method of supplementing one's research with the latest decisions interpreting a statute or rule (discussed in detail later in this text).

---

[19] See supra § 1D(3)(c)(vi) ("West's National Reporter System") in Chapter 1.

6. CITING EARLY LOWER FEDERAL CASES
(DECIDED PRIOR TO 1880)

Prior to 1880, decisions of the federal circuit courts, federal district courts, and U.S. Circuit Courts of Appeals were issued by over 230 different nominative reporters. In order to make these reports conveniently available to practicing attorneys and courts, West Publishing Company reprinted many of these decisions in a thirty volume set known as *Federal Cases*.

Unlike West's other reporters, the cases in this set were assigned arbitrary numbers and arranged in alphabetical order (except for ninety-one cases added to Volume 30). The Digest volume (Vol. 31) has an alphabetical "Table of Cases" and a "Table of Citations" (showing cross-references from the original nominative report to the Federal Case Number).

CITING CASES IN WEST'S FEDERAL CASES SET

In addition to the rules stated earlier, *The Bluebook* applies the following rules to citations of cases in the *Federal Cases*:

(1) If a decision has been reprinted in *Federal Cases* (F. Cas.), the original report should not be cited;

(2) Indicate the Federal Case Number at the end of the citation in a separate parenthetical. Note that a comma is not used when the Federal Case Number is less than 10,000 (e.g., 8180).

The following are examples of citations of opinions reprinted in West's *Federal Cases* in *Bluebook* form:

The Aalesund, 1 F. Cas. 1 (E.D.N.Y. 1877) (No. 1).

M'Grath v. Candalero, 16 F. Cas. 128 (D.S.C. 1794) (No. 8180).

Wilson v. Rousseau, 30 F. Cas. 162 (C.C.N.D.N.Y. 1845) (No. 17,832). (This citation is an opinion of one of the old federal circuit courts. Old circuit court decisions from the District of Columbia should be cited as "D.C. Cir." rather than "C.C.D.C.").

Windor v. McLellan, 30 F. Cas. 323 (C.C.D. Mass. 1843) (No. 17,887).

7. CITING STATE COURT DECISIONS

(a) Official Reports for State Court Decisions

An example of an official state report is shown in Figure 4-N below. This case appears in Volume 202 of *Michigan Reports*, the official state reporter for decisions of the Supreme Court of Michigan. Examine the first page of this case.

Unofficial syllabus prepared by the official reporter of <u>Michigan Reports</u>

In a few jurisdictions, "official" headnotes or syllabi are written by the judge or the court. In those instances, the reporter will ordinarily accompany the headnotes or syllabus with an appropriate notation, such as "Syllabus by the Court." In contrast to West's headnotes or summaries prepared by West's editors or by the official reporter, official headnotes prepared by the judge or the court may have value as authority.

1918]　　　　　　DENTON *v.* BOOTH.　　　　　　215

DENTON *v.* BOOTH.

1. SALES—UNIFORM SALES ACT—COMPLETED SALE—QUESTION FOR JURY.

   Where defendants orally agreed to purchase a number of horses from plaintiffs at a cash price, and, pending examination of papers as to the breeding of some of them, defendants were given possession, when a dispute arose over the papers and the purchase price was never paid, the court below, in an action to recover, was not in error in submitting to the jury the question as to whether there was a completed sale under the uniform sales law (chapter 228, 3 Comp. Laws 1915).

2. AMENDMENTS—PLEADING—FORM OF ACTION.

   Although plaintiffs commenced their action in assumpsit, the court below was not in error in regarding the action as one in tort, in view of the liberal provisions of the statute which permits amendments even in the Supreme Court.

3. PARTNERSHIP—REGISTRATION—CERTIFICATE—STATUTES.

   Although it has been held that the members of a copartnership who have not complied with the provisions of Act No. 164, Pub. Acts 1913 (3 Comp. Laws 1915, § 6354 *et seq.*), may not prosecute an action under a contract, *held*, that the effect of the statute should not be extended to actions founded on tort; it being in derogation of common law rights.

Error to Chippewa; Fead, J. Submitted January 30, 1918. (Docket No. 30.) Decided July 18, 1918.

Case by William L. Denton and another, copartners as W. L. Denton & Son, against Arthur Booth and others for the conversion of certain horses. Judgment for plaintiffs. Defendants bring error. Affirmed.

John A. McMahon and *Herbert L. Parsille*, for appellants.

FIGURE 4-N
MICHIGAN REPORTS

(b) Citing State Court Decisions
in Bluebook Form

The table below summarizes *Bluebook* rules for state court cases.

CITING STATE COURT CASES

According to *The Bluebook*, published[20] state court opinions should be cited as follows:

(1) Case Name. Appendix B sets out in detail how to cite case names using *Bluebook* rules.

(2) Reporters. (a) In documents submitted to a state court, all citations to cases decided by the courts of that state (but not other states) must include a citation to the official state reporter, if available, and West reporters. In all other situations, only the relevant regional reporter should be cited (assuming the case is reported therein) (Rule 10.3.1 and Practitioners' Note P.3). The official report should be cited first. Rule 10.3.1. Use the abbreviations in the "United States Tables" section, Table T.1. Special rules apply to certain early state court reports.[21]

(b) Adjacent single capitals should be closed up (no space between them). Numerals and ordinals (e.g., 3d) are treated as single capitals (e.g., N.E.2d). Single capitals (e.g., W.), however, should not be closed up with longer abbreviations (e.g., Va.). Thus, leave a space between single capitals and longer abbreviations (e.g., W. Va. and So. 2d). Rule 6.1(a).

---

[20]When a recent case has not yet appeared in the official state reporter (and the official reporter is being cited because the document will be submitted to the state court of that state), an official continuously paginated advance sheet service (e.g., Massachusetts Supreme Judicial Court Advance Sheets) should be cited if one exists and it is available. Bluebook Rule 10.3.1.

[21]Early state court reports, even official reports, were often named after their editors rather than after the courts whose cases they reported. Subsequently, most of the official nominative reports were combined into jurisdiction-named series with continuous volume numbering; those reports are now cited by the official series name and number only.

According to The Bluebook, citations of a few early (generally prior to 1880) state court decisions, however, must still include a reference to the original nominative report even though it has been incorporated into the official series. Rule 10.3.2. If you are using that citation form, the best method for determining how these early state court decisions should be cited is to consult the table in The Bluebook covering the relevant jurisdiction.

CITING STATE COURT CASES (CONTINUED)

(3) Court, Geographic Jurisdiction, and Date. When a decision of the highest court of the state is cited, only the jurisdiction and the date are indicated parenthetically. In addition, when the name of the report is the same as the name of the jurisdiction, it is assumed that the decision is that of the highest court in the jurisdiction without further notation. Thus, the indication of the jurisdiction also can be eliminated from the parenthetical. Rule 10.4(b).

The full abbreviated name of the lower or intermediate appellate state court, including its geographic jurisdiction, and the date must be indicated parenthetically. Information that otherwise would have to be noted parenthetically should be eliminated when the reporter title unambiguously conveys that information. Citations of intermediate state court decisions should not indicate the department, division, or district unless that information is of particular relevance. Rule 10.4(b).

The following are examples of state court citations in *Bluebook* form:

In re King's Estate, 183 Pa. Super. 190, 130 A.2d 245 (1957).
(*Bluebook* form for citation of this case in documents submitted to Pennsylvania state courts)
In re King's Estate, 130 A.2d 245 (Pa. Super. Ct. 1957).
(*Bluebook* form for all other situations)

Chicago & Calumet Dist. Transit Co. v. Vidinghoff, 122 Ind. App. 395, 103 N.E.2d 460 (1952). (*Bluebook* form for citation of this case in documents submitted to Indiana state courts)
Chicago & Calumet Dist. Transit Co. v. Vidinghoff, 103 N.E.2d 460 (Ind. Ct. App. 1952). (*Bluebook* form for all other situations)

George J. Kiebler Realty Co. v. Miller, 29 Ohio App. 130, 163 N.E. 51 (1927). (*Bluebook* form for citation of this case in documents submitted to Ohio state courts)
George J. Kiebler Realty Co. v. Miller, 163 N.E. 51 (Ohio Ct. App. 1927). (*Bluebook* form for all other situations)

<u>People v. Scalza</u>, 76 N.Y.2d 604, 563 N.E.2d 705, 562 N.Y.S.2d 14 (1990). (*Bluebook* form for citation of this case in documents submitted to New York state courts)[22]

<u>People v. Scalza</u>, 563 N.E.2d 705 (N.Y. 1990). (*Bluebook* form for all other situations)

<u>Williams v. Seaboard Air Line R.R.</u>, 9 A.D.2d 268, 193 N.Y.S.2d 588 (1959). (*Bluebook* form for citation of this case in documents submitted to New York state courts)

<u>Williams v. Seaboard Air Line R.R.</u>, 193 N.Y.S.2d 588 (App. Div. 1959). (*Bluebook* form for all other situations)

<u>Schwartz v. Zippy Mart</u>, 470 So. 2d 720 (Fla. Dist. Ct. App. 1985). (NOT "Fla. 1st Dist. Ct. App. 1985" unless for some reason the district number is of particular relevance) (*Bluebook* form for citation of this case in documents submitted to Florida and all other courts)

<u>Daar v. Yellow Cab Co.</u>, 67 Cal. 2d 695, 433 P.2d 732, 63 Cal. Rptr. 724 (1967). (*Bluebook* form for citation of this case in documents submitted to California state courts)[23]

<u>Daar v. Yellow Cab Co.</u>, 433 P.2d 732 (Cal. 1967). (*Bluebook* form for all other situations)

<u>General Fin. Corp. v. Archetto</u>, 93 R.I. 392, 176 A.2d 73 (1961). (*Bluebook* form for citation of this case in documents submitted to Rhode Island state courts)

<u>General Fin. Corp. v. Archetto</u>, 176 A.2d 73 (R.I. 1961). (*Bluebook* form for all other situations)

---

[22]New York decisions are given special treatment by West Publishing Company. West's regional reporter (<u>North Eastern Reporter</u>) contains decisions of the highest court in New York—the New York Court of Appeals. In addition, West Publishing Company publishes various New York decisions in its <u>New York Supplement</u> since 1887. In documents submitted to New York state courts, the official reporter and both of West's unofficial reporters (<u>North Eastern Reporter</u> and <u>New York Supplement</u>), if therein, should be cited. Table T.1 in <u>The Bluebook</u>, however, provides that in citations of the New York Court of Appeals cases prior to 1956, West's <u>New York Supplement</u> should not be cited because the first series of <u>New York Reports</u> was simply reprinted in West's <u>New York Supplement</u> without separate pagination. In all other documents, the <u>North Eastern Reporter</u> should be cited. See <u>Bluebook</u> Table T.1 ("United States Jurisdictions, New York").

[23]California decisions are given special treatment by West Publishing Company. Since 1960, California Supreme Court decisions reported officially in <u>California Reports</u> and California Court of Appeal decisions reported officially in <u>California Appellate Reports</u> are also reported in West's <u>California Reporter</u>. According to <u>The Bluebook</u>, in documents submitted to California state courts, California Supreme Court decisions should be cited to <u>California Reports</u>, the <u>Pacific Reporter</u>, and the <u>California Reporter</u> (if therein) in that order. California Court of Appeals cases should be cited to <u>California Appellate Reports</u> and either the <u>Pacific Reporter</u> if the case was decided prior to 1960, or the <u>California Reporter</u>, if decided thereafter.

Gelber v. Kugel's Tavern, 10 N.J. 191, 89 A.2d 654 (1952). (*Bluebook* form for citation of this case in documents submitted to New Jersey state courts)

Gelber v. Kugel's Tavern, 89 A.2d 654 (N.J. 1952).   (*Bluebook* form for all other situations)

Lawer v. Kline, 39 Wyo. 285, 270 P. 1077 (1928).   (*Bluebook* form for citation of this case in documents submitted to Wyoming state courts)

Lawer v. Kline, 270 P. 1077 (Wyo. 1928).   (*Bluebook* form for all other situations)

Gies v. Fischer, 146 So. 2d 361 (Fla. 1962).   (*Florida Reports* is no longer published.)   (*Bluebook* form for citation of this case in documents submitted to Florida and all other courts)

(c) Finding Parallel Citations when the Official State Reporter Citation is Known

Assume that you want to cite the case reproduced in Figure 4-N in a document to be submitted to the Michigan state courts in *Bluebook* form. In addition to the reference to the official *Michigan Reports* (202 Mich. 215), a proper citation to the case must include a reference to the unofficial West regional reporter. How can you find the parallel citation?

(i) *State Edition of Shepard's Citations.* One means of finding the unofficial reporter citation of a case when its official citation is known is to use the appropriate *state* edition of *Shepard's Citations.* The West citation is given in parentheses immediately after the page number.

(ii) *Digest Table of Cases.* If the name of the case is known, the unofficial citation can also be found by consulting the "Table of Cases" in the appropriate West regional or state digest.

(iii) *National Reporter Blue Book.* The *National Reporter Blue Book* is another means of finding the unofficial West citation when the official citation is known. The *National Reporter Blue Book* consists of a series of volumes that provide the parallel citations from the official report to the West Report. The approximate years of coverage are Vol. 1, years to 1928; Vol. 2, 1929 to 1936; Vol. 3, 1937 to 1948; Vol. 4, 1949 to 1960; Vol. 5, 1961 to 1970; Vol. 6, 1971 to 1980; Vol. 7, 1981 to 1990, and Cumulative Paper-Covered Supplements, 1991 to date.

PROBLEM 4.9 Because the year of the decision of the *Denton* case was 1918 (indicated in Figure 4-N), you would consult the first volume in the *National Reporter Blue Book* series. The relevant part of

the table for page 215 of Vol. 202 of *Michigan Reports* is reproduced below. What is the parallel *North Western Reporter* citation?

VOL. 202, MICHIGAN REPORTS

Mich. Rep. Pg.	N.W. Rep. Vol.	Pg.	Mich. Rep. Pg.	N.W. Rep. Vol.	Pg.	Mich. Rep. Pg.	N.W. Rep. Vol.	Pg.	Mich. Rep. Pg.	N.W. Rep. Vol.	Pg.	Mich. Rep. Pg.	N.W. Rep. Vol.	Pg.	Mich. Rep. Pg.	N.W. Rep. Vol.	Pg.	Mich. Rep. Pg.	N.W. Rep. Vol.	Pg.
1	167	1000	76	167	921	169	168	471	307	168	415	420	168	547	524	168	501	597	168	421
8	167	980	85	167	904	201	168	461	311	168	508	433	168	528	532	168	446	601	168	420
15	167	906	91	167	958	204	168	523	327	169	454	450	168	534	536	168	462	605	168	412
22	167	852	97	167	935	215	168	491	334	168	426	457	168	432	544	168	465	609	168	410
29	167	860	103	167	900	224	168	496	341	168	536	464	168	494	554	168	456	612	168	440
32	167	978	106	167	1010	232	168	531	346	168	444	469	168	558	558	168	411	615	168	457
37	167	919	111	167	1011	241	168	486	349	168	536	474	168	424	561	168	413	622	168	447
43	167	859	116	167	965	257	168	503	380	168	485	480	168	549	565	168	445	626	168	708
48	167	953	121	167	854	271	168	539	363	168	512	485	168	467	567	168	519	629	168	709
52	167	851	129	167	838	280	168	419	377	168	434	496	168	517	572	168	414	646	168	943

FIGURE 4-O
NATIONAL REPORTER BLUE BOOK

DISCUSSION OF PROBLEM 4.9 The entry for the *Denton* case is listed by the page number (215). Next to that page number is the parallel citation: [Vol.] 168 [at page] 491 of the *North Western Reporter*.

(iv) Insta-Cite and Auto-Cite. Insta-Cite and Auto-Cite can be used to find parallel citations when the official citation is known.[24]

PROBLEM 4.10 Based on the appropriate *Bluebook* rules, which of the following citations of the *Denton* case reproduced in Figure 4-N is correct (assuming that you are citing this case in a document that will be submitted to a Michigan state court)?

(a) Denton v Booth, 202 Mich 215, 168 NW 491 (S Ct 1918).

(b) Denton v. Booth, 168 N.W. 491, 202 Mich. 215 (1918).

(c) Denton v. Booth, 202 Mich. 215, 168 N.W. 491 (Sup. Ct. 1918).

(d) Denton v. Booth, 202 Mich. 215, 168 N.W. 491 (1918).

(e) Denton v. Booth, 168 N.W. 491, 202 Mich. 215 (Sup. Ct. 1918).

(f) Denton v Booth, 202 Mich 215, 168 NW 491 (1918).

DISCUSSION OF PROBLEM 4.10 When a case is cited to both an official and unofficial report, the reference to the official report must precede the reference to the unofficial report. Because the *North Western Reporter* is cited first in answers (b) and (e), those answers are incorrect.

In citing a state court case, the general rule is that the full abbreviated name of the court, including its geographical jurisdiction, must

---

[24] These services are discussed in Chapters 7 and 8.

be indicated parenthetically ("Mich. Sup. Ct. 1918"). Any information that is unambiguously conveyed by the reporter title, however, may be eliminated. Thus, all the answers properly deleted the reference to jurisdiction ("Mich.") because it is readily apparent from the citation to *Michigan Reports* ("202 Mich. 215"). In addition, when the name of the report is the same as the jurisdiction, it is assumed that the decision is that of the highest court in the jurisdiction. Because the Supreme Court of Michigan is the highest state court in Michigan, the reference to "Sup. Ct." is unnecessary and should be deleted. *Bluebook* Rule 10.4(b). Therefore, answer (d) is correct.

PROBLEM 4.11 Based on the appropriate *Bluebook* rules, which of the following citations of the *Denton* case reproduced in Figure 4-N is correct (assuming that you are citing this case in a document that will be submitted to the United States Supreme Court)?

    (a) <u>Denton v Booth</u>, 168 N.W. 491 (S. Ct. 1918).
    (b) <u>Denton v. Booth</u>, 168 N.W. 491 (1918).
    (c) <u>Denton v. Booth</u>, 168 N.W. 491 (Mich. Sup. Ct. 1918).
    (d) <u>Denton v. Booth</u>, 202 Mich. 215, 168 N.W. 491 (1918).
    (e) <u>Denton v. Booth</u>, 168 N.W. 491 (Mich. 1918).
    (f) <u>Denton v Booth</u>, 202 Mich 215, 168 NW 491 (1918).

DISCUSSION OF PROBLEM 4.11 As previously noted, the traditional rule has been that when state court decisions appear in both an official and unofficial reporter, a reference to the official and preferred unofficial reporter (parallel citations) had to be included in the citation of the case. The fifteenth edition of the *Bluebook* continues this requirement of parallel citation of state court reporters only in documents submitted to a state court (as in the preceding problem). In all other situations (such as the situation posed in this problem), only the relevant regional reporter should be cited (assuming the case is reported therein) (Rule 10.3.1 and Practitioners' Note P.3). Thus, answers (c) and (f) are incorrect because they provide parallel citations.

    The *North Western Reporter* contains decisions from the following states: Iowa, Michigan, Minnesota, Nebraska, North Dakota, South Dakota, and Wisconsin. Thus, the citation of the *North Western Reporter* fails to identify which court decided the case. "Mich." must be added to the parenthetical containing the date. No other identification is necessary because it will be assumed that the court deciding the case is the highest court in the jurisdiction *when* the name of the reporter is the same as the name of a jurisdiction and no other court is indicated. Therefore, answer (e) is correct.

(d) *Finding Parallel Citations for State Cases when the Unofficial West Reporter Citation is Known*

Examine the following page reproduced from the *North Eastern Reporter Second* in Figure 4-P.

STATE v. PIGOTT   Ohio   **911**
Cite as 197 N.E.2d 911

of the hearing on the 27th day of July, 1962.

"THE COURT: The defendant is to pay $70.00 a week through the Court to the Complainant. When is the payment supposed to be made? Any particular day?

(Discussion off the record)

"THE COURT: On the record. Defendant to pay costs.

(Thereupon, at 11:40 A.M., the proceedings were closed.)"

This bill of exceptions with the addition alluded to above was allowed and signed by the trial judge.

From the record before this court, it is patent that there was a denial to this defendant of his rights under Article I, Section 10, of the Constitution of Ohio, to defend in person and with counsel and to procure the attendance of witnesses in his behalf. In addition, the proceedings before the Juvenile Court did not meet the requirements of due process of law as contemplated by the Fourteenth Amendment to the United States Constitution.

The sequence of hearings as reflected by the record before us seems to relate to the general claim that the defendant was not supporting his children. However, he was charged with the specific crime of failure to support his children during the period from March 3, 1962, to April 19, 1962. He was not accorded a fair trial on this specific charge. We find that the trial court erred to the prejudice of the substantial rights of the defendant, as urged in each of the two assignments of error. This charge as set out in the affidavit before the Juvenile Court was the only charge before that court.

The trial court's denial of the rights secured to the defendant by the Constitution and laws of the State of Ohio and by the Fourteenth Amendment to the United States Constitution require that we

reverse the conviction and judgment of the Juvenile Court and remand the cause with instructions to accord the defendant a constitutional trial in accordance with the law on that particular charge.

Reversed and remanded.

KOVACHY, P. J., and ARTL, J., concur.

STATE of Ohio, Plaintiff Appellee,

v.

Harold L. PIGOTT, Defendant Appellant.

Court of Appeals of Ohio,

Cuyahoga County.

April 23, 1964.

Murder prosecution. The Court of Common Pleas of Cuyahoga County rendered judgment, and defendant appealed. The Court of Appeals, Artl, J., held that allowing jury view of scene of alleged offense, and of scenes of similar acts by defendant, evidence of such similar acts being properly admitted, was not error.

Affirmed.

1. Criminal Law ⬷651(1)

Court has judicial discretion to allow jury view when deemed proper. R.C. § 2945.16.

2. Criminal Law ⬷651(1)

Statute authorizing jury view does not limit place of view to place where crime occurred. R.C. § 2945.16.

3. Criminal Law ⬷369(1)

Statute authorizing admission of evidence of similar acts is merely expressive of common law. R.C. § 2945.59.

FIGURE 4-P
NORTH EASTERN REPORTER SECOND

Assume that you are going to cite this case shown in Figure 4-P in a document to be submitted to an Ohio state court in *Bluebook* form. To do so properly, a reference to the official report must be given in addition to the West reporter citation. The official citation of a state court case is supplied at the beginning of the case in West's regional reporters if it is available at the time of publication. In this instance, however, it was not. The official citation can also be found by consulting the "Table of Cases" in the appropriate West regional or state digest.[25]

Another method of determining the official citation is to consult the appropriate *Shepard's* regional reporter citation volume. As discussed previously, the official citation will be given in the first entry in parentheses following the page number on which the case begins. It should be noted that *Shepard's* abbreviations are often different than those commonly used in citation by courts and attorneys.

PROBLEM 4.12 Examine the portion of the page of *Shepard's Citations* reproduced in Figure 4-Q showing the parallel citations for the case reproduced in Figure 4-P. What parallel citations are listed? To which reporter do the parallel citations refer?

```
    —911—
   (1⊙A22)
  (94Abs335)
  (30⊙p56)
239NE⁸574
239NE⁹574
252NE⁹312
252NE¹⁰312
f255NE641
    Ariz
398P2d908
447P2d876
    Fla
261So2d860
```

FIGURE 4-Q
SHEPARD'S NORTH EASTERN REPORTER CITATIONS

DISCUSSION OF PROBLEM 4.12 *Shepard's Citations* provides three parallel citations. If you are not certain which reporters have been cited, you can consult the "Table of Abbreviations" at the beginning of each *Shepard's* volume. Examine the portions of table reproduced in Figure 4-R, and determine which reporters have been cited.

---

[25]West also publishes a <u>Blue and White Book</u> for about half of the states. The blue pages in a <u>Blue and White Book</u> for a particular state duplicates the information provided in the <u>National Reporter Blue Book</u> (parallel citations from the official state reporter to West's regional reporter). The white pages in a <u>Blue and White Book</u> for a particular state provides the opposite references (parallel citations from West's regional reporter to the official reporter). If a <u>Blue and White Book</u> is published for a state, it is generally only available in libraries located in that state.

> Abs–Ohio Law Abstract

> OA–Ohio Appellate Reports
> ⊘A –Ohio Appellate Reports,
>   Second Series
> OA3d–Ohio Appellate Reports, Third
>   Series
> OBR–Ohio Bar Reports
>
> OhM–Ohio Miscellaneous Reports
> OhM2d–Ohio Miscellaneous Reports,
>   Second Series
> Op–Ohio Opinions
> ⊘p –Ohio Opinions, Second Series
> Op3d–Ohio Opinions, Third Series
> OS–Ohio State Reports
> ⊘S–Ohio State Reports, Second Series
> OS3d–Ohio State Reports, Third Series

FIGURE 4-R

TABLE OF ABBREVIATIONS IN

SHEPARD'S NORTH EASTERN REPORTER CITATIONS

As indicated in "Table of Abbreviations" reproduced in Figure 4-R, the references are to *Ohio Appellate Reports, Second Series*, *Ohio Law Abstract*, and *Ohio Opinions, Second Series*.

The Insta-Cite service available through WESTLAW and the Auto-Cite service available through LEXIS can be used to find unofficial parallel citations when the official citation is known.[26]

PROBLEM 4.13   Assume that you are going to cite the case reproduced in Figure 4-P in a document to be submitted to an Ohio state court.   The case reproduced in Figure 4-P was decided by the Court of Appeals of Ohio, an intermediate appellate court in Ohio.

Table T.1 ("United States Jurisdictions, Ohio") in *The Bluebook* provides useful information about the Ohio courts and indicates which reporters should be cited. For citations of opinions decided by the Ohio Court of Appeals, *The Bluebook* states as follows: "In documents submitted to Ohio state courts, cite to Ohio App., Ohio App. 2d, or Ohio App. 3d, if therein, and to N.E. or N.E.2d if therein."

Based on this and other relevant *Bluebook* rules, which one of the following citations is correct?

---

[26]These services are discussed in Chapters 7 and 8.

(a) <u>State v. Pigott</u>, 1 Ohio App. 2d 22, 197 N.E. 2d 911 (1964).

(b) <u>State v. Pigott</u>, 1 Ohio App. 2d 22, 197 N.E.2d 911 (1964).

(c) <u>State v. Pigott</u>, 1 Ohio App. 2d 22, 197 N.E.2d 911 (Ct. App. 1964).

(d) <u>State v Pigott</u>, 1 Ohio App 2d 22, 197 NE2d 911 (1964).

(e) <u>State v Pigott</u>, 1 Ohio App 2d 22, 197 NE2d 911 (Ct App 1964).

(f) <u>State v. Pigott</u>, 197 N.E. 2d 911 (Ohio Ct. App. 1964).

DISCUSSION OF PROBLEM 4.13 The spacing of the abbreviation of the *North Eastern Reporter Second* reference is incorrect in the Answer (a); it should read "197 N.E.2d 911." How can you tell whether a space should be left between abbreviated letters in citations? Adjacent single capital letters should be closed up. Individual numbers are treated as single capitals, e.g., N.E.2d, P.2d, F.2d, etc. Single capitals with longer abbreviations, however, should not be closed up, e.g., Ohio St. 2d, Ill. App. 3d, Cal. 2d, F. Supp., So. 2d. *Bluebook* Rule 6.1(a). Answer (b) is correct. Answers (d) and (e), *inter alia*, incorrectly omit the periods in the abbreviations.

Answer (c) incorrectly includes a reference to the court. That reference is unnecessary because one of the reporters cited (Ohio App. 2d) unambiguously conveys that information. Answer (f) incorrectly omits the citation to the official reporter.

PROBLEM 4.14 Assume that you are going to cite the case reproduced in Figure 4-P in a document to be submitted to a Florida state court in *Bluebook* form. Which of the answer(s) listed in *Problem 4.13* would be correct?

DISCUSSION OF PROBLEM 4.14 According to the *Bluebook*, in all documents other than in those submitted to Ohio state courts, the case should be cited to *North Eastern Reporter* only. Thus, answer (f) is correct.

8. CITING ANNOTATED LAW REPORTS

American Law Reports (*A.L.R.*) is a good example of an annotated reporter. Figures 4-S and 4-T show the beginning two pages of a case in *A.L.R.3d*.[27]

---

[27] Recall that <u>A.L.R.</u> contains (1) selected cases and (2) annotations that discuss points of law involved in those cases. The annotations usually include historical background, current law, and probable future developments. In most instances, the annotations will cite
(continued...)

PROBLEM 4.15 Examine Figures 4-S and 4-T. (a) Determine on what page in the volume the accompanying annotation begins. (b) Determine which point(s) of law from this case have been annotated.

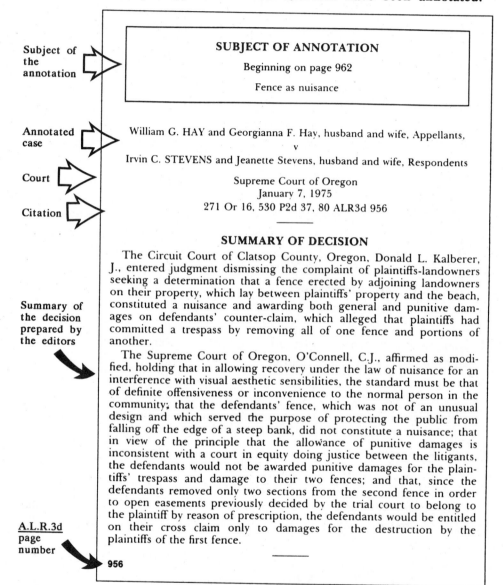

FIGURE 4-S
AMERICAN LAW REPORTS

---

[27](...continued)

all prior court decisions on the topic. The more recent A.L.R. volumes include practice pointers and cross-references. American Law Reports is published by Lawyers Cooperative Publishing Company. The case was selected for publication, in part, because it is a good illustration of the points of law covered in the accompanying annotation.

A.L.R.3d volume number

Headnotes from the reported case

The headnotes are classified to A.L.R. Digests.

Headnote 2 (A "2" in the text of the opinion indicates where this point of law is specifically discussed.

Not all points of law discussed in a case are annotated.

United States Supreme Court Reports, Lawyers' Edition, contains annotations of selected Supreme Court decisions that are similar to those contained in other A.L.R. series.

---

80 ALR3d   HAY v STEVENS
                          (Or) 530 P2d 37, 80 ALR3d 956

HEADNOTES

Classified to ALR Digests

Nuisances § 2.5 — what constitutes

1. Recovery will be permitted under the law of nuisance for an interference with visual aesthetic sensibilities; the standard for determining whether a nuisance exists is that of definite offensiveness, inconvenience or annoyance to the normal person in the community.

Nuisance § 57 — fence as nuisance

2. A fence of lumber and wire mesh constructed by the defendants across their undeveloped land between plaintiffs and the sea was not so unsightly or unusual in design as to be definitely offensive and where it served the utilitarian purpose of providing a barricade to deter the public from going down a steep bank and thereby suffering possible injury, it did not constitute a nuisance.

                    [Annotated]

Damages § 53 — exemplary — trespass

3. Punitive damages awarded against adjoining landowners, who trespassed upon the property of neighboring landowners and removed fences, were improper in view of the principle that the allowance of punitive damages is inconsistent with a court in equity doing justice between the litigants.

Damages § 254 — measure of compensation — injury to real property

4. Landowners were entitled to damages for the amount of the cost of materials of a fence destroyed by adjoining landowners trespassing on their property in the absence of a showing by the trespassers that the materials returned to the owners of the fence had salvage value; however, where the trespassers removed only two sections of a second fence and did so in order to open easements which a court decision had determined belonged to them by reason of prescription and where there was no evidence to establish the reduction in value of the fence caused by the removal of these two sections, the owners of the fence were not entitled to damages therefor.

BRIEF OF COUNSEL

Jeanyse R. Snow, MacDonald, Dean, McCallister & Snow, Astoria, argued the cause and filed briefs for appellants:

It was error to find for respondents in appellants' cause of suit, for respondents' fence unreasonably interferes with appellants' use and enjoyment of their land.

An unaesthetic sight, coupled with economic loss, can constitute a nuisance. 38 ALR3d 647; Parkersburg Builders Material Co. v Barrack, 118 W Va 608, 191 SE 368, 371.

Respondents' fence constitutes a nuisance: it unreasonably interferes with appellants' use and enjoyment of their land and has caused appellants economic loss.

Macca v General Tel. Co. 262 Or 414, 419, 495 P2d 1193; Amphitheaters, Inc. v Portland Meadows, 184 Or 336, 198 P2d 847; Loney v McPhillips, 521 P2d 340.

The asserted utility of respondents' fence must be balanced against the harm the fence causes appellants. The mere existence of a utility to respondents does not, as a matter of law, defeat appellants' nuisance suit. Gronn v Rogers Constr., Inc. 221 Or 226, 233, 350 P2d 1086.

Vawter Parker, Portland, argued the cause for respondents. With him on the brief were **Dezendorf, Spears, Lubersky & Campbell** and **Laurence F. Janssen,** Portland.

957

FIGURE 4-T
AMERICAN LAW REPORTS

DISCUSSION OF PROBLEM 4.15 The annotation accompanying this case begins on page 962. The point of law contained in headnote 2 has been annotated (indicated by the notation "[Annotated]" at the end of the headnote).

In *Bluebook* citations, a reference to *A.L.R.* is *not* included in the citation of a selected case appearing in that series.

Hay v. Stevens, 530 P.2d 37 (Or. 1975). (NOT Hay v. Stevens, 530 P.2d 37, 80 A.L.R.3d 956 (Or. 1975).)

9. SPECIAL SUBJECT REPORTERS

In addition to its regional and federal reporters, West Publishing Co. publishes several special subject reporters as part of its National Reporter System. In 1977, West's *Military Justice Reporter* began reporting decisions of the United States Courts of Military Appeals and the Courts of Military Review.

In 1979, West's *Bankruptcy Reporter* began reporting selected decisions from the federal courts dealing with bankruptcy matters. Federal district court decisions published in the *Bankruptcy Reporter* are not printed in the *Federal Supplement*. The *Bankruptcy Reporter* also reprints bankruptcy-related decisions of the U.S. Courts of Appeals and the U.S. Supreme Court, retaining respectively the pagination of the *Federal Reporter* and the *Supreme Court Reporter*. Because it provides a single source for bankruptcy decisions, West's *Bankruptcy Reporter* is a convenient source for bankruptcy research.

In 1982, West began publishing its *Education Law Reporter*, which reports selected state and federal court decisions on education law topics. It also includes various articles relating to that field. In 1983, West started a similar reporter on social security law (West's *Social Security Reporting Service*).

There are several other special subject reporters which report cases relating to particular topics. They generally are connected with current looseleaf services. The following are examples of special subject reporters:

U.S. Aviation Reports
Environment Reporter-Cases
Insurance Cases
  (Fire and Casualty, Negligence,
  Life, & Automobile Cases)
Labor Cases
Labor Relations Reference Manual
  (LRRM)
Employment Practices Decisions
Public Bargaining Cases

Labor Arbitration Reports
*Occupational Safety and Safety
  Health Cases*
Oil and Gas Reporter
*The United States Patents
  Quarterly*
American Federal Tax Reports
CCH's *Trade Cases*
Public Utility Reports

In *Bluebook* citations, parallel citations are not given to a special subject reporter when the case appears in an official or the preferred unofficial (West) reporter. *Bluebook* Rule 10.3.1. Otherwise, the special subject reporter should be cited. *See Bluebook* Rule 18. You will often see references to special subject reporters when you are using the computer legal research services.

10. ENGLISH COURT REPORTS

As the principal source of "received" law in the United States legal system, English common law has strongly influenced the development of American law in many areas, such as contracts, torts, and property law. Similarly, English cases have played an important role in legal scholarship and have been cited as persuasive authority in American courts. Because of the important relationship between English and American law, many American law libraries have English legal materials, including English reporters, and you may be called upon, on occasion, to refer to and cite English decisions.

Section 4C. Researching and Citing Recent Court Decisions

1. SLIP OPINIONS AND ADVANCE SHEETS

Judicial opinions do not appear immediately in bound volumes. For example, U.S. Supreme Court opinions first appear in pamphlet form. These "slip opinions" are published by the U.S. Government Printing Office. They are subject to correction and are not cumulatively paginated. Facsimile editions of these slip opinions are unofficially published by two looseleaf services, Bureau of National Affairs' *United States Law Week* (U.S.L.W.) and Commerce Clearing House's *U.S. Supreme Court Bulletin*. Opinions in these services usually reach subscribers within forty-eight hours after they have been handed down.

In addition to providing rapid publication of slip opinions, both *United States Law Week* and the *U.S. Supreme Court Bulletin* provide full coverage of the Court's calendar and docket. *United States Law Week* provides an extensive review of the work of the Supreme Court. This review includes several unique features, such as the reporting of arguments made in the more important cases heard by the Court and awaiting decision, including questions asked by the Court during oral argument. Both services have subject indexes and tables of cases. Furthermore, *United States Law Week* also has a docket number index.

Each of the three Supreme Court reporters (U.S., S. Ct., and L. Ed.) collect several slip opinions together for publication in paper-bound advance sheets (called "preliminary print" for *United States Reports*). Likewise, advance sheets are issued for all the other West reporters (*Federal Reporter Second, Federal Supplement*, etc.). Advance sheets are designed to provide attorneys and other legal researchers with the text of recent decisions in the reporter format without having to wait until enough opinions are accumulated to make an entire, permanently bound volume. The advance sheets have the same text and page numbering as the permanent reporter volumes so that cases in the advance sheets can be cited using the permanent reporter citation.

West's *Supreme Court Reporter* advance sheets have full editorial features, including headnotes classified according to topics and key numbers. *Lawyers' Edition* advance sheets, however, do not contain summaries of the briefs or annotations; these features are added in a separate section when the permanent volume is published. West's *Supreme Court Reporter* advance sheets (like advance sheets issued for other West reporters) have a "Judicial Highlights" section that notes current court decisions of special interest. The *Lawyers' Edition* advance sheets have a "Current Awareness Commentary" section that discusses recent developments in the Supreme Court.

Reporter advance sheets play an important role in updating an attorney's research. This updating is important because the researcher may otherwise miss critical recent legal developments.

2. WEST'S FEDERAL CASE NEWS

Although it is not a reporter, West's *Federal Case News* is another important source of recent developments involving federal cases. It provides lawyers with summaries of the latest federal cases before they are published in West's advance sheets. Each summary provides the essential points of the case, the case name, the court, the name of the judge deciding the case, the filing date, and the docket number.

3. CITING RECENT COURT DECISIONS

Rule 10.1 ("Basic Citation Forms") provides a listing of examples of how to cite numerous types of pending cases or recent decisions: filed but not decided; unpublished interim order; published interim order; unpublished decision; decision published in service only; decision published in newspaper only; decision available in electronic database; etc.

CITING RECENT U.S. SUPREME COURT DECISIONS

With respect to U.S. Supreme Court decisions, *The Bluebook* applies the following special rules:

(1) When a recent Supreme Court case has not yet appeared in *United States Reports*, *The Bluebook* establishes a priority of sources that should be cited. *Bluebook* Table T.1. West's *Supreme Court Reporter* advance sheets should be cited first if they are available (e.g., the *Montana* case reproduced in Figure 4-A would be cited: <u>Montana v. United States</u>, 99 S. Ct. 970 (1979).);

(2) If West's *Supreme Court Reporter* advance sheets are unavailable, the *Lawyers' Edition* advance sheets should be cited (e.g., <u>Montana v. United States</u>, 59 L. Ed. 2d 210 (1979).);

(3) If the case has not yet appeared in the *Supreme Court Reporter* or the *Lawyers' Edition* advance sheets, *United States Law Week* should be cited. Because the Supreme Court is the highest federal court, only the geographic jurisdiction (U.S.) is given in the parenthetical in citing Supreme Court cases to *United States Law Week* (U.S.L.W.); and

(4) *Bluebook* Rule 10.5 requires that the exact date of decision be given for cases cited to services such as *United States Law Week*. In giving the date, the month should be abbreviated as follows: Jan., Feb., Mar., Apr., May, June, July, Aug., Sept., Oct., Nov., and Dec. *Bluebook* Table T.12.

For example, assume that you had heard about a recent Supreme Court decision involving a Montana tax on the gross receipts of public contractors. Assume further that you were not sure of the names of the parties involved in the suit (Kiewit? the State of Montana? etc.). How could you find the decision in the looseleaf services?

One way to find the case is to consult the "Supreme Court Index" in the Supreme Court sections of *United States Law Week* covering the relevant Term (1978–1979). Another way is to consult the "Index to Opinions" in CCH's *U.S. Supreme Court Bulletin* covering the same Term. For example, the entry ("Taxation"-"Collateral estoppel") in the "Supreme Court Index" reproduced from *United States Law Week* directs you to page 4190 of *United States Law Week*. That page is shown below.

47 LW 4190   *The United States LAW WEEK*   **2-20-79**

tion that state-supervised care and programs designed to meet the special needs of neglected children cost more than basic AFDC care.[32] The legislative history of the amendment reveals no basis for distinguishing between related and unrelated foster homes.[34] Rather, it discloses a generalized concern for the plight of all dependent children who should be sheltered from their current home environments but are forced to remain in such homes because of the States' inability to finance substitute care. S. Rep. No. 744, at 163–165; H. R. Rep. No. 544, at 100–101. Significantly, the Committee Reports suggest that increasing federal matching payments would encourage relatives "not legally responsible for support" to undertake the care of foster children "in order to obtain the best possible environment for the child." S. Rep. No. 744, at 164; H. R. Rep. No. 544, at 101. The amendment is therefore described, without qualification, as providing "more favorable Federal matching . . . . for foster care for children removed from an unsuitable home by court order." S. Rep. No. 744, at 4; H. R. Rep. No. 544, at 4.

C

Our interpretation of the statute and its legislative history is buttressed by HEW Program Instruction APA–PI–75–9, which requires States to provide AFDC–FC benefits "regardless of whether the . . . foster family home in which a child is placed is operated by a relative." In reaching this conclusion, the Department of Health, Education, and Welfare reasoned:

> "A non-legally liable relative has no financial responsibility towards the child placed with him and the income and resources of such a relative are not factors in determining entitlement to a foster care payment. It must be noted, too, that the 1967 amendments to the Social Security Act liberalized Federal financial participation in the cost of foster care, recognizing foster family care is more costly than care in the child's own home." HEW Program Instruction APA–PI–75–9.

We noted in vacating the original three-judge District Court decision in this case that "[t]he interpretation of a statute by an agency charged with its enforcement is a substantial factor to be considered in construing the statute." 425 U. S., at 235–236, citing *New York Dept. of Social Services v. Dublino*, 413 U. S. 405, 421 (1973); *Columbia Broadcasting System, Inc.* v. *Democratic National Committee*, 412 U. S. 94, 121 (1973); *Investment Co. Institute* v. *Camp*, 401 U. S. 617, 626–627 (1971). Administrative interpretations are especially persuasive where, as here, the agency participated in developing the provision. *Adams* v. *United States*, 319 U. S. 312, 314–315 (1943); *United States* v. *American Trucking Associations*, 310 U. S. 534, 549 (1940). HEW's Program Instruction is fully supported by the statute, its legislative history, and the common sense observation that all dependent children are similarly in need of the protections and monetary benefits afforded by the AFDC–FC program.[35]

---

a Foster Care program. 81 Stat. 892 (1968), adding § 402 (a) (20) of the Act, 42 U. S. C. § 602 (a) (20).

[33] See S. Rep. No. 744, at 163–164; H. R. Rep. No. 544, 90th Cong., 1st Sess., 100–101 (1967) (hereinafter H. R. Rep. No. 544).

[34] Nor does the Illinois system indicate why such a distinction should be made. Since a related foster parent is subject to the same state-imposed responsibilities as a nonrelated foster parent, their costs must be equivalent.

[35] Relying on *General Electric Co.* v. *Gilbert*, 429 U. S. 125, 142–143 (1976), appellants maintain that the Program Instruction conflicts with an earlier HEW pronouncement and therefore deserves little weight. They refer to an inconsistent interpretation of § 408 sent to Illinois authorities in 1971 by a regional HEW official, which stated that foster children placed in related homes are not eligible for Foster Care benefits under the federal program. However, this correspondence was not approved by

III

We think it clear that Congress designed the AFDC–FC program to include foster children placed with relatives. The overriding purpose of § 408 was to assure that the most appropriate substitute care be given to those dependent children so mistreated that a court has ordered them removed from their homes. The need for additional AFDC–FC resources—both monetary and service-related—to provide a proper remedial environment for such foster children arises from the status of the child as a subject of prior neglect, not from the status of the foster parent.[36] Appellants attribute to Congress an intent to differentiate among children who are equally neglected and abused, based on a living arrangement bearing no relationship to the special needs that the AFDC–FC program was created to meet. Absent clear support in the statutory language or legislative history, we decline to make such an unreasonable attribution.

Accordingly, we hold that the AFDC–FC program encompasses foster children who, pursuant to a judicial determination of neglect, have been placed in related homes that meet a State's licensing requirements for foster homes.

The judgment below is

Affirmed.

MR. JUSTICE STEVENS took no part in the consideration or decision of this case.

PAUL J. BARGIEL, Assistant Attorney General, State of Illinois (WILLIAM J. SCOTT, Attorney General, and IMELDA R. TERRAZINO, Assistant Attorney General, with him on the brief) for appellants; ROBERT E. LEHRER, Chicago, Illinois (ROBERT P. BURNS, JAMES D. WEILL, and PATRICK KEENAN, with him on the brief) for appellees.

No. 77-1134

| State of Montana et al., Appellants, v. United States | On Appeal from the United States District Court for the District of Montana. |

[February 22, 1979]

Syllabus

Montana levies a 1% gross receipts tax upon contractors of public, but not private, construction projects. A public contractor may credit against the gross receipts tax its payments of personal property, corporate income, and individual income taxes. Any remaining gross receipts tax liability is customarily passed on in the form of increased construction costs to the governmental unit financing the project. In 1971, the contractor on a federal project in Montana brought a suit in state court contending that the gross receipts tax unconstitutionally discriminated against the Government and the companies with which it dealt. The litigation was directed and financed by the United States. Less than a month later, the Government brought this action in the

---

HEW's General Counsel or by any departmental official in the national office. See Letter from HEW's Assistant General Counsel to Illinois Special Assistant Attorney General Richard Ryan (Dec. 22, 1976), Brief for United States as *Amicus Curiae* 1a. Since the letter did not reflect an official position, we take the Program Instruction to be the Agency's first and only national interpretation concerning § 408's coverage of foster care by relatives. Appellants' reliance on *General Electric Co.* v. *Gilbert, supra*, is therefore misplaced, and we are bound by the "principle that the construction of a statute by those charged with its execution should be followed unless there are compelling indications that it is wrong." *Red Lion Broadcasting Co.* v. *FCC*, 395 U. S. 367, 381 (1969) (footnote omitted); see *Board of Governors of the Federal Reserve System* v. *First Lincolnwood Corp.*, — U. S. —, — (1978); *Zemel* v. *Rusk*, 381 U. S. 1, 11–12 (1965); *Udall* v. *Tallman*, 380 U. S. 1, 16–18 (1965).

[36] Illinois recognizes as much by providing special grants to some foster children placed with realtives which are not available to other basic AFDC recipients. See n. 12, *supra*.

FIGURE 4-U

REPRINTED WITH SPECIAL PERMISSION FROM U.S. LAW WEEK

Both *United States Law Week* and the *U.S. Supreme Court Bulletin* have case name indexes, which would be used if you knew the names of the parties involved in a recent Supreme Court case.

PROBLEM 4.16 Assuming that it is proper to cite the *Montana* case to *United States Law Week*, which of the following citations is correct (based on *Bluebook* form)?

    (a) <u>Montana v. United States</u>, 47 LW 4190 (U.S. 2-22-79).
    (b) <u>Montana v. United States</u>, 47 U.S.L.W. 4190 (Febr. 22, 1979).
    (c) <u>Montana v. United States</u>, 47 U.S.L.W. 4190 (U.S. Feb. 22, 1979).
    (d) <u>Montana v United States</u>, 47 USLW (BNA) 4190 (US 1979).

DISCUSSION OF PROBLEM 4.16 Special rules apply to citations of Supreme Court cases to *United States Law Week*. Answers (a) and (d) improperly abbreviate the name of the service. The date is properly given in answer (c). Note that February is abbreviated "Feb.," not "Febr."

Answer (c) also properly includes "U.S." in the parenthetical. "U.S." must be included because *United States Law Week* does not exclusively report cases from the United States Supreme Court (the name of the reporter does not unambiguously identify the court). Thus, answer (c) is correct.

Section 4D. Updating Case Research and Citing Prior and Subsequent History

Prior history of a case refers to earlier proceedings in the case relative to an opinion, such as an earlier appeal. In contrast, subsequent history refers to later proceedings relative to a reported opinion. As discussed in section B(4) of Chapter 3, *Shepard's Citations* provides the prior and subsequent history of a case immediately after the parallel citation is given (if there is one). A table in that section ("History of a Case in Shepard's") provides a listing of Shepard's symbols and their meanings. As part of noting the subsequent treatment of a case, *Shepard's Citations* also indicates when a case has been expressly overruled (using the symbol "o" in front of the subsequent citation).

There are several *Bluebook* rules that regulate when prior or subsequent history of a cited opinion should be included in a citation of an opinion.

CITING PRIOR AND SUBSEQUENT CASE HISTORY

(1) Prior Case History. According to *Bluebook* Rule 10.7, prior history of a case generally is not indicated in a citation. It should be given "only if significant to the point for which the case is cited or if the disposition cited does not intelligibly describe the issues in the case." Prior history is indicated by an explanatory phrase (aff'g, modifying, rev'g, enforcing, etc.). Bluebook Rule 10.7 and Table T.9.

(2) Subsequent Case History. Subsequent history, except for denial of rehearings and history on remands, must be shown when a case is cited in full. *Bluebook* Rule 10.7.

(3) Explanatory Phrases. The most frequently used phrases for indicating subsequent history in case citations are as follows:

Bluebook Abbreviation	Shepard's Abbreviation	Meaning
aff'd,	a	Affirmed
appeal dismissed,	D	Appeal dismissed
modified,	m	Modified on appeal
rev'd,	r	Reversed on appeal
vacated,	v	Vacated on appeal
cert. denied,	cert den	Certiorari denied
cert. dismissed,	cert dis	Certiorari dismissed

Note that these phrases are italicized (single underscored) and that some of them have a comma after them but others do not.

(4) Date. The year of decision is included only with the *last* cited decision when a case with several decisions in the *same* year is cited. If the exact date of decision is required for either case by *Bluebook* Rule 10.5 (for all unreported cases, all cases cited to newspapers, periodicals, and looseleaf services), however, include both dates. *Bluebook* Rule 10.5(c).

**CITING PRIOR AND SUBSEQUENT CASE HISTORY
(CONTINUED)**

(5) Case Names. When the name of a case differs in prior or subsequent history, both case names must be given in the citation; however, the second name should not be given when the parties' names are merely reversed or when the difference occurs in a citation to a denial of review by writ of certiorari or a rehearing. *Bluebook* Rule 10.7.2. A different name in subsequent history is introduced by "sub nom."

North Little Rock Transp. Co. v. Casualty Reciprocal Exch., 85 F. Supp. 961 (E.D. Ark. 1949), aff'd, 181 F.2d 174 (8th Cir.), cert. denied, 340 U.S. 823 (1950).

E.W. Wiggins Airways v. Massachusetts Port Auth., 362 F.2d 52 (1st Cir.), cert. denied, 385 U.S. 947 (1966).

American Thermos Prods. Co. v. Aladdin Indus., 207 F. Supp. 9 (D. Conn. 1962), aff'd sub nom. King-Seeley Thermos Co. v. Aladdin Indus., 321 F.2d 577 (2d Cir. 1963).

Section 4E. Parenthetical Comments and Signals in Legal Citations

1. PARENTHETICAL COMMENTS

"Parenthetical comments" are additional means of providing the reader information about a citation. The notation of dicta, dissenting opinions, statements of facts or rules, and brief quotations are typical examples. You should leave one space between adjoining parentheses.

Sears, Roebuck & Co. v. Stiffel Co., 376 U.S. 225 (1964) (unfair competition and the patent policy).

Community of Roquefort v. William Faehndrich, Inc., 303 F.2d 494, 497 (2d Cir. 1962) (dictum) (if an indication of regional origin registered as a certification mark becomes a generic term for a certain type of goods coming from any region, the mark is subject to cancellation).

According to *The Bluebook*, parentheticals noting the weight of authority (e.g., 5-4 decision, dictum, dissenting opinion, concurring opin-

ion, per curiam, by implication) should precede other parentheticals. When a case is cited for a proposition that is not the clear, single holding of the majority of the court, that fact must be indicated parenthetically.

The Bluebook provides that parenthetical information about a case should be given directly after the citation of the case, before any prior or subsequent history is cited. Furthermore, prior and subsequent history that can be properly included in an explanatory phrase should not be placed in a parenthetical. *Bluebook* Rule 10.6.

2. SIGNALS

In legal writing, introductory signals indicate the purpose for which an authority is cited or the degree of support the cited authority gives to a proposition. In legal writing, citations traditionally have served five possible purposes: (1) to provide authority for stated propositions; (2) to give illustrations; (3) to suggest profitable comparisons; (4) to note material contradictory to stated propositions; and (5) to refer to background materials. Signals are discussed in Rules 1.2-1.4 of *The Bluebook*. *The Bluebook* attaches specific meanings to a limited list of signals.

(a) No Signal

Generally speaking, when a case is cited without a signal (no signal), it means that the "[c]ited authority (i) *clearly states* the proposition, (ii) identifies the source of a quotation, or (iii) identifies an authority referred to in text." *Bluebook* Rule 1.2(a).

Assume, for example, that the text makes one of the following statements, based upon the case reproduced in Figure 1-I in Chapter 1.

Entries in a permanent record book of a trial court are admissible to prove a defendant's prior conviction without showing that the entries were made on or about the time the event occurred.

The circuit court's record book "was admissible without compliance with the Business Records Act."

The court in the Jones case held that a permanent record book of a circuit court is admissible without compliance with the Business Records Act to prove a defendant's prior conviction.

Each of these statements should be cited directly to the case without a signal:

State v. Jones, 579 S.W.2d 670, 670 (Mo. Ct. App. 1979).

Note that the preceding citation includes not only the page number on which the case begins (670), but also the page number (670) (a "pinpoint citation" or "jump cite") on which the specific support for the statement or the material cited can be found, separated by commas.

If citation in the text of a legal document is permitted, the citation would appear as follows:

The circuit court's record book "was admissible without compliance with the Business Records Act." State v. Jones, 579 S.W.2d 670, 670 (Mo. Ct. App. 1979).

In State v. Jones, 579 S.W.2d 670 (Mo. Ct. App. 1979), the Missouri Court of Appeals held that the trial court properly admitted a trial court's record book . . . .

The citation also could be placed in an appositive clause set off by commas in appropriate circumstances:

In Missouri, a permanent record book of a circuit court is admissible without compliance with the Business Records Act to prove a defendant's prior conviction, State v. Jones, 579 S.W.2d 670, 670 (Mo. Ct. App. 1979), but other courts have required compliance.

(b) Accord

Accord is a signal that indicates support for a statement. *The Bluebook* points out that this signal "is commonly used when two or more cases *state or clearly support* the proposition but the text quotes or refers to only one . . . ." The other authorities are introduced by accord. *Bluebook* Rule 1.2(a).

In the Jones case, a permanent record book of a circuit court was admitted without compliance with the Business Records Act to prove a defendant's prior conviction. State v. Jones, 579 S.W.2d 670, 670 (Mo. Ct. App. 1979); accord State v. Washington, 335 S.W.2d 23, 25 (Mo. 1960); State v. Winters, 525 S.W.2d 417, 422 (Mo. Ct. App. 1975).

(c) See

See is another signal that should be used when the "[c]ited authority *clearly supports* the proposition." This signal frequently is combined with "e.g.," preceded by a comma, to show that there are other examples directly supporting the textual statement, but citation to them would not be helpful. According to *The Bluebook*, see is used instead of

no signal "when the proposition is not directly stated by the cited authority but obviously follows from it . . . ." *Bluebook* Rule 1.2(a).

Several Missouri courts have permitted the introduction of record book entries into evidence without showing that the entries were made on or about the time the event occurred as a means of proving a defendant's prior conviction. See, e.g., State v. Jones, 579 S.W.2d 670, 670 (Mo. Ct. App. 1979).

(d) See also

Closely related to see is the see also signal. See also is used to introduce *"additional source material that supports"* a cited proposition. It is commonly used to cite additional authority when other supporting authority or authorities already have been cited or discussed. *The Bluebook* encourages the use of explanatory parentheticals to indicate the relevance of the cited additional sources. *Bluebook* Rule 1.2(a).

The signal cf. is used to indicate that the "[c]ited authority *supports a proposition different from the main proposition but [is] sufficiently analogous to lend support."* In other words, cf. is used to indicate direct support for a textual statement by analogy. *The Bluebook* strongly recommends the use of an explanatory parenthetical to make the relevance of the comparison clear to the reader. *Bluebook* Rule 1.2(a).

A permanent record book of a circuit court is admissible without compliance with the Business Records Act to prove a defendant's prior conviction. State v. Jones, 579 S.W.2d 670, 670 (Mo. Ct. App. 1979); cf. State v. Edmonds, 347 S.W.2d 158, 163-64 (Mo. 1961) (certified penitentiary records admissible without compliance with the Business Records Act).

Official entries in an appellate court docket book should be admissible without proof of compliance with the Business Records Act. Cf. State v. Jones, 579 S.W.2d 670, 670 (Mo. Ct. App. 1979) (entries in permanent record book of trial court admissible without compliance with the Business Records Act).

(e) Compare . . . [and] . . . with . . . [and]

Compare . . . [and] . . . with . . . [and] . . . is used to cite two or more authorities which, taken together, *"offer support for or illustrate"* a cited proposition. *The Bluebook* strongly recommends the use of an explanatory parenthetical to make clear to the reader the relevance of the

comparison.   Commas should not be used before "and" or "with."
Bluebook Rule 1.2(b).

Courts have made artificial and unworkable distinctions with respect to the classification of a trademarked word as "generic" or "descriptive."   For example, in one circuit an incipiently generic trademark
was classified as generic and in another the same term was viewed as
descriptive.   <u>Compare</u> <u>American Aloe Corp. v. Aloe Creme Laboratories</u>,
420 F.2d 1248, 1252-53 (7th Cir. 1970) ("Alo" generic for a type of
cosmetics) <u>with</u> <u>Aloe Creme Laboratories v. Milsan, Inc.</u>, 423 F.2d 845,
849 (5th Cir. 1970) ("Alo" descriptive of an ingredient in a type of
cosmetics).

(f) Contra, But See, and But Cf.

Three signals that indicate contradiction with the text are <u>contra</u>,
<u>but see</u>, and <u>but cf.</u>   <u>Contra</u> is used when no signal would be used for
support but when the "[c]ited authority *directly states the contrary* of the
[cited] proposition."   <u>But see</u> is used when the "[c]ited authority *clearly
supports a proposition contrary* to the main [cited] proposition."   <u>But see</u>
is used when "<u>see</u>" would be used for support.   <u>But cf.</u> is used to cite
authority that *"supports a proposition analogous to the contrary* of the
main proposition."   Again, *The Bluebook* strongly recommends the use of
an explanatory parenthetical to make clear to the reader the relevance of
the source material.   <u>But</u> should be omitted from <u>but see</u> and <u>but cf.</u>
whenever either follows another negative signal.   *Bluebook* Rule 1.2(c).

Loss of bargain damages for fraud can be awarded only in suits
against contracting parties; this measure does not apply when the fraud
is not that of one who has received consideration as a party to the
transaction.   <u>Sorensen v. Gardner</u>, 215 Or. 255, 264-67, 334 P.2d 471,
476 (1959).   <u>Contra</u> <u>Tillis v. Smith Sons Lumber Co.</u>, 188 Ala. 122, 137-
41, 65 So. 1015, 1019-20 (1914).

A trademark used on a number of different products cannot
become generic as to one of them.   <u>See</u> <u>Enders Razor Co. v. Christy Co.</u>,
85 F.2d 195, 197-98 (6th Cir. 1936).   <u>But see</u> <u>Dresser Indus. v. Heraeus
Engelhard Vacuum, Inc.</u>, 267 F. Supp. 963, 973-74 (W.D. Pa. 1967)
("Roots" generic even though it was used as a mark on several products).

In litigation to determine whether a trademark has become generic,
the question might be decided on what the mark has meant to <u>past</u>
buyers of the product.   <u>But cf</u> <u>Blisscraft v. United Plastics Co.</u>, 294 F.2d
694, 699 (2d Cir. 1961) (whether a trademark is entitled to legal protection immediately or entitled to legal protection only upon acquiring sec-

ondary meaning turns on the mark's descriptiveness to <u>prospective</u> purchasers at the time of its adoption).

(g) See Generally

<u>See generally</u> is used to indicate *"helpful background material related to the [cited] proposition."* *The Bluebook* encourages the use of a parenthetical indicating the relevance of the cited material. *Bluebook* Rule 1.2(d).

(h) Order of Signals in Citations

Cited material introduced by signals should be listed in the following order: (1) supportive—[no signal], <u>E.g.</u>, <u>Accord</u>, <u>See</u>, <u>See also</u>, <u>Cf.</u>; (2) comparative—<u>Compare</u> . . . [and] . . . <u>with</u> . . . [and] . . .; (3) contradictory—<u>Contra</u>, <u>But see</u>, <u>But cf.</u>; and (4) background—<u>See generally</u>. According to *Bluebook* Rule 1.3 ("Order of Signals"), "[s]ignals of the same basic type . . . must be strung together within a single citation sentence." In contrast, "[s]ignals of different types . . . must be grouped in different citation sentences." However, within a citation clause, citation strings may be strung together. *Bluebook* Rule 1.3.

<u>State v. Jones</u>, 579 S.W.2d 670, 670 (Mo. Ct. App. 1979); <u>see also</u> <u>State v. Washington</u>, 335 S.W.2d 23, 25 (Mo. 1960); <u>cf.</u> <u>State v. Edmonds</u>, 347 S.W.2d 158, 163-64 (Mo. 1961) (certified penitentiary record).

State governments have been permitted to sue for treble damages as "persons" under the Sherman Act. <u>See, e.g.</u>, <u>Georgia v. Evans</u>, 316 U.S. 159, 162 (1942). <u>But cf.</u> <u>United States v. Cooper Corp.</u>, 312 U.S. 600, 606, 614 (1941) (federal government not recognized as a "person" entitled to sue under the Sherman Act). (Different citation sentences were used because the citations were of different types—supportive and contradictive.)

Although the decisions on the point are split, <u>Sorensen v. Gardner</u>, 334 P.2d 471, 476-77 (Or. 1959); <u>contra</u> <u>Tillis v. Smith Sons Lumber Co.</u>, 65 So. 1015, 1019-20 (Ala. 1914), the better reasoned view is that loss of bargain damages for fraud can be awarded only in suits against contracting parties. (Different types of signals are permitted to be strung together within a citation clause.)

<u>State v. Jones</u>, 579 S.W.2d 670, 670 (Mo. Ct. App. 1979); <u>accord</u> <u>State v. Washington</u>, 335 S.W.2d 23, 25 (Mo. 1960); <u>cf.</u> <u>State v. Winters</u>, 525 S.W.2d 417, 422 (Mo. Ct. App. 1975). (These citations were strung together because they are all of the same basic type—supportive.)

(i) Signals Used as Ordinary Verbs

The above signals may be used as verbs in ordinary sentences. They should not be italicized (underlined) when they are used in this manner. *Bluebook* Rule 1.2(e) ("Signals as verbs").

Section 4F. Short Form Citations in Subsequent References to Cases

In briefs and memoranda, id. may be used when the immediately preceding case is cited again. *See Bluebook* Rule 4.1; Practitioners' Notes P.4(a).

In the Jones case, the court held that a volume of a circuit court's permanent record book is admissible without compliance with the Business Records Act to show a defendant's prior conviction. State v. Jones, 579 S.W.2d 670, 670 (Mo. Ct. App. 1979). The court in this case also held that the trial court did not abuse its discretion by permitting the prosecution to ask its own witnesses whether they were certain of their identification of the defendant. Id. at 670-71.

Note that the following use of id. is not allowed:

State v. Jones, 579 S.W.2d 670 (Mo. Ct. App. 1979); State v. Winters, 525 S.W.2d 417 (Mo. Ct. App. 1975). The court in the Jones case also held that the trial court did not abuse its discretion by permitting the prosecution to ask its own witnesses whether they were certain of their identification of the defendant. Id. at 670-71. (This example illustrates an IMPROPER USE OF Id. The citation is INCORRECT because the immediately preceding case was not the sole item in the prior citation sentence.)

The Bluebook generally does not permit the use of "supra" in citing previously cited cases when "id." would be inappropriate. *Bluebook* Rule 4.2 (recognizing a possible exception for case names that are "extremely long"). Instead, once a case has been textually named and fully cited, it may be referred to by one of the parties' names or by an established popular name.

The Jones case applied the general rule.

Furthermore, in subsequent references, a shortened citation, including the relevant page number, may be used. A shortened case name

(other than "United States" or another governmental litigant) can be used. *Bluebook* Rule 10.9.

> Jones, 579 S.W.2d at 670-71.
> Cooper, 312 U.S. at 602. (NOT United States, 312 U.S. at 602.)

The Bluebook provides additional rules for short form citations of other types of authority, such as periodical articles and books. *See Bluebook* Rule 13.7 (legislative materials), 14.9 (administrative materials), 15.8 (books), and 16.6 (periodicals).

Chapter 5
LEGISLATIVE LEGAL RESEARCH

Section 5A. Introduction

Recall from Chapter 1 that primary sources of law can be divided into three basic categories: (1) statutory law (legislation, such as constitutions, statutes, municipal ordinances, and treaties); (2) common law (judicial opinions); and (3) administrative law (regulations and agency decisions). Recall also from Chapter 1 that these primary sources are published (with a few exceptions) in two basic ways: (a) chronologically (e.g., by the date of enactment of a statute in session laws, such as in the *United States Statutes at Large*) and (b) topically (e.g., statutory collections arranged by subject, such as in the *United States Code*).

The preceding chapters focused on research primarily involving common-law sources. This chapter focuses on research primarily involving legislative sources.

Section 5B. Factual Contexts for Legislative Legal Research and Preliminary Problem Analysis

As discussed in Chapter 2, legal research is a problem-solving activity that ordinarily takes place in a factual context. Before you begin legal research, you should conduct a preliminary analysis of the facts and the legal research problem, including (1) the legal subjects involved; (2) the specific legal terms used to describe the parties, places, and things involved; (3) the specific legal issues involved; and (4) any research leads based on the material or information you have received.

This preliminary analysis is the same whether the factual context will eventually lead you to legislative primary sources rather than judicial (or administrative) ones. Sometimes, you will be provided a research lead that will readily indicate to you that legislative sources will be the principal sources of the legal rules that will apply to the factual situation that you are researching. In other situations, your general knowledge of the law will immediately suggest to you that legislative sources will provide the controlling legal rules.

PROBLEM 5.1 Consider the following factual situation. What legal subjects are involved? What terms describe the parties, places, and things involved? What legal issues appear to be involved? Are there any research leads based on the material or information that you have received? What aspects of this problem do you think might be controlled by legislative sources of law?

Assume that you are in practice in South Carolina and that you have received a long-distance call from John Slade. You represented Slade some years ago when he bought a mine and again two years ago when he purchased Acme, Inc., a licensed, local fireworks manufacturer. You have not had contact with Slade again until you received this call.

Slade is concerned that he may be charged with some kind of crime by state or federal authorities. Slade explained that he has strong political views and ties with certain "freedom fighters" in a Latin American country. Slade indicated that he shifted production of Acme away from minor fireworks such as Roman candles, bottle rockets, firecrackers, and sparklers into "larger fireworks." Slade calls his large fireworks "M-10,000." Slade has secretly been supplying his M-10,000 fireworks for "firework displays" by the freedom fighters. Slade said that he had a large supply of fireworks in a local warehouse and that he had not sold the M-10,000 fireworks to anyone in the United States or abroad. Slade indicated that representatives of the freedom fighters picked up the fireworks from the warehouse. Slade wasn't sure how the freedom fighters got the fireworks out of the country.

Slade indicated someone in the United States government had discovered that he was supplying the "rebels" with explosives. The United States government strongly supports the government of the Latin American country and regards the rebels as enemies. The United States has troops in the Latin American country to aid the Latin American country's government in its war against the "rebel scum." Slade admitted that some of the freedom fighters' actions have gone too far—engaging in political assassinations, cocaine trafficking, and kidnapping of Americans. However, Slade insists that the freedom fighters' cause is just. Slade wants to know what crimes he might be charged with. One of

Slade's sources indicated that the United States government was considering charging him with "treason" since some of the attacks were against United States military forces. Slade thinks that such a charge would surely be impossible because the attacks took place outside the United States and were directed against another government.

During the conversation, you asked Slade where he currently was. Slade said that he was in Spain on business. Slade wondered what action could be taken against him and whether he could be forced to return to the United States to face charges. Slade also wanted to know if there were any Latin American countries that did not have agreements to return persons charged with crimes.

DISCUSSION OF PROBLEM 5.1   In analyzing this situation, there are several words that can be used to describe the parties, places, and things involved. Two of the key words are fireworks and explosives. The principal subject involved is criminal law and procedure.

Slade may be facing a host of legal problems. For example, has Slade violated any criminal laws concerning the manufacture of fireworks or explosives? What are the legal requirements to manufacture explosives in the United States? To what extent can Slade be held responsible for the use of his explosives against United States armed forces? Is it possible to charge Slade with treason? Can Slade be forced to return to the United States? Is Slade shielded from any criminal liability because Slade's company (and technically not Slade personally) manufactured the explosives? Are any laws being violated by secretly storing the explosives in a local warehouse?

These issues are all principally controlled by federal or state statutes. Some also may involve other types of legislation as well. For example, treason has a federal constitutional dimension. Return of fugitives from foreign countries involves treaties. Municipal ordinances may restrict the location of manufacturing and storing of explosives. Federal and state administrative regulations (discussed in the next chapter) may also apply to various aspects of this situation. In terms of research leads, no specific statutes are mentioned. The manufacturing and storage of the explosives takes place in South Carolina. Thus, South Carolina state law is likely to be relevant. Furthermore, because many of the events take place in the United States, federal law is also likely to be relevant.

Section 5C. Basic Research Techniques and Starting Points

The basic research techniques discussed in the preceding chapters also apply to situations that are controlled by legislative primary sources

of law. The index and topic methods of search are the principal methods of search. In terms of starting points, most researchers would choose either (1) one or more secondary sources or (2) state or federal annotated statutes to begin researching *Problem 5.1*.

1. SECONDARY SOURCES

Secondary sources such as legal encyclopedias, treatises, and legal periodicals can be used to find useful background information and to provide you with the "big picture." These sources can also provide you with research leads to relevant authority, including statutes and constitutional provisions. These sources can also provide you with citations to judicial interpretations of legislative sources of law.

PROBLEM 5.2 In the context of *Problem 5.1*, assume that you have decided to consult a legal encyclopedia for purposes of developing some general background information and research leads to primary sources. Assume that you have decided to consult *American Jurisprudence Second*. What index entry or entries do you think would lead you to relevant discussion? Similarly, if you were going to use a topic approach, what topic or topics might you look for?

DISCUSSION OF PROBLEM 5.2 In the discussion of *Problem 5.1*, two key terms were identified: fireworks and explosives. Using the index method of search, entries under these terms in the General Index of *American Jurisprudence Second* lead you to the topic "Explosions and Explosives" in Volume 31A. Similarly, using the topic method of search, you would discover that there is no topic entitled "Fireworks" but the term explosives would lead you to the topic "Explosions and Explosives."

PROBLEM 5.3 Reproduced in Figures 5-A and 5-B on the following pages are the beginning pages of the topic "Explosions and Explosives" in Volume 31A of *American Jurisprudence Second*. (1) Using the "Scope of topic," "Federal aspects," and "Treated elsewhere" sections, determine whether this topic is likely to have material relevant to the factual situation presented in *Problem 5.1*. (2) Using the "Research References," identify (a) the sections of the *United States Code* that appear to be relevant to the research problem and (b) the part of the *Code of Federal Regulations* that applies to the regulation of commerce in explosives.

EXPLOSIONS AND EXPLOSIVES

by

Mitchell J. Waldman, J.D.

Scope of topic: This article includes discussions as to the regulation and control of explosives; civil liability, generally, and with regard to particular activities such as blasting; the use of fireworks; the transportation or storage of explosive materials; and matters of civil procedure and practice applicable in explosion cases. Also examined are criminal offenses with regard to explosives and prosecutions therefor.

Federal aspects: Federal statutes regulate and make criminal certain conduct with regard to the manufacture, storage, possession, use, placement, distribution, transportation, receiving in commerce, and other specific acts. (See "Federal Legislation," infra, for USCS citations). Federal statutes also prohibit certain activities pertaining to the use of explosives in furtherance of a civil disorder, (see 54 Am Jur 2d, MOBS AND RIOTS § 56), and prohibit the carrying of explosives aboard or while attempting to board an aircraft (see 8 Am Jur 2d, AVIATION § 164).

Treated elsewhere:

Act of God, explosion as, see 1 Am Jur 2d, ACT OF GOD § 8

Automobile liability policy, fire or explosion as within coverage of, see 7 Am Jur 2d, AUTOMOBILE INSURANCE §§ 201, 203

Atomic weapons, regulation and control of manufacture of atomic bombs, use of atomic energy for war purposes, and related activities, see 6 Am Jur 2d, ATOMIC ENERGY § 3

Nuclear explosions, civil liability for injuries from, see 6 Am Jur 2d, ATOMIC ENERGY §§ 47 et seq.

Aircraft, carrying weapons or explosives aboard, as criminal offense, see 8 Am Jur 2d, AVIATION § 164

Motorboat owners and operators, liability for injuries or damage resulting from explosions, see 12 Am Jur 2d, BOATS AND BOATING § 50

Burglary, lawfulness of possession of explosives or explosive devices under statutes proscribing possession of tools or implements for, see 13 Am Jur 2d, BURGLARY § 74

Carrier's liability for injuries from fires or explosions caused by articles of passengers, see 14 Am Jur 2d, CARRIERS § 1051

Gas, liability of gas companies for injury or damage from, see 26 Am Jur 2d, ELECTRICITY, GAS, AND STEAM §§ 195 et seq.

Shipowner's liability under Jones Act for negligently exposing crew members to danger of explosion, see 32 Am Jur 2d, FEDERAL EMPLOYERS' LIABILITY AND COMPENSATION ACTS § 54

Fire, liability for damage caused by spread of fire resulting from negligent storage of combustible materials on premises, see 35 Am Jur 2d, FIRES § 27

Filling station operator's duty to prevent injury from ignition or explosion of gasoline being furnished, see 38 Am Jur 2d, GARAGES, AND FILLING AND PARKING STATIONS § 125

Gas and oil, liability of refiners, storers, and sellers of, generally, see 38 Am Jur 2d, GAS AND OIL §§ 228 et seq.

Fire insurance, coverage of damages due to explosions and explosives, see 43 Am Jur 2d, INSURANCE §§ 483-487

Employer's duty and liability to employee for injury caused by explosives, see 53 Am Jur 2d, MASTER AND SERVANT § 209

Mine owners' or operators' duties, care, and negligence, as to injuries to persons or

401

FIGURE 5-A

AMERICAN JURISPRUDENCE SECOND

EXPLOSIONS AND EXPLOSIVES   31A Am Jur 2d

property from blasting or other mining activities, see 54 Am Jur 2d, MINES AND MINERALS §§ 184 et seq.

Civil disorder, teaching or demonstrating use, application, or making of explosive, or transportation or manufacture for transportation of explosive, in furtherance of, see 54 Am Jur 2d, MOBS AND RIOTS § 56

Liability of manufacturer or seller of explosives and fireworks, for injuries resulting therefrom, generally, see 63 Am Jur 2d, PRODUCTS LIABILITY §§ 827 et seq.

Exploding bottles or containers, liability of bottler, manufacturer, seller or related others, and application of doctrine of res ipsa loquitur, see 63 Am Jur 2d, PRODUCTS LIABILITY §§ 437, 843-846, 851, 854, 856

Weapons and firearms, generally, see 79 Am Jur 2d, WEAPONS AND FIREARMS

Employees' compensation under workmen's compensation acts for injuries resulting from explosion, see 82 Am Jur 2d, WORKMEN'S COMPENSATION § 320

Research References

Text References:
Speiser, Res Ipsa Loquitur Ch 17 (Explosions)

Annotation References:
ALR Digest to 3d, 4th, and Federal: Explosions and Explosives
Index to Annotations: Explosions and Explosives; Fireworks and Firecrackers

Practice References:
10 Am Jur Pl & Pr Forms (Rev), Explosions and Explosives
8 Am Jur Legal Forms 2d, Explosions and Explosives
12 Am Jur Proof of Facts 751, Water Heater Explosions; 24 Am Jur Proof of Facts 1, Blasting; Am Jur Proof of Facts/POF2d Fact Book 253, BOILERS § 1:82
11 Am Jur Trials 357, Trial of a Blasting Damage Case; 13 Am Jur Trials 343, Boiler Explosion Cases

Federal Legislation:
18 USCS § 836 (transportation of fireworks into state prohibiting sale or use)
18 USCS §§ 841-848 (importation, manufacture, distribution, and storage of explosive materials)
18 USCS § 1074 (flight to avoid prosecution for damage to property caused by explosives)

Administrative Rules and Regulations:
27 CFR Part 55 (Regulation by Bureau of Alcohol, Tobacco and Firearms of commerce in explosives)

VERALEX®:
Cases and annotations referred to herein can be further researched through the VERALEX electronic retrieval system's two services, **Auto-Cite®** and **SHOWME®**. Use Auto-Cite to check citations for form, parallel references, prior and later history, and annotation references. Use SHOWME to display the full text of cases and annotations.

Table of Parallel References
To convert General Index references to section references in this volume, or to ascertain the disposition (or current equivalent) of sections of articles in the prior edition of this publication, see the Table of References beginning at p ix.

Outline

I. IN GENERAL [§§ 1-16]

402

FIGURE 5-B
AMERICAN JURISPRUDENCE SECOND

DISCUSSION OF PROBLEM 5.3 It is readily apparent from the "Scope of topic," "Federal aspects," and "Treated elsewhere" sections that this topic is relevant to many of the questions raised by the facts of *Problem 5.1*. These entries also raise some continuing factual inquiries. For example, is Slade shipping the explosives to Latin America by airplane? If so, the discussion in "8 Am Jur 2d, Aviation § 164" may be relevant ("prohibit[ing] the carrying of explosives aboard or while attempting to board an aircraft"). Could the activities of the "freedom fighters" be characterized as a "civil disorder"? If so, the discussion in "54 Am Jur 2d, Mobs and Riots § 56" may be relevant ("prohibit[ing] certain activities pertaining to the use of explosives in furtherance of a civil disorder").

The "Research References" identify three sets of provisions in Title 18 of the *United States Code*: (1) § 836 (transporting fireworks into a state prohibiting sale or use thereof); (2) §§ 841-848 (importing, manufacturing, distributing, and storing explosive materials); (3) § 1074 (flight to avoid prosecution for damage to property caused by explosives). Note that this latter provision raises serious questions concerning Slade's planned avoidance of re-entry into the United States and search for countries that do not have extradition agreements with the United States.

The "Research References" also indicate that Part 55 of Title 27 of the *Code of Federal Regulations* covers the regulations promulgated by the Bureau of Alcohol, Tobacco, and Firearms relating to commerce in explosives.

PROBLEM 5.4 The Outline at the beginning of the topic "Explosions and Explosives" in *American Jurisprudence Second* indicates that the discussion of criminal offenses and prosecution begins with § 214. Reproduced in the following figures are §§ 214-215, § 223, §§ 226-227, and §§ 234-235. What preliminary conclusions can be drawn from the discussion in these sections?

§ 213   EXPLOSIONS AND EXPLOSIVES   31A Am Jur 2d

entitled to the weight of a jury verdict and will not be disturbed unless it is clearly wrong or without evidence to support it.[96]

VI. CRIMINAL OFFENSES AND PROSECUTION [§§ 214–251]

A. Particular Offenses [§§ 214–237]

Research References

18 USCS §§ 836, 841 et seq., 1074
ALR Digest to 3d, 4th, and Federal, Explosions and Explosives §§ 1.5, 1.7, 2, 8, 9
Index to Annotations, Explosions and Explosives; Fireworks and Firecrackers

1. Manufacture and Storage of Explosives [§§ 214, 215]

§ 214. Generally

The manufacture of explosive materials or compounds has been made a criminal offense by statute in some jurisdictions,[97] and it is a federal offense to manufacture for transportation in commerce an explosive, knowing or having reason to know or intending that such will be used unlawfully in furtherance of a civil disorder.[98] Furthermore, it has been made unlawful by federal statute for any person to store any explosive material in a manner not in conformity with regulations promulgated by the Secretary of the Treasury or his delegate[99] or to store any explosive materials knowing or having reasonable cause to believe that such materials were stolen.[1]

The manufacture and keeping of large quantities of explosives in, or dangerously near to, public places, such as towns and highways, are indictable as public nuisances, whether or not there is negligence in such manufacture or

96. M. W. Worley Constr. Co. v Hungerford, Inc., 215 Va 377, 210 SE2d 161, holding that trial court erred in finding construction company negligent since finding was not supported by evidence, in that both of witnesses whose testimony was relied upon to sustain court's finding of negligence had testified that the care and caution used in connection with the preparation and firing of the blasts which caused the damage was greater than the precautions which would ordinarily have been taken in the circumstances by those engaged in the trade of blasting.

As to negligence as the basis of liability for damage or injury from blasting, generally, see §§ 70 et seq.

97. Johnson v Lee (DC Conn) 281 F Supp 650 (statute making unlawful manufacture of explosive materials or compounds with knowledge or intent or reason to believe they are to be used for injury of person or property); Saunders v State (Del Sup) 275 A2d 564 (manufacture of

556

Molotov cocktail or any other device, instrument or object designed to explode or produce uncontained combustion made felony).

The corpus delicti of the making and procuring of dynamite with intent to use it for the unlawful destruction of the lives of certain persons is sufficiently proved by the facts that the defendant had such explosives in his possession, kept them concealed, and on different occasions threatened to take the lives of such persons. Hronek v People, 134 Ill 139, 24 NE 861.

98. 54 Am Jur 2d, Mobs and Riots § 56.

99. 18 USCS § 842(j); 18 USCS § 841(k).

1. 18 USCS § 842(h).

▌▌▌▌ Observation: The constitutionality of 18 USCS § 842(h) has been upheld despite its failure to require an evidential nexus between the prescribed activity and interstate commerce. United States v Dawson (CA8 Mo) 467 F2d 668, cert den 410 US 956, 35 L Ed 2d 689, 93 S Ct 1427.

FIGURE 5-C
AMERICAN JURISPRUDENCE SECOND

31A Am Jur 2d EXPLOSIONS AND EXPLOSIVES § 216

storage.[2] Upon the trial of such indictments, it is a question of fact for the jury whether the keeping and depositing or the manufacturing of such substances really does create danger to life and property as alleged; this question must be one of degree, depending on the circumstances of each particular case.[3]

§ 215. Violation of federal licensing and reporting requirements

A federal statute makes it unlawful for any person to engage in the business of manufacturing explosive materials without a license,[4] and, once licensed, it is unlawful to manufacture explosive materials without making such records as the Secretary of the Treasury or his delegate may by regulation require.[5]

2. OWNERSHIP, CONTROL, OR POSSESSION OF EXPLOSIVES OR MATERIALS THEREFOR [§§ 216–220]

§ 216. Generally

The legislature may prohibit the mere possession of explosives such as bombs or other devices which have no legitimate use, and which are used only in the unlawful destruction of property or lives.[6] Thus, state provisions sometimes make criminal the unlawful ownership,[7] custody,[8] control,[9] or possession,[10] of explosives,[11] explosive substances,[12] materials, compounds,[13] or devices,[14] bombs,[15] "Molotov cocktails,"[16] nitroglycerin, dynamite, or any other dangerous or violent explosives.[17] In some jurisdictions "criminal possession of explosives" has been defined broadly to encompass not only possession of

2. Rudder v Koopman, 116 Ala 332, 22 So 601; Kentucky Glycerine Co. v Commonwealth, 188 Ky 820, 224 SW 360, 11 ALR 715; Myers v Malcolm (NY) 6 Hill 292; Wilson v Phoenix Powder Manuf'g Co., 40 W Va 413, 21 SE 1035.

3. Kinney v Koopman, 116 Ala 310, 22 So 593; People v Sands (NY) 1 Johns 78.

4. 18 USCS § 842(a)(1).

5. 18 USCS § 842(f), 18 USCS § 841(k).

6. § 10.

7. Satterfield v State (Ind App) 468 NE2d 571.

8. State v Johnson (ND) 417 NW2d 365.

9. State v Johnson (ND) 417 NW2d 365; State v Lindway, 131 Ohio St 166, 5 Ohio Ops 538, 2 NE2d 490, cert den and app dismd 299 US 506, 81 L Ed 375, 57 S Ct 36.

10. Johnson v Lee (DC Conn) 281 F Supp 650; People v Westoby (1st Dist) 63 Cal App 3d 790, 134 Cal Rptr 97; Saunders v State (Del Sup) 275 A2d 564; Satterfield v State (Ind App) 468 NE2d 571; Hoey v State, 311 Md 473, 536 A2d 622; People v Dorris, 95 Mich App 760, 291 NW2d 196; State v Johnson (ND) 417 NW2d 365; State v Pelliccia, 109 RI 106, 280 A2d 330.

11. People v Westoby (1st Dist) 63 Cal App 3d 790, 134 Cal Rptr 97.

12. State v Pelliccia, 109 RI 106, 280 A2d 330.

13. Johnson v Lee (DC Conn) 281 F Supp 650; Saunders v State (Del Sup) 275 A2d 564.

14. People v Dorris, 95 Mich App 760, 291 NW2d 196 (devices designed to explode).

15. Satterfield v State (Ind App) 468 NE2d 571 (bombs loaded with dangerous gases or explosives); Hoey v State, 311 Md 473, 536 A2d 622 (firebomb); State v Lindway, 131 Ohio St 166, 5 Ohio Ops 538, 2 NE2d 490, cert den and app dismd 299 US 506, 81 L Ed 375, 57 S Ct 36 (bombs or similar devices); State v Pelliccia, 109 RI 106, 280 A2d 330.

Annotation: 42 ALR3d 1230 (possession of bomb, Molotov cocktail, or similar device as criminal offense).

16. Hoey v State, 311 Md 473, 536 A2d 622.

As to the definition of "Molotov cocktail," see § 5.

17. State v Johnson (ND) 417 NW2d 365, upholding validity of statute making felony custody, possession, or control of such substances, as being reasonably clear and definite.

557

FIGURE 5-D

AMERICAN JURISPRUDENCE SECOND

§ 222   EXPLOSIONS AND EXPLOSIVES   31A Am Jur 2d

making criminal damage or destruction to property by means of explosives.[52]

The elements constituting the crime of malicious use of explosives are the intent to injure, terrify, or intimidate a human being, and the placing or depositing or attempting to deposit an explosive in a place normally used by human beings.[53]

▌▌▌▌ *Practice guide:* One violates a statute making it a felony to maliciously deposit or explode or attempt to explode in, under or near any building, any explosive, with: (1) the intent to enter or destroy such building; or (2) with the intent to injure, intimidate or terrify a human being; or (3) by means of which a human being is injured or endangered, if he sets off an explosive intending to intimidate or terrify a human being, or damages a building while acting with a specific intent to do such damage, or deposits or explodes an explosive with or without the specific wrongful intents necessary for the first two types of violations, the result of which is to injure or endanger a human. In order to prove a violation of such statute it is insufficient to merely establish the detonation of explosives and resulting property damage therefrom.[54]

§ 223. Federal offenses

Under federal law, whoever uses an explosive to commit any felony which may be prosecuted in a court of the United States has committed a criminal offense.[55] Furthermore, whoever maliciously damages, or destroys, or attempts to damage or destroy, by means of an explosive, any building, vehicle, or other personal or real property which is in whole or in part owned, possessed or used by, or leased to the United States, any department or agency thereof, or any institution or organization receiving federal financial assistance,[56] such as, for example, the Planned Parenthood Association,[57] or which is used in interstate or foreign commerce or in any activity affecting interstate or foreign commerce,[58] is guilty of a federal offense. Furthermore, by combining a federal

494, cert den 370 US 903, 8 L Ed 2d 399, 82 S Ct 1247 (personal property); Koser v Smith, 12 Wash App 281, 529 P2d 893 (statute providing punishment for malicious destruction or damage to building, car, vessel, railroad track or structure, by explosion of gunpowder, or other explosive substances or materials).

52. § 223.

53. People v Kynette, 15 Cal 2d 731, 104 P2d 794, cert den 312 US 703, 85 L Ed 1136, 61 S Ct 806 and (ovrld on other grounds by People v Snyder, 50 Cal 2d 190, 324 P2d 1) and (ovrld on other grounds by People v Sharer, 61 Cal 2d 869, 40 Cal Rptr 851, 395 P2d 899) and (disagreed with on other grounds by People v Horn, 12 Cal 3d 290, 115 Cal Rptr 516, 524 P2d 1300) as stated in People v Buschbom (4th Dist) 189 Cal App 3d 1615, 234 Cal Rptr 914, op withdrawn by order of ct.

54. State v White, 102 Ariz 97, 425 P2d 424.

55. 18 USCS § 844(h)(1).

56. 18 USCS § 844(f).

57. United States v Brown (CA6 Mich) 557

F2d 541, 2 Fed Rules Evid Serv 312 (disagreed with on other grounds by United States v Downing (CA3 Pa) 753 F2d 1224, 17 Fed Rules Evid Serv 1, on remand (ED Pa) 609 F Supp 784, 19 Fed Rules Evid Serv 1305, affd without op (CA3 Pa) 780 F2d 1017 (upholding constitutionality of 18 USCS § 844(f) as applied to the Planned Parenthood Association).

58. 18 USCS § 844(i).

▌▌▌▌ *Reminder:* There has been some dispute as to what constitutes an "explosive," for purposes of prosecution under 18 USCS § 844(i). § 3.

In a prosecution for violations of 18 USCS § 844(i) for attempting to destroy, by means of an explosive, properties used in interstate commerce, by the alleged planting of a bomb on a commercial fishing boat, the prosecution was not barred for its failure to produce evidence of the specific effect which the injured party's boat had on interstate commerce, where there was ample evidence that the boat was used in commercial fishing and that the catch was

FIGURE 5-E

AMERICAN JURISPRUDENCE SECOND

statute making punishable conduct of a principal in willfully causing an act to be done which would be an offense against the United States,[59] with the statute making criminal malicious damage to property of the federal government by the use of explosives,[60] it is a federal offense to cause another person to destroy government property by means of an explosive.[61]

§ 224.   —What constitutes activity affecting interstate commerce

There has been some difference of opinion as to what constitutes an activity affecting interstate commerce for purposes of obtaining jurisdiction under the federal statute pertaining to malicious damage to property by means of explosives.[62] Thus, it has been said, generally, that the provision is to be interpreted in a broad, expansive manner in order to further Congress's intent in enacting the provision,[63] that the commerce requirement of the statute was intended to be broadly construed,[64] and that in using the words "affecting interstate commerce" Congress intended to exercise the full jurisdictional reach constitutionally permissible under the Commerce Clause.[65] On the other hand it has been said that the statute only applies to property that is used in an activity that affects commerce,[66] or only to property having certain de minimis interstate connections, and that only business-related activities constitute "commerce" for purposes of the provision.[67] Thus, the jurisdictional requirement is met under the applicable provision,[68] where in the regular course of a company's business, it received goods originating outside the state, and, at the time of the blast, the building in which the company was housed, contained items that were destined to be sold in interstate commerce.[69] Furthermore, where a commercial activity is being carried on in a building, the fact that food is served there which has traveled in interstate commerce or that the buildings are operated by means of fuel that has originated from out-of-

shipped interstate. United States v Keen (CA9 Wash) 508 F2d 986, cert den 421 US 929, 44 L Ed 2d 86, 95 S Ct 1655.

59. 18 USCS § 2(b).

60. 18 USCS § 844(f).

61. United States v Giese (CA9 Or) 597 F2d 1170, 4 Fed Rules Evid Serv 689, cert den 444 US 979, 62 L Ed 2d 405, 100 S Ct 480 and (disagreed with on other grounds by United States v Perez (CA9 Cal) 658 F2d 654, 9 Fed Rules Evid Serv 240.

62. 18 USCS § 844(i).

Annotation: 54 ALR Fed 752 (jurisdictional basis for prosecution under 18 USCS § 844(i), making it a federal offense to destroy, by means of explosive, property used in interstate commerce or in any activity affecting interstate commerce).

63. United States v Zabic (CA7 Ill) 745 F2d 464, 16 Fed Rules Evid Serv 692.

64. United States v Monholland (CA10 Okla) 607 F2d 1311.

65. United States v Grossman (CA4 NC) 608 F2d 534, 54 ALR Fed 747.

66. Russell v United States, 471 US 858, 85 L Ed 2d 829, 105 S Ct 2455.

67. United States v Mennuti (ED NY) 487 F Supp 539, affd (CA2 NY) 639 F2d 107 (disapproved by Russell v United States, 471 US 858, 85 L Ed 2d 829, 105 S Ct 2455) as stated in United States v Patterson (CA5 Tex) 792 F2d 531, cert den 479 US 865, 93 L Ed 2d 149, 107 S Ct 220.

The reach of 18 USCS § 844 is broad, applying even to commercial buildings used in activities that have only de minimis effect on interstate commerce. United States v Giordano (CA2 NY) 693 F2d 245.

68. 18 USCS § 844(i).

69. United States v Nashawaty (CA1 Mass) 571 F2d 71 (disagreed with on other grounds by United States v Muzychka (CA3 Pa) 725 F2d 1061, 14 Fed Rules Evid Serv 1538, cert den 467 US 1206, 81 L Ed 2d 348, 104 S Ct 2390).

FIGURE 5-F
AMERICAN JURISPRUDENCE SECOND

31A Am Jur 2d   EXPLOSIONS AND EXPLOSIVES   § 227

4. Dealing in, Buying, Procuring, Selling, Disposing of, or Distributing Explosives [§§ 226, 227]

§ 226. Generally

State provisions sometimes make criminal the disposal or transfer of explosive materials with knowledge, intent, or reason to believe that such materials or compounds are to be used to injure persons or property,[78] as well as the procuring of explosives with the intent to cause unlawful injury or destruction of property.[79] A sale of bombs, the seller having reasonable grounds to believe that the buyer intends an unlawful use, is a violation of law, even though the buyer's intention may be lawful.[80]

Furthermore, state statutory provisions have prohibited as criminal offenses the sale, offering or exposing for sale of fireworks.[81]

In addition, it is a federal offense for any person to barter, sell, or dispose of any explosive materials knowing or having reasonable cause to believe that such materials were stolen.[82]

▌▌▌▌ *Practice guide:* For purposes of a statute making criminal the procuring of explosives with intent to use them for unlawful purposes, the possession thereof with intent to use them for an unlawful purpose gives rise to a presumption that the explosives were procured for that purpose. Under such a statute, the date of procurement is material, and proof of procurement on some date within the statute of limitations is essential. But, where there was no direct evidence concerning the date on which the defendant procured the explosives, it was so highly improbable that possession of a bomb would be retained for more than 3 years—the period of limitations—as to amount to proof that it was in fact procured within that period.[83]

§ 227. Violations of federal licensing, permit, or reporting requirements

Federal provisions, in addition to making the businesses of manufacturing[84] or importing[85] explosives without a license unlawful, makes criminal the

---

78. Johnson v Lee (DC Conn) 281 F Supp 650 (statute making criminal disposal of explosive materials or compounds with knowledge, intent, or reason to believe that such materials or compounds are to be used to injure persons or property); Saunders v State (Del Sup) 275 A2d 564 (statute provided that whoever transfers Molotov cocktail or any other device, instrument or object designed to explode or produce uncontained combustion with intent to cause bodily or physical harm shall be guilty of a felony).

79. People v Catuara, 358 Ill 414, 193 NE 199.

80. People v Ficke, 343 Ill 367, 175 NE 543, holding that defendant's belief that the buyer intended unlawful use was evidenced by the price charged, the clandestine negotiations and methods of delivery, and the form of the bombs, which were apparently handmade and unusual for any lawful business, the buyer's intent (the buyer being employed by the state attorney's office) being immaterial.

81. People v Young, 139 Colo 357, 339 P2d 672; People v Ross (2d Dist) 82 Ill App 3d 158, 37 Ill Dec 509, 402 NE2d 399.

82. 18 USCS § 842(h).

The constitutionality of 18 USCS § 842(h) has been upheld despite its failure to require an evidential nexus between the prescribed activity and interstate commerce. United States v Dawson (CA8 Mo) 467 F2d 668, cert den 410 US 956, 35 L Ed 2d 689, 93 S Ct 1427.

83. People v Catuara, 358 Ill 414, 193 NE 199.

84. § 214.

85. § 228.

FIGURE 5-G
AMERICAN JURISPRUDENCE SECOND

business of dealing in explosive materials without a license,[86] and criminally prohibits the distribution of explosive materials to any person other than a licensee or permittee who the distributor knows or has reasonable cause to believe does not reside in the state in which the distributor resides.[87] Furthermore, it is a federal offense for any licensee—that is, a person who has obtained a license to engage in business of importing, manufacturing, or dealing in explosive materials—to knowingly distribute any explosive materials to any person except: a licensee;[88] a permittee;[89] or a resident of the state where distribution is made and in which the licensee is licensed to do business or a state contiguous thereto if permitted by law of the state of the purchaser's residence.[90] It is also a criminal offense for licensees to distribute explosive materials to persons who the licensee has reason to believe intends to transport such materials into a state where the purchase, possession or use thereof is prohibited or which does not permit its residence to transport or ship materials into or to receive explosive materials in it,[91] or to knowingly distribute explosive materials to particular types of individuals, including persons under 21 years of age,[92] persons under indictment[93] or convicted of a crime punishable by imprisonment for a term exceeding one year,[94] fugitives from justice,[95] unlawful users of specified drugs,[96] and persons who have been adjudicated metal defectives.[97] The statute also makes it unlawful for any licensee knowingly to distribute any explosive materials to any person in any state where the purchase, possession, or use by such person of such materials would be in violation of state law or published ordinance is applicable at the place of distribution,[98] and it is unlawful for a licensee or permittee willfully to purchase or distribute explosive materials without making such records as the secretary of the Treasury or his delegate, by regulation, requires.[99]

5. Transportation of Explosives; Receipt in Commerce [§§ 228–233]

§ 228. Generally

State statutory provisions sometimes make unlawful the transportation of explosive materials or compounds, knowing, intending, or having reason to believe that the same are to be used for the injury of any person or property.[1] Furthermore, under federal law, it is a crime to receive, transport, or ship any

---

86. 18 USCS § 842(a)(1).

87. 18 USCS § 842(a)(3)(B).

88. 18 USCS § 842(b)(1).

89. 18 USCS § 842(b)(2).

90. 18 USCS § 842(b)(3).

91. 18 USCS § 842(c).

92. 18 USCS § 842(d)(1).

93. 18 USCS § 842(d)(3).

94. 18 USCS § 842(d)(2).

▐▌ Observation: A federal statute provides for relief of persons who have been indicted or convicted from the disabilities imposed by statute with respect to their engaging in the business of dealing in explosive materials and in-

curred by reason of such indictment or conviction. 18 USCS § 845(b).

95. 18 USCS § 842(d)(4).

96. 18 USCS § 842(d)(5).

97. 18 USCS § 842(d)(6).

98. 18 USCS § 842(e).

99. 18 USCS § 842(f); 18 USCS § 841(k).

1. Johnson v Lee (DC Conn) 281 F Supp 650; Saunders v State (Del Sup) 275 A2d 564 (statute provided that whoever transports Molotov cocktail or any other device, instrument or object designed to explode or produce uncontained combustion with intent to cause bodily or physical harm shall be guilty of a felony).

566

FIGURE 5-H

AMERICAN JURISPRUDENCE SECOND

for a use prohibited by the laws of such state specifically prohibiting or regulating the use of fireworks.

There is authority for the view that the federal provision making unlawful the transportation of explosives in interstate or foreign commerce with the knowledge or intent that it will be used to intimidate any individual,[29] does not apply to the transportation of firecrackers, insofar as the word "intimidate", as used in the statute, does not encompass an effort to frighten someone with a firecracker.[30] But, on the other hand, there is authority for the view that M-80s and fireworks fall within the statutory definition of "explosives," for purposes of the criminal provisions of the Federal Explosive Control Act.[31]

6. OTHER OFFENSES [§§ 234–237]

§ 234. Encouraging or advocating use of explosives

Statutes in some jurisdictions make criminal conduct either directly or indirectly encouraging, inciting or advocating the use of explosive materials or compounds for the purpose of injuring persons or property, or soliciting or contributing money for any such purpose.[32] Furthermore, federal provisions make it unlawful to teach or demonstrate the use, application, or making of an explosive device, with knowledge or reason to know, or intent that it will be unlawfully employed in, or in furtherance of a civil disorder.[33]

§ 235. Avoiding prosecution or imprisonment for use of explosives

It is a federal offense to travel in interstate or foreign commerce to avoid prosecution or imprisonment for willfully damaging or destroying by explosives any building, structure, or vehicle, or attempting to do so, or to avoid giving testimony in cases arising out of such offenses.[34]

§ 236. Concealment of stolen explosives; failure to report theft or loss

Under federal statute, it is unlawful, subject to criminal penalty, for any person to conceal any explosive materials, knowing or having reasonable cause to believe that such materials were stolen.[35] It is also made unlawful for any person who has knowledge of the theft or loss of any explosive materials from his stock, to fail to report such theft or loss within 24 hours of discovery thereof to the Secretary of the Treasury or his delegate and to appropriate local authorities.[36]

§ 237. Bomb hoaxes, threats, or false reports

It has been made a criminal offense by statute in some states for a person to make a false report, with intent to deceive another, concerning the placing or

---

29. 18 USCS § 844(d), discussed, generally, in § 229.

30. United States v Norton (CA1 Me) 808 F2d 908.

31. § 3.

32. Johnson v Lee (DC Conn) 281 F Supp 650.

33. 18 USCS § 231(a), discussed in 54 Am Jur 2d, MOBS AND RIOTS § 56.

34. 18 USCS § 1074.

35. 18 USCS § 842(h).

The constitutionality of 18 USCS § 842(h) has been upheld despite its failure to require an evidential nexus between the prescribed activity and interstate commerce. United States v Dawson (CA8 Mo) 467 F2d 668, cert den 410 US 956, 35 L Ed 2d 689, 93 S Ct 1427.

36. 18 USCS §§ 841(k) and 842(k).

FIGURE 5-1

AMERICAN JURISPRUDENCE SECOND

DISCUSSION OF PROBLEM 5.4 It appears that Slade may face several potential criminal charges—although it is unclear from *American Jurisprudence Second* the exact terms of the potentially applicable federal statutes and regulations. Remember that while discussion in secondary authority is useful in gaining a broad perspective and for obtaining citations to primary authority, discussion in secondary authorities is not the law and is not binding. You will need to examine and analyze the statutory provisions themselves. Furthermore, no specific references to South Carolina statutes are given. It is clear, however, that state law is likely to provide additional prohibitions potentially affecting Slade's activities.

2. ANNOTATED STATUTES

Instead of starting with a secondary source such as a treatise or legal encyclopedia, researchers will sometimes start their research with annotated versions of the relevant statutes. When will they do so? Generally speaking, they will do so (1) when they have a research lead that points them to a specific statute (or constitutional provision, treaty, or municipal ordinance); and (2) when they are familiar enough with the area of law that beginning with the statutes (or other primary legislative source) is warranted. All state and federal statutes are now available on WESTLAW and LEXIS.[1] As noted in Chapter 1, many law libraries will have federal and state statutory compilations as part of their collections as well.

PROBLEM 5.5 In absence of a specific research lead, the principal approach to annotated statutes will be through the index. Assume, for example, that you want to find provisions of the South Carolina statutes dealing with fireworks and explosives. Examine the entries under the heading "Explosives and Explosions" from the General Index of *Code of Laws of South Carolina 1976 Annotated* reproduced in Figures 5-J and 5-K. What provisions might be applicable to Slade's situation?

---

[1] Computer searches for statutory materials are discussed in Chapters 7 (WESTLAW) and 8 (LEXIS).

SOUTH CAROLINA CODE—1976

962

FIGURE 5-J
CODE OF LAWS OF SOUTH CAROLINA (GENERAL INDEX)

GENERAL INDEX

EXPLOSIVES AND EXPLOSIONS —Cont'd
Fines and penalties—Cont'd
- fake bombs, use of, § 16-11-555
- false statements to obtain insurance benefits for fire or explosion loss, § 16-11-125
- stink bombs, illegal use of, § 16-7-160
Fire Commission, promulgation of regulations by, § 23-36-80
Fire marshal. **Fireworks** (this index)
Fireworks (this index)
Fish and Game (this index)
Infants or minors, no sale of dynamite to person under age twenty-one, § 23-35-170
Instruction, §§ 16-8-20, 16-8-30
Law Enforcement Division, reports and records of sales sent to, § 23-35-170
Liability insurance requirement, § 23-36-40
License and permit requirements, §§ 23-36-40 et seq.
Liquefied petroleum gas explosions, reporting of, § 39-43-140
Local governments, regulation of explosive materials by, § 23-36-150
Making or possession for use in commission of crime, § 16-11-20
Manner in which sold or delivered, § 23-35-170
Misdemeanor, violations as, § 23-35-170
Motor Vehicles (this index)
Municipal regulation of keeping explosives in city limits, § 5-25-50
Nitroglycerin
- crime, making or possession for use in, § 16-11-20
- public utilities, services, and carriers, meaning of term "explosive compound" in connection with, § 58-13-710
Notice of theft, illegal use, or illegal possession of explosive materials, § 23-36-70
Penalties. Fines and penalties, supra
Personal property, damaging or destroying of, § 16-11-540
Possession for use in commission of crime, § 16-11-20
Powerful explosives, sale or delivery of, § 23-35-170
Public buildings, use of explosives in, see lines throughout this topic
Public Utilities, Services and Carriers (this index)
Real property, damaging or destroying of, § 16-11-540
Records and Recording (this index)
Regulation of sale of dynamite and explosives, § 23-35-170
Revocation, suspension, or denial of license or permit, § 23-36-100
Safecracking, use in, § 16-11-390
Sales, reports and records of, § 23-35-170
State parks, unlawful possession of explosives in, § 51-3-145
Stink bombs or tear gas, illegal use in public building, § 16-7-160

EXPLOSIVES AND EXPLOSIONS —Cont'd
Storage
generally, §§ 23-9-40, 23-36-120
- **Fireworks** (this index)
Threatening to kill, injure or intimidate individual or damage or destroy property by means of explosive, § 16-11-550
Transportation
- automobile insurance rate, § 38-73-455
- carriers, generally. **Public Utilities, Services and Carriers** (this index)

EXPORTS
Imports and Exports (this index)

EXPOSITIONS
Fairs and Expositions (this index)

EX POST FACTO LAWS
Prohibited, US Const Art 1 § 9 cl 3, Art 1 § 10 cl 1, SC Const Art 1 § 4

EXPOSURE
Animals (this index)
Health (this index)
Indecent Exposure (this index)

EXPRESS COMPANIES
As to matters pertaining to all types of carriers, see topic **Public Utilities, Services and Carriers**
Conciliation of industrial disputes, chapter not applicable to express companies, § 41-17-30
Public service commission rules and regulations. **Public Utilities, Services and Carriers** (this index)
Taxation (this index)
Workers' compensation, exemption from provisions of Title, § 42-1-350

EXPRESS WARRANTIES
Warranties (this index)

EXPRESSWAYS
Highways and Streets (this index)
Motor Vehicles (this index)

EXPULSION
Banking and Financial Institutions (this index)
Ejection, Eviction, or Ouster (this index)

EXPUNGEMENT
Fraudulent checks, drawing and uttering, § 34-11-90
Suspension of hunting and fishing privileges, expungement of record and points after period of, § 50-9-1070

EX-SHIP DELIVERY OF GOODS
Uniform Commercial Code, § 36-2-322

EXTENSION DIVISION
University of South Carolina (this index)

EXTENSION OF TIME
Answer, time for, § 15-13-310
Civil Procedure, Rules of (this index)
Family Courts Rules (this index)
General Assembly (this index)
Health, certificate of need, § 44-7-210

EXTENSION OF TIME—Cont'd
Taxation, withholding of tax on sale of property by nonresidents, § 12-9-520

EXTENSIONS OR ADDITIONS
Abuse, order of protection from, § 20-4-70
Arbitration (this index)
Business corporations. **Corporations** (this index)
Cable television, issuance of continuing permit, § 58-12-130
Civil remedies and procedures, § 15-3-40
Commercial Code. **Uniform Commercial Code** (this index)
Commercial Paper (this index)
Corporations (this index)
Criminal procedures, extension of order for pen registers and trap and trace devices, § 17-29-30
Dams (this index)
Drainage (this index)
Electric Utilities and Cooperatives (this index)
Employment security. **Labor and Employment** (this index)
Environmental Protection and Conservation (this index)
Family court jurisdiction, § 20-7-420
Governor's Mansion and Lace House, approval of additions to, § 10-3-30
Highways and Streets (this index)
Insurance (this index)
Interchange of governmental employees, length of assignment, § 8-12-20
Landlords' liens, validity of extensions to subsequent purchasers and creditors without notice, § 30-7-10
Liens, §§ 30-7-10, 30-7-60
Local Government (this index)
Mitford Rural Water District of Fairfield and Chester Counties (this index)
Municipal Corporations (this index)
National forest, consent of National Forest Land Board to extension of, § 3-1-450
Neglected or abandoned orchard, removal of, § 46-35-50
Parks, Recreation and Tourism Commission, expansion of park system and recreational areas, § 51-1-60
Personal property, manner and form of recordation of instruments convey an interest in or lien on, § 30-7-80
Physical therapist registration, § 40-45-180
Probate code, personal representative's duties, § 62-3-704
Public Records (this index)
Public Utilities, Services and Carriers (this index)
Railroads (this index)
Retirement Systems (this index)
Revenue Bond Refinancing Act of 1937 (this index)
Rural electric cooperatives, extension of service in city or town after annexation of service area, § 33-49-250
Sewage (this index)
Soil and water conservation districts. **Environmental Protection and Conservation** (this index)

963

FIGURE 5-K
CODE OF LAWS OF SOUTH CAROLINA (GENERAL INDEX)

DISCUSSION OF PROBLEM 5.5 Entries in the General Index provide you with access to the South Carolina statutes dealing with explosives and fireworks. One set of entries leads you to the South Carolina Explosives Control Act (§§ 23-36-10 et seq.) as well as to other

various provisions. The subheading "fireworks" under "EXPLOSIVES AND EXPLOSIONS" directs you in a cross-reference to consult that entry in the General Index.

Section 5D. Reading, Working With, Citing, and Applying Legislative Sources

Secondary sources (such as *American Jurisprudence Second* in the preceding section) and statutory indexes (such as the General Index of the *Code of Laws of South Carolina 1976 Annotated* in the preceding section) have directed you to various federal and state statutes dealing with explosives. An essential part of the research process is reading and analyzing these primary sources and applying them to the facts.

Several mechanical and logical methods exist to help researchers read and understand legislation. These methods, such as key-element listing, flow charts, and logic trees, help researchers identify possible ambiguities. These methods are discussed in detail elsewhere.[2] Closely related to this analysis is the application of legislation. Ordinarily, statutes and other legislation are applied by deductive reasoning. The major premise of the syllogism is typically a rule of law derived from the legislation. Classification of the facts within or outside of the major premise derived from the legislation also plays an important role in the application process. These matters are also discussed in detail elsewhere.[3]

In the context of *Problem 5.1*, assume that you have decided to read §§ 841-848 (importing, manufacturing, distributing, and storing explosive materials) in the *United States Code*. Recall from Chapter 1 that because of the slow distribution of the *United States Statutes at Large* and the *United States Code* and their lack of convenient updating and editorial features, most lawyers consult one of the annotated versions of the *Code*, either West's *United States Code Annotated* (U.S.C.A.) or Lawyers Cooperative's *United States Code Service* (U.S.C.S.).

PROBLEM 5.6 Assume that you have decided to begin reading §§ 841-842 in the *United States Code Service* (reproduced in the following figures). Do any of the provisions appear to be applicable to Slade?

---

[2] See Larry L. Teply, Legal Writing, Analysis, and Oral Argument 215-27 (1990) ("Reading and Analyzing Statutes").

[3] Id. at 227-30 ("Applying Legislation").

The titles in the <u>United States Code</u> are organized into chapters and sections. Only the titles and sections are cited.

General history of this chapter

The text of the statute in the <u>United States Code Service</u> is the same as you would find if you consulted the official version of the <u>United States Code</u>.

Note that companies are included within the definition of "person" for purposes of these provisions.

CHAPTER 40.   IMPORTATION, MANUFACTURE, DISTRIBUTION AND STORAGE OF EXPLOSIVE MATERIALS

HISTORY; ANCILLARY LAWS AND DIRECTIVES

Explanatory notes:
Although the catchline to 18 USCS § 843, as added by Act Oct. 15, 1970, P. L. 91-452, Title XI, § 1102(a), 84 Stat. 955, reads "Licenses and user permits", item 843 as added by said said § 1102(a) reads "Licensing and user permits".

Amendments:
1970. Act Oct. 15, 1970, P. L. 91-452, Title XI, § 1102(a), 84 Stat. 952, added chapter 40 and items 841-848.

CROSS REFERENCES

This chapter is referred to in 42 USCS § 3795.

---

§ 841.   Definitions

As used in this chapter [18 USCS §§ 841 et seq.]—

(a) "Person" means any individual, corporation, company, association, firm, partnership, society, or joint stock company.

(b) "Interstate or foreign commerce" means commerce between any place in a State and any place outside of that State, or within any possession of the United States (not including the Canal Zone) or the District of Columbia, and commerce between places within the same State but through any place outside of that State. "State" includes the District of Columbia, the Commonwealth of Puerto Rico, and the possessions of the United States (not including the Canal Zone).

(c) "Explosive materials" means explosives, blasting agents, and detonators.

(d) Except for the purposes of subsections (d), (e), (f), (g), (h), (i), and (j) of section 844 of this title [18 USCS § 844(d)-(j)], "explosive" means any chemical compound mixture, or device, the primary or common purpose of

453

FIGURE 5-L
UNITED STATES CODE SERVICE

Statutory
definitions
(continued)

Several
titles of
the United
States
Code have
been
reenacted
into positive
law,
including
Title 18.
See 1
U.S.C.A. §
204 (West
1985).
If a title
has been
reenacted,
the wording
of the
United
States Code
will prevail
over the
wording of
the U.S.
Statutes at
Large when
a conflict
between the
two exists.

Citation to
the
original (and
any
amending)
acts in
the U.S.
Statutes
at Large.

18 USCS § 841   CRIMES

which is to function by explosion; the term includes, but is not limited to, dynamite and other high explosives, black powder, pellet powder, initiating explosives, detonators, safety fuses, squibs, detonating cord, igniter cord, and igniters. The Secretary shall publish and revise at least annually in the Federal Register a list of these and any additional explosives which he determines to be within the coverage of this chapter. For the purposes of subsections (d), (e), (f), (g), (h), and (i) of section 844 of this title [18 USCS § 844(d)-(j)], the term "explosive" is defined in subsection (j) of such section 844 [18 USCS § 844(j)].

(e) "Blasting agent" means any material or mixture, consisting of fuel and oxidizer, intended for blasting, not otherwise defined as an explosive: Provided, That the finished product, as mixed for use or shipment, cannot be detonated by means of a numbered 8 test blasting cap when unconfined.

(f) "Detonator" means any device containing a detonating charge that is used for initiating detonation in an explosive; the term includes, but is not limited to, electric blasting caps of instantaneous and delay types, blasting caps for use with safety fuses and detonating-cord delay connectors.

(g) "Importer" means any person engaged in the business of importing or bringing explosive materials into the United States for purposes of sale or distribution.

(h) "Manufacturer" means any person engaged in the business of manufacturing explosive materials for purposes of sale or distribution or for his own use.

(i) "Dealer" means any person engaged in the business of distributing explosive materials at wholesale or retail.

(j) "Permittee" means any user of explosives for a lawful purpose, who has obtained a user permit under the provisions of this chapter [18 USCS §§ 841 et seq.].

(k) "Secretary" means the Secretary of the Treasury or his delegate.

(l) "Crime punishable by imprisonment for a term exceeding one year" shall not mean (1) any Federal or State offenses pertaining to antitrust violations, unfair trade practices, restraints of trade, or other similar offenses relating to the regulation of business practices as the Secretary may be regulation designate, or (2) any State offense (other than one involving a firearm or explosive) classified by the laws of the State as a misdemeanor and punishable by a term of imprisonment of two years or less.

(m) "Licensee" means any importer, manufacturer, or dealer licensed under the provisions of this chapter [18 USCS §§ 841 et seq.].

(n) "Distribute" means sell, issue, give, transfer, or otherwise dispose of. (Added Oct. 15, 1970, P. L. 91-452, Title XI, § 1102(a), 84 Stat. 952.)

454

FIGURE 5-M
UNITED STATES CODE SERVICE

Historical note on § 841

Effective date

Congressional declaration of purpose

The editorial features in the other annotated version (United States Code Annotated) are similar but not identical to the ones shown here. The United States Code Annotated provides cross-references within the West system ("Library references" to West publications and the relevant topic and key number in West digest system).

Explosive Materials   **18 USCS § 841**

HISTORY; ANCILLARY LAWS AND DIRECTIVES

Effective date of section:
Section 1105(a), (b) of Title XI of Act Oct. 15, 1970, P. L. 91-452, 84 Stat. 959, provided: "(a) Except as provided in subsection (b), the provisions of chapter 40 of title 18, United States Code [18 USCS §§ 841 et seq.], as enacted by section 1102 of this title shall take effect one hundred and twenty days after the date of enactment of this Act [enacted Oct. 15, 1970]
"(b) The following sections of chapter 40 of title 18, United States Code [18 USCS §§ 841 et seq.], as enacted by section 1102 of this title shall take effect on the date of the enactment of this Act [enacted Oct. 15, 1970]: sections 841, 844(d), (e), (f), (g), (h), (i), and (j), 845, 846, 847, 848, and 849.". For full classification of this Title and this Act, consult USCS Tables volumes.

Other provisions:
Congressional declaration of purpose. Act Oct. 15, 1970, P. L. 91-452, Title XI, § 1101, 84 Stat. 952, provided: "The Congress hereby declares that the purpose of this title is to protect interstate and foreign commerce against interference and interruption by reducing the hazard to persons and property arising from misuse and unsafe or insecure storage of explosive materials. It is not the purpose of this title to place any undue or unnecessary Federal restrictions or burdens on law-abiding citizens with respect to the acquisition, possession, storage, or use of explosive materials for industrial, mining, agricultural, or other lawful purposes, or to provide for the imposition by Federal regulations of any procedures or requirements other than those reasonably necessary to implement and effectuate the provisions of this title.". For full classification of this Title consult USCS Tables volumes.

Modification of other provisions. Section 1104 of Title XI of Act Oct. 15, 1970, P. L. 91-452, 84 Stat. 959, provided: "Nothing in this title shall be construed as modifying or affecting any provision of—
"(a) The National Firearms Act (chapter 53 of the Internal Revenue Code of 1954) [26 USCS §§ 5801 et seq.];
"(b) Section 414 of the Mutual Security Act of 1954 (22 U.S.C. 1934), as amended, [22 USCS § 1934] relating to munitions control;
"(c) Section 1716 of title 18, United States Code, [18 USCS § 1716] relating to nonmailable materials;
"(d) Sections 831 through 836 of title 18, United States Code [18 USCS §§ 831-836]; or
"(e) Chapter 44 of title 18, United States Code [18 USCS §§ 921 et seq.].". For full classification of this Title consult USCS Tables volumes.

Continuation in business or operation of any person engaged in business or operation on October 15, 1970. Section 1105(c) of Title XI of Act Oct. 15, 1970 P. L. 91-452, 84 Stat. 959, provided: "Any person (as defined in section 841(a) of title 18, United States Code) [18 USCS § 841(a)] engaging in a business or operation requiring a license or permit under the provisions of chapter 40 of such title 18 [18 USCS

455

FIGURE 5-N

UNITED STATES CODE SERVICE

18 USCS § 841   CRIMES

History,
ancillary
laws, and
directives
(continued)

§§ 841 et seq.] who was engaged in such business or operation on the date of enactment of this Act [enacted Oct. 15, 1970] and who has filed an application for a license or permit under the provisions of section 843 of such chapter 40 [18 USCS § 843] prior to the effective date of such section 843 [see Effective date note] may continue such business or operation pending final action on his application. All provisions of such chapter 40 [18 USCS §§ 841 et seq.] shall apply to such applicant in the same manner and to the same extent as if he were a holder of a license or permit under such chapter 40 [18 USCS §§ 841 et seq.].".

Appropriation authorization. Section 1107 of Title XI of Act Oct. 15, 1970 P. L. 91-452, 84 Stat. 960, provided: "There are hereby authorized to be appropriated such sums as are necessary to carry out the purposes of this title.". For full classification of this Title, consult USCS Tables volumes.

Cross-
reference to
the Code of
Federal
Regulations

CODE OF FEDERAL REGULATIONS

Commerce in explosives, 27 CFR Part 181.

CROSS REFERENCES

Cross-
references
to other
provisions

Offenses classified, 18 USCS § 1.
United States defined, 18 USCS § 5.
Interstate commerce and foreign commerce defined, 18 USCS § 10.
Separability of provisions, 18 USCS § 1961 note.

RESEARCH GUIDE

Research
Guide
references

Am Jur:
31 Am Jur 2d, Explosions and Explosives § 125.5.

§ 842.   Unlawful acts

(a) It shall be unlawful for any person—

(1) to engage in the business of importing, manufacturing, or dealing in explosive materials without a license issued under this chapter;

§ 842 (the
principal
substantive
section)

(2) knowingly to withhold information or to make any false or fictitious oral or written statement or to furnish or exhibit any false, fictitious, or misrepresented identification, intended or likely to deceive for the purpose of obtaining explosive materials, or a license, permit, exemption, or relief from disability under the provisions of this chapter; and

(3) other than a licensee or permittee knowingly—

(A) to transport, ship, cause to be transported, or receive in interstate or foreign commerce any explosive materials, except that a person who lawfully purchases explosive materials from a licensee in a State contiguous to the State in which the purchaser resides may ship, transport, or cause to be transported such explosive materials to the State in which he resides and may receive such explosive materials in the State in which he resides, if such transportation, shipment, or receipt is permitted by the law of the State in which he resides; or

456

FIGURE 5-O
UNITED STATES CODE SERVICE

(B) to distribute explosive materials to any person (other than a licensee or permittee) who the distributor knows or has reasonable cause to believe does not reside in the State in which the distributor resides.

(b) It shall be unlawful for any licensee knowingly to distribute any explosive materials to any person except—

(1) a licensee;

(2) a permittee; or

(3) a resident of the State where distribution is made and in which the licensee is licensed to do business or a State contiguous thereto if permitted by the law of the State of the purchaser's residence.

(c) It shall be unlawful for any licensee to distribute explosive materials to any person who the licensee has reason to believe intends to transport such explosive materials into a State where the purchase, possession, or use of explosive materials is prohibited or which does not permit its residents to transport or ship explosive materials into it or to receive explosive materials in it.

(d) It shall be unlawful for any licensee knowingly to distribute explosive materials to any individual who:

(1) is under twenty-one years of age;

(2) has been convicted in any court of a crime punishable by imprisonment for a term exceeding one year;

(3) is under indictment for a crime punishable by imprisonment for a term exceeding one year;

(4) is a fugitive from justice;

(5) is an unlawful user of marihuana (as defined in section 4761 of the Internal Revenue Code of 1954 or any depressant or stimulant drug (as defined in section 201(v) of the Federal Food, Drug, and Cosmetic Act or narcotic drug (as defined in section 4721 (a) of the Internal Revenue Code of 1954); or

(6) has been adjudicated a mental defective.

(e) It shall be unlawful for any licensee knowingly to distribute any explosive materials to any person in any State where the purchase, possession, or use by such person of such explosive materials would be in violation of any State law or any published ordinance applicable at the place of distribution.

(f) It shall be unlawful for any licensee or permittee willfully to manufacture, import, purchase, distribute, or receive explosive materials without making such records as the Secretary may by regulation require, including, but not limited to, a statement of intended use, the name, date, place of birth, social security number or taxpayer identification number, and place of residence of any natural person to whom explosive materials are distributed. If explosive materials are distributed to a corporation or other business entity, such records shall include the identity and principal and

457

§ 842
(continued)

FIGURE 5-P
UNITED STATES CODE SERVICE

18 USCS § 842   CRIMES

local places of business and the name, date, place of birth, and place of residence of the natural person acting as agent of the corporation or other business entity in arranging the distribution.

§ 842
(continued)

(g) It shall be unlawful for any licensee or permittee knowingly to make any false entry in any record which he is required to keep pursuant to this section or regulations promulgated under section 847 of this title [18 USCS § 847].

(h) It shall be unlawful for any person to receive, conceal, transport, ship, store, barter, sell, or dispose of any explosive materials knowing or having reasonable cause to believe that such explosive materials were stolen.

(i) It shall be unlawful for any person—
     (1) who is under indictment for, or who has been convicted in any court of, a crime punishable by imprisonment for a term exceeding one year;
     (2) who is a fugitive from justice;
     (3) who is an unlawful user of or addicted to marihuana (as defined in section 4761 of the Internal Revenue Code of 1954) or any depressant or stimulant drug (as defined in section 201(v) of the Federal Food, Drug, and Cosmetic Act or narcotic drug (as defined in section 4731(a) of the Internal Revenue Code of 1954); or
     (4) who has been adjudicated as a mental defective or who has been committed to a mental institution;

to ship or transport any explosive in interstate or foreign commerce or to receive any explosive which has been shipped or transported in interstate or foreign commerce.

(j) It shall be unlawful for any person to store any explosive material in a manner not in conformity with regulations promulgated by the Secretary. In promulgating such regulations, the Secretary shall take into consideration the class, type, and quantity of explosive materials to be stored, as well as the standards of safety and security recognized in the explosives industry.

Citation to the original (and any amending) acts in the <u>U.S.</u> <u>Statutes</u> <u>at Large</u>.

(k) It shall be unlawful for any person who has knowledge of the theft or loss of any explosive materials from his stock, to fail to report such theft or loss within twenty-four hours of discovery thereof, to the Secretary and to appropriate local authorities.

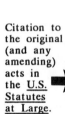 (Added Oct. 15, 1970, P. L. 91-452, Title XI, § 1102(a), 84 Stat. 953.)

HISTORY; ANCILLARY LAWS AND DIRECTIVES

History, ancillary laws and directives for § 842

References in text:
"Section 4761 of the Internal Revenue Code of 1954", referred to in subsecs. (d)(5) and (i)(3), was classified as 26 USCS § 4761, and repealed by Act Oct. 27, 1970, P. L. 91-513, Title III, § 1101(b)(3)(A), 84 Stat. 1292.

"Section 201(v) of the Federal Food, Drug, and Cosmetic Act", referred to in subsecs. (d)(5) and (i)(3), was classified as 21 USCS

FIGURE 5-Q
UNITED STATES CODE SERVICE

References for § 842

Pleading and practice forms

Notes of decisions provide you with access to decisions interpreting this section.

EXPLOSIVE MATERIALS   **18 USCS § 842, n 2**

§ 321(v), and was repealed by Act Oct. 27, 1970, P. L. 91-513, Title II, § 701(a), 84 Stat. 1281.

"Section 4721(a) of the Internal Revenue Code of 1954", referred to in subsec. (d)(5), probably was intended to refer to section 4731(a) of the Internal Revenue Code of 1954, which was classified as 26 USCS § 4731(a), and was repealed by Act Oct. 27, 1970, P. L. 91-513, Title III, § 1101(b)(3)(A), 84 Stat. 1292.

"Section 4731(a) of the Internal Revenue Code of 1954", referred to in subsec. (i)(3), was classified as 26 USCS § 4731(a), and was repealed by Act Oct. 27, 1970, P. L. 91-513, Title III, § 1101(b)(3)(A), 84 Stat. 1292.

Effective date of section:

This section became effective 120 days after Oct. 15, 1970; see Effective date note under 18 USCS § 841.

CODE OF FEDERAL REGULATIONS

Commerce in explosives, 27 CFR Part 181.

CROSS REFERENCES

United States defined, 18 USCS § 5.
Department and agency defined, 18 USCS § 6.
Penalties for violation of this section, 18 USCS § 844.
This section is referred to in 18 USCS §§ 843, and 844.

RESEARCH GUIDE

Forms:

Complaint in federal court for unlawful transporting, handling, and storing of explosives, 10 Am Jur Pl & Pr Forms (Rev ed), Explos, Form 45.

Allegation in complaint under Jones Act for injury resulting from carriage of prohibited cargo, 11 Am Jur Pl & Pr Forms (Rev ed), FELA, Form 155.1 (supp).

INTERPRETIVE NOTES AND DECISIONS

1. Constitutionality
2. Relationship with other laws
3. Knowledge
4. Defenses
5. Evidence
6. Instructions
7. Stipulation to prior conviction
8. Expungement of prior conviction
9. Mistrial

1. Constitutionality

Since defendant failed even to suggest that his own conduct fell within either of hypothetical situations which he urged as showing that 18 USCS § 842 was overbroad and in view of trial court's instruction requiring proof of willfulness, it was clear that § 842 had operated constitutionally in his particular case; § 842 was not rendered invalid where Congress failed to specify manner in which misuse of explosives affects interest in commerce when there was a rational basis for determining that the misuse of explosive materials is one act of a class of activity which affects commerce. United States v Dawson (1972, CA8 Mo) 467 F2d 668, cert den 410 US 956, 35 L Ed 2d 689, 93 S Ct 1427.

2. Relationship with other laws

Defendant could not be prosecuted under 18 USCS § 842(a)(3) for transporting explosives across state lines without a permit required by law, because of the explicit exception in 18

459

FIGURE 5-R

UNITED STATES CODE SERVICE

18 USCS § 842, n 2 CRIMES

Notes of
decisions
(continued)

USCS § 845(a)(1) to § 842's application; explosives are regulated by the administrator of the Federal Aviation Administration, an agency of the Department of Transportation, in regard to their transportation by air. United States v Illingworth (1973, CA10 Colo) 489 F2d 264.

3. Knowledge

Although 18 USCS § 842(a)(3)(A) requires that the violator "knowingly" transport explosives in interstate commerce, nevertheless there is no requirement that violator know that such transportation violates federal statute. United States v Franks (1975, CA6 Tenn) 511 F2d 25, cert den 422 US 1042, 45 L Ed 2d 693, 95 S Ct 2654, 2656, and cert den 422 US 1048, 45 L Ed 2d 701, 95 S Ct 2667 and (disagreed with on other grounds United States v McDaniel, 176 App DC 60, 538 F2d 408).

4. Defenses

Neither double jeopardy clause of Fifth Amendment and Fourteenth Amendment nor doctrine of collateral estoppel foreclosed prosecution by Federal Government of defendant for possession and illegal transfer of sawed-off shotgun and unlawful receipt of dynamite and state prosecution for sale of cocaine, even though sales of dynamite and cocaine were contemporaneous and were made to same person; since federal funds were used in purchase of firearm and dynamite, and state funds were used for purchase of cocaine, it was not irrational or essentially manipulative for prosecution to be separated on such basis, as sales comprised essentially two acts. United States v Worth (1974, CA10 Kan) 505 F2d 1206, cert den 420 US 964, 43 L Ed 2d 443, 95 S Ct 1358.

5. Evidence

Evidence that phone call to defendant meant only car trouble, but another defendant's name and "the stuff", that two calls, 15 minutes apart, were required to get defendant to come to motel, and that defendant came armed, and hailed by police after caller had entered defendant's car with pills, defendant fled, firing shot behind him and tried to clear impassable ditch in car, supported conviction for smuggling benzadrine and dexedrine tablets into United States and conspiracy to commit that offense. United States v Sullivan (1971, CA5 Tex) 443 F2d 813, cert den 404 US 861, 30 L Ed 2d 105, 92 S Ct 163.

Since in order to prove a violation of 18 USCS § 842(h), the government had to show that defendants knew or had reasonable cause to believe that the blasting caps were stolen, evidence that defendants committed burglary of blasting caps

from a construction company's magazine was properly admissible as proof of scienter required by § 842(h). United States v Lewis (1974, CA6 Ky) 504 F2d 92, cert den 421 US 975, 44 L Ed 2d 466, 95 S Ct 1974.

Where defendant was charged with possession and illegal transfer of sawed-off shotgun and unlawful receipt of dynamite, and was charged in state court with sale of cocaine, and where sales had been to same government informant within few days of each other, evidence of sale of cocaine was directly relevant to contemporaneous dynamite sale and, in view of defense of entrapment, to predisposition of defendant to commit each of offenses charged in federal indictment. United States v Worth (1974, CA10 Kan) 505 F2d 1206, cert den 420 US 964, 43 L Ed 2d 443, 95 S Ct 1358.

Evidence that defendant gave explosive devices to one he knew will cross state lines was sufficient to show that he "caused" the interstate transportation of such devices within meaning of 18 USCS § 842(a)(3)(A). United States v Franks (1975, CA6 Tenn) 511 F2d 25, cert den 422 US 1042, 45 L Ed 2d 693, 95 S Ct 2654, 2656, and cert den 422 US 1048, 45 L Ed 2d 701, 95 S Ct 2667 and (disagreed with United States v McDaniel 176 App DC 60, 538 F2d 408).

Evidence in prosecution for interstate transportation of explosive materials was sufficient to support finding that defendant took part in transporting dynamite between New Hampshire and Vermont. United States v Harvey (1975, CA2 Vt) 526 F2d 529, cert den 424 US 956, 47 L Ed 2d 362, 96 S Ct 1432.

Testimony from National Guard officer that removal of ordnance materials from guard posts was not authorized was sufficient to permit defendant's conviction for illegal possession of unregistered and improperly identified firearms and unlawful storage of explosive materials, over his argument that he came into possession of materials legally while on active duty as member of National Guard. United States v Crumpler (1976, CA5 Tex) 536 F2d 1063, cert den 429 US 1039, 50 L Ed 2d 750, 97 S Ct 736.

Jury could validly infer that explosives were stolen from concealment of explosives in defendant's basement, lack of evidence of purchase, and evidence concerning lack of alternative available sources for such explosives. Ramos Colon v United States Attorney (1978, CA1 Puerto Rico) 576 F2d 1.

6. Instructions

Where unlawful entrapment was principal defense made to charges of selling, storing and disposing of stolen explosive materials knowing

FIGURE 5-S
UNITED STATES CODE SERVICE

DISCUSSION OF PROBLEM 5.6 Section 842 establishes criminal liability in several situations. For example, subsection (b) prohibits any licensee (defined to include manufacturers, dealers, and importers in § 841(m)) from distributing (defined to include gifts or other transfers in addition to sales in § 841(n)) to any person except "(1) a licensee; (2) a permittee; or (3) a resident of the State where distribution is made and in which the licensee is licensed to do business or a State contiguous thereto . . . ." Since the "freedom fighters" are not "permitees" ("any user of explosives for a lawful purpose who has obtained a user permit under the provisions of this chapter"), licensees, or "residents" (?) of the state, Slade's transfer appears to violate this provision. Furthermore, because Slade's activities have been kept secret, Slade may have violated the record-keeping and reporting provisions.

CITING PROVISIONS IN THE UNITED STATES CODE AND ITS ANNOTATED VERSIONS

According to *Bluebook* Rule 12, provisions in the *United States Code* should be cited as follows:

(1) Cite the *United States Code* by title, section, and edition or supplement date. Include the supplement number of the official version of the *Code* if you are citing it. Include the publisher's name (West or Law. Co-op.) if you are citing an unofficial version. *See Bluebook* Table T.1: United States Jurisdiction, Federal. Give the name and original section number only if the statute is commonly cited that way or the information would otherwise aid in identification. Bluebook Rules 12.2 and 12.3.

(2) Statutes no longer in force to the current *Code* if they still appear therein. Otherwise, cite them to the *U.S. Statutes at Large* or another secondary source. *Bluebook* Rule 12.2.1 In any event, indicate parenthetically that they are no longer in force (e.g., repealed 1992) or add a full citation to the repealing statutes, introduced by "repealed by." *Bluebook* Rule 12.6.1.

(3) Cite consecutive sections or subsections of a statute by inclusive numbers. Identical digits or letters may be omitted when they are preceded by a punctuation mark

---

**CITING PROVISIONS IN THE UNITED STATES CODE
AND ITS ANNOTATED VERSIONS (CONTINUED)**

"unless doing so would create confusion"; all other digits should be retained. *Bluebook* Rule 3.4(b) (discussing the citation of multiple sections and subsections).

    (4) The current Internal Revenue Code (I.R.C.) is often cited as a separate codification even though it does appear in Title 26 of the *United States Code*. In memoranda and briefs, citations to the current Internal Revenue Code may omit the date and the publisher's name. *See Bluebook* Rule 12.8.1 and Practitioners' Notes P.5.

    PROBLEM 5.7 Assume that you want to cite sections 841 and 842 reproduced in the preceding figures in *Bluebook* form. Assume that the copyright date of the volume of Lawyers Cooperative's *United States Code Service* in which the section appears is 1979. Which of the following citations would be correct?

    (a)   18 U.S.C.S. § 841, § 842 (1979).
    (b)   18 U.S.C.S. §§ 841-842 (1979).
    (c)   18 U.S.C.S. §§ 841-42 (1979).
    (d)   18 USCS §§ 841-842 (1979).
    (e)   18 U.S.C.S. §§ 841-842 (Law. Co-op. 1979).
    (f)   18 U.S.C.S. §§ 841-42 (Law. Co-op. 1979).
    (g)   18 USCS §§ 841-842 (Law Co-op 1979).

    DISCUSSION OF PROBLEM 5.7 The *Bluebook* requires the publisher's name (West or Law. Co-op.) be included if you are citing an unofficial version of the *United States Code*. Because that reference is omitted from the first three answers, those answers are incorrect. Answers (d) and (g) do not use proper abbreviations. Furthermore, *The Bluebook* states that consecutive sections or subsections of a statute should be cited by inclusive numbers (§§ 841-842). Identical digits or letters may be omitted when they are preceded by a punctuation mark. In this instance, there is no punctuation mark in the designation of the provision. Thus, answer (e) is correct.

    PROBLEM 5.8 The text of § 844 in West's *United States Code Annotated* is shown in the following figures. Are there significant penalties for violation of federal law relating to explosives?

18 § 843 CRIMES Pt. 1

Historical Note

References in Text. Sections 701 to 706 of title 5, United States Code, referred to in subsec. (e)(2), are sections 701 to 706 of Title 5, Government Organization and Employees.

Effective Date. Section effective 120 days after Oct. 15, 1970, see section 1105(a) of Pub.L. 91–452, set out as a note under section 841 of this title.

Continuation in Business or Operation of Any Person Engaged in Business or Operation on October 15, 1970. Filing of application for a license or permit prior to the effective date of this section as authorizing any person engaged in a business or operation requiring a license or a permit on Oct. 15, 1970 to continue such business or operation pending final action on such application, see section 1105(c) of Pub.L. 91–452, set out as a note under section 841 of this title.

Legislative History. For legislative history and purpose of Pub.L. 91–452, see 1970 U.S.Code Cong. and Adm.News, p. 4007.

Library References

Explosives ☞4. C.J.S. Explosives § 4 et seq.

West's Federal Forms

Enforcement and review of decisions and orders of administrative agencies, see § 851 et seq.

§ 844
(another
key part
of the
statutes)

§ 844. Penalties

(a) Any person who violates subsections (a) through (i) of section 842 of this chapter shall be fined not more than $10,000 or imprisoned not more than ten years, or both.

(b) Any person who violates any other provision of section 842 of this chapter shall be fined not more than $1,000 or imprisoned not more than one year, or both.

(c) Any explosive materials involved or used or intended to be used in any violation of the provisions of this chapter or any other rule or regulation promulgated thereunder or any violation of any criminal law of the United States shall be subject to seizure and forfeiture, and all provisions of the Internal Revenue Code of 1954 relating to the seizure, forfeiture, and disposition of firearms, as defined in section 5845(a) of that Code, shall, so far as applicable, extend to seizures and forfeitures under the provisions of this chapter.

(d) Whoever transports or receives, or attempts to transport or receive, in interstate or foreign commerce any explosive with the knowledge or intent that it will be used to kill, injure, or intimidate any individual or unlawfully to damage or destroy any building, vehicle, or other real or personal property, shall be imprisoned for not more than ten years, or fined not more than $10,000, or both; and if personal injury results shall be imprisoned for not more than twenty years or fined not more than $20,000, or both; and if death results, shall be subject to imprisonment for any term of years, or to the death penalty or to life imprisonment as provided in section 34 of this title.

(e) Whoever, through the use of the mail, telephone, telegraph, or other instrument of commerce, willfully makes any threat, or mali-

116

FIGURE 5–T
UNITED STATES CODE ANNOTATED

Ch. 40   EXPLOSIVE MATERIALS   **18 § 844**

ciously conveys false information knowing the same to be false, concerning an attempt or alleged attempt being made, or to be made, to kill, injure, or intimidate any individual or unlawfully to damage or destroy any building, vehicle, or other real or personal property by means of an explosive shall be imprisoned for not more than five years or fined not more than $5,000, or both.

(f) Whoever maliciously damages or destroys, or attempts to damage or destroy, by means of an explosive, any building, vehicle, or other personal or real property in whole or in part owned, possessed, or used by, or leased to, the United States, any department or agency thereof, or any institution or organization receiving Federal financial assistance shall be imprisoned for not more than ten years, or fined not more than $10,000, or both; and if personal injury results shall be imprisoned for not more than twenty years, or fined not more than $20,000, or both; and if death results shall be subject to imprisonment for any term of years, or to the death penalty or to life imprisonment as provided in section 34 of this title.

(g) Whoever possesses an explosive in any building in whole or in part owned, possessed, or used by, or leased to, the United States or any department or agency thereof, except with the written consent of the agency, department, or other person responsible for the management of such building, shall be imprisoned for not more than one year, or fined not more than $1,000, or both.

(h) Whoever—

(1) uses an explosive to commit any felony which may be prosecuted in a court of the United States, or

(2) carries an explosive unlawfully during the commission of any felony which may be prosecuted in a court of the United States,

shall be sentenced to a term of imprisonment for not less than one year nor more than ten years. In the case of his second or subsequent conviction under this subsection, such person shall be sentenced to a term of imprisonment for not less than five years nor more than twenty-five years, and, notwithstanding any other provision of law, the court shall not suspend the sentence of such person or give him a probationary sentence.

(i) Whoever maliciously damages or destroys, or attempts to damage or destroy, by means of an explosive, any building, vehicle, or other real or personal property used in interstate or foreign commerce or in any activity affecting interstate or foreign commerce shall be imprisoned for not more than ten years or fined not more than $10,000, or both; and if personal injury results shall be imprisoned for not more than twenty years or fined not more than $20,000, or both; and if death results shall also be subject to imprisonment for any term of years, or to the death penalty or to life imprisonment as provided in section 34 of this title.

117

§ 844
(continued)

FIGURE 5-U
UNITED STATES CODE ANNOTATED

§ 844
(continued)

Note the differences in format and editorial features between West's United States Code Annotated and Lawyers Cooperative's United States Code Service.

---

18 § 844   CRIMES   **Pt. 1**
Note I

(j) For the purposes of subsections (d), (e), (f), (g), (h), and (i) of this section, the term "explosive" means gunpowders, powders used for blasting, all forms of high explosives, blasting materials, fuzes (other than electric circuit breakers), detonators, and other detonating agents, smokeless powders, other explosive or incendiary devices within the meaning of paragraph (5) of section 232 of this title, and any chemical compounds, mechanical mixture, or device that contains any oxidizing and combustible units, or other ingredients, in such proportions, quantities, or packing that ignition by fire, by friction, by concussion, by percussion, or by detonation of the compound, mixture, or device or any part thereof may cause an explosion.

Added Pub.L. 91–452, Title XI, § 1102(a), Oct. 15, 1970, 84 Stat. 956.

Historical Note

References in Text. The Internal Revenue Code of 1954, referred to in subsec. (c), is set out as Title 26, Internal Revenue Code.

Section 5845(a) of that Code, referred to in subsec. (c), is section 5845(a) of Title 26.

Effective Date. Subsecs. (a) to (c) of this section effective 120 days after Oct.

15, 1970, and subsecs. (d) to (j) of this section effective on Oct. 15, 1970, see section 1105(a), (b), set out as a note under section 841 of this title.

Legislative History. For legislative history and purpose of Pub.L. 91–452, see 1970 U.S.Code Cong. and Adm.News, p. 4007.

Library References

Explosives ☞4.

C.J.S. Explosives § 4 et seq.

West's Federal Forms

Information, see § 7181.
Sentence and fine, see § 7531 et seq.

Notes of Decisions

Bill of particulars 9
Defenses 11
Discovery and inspection 12
Evidence 14
Findings 16
Harmless or prejudicial error 18
Indictment 8
Inferences 13
Instructions 15
Jurisdiction 7
Knowledge 5
Mistrial 17
Organizations within section 3
Power of Congress 2
Prejudicial error 18
Purpose 1
Separate offenses 6
Separate trials 10
Threats 4

---

1. Purpose

This section making it a federal offense to use explosives against any organization receiving federal financial assistance was intended to cover the bombings of any real or personal property of any institution receiving federal financial assistance in whatever capacity, for whatever purpose, and in whatever amount. U. S. v. Brown, D.C.Mich.1974, 384 F. Supp. 1151.

2. Power of Congress

Congress had power to enact this section making it a crime to destroy or damage property used in interstate or foreign commerce. U. S. v. Keen, C.A. Wash.1974, 508 F.2d 986, certiorari denied 95 S.Ct. 1655, 421 U.S. 929, 44 L.Ed.2d 86.

Where the federal government has no property interest in a planned parenthood league or in any of the league's property and the sole interest of the federal government is in the partial funding of the league's programs, application of this section making it a federal offense

118

FIGURE 5-V
UNITED STATES CODE ANNOTATED

DISCUSSION OF PROBLEM 5.8 Section 844 provides significant penalties for violation of federal law relating to explosives. The penalties range from fines and imprisonment for violation of section 842 to the death penalty for violation of §§ 844(d), (f), and (i). Section 844(c) provides for seizure and forfeiture of explosives involved, used, or intended to be used in violation of federal law.

CITING STATE STATUTORY CODES

Citations of state statutes follow the same basic rules that were outlined for federal statutes.

In general, cite state statutes to the current official code (if available) or to a current unofficial code, session laws, legislative advance sheets, or other available sources. Cite codified provisions by section numbers (title or chapter designations are also used when necessary to identify the particular section), but session laws usually are cited by page number. Follow the abbreviations and include the publisher as provided in Table T.1 *The Bluebook*.

The appropriate subject-matter code should be included in the citation of subject-matter codes. The various abbreviations of the subject-matter codes are set forth in Table T.1.

For codified state statutes, give (1) the year that appears on the spine of the volume, (2) the year that appears on the title page, or (3) the latest copyright year, in that order of preference. If the volume is a "replacement" of an earlier edition, the date of the replacement volume is used, not the year of the original. If the date on the spine or title page spans more than one year, all years are given (e.g., 1991-1992). *Bluebook* Rule 12.3.2.

Some state codifications are in looseleaf form. In citing those codifications, use (1) the date on the page on which the material is printed or (2) the date on the first page of the subdivision within which the cited material appears, if any, in that order of preference (in lieu of the dates stated above). *Bluebook* Rule 12.3.2.

Examine the provision of the *Code of Laws of South Carolina 1976 Annotated* published by Lawyers Cooperative in Figure 5-W.

As indicated in the background reading in American Jurisprudence Second, states also have laws regulating the sale and delivery of explosives. States impose recordkeeping and reporting requirements as well.

§ 23–35–160   LAW ENFORCEMENT AND PUBLIC SAFETY

For a local law making it unlawful to use truck or trailer for storing or selling fireworks in Charleston County, see Local Law Index.

For a local law requiring written permission of governing body for discharge of fireworks after a certain time in Georgetown County, see Local Law Index.

§ 23–35–170. Manner in which powerful explosives shall be sold or delivered; reports; penalties.

No person shall sell, deliver or dispose of dynamite or similar powerful explosives, except ordinary gunpowder, unless such person knows the purchaser or the person to receive such explosive and is satisfied that the explosive is not to be used for killing fish, and then only upon a written application from the person desiring to purchase, stating the purpose for which he desires to use such explosives. A person selling, delivering or disposing of such explosives shall keep a book in which shall be recorded the name of the purchaser or person to whom the explosive is delivered, the quantity sold or so delivered and the date of such sale or delivery. No sale shall be made to a person under the age of eighteen or a person who has been convicted of a felony. Such person selling or keeping for sale the explosives mentioned in this section shall make sworn quarterly reports of such sales, the name and race of the purchaser, the amount sold and the date of sale to the county auditor of each county. The auditor of each county shall forward a copy of all reports to the South Carolina Law Enforcement Division. Any person violating this section shall be guilty of a misdemeanor, punishable by fine not to exceed one hundred dollars or imprisonment not to exceed thirty days.

History of this provision ➤

HISTORY: 1962 Code § 66-4; 1952 Code § 66-4; 1942 Code § 1304; 1932 Code § 1304; Cr. C. '22 § 197; Cr. C. '12 § 491; 1903 (24) 124; 1971 (57) 887; 1976 Act No. 695 § 1.

Related Local Laws—

For a local law to as to operating a filling station within 100 feet of school or church in Union County, see Local Law Index.

Research and Practice References—

2 Am Jur Proof of Facts, Blasting, Proof No. 1 (testimony of expert as to damage by blasting).

ALR and L Ed Annotations—

Meaning of term "explosive" within 18 USCS § 844(i) prohibiting damage for destruction of property used in interstate commerce by means of explosive. 61 ALR Fed 899.

Admissibility, in trial for federal offense involving malicious use of explosives (under 18 USCS § 844), of evidence of taggants embedded in explosives. 70 ALR Fed 906.

338

FIGURE 5-W

CODE OF LAWS OF SOUTH CAROLINA 1976 ANNOTATED

PROBLEM 5.9 Assume that you want to cite section 23-35-170 in *Bluebook* form. The date on the spine and title page of the bound volume containing this section is "Revised 1989"; the copyright date for the volume is 1989. Which one of the following citations would be correct?

> (a) S.C. Code Ann. § 23-35-10 (Law. Co-op. 1989).
> (b) S.C. Code Ann. § 23-35-10 (Law. Co-op. 1976).
> (c) SC Code Ann § 23-35-10 (Law Co-op 1989).
> (d) 23 SC Code Ann § 10 (Law Co-op 1976).

DISCUSSION OF PROBLEM 5.9 The *Code of Laws of South Carolina 1976 Annotated* is a bound replacement volume. The year on the spine of the volume ("Revised 1989") is the year which should be used rather than the original year (1976). The first answer is thus correct. Answers (c) and (d) do not properly designate the *Code*; nor does answer (d) properly designate the section.

The facts of *Problem 5.1* raised a possible charge of treason. Investigation of this charge involves, in part, a constitutional dimension.[4] You may recall that a provision of the United States Constitution defines treason and limits proof of the crime in certain ways. Assume that you want to find this provision. The United States Constitution can be found in several publications. One of the best publications for legal research purposes is West's *United States Code Annotated* (17 volumes covering the Constitution). The constitutional volumes of Lawyers Cooperative's *United States Code Service* are also a good source. These two sets provide references to cases that have interpreted a constitutional provision. Another good source is *The Constitution of the United States of America* prepared by the Library of Congress' Congressional Research Service.[5]

PROBLEM 5.10 Slade believes that treason cannot occur because the attacks took place outside the United States and were directed against another government. Examine the following text and notes of decisions. Does Slade appear to be correct?

---

[4] Recall from Chapter 1 that a constitution establishes the structure and powers of a government. The United States Constitution is "the supreme law of the land," and any federal law, state constitutional provision, state law, or judicial decision conflicting with it is invalid. See supra § 1D(2)(a)(i) ("Constitutions as Sources of Law").

[5] For research on the original meaning of federal constitutional provisions, M. Farrand's The Records of the Federal Convention of 1789 and J. Elliot's The Debates in the Several State Conventions of the Adoption of the Federal Constitution Together with the Journal of the Federal Convention (variously titled and generally known as "Elliot's Debates") are recommended. Other sources can be found through the card catalog.

The provision(s) of the United States Constitution dealing with treason could be found by consulting the index or by using a topic method of search.

Art. 3 TREASON   **Sec. 3, cl. 1**

Right of a defendant to be tried in the district in which the crime was committed is a privilege that may be waived by failure to make timely objection. U.S. v. Polin, C.A.N.J.1963, 323 F.2d 549.

Rule 20, Federal Rules of Criminal Procedure, 18 U.S.C.A., under which defendant consented to transfer of case to another district for plea and sentence does not violate this clause relating to place of trial on theory that jurisdictional limitations may not be waived, and hence conviction pursuant to such consent was valid. Hilderbrand v. U.S., C.A. Kan.1962, 304 F.2d 716.

Where federal indictment was returned in Kentucky, and case was transferred to Tennessee, and accused pleaded guilty, accused waived his privilege under this clause and Amend. 6, to be tried by jury in state where crime was committed, and sentence under judgment entered on guilty plea would not be vacated. Earnest v. U.S., C.A.Tenn. 1952, 198 F.2d 561.

Rule 20, Federal Rules of Criminal Procedure, 18 U.S.C.A., permitting a defendant who is arrested in a district other than that in which indictment is pending, to consent to disposition of case, upon a plea of guilty, in district of arrest, only upon express written waiver, does not violate constitutional right to trial in district in which offense has been committed. U.S. v. Gallagher, C.A. N.J.1950, 183 F.2d 342, certiorari denied 71 S.Ct. 283, 340 U.S. 913, 95 L.Ed. 659.

This provision respecting place of criminal trials is a "personal privilege" which may be waived. Mahaffey v. Hudspeth, C.C.A.Kan.1942, 128 F.2d 940, certiorari denied 63 S.Ct. 76, 317 U.S. 666, 87 L.Ed. 535.

The jurisdictional requirement of this clause that trial of all crimes shall be held in state where crime was committed may not be waived by any action of defendant or rendered inoperative by any action of court in disregard of such requirement. U.S. v. Holdsworth, D.C. Me.1949, 9 F.R.D. 198, appeal dismissed 179 F.2d 933.

The principal constitutional provision (Article III, § 2, cl. 1) dealing with treason

Section 3, Clause 1. Treason

Section 3. Treason against the United States, shall consist only in levying War against them, or in adhering to their Enemies, giving them Aid and Comfort. No Person shall be convicted of Treason unless on the Testimony of two Witnesses to the same overt Act, or on Confession in open Court.

CROSS REFERENCES

Treason as ground for impeachment and removal of President, Vice President, and civil officers of United States, see section 4 of Art. 2.

Library references

LIBRARY REFERENCES

American Digest System

Evidence required to convict of treason, see Treason ⊂⇒13.
General nature and constitutional provisions as to treason, see Treason ⊂⇒1, 2.

Encyclopedias

Constitutional definition of treason, see C.J.S. Treason §§ 1, 2.
Constitutional requirement of evidence, see C.J.S. Treason § 13.

Texts and Treatises

Special verdicts, limited use of, see Criminal Procedure § 23.7.
Treason and corruption of blood, see Rotunda, Nowak & Young, Treatise on Constitutional Law: Substance and Procedure §§ 6.14 to 6.16.
Ultimate remedy: impeachment for high crimes and misdemeanors, see Tribe, American Constitutional Law § 4–16.

255

FIGURE 5-X

UNITED STATES CODE ANNOTATED

Sec. 3, cl. 1 THE JUDICIARY **Art. 3**

The "Notes of Decisions" will help you understand the meaning and application of this provision.

This internal index directs you to the topic covered in each note.

WESTLAW ELECTRONIC RESEARCH

See WESTLAW guide following the Explanation pages of this volume.

NOTES OF DECISIONS

Abuse of American prisoners, aid and comfort to enemies 13
Adherence to enemy 9
Aid and comfort to enemies
    Generally 10
    Abuse of American prisoners 13
    Delivery of prisoners 14
    Escape of captured enemies 15
    Intent generally 11
    Overt acts generally 12
    Speeches 16
Assembly of force, levying war against United States 6
Confession in open court, proof for conviction of treason 19
Conspiracy, levying war against United States 7
Delivery of prisoners, aid and comfort to enemies 14
Enemies within clause 3
Escape of captured enemies, aid and comfort to enemies 15
Intent generally, aid and comfort to enemies 11
Levying war against United States
    Generally 5
    Assembly of force 6
    Conspiracy 7
    Use of force 8
Overt acts generally, aid and comfort to enemies 12
Place of act 4
Power of Congress 1
Proof for conviction of treason
    Generally 17
    Confession in open court 19
    Testimony of two witnesses 18
Speeches, aid and comfort to enemies 16
Syndicalism 20
Testimony of two witnesses, proof for conviction of treason 18
Treason defined 2
Use of force, levying war against United States 8

1. Power of Congress

Under this clause, Congress has power to punish treason committed abroad. Chandler v. U.S., C.A.Mass.1948, 171 F.2d 921, certiorari denied 69 S.Ct. 640, 336 U.S. 918, 93 L.Ed. 1081, rehearing denied 69 S.Ct. 809, 336 U.S. 947, 93 L.Ed. 1103.

This clause defining treason has left no room for constructive treason, and Congress could not and has not undertaken to restrict or enlarge the definition. Stephan v. U.S., C.C.A.Mich.1943, 133 F.2d 87, certiorari denied 63 S.Ct. 858, 318 U.S. 781, 87 L.Ed. 1148, rehearing denied 63 S.Ct. 1172, 319 U.S. 783, 87 L.Ed. 1727.

Congress can neither extend, nor restrict, nor define the crime of treason; its power over the subject is limited to prescribing the punishment. U.S. v. Greathouse, C.C.Cal.1863, 4 Sawy., U.S., 457, 26 Fed.Cas. No. 15,254. See, also, U.S. v. Hoxie, C.C.Vt.1808, 1 Paine, U.S., 265, 26 Fed.Cas. No. 15,407; U.S. v. Fries, C.C.Pa.1799, 3 Dall. 515, 9 Fed.Cas. No. 5,126.

2. Treason defined

Treason is a breach of allegiance, and can be committed by him who owes allegiance either perpetual or temporary. U.S. v. Wiltberger, Pa.1820, 18 U.S. 76, 5 Wheat. 76, 5 L.Ed. 37. See, also, Charge to Grand Jury, C.C.Pa.1851, 2 Wall.Jr., C.C., 134, 30 Fed.Cas. No. 18,276.

While the crime of treason, as defined in Constitution, is not classified as to degree, its common law counterpart is called high treason. U.S. v. Tomoya Kawakita, D.C.Cal.1952, 108 F.Supp. 627.

The abuses of the tyrannical reigns of the Tudors and the Stuarts were well known to the founders of our government, and doubtless led to the peculiar phraseology observable in the definition of the crime, namely, that it shall consist only in levying war against the United States, or in adhering to their enemies, giving them aid and comfort, and to the other equally stringent feature, that no person shall be convicted of the offense except on the testimony of two witnesses to the same overt act. Law of Treason, C.C.N.Y.1861, 5 Blatchf., U.S., 549, 30 Fed.Cas. No. 18,271. See, also, Druecker v. Salomon, 1867, 21 Wis. 626.

Successfully to instigate treason is to commit it. Charge of Grand Jury, C.C. Pa.1851, 2 Wall.Jr., C.C., 134, 30 Fed.Cas. No. 18,276.

Word "treason", in its criminally acceptable meaning consists only in

FIGURE 5-Y

UNITED STATES CODE ANNOTATED

Art. 3 TREASON

Sec. 3, cl. 1

Note 5

levying war against the United States or adhering to their enemies, giving aid and comfort to them. Bennett v. Seimiller, 1954, 267 P.2d 926, 175 Kan. 764.

3. Enemies within clause

The Confederate government was never acknowledged by the United States as a de facto government in the sense that adherents to it in war against the government de jure did not incur the penalties of treason; from a very early period of the Civil War to its close, it was regarded as simply the military representative of the insurrection against the authority of the United States. Thorington v. Smith, Ala.1869, 75 U.S. 1, 8 Wall. 1, 19 L.Ed. 361. See, also, Sprott v. U.S., 1874, 87 U.S. 459, 20 Wall. 459, 22 L.Ed. 371.

The subject of a foreign power in a state of open hostility with the United States was an "enemy", within this clause defining treason. Stephan v. U.S., C.C.A.Mich.1943, 133 F.2d 87, certiorari denied 63 S.Ct. 858, 318 U.S. 781, 87 L.Ed. 1148, rehearing denied 63 S.Ct. 1172, 319 U.S. 783, 87 L.Ed. 1727.

Upon declaration of war with Germany, all subjects of the German Government, all members of German military and naval forces, and all persons engaged by or working for German Government as agents, spies or saboteurs to assist in prosecution of war or hamper United States in prosecution of war, were "enemies" of the United States within terms of this clause and 18 U.S. C.A. § 2381 defining treason as giving aid and comfort to enemies. U.S. v. Haupt, D.C.Ill.1942, 47 F.Supp. 836.

The term "enemies," as used in this clause, according to its settled meaning at the time the Constitution was adopted, applies only to the subjects of a foreign power in a state of open hostility with us; it does not embrace rebels in insurrection against their own government. U.S. v. Greathouse, C.C.Cal.1863, 4 Sawy., U.S., 457, 26 Fed.Cas. No. 15,254.

German widows, orphans and invalids of World War were not "enemies" after the signing of the Armistice. In re Rahn's Estate, 1927, 291 S.W. 120, 316 Mo. 492, certiorari denied 47 S.Ct. 591, 274 U.S. 745, 71 L.Ed. 1325.

4. Place of act

Treason can be committed by American citizen though he is living beyond territorial limits of the United States. Tomoya Kawakita v. U.S., Cal.1952, 72

S.Ct. 950, 343 U.S. 717, 96 L.Ed. 1249, rehearing denied 73 S.Ct. 5, 344 U.S. 850, 97 L.Ed. 660.

Treason may be committed by a citizen of the United States while residing in the territory of an enemy. Gillars v. U.S., 1950, 182 F.2d 962, 87 U.S.App.D.C. 16.

An act of treason by a United States citizen, though committed outside the United States, is an offense punishable here. U.S. v. Stephan, D.C.Mich.1943, 50 F.Supp. 738.

Treason may be committed at places remote from the seat of the rebellion, by co-operating with the rebels and sending them arms or intelligence, or intentionally rendering other assistance, and the trial of such offense will be had in the state and district where committed. Charge of Grand Jury, D.C.Mass.1861, 1 Sprague, U.S., 602, 30 Fed.Cas. No. 18,273.

5. Levying war against United States—Generally

In treason there are no accessories; all who engage in the rebellion at any stage of its existence, or who designedly give it any species of aid and comfort, in whatever part of the country they may be, stand on the same platform; they are all principals in the commission of the crime; they are all levying war against the United States. U.S. v. Greathouse, C.C.Cal.1863, 4 Sawy., U.S., 457, 26 Fed. Cas. No. 15,254. See, also, Fries's Case, C.C.Pa.1800, 9 Fed.Cas. No. 5,127.

If the purpose be entirely to overthrow the government at any one place, by force, that is a treasonable purpose. Charge of Grand Jury, D.C.Mass.1861, 1 Sprague, U.S., 602, 30 Fed.Cas. No. 18,273. See, also, Charge of Grand Jury, D.C.Mass.1863, 2 Sprague, U.S., 292, 30 Fed.Cas. No. 18,274.

The two species of treason mentioned in the Constitution are described in it in language borrowed from that of the English Statute of treasons; the phrase "levying war" is therefore understood and applied in the United States in the sense in which it has been used in England. U.S. v. Greiner, D.C.Pa.1861, 4 Phila., Pa., 396, 18 Leg.Int., Pa., 149, 26 Fed.Cas. No. 15,262.

The term "levying war" should be confined to insurrections and rebellions for the purpose of overturning the government by force and arms. U.S. v. Han-

257

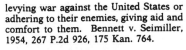

FIGURE 5-Z

UNITED STATES CODE ANNOTATED

DISCUSSION OF PROBLEM 5.10 Note 1 ("Power of Congress"), indicates that Congress has the power to punish acts of treason committed abroad. Similarly, Note 4 ("Place of act") indicates that acts of treason committed abroad may be punished. Note 4 also indicates that treason may be committed at places remote from the rebellion by cooperating with the rebels and sending them arms or intentionally rendering other assistance. Thus, Slade is clearly incorrect that treason cannot occur because the attacks took place outside the United States.

On the other hand, Slade may be correct that treason cannot occur because the attacks were directed at a foreign government. Further legal and factual investigation would be necessary. To what extent are the attacks directed at United States forces? On what basis are United States forces present in the foreign country? To what extent are the United States forces directly involved in the fighting? Is this situation similar to an undeclared war, such as the Viet Nam War?

CITING CONSTITUTIONS IN BLUEBOOK FORM

According to Rule 11 of *The Bluebook*, the United States Constitution should be cited as follows:

(1) Cite the U.S. Constitution by article, section, and, if appropriate, by clause. Abbreviate "United States" to "U.S." and "Constitution" to "Const." Abbreviate "Article" to "art." Abbreviate "Section" to "§" and "Clause" to "cl." Do not capitalize "art." or "cl."

(2) Amendments. Cite amendments by Roman number. Abbreviate "Amendment" to "amend." Do not capitalize "amend."

(3) State Constitutions. State constitutional provisions are cited in the same manner as the U.S. Constitution.[6]

PROBLEM 5.11 Assume that you want to cite the constitutional provision reproduced in Figure 5-EE in *Bluebook* form. Which of the following citations would be correct?

---

[6] State constitutions usually are included in state statutory compilations. A good comparative source for state constitutions is the Legislative Research Fund's <u>Constitutions of the United States: National and State</u>.

    (a)   US Constitution Art III, Sec 3, Cl 1.

    (b)   US Const Art III, § 3, cl 1.

    (c)   United States Constitution art. III, § 3, cl. 1.

    (d)   U.S. Const. art. III, § 3, cl. 1.

    DISCUSSION OF PROBLEM 5.11   The U.S. Constitution should be cited by article, section, and, if applicable, clause. The correct citation is given in the last answer. Note that "Constitution" should be abbreviated and that "art." and "cl." are not capitalized.

    Another matter raised by Slade in the facts of *Problem 5.1* relates to whether Slade could be forced to return to the United States to face charges. As mentioned earlier, return from a foreign country involves matters that are normally covered by treaty agreements between the United States and foreign governments.[7]

    All treaties before 1950 to which the United States was a party were officially published in the *United States Statutes at Large* (Stat.). Since 1950, those treaties and other international agreements have been officially published in *U.S. Treaties and Other International Agreements* (U.S.T.). Other sources for international agreements include the *League of Nations Treaty Series* (L.N.T.S., 1920-1945), the *United Nations Treaty Series* (U.N.T.S., 1945 to date), the *Pan American Union Treaty Series* (Pan-Am. T.S.), and the *European Treaty Series* (Europ. T.S.).

    The State Department also has published treaties and other international agreements in several series: *Treaty Series* (T.S., to 1945), *Treaties and Other International Act Series* (T.I.A.S., 1945 to date), and *Executive Agreement Series* (E.A.S., to 1945).

    The beginning page of the Extradition Treaty between the United States and Spain was reproduced in Figure 1-G in Chapter 1 (the President's proclamation precedes the text of the treaty). Citation of treaties and other international agreements is covered in Rule 20.4 of *The Bluebook*. The citation of the Extradition Treaty is given as an example in the text immediately preceding Figure 1-G.

    PROBLEM 5.12   The next two pages of the Extradition Treaty are shown in Figures 5-AA and 5-BB. Will Spain extradite Slade?

---

[7]Recall from Chapter 1 that the United States Constitution provides that the President has the authority to make "treaties" with the advice and consent of Congress and two-thirds approval by the Senate. U.S. Const. art. II, § 2, cl. 2. Under Article VI of the Constitution, treaties made under the authority of the United States are declared the supreme law of the land, and state laws inconsistent with such treaties are invalid. In contrast to treaties, "international agreements" or "executive agreements" are entered into under the President's own constitutional power. Also classified in this same way are those agreements entered into by the President based upon authority granted by an act of Congress. See supra § 1D(2)(c)(i) ("Treaties as Sources of Law").

IN TESTIMONY WHEREOF, I have signed this proclamation and caused the Seal of the United States of America to be affixed.

DONE at the city of Washington this second day of July in the year of our Lord one thousand nine hundred seventy-one and of [SEAL] the Independence of the United States of America the one hundred ninety-fifth.

RICHARD NIXON

By the President:
WILLIAM P ROGERS
Secretary of State

TREATY ON EXTRADITION BETWEEN THE UNITED STATES OF AMERICA AND SPAIN

TREATY ON EXTRADITION BETWEEN THE UNITED STATES OF AMERICA AND SPAIN

The President of the United States of America and the Chief of State of Spain, desiring to make more effective the cooperation of the two countries in the repression of crime through the rendering of maximum assistance in matters of extradition,

Have decided to conclude a Treaty and to this end have named as their representatives:

The President of the United States of America, The Honorable William P. Rogers, Secretary of State,

The Chief of State of Spain, His Excellency Señor Gregorio Lopez Bravo de Castro, Minister of Foreign Affairs, who have agreed as follows:

ARTICLE I

In accordance with the conditions established in this Treaty, each Contracting Party agrees to extradite to the other, for prosecution or to undergo sentence, persons found in its territory who have been charged with or convicted of any of the offenses mentioned in Article II of this Treaty committed within the territory of the other, or outside thereof under the conditions specified in Article III.

ARTICLE II

A. Persons shall be delivered up according to the provisions of this Treaty for any of the following offenses provided that these offenses

TIAS 7136

FIGURE 5-AA

U.S. TREATIES AND OTHER INTERNATIONAL AGREEMENTS

are punishable by the laws of both Contracting Parties by a term of imprisonment exceeding one year:

1. Murder; infanticide; parricide; manslaughter.
2. Abortion.
3. Rape; statutory rape; indecent assault, including sodomy and unlawful sexual acts with or upon minors under the age specified by the penal laws of both Contracting Parties.
4. Aggravated injury or mutilation.
5. Procuration.
6. Willful nonsupport or willful abandonment of a child or spouse when for that reason the life of that child or spouse is or is likely to be endangered.
7. Bigamy.
8. Kidnapping or abduction; child stealing; false imprisonment.
9. Robbery or larceny or burglary; housebreaking.
10. Embezzlement; malversation; breach of fiduciary relationship.
11. Obtaining money, valuable securities or property, by false pretenses, by threat of force or by other fraudulent means including the use of the mails or other means of communication.
12. Any offense relating to extortion or threats.
13. Bribery, including soliciting, offering and accepting.
14. Receiving or transporting any money, valuable securities or other property knowing the same to have been obtained pursuant to a criminal act.
15. Any offense relating to counterfeiting or forgery; making a false statement to a government agency or official.
16. Any offense relating to perjury or false accusation.
17. Arson; malicious injury to property.
18. Any malicious act that endangers the safety of any person in a railroad train, or aircraft or vessel or bus or other means of transportation.
19. Piracy, defined as mutiny or revolt on board an aircraft or vessel against the authority of the captain or commander of such aircraft or vessel, any seizure or exercise of control, by force or violence or threat of force or violence, of an aircraft or vessel.
20. Any offense against the bankruptcy laws.
21. Any offense against the laws relating to narcotic drugs, psychotropic drugs, cocaine and its derivatives, and other dangerous drugs, including cannabis, and chemicals or substances injurious to health.
22. Any offense relating to firearms, explosives, or incendiary devices.
23. Unlawful interference in any administrative or juridical proceedings by bribing, threatening, or injuring by any means, any officer, juror, witness, or duly authorized person.

TIAS 7136

FIGURE 5-BB

U.S. TREATIES AND OTHER INTERNATIONAL AGREEMENTS

DISCUSSION OF PROBLEM 5.12 Article I of the Treaty establishes that the United States and Spain will extradite persons found in
their respective territories when they have been charged with any of the
offenses listed in Article II. Item 22 in Article II covers "[a]ny offense
relating to firearms, explosives, or incendiary devices" (provided the
offense is punishable by a term of imprisonment exceeding one year).
As seen earlier in 18 U.S.C.A. § 844, the basic prison terms for violation
of federal laws relating to explosives far exceed one year. Thus, Slade
would be subject to extradition from Spain to the United States to face
trial.

In the discussion of *Problem 5.1*, it was also noted that municipal
ordinances may restrict the location of manufacturing and storage of
explosives. Most law libraries will have ordinances of cities within their
locality. *Bluebook* Rule 12.8.2 states that ordinances are cited by analogy
to statutes.

A special kind of legislative research involves uniform acts. As
noted in Chapter 1, The National Conference of Commissioners of Uniform State Laws is responsible for encouraging the drafting and adoption
of uniform state legislation on a variety of subjects. Research on a
particular uniform law can be greatly aided by consulting *Uniform Laws
Annotated Master Edition*, 1969—). It provides citations to relevant periodical literature, official comments, and digests of state and federal decisions interpreting or citing particular provisions of a uniform law. Devi-
ations in particular states from the text of a uniform law are also noted.
It is kept current by pocket parts, which also contain a "Table of Jurisdictions Wherein Act Has Been Adopted."

PROBLEM 5.13 Assume that in the context of *Problem 5.1*, your
client wants to know what would happen if he abandoned the fireworks
that he has in a public warehouse. From your research, it is apparent
that illegal fireworks may be subject to seizure and forfeiture. However,
Acme's legal fireworks might be treated differently. What happens to
them if they are abandoned? Assume that you remember that some
states have adopted the Uniform Disposition of Unclaimed Property Act
and that you want to determine whether South Carolina has adopted this
Act. You could determine the answer to this question by consulting the
Index to the *Code of Laws of South Carolina (1976) Annotated*. You
can also determine this information by consulting West's *Uniform Laws
Annotated*. Examine the following table in Figure 5-JJ and determine
whether South Carolina has adopted this uniform act.

UNIFORM UNCLAIMED PROPERTY ACT (1981 ACT)

See, also, material relating to the Uniform Disposition of Unclaimed Property Acts of 1966 and 1954, supra, this supplement.

Tables of Jurisdictions Wherein Act Has Been Adopted

Jurisdiction	Laws	Effective Date	Statutory Citation
Alaska	1986, c. 133	9–19–1986	AS 34.45.110 to 34.45.780.
Arizona	1983, c. 240	1–1–1984	A.R.S. §§ 44–301 to 44–340.
Colorado	1987, c. 274	7–1–1987	West's C.R.S.A. §§ 38–13–101 to 38–13–134.
Hawaii	1983, c. 37	5–18–1983	HRS §§ 523A–1 to 523A–41.
Florida.........	1987, c. 87–105	7–1–1987	West's F.S.A. §§ 717.001 to 717.1401.
Georgia	1990, p. 1506	7–1–1990	O.C.G.A. §§ 44–12–190 to 44–12–235.
Idaho	1983, c. 209	7–1–1983	I.C. §§ 14–501 to 14–542.
Iowa[3].........	1967, c. 391	7–1–1967	I.C.A. §§ 556.1 to 556.29.
Louisiana.......	1986, Act 829	7–10–1986 *	LSA—R.S. 9:151 to 9:188.
Maine	1987, c. 691	4–7–1988 *	33 MRSA §§ 1801 to 1875.
Maryland[6]	1966, c. 611	6–1–1966	Code, Commercial Law, §§ 17–101 to 17–326.
Minnesota[5]	1969, c. 725	7–1–1969	M.S.A. §§ 345.31 to 345.60.
Montana	1983, c. 269	7–1–1983	MCA 70–9–101 to 70–9–316.
Nevada[1]	1979, c. 682	1–1–1980	N.R.S. 120A.010 to 120A.450.
New Hampshire ..	1986, c. 204.1	1–1–1987	RSA 471–C:1 to 471–C:43.
New Jersey......	1989, c. 58	4–14–1989	N.J.S.A. §§ 46:30B–1 to 46:30B–109.
New Mexico	1989, c. 293	11–1–1989	NMSA 1978, §§ 7–8–1 to 7–8–40.
North Dakota....	1985, c. 510		NDCC 47–30.1–01 to 47–30.1–38.
Oregon[2]	1957, c. 670	8–20–1957	ORS 98.302 to 98.436.
Rhode Island.....	P.L.1986, c. 500	7–1–1987	Gen.Laws 1956, §§ 33–21.1–1 to 33–21.1–41.
South Carolina ...	1988, Act No. 658, Pt. II, § 34A	7–1–1988	Code 1976, §§ 27–18–10 to 27–18–400.
Tennessee[4]	1978, c. 561	3–6–1978	T.C.A. §§ 66–29–101 to 66–29–134.
Utah	1983, c. 164	7–1–1983	U.C.A.1953, 78–44–1 to 78–44–40.
Vermont[7]	1964, No. 35	1–1–1965	27 V.S.A. §§ 1208 to 1238.
Virgin Islands	1988, Act 5341	6–6–1988 *	29 V.I.C. §§ 651 to 687.
Virginia	1984, c. 121		Code 1950, §§ 55–210.1 to 55–210.30.
Washington......	1983, c. 179	6–30–1983	West's RCWA 63.29.010 to 63.29.905.
Wisconsin	1983, Act 408	12–31–1984	W.S.A. 177.01 to 177.41.

* Date of approval.

[1] The Nevada act, as amended by L.1983, c. 520, retains the basic format and many of the provisions of the Uniform Disposition of Unclaimed Property Act of 1966, but now also contains many of the major provisions of the Uniform Unclaimed Property Act of 1981. Accordingly, the citation of the Nevada act is set forth in the tables for both of these acts.

[2] The Oregon act, as amended by L.1983, c. 716, now contains the basic format and many of the provisions of the Uniform Disposition of Unclaimed Property Act of 1966, but now also contains many of the major provisions of the Uniform Unclaimed Property Act of 1981. Accordingly, the citation of the Oregon act is set forth in the tables for both acts.

[3] The Iowa act, as amended by L.1984, H.F. 2522, retains the basic format and many of the provisions of the Uniform Disposition of Unclaimed Property Act of 1966, but now also contains many of the major provisions of the Uniform Unclaimed Property Act of 1981. Accordingly, the citation of the Iowa act is set forth in tables for both acts.

[4] The Tennessee act, as amended by L.1984, c. 544, retains the basic format and many of the provisions of the Uniform Disposition of Unclaimed Property Act of 1966, but now also contains many of the provisions of the Uniform Unclaimed Property Act of 1981. Accordingly, the citation of the Tennessee act is set forth in tables for both acts.

[5] The Minnesota act, as amended, retains the basic format and many of the provisions of the Uniform Disposition of Unclaimed Property Act of 1966, but now also contains many of the major provisions of the Uniform Unclaimed Property Act of 1981. Accordingly, the citation of the Minnesota act is set forth in the tables for both acts.

292

FIGURE 5-CC
UNIFORM LAWS ANNOTATED POCKET PART

DISCUSSION OF PROBLEM 5.13 From the table reproduced in Figure 5-CC, it is apparent that South Carolina adopted this uniform act in 1988. It become effective on July 1, 1988. The text of the act can be found in §§ 27-18-10 to 27-18-400 of the *Code of Laws of South Carolina*. Although South Carolina has adopted this uniform law, upon further reading, you would discover that this law applies only to intangible property. You would want to pursue other theories, including the provisions of the contract between Acme and the warehouse. You would also want to explore possible practical solutions, such as simply selling the legal fireworks to another licensed manufacturer or dealer.

CITING UNIFORM ACTS IN BLUEBOOK FORM

In general, uniform acts are cited as separate codes. The Uniform Commercial Code should be abbreviated to "U.C.C." A citation to West's *Uniform Laws Annotated* (U.L.A.) may be given. Use the year the act was last amended in the citation (even if the cited section was not amended at that time. *Bluebook* Rule 12.8.4. The following are examples of the citation of uniform acts: U.C.C. § 2-719 (1977); Uniform Parentage Act § 10 (1973); Uniform Parentage Act § 10, 9A U.L.A. 600-01 (1973).

When a uniform act is cited as the law of a particular state, however, it should be cited as a state statute. *Bluebook* Rule 12.8.4. Colo. Rev. Stat. § 4-8-401 (1973).

Section 5E. Developing and Updating Legislative Research

This section discusses the various ways in which legislative research can be developed and updated.

1. PUBLISHER'S CROSS-REFERENCES

One reason for using annotated versions of statutory codes is the availability of cross-references to other publications within the publisher's "system" (in addition to providing relevant case references). For example, Lawyers Cooperative's *United States Code Service* provides references to relevant *A.L.R. Annotations*, *American Jurisprudence Second* topics and sections, and form books. Similarly, West's *United States Code Annotated* provides "Library References" to *Corpus Juris Secundum*, West treatises,

relevant topics and key numbers in its digest system, and form books. These references can be readily used to develop one's initial research.

2. REFERENCES TO LEGISLATIVE HISTORY

Annotated versions of the statutory codes provide references to the legislative history of the provisions (discussed in the next section).

3. FINDING RECENT LEGISLATION AND RECENT CASES INTERPRETING A STATUTORY PROVISION

(a) Supplements, Session Laws, and Slip Laws

The *United States Code* is reissued by the U.S. Government Printing Office every six years. The *Code* is supplemented by annual cumulative supplement volumes. West's *United States Code Annotated* and Lawyers Cooperative's *United States Code Service* provide the text of permanent public laws in force with annotations of judicial opinions construing those laws. These sets are both supplemented by cumulative annual pocket parts, pamphlet supplements, and replacement volumes.

Thus, one means of updating a section that you have consulted is to check the supplements of the *Code*. Most lawyers use the annotated versions of the *Code* for this purpose because of their speed of supplementation. Very recent federal laws can be found in West's *U.S. Code Congressional & Administrative News*. Lawyers Cooperative's *United States Code Service Advance Sheets* performs a similar function. West's *U.S. Code Congressional & Administrative News* and Lawyers Cooperative's *Advance Sheets* both have (1) a cumulative table showing *United States Code* sections added, amended, repealed, or otherwise affected and (2) a cumulative subject index for the most recent session of Congress.

(b) Updating Case Annotations in Annotated Codes

For the annotations in the *United States Code Annotated* and *United States Code Service*, a closing table[8] is provided. This table informs you what latest reporter volumes were checked for cases relating to the statutory provisions covered by the volume. To find later cases you would check the "Table of Statutes Construed" in the front of all reporter volumes and advance sheets issued after the closing date.

Another means of checking the current status of legislation and finding cases that have cited a particular statute is *Shepard's Statute*

---

[8]Closing tables are discussed and illustrated in section B(3) of Chapter 3.

Citations. Federal statutes are covered in *Shepard's United States Citations Statute Edition.* Like the case editions, statute editions of *Shepard's* use various symbols to indicate the legislative and judicial "Operation of the Statute." These symbols are shown in the Figure 5-DD.

Operation of Statute

Legislative

A	(amended)	Statute amended.
Ad	(added)	New section added.
E	(extended)	Provisions of an existing statute extended in their application to a later statute, or allowance of additional time for performance of duties required by a statute within a limited time.
L	(limited)	Provisions of an existing statute declared not to be extended in their application to a later statute.
R	(repealed)	Abrogation of an existing statute.
Re-en	(re-enacted)	Statute re-enacted.
Rn	(renumbered)	Renumbering of existing sections.
Rp	(repealed in part)	Abrogation of part of an existing statute.
Rs	(repealed and superseded)	Abrogation of an existing statute and substitution of new legislation therefor.
Rv	(revised)	Statute revised.
S	(superseded)	Substitution of new legislation for an existing statute not expressly abrogated.
Sd	(suspended)	Statute suspended.
Sdp	(suspended in part)	Statute suspended in part.
Sg	(supplementing)	New matter added to an existing statute.
Sp	(superseded in part)	Substitution of new legislation for part of an existing statute not expressly abrogated.
Va	(validated)	

Judicial

C	Constitutional.		V	Void or invalid.
U	Unconstitutional.		Va	Valid.
Up	Unconstitutional in part.		Vp	Void or invalid in part.

FIGURE 5-DD

SHEPARD'S UNITED STATES CITATIONS STATUTE EDITION

    PROBLEM 5.14 Shown in Figure 5-EE is a page from *Shepard's United States Citations Statute Edition* covering § 844 of Title 18. Has subsection (i) been held to be constitutional? Has it been amended?

UNITED STATES CODE '82 Ed.

T. 18 § 841

Subsec. f	**¶ B**	505F2d1207	742F2d845	**Subsec. e**	58FRD627	646F2d1325
Cir. 8	Cir. 4	67FRD233	770F2d476	A96St1319	Cir. 8	662F2d1292
656F2d351	626F2d365	**Subsec. j**	545FS989	Cir. DC	496F2d351	676F2d1247
Cir. 9	Cir. 11	449US122	495F2d137	495F2d1125	551F2d1125	685F2d1095
487F2d273	710F2d734	66L╚336	482F2d454	Cir. 2	Cir. 9	726F2d572
§ 842	**Subsec. b**	101SC429	710F2d277	700F2d883	629F2d575	739F2d489
et seq.	**Subd. 1**	Cir. 1	522FS1194	Cir. 4	Cir. 11	773F2d1069
Cir. 5	Cir. 1	576F2d3	531FS462	565F2d868	663F2d1383	487FS992
465F2d810	576F2d2	Cir. 2	Cir. 10	543FS727	**Subd. 1**	Cir. 10
359FS862	**Subsec. d**	604F2d771	560F2d1004	Cir. 5	A96St1319	560F2d1004
Cir. 9	Cir. 11	Cir. 5	631F2d666	487F2d634	Cir. 2	598F2d575
482F2d1019	724F2d926	536F2d1064	Cir. 11	562F2d960	547F2d746	607F2d1312
§ 842	**Subd. 2**	Cir. 6	710F2d1518	Cir. 6	404FS1362	667F2d940
Cir. 2	Cir. 2	509F2d887	724F2d924	450FS249	Cir. 3	692F2d1280
639F2d110	526F2d530	689F2d1267	**Subsec. b**	Cir. 7	717F2d802	705F2d379
658F2d34	**Subsec. e**	710F2d277	449US122	563FS1087	Cir. 5	726F2d602
Cir. 5	Cir. 3	531FS462	66L╚336	Cir. 8	670F2d36	528FS83
586F2d422	523FS265	Cir. 11	101SC429	462F2d617	Cir. 7	Cir. 11
654F2d1038	**Subsec. f**	674F2d844	Cir. 3	543F2d1247	537F2d261	697F2d925
706F2d515	Cir. 3	**§ 843**	595F2d158	576F2d224	559F2d1094	699F2d1056
Cir. 6	C523FS265	Cir. 5	Cir. 6	588F2d670	738F2d779	700F2d621
531FS465	Cir. 4	706F2d515	710F2d277	629F2d575	768F2d203	721F2d343
Cir. 7	726F2d1021	Cir. 6	**Subsecs. d to j**	704F2d1130	558FS330	**Subsec. j**
560F2d281	**Subsec. h**	531FS466	Cir. 5	Cir. 10	**Subd. 2**	Cir. 2
Cir. 8	Cir. 1	Cir. 8	706F2d515	496FS285	Cir. 2	639F2d108
656F2d351	576F2d2	656F2d351	Cir. 8	12MJ287	586F2d979	700F2d876
497FS349	Cir. 2	497FS349	656F2d351	13MJ739	Cir. 3	713F2d935
Cir. 9	526F2d53d	Cir. 10	497FS349	17MJ216	424FS996	715F2d772
487F2d272	647F2d22?	457F2d1121	**Subsecs. d to i**	95╚414n	Cir. 5	733F2d212
629F2d575	694F2d899	**Subsec. b**	Cir. 5	**Subsec. f**	488F2d854	Cir. 3
Cir. 10	Cir. 3	Cir. 6	737F2d453	A96St1319	Cir. 6	717F2d802
489F2d264	523FS275	642F2d1040	Cir. 7	A98St2142	354FS370	Cir. 4
10A╚F844s	Cir. 4	**§ 844**	675F2d908	408US385	Cir. 8	726F2d130
Subsec. a	632F2d1150	Cir. 2	**Subsec. d**	33L╚434	496F2d352	Cir. 5
Subd. 1	Cir. 6	639F2d110	A98St2142	92SC2802	**Subsec. i**	483F2d318
Cir. 2	482F2d454	700F2d55	408US412	Cir. 1	A96St1319	706F2d515
526F2d530	504F2d93	700F2d881	455US659	470F2d1202	A98St2142	737F2d453
Cir. 3	509F2d887	715F2d772	33L╚449	Cir. 2	408US385	742F2d843
523FS276	513F2d331	560FS324	71L╚536	639F2d111	444US194	Cir. 6
Cir. 5	689F2d1268	Cir. 3	92SC2815	700F2d883	33L╚434	717F2d1022
654F2d1036	700F2d1077	652F2d325	102SC1341	Cir. 3	62L╚358	486FS138
Cir. 6	Cir. 8	717F2d803	Cir. 1	53FRD195	85L╚831	522FS1194
689F2d1265	C467F2d669	424FS1004	470F2d1202	Cir. 5	92SC2802	Cir. 7
710F2d277	Cir. 9	Cir. 4	561F2d105	493F2d30	100SC404	675F2d907
531FS462	742F2d495	726F2d131	568F2d224	764F2d1036	105SC2456	704F2d978
Cir. 8	Cir. 10	Cir. 5	575F2d27	418FS574	53USLW	745F2d469
494F2d895	560F2d1003	586F2d422	Cir. 2	Cir. 6	[4652	591FS865
Cir. 11	631F2d666	588F2d1119	526F2d530	482F2d454	Cir. DC	Cir. 8
724F2d923	5MJ839	706F2d515	567F2d192	C557F2d544	636F2d629	656F2d352
Subd. 2	**Subsec. i**	737F2d453	700F2d55	C384FS1151	Cir. 2	497FS349
Cir. 4	404US341	Cir. 6	743F2d64	Cir. 9	470F2d1202	564FS1087
726F2d1019	30L╚493	713F2d1196	460FS668	597F2d1170	571F2d72	Cir. 9
Cir. 10	92SC519	736F2d321	508FS1039	629F2d575	646F2d5	662F2d1295
505F2d1207	Cir. 5	486FS138	Cir. 4	499FS49	Cir. 2	676F2d1248
Subd. 3	565F2d1311	Cir. 7	626F2d365	Cir. 10	465F2d803	C726F2d572
Cir. 6	Cir. 6	557F2d100	682F2d470	522F2d569	482F2d39	739F2d489
531FS467	583F2d273	560F2d281	540FS692	556F2d480	520F2d600	Cir. 10
Cir. 10	Cir. 7	704F2d979	Cir. 7	598F2d578	550F2d820	457F2d1121
489F2d264	503F2d316	Cir. 8	703F2d1005	**Subsec. g**	639F2d108	607F2d1312
10A╚F844s	448FS577	656F2d351	Cir. 9	Cir. 5	647F2d227	C667F2d941
¶ A	Cir. 9	368FS1249	629F2d575	764F2d1036	679F2d1033	705F2d379
Cir. 2	487F2d270	Cir. 9	723F2d673	Cir. 9	693F2d247	726F2d602
743F2d64	497F2d1107	646F2d1327	767F2d1325	629F2d575	700F2d55	Cir. 11
Cir. 4	Cir. 10	487FS995	Cir. 10	**Subsec. h**	700F2d876	663F2d1389
626F2d365	560F2d1003	Cir. 10	457F2d1121	Cir. DC	713F2d935	16A╚F906s
Cir. 5	**Subd. 1**	692F2d1280	598F2d578	516F2d688	715F2d771	**§ 845**
582F2d953	Cir. 2	705F2d381	607F2d1312	Cir. 2	733F2d212	Cir. 5
Cir. 6	526F2d530	18A╚F875s	631F2d666	550F2d820	487FS540	443F2d814
511F2d26	Cir. 4	29A╚F826s	705F2d381	700F2d876	508FS1039	Cir. 6
531FS462	626F2d365	**Subsec. a**	739F2d511	715F2d771	535FS257	531FS466
Cir. 8	Cir. 6	Cir. 2	Cir. 11	Cir. 3	Cir. 3	Cir. 9
713F2d390	689F2d1268	526F2d530	700F2d621	717F2d802	479F2d726	487F2d273
	528F2d884	Cir. 4	57ABA588	424FS998	652F2d329	C508F2d987
	629F2d574	626F2d365		Cir. 5	686F2d149	587F2d949
	Cir. 10	Cir. 5		468F2d737	717F2d803	629F2d575
		737F2d453		514F2d796	424FS998	644F2d1271

620

FIGURE 5-EE

SHEPARD'S UNITED STATES CITATIONS STATUTE EDITION

DISCUSSION OF PROBLEM 5.14   The entries in *Shepard's* indicate that the Seventh Circuit ("C548F2d198") and the Ninth Circuit ("C508F2d987") have held subsection i to be constitutional. *Shepard's* also indicates that this subsection was amended twice ("A96St1319") and ("98St2142") ("St" is a reference to *United States Statutes at Large*). To fully update this section, you would need to consult later *Shepard's* pamphlets in the same manner that you would for updating case research.[9]

    Shepard's also covers treaties and other "legislative" sources. For example, state statutes and constitutions are covered in state *Shepard's* volumes.[10] Most law libraries, however, will only carry these state *Shepard's* volumes for the state in which they are located and perhaps for the adjoining states. *Shepard's* notes amendments, repeals, and other statutory modifications in the same manner previously noted for *Shepard's* volumes covering federal statutes. *Shepard's* also indicates state and federal court opinions, attorney general opinions, and legal periodicals that have cited the state statute.

    Municipal ordinances and city charters are covered in the relevant state edition of the *Shepard's Statute Citation* volume. Citations of court decisions that have cited or construed ordinances of cities or counties within the state are listed under (1) the name of the city, subdivided by topics commonly covered by municipal codes or (2) an alphabetical listing of topics commonly covered by municipal codes.

    In addition, municipal ordinances are covered in *Shepard's Ordinance Law Annotations*. This *Shepard's* set is organized differently from other *Shepard's* units. It contains case annotations arranged alphabetically by subject. It also has a general index and a table of cases. Figure 5-FF shows typical annotations in this *Shepard's* volume.

---

[9]This process is described in both Chapters 3 and 4 in conjunction with case editions of Shepard's.

[10]Recall from Chapter 3 that Shepard's volumes are issued for the regional reporters and for individual states (e.g., South Carolina). See supra § 3B(4) ("Using Shepard's Citations to Develop Your Reach and to Find Cases in Specific Jurisdictions").

EXPLOSIVES

EDITORIAL COMMENT. There are not as many cases dealing with local regulation of explosives as might have been expected. This may partly be because we have given separate treatment to such things as FIREWORKS, and GAS, NATURAL, and GASOLINE BUSINESS. Even in the present topic, however, we find such interesting holdings a prohibition against storage of ammonia (§4), the transportation of propane gas (§10), and that gasoline may be deemed an explosive, even in the face of a state law that specifically says "explosive" does not mean gasoline.

I. DEFINITIONS

§1. Gasoline

Under a zoning ordinance prohibiting the storage of explosives a city may deny a permit for storage of gasoline, since under certain conditions gasoline may be deemed an explosive, though by statutory definition "explosive" does not mean gasoline.

    NY Attica v Day (1929) 134 Misc 882, 236 NYS 607.

§2. Combustibles

A municipal provision prohibiting storage of combustible material without a permit is construed to include burlap bags and bagging.

    NY People v Freedman (1941) 31 NYS2d 82.

107

FIGURE 5-FF
SHEPARD'S ORDINANCE LAW ANNOTATIONS

4. TABLES

Accompanying statutory compilations are various tables that will sometimes be needed to develop one's research. Tables called "parallel reference tables" accompany the *United States Code* and its annotated versions. These tables allow a researcher to translate an outdated or *United States Statutes at Large* citation into a current *Code* reference. For example, these parallel reference tables provide cross-references between the public law number or *United States Statutes at Large* citation to the sections where the law has been codified. These tables translate citations from the early *Revised Statutes*[11] sections to *United States Code* sections. These tables also explain the disposition of sections of the *Code* titles that have been revised. Because of the more frequent updating of the annotated versions, most researchers prefer to use the tables accompanying the annotated versions of the *Code*.

Another type of table called a "popular name table" allows a researcher to find the citation of a statute when you only have a reference to the name of a statute. Such tables accompany the various versions of the *United States Code*.[12] Shepard's also has a set providing the same function for both state and federal legislation called *Shepard's Acts and Cases by Popular Names: State and Federal*.[13]

PROBLEM 5.15 Assume for purposes of this problem that someone has told you that the Organized Crime Control Act of 1970 dealt, in part, with explosives. Using *Shepard's* Popular Name Table in Figure 5-GG, find its citation.

---

[11]The first codification of federal statutes, United States Revised Statutes of 1875, compiled by subject the then-current text of public laws of general interest which had been previously published in the Statutes at Large. It was then reenacted by Congress. A second edition of the Revised Statutes of 1875, published in 1878, corrected errors and updated the first edition; brackets and italics in the second edition were used to indicate changes made in the text of the first edition. Congress never reenacted the second edition, and thus the changes indicated in the second edition are technically only prima facie evidence of the law. The first edition of the current United States Code (U.S.C.) was published in 1926. The 1926 edition of the Code compiled all sections of the Revised Statutes of 1875 which had not been repealed and all public laws from the Statutes at Large enacted after 1873 that were still in force; those laws were arranged by subject under fifty titles.

[12]West's United States Code Annotated popular name table is printed in the last index volume (reissued annually). This table is further updated by an "Alphabetical Table of Laws" in the front of each quarterly pamphlet and a table in each issue of U.S. Code Congressional and Administrative News, which cumulates each month during each congressional session. Lawyers Cooperative's United States Code Service popular name table appears in a bound volume with other tables. It is updated by an annual pocket part. This table is further updated in the back of every quarterly Cumulative Later Case and Statutory Service and monthly Advance pamphlet.

[13]This set also provides citations to cases when only the popular case name is known.

Org	FEDERAL AND STATE ACTS CITED BY POPULAR NAMES

Organizations Registration Act
Ark. Stat. 1947, 6-817 et seq.

Organized Crime Act
N.M. Stat. Anno. 1978, 29-9-1 et seq.

Organized Crime Control Act
Colo. Rev. Stat. 1973, 18-17-101 et seq.
Wis. Stat. 1981, 946.80 et seq.

Organized Crime Control Act of 1970
See U.S. Code tables
Oct. 15, 1970, P.L. 91-452, 84 Stat. 922

Organized Crime Profits Act (Control)
Cal. Penal Code §186 et seq.

Original Investment Act (Trustees)
Okla. Stat. 1981, Title 60, §163

Original Packages Act (Intoxicating Liquors)
U.S. Code 1982 Title 27, §121
Aug. 8, 1890, c. 728, 26 Stat. 313

Orland Park Civic Center Act
Ill. Laws 1984, P.A. 83-1456, §§4-1 to 4-30

Orlando Central City Neighborhood Development Board Act
Fla. Special Laws 1971, Ch. 71-810

Orlando Downtown Development Board Act
Fla. Special Laws 1969, Ch. 69-1390

Orlando-Orange County Expressway Authority Act
Fla. Stat. 1983, 348.751 et seq.

Osage Act (Indians)
U.S., June 21, 1906, c. 3504, 34 Stat. 363, 365
U.S., June 28, 1906, c. 3572, 34 Stat. 539
U.S., Mar. 1, 1907, c. 2285, 34 Stat. 1043
U.S., Apr. 18, 1912, c. 83, 37 Stat. 86
U.S., Feb. 6, 1921, c. 36, 41 Stat. 1097
U.S., Mar. 3, 1921, c. 120, 41 Stat. 1249
U.S., Feb. 27, 1925, c. 359, 43 Stat. 1008

Osage Allotment Act
U.S., June 28, 1906, c. 3572, 34 Stat. 539

Osage Indians Citizenship Act
U.S., Mar. 3, 1921, c. 120, 41 Stat. 1249, §3

Osage Town Site Act
U.S., Mar. 3, 1905, c. 1479, 33 Stat. 1061, §1

Osage Tribe of Indians Technical Corrections Act of 1984
U.S., Oct. 30, 1984, P.L. 98-605, 98 Stat. 3163

Osborn Act (Area of State)
Mich. Comp. Laws 1979, 2.1, 2.2

Ossining Housing and Property Maintenance Code
N.Y. Local Laws 1973, Village of Ossining, p. 3660

Osteopathic and Medical Practice Act
Ky. Rev. Stat. 1971, 311.530 et seq.

FIGURE 5-GG
SHEPARD'S ACTS AND CASES BY POPULAR NAMES

DISCUSSION OF PROBLEM 5.15 *Shepard's Acts and Cases by Popular Names: State and Federal* lists the following as the citation for the Organized Crime Control Act of 1970: Oct. 15, 1970, P.L. 91-452, 84 Stat. 922. Note that instead of providing a *United States Code* citation, *Shepard's* directs you to "See U.S. Code tables." The reason for this direction is that this Act covered multiple topics and thus the various provisions of this Act were codified in diverse locations—too numerous to conveniently list in this table.

PROBLEM 5.16 Assume that you have located volume 84 of the *United States Statutes at Large*. Assume that you have examined this Act and found that Title XI of this Act deals with Explosives. Section 1101 of Title XI is a declaration of purpose of the title. Section 1102(a) adds Chapter 40 to Title 18 of the *United States Code*. Using the "Statutes at Large" table reproduced in Figure 5-HH from the Tables volume of *United States Code Annotated*, determine where § 1101 and § 1102(a) have been codified in the *United States Code*.

Statutes at Large page number

Date

Public Law
No.

The entry
"Rev. T."
in the
"Status"
column for
this entry.
When that
status is
indicated, it
means that
the reference
given is to
the United
States Code
title and
section as
originally
allocated.
To find
where sec-
tions of the
earlier ver-
sion have
been placed,
the "Revis-
ed Titles"
table must
then be
consulted.

Relevant
entries

STATUTES AT LARGE						1970
1970—91st Cong.—84 Stat.				U S C A		
Oct.	P.L.	Sec.	Page	Tit.	Sec.	Status
13	91–452	239	930	45	362	
		241	930	46	1124	
		242	930	47	409	
		243(a)	931	49	9	Rev. T.
		243(b)	931	49	916	Rev. T.
		243(c)	931	49	1017	Rev. T.
		244	931	49	43	Rev. T.
		245	931	49	46	Rev. T.
		246	931	49	1484	
		247	931	50	792	
		248	931	50 App.	643a	Elim.
		249	931	50 App.	1152	Elim.
		250	931	50 App.	2026	
		251	931	50 App.	2155	
		259	931	18	6001 nt	
		260	931	18	6001 nt	
		301(a)	932	28	1826	
		301(b)	932	28	Prec. 1821	
		302(a), (b)	932	18	1073	
		401(a)	932	18	1623	
		401(b)	933	18	Prec. 1621	
		501	933	18	Prec. 3481 nt	
		601(a)	934	18	3503	
		601(b)	935	18	Prec. 3481	
		701	935	18	3504 nt	
		702(a)	935	18	3504	
		702(b)	936	18	Prec. 3481	
		703	936	18	3504 nt	
		801	936	18	1511 nt	
		802(a)	936	18	1511	
		802(b)	937	18	Prec. 1501	
		803(a)	937	18	1955	
		803(b)	938	18	Prec. 1951	
		804(a)–(d)	938	18	1955 nt	
		805(a)–(c)	939	18	1955 nt	
		806(a)–(d)	939	18	1955 nt	
		807(a), (b)	940	18	1955 nt	
		808(a), (b)	940	18	1955 nt	
		809	940	18	1955 nt	
		810	940	18	2516	
		811	940	18	1511 nt	
		901(a)	941– 947	18	prec. 1961, 1961–1968	
		901(b)	947	18	prec. 1	
		902(a)	947	18	2516	
		902(b)	947	18	2517	
		903	947	18	1505	
		904	947	18	1961 nt	
		1001(a)	948– 952	18	3575–3578	
		1001(b)	952	18	prec. 3561	
		1002	952	18	3148	
		1101	952	18	841 nt	
		1102(a)	952– 959	18	prec. 841, 841–848	
		1102(b)	959	18	prec. 1	
		1103	959	18	2516	
		1104	959	18	841 nt	
		1105	959	18	841 nt	
		1106(b) (2)	960	18	prec. 831	
		1107	960	18	841 nt	
		1201–1211	960, 961	18	prec. 3331 nt	
		1212	961	18	2510 nt Rep.	
		1301	962	18	1961 nt	
	91–453	1	962	49	1601a	
		2	962	49	1602	
		3	965	49	1603	
		4	966	49	1604	
		5	966	49	1608	
		6	966	49	1610	
		7	967	49	1611	
		8	967	49	1612	
		9, 10	968	49	1602 nts	
		11	968	49	1605 nt	

377

FIGURE 5-HH
UNITED STATES CODE ANNOTATED

DISCUSSION OF PROBLEM 5.16   The "Statutes at Large" table reproduced in Figure 5-HH from the Tables volume of *United States Code Annotated* indicates that § 1101 has been codified as a note ("nt") to § 841 of Title 18 of the *United States Code*.   That note appears in Figure 5-N above.   The table indicates that § 1102(a) has become §§ 841-848 and material preceding the beginning of § 841.

5. FINDING DISCUSSIONS OF STATUTES IN LEGAL PERIODICALS

The publishers of annotated versions of statutes often provide you with references to secondary sources, particularly law articles and treatises. *Shepard's Federal Law Citations in Selected Law Reviews* is another source for treatment of federal statutes in legal periodicals.   This unit searches the twenty "national" periodicals citations to federal statutes.

PROBLEM 5.17   In *Problem 5.1*, it was mentioned that you had originally represented Slade in the purchase of a mine.   Assume that Slade has called you again and has asked you to help him with a problem involving a warrantless mine inspection under the Federal Mine Safety and Health Amendment Act of 1977.   Assume that as part of your research you would like to find law review articles that have discussed § 811 of Title 30 of the *United States Code* (one of the provisions of this Act).   Shown in Figure 5-II is a page from *Shepard's Federal Law Citations in Selected Law Reviews* covering Title 30.   Find the relevant entries for § 811.   What law reviews have cited this section?

For purposes of answering this question, assume (as indicated in *Shepard's* Table of Abbreviations) that "McL" is the abbreviation for the *Michigan Law Review*, "MnL" is the abbreviation for the *Minnesota Law Review*, and "NwL" is the abbreviation for the *Northwestern Law Review*.

T. 29 § 1132 **UNITED STATES CODE** '76 Ed. & '81 Supp.

Subsec. c
46ChL34
25CLA517
Subsec. d
Subd. 1
46ChL34
86YLJ84
Subd. 2
46ChL34
Subsec. e
46ChL34
25CLA515
Subd. 1
25CLA517
86YLJ84
Subd. 2
128PaL [1380
Subsec. f
128PaL [1380
Subsec. g
46ChL34
126PaL304
128PaL [1380
86YLJ84
Subsec. h
86YLJ84
Subsec. i
128PaL [1382
86YLJ84
§ 1134
86YLJ83
§ 1135
80WLR693
§ 1136
46ChL34
§ 1140
50NYL1191
86YLJ84
§ 1141
86YLJ84
§ 1144
46ChL39
67Cor1021
31StnL164
86YLJ84
Subsec. a
46ChL38
25CLA513
63Cor832
128PaL [1350
84WLR746
Subsec. b
46ChL38
Subd. 1
46ChL39
Subd. 2
¶ A
46ChL39
¶ B
46ChL39
Subd. 4
46ChL39
Subsec. c
Subd. 2
25CLA513
Subsec. d
46ChL39

128PaL [1349
§ 1145
30CLA316
§§ 1201 to 1242
46ChL34
§ 1202
Subsec. d
86YLJ84
§ 1203
86YLJ84
§ 1232
Subsec. d
Subd. 1
¶ B
52NYL457
§ 1301
et seq.
64Cor962
§§ 1301 to 1381
70VaL424
86YLJ87
§§ 1301 to 1323
79McL91
§§ 1301 to 1304
86YLJ9
§§ 1302 to 1368
80WLR645
§ 1302
Subsec. a
46ChL31
Subd. 2
46ChL31
§ 1306
53NYL [1157
§ 1307
53NYL [1157
§§ 1321 to 1323
86YLJ9
§ 1321
80WLR643
Subsec. a
46ChL31
82WLR732
Subsec. b
Subd. 1
82WLR732
§ 1322
53NYL [1157
32StnL263
82WLR732
Subsec. a
80WLR671
86YLJ21
Subsec. b
80WLR671
Subd. 3
46ChL32
86YLJ21
Subd. 6
86YLJ21

§ 1323
Subsecs. a to f
64MnL946
§ 1341
53NYL [1157
82WLR750
Subsec. f
82WLR812
§ 1342
53NYL [1157
Subsec. f
86YLJ89
§ 1362
46ChL32
70VaL423
80WLR645
86YLJ92
Subsec. a
86YLJ48
Subsec. b
46ChL32
80WLR646
86YLJ48
§§ 1363 to 1368
53TxL1426
§ 1364
80WLR643
§ 1368
82WLR813
86YLJ48
§ 1381
Subsec. c
Subd. 1
80WLR647
Subsec. d
80WLR648

TITLE 30

§ 21
et seq.
74CR1233
§§ 21 to 54
49ChL1026
75McL263
§ 21
74CR1245
§ 21a
64CaL1303
§§ 22 to 39
70Geo1514
§§ 22 to 26
60MnL630
§ 22
74CR1234
70Geo1515
60MnL625
§ 23
74CR1260

§ 26
74CR1234
§ 28
74CR1234
§ 35
74CR1234
§ 51
30StnL [1112
§ 52
30StnL [1112
§ 181
et seq.
74CR1260
60MnL625
§§ 181 to 287
32StnL375
§ 181
43ChL768
60MnL630
§ 185
70CaL584
63Cor182
67Geo711
39LCP(4) [226
27StnL345
§ 187
57TxL935
§ 193
74CR1262
§ 201
Subsec. a
Subd. 3
¶ C
67Geo717
§ 208
61VaL23
§ 226
Subsec. e
43CLA768
§ 241
74CR1242
§ 298
29StnL73
§ 351
et seq.
75CR1313
§ 352
60MnL630
§ 422
62CaL1056
§ 541
et seq.
74CR1236
§ 541i
74CR1236
§ 611
74CR1260
§ 612
74CR1249
70Geo1515
§ 621
et seq.
74CR1236
§ 621
74CR1249
§ 623
74CR1250

§ 721
et seq.
38LCP608
59MnL656
§§ 721 to 740
84CR584
§ 801
et seq.
66Cor244
80McL1472
59MnL656
29StnL5
63VaL307
86YLJ1025
§§ 801 to 962
69VaL1026
§§ 801 to 961
64MnL128
64MnL1076
64VaL993
§§ 801 to 960
64CaL702
44ChL330
78CR303
81McL1430
65MnL635
30StnL286
85YLJ38
§§ 801 to 825
65Cor502
§§ 801 to 823
80McL1484
§ 801
64CaL704
75CR24
59MnL655
§ 811
71McL169
59MnL655
Subsecs. c to f
72NwL106
Subsec. g
72NwL106
§ 811
(91St1291)
Subsec. c
80McL1484
§ 812
72NwL106
§ 813
Subsec. i
59MnL685
§ 813
(91St1297)
Subsec. a
67MnL137
§ 814
Subsec. a
64MnL123
§ 814
(91St1300)
Subsec. a
79CR1480

§ 815
(91St1303)
Subsec. a
79CR1450
Subsec. c
Subd. 1
64MnL127
Subd. 3
79CR1443
Subsec. d
79CR1447
§ 816
Subsec. b
60VaL218
§ 816
(91St1306)
Subsec. a
Subd. 1
79CR1448
65MnL67
Subsec. b
79CR1448
§ 819
64VaL993
Subsec. a
Subd. 3
79CR1439
§ 820
64VaL993
Subsec. b
Subd. 1
59MnL707
50NYL1191
§ 820
(91St1311)
79CR1438
Subsec. a
79CR1447
Subsec. i
79CR1447
Subsec. k
79CR1451
§ 823
79CR1447
81CR761
71Geo13
Subsec. d
Subd. 1
79CR1447
§§ 824 to 902
80McL1484
§ 861
Subsec. a
95HLR420
§ 863
59MnL671
Subsec. d
Subd. 1
59MnL685
§ 901
et seq.
75CR37
40LCP(4) [127
27StnL340
29StnL5
§§ 901 to 960
91HLR337

§§ 901 to 945
97HLR926
§§ 901 to 941
91HLR [1782
40LCP(4) [122
§§ 901 to 936
40LCP(4) [122
§ 901
44ChL31
62Cor523
§ 902
44ChL31
62Cor523
57TxL935
Subsec. a
Subd. 2
57TxL935
Subsec. e
57TxL935
§§ 921 to 924
44ChL31
62Cor523
80McL1484
§ 921
Subsec. c
70CaL890
§ 923
Subsec. b
50NYL1334
§ 924
75CR24
57TxL935
§§ 925 to 934
80McL1484
§§ 931 to 934
44ChL31
62Cor523
§ 931
75CR24
57TxL935
§ 932
75CR24
Subsec. a
55TxL975
§ 934
57TxL935
§§ 936 to 960
80McL1484
§§ 936 to 940
44ChL31
62Cor523
§§ 951 to 955
46LCP(3) [59
§ 951
44ChL31
62Cor523
§ 953
Subsec. d
63Geo8

§ 1001
et seq.
74CR1254
60MnL630
§ 1015
60MnL626
§ 1201
et seq.
68VaL450
§§ 1201 to 1328
30CLA613
79CR869
69Geo1083
67MnL300
132PaL300
67VaL329
89YLJ1536
§ 1202
Subsec. d
132PaL300
§§ 1211 to 1213
84CR590
§ 1253
Subsec. a
132PaL300
§ 1254
Subsec. a
132PaL301
Subsec. b
132PaL301
§ 1265
Subsec. d
35StnL1111
Subsec. e
35StnL1111
§ 1270
72CaL84
30CLA564
95HLR1216
Subsec. f
69Cor233
§ 1272
67Geo717
§§ 1401 to 1428
70Geo1514
§ 1401
46LCP(2) [33
§ 1411
70Geo1514

TITLE 31

91HLR [1771
80McL221
§ 1
et seq.
44ChL272
80CR963
37LCP135
40LCP(2) [53
124PaL615

556

FIGURE 5-II
SHEPARD'S FEDERAL LAW CITATIONS
IN SELECTED LAW REVIEWS

DISCUSSION OF PROBLEM 5.17   Under section 811, "71 McL 169" (*Michigan Law Review*) and "59 Mn L 655" (*Minnesota Law Review*) are cited.   Subsections c to f of that section were cited in "72 NwL 106" (*Northwestern Law Review*).   Subsection g was also cited in "72 NwL 106."   Also, "91 St 1291" (§ 811) was cited in "80 McL 1484."

Another way to find law review treatment of recent statutes is to consult the various indexes to legal periodicals.   Both the *Index to Legal Periodicals* and the *Current Law Index* have sections that cite legal literature commenting on particular statutes.

PROBLEM 5.18   Examine the entries reproduced from the *Current Law Index* in Figure 5-JJ from two years of this *Index* covering the Federal Mine Safety and Health Amendment Act of 1977.   (You would, of course, consult others years in the *Index* to find other articles.)   Does this research tool duplicate *Shepard's Federal Law Citations in Selected Law Reviews*?   In other words, what are the differences between the two?

FEDERAL Mine Safety and Health Amendment Act of 1977
30 U.S.C. 801-961 Warrantless administrative searches permissible under the Federal Mine Safety and Health Act of 1977. (case note)
64 Minn. L. Rev. 1076-1093 June '80

30 U.S.C. 801-960 Testing the constitutionality of warrantless administrative inspections. (case note)   11 U. Tol. L. Rev. 567-593 Spr '80

30 U.S.C. 801 et seq. Federal Mine Safety and Health Act of 1977 - an overview.
16 Law Notes 85-93 Summ '80

FEDERAL Mine Safety and Health Amendment Act of 1977
Federal mine health and safety.
38 J. Mo. B. 245-256 June '82

Administrative law: constitutionality of warrantless inspections authorized by the Federal Mine Safety and Health Act of 1977.
21 Washburn L.J. 652-663 Spr; '82

Donovan v. Dewey. (constitutionality of warrantless mine inspections) (case note)
10 Ecology L.Q. 139-149 Wntr '82

Fourth Amendment - warrantless administrative inspections of commercial property. (Supreme Court review) (case note)
72 J. Crim. L. & Criminology 1222-1245 Wint '81

FIGURE 5-JJ
CURRENT LAW INDEX

DISCUSSION OF PROBLEM 5.18   These two publications overlap in some ways but have important differences.   First, *Shepard's Federal Law Citations in Selected Law Reviews* is limited to twenty "national" reviews while the periodical indexes cover a much wider range of publi-

cations. Second, *Shepard's* provides detailed information about which section or sections were cited. On the other hand, the *Current Law Index* does not always identify the particular sections commented upon. Third, unlike the *Current Law Index*, *Shepard's* does not give the title of the article in which the statute was cited. You can also use the CD-ROM version of the *Current Law Index* ("LegalTrac") for this purpose.

6. PENDING LEGISLATION

The *CCH Congressional Index*, the *Congressional Information Service*, and the *Congressional Monitor* are good sources for determining the status of pending legislation. Of these, the *CCH Congressional Index* is probably the best because of its weekly supplementation. Computer databases are also useful for this purpose.

Section 5F.   Legislative History

Legislative intent is often regarded as the controlling factor in interpreting legislation.[14] Legislative history is often used to identify that legislative intent.[15]

1. THE LEGISLATIVE PROCESS AND THE SOURCES OF LEGISLATIVE HISTORY

The legislative process generates various sources that can be consulted to determine the legislative intent of Congress, such as Presidential messages that accompany proposed legislation, differences in congressional bills, testimony presented at hearings, congressional committee reports, debates on the floor of the House and Senate, proposed or adopted amendments, and other various documents. Legislative history of state legislation is generally difficult to obtain because many items, such as debates or hearings, are rarely published. A few states, however, now have commercial legislative history services. In absence of such a service, official information services through the legislature must be utilized as well as other local sources.

---

[14] See, e.g., United States v. Stone & Downer Co., 274 U.S. 225, 239 (1927) ("In this case, as in every other involving the interpretation of a statute, the intention of Congress is an all-important factor"); Carr v. New York State Bd. of Elections, 356 N.E.2d 713, 715 (N.Y. 1976) ("In statutory interpretation, legislative intent is the great and controlling principle").

[15] See Larry L. Teply, Legal Writing, Analysis, and Oral Argument 230-44 (1990) (discussing the various intrinsic and extrinsic means of determining legislative intent, including the use (and abuse) of legislative history).

A key to understanding the sources of legislative history is the legislative process, shown in Figure 5-KK (for federal legislation).

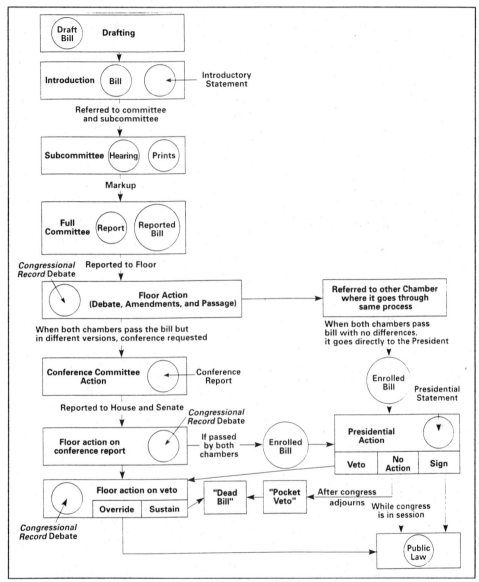

FIGURE 5-KK
WINNING RESEARCH SKILLS (WEST PUBLISHING CO.)

2. FINDING LEGISLATIVE HISTORY

(a) References in the Statutes at Large

One way to find the legislative history of a federal statute is to find the *United States Statutes at Large*. The basic legislative history of

enacted bills has been included in this source since the 88th Congress (1963).

(b) Compiled Legislative Histories

In a few instances, the legislative histories of statutes have been compiled by agencies that enforce statutes, law review authors, or special interest groups.   To determine if one exists for a particular statute, consult Nancy Johnson's *Sources of Compiled Legislative Histories* (AALL Pub. Ser. No. 14, 1988).   For most statutes, no such compilation exists.

(c) West's U.S. Code Congressional and Administrative News

Another source is West's *U.S. Code Congressional & Administrative News*.   This source is especially convenient because it not only provides references to the legislative history of an act but also reprints selected committee reports in the volume itself.

PROBLEM 5.19   Assume now that you want to determine the legislative history of the Federal Mine Safety and Health Amendments Act of 1977.   To find the legislative history of the Federal Mine Safety and Health Amendments Act of 1977, you would consult the index in the volumes of the *U.S. Code Congressional & Administrative News* (USCCAN) covering legislation enacted in 1977.   The relevant portion of the index entry for "Mines and Minerals" is reproduced in Figure 5-LL.   On what page in that volume can the legislative history be found?

MINES AND MINERALS
Coal, generally, this index
Federal Mine Safety and Health Act of 1977, 91 Stat. 1290
    Legislative history, 3401
Surface Mining Control and Reclamation Act of 1977, 91 Stat. 445
    Legislative history, 593

FIGURE 5-LL
U.S. CODE CONGRESSIONAL & ADMINISTRATIVE NEWS INDEX

DISCUSSION OF PROBLEM 5.19   The relevant index entry indicates that the legislative history of the Act begins on page 3401 of *U.S. Code Congressional & Administrative News*.

PROBLEM 5.20   Page 3401 of *U.S. Code Congressional & Administrative News* (USCCAN) is reproduced in Figure 5-MM.   Based on the information shown, what is the legislative history of this statute?

Title of
the
Act

Public
law
number

Commit-
tee
reports
relevant
to this
law

Dates
this
legisla-
tion
was
consid-
ered and
passed

Reprint-
ed
reports

Page
number
of the
original
report

Full text
of the
report

USCCAN
page
number

MINE SAFETY AND HEALTH ACT
P.L. 95-164

FEDERAL MINE SAFETY AND HEALTH AMEND-MENTS ACT OF 1977

P.L. 95-164, see page 91 Stat. 1290

Senate Report (Human Resources Committee) No. 95-181,
May 16, 1977 [To accompany S. 717]

House Report (Education and Labor Committee) No. 95-312,
May 13, 1977 [To accompany H.R. 4287]

Senate Conference Report No. 95-461, Oct. 3, 1977
[To accompany S. 717]

House Conference Report No. 94-655, Oct. 3, 1977
[To accompany S. 717]

Cong. Record Vol. 123 (1977)

DATES OF CONSIDERATION AND PASSAGE

Senate June 21, October 6, 1977

House July 15, October 27, 1977

The Senate bill was passed in lieu of the House bill. The Senate
Report and the House Conference Report are set out.

SENATE REPORT NO. 95-181

[page 1]

The Committee on Human Resources, to which was referred
the bill (S. 717) to promote safety and health in the mining industry, to prevent recurring disasters in the mining industry, and for
other purposes, having considered the same, reports favorably thereon
with an amendment and recommends that the bill (as amended)
do pass.

INTRODUCTION

The hazards involved with the mining of coal and other materials
and the need to provide for the health and safety of the nation's min-
ers have long been a matter of Federal law.

As early as 1865, a bill was introduced in the Congress to create a
Federal Mining Bureau. However, little was done until a series of
serious mine disasters occurred after the turn of the century, causing
public demand for Federal action to stop excessive loss of life. In July
1910, an act of Congress established a Bureau of Mines in the Department of the Interior which was charged with making:

> Diligent investigation of the methods of mining especially
> related to the safety of miners and the appliances best
> adapted to prevent accidents, the possible improvement of

3401

FIGURE 5-MM
U.S. CODE CONGRESSIONAL & ADMINISTRATIVE NEWS

DISCUSSION OF PROBLEM 5.20   The information given in Figure 5-MM indicates that the Senate bill, S. 717, was the bill ultimately enacted by Congress. The Act's public law number is 95-164. The text of the law as enacted can be found at 91 Stat. 1290 and on a similarly numbered page in the *U.S. Code Congressional and Administrative News*.

Four committee reports on this legislation are cited: Senate Report No. 95-181, House Report No. 95-312, Senate Report No. 95-461 (Conference Report), and House Report No. 94-655 (Conference Report). *U.S. Code Congressional & Administrative News* has reprinted the text of two of them.

The dates of consideration and passage by the Senate were June 21 and October 6, 1977. The House considered and passed the legislation on July 15 and October 27, 1977. The debate and vote can be found by consulting those dates in Volume 123 of the *Congressional Record* (1977).

PROBLEM 5.21   Many volumes of West's *U.S. Code Congressional & Administrative News* also have a "Legislative History Table." Two pages from that table have been reproduced in Figures 5-NN and 5-OO. Find the entry for the Federal Mine Safety and Health Amendments Act of 1977. What information do you need to know to use this table?

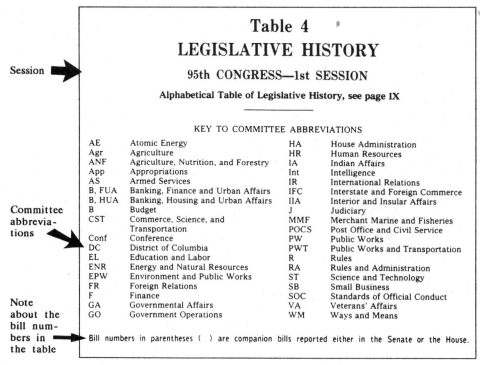

FIGURE 5-NN

U.S. CODE CONGRESSIONAL & ADMINISTRATIVE NEWS

TABLE 4—LEGISLATIVE HISTORY

Public Law No.95-	Date App.	91 Stat. Page	Bill No.	Report No. 95- House	Report No. 95- Senate	Comm. Reporting House	Comm. Reporting Senate	Cong.Rec.Vol.123 (1977) Dates of Consideration and Passage House	Senate
152	Nov. 4	1254	H.R. 2817	253	185	MMF	EPW (S. 1237)	May 10	Oct. 19
153	Nov. 4	1255	H.R. 4297	325(I) 325(II)	189 216	MMF ST	EPW CST (S. 1527, 1425)	Oct. 14 Oct. 14	Oct. 20 Oct. 20
154	Nov. 7	1256	H.J.Res. 611	none	none	none	none	Oct. 31	Nov. 3
155	Nov. 8	1257	H.R. 5101	157 722	188	ST Conf	EPW (S. 1417)	Apr. 19, Oct. 25	May 27, Oct. 20
156	Nov. 8	1264	H.R. 9090	638(I) 638(II)	none	Agr App	none	Oct. 17	Oct. 25
157	Nov. 8	1265	S. 2149	none	475	none	J	Oct. 25	Oct. 13
158	Nov. 8	1268	H.J.Res. 621	739(I) 739(II)	567	IIA IFC	ENR (S.J.Res. 82)	Nov. 2	Nov. 2
159	Nov. 8	1269	H.R. 3259	79	422	WM	F	Mar. 21, Oct. 25	Sept. 15
160	Nov. 8	1271	H.R. 2850	423	419	WM	F	July 18, Oct. 25	Sept. 15
161	Nov. 8	1273	H.R. 2982	424	420	WM	F	July 18, Oct. 25	Sept. 16
162	Nov. 8	1275	H.R. 3093	425	421	WM	F	July 18, Oct. 25	Sept. 15
163	Nov. 9	1278	H.R. 6010	301 14 15 773	199	PWT PWT PWT Conf (H.R. 26, 27)	CST (S. 1325)	May 17, June 8, Nov. 2	May 27, Oct. 20, 28
164	Nov. 9	1290	S. 717	312 655	181 461	EL Conf (H.R. 4287)	HR Conf	July 15, Oct. 27	June 21, Oct. 6
165	Nov. 9	1323	H.J.Res. 643	792	none	App	none	Nov. 3	Nov. 4
166	Nov. 10	1325	H.R. 1139	281 708	277 504	EL Conf (S. 1420)	ANF	May 18, Oct. 27	June 30, Oct. 28
167	Nov. 11	1347	S. 2208	750	510	J (H.R. 7249)	J	Oct. 31	Oct. 20
168	Nov. 11	1349	S. 810	745	152	J	J	Oct. 31	May 13
169	Nov. 12	1350	H.R. 2527	192	518	IIA	ENR	May 2	Oct. 28
170	Nov. 12	1351	H.R. 2849	422	433	WM	F	July 18, Oct. 25	Sept. 21, Oct 27
171	Nov. 12	1353	H.R. 3387	439	456	WM	F	July 18, Oct. 25	Oct. 17, 27
172	Nov. 12	1358	H.R. 3373	426	434	WM	F	July 18, Oct. 25	Sept. 21, Oct. 27
173	Nov. 12	1359	S. 1019	332 747	160	MMF Conf (H.R. 4963)	CST	July 13, Oct. 31	May 24, Nov. 1
174	Nov. 12	1361	S. 2118	none	527	none	ENR	Oct. 31	Oct. 28
175	Nov. 14	1362	S. 2052	735	451	PWT	RA	Nov. 1	Sept. 30
176	Nov. 14	1363	H.R. 4458	761	none	WM	none	Oct. 31	Nov. 1
177	Nov. 15	1368	H.R. 7278	727	none	MMF	none	Oct. 25	Nov. 1
178	Nov. 15	1369	H.R. 8499	712	none	IIA	none	Oct. 31, Nov. 3	Nov. 1

Rele- vant entry

FIGURE 5-OO
U.S. CODE CONGRESSIONAL & ADMINISTRATIVE NEWS

DISCUSSION OF PROBLEM 5.21 The relevant entry is listed under 95-164, the public law number. Note the committee abbreviations (EL and HR). The key to abbreviations in Figure 5-NN identifies the reporting committees as the House Education and Labor Committee and the Senate Human Resources Committee. To find documents not reprinted in *U.S. Code Congressional and Administrative News*, you would need to obtain those documents from the *Serial Set*, the *Monthly Catalog of U.S. Government Publications*, or other published sources. Some of these documents may be available in depository libraries.

(d) Congressional Information Service

Another excellent source for finding the legislative history of federal statutes enacted since 1970[16] is the *Congressional Information Service (CIS Index)*. This service indexes and abstracts relevant legislative documents for each session.

PROBLEM 5.22 The legislative history for the Federal Mine Safety and Health Amendments Act of 1977 in the *Congressional Information Service* is shown in Figure 5-PP. (1) Compare the legislative history shown in Figures 5-MM and 5-OO with that shown in Figure 5-PP. What are some of the differences between the two? (2) Assume that you want to find the Presidential statement on the Federal Mine Safety and Health Act Amendments Act of 1977. Where can that statement be found?

---

[16]The Congressional Information Service has also begun to index older congressional materials.

Abstracts of the various reports can be found in the annual volumes (e.g., 1976 CIS/Annual).

Complete legislative histories, including the slip laws, reports, debates, hearings, committee prints, Presidential messages, and other documents are available through Congressional Information Service's CIS Legislative History Service. The legislative histories may be purchased individually in paper or microfiche copies or as part of a microfiche subscription service.

Each CIS legislative history is accompanied by an "Annotated Directory" that contains a "Table of Contents and Guide to Microfiche" and a list of "Citations and Annotations to Official Publications." The annotated directories that accompany each history in the service are published in a bound "Legislative History Annual" at the end of each congressional session.

> **PL95-164   FEDERAL MINE SAFETY AND HEALTH AMENDMENTS ACT OF 1977.**
> Nov. 9, 1977. 95-1.   34 p.
> • CIS/MF/3   eItem 575.
> 91 STAT. 1290.
>
> "To promote safety and health in the mining industry, to prevent recurring disasters in the mining industry, and for other purposes."
>
> Title I changes title of the Federal Coal Mine Health and Safety Act of 1969 to the Federal Mine Safety and Health Act and brings mining and milling under the act's jurisdiction. Title II contains revised provisions relating to standards enforcement by DOL and HEW, and establishes the Federal Mine Safety and Health Review Commission. Title III transfers administration of mine safety and health programs from Interior Dept to DOL under a new Mine Safety and Health Administration, and repeals the Federal Metal and Nonmetallic Mine Safety Act of 1966.
>
> Legislative history: (S. 717 and related bills):
> **1971 CIS/Annual:**
> Senate Hearings: S541-17.
> **1973 CIS/Annual:**
> House Hearings: H341-9.
> Senate Hearings: S541-4.
> Senate Committee Print: S542-29.
> **1974 CIS/Annual:**
> House Hearings: 401-19.
> **1975 CIS/Annual:**
> Senate Hearings: S401-39.
> Senate Committee Print: S542-8.
> Senate Report: S403-3 (No. 95-217, accompanying S. 1774).
> **1976 CIS/Annual:**
> House Hearings: H341-52; H341-68.
> Senate Hearings: S541-79.
> House Reports: H343-12 (No. 94-1147, accompanying H.R. 13555); H343-13 (No. 94-1147, pt. 2, accompanying H.R. 13555); H343-14 (No. 94-1147, pt. 3, accompanying H.R. 13555).
> Senate Reports: S543-29 (No. 94-1197, accompanying H.R. 13555); S543-30 (No. 94-1198, accompanying S. 1302).
> **1977 CIS/Annual:**
> House Hearings: H341-56; H341-57.
> Senate Hearings: S411-25.
> House Reports: H343-11 (No. 95-312, accompanying H.R. 4287); H343-22 (No. 95-655, Conference Report).
> Senate Reports: S413-16 (No. 95-181); S413-28 (No. 95-461, Conference Report).
> Congressional Record Vol. 123 (1977):
> June 20, 21, considered and passed Senate.
> July 14, 15, considered and passed House, amended, in lieu of H.R. 4287.
> Oct. 6, Senate agreed to conference report.
> Oct. 27, House agreed to conference report.
> Weekly Compilation of Presidential Documents Vol. 13, No. 46 (1977):
> Nov. 9, Presidential statement.

FIGURE 5-PP
CIS 1977 ANNUAL ABSTRACTS

DISCUSSION OF PROBLEM 5.22 (1) The *Congressional Information Service* provides a more detailed legislative history than West's *U.S. Code Congressional & Administrative News.* (2) The last entry of

the relevant legislative history in Figure 5-PP indicates that the President's statement can be found in Volume 13, No. 46 of the *Weekly Compilation of Presidential Documents* covering November 9th, 1977.

3. CITING COMMITTEE REPORTS

CITING CONGRESSIONAL COMMITTEE REPORTS IN BLUEBOOK FORM

According to *Bluebook* Rule 13.4, numbered federal committee reports should be cited as follows:

Cite committee reports by number, Congress, session, page, and year. Do not include as a part of the report number the identification of the Congress. Add a parallel citation to the *U.S. Code Congressional and Administrative News* whenever possible (U.S.C.C.A.N.). Titles and authors of reports may be given.

The following are citations of congressional committee reports:

S. Rep. No. 2107, 87th Cong., 1st Sess., <u>reprinted in</u> 1962 U.S.C.C.A.N. 2844.

H.R. Rep. No. 390, 100th Cong., 1st Sess., <u>reprinted in</u> 1987 U.S.C.C.A.N. 2137, 2138. (Page 2 of the report is cited; the cited material is reprinted on page 2138).

PROBLEM 5.23 Assume that you have just quoted the following two sentences from the third paragraph of the Senate Report reproduced in Figure 5-OO: "As early as 1865, a bill was introduced in the Congress to create a Federal Mining Bureau. However, little was done until a series of serious mine disasters occurred after the turn of the century, causing public demand for Federal action to stop excessive loss of life." Which of the following is the correct citation for this quoted sentence?

(a) S. Rep. No. 95-181, 95th Cong., 1st Sess. 1, <u>reprinted in</u> 1977 U.S.C.C.A.N 3401.

(b) Federal Mine Safety and Health Amendments Act of 1977, S Rep No 95-181, 95th Cong, 1st Sess 1 (1977), reprinted in 1977 USCCAN 3401, 3401.

(c) Federal Mine Safety and Health Amendments Act of 1977, S Rep No 181, 95th Cong, 1st Sess 1, reprinted in 1977 USCCAN 3401.

(d) S. Rep. No. 181, 95th Cong., 1st Sess. 1, reprinted in 1977 U.S.C.C.A.N. 3401, 3401.

DISCUSSION OF PROBLEM 5.23 Unlike answer (d), answer (a) erroneously includes the Congress in the report number (95-181). Answers (b) and (c) improperly omit the periods from the abbreviations. Another difference between answer (a) and answer (d) is the repetition of the page number (3401) in answer (d). In referring to specific material within a source that is not separately paginated, both the page on which the material begins and the page on which the specific material appears should be indicated; when the first page is referred to, the page number should be repeated. *Bluebook* Rule 3.3(a). Unlike the original Senate Report, which is a separately paginated work, the reprinted committee reports in *U.S. Code Congressional & Administrative News* are not separately paginated. Therefore, the page number must be repeated, and answer (d) is the preferred citation. Note that the original page numbers of the Senate Report are indicated in brackets, e.g., [page 1] in the reprinted report.

4. CITING CONGRESSIONAL DEBATES

Legislative debates and proceedings are reported verbatim (subject to revision by members of Congress) in the *Congressional Record* (Cong. Rec.) (1873 to date). The *Congressional Record's* predecessors were the *Congressional Globe* (Cong. Globe) (1833-1873), the *Register of Debates* (Cong. Deb.) (1824-1837), and the *Annals of Congress* (Annals of Cong.) (1789-1824).

CITING THE CONGRESSIONAL RECORD

The Congressional Record is cited by volume, page, and date (e.g., 119 Cong. Rec. 741 (1973). The *Congressional Record* is repaged when it is bound. If the daily edition of the *Record* is being cited, "daily ed." should be inserted before the full date, e.g., 122 Cong. Rec. H2086 (daily ed. Mar. 18, 1976). *Bluebook* Rule 13.5.

The *Congressional Record* has a Daily Digest (status table of bills acted upon) and an Index. The bound version has a cumulative index, a table of the history of bills and resolutions for the session, and a cumulation of the Daily Digest.

Chapter 6

ADMINISTRATIVE LEGAL RESEARCH AND RULES OF EVIDENCE, PRACTICE, PROCEDURE, AND ETHICS

Section 6A. Introduction

This chapter focuses primarily on administrative legal research. It also discusses rules of evidence, practice, procedure, and ethics. Recall from Chapter 1 that administrative law is a major source of law (in addition to legislative and judicial sources). Administrative law is created by governmental agencies in the form of administrative regulations and agency rulings.

The same basic research techniques described in prior chapters (e.g., index and topic method of search, *Shepard's Citations*, etc.) are used in administrative law research. Administrative regulations are published (1) chronologically in administrative registers by the date that the rules and regulations were issued and (2) by subject in administrative codes of regulations and rules currently in force by subject matter—without regard to the date they were issued. Similarly, agency rulings are published (1) chronologically in reporters (e.g., decisions of the Federal Trade Commission are reported in the *Federal Trade Commission Reports* (1915 to date)) and (2) by subject (most often in looseleaf services in summary form) (e.g., in Commerce Clearing House's *Trade Regulation Reporter*). In many ways, agency decisions are similar to court decisions.

Like other research situations, administrative law research is likely to arise in a factual context. Several examples have already arisen in the various fact patterns presented in prior chapters.

Section 6B. Finding, Working With, Citing, and Updating Administrative Rules and Regulations

1. FINDING ADMINISTRATIVE RULES AND REGULATIONS

Federal administrative rules and regulations have been published in the *Federal Register* (Fed. Reg.) since 1936. The *Federal Register* is published daily, except Saturday, Sunday, and official holidays. It is analogous to the *United States Statutes at Large*. Rules and regulations published in the *Federal Register* are codified in the *Code of Federal Regulations* (C.F.R.).

Many states now officially codify and publish state administrative regulations in state registers and sets similar to the *Code of Federal Regulations*. In other states, each agency issues its own regulations, and, in such instances, you will have to contact the agency to obtain the regulations. Generally speaking, state administrative regulations are not widely available beyond the state of their applicability—although the trend is clearly toward making state administrative regulations more widely available.

How would you find the regulations (if any) that have been issued in a particular context? The focus of the following discussion is on federal regulations. Not all of these approaches are possible with state administrative regulations.

(a) Cross-References to Regulations

One way to find federal regulations would be to consult an annotated version of the *United States Code*. The annotated versions provide cross-references to the *Code of Federal Regulations*. Other sources also provide cross-references.

PROBLEM 6.1 Assume that you want to find federal regulations governing the storage of explosives. Examine the "Research References" in *American Jurisprudence Second* reproduced in Figure 5-B in Chapter 5. To what title and part of the *Code of Federal Regulations* are you directed?

DISCUSSION OF PROBLEM 6.1 The "Research References" in *American Jurisprudence Second* direct you to the following federal regulations: "27 CFR Part 55 (Regulation by Bureau of Alcohol, Tobacco and Firearms of commerce in explosives)."

(b) Indexes

The *Code of Federal Regulations* has an Index section in its *CFR Index and Finding Aids* volume. The *Federal Register* has annual, quarterly, and weekly indexes. National Standards Association publishes the *Federal Index*. This index provides monthly indexing of the *Federal Register*, the *Congressional Record*, and the *Weekly Compilation of Presidential Papers*. It also has a cumulative annual volume. *Federal Regulatory Week*, published by Prentice Hall, provides a weekly summary of proposed, interim, and final regulations. It also has a calendar of hearing dates and deadlines.

PROBLEM 6.2 Assume that you want to find federal regulations dealing with explosives and fireworks and that you do not have any direct references to those regulations. One way to find these rules and regulations is to consult the *CFR Index and Finding Aids* volume. The beginning entries under "Explosives" are shown in Figure 6-A. To what titles and parts of the *Code of Federal Regulations* are you directed?

Explosives

See also Hazardous materials
            transportation
            Hazardous substances
Airplane operator security, 14 CFR 108
Blasters, surface coal mining and
        reclamation operations
    Certification in Federal program States
        and on Indian lands, 30 CFR 955
    Certification standards, permanent
        regulatory program requirements,
        30 CFR 850
Explosives, commerce, 27 CFR 55
Explosives and other dangerous cargoes
        within or contiguous to waterfront
        facilities, handling, 33 CFR 126
Fireworks devices, 16 CFR 1507
Manufacturing, water pollution, effluent
        guidelines and standards, point source
        categories, 40 CFR 457
Mine safety and health
    Explosives and sheathed explosive units
        used in underground mines,
        approval requirements, 30 CFR 15

FIGURE 6-A

CFR INDEX AND FINDING AIDS VOLUME

DISCUSSION OF PROBLEM 6.2   The entry "Explosives, commerce" in the *CFR Index and Finding Aids* volume directs you to Part 55 of Title 27 of the *Code of Federal Regulations*.   Title 27 covers "Alcohol, Tobacco Products and Firearms."   The entry "Fireworks devices" directs you to Part 1507 of Title 16.

(c) Parallel Table of Authorities and Rules

If the authority for promulgating regulations is known, you can find the relevant regulations by consulting the "Parallel Table of [Statutory] Authorities and Rules" in the *CFR Index and Finding Aids* volume accompanying the *C.F.R.* pamphlets.   Read the following description of this table.

The following table lists rulemaking authority (except 5 U.S.C. 301) for regulations codified in the *Code of Federal Regulations*. Also included are statutory citations which are noted as being interpreted or applied by those regulations.

The table is divided into four segments: United States Code citations, United States Statutes at Large citations, public law citations, and Presidential documents citations. Within each segment the citations are arranged in numerical order:

For the United States Code, by title and section;

For the United States Statutes at Large, by volume and page number;

For public laws, by number; and

For Presidential documents (Proclamations, Executive orders, and Reorganization plans), by document number.

Entries in the table are taken directly from the rulemaking authority citation provided by Federal agencies in their regulations. Federal agencies are responsible for keeping these citations current and accurate. Because Federal agencies sometimes present these citations in an inconsistent manner, the table cannot be considered all inclusive.

The portion of the table listing the United States Code citations is the most comprehensive, as these citations are picked up and carried in the table whenever they are given in the authority citations provided by the agencies. United States Statutes at Large and public law citations are carried in the table only when there are no corresponding United States Code citations given.

For a list of current public laws cited as rulemaking authority, see Table I-- Parallel Table of Authorities and Rules in the monthly "List of CFR Sections Affected" (LSA).

This table is revised as of January 1, 1990. Additions and removals to the table resulting from regulations published in the *Federal Register* since January 1, 1990, are found in the current month's edition of the LSA.

FIGURE 6-B

CFR INDEX AND FINDING AIDS VOLUME

PROBLEM 6.3   Assuming that you know the statutory authority for promulgating regulations governing explosives is 18 U.S.C. §§ 841 et seq.   Find the entry for these sections in the Parallel Table of [Statutory] Authorities and Rules reproduced in Figure 6-D.   To what title and *CFR* parts are you directed?

Sections of Title 18 of the <u>United States Code</u> are listed in this column →

Relevant entry →

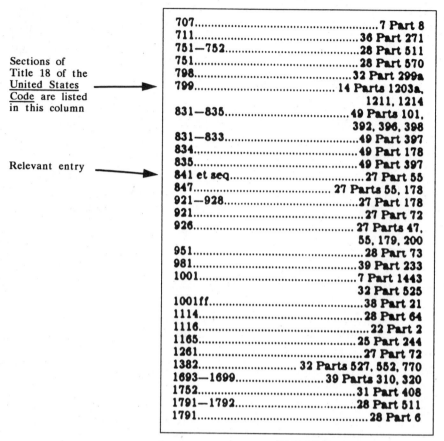

707	7 Part 8
711	36 Part 271
751—752	28 Part 511
751	28 Part 570
798	32 Part 299a
799	14 Parts 1203a, 1211, 1214
831—835	49 Parts 101, 392, 396, 398
831—833	49 Part 397
834	49 Part 178
835	49 Part 397
841 et seq	27 Part 55
847	27 Parts 55, 178
921—928	27 Part 178
921	27 Part 72
926	27 Parts 47, 55, 179, 200
951	28 Part 73
981	39 Part 233
1001	7 Part 1443 / 32 Part 525
1001ff	38 Part 21
1114	28 Part 64
1116	22 Part 2
1165	25 Part 244
1261	27 Part 72
1382	32 Parts 527, 552, 770
1693—1699	39 Parts 310, 320
1752	31 Part 408
1791—1792	28 Part 511
1791	28 Part 6

FIGURE 6-C

CFR INDEX AND FINDING AIDS VOLUME

DISCUSSION OF PROBLEM 6.3 You are again directed to Part 55 of Title 27.

2. READING, APPLYING, AND CITING ADMINISTRATIVE RULES AND REGULATIONS

Reading and applying administrative regulations is similar to reading and applying legislation. In fact, valid administrative rules and regulations have the same binding force as statutes. Other issues relating to administrative regulations relate to their promulgation[1] and delegation of authority.[2]

---

[1] *See* Larry L. Teply, <u>Legal Writing, Analysis, and Oral Argument</u> 210-11 (1990) ("Promulgation of Regulations").

[2] *See id.* at 214 ("Delegated Authority").

PROBLEM 6.4 Examine the following figures showing the beginning pages of Part 55 of Title 27. Which subpart and sections deal with licensing and permits?

Pt. 55   **27 CFR Ch. I (4-1-91 Edition)**

27 CFR part 53 section number	OMB control number(s)
§ 53.1	1545-0723
§ 53.3	1545-0685
§ 53.11	1545-0723
§ 53.92	1545-0023
§ 53.93	1545-0023
§ 53.99	1545-0023
§ 53.131	1545-0023
§ 53.132	1545-0023
§ 53.133	1545-0023
§ 53.134	1545-0023
§ 53.136	1545-0023
§ 53.140	1545-0023
§ 53.141	1545-0023
§ 53.142	1545-0023
§ 53.143	1545-0023
§ 53.151	1545-0023, 1545-0723
§ 53.152	1545-0723
§ 53.153	1545-0257, 1545-0723
§ 53.155	1545-0723
§ 53.157	1545-0257
§ 53.171	1545-0023, 1545-0723
§ 53.172	1545-0723
§ 53.173	1545-0723
§ 53.174	1545-0723
§ 53.175	1545-0723
§ 53.176	1545-0723
§ 53.177	1545-0723
§ 53.178	1545-0723
§ 53.179	1545-0723
§ 53.180	1545-0723
§ 53.181	1545-0723
§ 53.182	1545-0723
§ 53.183	1545-0723
§ 53.184	1545-0023, 1545-0723
§ 53.185	1545-0023, 1545-0723
§ 53.186	1545-0723

PART 55—COMMERCE IN EXPLOSIVES

Subpart A—Introduction

Sec.
55.1 Scope of regulations.
55.2 Relation to other provisions of law.

Subpart B—Definitions

55.11 Meaning of terms.

Subpart C—Administrative and Miscellaneous Provisions

55.21 Forms prescribed.
55.22 Alternate methods and procedures; emergency variations from requirements.
55.23 List of explosive materials.
55.24 Right of entry and examination.
55.25 Disclosure of information.
55.26 Prohibited shipment, transportation, or receipt of explosive materials.

Sec.
55.27 Out-of-State disposition of explosive materials.
55.28 Stolen explosive materials.
55.29 Unlawful storage.
55.30 Reporting theft or loss of explosive materials.
55.31 Inspection of site of accidents or fires; right of entry.
55.32 Special explosive devices.

Subpart D—Licenses and Permits

55.41 General.
55.42 License fees.
55.43 Permit fees.
55.44 License or permit fee not refundable.
55.45 Original license or permit.
55.46 Renewal of license or permit.
55.47 Insufficient fee.
55.48 Abandoned application.
55.49 Issuance of license or permit.
55.50 Correction of error on license or permit.
55.51 Duration of license or permit.
55.52 Limitations on license or permit.
55.53 License and permit not transferable.
55.54 Change of address.
55.55 Change in class of explosive materials.
55.56 Change in trade name.
55.57 Change of control.
55.58 Continuing partnerships.
55.59 Right of succession by certain persons.
55.60 Certain continuances of business or operations.
55.61 Discontinuance of business or operations.
55.62 State or other law.
55.63 Explosives magazine changes.

Subpart E—License and Permit Proceedings

55.71 Opportunity for compliance.
55.72 Denial of initial application.
55.73 Hearing after initial application is denied.
55.74 Denial of renewal application or revocation of license or permit.
55.75 Hearing after denial of renewal application or revocation of license or permit.
55.76 Action by regional director (compliance).
55.77 Designated place of hearing.
55.78 Representation at a hearing.
55.79 Appeal on petition to the Director.
55.80 Court review.
55.81 Service on applicant, licensee, or permittee.
55.82 Provisions of Part 200 made applicable.
55.83 Operations by licensees or permittees after notice of denial or revocation.

658

FIGURE 6-D
CODE OF FEDERAL REGULATIONS (4-1-91)

Bureau of Alcohol, Tobacco and Firearms, Treasury   **§ 55.1**

Sec.

Subpart F—Conduct of Business or Operations

55.101   Posting of license or permit.
55.102   Authorized operations by permittees and certain licensees.
55.103   Transactions among licensees/permittees.
55.104   Certified copy of license or permit.
55.105   Distributions to nonlicensees and nonpermittees.
55.106   Certain prohibited distributions.
55.107   Record of transactions.
55.108   Importation.
55.109   Identification of explosive materials.

Subpart G—Records and Reports

55.121   General.
55.122   Records maintained by licensed importers.
55.123   Records maintained by licensed manufacturers.
55.124   Records maintained by licensed dealers.
55.125   Records maintained by licensed manufacturers-limited and permittees.
55.126   Explosives transaction record.
55.127   Daily summary of magazine transactions.
55.128   Discontinuance of business.
55.129   Exportation.
55.130   [Reserved]

Subpart H—Exemptions

55.141   Exemptions.
55.142   Relief from disabilities incurred by indictment, information or conviction.

Subpart I—Unlawful Acts, Penalties, Seizures, and Forfeitures

55.161   Engaging in business without a license.
55.162   False statement or representation.
55.163   False entry in record.
55.164   Unlawful storage.
55.165   Failure to report theft or loss.
55.166   Seizure or forfeiture.

Subpart J—[Reserved]

Subpart K—Storage

55.201   General.
55.202   Classes of explosive materials.
55.203   Types of magazines.
55.204   Inspection of magazines.
55.205   Movement of explosive materials.
55.206   Location of magazines.
55.207   Construction of type 1 magazines.
55.208   Construction of type 2 magazines.
55.209   Construction of type 3 magazines.
55.210   Construction of type 4 magazines.
55.211   Construction of type 5 magazines.

Sec.

55.212   Smoking and open flames.
55.213   Quantity and storage restrictions.
55.214   Storage within types 1, 2, 3, and 4 magazines.
55.215   Housekeeping.
55.216   Repair of magazines.
55.217   Lighting.
55.218   Table of distances for storage of explosive materials.
55.219   Table of distances for storage of low explosives.
55.220   Table of separation distances of ammonium nitrate and blasting agents from explosives or blasting agents.
55.221   Requirements for special fireworks, pyrotechnic compositions, and explosive materials used in assembling fireworks.
55.222   Table of distances between fireworks process buildings and between fireworks process and fireworks nonprocess buildings.
55.223   Table of distances between fireworks process buildings and other specified areas.
55.224   Table of distances for the storage of special fireworks (except bulk salutes).

AUTHORITY: 18 U.S.C. Chapter 40, 847, 926; 44 U.S.C. 3504(h).

SOURCE: T.D. ATF-87, 46 FR 40384, Aug. 7, 1981, unless otherwise noted.

Subpart A—Introduction

§ 55.1   Scope of regulations.

(a) *In general.* The regulations contained in this part relate to commerce in explosives and implement Title XI, Regulation of Explosives (18 U.S.C. Chapter 40; 84 Stat. 952), of the Organized Crime Control Act of 1970 (84 Stat. 922).

(b) *Procedural and substantive requirements.* This part contains the procedural and substantive requirements relative to:

(1) The interstate of foreign commerce in explosive materials;

(2) The licensing of manufacturers and importers of, and dealers in, explosive materials;

(3) The issuance of user permits;

(4) The conduct of business by licensees and operations by permittees;

(5) The storage of explosive materials;

(6) The records and reports required of licensees and permittees;

(7) Relief from disabilities under this part; and

659

FIGURE 6-E

CODE OF FEDERAL REGULATIONS (4-1-91)

DISCUSSION OF PROBLEM 6.4   Licensing and permits are covered in Subpart D (§§ 55.41 to 55.63).   Proceedings relating to licensing and permits are covered in Subpart E.   Section 55.161 specifically prohibits engaging in a business (involving explosive materials) without a license.

CITING FEDERAL RULES AND REGULATIONS

The *Federal Register* is cited by volume, page, and date. When the *Federal Register* (Fed. Reg.) indicates where the regulation will appear in the *Code of Federal Regulations*, that information should be given parenthetically. *Bluebook* Rule 14.2(a).

The *Code of Federal Regulations* (C.F.R.) is cited by title, section, and year. The date of the volume is given in parentheses. *Bluebook* Rule 14.2(a). Note that the section number is formed from a part number and subsection; thus, § 55.161 is subsection 161 of Part 55.

Examples of typical citations of these sources were given in § D(4)(a) in Chapter 1.

3. UPDATING FEDERAL ADMINISTRATIVE RULES AND REGULATIONS

The regulations shown in Figure 6-D and 6-E are in the 1991 volume of the *Code of Federal Regulations*. Before you can be assured that these regulations are the ones currently in force, you must update the *Code of Federal Regulations* volume. Federal rules and regulations are updated in two basic ways: (a) using the *Federal Register*; and (b) using *Shepard's Code of Federal Regulations Citations*.

(a) Updating Using the Federal Register

New or revised regulations issued since the latest *Code of Federal Regulations* volume can be located by examining (1) the "Cumulative List of CFR Sections Affected" table in the latest *List of CFR Sections Affected* ("LSA") pamphlet (issued monthly) accompanying the *Code of Federal Regulations*, and then (2) the "Cumulative List of Parts Affected" table appearing in the "Reader Aids" section at the end of the latest issue of the *Federal Register*.

PROBLEM 6.5 Examine the title page and explanation of how to use the LSA given at the beginning of the pamphlet shown in Figures 6-F and 6-G. Review the discussion of how the LSA is issued, and determine when Title 27 volumes are reissued each year. This LSA pamphlet was issued at the end of August, 1991.

LSA

List of CFR Sections Affected

August 1991

Title 1–16
Changes January 2, 1991
through August 30, 1991

Title 17–27
Changes April 1, 1991
through August 30, 1991

Title 28–41
Changes July 1, 1991
through August 30, 1991

Title 42–50
Changes October 1, 1990
through August 30, 1991

FIGURE 6-F
LIST OF CFR SECTIONS AFFECTED (LSA)

1

LSA—LIST OF CFR SECTIONS AFFECTED

The LSA (List of CFR Sections Affected) is a monthly publication designed to lead users of the Code of Federal Regulations (CFR) to amendatory actions published in the Federal Register (FR). It should be shelved with current CFR volumes. Entries are by CFR title, chapter, part, and section. Proposed rules are listed at the end of appropriate titles.

HOW TO USE THIS FINDING AID

The CFR is revised annually according to the following schedule:

Titles 1-16—as of Jan. 1
17-27—as of April 1
28-41—as of July 1
42-50—as of Oct. 1

To bring these regulations up to date, consult the most recent LSA for any changes, additions, or removals published after the revision date of the volume you are using. Then check the CUMULATIVE LIST OF PARTS AFFECTED appearing in the Reader Aids of the latest Federal Register for less detailed but timely changes published after the final date included in this publication.

Boldface entries are used to distinguish current month amendments from previous entries. Example: **1413.23 Amended......12345. Boldface** page numbers under a particular title indicate that the page numbers span 2 years.

Cite a page reference from this publication using the volume number (i.e. 56 FR for 1991) and the page number. Example: 24727 cite as 56 FR 24727. For your convenience, the volume number has been included in the Table of Federal Register Issue Pages and Dates.

ISSUES TO BE SAVED

There is no single annual issue of the LSA. Four ANNUAL ISSUES must be saved; the DECEMBER issue is the ANNUAL for Titles 1-16; the MARCH issue is the ANNUAL for Titles 17-27; the JUNE issue is the ANNUAL for Titles 28-41; the SEPTEMBER issue is the ANNUAL for Titles 42-50. ANNUAL ISSUES to be saved are clearly designated on the cover.

PARALLEL TABLE OF AUTHORITIES AND RULES

Following Title 50 is an update to Table I—Parallel Table of Authorities and Rules found in the CFR Index and Finding Aids. This table contains authority citations added to or removed from Table I as a result of documents published in the Federal Register since January 1, 1991.

TABLE OF FEDERAL REGISTER ISSUE PAGES AND DATES

A table is included at the end of this publication which identifies the volume number, the inclusive page numbers, and the corresponding Federal Register issue dates for the period covered.

INDEXES

An INDEX to the daily Federal Register is published monthly and is cumulated for 12 months. A separate volume, the CFR Index and Finding Aids to the entire Code of Federal Regulations, is revised as of January 1 each year.

FIGURE 6-G

LIST OF CFR SECTIONS AFFECTED (LSA)

DISCUSSION OF PROBLEM 6.5 The volumes of the *Code of Federal Regulations* covering Title 27 are reissued as of April 1st of each year.

PROBLEM 6.6 Assume that you now want to check whether any provisions in this part have been modified, amended, or removed since it appeared in the latest *C.F.R.* pamphlet. Assume that the last *C.F.R.* volume was revised through April 1st for purposes of this problem. Based on the information provided in Figure 6-G, determine which of the following sources you would need to consult. Assume the latest available issue of the *Federal Register* is September 30th. The discussion below will show you the correct source(s).

(a) The latest *C.F.R. Index and Finding Aids* volume.
(b) The latest *List of CFR Sections Affected* (LSA) pamphlet.
(c) The "Cumulative List of CFR Parts Affected" in the last issue of the *Federal Register* for the month subsequent to the date of the latest LSA pamphlet.
(d) The "List of CFR Parts Affected" in each *Federal Register* issue that has appeared after the latest LSA pamphlet.

DISCUSSION OF PROBLEM 6.6 Assuming the latest available *Federal Register* is September 30th, you would first consult the latest *List of CFR Sections Affected* (LSA) pamphlet, answer (b). The latest LSA pamphlet available would be the one issued at the end of August. The cover of that pamphlet was shown in Figure 6-F. Note that the pamphlet in Figure 6-F covers changes in Title 27 (the relevant title) from April 1st through August 30th. To check for changes during this period, you would turn to the pages of the *List of CFR Sections Affected* (LSA) that cover Title 27. You would look to see whether any changes for the relevant part (55) are listed. The relevant page of the August LSA pamphlet is shown in Figure 6-H.

CHANGES APRIL 1, 1991 THROUGH AUGUST 30, 1991

TITLE 27—ALCOHOL, TOBACCO PRODUCTS AND FIREARMS

Chapter I—Bureau of Alcohol, Tobacco and Firearms, Department of the Treasury (Parts 1—299)

	Page
4.21 (f)(1)(i) amended	31076
4.25a (a)(1)(v) amended	31076
4.32 (a) introductory text amended	31076
(f) removed	31077
4.34 (a) amended	31097
4.38 (b)(1) and (2) amended	31077
5.32 (d) removed	31077
6.31—6.35 Undesignated center heading revised	31077
7.22 (c) removed	31077
19.906 (a) authority citation removed	31077
24.10 Amended	31077
24.25 (a)(3) redesignated in part as (a)(4)	31077
24.82 Amended	31077
24.125 (a) amended	31077
24.131 Amended	31077
24.148 Revised	31078
24.167 (b)(1) amended; (b)(4) revised	31078
24.176 Revised	31078
24.177 Amended	31078
24.179 (d) amended	31078
24.181 Amended	31078
24.182 (a) and (c) revised	31078
24.190 Amended	31078
24.215 (b) revised	31079
24.225 Amended	31079
Corrected	38486
24.227 Amended	31079
24.228 Heading amended	31079
24.240 Amended	31079
24.246 (b) table amended	31079
24.248 Table amended	31081
24.257 (b) amended	31082
24.259 (a) introductory text revised; (a)(4) and (b) amended	31082
24.260 Amended	31082
24.266 (a) amended	31082
24.273 (a) amended	31082
24.281 Amended	31082
24.293 (b) authority citation amended	31082

	Page
24.295 Undesignated center heading revised; heading, (b) and (c) amended	31082
24.301 (c) amended	31082
24.302 (f) revised	31082
24.304 (a) amended	31082
24.306 Amended	31083
24.308 (c) revised	31083
24.309 (f) revised	31083
24.310 Amended	31083
24.311 (a)(6) and (b)(4) revised	31083
24.312 Heading amended	31083
24.316 Amended	31083
24.320 Amended	31083
53.11 Amended	31083
53.91 (e) amended	31083
53.96 (a) introductory text amended; (a)(3) redesignated in part as (a)(4)	31083
53.97 (a) and (d) amended; (c)(3) redesignated in part as (c)(4); new (c)(4)(ii) redesignated in part as (c)(4)(iii)	31083
53.100 (b)(2) concluding text amended	31083
53.101 (c) Example 1 amended	31084
53.102 (b) heading and (2) amended	31084
53.103 Amended	31084
53.111 Heading, (a)(2) and (3) amended	31084
53.113 Amended	31084
53.114 Amended	31084
53.115 (a) and (c)(3) amended	31084
53.141 (d) amended	31084
53.156 (d) amended	31084
53.157 (b)(2) introductory text revised	31084
53.172 (a)(3)(ii)(A) and (B) revised; (a)(3)(ii)(C) amended	31084
53.173 Concluding text amended	31084
53.181 (b) amended	31084
53.182 (b)(1) heading revised	31085
70.41 (c) and (f) amended	31085
178.11 Amended	32508
178.30 Revised	32508
178.33 Revised	32508
178.34 Revised	32508
178.125 (f) revised	32508
178.125a (a)(4) revised	32509

Note: **Boldface entries indicate August changes.**

FIGURE 6-H

LIST OF CFR SECTIONS AFFECTED (LSA)

After examining the LSA, you would then need to examine the "Cumulative List of CFR Parts Affected" in the last available issue of the *Federal Register* for the month subsequent (September) to the date of the latest LSA pamphlet (August) (answer (c)). The relevant part of that list is shown in Figure 6-I.

Federal Register / Vol. 56. No. 189 / Monday, September 30, 1991 / Reader Aids

Proposed Rules:
130.............48270
308.............46354
318.............48131
381.............48131

10 CFR
13.............47132
73.............47671
1048.............43096
1705.............47144
Proposed Rules:
2.............46739
11.............49435
30.............48445
40.............46739, 48445
50.............46739, 48445
51.............46739, 47016
70.............46739, 48445
72.............48445
75.............46739
110.............46739
140.............46739
150.............46739
170.............46733

12 CFR
19.............46667
201.............48730
207.....46109, 46110, 46227
220.............46109
221.....46110, 46227
611.............46111
612.............48097
620.............46111
621.............46111
701.............48421
741.............44128
1507.............43997
Proposed Rules:
203.............47703
323.............47035
534.............47919
613.............45902
618.............45902
1608.............47164

13 CFR
108.............43867
121.............43869
Proposed Rules:
121.............43891, 47920

14 CFR
21.........45886, 45883, 47900, 48097, 49396
23.............47900, 49396
25.........45886, 45888, 48097
39.........43548–43550, 45891–45893, 46112, 46228–46233, 46725, 46985, 47376–47378, 47671, 47672, 47901, 49408
61.............43970, 47833
71.........43691, 46113, 46523, 45727, 47902, 47903, 48427, 48428, 49136
73.............46523
75.............46113
91.............48088, 48628
93.........43692, 43965, 46235, 48092
97.........48100–48101
108.............48370
121.............43974
129.............48370
135.............43974

161.............48661
221.............44000
1214.......47146–47148
1217.............47148
1266.............48429
Proposed Rules:
Ch. I.............46585
21.............49660
36.............49660
39.......45304, 45587, 46588, 49437–49439
43.............49660
71.......45906, 47036, 48768, 48769
75.............46747
91.............49660
93.............46674
141.............49660
147.............49660

15 CFR
779.............49137
Proposed Rules:
925.............47836
799.............49441

16 CFR
4.............49138
305.......43593, 46524, 46728
1000.............46235
1500.............49139
1501.............46986
Proposed Rules:
Ch. II.............47166
435.......46133, 48270

17 CFR
5.............43694
15.............43694
33.............43694
229.............48103
230.............48103
249.............45894
Proposed Rules:
5.............43726
32.............43560
240.......44014, 46748
249.......44014, 44029

18 CFR
Proposed Rules:
1312.......46259, 46261

19 CFR
Ch. I.......46114, 47268
10.............48823
146.............46371
171.............48823
172.............48823
177.............46372
Proposed Rules:
4.............48448
10.............48448
102.............48448
134.............48448
177.......46134, 48448

20 CFR
10.............4767?
367.............4637?
Proposed Rules:
10.............47713
255.............47426
335.............47430

21 CFR
14.............48103
172.............46667
173.............46667
178.............43697
310.............46823
510.......43698, 49409
520.............43698
529.............43698
558.......48732, 49410
878.............47150
1310.............48732
Proposed Rules:
101.............43954
356.............48302
369.............48302

22 CFR
40.............43551
41.............46716
43.............46904
302.............43699
Proposed Rules:
41.............43565
120.............43894
121.......43894, 43896, 46753, 46754

24 CFR
203.............46964
291.......46952–46964
577.............46952
578.............46952
882.............49588
887.............49588
888.............49024
905.......46356, 47852
906.............47852
965.............46356
990.............46356
Proposed Rules:
Subtitle B.............49592
905.............45814
963.............48453
990.............45814

25 CFR
Proposed Rules:
83.............47320
101.............48082
103.............48082

26 CFR
1.......47379, 47524–47659, 47904, 48443, 48733, 49512
5c.............49512
35a.............47904
602.......47379, 49512
Proposed Rules:
1.......43571, 47921–47928, 48457–48465, 49151, 49524–49545
7.............49151
20.......46244, 46245
25.......46244, 46245
31.............47929
53.............43571
301.......49526–49545
602.............47928

27 CFR
55.............49139
178.............43649
Proposed Rules:
4.............46393

5.......46393, 49152
9.......46135, 47039, 47044

28 CFR
0.............48734
Proposed Rules:
16.......44049, 48469
76.............45907

29 CFR
92.............46116
102.............49141
541.............45624
1910.............43699
1926.............43699
2619.............46525
2676.............46526
Proposed Rules:
541.............45828
1910.......47348, 47592, 48133
1926.............47348
1952.............49444

30 CFR
56.............46500
57.............46500
206.............46527
705.............46987
706.............46987
916.............46531
917.............47907
Proposed Rules:
Ch. II.............47049
46.............48720
48.............48376
56.............48720
57.............48720
75.............48376
77.......48376, 48720
218.............46396
230.............46396
701.......44049, 45780, 48714
724.............48924
740.............46396
761.............46396
772.............46396
773.............45780
778.............45780
780.............44049
784.............44049
785.............48714
816.............44049
817.............44049
840.............45780
843.............45780
846.............48924
901.............44050
914.............47051
934.............47929
935.......46588, 48470

31 CFR
505.............45894
520.............45894
575.............48104

32 CFR
163.............43871
199.............44001
518.............48932
619.............45895
706.......47151–47153
Proposed Rules:
199.......48134, 48135
229.......46259, 4626

FIGURE 6-I
FEDERAL REGISTER

Thus, answers (b) and (c) are the correct answers to *Problem 6.6*. Note that the list indicates that Part 55 was affected by material appearing on page 49,139 of the *Federal Register*. You could find that materi-

al by locating page 49,139 in the *Federal Register* (in this instance, the issue issued on September 27th).

(b) Using Shepard's Code of Federal
Regulations Citations

In addition to using the *Federal Register* to update federal rules and regulations, you can also use *Shepard's Code of Federal Regulations Citations* to find judicial, selected law review, and *A.L.R.* treatment of a *C.F.R.* section. For example, *Shepard's* indicates whether a section has been held constitutional (C), unconstitutional (U), void or invalid (V), valid (Va), or void or invalid in part (Vp). *Shepard's Code of Federal Regulations Citations* does not indicate how the administrative agency itself has treated the regulation—for example, the agency may have amended, renumbered, or rescinded the regulation after it has appeared in the latest *C.F.R.* volume.

Shepard's indicates the date of each citation reference in one of two ways. When the *citing* source referred to the date of the cited *C.F.R.* provision, the cited year is shown, preceded by an asterisk. On the other hand, when the *citing* source did not refer to a *C.F.R.* date, the year of the citing reference is shown, preceded by a small triangle. These indications of currentness are necessary because of the frequent revisions of *C.F.R.* By noting the year in the citation entry, the researcher can determine whether the citations are to current or superseded provisions of *C.F.R.*

PROBLEM 6.7 The page of *Shepard's Code of Federal Regulations Citations* covering Title 27 is reproduced in Figure 6-J. Have any of the regulations in Part 55 been cited in judicial decisions?

CODE OF FEDERAL REGULATIONS TITLE 27

§§19.189 to 19.192 AEn§30.04	§19.957(a) AEn§30.12	§71.25(d)(1)(iii) 577FS1216 △1983	§178.25 545F2d765 *1976
§19.211 AEn§30.04	§19.959 AEn§30.12	§71.27 214Neb530 *1982 Nebr 335NW277 *1982	§178.27 722F2d28 △1983
§19.231 739F2d432 *1983 AEn§30.05	§19.960 AEn§30.12	§71.41(d)(2)(iii)(B) 515FS520 △1981	§178.30 719F2d299 △1983 729F2d596 *1983 753F2d1506 *1984 754F2d659 △1985
§19.243 AEn§30.05	§§19.972 to 19.974 AEn§30.13	§72.22 444FS308 △1977	
§19.244 AEn§30.05	§19.975 AEn§30.18	§170.51 571F2d925 △1978	§178.31 719F2d299 △1983 729F2d596 *1983 753F2d1506 *1984
§19.245 AEn§30.05	§§19.982 to 19.986 AEn§30.14	§172.1 et seq. 489FS23 △1980	§178.31(a) 754F2d659 △1985
§§19.271 to 19.274 AEn§30.06	§19.988 AEn§30.14	Part 173 715F2d645 *1982	§§178.41 to 178.60 193Ct11 △1984 Conn 475A2d259 △1984
§19.279 AEn§30.06	§19.989 AEn§30.15	§173.32 715F2d645 △1983	§178.41 193Ct10 △1984 89Wis2d237 △1979 Conn 475A2d259 △1984 Wis 278NW243 △1979
§19.281 AEn§30.06	§19.990 AEn§30.15	Part 178 435FS453 △1977 601FS409 △1984 65H67 △1982 Haw 647P2d720 △1982	
§§19.311 to 19.350 AEn§30.07	§19.992 AEn§30.16		
§§19.454 to 19.458 AEn§30.09	§19.993 AEn§30.16		§178.41(d) 463FS370 △1978 493FS1357 △1980
§19.536 AEn§30.08	§§19.994 to 19.999 AEn§30.17	§178.1 et seq. 481FS803 △1979	§178.47 715F2d637 *1982 89Wis2d248 △1979 Wis 278NW248 △1979
§19.540 AEn§30.08	Part 55 545FS988 △1982	§178.2 435FS453 △1977	
§19.632 C488FS160 *1980	§55.1 545FS988 △1982	§178.11 715F2d636 *1975 724F2d927 △1984 463FS370 △1978 493FS1356 △1980 601FS409 △1984 193Ct11 △1984 Conn 475A2d259 △1984 State of residence 629F2d1257 △1980	§178.47(b)(3) 505FS696 △1980
§§19.741 to 19.786 AEn§30.07	§55.11 710F2d277 △1983 724F2d925 *1983 545FS988 △1982		§178.47(b)(5) 193Ct11 △1984 Conn 475A2d259 △1984
§19.932(b) AEn§30.11	§55.41 545FS987 △1982		§178.49 89Wis2d248 △1979 Wis 278NW248 △1979
§19.934 AEn§30.10	§55.141 700F2d883 △1983		
§§19.935 to 19.937 AEn§30.11	§55.182(c) 710F2d277 △1983		§178.50 505FS698 △1980
§19.938 AEn§30.12		§178.23 545F2d765 *1976 34ARF436n △1977	§178.58 601FS409 △1984
§§19.939 to 19.941 AEn§30.11	Part 71 572FS1098 *1981	§178.24 545F2d765 *1976	§§178.71 to 178.82 89Wis2d248 △1979 Wis 278NW248 △1979
§§19.946 to 19.953 AEn§30.11	§71.25(d)(1)(ii) 577FS1215 △1983		

* followed by a year refers to the CFR edition, if cited. If not cited,
△ followed by a year indicates the date of the citing reference

701

FIGURE 6-J

SHEPARD'S CODE OF FEDERAL REGULATIONS CITATIONS

DISCUSSION OF PROBLEM 6.7 The entries in *Shepard's* indicate that several sections in Part 55 of Title 27 of the *Code of Federal Regulations* have been cited in judicial decisions. The validity of those sections does not appear to have been litigated.

Section 6C. Agency Decisions

Agency decisions are reported in the same basic manner as court decisions. For example, decisions of the National Labor Relations Board (NLRB) are reported officially in *Decisions and Orders of the National Labor Relations Board* (1935 to date). Looseleaf services often report administrative decisions unofficially. For example, NLRB decisions can be found in Commerce Clearing House's *NLRB Decisions* (the bound version of CCH's *Labor Law Reports* looseleaf service). Looseleaf services also provide subject (topical) access to administrative decisions.

Administrative decisions are updated in the same manner as cases—by using *Shepard's Citations* volumes covering these decisions. Administrative decisions are generally cited like court opinions, except that *Bluebook* Rule 14.3.1 requires that the decision be cited by the "full reported name of the first-listed private party or by the official subject-matter title."

Section 6D. Executive Orders and Other Presidential Documents

Presidential executive orders are used to direct action by federal agencies and officials. Presidential proclamations customarily are used to make announcements or declarations that carry with them no legal effect. Presidential reorganization plans make changes to carry out better management of the executive branch of government. Other Presidential papers and speeches are sometimes useful for legal research.

Presidential proclamations and executive orders are published in the *Federal Register* and are compiled in Title 3 of the *Code of Federal Regulations*. Some are included in the *United States Code*. Other sources for executive orders are West's *U.S. Code Congressional and Administrative News* and Lawyers Cooperative's *United States Code Service*.

Reorganization plans are proposed by executive orders and are submitted to Congress. If neither house of Congress objects, they go into effect and are published (as approved) in an Appendix to Title 5 of the *United States Code*. Presidential papers, speeches, and documents are published in the *Public Papers of the Presidents* (since 1945). There is also a *Weekly Compilation of Presidential Documents* available. *See Bluebook* Rule 14.7.

Section 6E. Court Rules

Court rules govern the practice before the courts issuing them. Unlike rules (such as the Federal Rules of Civil Procedure) governing proceedings of an entire class of courts (e.g., all federal district courts), the court rules referred to here apply only to the particular court issuing them. These rules regulate such matters as motion practice, filing procedures, preparation of briefs or memoranda, etc.

Rules of the U.S. Supreme Court are published with annotations in the *United States Code Annotated*, West's *U.S. Supreme Court Digest*, Lawyers Co-operative's *U.S. Supreme Court Digest*, the *United States Code Service*, and Bender's *Federal Practice Manual*.

Convenient sources for the rules of each of the U.S. Courts of Appeals are the *Federal Rules Service* and the annotated versions of the *United States Code*.

Local federal court rules can be found in the *Federal Rules Service* and in separate pamphlet form. Rules of state and local courts are usually available in pamphlet form or in local practice manuals.

Section 6F. Rules of Practice, Procedure, and Evidence

The text of the Federal Rules of Civil and Criminal Procedure can be found in a large number of publications. Most often consulted are those with annotations and current supplementation, such as the *Federal Rules Service*, *United States Code Annotated*, and *United States Code Service*. Secondary sources discussing the federal rules can be found in the card catalog.

Federal district court decisions that involve the Federal Rules of Civil Procedure (since 1939) and the Federal Rules of Criminal Procedure (since 1946) are selectively reported in West's *Federal Rules Decisions*. *Federal Rules Decisions* is part of West's National Reporter System and uses its key-number indexing. *Federal Rules Decisions* also contains articles on topics of general interest.

Several states have enacted civil practice acts and other laws governing civil and criminal practice and procedure. For these laws, the state statutes should be consulted. The state court rules are often published with the state statutes and are also published periodically in West's regional reporters. Volumes containing those rules are marked on the binding. In addition, state court rules sometimes appear in local practice manuals and in pamphlet form.

The Federal Rules of Evidence were adopted in 1974 for use in federal courts, and similar rules have been adopted by many states. The

Federal Rules of Evidence can be found in several sources. Good sources include an Appendix to Title 28 in the annotated versions of the *United States Code*, Weinstein and Burger's *Weinstein's Evidence*, and the *Federal Rules of Evidence Service*.

    Shepard's Federal Rules Citations and the Statute Edition of *Shepard's United States Citations* provide citations to cases and other sources construing the Federal Rules of Civil and Criminal Procedure as well as the Federal Rules of Evidence.

CITING RULES OF PROCEDURE OR EVIDENCE

    According to *Bluebook* Rule 12.8.3, you should cite current rules of procedure or evidence by name and rule number without giving a date. Abbreviate "Federal" to "Fed.," "Rules" to "R.," "Procedure" to "P.," "Evidence" to "Evid.," "Civil" to "Civ.," and "Criminal" to "Crim."

The following are examples of citations of rules of procedure or evidence:

> Fed. R. Civ. P. 15(d).
> Fed. R. Crim. P. 10.
> Fed. R. Evid. 703.

Section 6F. Researching Ethics Questions

    Section 1G of Chapter 1 highlighted various ethical aspects of legal research. Recall that the two principal sources for rules governing the professional conduct of lawyers are (1) the American Bar Association's *Model Rules of Professional Conduct* (1983) (the current ethical standards of the American Bar Association which have been adopted in a majority of jurisdictions) and (2) the American Bar Association's *Model Code of Professional Responsibility* (1980) (still used for professional discipline in some jurisdictions).[3]

---

[3]The American Bar Association (ABA) has adopted three different sets of ethical rules this century. In 1908, the ABA adopted Canons of Professional Ethics (Canons), which contained 32 hortatory statements. In 1969, the ABA replaced the Canons with a much more extensive Code of Professional Responsibility (Model Code), which consisted of nine Canons (axiomatic norms expressing in general terms the standard of professional conduct expected of lawyers), 138 Ethical Considerations (aspirational objectives toward which every member of the profession should strive), and 41 Disciplinary Rules (the minimum level of conduct below which no lawyer may fall without being subject to disciplinary action such

(continued...)

Ethical issues arise in a wide range of contexts. For example, the client in *Problem 5.1* wanted to know whether he could be forced to return to the United States to face charges. The client also wanted to know if there were any Latin American countries that did not have agreements to return persons charged with crimes. Is there an ethical problem about answering the client's questions? How would you find the answer?

Like other areas of legal research, a secondary source dealing with professional ethics is a good starting point for researching ethical questions. Secondary sources on ethics can be found by using the card catalog and periodical indexes. Wolfram's treatise on *Modern Legal Ethics* is an excellent source. Issues involving ethics and professional responsibility are often discussed in legal periodicals.

The Standing Committee on Ethics and Professional Responsibility of the American Bar Association issues both formal and informal opinions interpreting the American Bar Association's ethical rules.[4] Although they do not have the force of law, these opinions are regarded as persuasive authority concerning matters of professional conduct. An excellent source for these opinions and other aspects of professional ethics is the *ABA/BNA Lawyer's Manual on Professional Conduct*. A source for all the state rules and codes is the *National Reporter on Legal Ethics and Professional Responsibility*.

Cases construing the disciplinary rules can be found in several sources, including the *National Reporter on Legal Ethics and Professional Responsibility*. *Shepard's Professional and Judicial Conduct Citations* set covers a large number of sources that cite the ABA *Model Code* and the *Model Rules*.

PROBLEM 6.8 Assume that you have decided to consult § 13.3.2 "Advising on the Limits of the Law: Client Crimes" in Wolfram's treatise on *Modern Legal Ethics* to determine if there is an ethical problem in answering the questions raised by the client in *Problem 5.1*. Examine the page reproduced from § 13.3.2 in Figure 6-K. Does there appear to be a problem?

---

[3](...continued)
as censure or disbarment). The Model Code was adopted (with some modifications or omissions) as the basis for professional discipline in every state but California. In 1983, the ABA again revised its standards governing professional conduct in the form of Model Rules of Professional Conduct (Model Rules) (consisting of a Terminology section, 52 Model Rules, and explanatory Comments). See Charles W. Wolfram, Modern Legal Ethics § 2.6 (1986). The Model Rules have now been adopted by a majority of the states as the basis for professional discipline.

[4]"Formal" opinions cover matters of general interest to the bar. "Informal" opinions respond to specific questions involving particular factual situations.

other respects seems merely congruent with the criminal law that would apply to all lawyers in any event.

1969 Code. In the Code, DR 7–102(A)(7) broadly provides that a lawyer representing a client shall not "counsel or assist his client in conduct that the lawyer knows to be illegal or fraudulent." [25] The California rule is similar. [26] Nowhere does the Code suggest that "illegal" is limited to criminal violations alone, [27] although the few disciplinary decisions under DR 7–102(A)(7) involve lawyers who assisted a client in criminal conduct. [28] And EC 7–5 makes it clear that a lawyer should not counsel a client on how to avoid punishment for violations of the law. No authority, apparently, has interpreted "counsel or assist" in DR 7–102(A)(7), particularly with respect to the question whether it requires something more than a lawyer's passive participation in illegality. [29]

1983 Model Rules. Rule 1.2(d) of the 1983 Model Rules provides a rule similar to DR 7–102(A)(7), but the rule is limited to "criminal and fraudulent" client conduct and introduces a potentially confusing exception. Rule 1.2(d) states that

> (d) A lawyer shall not counsel a client to engage, or assist a client, in conduct that the lawyer knows is criminal or fraudulent, but a lawyer may discuss the legal consequences of any proposed course of conduct with a client and may

counsel or assist a client to make a good faith effort to determine the validity, scope, meaning or application of the law.

As will be discussed at a later point, [30] MR 1.2(d) clearly is a narrower rule than DR 7–102(A)(7).

The narrowness of MR 1.2(d) is evident in one situation that was clearly intended and in a second, possible, situation that is shocking and might well be inadvertent. First, the rule is limited to advice about "criminal or fraudulent" client conduct, whereas DR 7–102(A)(7) extends to "illegal" conduct. [31] Second, and shockingly, if so, the exception in MR 1.2(d) stating that a lawyer may "discuss" legal consequences of "any proposed course of conduct" on its face is open to the interpretation that a lawyer may give legal advice to a client about various methods of operating a proposed drug-smuggling ring, murdering a political rival or disgruntled spouse, or cheating a trusting business partner. The essential condition would be that the lawyer's advice remain at the personally uncommitted level of "discuss" and not heat up to the level of "counsel" or "assist." That reading of the rule is supported by a comment to Rule 1.2(d) that states that "[t]here is a critical distinction between presenting an analysis of legal aspects of questionable conduct and recommending the means by which a crime or fraud might be committed with impunity," [32] al-

---

[25] An ambiguity lurks in DR 7–102(A)(7) that has potential for strange results. In re Connaghan, 613 S.W.2d 626 (Mo.1981), a lawyer accepted $20,000 from a client as a fee and, without the client's knowledge, used part to bribe a legislator. The court held that because the client did no wrong, the lawyer did not violate DR 7–102(A)(7). But the court found that several other, more general disciplinary rules were violated.

[26] Calif.R. 7–101:

> A member of the State Bar shall not advise the violation of any law, rule or ruling of a tribunal unless he believes in good faith that such law, rule or ruling is invalid. A member of the State Bar may take appropriate steps in good faith to test the validity of any law, rule or ruling of a tribunal.

[27] The California rule, supra, which refers globally to "law, rule or ruling of a tribunal" is also clearly not limited to criminal law violations.

[28] In re Nulle, 127 Ariz. 299, 620 P.2d 214 (1980)(advising client to file false application for liquor license); In re Schneider, 98 Ill.2d 215, 74 Ill.Dec. 500, 456 N.E.2d 2

(1983)(counseling clients to provide false information to prosecutor); In re Agnew, 311 N.W.2d 869 (Minn.1981) (advising client facing several misdemeanor charges that he had "49 options" (to flee the state)); Toledo Bar Ass'n v. Kitchen, 69 Ohio St.2d 338, 432 N.E.2d 195 (1982) (persistence in negotiating sale of machine after forming accurate belief that machine was stolen).

[29] Cf. In re Prescott, 271 N.W.2d 822, 823–24 (Minn. 1978)(DR 1–102(A)(4) on dishonesty, fraud, deceit, and misrepresentation prohibits both active as well as passive participation in process of obtaining loans by false pretenses). But cf. M.Freedman, Lawyers Ethics in an Adversary System 60 (1975)("counsel or assist" in Code refers to "an active kind of participation in the client's illegal act, going beyond merely giving advice about the law").

[30] § 13.3.9.

[31] Id.

[32] MR 1.2 comment (Criminal, Fraudulent and Prohibited Transactions; first paragraph). A further comment indicates that suggesting how a client's wrongdoing can

---

FIGURE 6-K

CHARLES W. WOLFRAM, MODERN LEGAL ETHICS

DISCUSSION OF PROBLEM 6.8 Disciplinary Rule 7–102(A)(7) of the 1969 *Model Code* states that lawyers cannot "counsel or assist" their clients "in conduct that the lawyer knows to be illegal or fraudu-

lent." Wolfram also points out that Ethical Consideration 7-5 specifically provides that lawyers should not counsel their clients "on how to avoid punishment for violations of the law." Footnote 28 cites the case of In re Agnew, 311 N.W.2d 869 (Minn. 1981), in which a lawyer was disciplined for "advising [a] client facing several misdemeanor charges that he had '49 options' (to flee the state)."

Wolfram states that Rule 1.2(d) of the 1983 *Model Rules* establishes a rule similar to DR 7-102(A)(7), but introduces an exception that might be applicable: "[A] lawyer may discuss the legal consequences of any proposed course of conduct with a client and may counsel or assist a client to make a good faith effort to determine the validity, scope, meaning or application of the law." Note that at least one writer suggests (in footnote 29) that "counsel or assist" refers to "an active kind of participation in the client's illegal act, going beyond merely giving advice about the law."

The discussion in Wolfram leaves several questions unanswered. Is merely telling the client the law "counseling or assisting" the client in an illegal act? Recall that the excerpt shown in Figure 5-I from *American Jurisprudence Second* indicates that 18 U.S.C. § 1074 makes it a federal offense to travel in interstate or foreign commerce to avoid prosecution or imprisonment for willfully damaging or destroying by explosive any building, structure, or vehicle, or attempting to do so. Assuming that supplying the explosives is sufficient to make the client a principal or a co-conspirator, is it important that the client has not yet been charged with a crime? Or does 18 U.S.C. § 1074 apply to the client even if he has not been charged yet? Further research on these and other questions would be necessary.

Chapter 7
WESTLAW COMPUTER LEGAL RESEARCH SERVICE

Section 7A. Introduction to Using the WESTLAW Service

WESTLAW is the computer-assisted legal research service provided by West Publishing Company. This section introduces the following aspects of the WESTLAW service: (1) accessing WESTLAW; (2) signing on WESTLAW; (3) determining the available sources and database coverage; (4) using EZ ACCESS menus; (5) retrieving known cases, statutes, and other sources using FIND; (6) printing screens and documents; and (7) signing off WESTLAW.

1. ACCESSING WESTLAW

To begin using the WESTLAW service, you must first access the service.[1] How you access the service depends on what kind of computer terminal you are using.[2]

---

[1] Before you can use WESTLAW, you must first have access to the service. The WESTLAW service charges varying time-related fees.

[2] Research on WESTLAW is conducted by means of a terminal, consisting of a video display and a keyboard. The terminal ordinarily is connected to the central computer by a phone line. Some WESTLAW terminals have custom keyboards. Other terminals, including personal computers, can be used with the WESTLAW service. WESTLAW supplies templates for personal computer keyboards to facilitate using the service. The technical aspects of connecting the terminal and accessing WESTLAW can be determined by consulting WESTLAW publications and WESTLAW Customer Service.

After the initial connection with the computer has been made with WESTLAW, the WESTLAW logo shown in Figure 7-A will be displayed.

```
=================================================================
  **        **  ******      ****  ******** **        *  **        **
  **   *   **  **            **        **  **       *** **    *  **
  ** *** **   *****         **        **  **      ** **  ** ** *** **
  *** *** **   **            **        **  **      **  **  ** *** ***
   *   *     ****** *****      **     ****** **      ** *  *

    A COMPUTER-ASSISTED LEGAL RESEARCH SERVICE OF WEST PUBLISHING COMPANY

    COPYRIGHT (C) 1992 BY WEST PUBLISHING COMPANY.  COPYRIGHT IS NOT CLAIMED AS
    TO ANY PART OF THE ORIGINAL WORK  PREPARED BY A U. S. GOVERNMENT OFFICER OR
    EMPLOYEE  AS PART  OF THAT PERSON'S OFFICIAL DUTIES.    ALL RIGHTS RESERVED.
    NO  PART  OF A  WESTLAW TRANSMISSION MAY BE COPIED, DOWNLOADED, STORED IN A
    RETRIEVAL  SYSTEM, FURTHER  TRANSMITTED  OR  OTHERWISE  REPRODUCED, STORED,
    DISSEMINATED, TRANSFERRED  OR  USED, IN ANY FORM  OR  BY ANY MEANS, WITHOUT
    WEST'S PRIOR WRITTEN AGREEMENT.  EACH REPRODUCTION OF ANY PART OF A WESTLAW
    TRANSMISSION MUST  CONTAIN NOTICE  OF  WEST'S COPYRIGHT AS  FOLLOWS: "COPR.
    (C) WEST 1992 NO CLAIM TO ORIG. U.S. GOVT. WORKS".  WESTLAW AND WESTNET ARE
    REGISTERED SERVICE MARKS OF WEST PUBLISHING CO. REG. U.S. PAT. AND TM. OFF.

                    AVAILABLE 24 HOURS MONDAY THROUGH SATURDAY
                         AND SUNDAY FROM 8 AM, CST
        PLEASE TYPE YOUR PASSWORD AND PRESS ENTER:  (PASSWORD MAY NOT BE DISPLAYED)
```

FIGURE 7-A
WESTLAW PRINTOUT

2. SIGNING ON WESTLAW

After you have properly accessed WESTLAW, you must type your password and press the ENTER key. (See the last sentence on the screen shown in Figure 7-A). The password is unique to the user and is the only method by which a user can gain access to WESTLAW. The password does not appear as it is typed.[3]

Next, the computer may display screens containing information about recent developments and other matters. The computer will then ask the user to identify the research. These identifiers are designated by the WESTLAW account and can be totally customized (provided no more than thirty-two characters and no semi-colons are used).

Assume that the computer has now accepted your research identifier. The next display shown on WESTLAW will be a list of available databases (WESTLAW DIRECTORY WELCOME SCREEN) shown in Figure 7-B. You are now ready to select the database or service you want to use.

---

[3]WESTMATE software allows you to enter your password automatically.

```
_____ WELCOME TO THE WESTLAW DIRECTORY _____P1_____

GENERAL MATERIAL      TEXT & PERIODICAL       CITATORS          SPECIALIZED MAT'L
Federal        P2     Law Reviews,   P320  Insta-Cite,   P357  ABA            P359
State          P6      Texts & CLEs        Shepard's,          BNA            P361
DIALOG         P145   Restatements         Shepard's PreView   C. Board. Cal. P365
News & Info.   P183    & Unif. Laws P356   & QuickCite         Dictionary     P367
------------------- TOPICAL MATERIAL -------------------       Directories    P368
Antitrust      P191   Family Law     P232  Legal Ser.    P279  Gateways (D&B, P372
Bankruptcy     P194   Financial Ser  P235  Maritime Law  P283   Dow Jones, etc.)
Business       P197   First Amend.   P240  Military Law  P285  Historical     P373
Civil Rights   P203   Gov't Benefit  P242  Product Liab  P287  Other Pub's    P390
Commun. Law    P206   Gov't Cont.    P245  Real Prop.    P290  TaxSource      P401
Corporations   P208   Health Ser.    P251  Sci. & Tech.  P293  WESTLAW        P402
Crim. Just.    P213   Immigration    P257  Securities    P296   Highlights
Education      P217   Insurance      P259  Soc. Science  P304  Other Serv.    P404
Energy         P220   Intell. Prop.  P263  Taxation      P307   (NEW, FIND, etc.)
Environment    P225   International  P267  Transport.    P315  EZ ACCESS      P405
                      Labor          P272  Worker Comp.  P317  Customer Info  P406

If you wish to:
   View another Directory page, type P followed by its NUMBER and press ENTER
   Select a known database, type its IDENTIFIER and press ENTER
   Obtain further information, type HELP and press ENTER
```

FIGURE 7-B
WESTLAW PRINTOUT

3. WESTLAW DATABASES

To use the computer resources effectively, you must know how WESTLAW is organized and how you can determine the coverage of the various databases or files. The WESTLAW DIRECTORY WELCOME SCREEN shown in Figure 7-B provides a list of available databases and services. It is constantly updated to reflect changes in services and coverage.

PROBLEM 7.1 (a) By examining Figure 7-B, determine the five basic categories of sources on WESTLAW. (The five categories appear as capitalized headings.) (b) Assume that you want more information about the databases that include state court opinions. Determine what you should type and enter to see that information.

DISCUSSION OF PROBLEM 7.1 (a) The five basic categories are GENERAL MATERIAL (e.g., state and federal cases, statutes, regulations, and administrative law), TEXT & PERIODICAL (e.g, bar journals, law reviews, and texts, restatements, and uniform laws), CITATORS (e.g., services that provide the current status, subsequent judicial history, and subsequent interpretation of reported decisions and lists of cases construing or applying statutory sources), TOPICAL MATERIAL (e.g., databases organized by topic), and SPECIALIZED MATERIAL (e.g., dictionaries and databases supplied by other publishers).

(b) More information on the state databases can be determined by entering the relevant page number. In this instance, you would type: **p6** (which would request information on GENERAL MATERIAL—State).[4]

PROBLEM 7.2 Assume now that you have typed and entered **p6** to see more information on the databases containing state court opinions. A printout of that screen (p6) is shown in Figure 7-C. Examine Figure 7-C and determine what you would type and enter to see more information about Missouri databases.

```
____WESTLAW DIRECTORY WELCOME SCREEN_____P1_____
____GENERAL STATE DATABASES                                P6_____

------------------- STATE DATABASES: DOCUMENT INDEX ------------------
Multistate ....... Next Page   Court Orders .... P14    Regional Rptrs .P19
Admin. Law/Code .. P8          Court Rules ..... P15    Reg. Tracking ..P8
At. Gen. Op. ..... P10         Indices ......... P16    Statutes-Anno. .P20
Bill Tracking .... P11         Legis. Service .. P17    Statutes-Unanno.P21
Case Law ......... P13
-------------- STATE AND TERRITORY DATABASES: DIRECTORY LOCATIONS ------------
   AL..P22   DC..P44   KS..P64   MS..P86   NY..P106   PR..P126   VI..P143
   AK..P25   FL..P46   KY..P66   MO..P88   NC..P109   RI..P127   VA..P146
   AZ..P28   GA..P49   LA..P69   MT..P91   ND..P111   SC..P130   WA. P149
   AR..P31   HI..P52   ME..P72   NE..P94   MP..P113   SD..P133   WV. P152
   CA..P33   ID..P54   MD..P74   NV..P97   OH..P114   TN..P135   WI. P154
   CO..P36   IL..P56   MA..P77   NH..P99   OK..P117   TX..P137   WY. P157
   CT..P39   IN..P59   MI..P80   NJ..P101  OR..P120   UT..P140
   DE..P42   IA..P61   MN..P83   NM..P104  PA..P123   VT..P142
-------------------------------------------------------------------------
If you wish to:
   Select a database, type its identifier, e.g., ALLSTATES and press ENTER
   View information about a database, type SCOPE followed by its identifier
      and press ENTER
```

FIGURE 7-C
WESTLAW PRINTOUT

DISCUSSION OF PROBLEM 7.2 As the printout in Figure 7-C indicates, to view the Missouri state database information, you would type **p88** and then press the ENTER key.

PROBLEM 7.3 Assume that you have typed and entered the correct information to view the Missouri state databases. The screen that would appear is shown in Figure 7-D. Examine Figure 7-D and answer the following questions. (a) What would you type and enter to select the Missouri Courts database for the purpose of entering a search query? (b) What could you do to view more information about the database containing opinions of the Missouri courts?

---

[4] There are other ways to obtain information on WESTLAW databases. For example, you could consult West's published <u>WESTLAW Database List</u> (which is usually kept near the terminal for reference).

```
_____WESTLAW DIRECTORY WELCOME SCREEN_____P1_____
_____GENERAL STATE DATABASES:  MISSOURI                              P88_____

          GENERAL CASE LAW                    GENERAL STATUTES
   MO-CS     Missouri Courts          MO-ST-ANN    Annotated Statutes
                                      MO-ST        Unannotated Statutes
      GENERAL ADMINISTRATIVE LAW      MO-ST-IDX    General Index
   MO-AG     Attorney General Opinions MO-LEGIS    Legislative Service
   MO-REGTRK Regulation Tracking
                                          HISTORICAL STATUTES
   TOPICAL/SPECIALIZED DATABASES INDEX Annotated Statutes  1989-91
   Topical Case Law ........ Next Page e.g., MO-STANN89
   Topical Admin. Law ...... Next Page Legislative Service 1988-91
   Specialized Databases ... Enter P90 e.g., MO-LEGIS88

                                              COURT RULES
                                      MO-RULES     Court Rules
                                      MO-ORDERS    Court Orders
   If you wish to:
      Select a database, type its identifier, e.g., MO-CS and press ENTER
      View information about a database, type SCOPE followed by its identifier
        and press ENTER
      View the Index to State Databases, type P6 and press ENTER
```

FIGURE 7-D
WESTLAW PRINTOUT

DISCUSSION OF PROBLEM 7.3   (a) To select the Missouri Courts database, you would type **mo-cs** and then press the ENTER key. You would then be ready to type your search query. (b) To find more information about the coverage of the Missouri Courts database, **scope mo-cs** could be typed and entered.

PROBLEM 7.4 Assume that you have instructed the computer to provide you with more information about the Missouri Courts database by using the scope command. The first page of the printout of that information is shown in Figures 7-E. (a) What are the dates of coverage of the reporters in this database? (b) What are "quick opinions"?

```
SCOPE: MO-CS                                    Page  1 of  7
                        MISSOURI CASES

   The MO-CS database contains documents from the Missouri state
 courts.  A document is a case (a decision or order) decided by the courts.

 DERIVATION:
   This database includes documents released for publication in West's South
 Western Reporter (see below) and "quick opinions" (cases available online
 prior to West advance sheets and which do not contain editorial enhancements).

                                    COVERAGE BEGINS:
   South Western Reporter            257 S.W. - 300 S.W.  (1923-1928)
   South Western Reporter, 2nd Series  1 S.W.2d  (1928)

 SOURCE(S):
   (1) Supreme Court

 If you wish to:
   Select this database, type MO-CS and press ENTER
   View a different page, type P followed by its NUMBER and press ENTER
   Continue in the WESTLAW Directory, press ENTER
```

FIGURE 7-E
WESTLAW PRINTOUT

DISCUSSION OF PROBLEM 7.4 (a) The printout shown in Figure 7-E indicates that volumes 257-300 of the *South Western Reporter* (1923-1928) and volume 1 to the present of the *South Western Reporter Second* (1928 to date) are covered. (b) "Quick opinions" are also included in this database. As the printout indicates, quick opinions are cases available online prior to their publication in West's advance sheets. They do not have "editorial enhancements," such as West's headnotes.

The printout in Figure 7-E indicates that this page is one of seven pages dealing with the scope of MO-CS database. To see the next page, you could type **p2** and then press the ENTER key. A printout of that screen is shown in Figure 7-F.

PROBLEM 7.5 Determine when coverage of the Missouri Supreme Court and the Missouri Court of Appeals begins by examining Figures 7-E (above) and 7-F (below).

```
SCOPE: MO-CS                              Page  2 of  7

        from 257 S.W. (1923) through quick opinions
  (2) Courts of Appeals
        from 180 S.W.2d (1944) through quick opinions

  A limited number of selected opinions from trial courts may be included.
  Check the local court rules to find out whether or not these cases may be
  cited.  Check with the court to find out whether there has been subsequent
  history.
     Check court rules, statutes, and case law to determine the authoritative
  nature of court syllabi.

  PARALLEL CITATIONS:                              CITE AS:
     American Law Reports (Law. Co-op)             A.L.R.
     American Law Reports 2nd Series (Law. Co-op)  A.L.R.2d
     American Law Reports 3rd Series (Law. Co-op)  A.L.R.3d
     American Law Reports 4th Series (Law. Co-op)  A.L.R.4th

  If you wish to:
     Select this database, type MO-CS and press ENTER
     View a different page, type P followed by its NUMBER and press ENTER
     Continue in the WESTLAW Directory, press ENTER
```

FIGURE 7-F

WESTLAW PRINTOUT

DISCUSSION OF PROBLEM 7.5   The screens shown in Figures 7-E and 7-F provide specific information about the coverage of the Missouri Supreme Court and Missouri Court of Appeals. In this instance, coverage of the Missouri Supreme Court begins with volume 257 of the *South Western Reporter* in 1923. Coverage of the Missouri Court of Appeals begins with volume 180 of the *South Western Reporter Second* in 1944.

Assume that you have decided to select the Missouri Courts database by typing **mo-cs** and then pressing the ENTER key. Figure 7-G shows the next screen that would be displayed. You would now be ready to entry your search query.

```
Please enter your query.

Your database is MO-CS




If you wish to:
    Enter your query, type it as desired and press ENTER
    View a list of available fields, type F and press ENTER
    View detailed information about this database, type SCOPE and press ENTER
COPR. (C) WEST 1992 NO CLAIM TO ORIG. U.S. GOVT. WORKS
```

FIGURE 7-G
WESTLAW PRINTOUT

4. USING EZ ACCESS MENUS

EZ ACCESS is a menu-driven approach to retrieving information stored in WESTLAW databases. This approach provides simple menu choices. When you are unsure of the next step or when the choice you want is not listed, you can generate additional choices by typing **ez** and then pressing the ENTER key.

PROBLEM 7.6 The EZ ACCESS Welcome screen is shown in Figure 7-H. Assume that you want to retrieve a case and that you know its citation is 579 S.W.2d 670. Which number on the EZ ACCESS menu would you type and enter?

```
                COPR. (C) 1992 West Publishing Co. All Rights Reserved

                *** WELCOME TO EZ ACCESS ***

EZ ACCESS is West Publishing Company's easy-to-use menu driven research system.
You can quickly retrieve information by making a selection from a list of
options.  When you are unsure of the next step, type EZ to see available
choices.

    What would you like to do?

              RETRIEVE CASES, STATUTES OR OTHER DOCUMENTS USING:

                  1.  A Title or Citation
                  2.  A West Topic and Key number
                  3.  Significant words

              RETRIEVE REFERENCES TO YOUR DOCUMENT CITATION USING:

                  4.  Insta-Cite, Shepard's, Shepard's PreView or WESTLAW

        Type a NUMBER and press ENTER
```

FIGURE 7-H
WESTLAW PRINTOUT

DISCUSSION OF PROBLEM 7.6 It is readily apparent that you would type **1** and then press the ENTER key.

Figure 7-I shows the next screen that would appear.

```
                    COPR. (C) 1992 West Publishing Co. All Rights Reserved
    FIND:  Document Type

        What type of document would you like to find?

              1. Case Law
              2. State Statute or Session Laws
              3. Federal Statute, Rule or Regulation

        Type a NUMBER and press ENTER



            For more choices, type EZ and press ENTER
```

FIGURE 7-I
WESTLAW PRINTOUT

You would again choose the first option by typing **1** and then pressing the ENTER key. You would then type **579 SW2d 670** on the CITATION line on the screen shown in Figure 7-J and press the ENTER key.

```
FIND Case Law:  Citation or Party Names

        What do you know about the case you want to find?

                 Press TAB to move to a choice
          CITATION:  579 SW2D 670_____

                            OR

     PARTY NAMES:   _____
                            First party

                    _____
                    Second party (optional)

        Type a CITATION or PARTY NAME and press ENTER

            For more choices, type EZ and press ENTER
```

FIGURE 7-J
WESTLAW PRINTOUT

WESTLAW will then ask you to confirm your choice, as shown in the next menu reproduced in Figure 7-K.

```
FIND Case Law:  Final Request

You want to retrieve cases using FIND.  To retrieve a case with a citation, use
the FIND command.

        Your request is:  FIND 579 SW2D 670

        To send this request, press ENTER




            For more choices, type EZ and press ENTER
```

FIGURE 7-K
WESTLAW PRINTOUT

Assume that you wanted to retrieve § 4980 of the California Business and Professions Code. Instead of choosing option 1 ("Case Law") in Figure 7-I, you would choose option 2 ("State Statute or Session Laws"). Similarly, if you wanted to retrieve 15 U.S.C. § 1242, you would choose option 3 ("Federal Statute, Rule or Regulation"). In each instance, you would simply follow the directions in the EZ ACCESS menus provided.

5. USING FIND TO RETRIEVE KNOWN CASES, STATUTES, AND OTHER SOURCES

Assume that you know the citation of a case that is unavailable to you because the library does not carry the relevant reporter, the needed volume is missing, the case is a very recent one that has not reached you yet, or the case is simply one that you would like to view on the computer. The most basic use of a computer database is to access a known source. The EZ ACCESS menus illustrated the steps to develop such a request. As indicated in Figure 7-K, that request was a "FIND" request: **FIND 579 SW2D 670.**

FIND allows you to view a document by typing the word find followed by the citation. A more detailed description of FIND is given in the following WESTLAW informational screens. Note the types of documents that can be retrieved using the FIND service as well as the tips for using the FIND service.

```
 SCOPE: FIND                           Page  1 of  3
                           FOUND DOCUMENTS
    The FIND service makes documents with a known citation available with
 a single command.  Use FIND to view documents cited within documents in
 your search result without losing the result, or to read any document with
 a known citation.

 COVERAGE:
    The WESTLAW FIND service is available for the following types of documents:

    Federal Case Law                Congressional Record
    State Case Law                  Code of Federal Regulations
    United States Code Annotated    Federal Register
    State Statutes                  Federal Administrative Material
    Federal Public Laws             State Administrative Material
    State Public Laws

 If you wish to:
    Select this database, type FIND and press ENTER
    View a different page, type P followed by its NUMBER and press ENTER
    Continue in the WESTLAW Directory, press ENTER
```

FIGURE 7-L
WESTLAW PRINTOUT

```
SCOPE: FIND                              Page  2 of  3

FIND is also available for Topical Materials, including parallel citations to,
and full text documents prepared by, The Bureau of National Affairs, Inc.
(BNA), Tax Management, Inc., and other publishers.

   TIP:  To view a document, type FIND followed by the CITATION and press
ENTER, e.g., find 105 S.Ct. 1005.  Parallel citations to the same document
can usually be used, e.g., use either find 469 U.S. 528 or find 102 Lab.Cas.
34,633.  Parallel citations cannot be used to retrieve Revenue Rulings or
Revenue Procedures.

   TIP:  To view a United States Public Law type FIND followed by the citation
and press ENTER, e.g., fi us pl 102-39.

   TIP:  To view a State Legislative Service document which has been assigned
a chapter, act, public act or public law number, type FIND followed by the

If you wish to:
   Select this database, type FIND and press ENTER
   View a different page, type P followed by its NUMBER and press ENTER
   Continue in the WESTLAW Directory, press ENTER
```

FIGURE 7-M
WESTLAW PRINTOUT

```
SCOPE: FIND                              Page  3 of  3

CITATION and press ENTER, e.g., fi tx legis 1.

   TIP:  Punctuation and spacing in the citation do not affect FIND,
and quotation marks are not necessary.  Thus, a citation may be typed
105 S.CT. 1005 or 105SCT1005 with the same result.

   TIP:  FIND cannot be used to view particular U.S. Code subsections.

   TIP:  To view abbreviation examples and a complete list of publications
recognized by FIND type FI PUBS and press ENTER.




If you wish to:
   Select this database, type FIND and press ENTER
   View a different page, type P followed by its NUMBER and press ENTER
   Continue in the WESTLAW Directory, press ENTER
```

FIGURE 7-N
WESTLAW PRINTOUT

WESTLAW has a list of publications that are available with FIND. To see this list (as indicated in Figure 7-N above), you would type **fi pubs** (or **find pubs**) and then press the ENTER key. After typing and entering this request, WESTLAW will display an index of publications shown in Figure 7-O.

```
                                                        Page  1 of 98
                       FIND PUBLICATIONS INDEX

Beginning With      Page    Beginning With      Page    Beginning With      Page

A..............       2      J..............      35      S..............      62
B..............       5      K..............      35      T..............      63
C..............      11      L..............      35      U..............      68
D..............      22      M..............      37      V..............      95
E..............      24      N..............      42      W..............      96
F..............      26      O..............      55      X..............      --
G..............      30      P..............      57      Y..............      --
H..............      31      Q..............      --      Z..............      --
I..............      32      R..............      60



If you wish to:
   View a page of publication abbreviations, type P followed by its NUMBER
     and press ENTER
   FIND a document, type its CITATION and press ENTER
   Leave the FIND Publications List, press ENTER
```

FIGURE 7-O
WESTLAW PRINTOUT

PROBLEM 7.7   Assume that you want to retrieve § 4980 of the California Business and Professions Code using the FIND service. Assume that you want to know the format for this publication. By typing **p11** and then pressing the ENTER key, you would see the screen reproduced in Figure 7-P. What is the proper format?

```
                                                       Page 11 of 98
PUBLICATION                                           ABBREVIATION
Board of Immigration Appeals Interim Decisions . . . . Interim Decision
Board of Tax Appeals . . . . . . . . . . . . . . . . . B.T.A.
California Appellate Reports . . . . . . . . . . . . . Cal.App.
California Appellate Reports 2nd . . . . . . . . . . . Cal.App.2d
California Appellate Reports 3rd . . . . . . . . . . . Cal.App.3d
California Appellate Reports Supplement 2nd  . . . . . Cal.App.2d Supp.
California Appellate Reports Supplement 3rd  . . . . . Cal.App.3d Supp.
California Business & Professions . . . . . . . . . . CA BUS & PROF
California Civil . . . . . . . . . . . . . . . . . . . CA CIVIL
California Civil Procedure . . . . . . . . . . . . . . CA CIV PRO
California Code of Regulation . . . . . . . . . . . . CA ADC
California Code of Regulations (Barclays)  (e.g., 1 CA
     ADC s 125) . . . . . . . . . . . . . . . . . . . CA ADC
California Commercial . . . . . . . . . . . . . . . . CA COML

If you wish to:
   View a page of publication abbreviations, type P followed by its NUMBER
     (e.g., P2) and press ENTER
   Return to the Index of Publication Abbreviations, type P1 and press ENTER
   Find a document, type its CITATION (e.g.,98 SCT 1) and press ENTER
   Continue, press ENTER
```

FIGURE 7-P
WESTLAW PRINTOUT

DISCUSSION OF PROBLEM 7.7 As indicated in Figure 7-P, the proper format for the California Business and Professions Code is CA BUS & PROF. Thus, to retrieve § 4980, you would type **find ca bus & prof s 4980**. Note that "s" can be used to represent the section sign and that all capital letters could have been used.

After you have entered FIND with a proper citation, the computer will retrieve the document. The first page of the case that would be retrieved by entering the request developed in the EZ ACCESS menus in the preceding subsection (**find 579 SW2d 670**) is shown in Figure 7-Q.

```
                    COPR. (C) WEST 1992 NO CLAIM TO ORIG. U.S. GOVT. WORKS
  Citation                            Page(P)           Database   Mode
  579 S.W.2d 670          FOUND DOCUMENT P 1 OF 5       MO-CS        P
  (CITE AS: 579 S.W.2D 670)
                    STATE of Missouri, Plaintiff-Respondent,
                                     v.
                  Charles Bernard JONES, Defendant-Appellant.
                                No. 39630.
            Missouri Court of Appeals, Eastern District, Division Three.
                              Feb. 14, 1979.
        Defendant was convicted in the Circuit Court, City of St. Louis, Murry L.
      Randall, J., of first-degree robbery and first-degree burglary.  Defendant
      appealed, and the Court of Appeals, Reinhard, P. J., held that: (1) a permanent
      record book of the circuit court was admissible to prove defendant's prior
      conviction without compliance with the Business Records Act, and (2) the trial
      court did not abuse discretion by permitting the State to ask its own witnesses
      whether they were certain of their identification of defendant as the culprit.
       Affirmed.
```

FIGURE 7-Q
WESTLAW PRINTOUT

Note that the *Jones* case is contained on five pages. To examine the next page of this case, you could type **p2** and then press the ENTER key. To move to page 5, you could type **p5** and then press the ENTER key. To see where specific terms appear in the document, you could use LOCATE. Thus, you could type **loc records** and then press the ENTER key to find each instance where this term appears in the document.

The remaining pages of the *Jones* case are shown in the following figures.

```
                    COPR. (C) WEST 1992 NO CLAIM TO ORIG. U.S. GOVT. WORKS
579 S.W.2d 670              FOUND DOCUMENT P 2 OF 5        MO-CS      P
(CITE AS: 579 S.W.2D 670)
 110k444
CRIMINAL LAW
k. Authentication of documents.
Mo.App. 1979.
For purpose of proving defendant's prior conviction under the Second Offender
Act, a volume of the circuit court's permanent record book was admissible
without compliance with the Business Records Act.  V.A.M.S. ss 490.660 et seq.,
556.280, Laws 1959, S.B. 117.
State v. Jones
579 S.W.2d 670
```

FIGURE 7-R
WESTLAW PRINTOUT

```
                    COPR. (C) WEST 1992 NO CLAIM TO ORIG. U.S. GOVT. WORKS
579 S.W.2d 670              FOUND DOCUMENT P 3 OF 5        MO-CS      P
(CITE AS: 579 S.W.2D 670)
 410k245
WITNESSES
k. Repetition of questions.
Mo.App. 1979.
In prosecution for first-degree burglary and first-degree robbery, the trial
court did not abuse discretion by permitting the State to ask its own witnesses
whether they were certain of their identification of defendant.
State v. Jones
579 S.W.2d 670
```

FIGURE 7-S
WESTLAW PRINTOUT

```
                         COPR. (C) WEST 1992 NO CLAIM TO ORIG. U.S. GOVT. WORKS
 579 S.W.2d 670               FOUND DOCUMENT P 4 OF 5        MO-CS      P
(CITE AS: 579 S.W.2D 670, *670)
 *670 Erica Leisenring, Asst. Public Defender, St. Louis, for defendant-
 appellant.
 Richard Thurman, Asst. Atty. Gen., Jefferson City, for plaintiff-respondent.

 REINHARD, Presiding Judge.
 Defendant appeals from a conviction by a jury of Burglary First Degree and
Robbery First Degree.  Under the Second Offender Act the Court sentenced him to
20 years on each charge, the sentences to run concurrently.
 Because of the nature of defendant's complaints it is unnecessary for us to
recite the facts.  As to both of defendant's allegations of error, the Supreme
Court of Missouri has previously ruled adversely to defendant's position.
 Defendant's first point involves the proof of a prior conviction under the
Second Offender Act.  He alleges that the court improperly admitted State's
Exhibit 14, which was Volume 62 of the Permanent Record Book of the Circuit
Court.  Defendant specifically claims that "The state failed to show entries
were made on or about the time the event occurred," and therefore did not
qualify under the Business Records Act.
 In State v. Washington, 335 S.W.2d 23 (Mo.1960) the deputy circuit clerk
produced and read from the original circuit court records, as was done here.
Defendant objected that the state had not complied with the Business Records
Act.  The court rejected defendant's argument, saying that these court records
```

FIGURE 7-T
WESTLAW PRINTOUT

```
                         COPR. (C) WEST 1992 NO CLAIM TO ORIG. U.S. GOVT. WORKS
 579 S.W.2d 670               FOUND DOCUMENT P 5 OF 5        MO-CS      P
(CITE AS: 579 S.W.2D 670, *670)
 were required to be kept before the adoption of the Business Records Act and
 were admissible in evidence even though they failed to meet the requirements of
 that law.  In this case Exhibit 14 was admissible without compliance with the
 Business Records Act.  This point is without merit.
 Defendant also alleges that "(T)he trial court erred in permitting the State
 to ask its own witnesses whether they were certain of their identification of
 appellant as the culprit," contending that such questions invade the province
 of the jury.  The complaint involved the testimony of witnesses Malone and
 Levenberry.  Similar questions were asked and the same point raised in State v.
 Taylor, 496 S.W.2d 822 *671 (Mo.1973).  The Supreme Court said at 824, "The
 propriety of the question was for the trial court . . ." and, as in Taylor, we
 find no abuse of discretion.
 Affirmed.

 CLEMENS and GUNN, JJ., concur.
END OF DOCUMENT
```

FIGURE 7-U
WESTLAW PRINTOUT

6. PRINTING WESTLAW SCREENS AND DOCUMENTS

Several printing, storing, and downloading options are available on WESTLAW. Your options will depend on the equipment or software that you are using. Generally speaking, three basic types of printing, storing,

and downloading are possible: (1) online printing;[5] (2) online storing;[6] and (3) offline printing[7] and downloading.[8]

Many personal computers allow you to print the screen that you are viewing by pressing the PRINT SCREEN (PrtSc) key. Some require you to simultaneously press the SHIFT and PRINT SCREEN (PrtSc) keys. If you want to print or store several pages, an entire document, or several documents, offline printing or downloading will be the most efficient method. On custom terminals, look for the specialized print keys. In most other situations, to access these functions (to the extent that they are available to you), you can type **pr** and then press ENTER.

7. EXITING A SERVICE AND SIGNING OFF WESTLAW

At some point you will want to exit a service or to sign off WESTLAW. For example, to exit the FIND service, you would type **go back** or **gb** and then press the ENTER key. To sign off on the WESTLAW service, you could type the word **off** and then press the ENTER key. If the option is available to you, WESTLAW can save your search result for later use.

The net chargeable time will then be displayed. Note that you do not have to sign-off to change research projects. After you have finished with one client's research, you can change the research identifier and set the time to zero by typing the word **client** and pressing the ENTER key. You then will be asked to enter the new research identifier.

Section 7B. The Basics of Formulating and Executing Search Queries

This section discusses the formulation of WESTLAW search queries.[9] It applies these search principles to searches in secondary

---

[5]In this situation, you are printing on paper while you are signed on WESTLAW.

[6]In this situation, you are copying information to a floppy or hard disk while you are signed on WESTLAW.

[7]When you are printing information after you have signed off WESTLAW, you are printing offline.

[8]When you are copying information to a floppy or hard disk after you sign off WESTLAW, you are downloading offline.

[9]For a more detailed discussion, you should consult the WESTLAW Reference Manual (4th ed. 1990).

sources. In particular, this section discusses the following topics: (1) search terms on WESTLAW; (2) WESTLAW connectors; (3) phrase searching, root expansion, and universal characters; (4) using EZ ACCESS in formulating a search; (5) executing search queries and viewing the results; (6) using *Black's Law Dictionary*; (7) star paging; and (8) editing your query and conducting new searches.

1. SEARCH TERMS ON WESTLAW

On WESTLAW, a database can be searched by entering one or more search terms. For example, if you entered formica as your search query, you would retrieve all documents in a database in which the word formica appears.

The following chart summarizes how WESTLAW searches singular terms, plurals, possessives, compound terms, acronyms, abbreviations, and equivalencies (states, numbers, calendar terms, legal terms, and other common abbreviations).[10] Some words, such as "an," "the," "but," "to," and several others, are too common to be searched efficiently on WEST-LAW. These words are called "stop words" and will generate the following message when your query contains a stop word: "Your query contains term(s) too common to be searched."[11]

---

[10] See id. §§ 3.2-3.4 (discussing plurals and possessives, automatic equivalencies, compound words, and acronyms). Appendix E lists the automatic equivalencies for the states, calendar abbreviations, numbers, common abbreviations, and spelling variations. Id. app. E.

[11] See id. § 3.7 & app. D.

SEARCH TERMS ON WESTLAW

Type of Term	Example	What WESTLAW Retrieves
Singular and both regular and irregular plurals	house	Both the singular and plural (house and houses)
	houses	Plural (houses), but not the singular (note that **#house** retrieves only house)
Possessives	court	Possessive forms (court's) but court's does not retrieve court
Compound words	post-man	All forms (postman, post man, post-man, post-men, post men, and postmen) (but postman does not retrieve post-man)
Acronyms and abbreviations	f.t.c	Any form, regardless of spaces and periods (F.T.C., F. T. C., FTC, F T C)
	ftc	Only ftc and FTC
Equivalent terms on WESTLAW	Alabama 10, Jan cert	The equivalent (Alabama = Ala, 10 = ten, jan = January, cert = certiorari) (# in front of the term turns off equivalencies)

2. WESTLAW CONNECTORS

On WESTLAW, you can specify the relationship of your search terms by using connectors. The following chart shows the function of the connectors that you can use in formulating your search queries.[12]

---

[12] See id. § 4 ("Connectors").

WESTLAW CONNECTORS

Connector	Function
space (or)	retrieves documents containing either of the search terms (e.g., entering **house or home** retrieves all documents containing the word house or the word home). A space between search terms is treated as meaning or.
& (and)	retrieves documents containing both search terms (e.g., entering **dog & bite** retrieves all documents containing the word dog and the word bite).
/p	retrieves documents containing both of the search terms in the same paragraph (e.g., entering **dog /p bite** retrieves all documents containing the word dog and the word bite in the same paragraph).
/s	retrieves documents containing both of the search terms in the same sentence (e.g., entering **dog /s house** retrieves all documents containing the word dog and house in the same sentence)
/n	retrieves documents in which both of the search terms are within a specified number of words of each other (e.g., entering **personal /3 jurisdiction** retrieves all documents in which these terms are within three words of each other).
+n	retrieves documents in which the term on the left precedes the term on the right by no more than the specified number of words (e.g., **50 + 5 16.11** could be used to retrieve citations to 50 C.F.R. s 16.11).
%	excludes documents containing terms and relations listed after the % symbol.

WESTLAW processes these connectors in the following order: space (or), +n, /n, +s, /s, /p, &, %. The order of processing will affect your search results. The *WESTLAW Reference Manual* gives the following

example.   Suppose you want to retrieve cases containing the term frisk or the phrase search and seizure.   If **frisk! search! /3 seiz!** was used, the "or" relationship between frisk! and search! would be processed first. The query thus requires that frisk! or search! appear within three words of seiz!   To change the order of processing you would place search! /3 seiz! in parentheses: **frisk! (search! /3 seiz!).**   WESTLAW would then search for two alternative sets—(1) documents with frisk! or (2) documents with search! /3 seiz!.[13]

3. PHRASE SEARCHING, ROOT EXPANSION, AND UNIVERSAL CHARACTERS ON WESTLAW

To search for phrases on WESTLAW, you can enclose the phrase in quotation marks.   For example, to search for the phrase attractive nuisance, you could enter **"attractive nuisance"** as your query.   This query would retrieve documents containing these search terms in the same order as they appear within the quotation marks.

If you do not use quotation marks to enclose the phrase, the computer will treat the space between as an "or" and will retrieve all documents containing either the word attractive or the word nuisance.

On WESTLAW, you can use ! as a root expander. **Negligen!** would retrieve negligent, negligence, and negligently.   The * is the universal character, which would retrieve any character in the position the asterisk is typed. **Bec*me** would retrieve become and became.[14]

PROBLEM 7.8   Based on the preceding discussion, formulate a search query for the following situations.   Unless otherwise stated, assume that you want the plurals of any search words.

(a) Formulate a query in which the words *comparative* and *negligence* appear in the same sentence of a document.

Your Query: _____

(b) Formulate a query in which the words *narcotics* and *informer* appear in the same paragraph of a document.

Your Query: _____

---

[13] See id. § 4.7 & app. F.

[14] See id. § 3.5 ("Searching for Various Forms of Words").

(c) Formulate a query that would retrieve documents containing the phrase *attractive nuisance* and the word *culvert*.

Your Query: _____

(d) Formulate a query that would retrieve documents containing the word *nuisance*, the word *water*, and any form of the word *child* in the same paragraph.

Your Query: _____

(e) Formulate a query that would retrieve documents containing the words *license* and *fireworks* in the same paragraph but excluding those documents in which either the word *laches* or the phrase *res judicata* occurs. In formulating your query, you should anticipate that fireworks may appear in varying ways.

Your Query: _____

DISCUSSION OF PROBLEM 7.8   These are the proper queries:
(a) comparative /s negligence
(b) narcotics /p informer
(c) "attractive nuisance" & culvert
(d) nuisance /p water /p child!
(e) license /p fire-work % laches "res judicata"

PROBLEM 7.9   Assume that you want to search the text of law journals for articles that discuss "John Doe" defendants in conjunction with subject-matter jurisdiction. Evaluate the following search query for this purpose:

john +1 doe /p defendant /p jurisdiction

DISCUSSION OF PROBLEM 7.9   The above search query is a good start on formulating a search query. This query will retrieve all documents in which the word "john" immediately precedes the word "doe" in paragraphs in which "defendant" and "jurisdiction" appear. Note that the word "defendant" will also retrieve the plural "defendants." A technical improvement to this search query would be to limit "doe" to the singular by adding # in front of doe (#doe) to prevent the retrieval of the plural, which also is the verb "does."
    Depending on what this query retrieves, you want to restrict it further—for example, by adding the concept of subject matter to the

query—or you may want to broaden it—for example, by dropping the word defendant from the query.

4. USING EZ ACCESS IN FORMULATING A SEARCH

Reexamine Figure 7-H showing the Welcome Screen for EZ AC-CESS. If you wanted to search by significant words, you would select the third choice: "Significant words." The menus would assist you in formulating your search query.

5. EXECUTING SEARCH QUERIES AND VIEWING THE RESULTS

PROBLEM 7.10 Assume that you have decided to use the query formulated in *Problem 7.9*. Reexamine the "Welcome to WESTLAW Screen" shown in Figure 7-B. What would you type to view the directory page providing information about law review databases?

DISCUSSION OF PROBLEM 7.10 To view the relevant directory page, you would type **p320** and then press the ENTER key.

PROBLEM 7.11 Page 320 is below. What is the database identifier for the database that contains journals and law reviews?

```
 _____WESTLAW DIRECTORY WELCOME SCREEN_____P1_____
 _____TEXTS & PERIODICALS                                          P320_____

            GENERAL DATABASES            INDIVIDUAL PUBLICATION DATABASES
 TP-ALL    All law reviews, texts, bar   Databases of individual text, law
           journals and CLE              review, journal & CLE publications
 JLR       Journals & Law Reviews        are listed on the following pages.
 TEXTS     Texts & Treatises             A . . . . P326    N . . . . P340
 AMBAR-TP  ABA Journals                  B . . . . P328    O and P . P342
 ----------------------------------      C . . . . P329    Q and R . P343
     INDEX TO INDICES, TOPICAL TP AND    D and E . P331    S . . . . P344
        SPECIALIZED TP DATABASES         F . . . . P332    T . . . . P346
 Indices to Texts/Periodicals ...P321    G . . . . P333    U . . . . P347
   DIALOG Databases .............P321     H . . . . P334    V . . . . P349
 DIALOG Periodical Databases ....P323     I . . . . P335    W . . . . P350
 Topical Texts & Periodicals ....P324     J . . . . P336    X Y and Z P351
 ----------------------------------      K and L . P338    CLE . . . P352
                                         M ....... P339    TEXTS . . P353

 If you wish to:
   Select a database, type its IDENTIFIER, e.g., TP-ALL and press ENTER
   View information about a database, type SCOPE followed by its IDENTIFIER
      and press ENTER
```

FIGURE 7-V
WESTLAW PRINTOUT

DISCUSSION OF PROBLEM 7.11 The database identifier is jlr. Assume that the query has now been entered as shown in Figure 7-W.

```
       JOHN +1 #DOE /P DEFENDANT /P JURISDICTION


    Please enter your query.

    Your database is JLR




    If you wish to:
       Enter your query, type it as desired and press ENTER
       View a list of available fields, type F and press ENTER
       View detailed information about this database, type SCOPE and press ENTER
    COPR. (C) WEST 1992 NO CLAIM TO ORIG. U.S. GOVT. WORKS
```

FIGURE 7-W
WESTLAW PRINTOUT

Assume that your search is proceeding. WESTLAW "updates" the progress of your search and gives you the opportunity to cancel your search by typing x and pressing ENTER. After your search has been completed, the highest ranked document will appear on the screen.

```
Citation              Rank(R)          Page(P)        Database   Mode
18 HSTCLQ 745         R 1 OF 6         P 1 OF 83       JLR        T
 18 Hastings Const. L.Q. 745


                SECRET JUSTICE AND THE ADVERSARY SYSTEM

            University of California, Hastings College of the Law

                          Summer, 1991

                        Frank Askin [FNa]

      Copyright 1991 by the Hastings College of the Law; Frank Askin

                             ARTICLES

                           Introduction
    For years, The Trial, by Franz Kafka, has served as the literary model for
    totalitarian justice. Kafka's protagonist, Joseph K., stumbles through a
    nightmarish judicial proceeding in a shadowy forum without ever discovering the
    nature of the charges against him or the evidence upon which they are based. In
    a passage that probably best explains the derivation of the adjective
                COPR. (C) WEST 1992 NO CLAIM TO ORIG. U.S. GOVT. WORKS
```

FIGURE 7-X
WESTLAW PRINTOUT

This document is one of six found ("R 1 of 6"). To see a list of citations, you would type L and press ENTER (shown below).

```
CITATIONS LIST (Page 1)                    Total Documents:  6
Database: JLR

    1.    18 Hastings Const. L.Q. 745    SECRET JUSTICE AND THE ADVERSARY SYSTEM
Summer, 1991   Frank Askin [FNa]    18 HSTCLQ 745

    2.    38 U. Kan. L. Rev. 863
POSTREMOVAL CHANGES IN THE PARTY STRUCTURE OF DIVERSITY CASES: THE OLD LAW, THE
NEW LAW, AND RULE 19   Summer, 1990   Joan Steinman [FNa]    38 UKSLR 863

    3.    123 F.R.D. 399
CHANGES IN FEDERAL JURISDICTION AND PRACTICE UNDER THE NEW JUDICIAL
IMPROVEMENTS AND ACCESS TO JUSTICE ACT [FN*]    1989   David D. Siegel%n**%n
123 FEDRDTP 399

    4.    85 Mich.L.Rev. 1507
THE EXCESSIVE HISTORY OF FEDERAL RULE 15(c) AND ITS LESSONS FOR CIVIL RULES
REVISION   June, 1987   Harold S. Lewis, Jr. [FN*]

    5.    80 Nw.U.L.Rev. 1066
POLYPLASTICS, INC. V. TRANSCONEX, INC.: ANTISUIT ORDERS AS INTERLOCUTORY
INJUNCTIONS UNDER 28 U.S.C. s 1292(a)(1)   Winter, 1986   Robert A. Mackey

                COPR. (C) WEST 1992 NO CLAIM TO ORIG. U.S. GOVT. WORKS
```

FIGURE 7-Y
WESTLAW PRINTOUT

To see the fourth ranked document, you would type **r4** and then press ENTER. The beginning page of that document is shown below.

```
                     COPR. (C) WEST 1992 NO CLAIM TO ORIG. U.S. GOVT. WORKS
Citation             Rank(R)        Page(P)        Database   Mode
85 MILR 1507         R 4 OF 6       P 1 OF 158     JLR        T
85 Mich.L.Rev. 1507


    THE EXCESSIVE HISTORY OF FEDERAL RULE 15(c) AND ITS LESSONS FOR CIVIL RULES
                                   REVISION

                     The Michigan Law Review Association

                               June, 1987

                         Harold S. Lewis, Jr. [FN*]

                   Copyright 1987 by Harold S. Lewis, Jr.

                               INTRODUCTION

    What role remains for traditional doctrinal analysis?  Bounded on one side by
the neo-nihilism of critical legal studies, and on the other by the
unabashedly 'cold-blooded' [FN1] latter-day Darwinism of law and economics, can
traditional analysts still make a valuable contribution?  In the midst of these
curve-ball throwing southpaws and hard-throwing right-handers, can today's
```

FIGURE 7-Z
WESTLAW PRINTOUT

Note that WESTLAW is in the Term Mode (T). In this mode, pressing the ENTER key would display the next page with query terms.

In contrast, pressing the ENTER key in the Page Mode (P) would display the next page.

6. USING BLACK'S LAW DICTIONARY ONLINE

While you are viewing your results, you may want to check the meaning of a term by consulting *Black's Law Dictionary*. To do so, you could type **di** and the word or phrase that you want to look up. For example, assume that you want to look up the phrase "john doe." You would type **di john doe** and then press the ENTER key. In this context, you do not need to enclose the phrase in parentheses. To leave the dictionary system, you would type **goback** or **gb** and then press the ENTER key. Figure 7-AA shows a page from *Black's Law Dictionary*.

```
BLACK'S LAW DICTIONARY  6TH EDITION                      P. 1 OF  1
JOHN DOE.

    A fictitious name frequently used to indicate a person for the purpose of
argument or illustration, or in the course of enforcing a fiction in the law.
The name which was usually given to the fictitious lessee of the plaintiff in
the mixed action of ejectment.  He was sometimes called ''Goodtitle.''  So the
Romans had their fictitious personages in law proceedings, as Titius, Seius.
    The name ''John Doe'' is, and for some centuries has been, used in legal
proceedings as a fictitious name to designate a party until his real name can
be ascertained.  State v. Rossignol, 22 Wash.2d 19, 153 P.2d 882, 885.  When
''John Doe'' is used in a search warrant, case report, textbook, or other
legal document, it refers to an unknown or nonexistent person.  Garner v.
State, 220 Tenn. 680, 423 S.W.2d 480, 482.

John Doe summons.  A summons used when the defendant's name is unknown and
which is therefore made out to John Doe.  After the true name of the defendant
is known, it is substituted.

To leave th  Dictionary system. . . . . . . . . . . Enter GOBACK or GB
COPR. (C) WEST 1992 NO CLAIM TO ORIG. U.S. GOVT. WORKS
```

FIGURE 7-AA
WESTLAW PRINTOUT

7. STAR PAGING

The Bluebook has special rules for citing cases in electronic databases such as WESTLAW. In general, enough information must be given to identify the database and find the case. Screen or page numbers, if assigned, should be preceded by an asterisk. *See Bluebook* Rule 10.8.1(b).

Furthermore, WESTLAW provides star paging to original sources. The star paging allows you to see both electronic pagination and print pagination.

PROBLEM 7.12 Reexamine Figure 7-U showing the *Jones* case. What are the first words on page 671 of the opinion?

DISCUSSION OF PROBLEM 7.12   The first words on page 671 is the parenthetical of the citation of the *Taylor* case: "(Mo.1973)."

8. EDITING YOUR QUERY AND CONDUCTING NEW SEARCHES

After reviewing the result of your search, you may want to edit your query or you may want to conduct a new search. The following summarizes your options:

q displays the last query for editing. You can then expand or restrict your query;

s displays an Enter Query screen. You can then begin a completely new search in the same database;

sdb *xxx* (where *xxx* is the database identifier) runs the same query in a different database;

qdb xxx (where xxx is the database identifier) displays the query for editing in a different database);

db returns you to the WESTLAW Directory from a database; and

db xxx (where xxx is the database identifier) accesses a database.

Section 7C. Field Restrictions in Databases Containing Case Law and Secondary Sources

Almost all WESTLAW documents contain "fields." Such fields reflect the "naturally occurring divisions of a document."[15] For example, the fields in texts and periodicals such as the ones shown in the preceding figures include the citation (ci), title (ti), source (so), author (au), and the text (te).

Rather than searching the entire document, you can limit your search to one or more of these fields. For example, if you wanted to find all articles by a certain author in the database, you could (as discussed below) restrict your search to only the author (au) field.

To display the fields available in a particular database, you could type **f** and press the ENTER key while you are in that database. The SCOPE information for a database also contains this information. The following discussion will focus on field restrictions in case law databases. For case law databases, your search may be limited to one or more of the following fields.

---

[15] See id. § 5.1 (discussing field restrictions).

WESTLAW FIELDS FOR CASE LAW DATABASES

Field	Description
Title ti	Title of the case
Citation ci	Case citation (but you would ordinarily use FIND if you knew the citation)
Judge ju	Author of the majority opinion
Synopsis sy	Brief description of the facts and the holding of the case written by West editors
Digest di	Combination of the headnote, court, topic, title, and citation fields
Topic to	West digest topic name, number, and key line
Headnote he	West's summary of a point of law
Opinion op	Text of the case written by the court (in reported cases, the opinion is enhanced by the addition of parallel citations and corrections by the court; all citations and quoted materials are also verified; thus, the text is superior to what is received from the court in slip opinion form.)

The following chart shows sample formats for selected field restrictions in case law databases. Note that you can either use the full name of the field (e.g., title) or its short form (e.g., ti). You may also leave a space between the name of the field and the parenthesis. Thus, for the first sample format below, you could enter either **title(smith & jones), ti(smith & jones), title (smith & jones),** or **ti (smith & jones).**

Note that court, date, and topic/key number field restrictions can be used. EZ ACCESS can help you formulate field searches using West's topics and key numbers. Reexamine Figure 7-H showing the Welcome Screen for EZ ACCESS. If you wanted to search by a topic and key number, you would select the second choice: "A West Topic and Key number." The menus would assist you in formulating your search query.

SAMPLE FORMATS FOR WESTLAW CASE LAW FIELD SEARCHES

Field	Sample Format
Title ti	**ti(smith & jones)**
Citation ci	**ci(294 +5 415)** in the relevant database (better still, use FIND)
Judge ju	**ju(brennan)**
Attorney at	**at(teply)**
Synopsis sy	**sy(stevens +s dissent!)**
Topic to	**to(402)** (The *WESTLAW Reference Manual (4th ed. 1990)* lists numerical topic designations in Appendix A). You could also use the topic name and other words (e.g., **to("work*** compensation")** or **to(mental! /s suffer!))**. Using words enhances the utility of a topic search.
Date da	**da(1992) & search terms** **da(after 1991) & search terms** **da(date after 1988 & before 1990) & search terms** **added da(after 1-1-92) & search terms** (retrieves documents added after the date)
Court co	**co(ny)** (run in the database containing federal district court opinions restricts the cases retrieved to New York federal district court opinions); **co(high)** retrieves cases involving only the highest court; **co(low)** retrieves cases involving lower courts.
Topic and Key Number k	**272k105** (retrieves cases under digest topic 272 (Negligence) and key number 105)—West's summary of a point of law

PROBLEM 7.13 Based on the preceding discussion, formulate a search query for the following situations. Unless otherwise stated, assume that you want the plurals of any search words.

(a) Formulate a query that would retrieve only cases decided after 1990 that contain the words *release* and *prisoner* in the same paragraph.

Your Query: _____

(b) Formulate a query that would retrieve New York cases with at least one headnote digested under the topic Assault and Battery. Assume that Appendix A of the *WESTLAW Reference Manual* indicates that this digest topic is WESTLAW digest topic number 37. Assume also that you want to find cases decided before 1992.

Your Query: _____

(c) Formulate a search query that would retrieve cases which have a headnote classified under the WESTLAW digest topic number 272 (Negligence) and key number 63 and which mention the word *toilet* or the word *restroom* in the case. In formulating your query, you should anticipate that restroom may appear in varying ways.

DISCUSSION OF PROBLEM 7.13 Compare your answers with these:

(a) date(after 1990) & release /p prisoner
(b) court(ny) & topic(37) & date(before 1992)
(c) 272k63 & toilet rest-room

Section 7D. Online Use of Insta-Cite and Shepard's Citations

1. INSTA-CITE

West Publishing Company's case history and citation service is called "Insta-Cite." It is useful for finding parallel citations, identifying cases having a negative impact on the precedential value of the case, and checking the accuracy of your citations.[16]

To use Insta-Cite, you simply type **ic** and the citation. For example, to view the Insta-Cite information for *United States v. Montana*,

---

[16] See id. § 12 (discussing Insta-Cite).

reported at 99 S. Ct. 970, you would type **ic 99 s ct 970** and then press the ENTER key. If you were viewing this case on WESTLAW, you could simply enter **ic** to activate the Insta-Cite service. The Insta-Cite screens for this case are shown in the following two figures.

```
                                    INSTA-CITE                 Page   1 of   2
        CITATION: 99 S.Ct. 970
                                  DIRECT HISTORY

            1  U. S. v. State of Mont., 437 F.Supp. 354,
                  24 Cont.Cas.Fed. (CCH) P 81,804 (D.Mont., Aug 19, 1977)
                  (NO. CIV. 1989)
                  Probable Jurisdiction Noted by
            2  Montana v. U.S., 436 U.S. 916, 98 S.Ct. 2260, 56 L.Ed.2d 756
                  (U.S.Mont., May 22, 1978) (NO. 77 1134)
                  AND Judgment Reversed by
        =>  3  MONTANA V. U. S., 440 U.S. 147, 99 S.Ct. 970, 59 L.Ed.2d 210,
                  25 Cont.Cas.Fed. (CCH) P 82,034 (U.S.Mont., Feb 22, 1979)
                  (NO. 77-1134)

        Note: This result is for the highlighted citation.  To view history for another
              case in this display, type IC and its NUMBER and press ENTER.  For
              indirect history prior to 1972 use Shepard's.  See SCOPE for more info.
        (C) Copyright West Publishing Company 1992
```

FIGURE 7-BB
WESTLAW PRINTOUT

```
                                    INSTA-CITE                 Page   2 of   2
        CITATION: 99 S.Ct. 970
                              NEGATIVE INDIRECT HISTORY

          Disagreed With by
            4  U. S. v. State of Wash., 654 F.2d 570, 29 Cont.Cas.Fed. (CCH) P 81,852
                  (9th Cir.Wash., Aug 24, 1981) (NO. 78-1424)

        (C) Copyright West Publishing Company 1992
```

FIGURE 7-CC
WESTLAW PRINTOUT

2. SHEPARD'S CITATIONS

As discussed in earlier chapters, *Shepard's Citations* provides you with parallel citations, judicial history of a case, verification of the status of a case, later cases that have cited a case, and research leads to other sources, such as *A.L.R. Annotations*. *Shepard's Citations* is available online on WESTLAW.[17]

You can "shepardize" a case by entering **sh** and the citation. If you are currently viewing a case on WESTLAW, you can simply type **sh** and then press the ENTER key. Assume that you want to shepardize *United States v. Montana*, reported at 99 S. Ct. 970. The printout of the first page of the *Shepard's* display is shown in Figure 7-DD.

```
                      SHEPARD'S  (Rank 1 of 1)      Page 1 of 58
CITATIONS TO: 99 S.Ct. 970
CITATOR: UNITED STATES CITATIONS
DIVISION: Supreme Court Reporter
COVERAGE: 1943-1988 Bound Supplement through Dec 1991 Supp; for more see SCOPE
Retrieval                                     Headnote
  No.    -----Analysis----- ------Citation------   No.
          Same Text        (440 U.S. 147)
   1     SC Same Case       437 F.Supp. 354
   2                        547 F.Supp. 988, 993     2
         CC Connected Case  161 Mont. 140
         CC Connected Case  166 Mont. 260

                                   Mont
         CC Connected Case  505 P.2d 102
         CC Connected Case  531 P.2d 1327
   3                         99 S.Ct. 2205, 2209
   4                         99 S.Ct. at 2213        2
   5     E  Explained      101 S.Ct. 411, 415        2
   6     J  Dissenting Opin 101 S.Ct. 411, 424

NOTE:  Check Shepard's PreView (SP), Insta-Cite (IC), and QuickCite (QC).
Copyright (C) 1992 McGraw-Hill, Inc.; Copyright (C) 1992 West Publishing Co.
```

FIGURE 7-DD
WESTLAW PRINTOUT

Note that the printout in Figure 7-DD indicates the citator ("United States Citations"), the Division ("Supreme Court Reporter"), and the coverage of the display ("1943-1988 Bound Supplement through Dec 1991 Supp"). It also indicates that this information covers 58 screens. You can limit the display to particular items, such as cases that have cited a particular headnote or have treated the case in a certain way. By typing **locate 1** (or **loc 1**), you would limit the display to those cases that have cited headnote 1 of the case in the *Supreme Court Reporter*. The first page of that display in shown in Figure 7-EE.

---

[17] *See id.* § 13 (discussing Shepard's Citations).

```
                        SHEPARD'S   (Rank 1 of 1)        Page 1 of 9
CITATIONS TO: 99 S.Ct. 970
CITATOR: UNITED STATES CITATIONS
DIVISION: Supreme Court Reporter
COVERAGE: 1943-1988 Bound Supplement through Dec 1991 Supp; for more see SCOPE
LOCATED:    1
Retrieval                                       Headnote
    No.    ----Analysis----  ------Citation-------  No.
    1                        103 S.Ct. 2906, 2917    1
    2      D  Distinguished 104 S.Ct. 568, 571       1
    3      F  Followed      104 S.Ct. 575, 577       1
    4      E  Explained     104 S.Ct. 575, 581       1

                              Cir. DC
    5                        658 F.2d 835, 851        1
    6                        803 F.2d 1197, 1201      1
    7                        835 F.2d 1458, 1462      1
    8                        579 F.Supp. 967, 973     1
    9                        594 F.Supp. 997, 1003    1

NOTE:  Check Shepard's PreView (SP), Insta-Cite (IC), and QuickCite (QC).
Copyright (C) 1992 McGraw-Hill, Inc.; Copyright (C) 1992 West Publishing Co.
```

FIGURE 7-EE

WESTLAW PRINTOUT

By typing **locate cir1** (or **loc cir1**), you would limit the display to cases from the First Circuit that have cited the case. The first page of that display in shown in Figure 7-FF.

```
                        SHEPARD'S   (Rank 1 of 1)        Page 1 of 3
CITATIONS TO: 99 S.Ct. 970
CITATOR: UNITED STATES CITATIONS
DIVISION: Supreme Court Reporter
COVERAGE: 1943-1988 Bound Supplement through Dec 1991 Supp; for more see SCOPE
LOCATED:    CIR1
Retrieval                                       Headnote
    No.    --Analysis--  ----Citation-----    No.
                            Cir. 1
                         Dk1 87-1800
                         Dk1 89-1353
    1                    630 F.2d 864, 868
    2                    727 F.2d 7, 11          1
    3                    745 F.2d 100, 104
    4                    746 F.2d 87, 92
    5                    787 F.2d 748, 750       2
    6      E  Explained  800 F.2d at 8           2
    7                    801 F.2d 1, 4           2
    8      F  Followed   817 F.2d 161, 172       2
    9                    817 F.2d 894, 905

NOTE:  Check Shepard's PreView (SP), Insta-Cite (IC), and QuickCite (QC).
Copyright (C) 1992 McGraw-Hill, Inc.; Copyright (C) 1992 West Publishing Co.
```

FIGURE 7-FF

WESTLAW PRINTOUT

You can also limit a *Shepard's* display to a particular type of treatment, e.g., "followed" by entering **loc f** as shown in Figure 7-GG.

```
                           SHEPARD'S  (Rank 1 of 1)        Page 1 of 5
CITATIONS TO: 99 S.Ct. 970
CITATOR: UNITED STATES CITATIONS
DIVISION: Supreme Court Reporter
COVERAGE: 1943-1988 Bound Supplement through Dec 1991 Supp; for more see SCOPE
LOCATED:  F
Retrieval                                      Headnote
  No.      -Analysis-- -------Citation-------   No.
   1        F  Followed 104 S.Ct. 575, 577       1

                             Cir. DC
   2        F  Followed 677 F.2d 118, 120         2
   3        F  Followed 747 F.Supp. 760, 766

                             Cir. 1
   4        F  Followed 817 F.2d 161, 172         2
   5        F  Followed 836 F.2d 31, 37           2

                             Cir. 2
   6        F  Followed 699 F.Supp. 1025, 1036    2

NOTE:  Check Shepard's PreView (SP), Insta-Cite (IC), and QuickCite (QC).
Copyright (C) 1992 McGraw-Hill, Inc.; Copyright (C) 1992 West Publishing Co.
```

FIGURE 7-GG
WESTLAW PRINTOUT

You can retrieve a case from a *Shepard's* screen by entering its "Retrieval No." Not all cases cited by *Shepard's* are available on WEST-LAW, but any case with a "Retrieval No." *is* on WESTLAW.

3. SHEPARD'S PREVIEW

Shepard's PreView (sp) citator service (jointly developed by Shepard's/ McGraw-Hill, Inc. and West Publishing Co.) provides a "preview" of citing references that will later appear in *Shepard's Citations* online. To access *Shepard's PreView* while you are viewing any *Shepard's* display, any Insta-Cite display, or any page of a case on WESTLAW, you would type **sp** and then press the ENTER key. You can also type **sp** followed by a citation (e.g., **sp 99 s ct 970**).

The initial *Shepard's PreView* screen for 99 S. Ct. 970 is shown in Figure 7-HH.

```
┌─────────────────────────────────────────────────────────────────────┐
│                                                                       │
│                     SHEPARD'S PREVIEW              Page 1 of 3         │
│     Citations to:  99 S.CT. 970                                       │
│                    Montana v. U. S., (U.S.Mont.  1979)                │
│                                                                       │
│     Retrieval                                                         │
│        No.    -------Citation-------                                  │
│               (440 U.S. 147)               Same Text                  │
│               ( 59 L.Ed.2d 210)            Same Text                  │
│                                                                       │
│                    Cir. DC                                            │
│          1    763 F.Supp. 645, 648                                    │
│                                                                       │
│                    Cir. 2                                             │
│          2    942 F.2d 151, 156                                       │
│          3    764 F.Supp. 864, 870                                    │
│          4    133 B.R. 569, 573                                       │
│                                                                       │
│                    Cir. 3                                             │
│          5    771 F.Supp. 1390, 1400                                  │
│                                                                       │
│     NOTE:  Citing references are only from West Reporters.  See SCOPE for a list.│
│          Check Shepard's (SH), Insta-Cite (IC), and QuickCite (QC).   │
│     Copyright (C) 1992 Shepard's/McGraw-Hill, Inc. and West Publishing Company│
│                                                                       │
└─────────────────────────────────────────────────────────────────────┘
```

FIGURE 7-HH

WESTLAW PRINTOUT

4. USING WESTLAW AS A CITATOR

You can also use WESTLAW as a citator. To do so, you would conduct a WESTLAW search designed to retrieve documents that cite a given authority.[18] For example, the following query would retrieve documents in which *Montana v. United States* had been cited: **Montana & 99 +5 970.**

The "QuickCite" (qc) function automates this updating process in conjunction with a *Shepard's Preview* or *Insta-Cite* display. For example, **qc 99 s ct 970** retrieves the very latest citing cases and dispositions for the *Montana* case.

5. THE MAP COMMAND

After you have viewed a document, you can type **goback** or **gb** to return to your previous search result or service. If you have used several services, you may have to enter goback several times to return through the levels of your research. To avoid multiple goback commands, you can type **map** and press the ENTER key. Examine Figure 7-II illustrating how the map command works.

---

[18]This approach is discussed in detail in section 15 of the fourth edition of the WESTLAW Reference Manual.

```
Service or Database          Request                  Page 1 of 1

  1. WESTLAW Directory          ...
  2. Found Document             99 S.Ct. 970
  3. Insta-Cite                 99 S.Ct. 970
  4. Shepard's                  99 S.Ct. 970
  5. Shepard's PreView          99 S.Ct. 970




      NOTE:  If you go back to one of the above saved results,
             all requests with a larger number will be discarded.

  If you wish to:
      Go back to one of the above services, type its NUMBER and press ENTER
      Return to the last substantive screen, press ENTER
      Receive further information on Map, type HELP and press ENTER
```

FIGURE 7-II
WESTLAW PRINTOUT

Section 7E. Searching for Legislative and Administrative Sources

Research involving legislative and administrative sources on WEST-LAW follows the same basic pattern as described in preceding sections. You can use the FIND service to retrieve legislative and administrative sources, such as code provisions or administrative regulations. You can use EZ ACCESS to retrieve statutes and constitutional provisions. You can also use field restrictions in legislative and administrative searches.

After you have found the text of a state statute, *United States Code* section, or *Code of Federal Regulations* section, you can find amending and repealing provisions in session laws or the *Federal Register* by using the "UPDATE" command.

The following chart shows the fields in the United States Code Annotated database.

WESTLAW FIELDS FOR THE UNITED STATES CODE ANNOTATED DATABASE

Field	Description
Caption ca	Section number and heading
Citation ci	Reference for citing a specific statutory section (but use FIND instead)
Prelim pr	*United States Code* title and other headings that precede the caption
Text te	Text of a *United States Code* section
Credit cr	Statutory credits
Historical and Statutory Notes hn	Historical and statutory notes following the document
Annotations an	Notes of decision
References re	Miscellaneous references relating to the document

State statutes and administrative law sources have slightly different fields. To see the available fields when you are using WESTLAW, you would type **f** after you have accessed a database or when you are viewing scope information for a database.

You can also access various legislative history sources and *Uniform Laws Annotated* through WESTLAW.

Section 7F. Other Sources Accessible Through WESTLAW

Reexamine the WESTLAW DIRECTORY WELCOME SCREEN shown in Figure 7-B. Note particularly the SPECIALIZED MATERIAL listing, which allows you (depending on your account agreement) to access databases supplied by other publishers. Databases such as the DIALOG database will often be useful resources for finding nonlegal discussion of particular topics and other information.

Chapter 8
LEXIS COMPUTER LEGAL RESEARCH SERVICE

Section 8A. Introduction to Using the LEXIS Service

LEXIS is the computer-assisted legal research service provided by Mead Data Central, Inc. This section introduces the following aspects of the LEXIS service: (1) accessing LEXIS; (2) signing on LEXIS; (3) determining the available sources and file coverage; (4) retrieving a known case or statute using LEXSEE and LEXSTAT; (5) printing LEXIS screens and documents; and (6) signing off LEXIS.

1. ACCESSING LEXIS

To begin using the LEXIS service, you must first make contact with Mead Data Central's computers through a phone connection.[1] How that connection is made depends on the equipment that you are using.[2]

2. SIGNING ON LEXIS

After you have accessed LEXIS, you will be requested (1) to type your personal LEXIS identification number (unless you have prearranged

---

[1]Before you can use LEXIS, you must first have access to the service. The LEXIS service has monthly and "research session" charges.

[2]Research on LEXIS is conducted by means of a terminal, consisting of a video display and a keyboard. Some LEXIS terminals have custom keyboards. Other terminals, including personal computers, can be used with the LEXIS service. LEXIS supplies templates for personal computer keyboards to facilitate using the service. The technical aspects of connecting the terminal and accessing LEXIS can be determined by consulting LEXIS publications and LEXIS Customer Service.

to have the software transmit it for you automatically) and then (2) to press the TRANSMIT key (equivalent to the ENTER key). After you have entered your personal LEXIS identification number, you will be asked to identify your research and then to press the TRANSMIT key. The identifying information given depends on the arrangement for the use of LEXIS—such as in a law school or a law office.

You will then be shown the first page of the list of LEXIS Libraries. A printout of that screen is shown in Figure 8-A.

```
                         LIBRARIES -- PAGE 1 of 2
         Please TRANSMIT the NAME (only one) of the library you want to search.
          - For more information about a library, TRANSMIT its page (PG) number.
          - To see a list of additional libraries, press the NEXT PAGE key.
           NAME    PG NAME   PG NAME   PG NAME   PG NAME   PG NAME    PG NAME    PG

           - - - - - L E X I S - U S - - - - - - - - - - - PUBLIC       FINANCIAL  --NEXIS--
            GENFED   1 CODES   1 LEGIS   1 STATES  1 CITES   6 RECORDS      COMPNY 15 NEXIS  13
                                                            ASSETS   6 MERGER 15 BACKGR 13
            ADMRTY   2 FEDCOM  3 MILTRY  4 CORP    2 LAWREV  6 DOCKET   6 NAARS  15 BANKS  14
            BANKNG   2 FEDSEC  3 PATENT  4 EMPLOY  2 MARHUB  6 INCORP   6            CMPCOM 13
            BKRTCY   2 FEDTAX  3 PENBEN  4 HEALTH  3 LEXREF  6 LIENS    6 --INT'L-- CONSUM 13
            COPYRT   2 IMMIG   3 PUBCON  4 INSRLW  3 ABA     6            WORLD  16 ENRGY  14
            ENERGY   2 INTLAW  3 PUBHW   4 MEDMAL  3 BNA     6 --MEDIS-- ASIAPC 16 ENTERT 13
            ENVIRN   2 ITRADE  3 REALTY  4 PRLIAB  4 TAXRIA  6 GENMED 12 EUROPE 16 INSURE 13
            ESTATE   2 LABOR   3 TRADE   5 STENV   4 ALR     6 MEDEX  12 MDEAFR 16 LEGNEW 14
            ETHICS   2 LEXPAT  3 TRDMRK  5 STSEC   4            MEDLNE 12 NSAMER 16 MARKET 14
            FAMILY   2 M&A     4 TRANS   5 STTAX   4 -ASSISTS-                      PEOPLE 14
            FEDSEN   3 MSTORT  5            UCC     5 PRACT  12 POLITICAL           SPORTS 13
                                          UTILTY  5 GUIDE  12 CMPGN  14             TRAN   14
                                                              EXEC   14
               AC for AUTO-CITE       LXE (LEXSEE) to retrieve a case/document by cite
               SHEP for SHEPARD'S     LXT (LEXSTAT) to retrieve a statute by cite
            Press <ESC> for Local Help                                          CD
```

FIGURE 8-A
LEXIS PRINTOUT

3. LEXIS DATABASES AND SERVICES

LEXIS is organized by libraries. A LEXIS library contains all related materials for a particular area of research. For example, the General Federal Library contains federal cases, federal statutes, federal rules of procedure and evidence, federal regulations, United States Supreme Court briefs, opinions of the U.S. Attorney General, and other federal materials. Similarly, the States Library contains state court cases, state statutes, state attorney general opinions, and other state materials. The Codes Library contains state and federal statutory, administrative, and related materials.

PROBLEM 8.1 Reexamine the printout of the first page of the screen showing the LEXIS libraries in Figure 8-A. Determine what basic categories of libraries are available through LEXIS.

DISCUSSION OF PROBLEM 8.1   The materials available through LEXIS are broadly divided in "LEXIS - US," "PUBLIC RECORDS," "FINANCIAL," "NEXIS" (containing the full text of news and business publications),[3] "MEDIS" (containing medical related publications), "POLIT-ICAL," "INT'L" (International publications), and "ASSISTS" (for learning LEXIS and practice).   Note that there are specialized libraries listed on such subjects as admiralty ("ADMRTY"), copyright ("COPYRT"), and immigration ("IMMIG").   Other libraries include *American Law Reports Annotated* ("ALR") and legal periodicals ("LAWREV").

PROBLEM 8.2   Reexamine the printout of the first page of the screen showing the LEXIS libraries in Figure 8-A.   (a) What would you type and transmit to select the General Federal Library?   (b) What would you type and transmit to select the States Library?

DISCUSSION OF PROBLEM 8.2   (a) To select the General Federal Library, you would type **genfed** and then press the TRANSMIT (ENTER) key.   (b) To select the States Library, you would type **states** and then press the TRANSMIT key.

Figure 8-A showed the first page of the available LEXIS Libraries. To move to the next page, you could use the NEXT PAGE key on a custom terminal, "dot commands" (e.g., by typing **.np** and then pressing the TRANSMIT key), or designated function keys on a personal computer (easily identified by using a template) (e.g., on IBM and IBM-compatible personal computers, F1 for next page, F2 for previous page, etc.).   For purposes of further discussion, keys will be referred to by their function (e.g., NEXT PAGE, PREV PAGE, etc.).

Assume that you have pressed the NEXT PAGE key while viewing the screen shown in Figure 8-A.   The next page showing the available LEXIS Libraries is shown in Figure 8-B.   Note that this screen allows you to select specific state libraries and various libraries containing materials from the United Kingdom, Ireland, Commonwealth countries, France, and the European Community.

---

[3]NEXIS is the world's largest database.

```
                        LIBRARIES -- PAGE 2 of 2
    Please TRANSMIT the NAME (only one) of the library you want to search.
      - For more information about a library, TRANSMIT its page (PG) number.
      - To see a list of additional libraries, press the PREV PAGE key.
    NAME   PG NAME    PG NAME    PG NAME    PG NAME    PG NAME     PG NAME    PG

    - - - - - - - L E X I S - U S - - - - - - - -    LEXIS-UK  LEXIS-CW   LEXIS-FR
    ALA    7 GA      7 MD      7 NJ    8 SD    8  ENGGEN 10  COMCAS 10  INTNAT 11
    ALAS   7 HAW     7 MASS    7 NM    8 TENN  8  UKTAX  10  AUST   10  LOIREG 11
    ARIZ   7 IDA     7 MICH    7 NY    8 TEX   8  SCOT   10  NZ     10  PRIVE  11
    ARK    7 ILL     7 MINN    7 NC    8 UTAH  8  UKJNL  10             PUBLIC 11
    CAL    7 IND     7 MISS    8 ND    8 VT    9  NILAW  10             REVUES 11
    COLO   7 IOWA    7 MO      8 OHIO  8 VA    9
    CONN   7 KAN     7 MONT    8 OKLA  8 VI    9            EC-LAW
    DEL    7 KY      7 NEB     8 ORE   8 WASH  9          EURCOM 10
    DC     7 LA      7 NEV     8 PA    8 WVA   9
    FLA    7 MAINE   7 NH      8 PR    8 WISC  9           LEXIS-IR
                              RI    8 WYO   9           IRELND 10

    Press <ESC> for Local Help                                            CD
```

FIGURE 8-B
LEXIS PRINTOUT

Each LEXIS Library is divided into files containing "documents" that can be searched.

PROBLEM 8.3 Assume that you have selected the General Federal Library by typing **genfed** and then pressing the TRANSMIT key. The following figures show part of the contents of the General Federal Library. Based on information provided in these figures, what would you transmit to select a file (or files) containing

    (a) only United States Supreme Court cases;

    (b) all federal and state court cases;

    (c) only cases decided by the First and Second Circuits of the Courts of Appeals;

    (d) the *Congressional Record* for the 102nd Congress; and

    (e) the *United States Code Service*.

The relevant figures are shown on the following pages.

```
Please TRANSMIT, separated by commas, the NAMES of the files you want to search.
You may select as many files as you want, including files that do not appear
below, but you must transmit them all at one time.  To see a description of a
file, TRANSMIT its page (PG) number.
          FILES - PAGE 1 of 8 (NEXT PAGE for additional files)

NAME  PG DESCRIP          NAME   PG DESCRIP          NAME   PG DESCRIP

   ---COURT GROUP FILES--   ----ADMINISTRATIVE-----    ---LEGAL DEVELOPMENTS--
MEGA   11 Fed & State Cts ALLREG 16 FEDREG & CFR     USLIST 12 Sup.Ct Summaries
COURTS  1 Fed Cases & ALR FEDREG 16 Fed. Register    APPSUM 13 Ct App Summaries
CURRNT  1 Cases aft 1990  CFR    16 Code of Fed.Reg  USLW   12 US Law Week
NEWER   3 Cases aft 1944  COMGEN 14 Comp.Gen.Decs.   USLWD  12 US Law Wk Daily
SUPCIR  1 US,USAPP & CAFC  --SUPREME COURT BRIEFS-   PUBS   37 Legal Pubs
   ---U.S. COURT FILES---  BRIEFS 12 Argued aft 9/79    ------LEGISLATIVE------
US      1 US Supreme Ct    ---------RULES---------   RECORD 26 CongRec aft 1984
USAPP   1 Cts of Appeal   RULES  31 Federal Rules    USCODE 15 USCS & PUBLAW
DIST    1 District Courts CIRRUL 33 Circuit Ct Rules BLREC  26 CongRec & BLTEXT
CLCT    2 Claims Court

To search by Circuits press NEXT PAGE.  NOTE:  Only court files can be combined.
Press <ESC> for Local Help                                              CD
```

FIGURE 8-C
LEXIS PRINTOUT

```
Please TRANSMIT, separated by commas, the NAMES of the files you want to search.
You may select as many files as you want, including files that do not appear
below, but you must transmit them all at one time.  To see a description of a
file, TRANSMIT its page (PG) number.
          FILES - PAGE 2 of 8 (NEXT PAGE or PREV PAGE for additional files)

NAME   PG NAME    PG        NAME   PG NAME   PG        NAME   PG NAME   PG

   C I R & D I S T              C I R C U I T            D I S T R I C T

1ST     5 8TH      6        1CIR    9 8CIR    9        1DIST  10 10DIST 10
2ND     5 9TH      7        2CIR    9 9CIR    9        2DIST  10 11DIST 10
3RD     5 10TH     7        3CIR    9 10CIR   9        3DIST  10 DCDIST 10
4TH     5 11TH     8        4CIR    9 11CIR   9        4DIST  10 CIT     2
5TH     6 CADC     8        5CIR    9 DCCIR   9        5DIST  10 CVA     2
6TH     6 FED      8        6CIR    9 CAFC    9        6DIST  10 TC      2
7TH     6                  7CIR    9 CCPA    2        7DIST  10 BANKR   2
           MILTRY   2                                  8DIST  10 CUSTCT  2
                                                       9DIST  10 COMCT   2
-----------------------CASES BY CIRCUIT AFTER 1911-----------------------

Press NEXT PAGE for Cong. Record.  Note:  Only court files can be combined.
Press <ESC> for Local Help                                              CD
```

FIGURE 8-D
LEXIS PRINTOUT

```
        FILES - PAGE 3 of 8 (NEXT PAGE or PREV PAGE for additional files)

NAME   PG DESCRIP         NAME   PG DESCRIP         NAME   PG DESCRIP

 -CONGRESSIONAL RECORD-   -----------LEGISLATIVE MATERIAL------------------
RECORD 26 1985 - 1991    BILLS  27 All Bills Files BLREC  26 CongRec & BLTEXT
102ND  26 102nd Congress BLTRCK 27 Bill Tracking
101ST  26 101st Congress BLCAST 27 Billcast        CNGRES 28 All CNGRES Files
100TH  26 100th Congress BLTEXT 27 Full Text Bills CNGVOT 28 CNGRES Votes
99TH   26 99th Congress  CMTRPT 27 Committee Rpts. CNGFIN 28 CNGRES Financial
102SEN 26 102nd Senate   ROLLCL 27 Roll Call       CNGMEM 28 CNGRES Backgrnd
102HSE 26 102nd House    BNAWI  27 Wash. Insider
102RMK 26 102nd Remarks   -LEGISLATIVE ARCHIVES---   -LEGISLATIVE HISTORIES--
102DIG 26 102nd Digest   BLARCH 27 Archived Bills  BKRLH  29 Bkrtcy Leg. Hist
SENATE 26 102 - 99 Senate BTX101 27 BLTEXT Archive ENVLH  29 *Envirn Leg. Hist
HOUSE  26 102 - 99 House  BLT101 27 BLTRCK Archive FIRLH  30 *FIRREA Leg. Hist
REMARK 26 102 - 99 Remark                          TAXLH  30 Tax Leg. Hist
DIGEST 26 102 - 99 Digest          *Compiled by Wilmer, Cutler & Pickering.
Press <ESC> for Local Help                                              CD
```

FIGURE 8-E
LEXIS PRINTOUT

```
          FILES - PAGE 4 of 8 (NEXT PAGE or PREV PAGE for additional files)

NAME    PG DESCRIP                    NAME   PG DESCRIP

 ------------U.S. CODE-------------   ---- CODE OF FEDERAL REGULATIONS ----
USCODE 15 USCS & PUBLAW              LSA    16 List of CFR Sections Affected
USCS   15 US Code Service            INDEX  16 CFR Index
PUBLAW 15 US Public Laws             CFR    17 Title  1 through Title  8
USCNST 15 US Constitution            CFR    18 Title  9 through Title 15
                                     CFR    19 Title 16 through Title 21
 --------FEDERAL REGISTER----------  CFR    20 Title 22 through Title 27
FEDREG 16 From 07/01/80 - 01/24/92   CFR    21 Title 28 through Title 33
                                     CFR    22 Title 34 through Title 38
                                     CFR    23 Title 39 through Title 44
                                     CFR    24 Title 45 through Title 50

NOTE: Only court files can be combined. NEXT PAGE for Archived CFR and FARS.
Press <ESC> for Local Help                                              CD
```

FIGURE 8-F
LEXIS PRINTOUT

DISCUSSION OF PROBLEM 8.3   To select the relevant file (or files), you would transmit the following:

(a) **us**   for only United States Supreme Court cases;

(b) **mega**   for all federal and state court cases;

(c) **1cir,2cir**   for only cases decided by the First and Second Circuits of the Courts of Appeals;

(d) **102nd** for the *Congressional Record* for the 102nd Congress; and

(e) **uscs** for the *United States Code Service.*

Assume that instead of selecting the General Federal Library, you have typed **states** to select the States Library. The first screen showing the files in the States Library is shown in Figure 8-G.

PROBLEM 8.4 Assume that you are interested in searching for Missouri cases that are relevant to a problem. (a) What would you type and transmit to see a description of the Missouri Cases file? (b) What would you type and transmit to select the Missouri Cases file for the purpose of entering a search request?

```
Please TRANSMIT, separated by commas, the NAMES of the files you want to search.
You may select as many files as you want, including files that do not appear
below, but you must transmit them all at one time.  To see a description of a
file, TRANSMIT its page (PG) number.
          FILES - PAGE 1 of 6 (NEXT PAGE for additional files)

NAME   PG NAME   PG NAME   PG NAME   PG NAME   PG NAME   PG NAME   PG NAME   PG

- - - - - - - - - - - - C A S E S - - - - - -  - - - - ---- C O D E S -----
ALA     1 HAW    13 MICH   25 NC     37 UTAH   47 ALLAG  63 STTRCK 55 DCCODE 10
ALAS    2 IDA    14 MINN   27 ND     37 VT     48 ALLENV 63 ALLCDE 64 FLCODE 11
ARIZ    3 ILL    15 MISS   28 OHIO   38 VA     49 ALLPUC 63 STRGTR 64 GACODE 12
ARK     4 IND    16 MO     29 OKLA   39 VI     50 ALLSEC 63 ALCODE  1 HICODE 13
CAL     5 IOWA   17 MONT   30 ORE    40 WASH   51 ALLSOS 63 AKCODE  2 IDCODE 14
COLO    7 KAN    18 NEB    31 PA     41 WVA    52 ALLTAX 63 AZCODE  3 ILCODE 15
CONN    8 KY     20 NEV    32 RI     43 WISC   53                ARCODE  4 INCODE 16
DEL     9 LA     21 NH     33 SC     44 WYO    54                CACODE  5 IACODE 17
DC     10 ME     22 NJ     34 SD     44                          COCODE  7 KSCODE 18
FLA    11 MD     23 NM     35 TENN   45 MEGA   64 OMNI2  64 CTCODE  8 KYCODE 20
GA     12 MASS   24 NY     36 TEX    46 OMNI   64 HIGHCT 64 DECODE  9 KYSTAT 20
NOTE:  The CODE files cannot be combined using Custom File Selection.
SEE NEXT PAGE FOR ADDITIONAL CODE FILES.
Press <ESC> for Local Help                                          CD
```

FIGURE 8-G
LEXIS PRINTOUT

DISCUSSION OF PROBLEM 8.4 (a) To see a description of the Missouri cases file, you would type the number **29** and press the TRANSMIT key. Note that you do not type "p29" (as you would do using WESTLAW). If you did, the computer would respond: "P29 is not a correct file name."

(b) To select a file, you would type its name. Thus, to select the file containing Missouri court opinions, you would type **mo** and press the TRANSMIT key.

Assume that you have typed the correct page number to see a description of the Missouri cases file. A printout of that screen is shown in Figure 8-H.

PROBLEM 8.5 What is the beginning coverage in the file for opinions of the Missouri Supreme Court and the Missouri Court of Appeals?

```
Please TRANSMIT, separated by commas, the NAMES of the files you want to search.
You may select as many files as you want, including files that do not appear
below, but you must transmit them all at one time.  To see the menu page
containing the first file described below, press the TRANSMIT key.
    DESCRIPTIONS - PAGE 29 of 69 (NEXT PAGE or PREV PAGE for additional files)

NAME    FILE                              NAME    FILE

MO      -Sup. Ct.          1/24 to  1/92  MOCODE -Revised Statutes of Missouri
         App. Ct.          1/44 to  1/92          (All Statutes enacted through
MOTAX   -Tax Comm. Dec.    8/80 to 12/91          the 1990 Cumm. Supp.; 2nd Reg.
         Adm Hearing Comm  2/80 to 12/91          Sess.; 85th Gen. Assembly,
MOSEC   -Sec. Comm.        3/71 to 11/91          State Constitution and Supreme
MOPUC   -Pub.Serv.Comm.    3/72 to  8/91          Ct. Rules through 12/18/90.)
MOAG    -Att'y Gen. Ops.   1/77 to 12/91         -Missouri Adv. Legis. Service,
MOINC   -Missouri Secretary of State             including acts from 1991.
         Corporation Information         *Mead Data Central acknowledges the
         Updated Weekly                  Revisor of Statutes, State of Missouri,
                                         as compiler and editor of the Rev.
                                         Stats. of Missouri.
                                         *Mead Data Central is compiler & editor
                                         of the S.CT. Rules in the MOCODE file.
                                                                             CD
Press <ESC> for Local Help
```

FIGURE 8-H
LEXIS PRINTOUT

DISCUSSION OF PROBLEM 8.5 Figure 8-H indicates that coverage of the Missouri Supreme Court begins on January, 1924. The coverage of the Missouri Court of Appeals begins in January, 1944.

After you have selected the library and file(s) that you want to search, you are ready to enter your search request. For this purpose, the following screen will appear.

```
Please type your search request then press the TRANSMIT key.
What you transmit will be Search Level 1.

For further explanation, press the H key (for HELP) and then the TRANSMIT key.
  Press <ESC> for Local Help                                           CD
```

FIGURE 8-I
LEXIS PRINTOUT

4. USING LEXSEE AND LEXSTAT

The LEXSEE (or LXE) Citation Service on LEXIS allows you to retrieve the full text of a case (and certain other documents) based on a known citation to it. Similarly, the LEXSTAT (or LXT) Citation Service on LEXIS allows you to retrieve statutory materials based on known citations. You may use LEXSEE and LEXSTAT at any time after you have properly signed on. The easiest approach is to type the word **lexsee** or **lexstat** followed by the citation.[4]

Assume that you want to see a United States Supreme Court opinion published in volume 99 of West's *Supreme Court Reporter* at page 970. Which of the following, if any, would retrieve this case? (a) **lexsee 99 S.C. 970** (b) **lexsee 99 S.Ct. 970** (c) **lexsee 99 s ct 970** or (d) **lexsee 99S.Ct.970**. Can you tell from the information you know so far?

Assume (without finally resolving the answer to this question) that you transmitted (d) above. The computer would respond with the message shown in Figure 8-J. Examine that message and determine why answer (d) is an improper format.

```
99S.CT.970
LEXSEE Service:




The above citation is not in the correct LEXSEE format.

You may edit the above citation, or type a new one, and press the TRANSMIT key.

To see examples of correct citation formats and related information, press the
H key (for HELP) and then the TRANSMIT key.

To return to LEXIS, press the EXIT SERV key.

For further explanation, press the H key (for HELP) and then the TRANSMIT key.
 Press <ESC> for Local Help
                                                                    CD
```

FIGURE 8-J
LEXIS PRINTOUT

[4]You can type LXE or LXT, as indicated in Figure 8-A. You can also use the SELECT SERV key to enter the LEXSEE (LXE) or LEXSTAT (LXT) services. To exit these services, you would use the EXIT SERV key.

PROBLEM 8.6   Assume that you have decided to type and transmit **h** (for HELP) to see examples of the correct citation formats and related information.   The screen that would next appear is shown in Figure 8-K.   Examine that screen and decide what the error in (d) above might be.

```
        Some reasons for an incorrect citation format are:

              *Omitting spaces between parts of the citation --
               for example, between reporter and page number.

              *Mistyping a character--for example, a letter
               instead of a number.

              *Pressing the TRANSMIT key when the cursor is
               not at the end of the complete citation.

      ---->For more HELP on citation formats, transmit H.

              To resume your work in another citation service,
              transmit RESUME and the name of the service.  For
              example:
                            RESUME AC

      --------------------------------------------------------------------
      To choose from the master list of LEXSEE tutorial topics, transmit M.
      To return to the point where you requested HELP, press TRANSMIT.
      To return to LEXIS, press the EXIT SERV key (or transmit .ES).
       Press <ESC> for Local Help                                    CD
```

FIGURE 8-K

LEXIS PRINTOUT

DISCUSSION OF PROBLEM 8.6   The HELP screen in Figure 8-K indicates that spaces should be left between the various parts of the citation.   Assume that you again type and transmit **h** for more help on citation formats.   The next HELP screen is shown in Figure 8-L.

```
LEXSEE citation requests for most kinds of documents must be
in the following format:

        NUMBER          ABBREVIATION          NUMBER
        (volume         (reporter, forum,     (page/paragraph
        or year)         or jurisdiction)     or document number)


Note that the single spaces between the abbreviations and numbers
are required. Abbreviations do not need spaces or periods (U.S. = US;
A.L.R. 3d = ALR3D).

Examples:    300 US 1      1987 US LEXIS 24        81 L Ed 463


For more information on documents with unique citation formats, transmit H.

For a list of LEXSEE citation formats, transmit L.

--------------------------------------------------------------------------------
To choose from the master list of LEXSEE tutorial topics, transmit M.
To return to the point where you requested HELP, press TRANSMIT.
To return to LEXIS, press EXIT SERV (or TRANSMIT .ES).
 Press <ESC> for Local Help                                           CD
```

FIGURE 8-L
LEXIS PRINTOUT

This HELP screen confirms that an error in (d) was the failure to leave spaces between the different parts of the citation: the volume number, the reporter, and the page. At this point, however, you still cannot determine whether any of the other forms shown in (a)-(c) would work. Reconsider these possibilities:

(a) lexsee 99 S.C. 970

(b) lexsee 99 S.Ct. 970

(c) lexsee 99 s ct 970

PROBLEM 8.7 Based on the information you learned from the HELP screens, how could you determine the proper format for the *Supreme Court Reporter*?

DISCUSSION OF PROBLEM 8.7 As indicated in Figure 8-L, to determine the proper format for West's *Supreme Court Reporter*, you could type and transmit the letter L to see a list of LEXSEE reporter abbreviations. A printout of the screen that would appear is shown in Figure 8-M. Examine this printout.

```
    LEXSEE citation formats are listed in alphabetical order.  The index
    below indicates the beginning page number for abbreviations that
    start with a particular letter.

                         LEXSEE CITATION FORMATS

        abbrev    page    abbrev    page    abbrev    page
          A         1       K        12       U        22
          B         3       L        12       V        23
          C         4       M        13       W        24
          D         6       N        15       X
          E         6       O        17       Y        24
          F         7       P        18       Z
          G         9       Q
          H         9       R        19
          I        10       S        20
          J        11       T        21

------------------------------------------------------------------------
To go to the beginning of any letter, type the letter and press TRANSMIT.
You may transmit the numbers (1 through 24) of the page you want to see.
To choose from the master list of LEXSEE tutorial topics, transmit MA.
To return to the point where you requested HELP, press TRANSMIT.
  Press <ESC> for Local Help                                      CD
```

FIGURE 8-M
LEXIS PRINTOUT

To see the abbreviation for West's *Supreme Court Reporter*, you would type and transmit the number of the relevant page. In this instance, you would type the number **20** and then press the TRANSMIT key. The next screen that would appear is shown in Figure 8-N.

```
                    LEXSEE Citation Formats -- page 20 of 24

    Abbreviation        Reporter, Forum or Jurisdiction

    S.C.                South Carolina Reports
    S.Ct.               Supreme Court Reporter
    S.D.                South Dakota Reports
    S.E.2d              Southeastern Reporter, Second Series
    S.E.C.JudDec        Securities and Exchange Commission Judicial Decisions
    S.W.2d              Southwestern Reporter, Second Series
    S. Cal. L. Rev.     Southern California Law Review
    So.                 Southern Reporter
    So.2d               Southern Reporter Second Series
    Stan.L.Rev.         Stanford Law Review

------------------------------------------------------------------------
To continue viewing the INDEX, press the NEXT PAGE key or the PREV PAGE key.
To review the LEXSEE Browse HELP Menu, transmit LI.
To choose from the master list of LEXSEE tutorial topics, transmit MA.
To return to the point where you requested HELP, press the TRANSMIT key.
  Press <ESC> for Local Help                                      CD
```

FIGURE 8-N
LEXIS PRINTOUT

PROBLEM 8.8 Based on the information shown in Figure 8-N, decide which of the following answers uses the correct format:

(a) lexsee 99 S.C. 970
(b) lexsee 99 S.Ct. 970
(c) lexsee 99 s ct 970

DISCUSSION OF PROBLEM 8.8 If you would use S.C. for the abbreviation, the computer would treat that abbreviation as a reference to *South Carolina Reports*. As indicated in Figure 8-N, the correct abbreviation is S.Ct. LEXIS will also accept this abbreviation with a space between the S. and Ct. (S. Ct.), with or without periods (S Ct), or in lower case letters (s ct). Thus, answers (b) and (c) will retrieve this case using LEXSEE.

Assume that you now want to retrieve the opinion reported at 579 S.W.2d 670. This case could be retrieved by typing and transmitting the following (or an acceptable variant):

lexsee 579 S.W.2d 670

The computer would respond by showing you the beginning page of this case. Figure 8-O shows a printout of that screen.

```
            State of Missouri, Plaintiff-Respondent, vs. Charles Bernard
                           Jones, Defendant-Appellant.

                                    No. 39630

                      Missouri Court of Appeals Eastern District

                                 579 S.W.2d 670


                                   02/14/79

     PRIOR HISTORY: From the Circuit Court of the City of St. Louis

        Criminal Appeal

        Judge Murry L. Randall

        Affirmed

     COUNSEL: Erica Leisenring, St. Louis, Missouri, Attorney for Appellant; Richard
     Thurman, Jefferson City, Missouri, Attorney for Respondent.
     Press <ESC> for Local Help
                                                                          CD
```

FIGURE 8-O
LEXIS PRINTOUT

The remaining pages of the *Jones* case are shown in the following figures.[5]

```
                           579 S.W.2d 670                        LEXSEE

JUDGES: Before Reinhard, P.J., Clemens, Gunn, JJ.

OPINIONBY: Reinhard, P.J.

OPINION: Defendant appeals from a conviction by a jury of Burglary First Degree
and Robbery First Degree. Under the Second Offender Act the Court sentenced him
to 20 years on each charge, the sentences to run concurrently.

    Because of the nature of defendant's complaints it is unnecessary for us to
recite the facts. As to both of defendant's allegations of error, the Supreme
Court of Missouri has previously ruled adversely to defendant's position.

    Defendant's first point involves the proof of a prior conviction under the
Second Offender Act. He alleges that the court improperly admitted State's
Exhibit 14, which was Volume 62 of the Permanent Record Book of the Circuit
Court. Defendant specifically claims that "The state failed to show entries were
made on or about the time the event occurred," and therefore did not qualify
under the Business Records Act.

    In State v. Washington, 335 S.W.2d 23 (Mo. 1960) the deputy circuit clerk
produced and read from the original circuit court records, as was done here.
Defendant objected that the state had not complied with the Business Records
  Press <ESC> for Local Help                                        CD
```

FIGURE 8-P

LEXIS PRINTOUT

```
                           579 S.W.2d 670                        LEXSEE

Act. The court rejected defendant's argument, saying that these court records
were required to be kept before the adoption of the Business Records Act and
were admissible in evidence even though they failed to meet the requirements of
that law. In this case Exhibit 14 was admissible without compliance with the
Business Records Act. This point is without merit.

    Defendant also alleges that "[The] trial court erred in permitting the State
to ask its own witnesses whether they were certain of their identification of
appellant as the culprit," contending that such questions invade the province of
the jury. The complaint involved the testimony of witnesses Malone and
Levenberry. Similar questions were asked and the same point raised in State v.
Taylor, 496 S.W.2d 822 (Mo. 1973). The Supreme Court said at 824, "The propriety
of the question was for the trial court . . ." and, as in Taylor, we find no
abuse of discretion.

    Affirmed.

    All concur




  Press <ESC> for Local Help                                        CD
```

FIGURE 8-Q

LEXIS PRINTOUT

---

[5] To see the next computer page of this case, you would press the NEXT PAGE key. To go back one page, you would press the PREV PAGE key. To return to the first page, you would press the FIRST PAGE key.

LEXSTAT (LXT) is used in the same basic way as LEXSEE. Similar help screens are available to assist you in using the proper format for your request.

5. PRINTING LEXIS SCREENS AND DOCUMENTS

Several printing, storing, and downloading[6] options are generally available. The PRINT key prints the text on individual screens. To print successive pages of text, you would press the PRINT key as each page is displayed. Many personal computers also allow you to print the screen that you are viewing by pressing the PRINT SCREEN (PrtSc) key. Some require you to simultaneously press the SHIFT and PRINT SCREEN (PrtSc) keys.

Depending on the equipment and service available to you, you would press the PRINT DOC key to print an entire document that has been displayed. A screen will tell you how many printed pages the document contains. To confirm the printing order, you would press the Y key (for yes) and then the TRANSMIT key. Similarly, you may be able to use the MAIL IT key. This service prints all the text of all the documents that you have found. Printing will be done on a local printer you designate or at the Mead Data Central computer center in Ohio.[7]

6. SIGNING OFF LEXIS

When you have completed your research, you would press the SIGN OFF key. You will be shown a summary of your last search request and will be given an opportunity to store the results of your LEXIS search for use later in the same day. The computer will then indicate the time used or charged.

Section 8B. The Basics of Formulating and Executing Search Requests

This section discusses the following topics: (1) search terms on LEXIS; (2) phrase searching, root expansion, and universal characters; (3) "segments" of documents; (4) LEXIS connectors and search levels; and (5) examining search results.

---

[6]Downloading is copying information from LEXIS to a floppy or hard disk.

[7]A similar service is available for WESTLAW through OFF-LINE PRINT.

1. SEARCH TERMS ON LEXIS

On LEXIS, you can search a file in a library by entering a search request, which consists of one or more search terms. For example, assume that you entered the following search request: **plexiglass.** This query would retrieve all documents in the file in which the word plexiglass appears.

The following chart summarizes how LEXIS searches singular terms, numbers, compound terms, abbreviations, and equivalent terms (states, numbers, calendar abbreviations, legal terms, acronyms, and other common abbreviations).

SEARCH TERMS ON LEXIS		
Type of Term	**Example**	**What LEXIS Retrieves**
Singular or plural terms	house or houses	Both the singular and plural (house and houses) EXCEPT when the word ends in -us or -is or when the plural is irregular (in which case only the form transmitted is retrieved)
Possessives	court	Possessive forms (court's) but not court's does not retrieve court
Numbers and sections	16.11	16.11 and s 16.11, but it does not retrieve s16.11
Compound words	post-man	post man and post-man, but not postman
Abbreviations	f.t.c	F.T.C. and FTC (if the abbreviation is on LEXIS' list of equivalents) but not f t c
Equivalent terms on LEXIS (see LEXIS publications)	Alabama 10, Jan cert	The equivalent (Alabama = Ala, 10 = ten, jan = January, cert = certiorari) (if it is one of LEXIS' equivalencies)

2. PHRASE SEARCHING, ROOT EXPANSION, AND UNIVERSAL CHARACTERS ON LEXIS

To search for phrases on LEXIS, you type the phrase. For example, to search for the phrase attractive nuisance, you would simply transmit the words **attractive nuisance** as your request. On LEXIS, you can use **!** as a root expander. **Negligen!** would retrieve negligent, negligence, and negligently. The ***** is the universal character, which would retrieve any character in the position the asterisk is typed. **Bec*me** would retrieve become and became.

3. DOCUMENT SEGMENTS

Documents on LEXIS are divided into segments. LEXIS allows you to restrict a search based on the segments in a document. To see a list of the segments that can be searched in a particular file, you can use the online GUIDE files. When you have already selected a particular file, you can use the SEGMTS key to display the list. The following figures show the segments for various types of files. Figure 8-R shows the segments available for a case law search.

```
    The following names may be used as a segment name in your search request:

    NAME            NUMBER          COURT           CITE
    DATE            NOTICE          HISTORY         DISPOSITION
    HEADNOTES       SYLLABUS        COUNSEL         JUDGES
    OPINIONBY       OPINION         CONCURBY        CONCUR
    DISSENTBY       DISSENT         OPINIONS        WRITTENBY

    The following name may be used with the arithmetic operators:

    DATE


    Please type your search request then press the TRANSMIT key.
    What you transmit will be Search Level 1.

    For further explanation, press the H key (for HELP) and then the TRANSMIT key.
      Press <ESC> for Local Help                                            CD
```

FIGURE 8-R
LEXIS PRINTOUT

Figure 8-S shows the segments available for searches in files containing law journal articles.

```
The following names may be used as a segment name in your search request:

PUBLICATION          DATE              CITE              LENGTH
TITLE                NAME              AUTHOR            HIGHLIGHT
TEXT                 GRAPHIC           PAGES

The following names may be used with the arithmetic operators:

DATE                 LENGTH


Please type your search request then press the TRANSMIT key.
What you transmit will be Search Level 1.

For further explanation, press the H key (for HELP) and then the TRANSMIT key.
 Press <ESC> for Local Help                                              CD
```

FIGURE 8-S
LEXIS PRINTOUT

Figure 8-T shows the segments available for files containing *A.L.R. Annotations*.

```
The following names may be used as a segment name in your search request:

PUBLICATION          CITE              CONTENTS          TABLE-OF-CASES
TITLE                TCSL-REFS         JUR-TABLE         INDEX
BYLINE               REFERENCES        TEXT

Please type your search request then press the TRANSMIT key.
What you transmit will be Search Level 1.

For further explanation, press the H key (for HELP) and then the TRANSMIT key.
 Press <ESC> for Local Help                                              CD
```

FIGURE 8-T
LEXIS PRINTOUT

4. LEXIS CONNECTORS AND SEARCH LEVELS

On LEXIS, you can specify the relationship of your search terms by using connectors in your search request. The following chart shows the principal connectors that can be used on LEXIS:

PRINCIPAL LEXIS CONNECTORS

Connector	Function
OR	retrieves documents containing either of the search terms (e.g., entering **house or home** retrieves all documents containing the word house or the word home).
W/n	retrieves documents in which both of the search terms are within a specified number of words of each other in the SAME SEGMENT (e.g., entering **personal w/3 jurisdiction** retrieves all documents in which these terms are within three words of each other in the same segment).
AND	retrieves documents containing both search terms (e.g., entering **dog & bite** retrieves all documents containing the word dog and the word bite).
W/SEG	retrieves documents containing both of the search terms in the SAME SEGMENT (e.g., entering **dog w/seg bite** retrieves all documents containing the word dog and the word bite in the same segment).
PRE/n	retrieves documents in which the term on the left precedes the term on the right by no more than the specified number of words in the document (e.g., **50 pre/5 16.11 or §16.11** could be used to retrieve citations to 50 C.F.R. § 16.11).

Other LEXIS connectors are NOT W/n, NOT W/SEG, and AND NOT (which are used to exclude specified search terms). LEXIS processes these connectors in the following order: or, w/n, pre/n, not w/n,

w/seg, not w/seg, and, and not. If the w/n connectors have different numbers, the smallest number is processed first. If the w/n connectors have the same numbers, they are processed left to right.[8]

The order in which the connectors are processed affects search results. The *Learning Lexis* handbook provides the following example:[9] **move* or motion w/3 dismiss! or rule 12.** LEXIS would process this request by looking for

> move* w/3 dismiss! OR
> move* w/3 rule 12 OR
> motion w/3 dismiss! OR
> motion w/3 rule 12.

To change the order of processing, you can use parentheses: **(move* or motion w/3 dismiss!) or rule 12.** LEXIS would process this request by looking for

> move* w/3 dismiss! OR
> motion w/3 dismiss! OR
> rule 12.

PROBLEM 8.9 Based on the preceding discussion, formulate search requests for the following situations. Unless otherwise stated, assume that you want the plurals of any search words.

(a) Formulate a request that would retrieve documents containing the word *automobile*, *auto*, *vehicle*, *bus*, *truck*, or *car* within the same segment as the word *cliff*.

Your Request: _____

_____

(b) Formulate a request that would retrieve documents containing the phrase *attractive nuisance* within 15 words of the word *culvert* in the same segment.

Your Request: _____

_____

---

[8]Mead Data Central, Inc., <u>Learning Lexis: A Handbook for Modern Legal Research</u> 17 (1991).

[9]<u>See id.</u> at 18.

(c) Formulate a request that would retrieve documents containing all forms of the word *child* when one of those forms appears within 15 words of the word *fireworks* in the same segment.

Your Request: _____

DISCUSSION OF PROBLEM 8.9   These are the proper queries:

(a) automobile or auto or vehicle or bus or truck or car w/seg cliff

(b) attractive nuisance w/15 culvert

(c) child! w/15 fireworks or fire works

LEXIS allows you to transmit a search request in "levels"—so that each level searches for one basic idea. Thus, to search by levels, you would transmit your broadest idea first (Search Level 1). You could then review the first few documents retrieved.

You then could press the letter **M** key and the TRANSMIT key to modify your search. You could then enter the next more specific part of your search request (Search Level 2), beginning the new level with a connector. You could continue to narrow the focus of your research by adding more levels. To change the search itself, you could transmit, for example, **2m** (the number of the level you want to modify, followed by "m" for modify). Then you could move the cursor to insert or delete words. When you transmit this modified request, it becomes your new Level 1. To view a different level of your search results, you may type the number of a prior level and then press the DIFF LEVEL key.

PROBLEM 8.10   Assume that the computer has displayed: "Please type your search request and then press the TRANSMIT key. What you type will be Search Level 1."

(a) Formulate a search request that would retrieve documents in which the words *warrant* and *informer* appear.

Your Request: _____

(b) Assume that you have entered this search request, the results have been displayed, and you have transmitted "m" to modify your search request (Level 2). What would you transmit to require that the word *narcotics* also appear in the documents retrieved.

Your Request: _____

DISCUSSION OF PROBLEM 8.10   (a) The request would be as follows: warrant and informer.   (b) After transmitting "m" to modify the request, you would begin Level 2 with the connector (in this instance, "and")   and narcotics.

5. EXAMINING SEARCH RESULTS

Assume that you have transmitted a search request in the ALLREV file of the LAWREV library. Assume that LEXIS has reported as follows: "Your search request has found 12 ITEMS through Level 2. To DISPLAY these ITEMS press the KWIC, FULL, CITE or SEGMTS key."   This message indicates your basic options for examining search results.

The FULL key displays the document in full.   In contrast, the KWIC key displays portions of the document containing one or more of your search words—a "window" of text around your search words.[10] The SEGMTS key displays the segments available and allows you to view a specific part or parts of the document.   The CITE key displays the citations or references for the documents found by your search.   Assume that you have chosen the KWIC mode of display for your search.   The first screen displayed is shown in Figure 8-U.

```
                    LEVEL 2 - 1 OF 12 ITEMS

              Copyright (c) 1987 The Columbia Law Review.
                         Columbia Law Review

                            JANUARY, 1987

                          87 Colum. L. Rev. 55

LENGTH: 27965 words

ARTICLE: NEIGHBORS IN AMERICAN LAND LAW.

Stewart E. Sterk *

   * Professor of Law, Benjamin Cardozo School of Law, Yeshiva University;
Visiting Professor of Law, Columbia University.  I would like to thank William
Bratton, David Carlson, Richard Friedman, Carol Rose, Paul Shupack, and Charles
Yablon for their helpful criticisms of earlier drafts.  Heidi Bettini, Vivien
Naim, and Candace Reid provided invaluable research assistance.

   TEXT:
   ... [*56]  two principal forms.  First, rights are sometimes allocated
across boundary lines, giving one landowner the right to use his neighbor's        CD
Press <ESC> for Local Help
```

FIGURE 8-U
LEXIS PRINTOUT

---

[10] See id. at 12 (ordinarily 25 words on either side of a search word).

Pressing the NEXT PAGE key in the KWIC format moves you to the next page where your search terms are found—in this instance, page 63 and 64. That page is shown in Figure 8-V.

```
                     87 Colum. L. Rev. 55, *63

    n34 See  Prah  v. Maretti, 108 Wis. 2d 223, 321 N.W.2d 182 (1982)
(obstruction of a neighbor's solar collector could produce actionable nuisance).
Compare, e.g., Sundowner, Inc. v. King, 95 ...

    ... [*63]  academic commentary commonly justify many of the doctrinal rules
just outlined (albeit not all of them -- spite-fence rules are an exception) as
rules designed to effectuate party intent. n36 Thus, the intent-enforcing
justification for  easements  by implication runs like this: Suppose, prior to
severance, one of two nowdivided parcels had been used for the benefit of the
other, and, at severance, the use was evident to all parties and evidently
"necessary" for the enjoyment of the dominant land.  The " ...

    ... [*63]  wished at severance to terminate the existing use, one would have
expected him to express his   [*64]   wishes at that time.  The servient owner's
silence, then, must be taken either as an attempt to "put one over" on the
dominant owner, or as an assent to the existing use.  The
 easement -by-implication rule presumes, perhaps based on experience, perhaps on
moral preference, that the servient owner's silence constitutes assent.

    n36 With respect to  easements  by implication, see, e.g., Granite Properties
Ltd. v. Manns, 487 N.E.2d 1230, 1238 (App. Ct. 1986) ("implied  easements  arise
as an inference of the parties' intent as derived from the circumstances of a
 Press <ESC> for Local Help                                              CD
```

FIGURE 8-V

LEXIS PRINTOUT

To see a list of citations, you would press the CITE key. Figure 8-W shows the first page of the citation list.

```
                     LEVEL 2 - 12 ITEMS

1. Copyright (c) 1987 The Columbia Law Review. Columbia Law Review, JANUARY,
1987, 87 Colum. L. Rev. 55, 27965 words, ARTICLE: NEIGHBORS IN AMERICAN LAND
LAW., Stewart E. Sterk *

2. Copyright (c) Cornell Law Review 1983. Cornell Law Review, August, 1983, 68
Cornell L. Rev. 941, 24668 words, RECENT DEVELOPMENT: CASTING A SHADOW ON A
SOLAR COLLECTOR -- A CAUSE OF ACTION RECOGNIZED; AN ALTERNATIVE RESOLUTION
FRAMEWORK SUGGESTED: Prah v. Maretti., Steven M. Cherin

3. Copyright (c) Environmental Law 1988. Northwestern School of Law of Lewis &
Clark College, WINTER, 1988, 19 Envtl. L. 167, 17193 words, ARTICLE: FUTURE
DIRECTIONS IN SOLAR ACCESS PROTECTION., BY ADRIAN J. BRADBROOK *

4. Copyright (c) Environmental Law 1983. Northwestern School of Law of Lewis &
Clark College, FALL, 1983, 14 Envtl. L. 223, 6520 words, RECENT DEVELOPMENT:
Prah v. Maretti, 108 Wis. 2d 223, 321 N.W.2d 182 (1982)., LAURIE BENNETT

5. Copyright (c) Georgetown Law Journal 1991, Georgetown Law Journal, June, 1991
79 Geo. L.J. 1447, 25318 words, ARTICLE ARTICLE: Status and Incentive Aspects of
Judicial Decisions., JEFFREY EVANS STAKE *


 Press <ESC> for Local Help                                              CD
```

FIGURE 8-W

LEXIS PRINTOUT

To see an item on your citation list, you would transmit its number. For example, if you typed **4** and then pressed the TRANS-MIT key, the following screen would be displayed.

```
                        LEVEL 2 - 4 OF 12 ITEMS

                    Copyright (c) Environmental Law 1983.
            Northwestern School of Law of Lewis & Clark College

                            FALL, 1983

                          14 Envtl. L. 223

    LENGTH: 6520 words

    RECENT DEVELOPMENT:  Prah  v. Maretti, 108 Wis. 2d 223, 321 N.W.2d 182 (1982).

    LAURIE BENNETT

     HIGHLIGHT:
       In  Prah  v. Maretti, the Wisconsin Supreme Court extended the protection of
    the nuisance doctrine to owners of solar collectors whose sunlight is blocked by
    neighboring structures.  Meanwhile, the Wisconsin Legislature enacted solar
    access legislation, providing ...

     TEXT:
       ... [*223]    insurmountable barrier to owners of solar heated or solar
    powered homes whose source of energy disappears when a neighbor constructs a
     Press <ESC> for Local Help                                              CD
```

FIGURE 8-X
LEXIS PRINTOUT

The Bluebook has special rules for citing cases in electronic databases such as LEXIS. In general, enough information must be given to identify the database and find the case. Screen or page numbers, if assigned, should be preceded by an asterisk. *See Bluebook* Rule 10.8.1(b).

Section 8C. LEXIS Date Restrictions and Segment Searches

The following chart shows sample formats for selected segment and date searches in case law files on LEXIS.[11]

---

[11]Figure 8-R shows all the segments available for searching in case law databases on LEXIS.

SAMPLE FORMATS FOR LEXIS CASE LAW SEGMENT SEARCHES

Segment	Sample Format
Name	**name (smith and jones)**
Cite	**cite (294 +5 415)** in the relevant database (better still, you would transmit **lexsee 294 f.2d 415**)
Opinionby	**opinionby (brennan)** (wrote or joined in the majority opinion)
Dissentby	**dissentby (holmes)** (wrote or joined in the dissenting opinion)
Concurby	**concurby (story)** (wrote or joined in the concurring opinion)
Counsel	**counsel (teply)** (lawyer or law firm)
Date	**date is 4-1-92 and search terms** **date aft 1990 and search terms** **date bef 1/1/92 and search terms** **date aft 1965 and date bef jan 1992 and search terms**

Segment searches are also possible in statutory files on LEXIS. For example, a search of the United States Code file on LEXIS could be restricted to the heading, cite, section, text, or history segments. Additional segments may be searched in files containing state statutes.

PROBLEM 8.11 Formulate a search request that would retrieve documents in which *comparative* occurs in the same segment within 15 words of the word *negligence*; limit the search to documents before 1992.

Your Request: _____

DISCUSSION OF PROBLEM 8.11   The proper request would be as follows: comparative w/15 negligence and date before 1992 .

Section 8D. Online Use of Auto-Cite and Shepard's Citations

1. AUTO-CITE

"Auto-Cite" is a case history and citation service offered by Lawyers Cooperative Publishing Co. through LEXIS. To use Auto-Cite, you simply type   **ac**   and the citation. For example, to view the Auto-Cite information for *United States v. Montana*, reported at 99 S. Ct. 970, you would type   **ac 99 s ct 970**   and then you would press the TRANSMIT key. If you were viewing this case on LEXIS, you could simply transmit   **ac**   to activate the Auto-Cite service.[12] To leave the Auto-Cite service, you would press the EXIT SERV key. To resume a LEXIS search, you could transmit   **resume lexis.**[13]

The Auto-Cite screens for the *Montana* case are shown in the following two figures.

```
Auto-Cite (R) Citation Service, (c) 1992 Lawyers Cooperative Publishing

99 S CT 970:                                          Screen 1 of 2

CITATION YOU ENTERED:

Montana v United States*1, 440 US 147, 59 L Ed 2d 210, 99 S Ct 970 (1979)

PRIOR HISTORY:

United States v Montana, 437 F Supp 354, 24 CCF P 81804 (DC Mont 1977),

    revd (BY CITATION YOU ENTERED)

CITATION YOU ENTERED MAKES NEGATIVE REFERENCE TO:

Commissioner v Sunnen, 333 US 591, 92 L Ed 898, 68 S Ct 715, 77 USPQ 29, 48-1
USTC P 9230, 36 AFTR 611 (1948)

-----------------------------------------------------------------------
Alternate presentation formats are available.
For further explanation, press the H key (for HELP) and then the TRANSMIT key.
To return to LEXIS, press the EXIT SERV key.
 Press <ESC> for Local Help                                          CD
```

FIGURE 8-Y
LEXIS PRINTOUT

---

[12]On custom terminals, you can also press the AUTO-CITE key.

[13]On custom terminals, you can also press the RESUME LEXIS key.

```
99 S CT 970:                                           Screen 2 of 2


ANNOTATIONS CITING THE CASE(S) INDICATED ABOVE WITH ASTERISK(S):

*1  Supreme Court's views as to res judicata or collateral estoppel effect of
    state court judgments on federal courts, 72 L Ed 2d 911, secs. 2, 5, 8, 10,
    11.

To search for collateral annotations referring to the annotation(s) above, type
the citation and press the TRANSMIT key.




-------------------------------------------------------------------------------
To return to LEXIS, press the EXIT SERV key.
  Press <ESC> for Local Help                                              CD
```

FIGURE 8-Z
LEXIS PRINTOUT

The Auto-Cite service can also be used to find related annotations when an *A.L.R.* citation is known. The following screens illustrate the type of information retrieved.

```
8 ALR FED 675:                                         Screen 2 of 3

    ALR2d 717, supp sec. 1 (superseded by What constitutes improper or
    collusive making or joining of parties, under 28 USCS sec. 1359, for
    purpose of invoking Federal District Court jurisdiction, 67 ALR Fed 463).

    Comment Note.--Right to join master and servant as defendants in tort
    action based on respondeat superior, 59 ALR2d 1066, supp.

    Construction and effect of statute as to doing business under an assumed or
    fictitious name or designation not showing the names of the persons
    interested, 42 ALR2d 516, supp sec. 2.

    Federal court's jurisdiction as affected by common citizenship of third
    party defendant with either or both of original parties, 37 ALR2d 1411,
    supp sec. 1.

    Federal diversity of citizenship jurisdiction where one of the states in
    which multistate corporation party litigant is alleged to be incorporated
    is also state of citizenship of opponent, 27 ALR2d 745, supp sec. 1.

-------------------------------------------------------------------------------
To return to LEXIS, press the EXIT SERV key.
  Press <ESC> for Local Help                                              CD
```

FIGURE 8-AA
LEXIS PRINTOUT

```
8 ALR FED 675:                                     Screen 2 of 3

  ALR2d 717, supp sec. 1 (superseded by What constitutes improper or
  collusive making or joining of parties, under 28 USCS sec. 1359, for
  purpose of invoking Federal District Court jurisdiction, 67 ALR Fed 463).

  Comment Note.--Right to join master and servant as defendants in tort
  action based on respondeat superior, 59 ALR2d 1066, supp.

  Construction and effect of statute as to doing business under an assumed or
  fictitious name or designation not showing the names of the persons
  interested, 42 ALR2d 516, supp sec. 2.

  Federal court's jurisdiction as affected by common citizenship of third
  party defendant with either or both of original parties, 37 ALR2d 1411,
  supp sec. 1.

  Federal diversity of citizenship jurisdiction where one of the states in
  which multistate corporation party litigant is alleged to be incorporated
  is also state of citizenship of opponent, 27 ALR2d 745, supp sec. 1.

----------------------------------------------------------------------------
To return to LEXIS, press the EXIT SERV key.
 Press <ESC> for Local Help
                                                                      CD
```

FIGURE 8-BB
LEXIS PRINTOUT

```
8 ALR FED 675:                                     Screen 3 of 3

  Effect upon jurisdiction of state court of 28 USC sec. 1446 relating to
  removal of cause to federal court, 25 ALR2d 1045, supp (superseded by
  Effect, on jurisdiction of state court, of 28 USCS sec. 1446(e), relating
  to removal of civil case to federal court, 38 ALR Fed 824).

  Rule 15(c), Federal Rules of Civil Procedure, or state law as governing
  relation back of amended pleading, 100 ALR Fed 880, sec. 1.

  Fetus as person on whose behalf action may be brought under 42 USCS sec.
  1983, 64 ALR Fed 886.

  Status, in federal court, of judgment or order rendered by state court
  before removal of case, 2 ALR Fed 760, supp sec. 1.

To search for collateral annotations referring to the annotation(s) above, type
the citation and press the TRANSMIT key.



----------------------------------------------------------------------------
To return to LEXIS, press the EXIT SERV key.
 Press <ESC> for Local Help
                                                                      CD
```

FIGURE 8-CC
LEXIS PRINTOUT

2. SHEPARD'S CITATIONS

Recall that *Shepard's Citations* provides you with parallel citations, judicial history of a case, verification of the status of a case, later cases that have cited a case, and research leads to other sources, such as *A.L.R. Annotations*. *Shepard's Citations* is available online on LEXIS.

To "shepardize" a case, you would type **sh** followed by the citation. If you are currently viewing a case on LEXIS, you can simply type **sh** and then press the TRANSMIT key.[14] Assume that you want to "shepardize" *United States v. Montana*, reported at 99 S. Ct. 970. The printout of the first page of the *Shepard's* display is shown in Figure 8-DD.

```
          (c) 1992 McGraw-Hill, Inc. - DOCUMENT 1 (OF 1)

CITATIONS TO: 99 S.Ct. 970
SERIES: SHEPARD'S UNITED STATES CITATIONS
DIVISION: SUPREME COURT REPORTER
COVERAGE: Shepard's 1943-1986 Supplements Through 01/92 Supplement.

NUMBER  ANALYSIS              CITING REFERENCE              PARA   NOTES
------  ----------------     -------------------------    ----   ----------
   1    parallel citation    (440 U.S. 147)
   2    same case            437 F.Supp. 354
   3                         547 F.Supp. 993                2
   4    connected case       161 Mont. 140
   5    connected case       166 Mont. 260
                             Mont
   6    connected case       505 P.2d 102
   7    connected case       531 P.2d 1327
   8                          99 S.Ct. 2209
   9                          99 S.Ct. 2213                 2
  10    explained            101 S.Ct. 415                  2
-----------------------------------------------------------------------------
To see the text of a citing case, press the citing reference NUMBER and then
the TRANSMIT key.
For further explanation, press the H key (for HELP) and then the TRANSMIT key.
 Press <ESC> for Local Help                                              CD
```

FIGURE 8-DD
LEXIS PRINTOUT

Note that the printout in Figure 8-DD indicates the citator ("Shepard's United States Citations"), the Division ("Supreme Court Reporter"), and the coverage of the display ("1943-1986 Supplements through 01/92 Supplement"). To see the number of screens that the *Shepard's* display occupies, you would type **p** and then press the TRANSMIT key. To see the text of a citing case, you would type the number of the citing reference and then press the TRANSMIT key.

Shepard's allows you to limit the display to cases treating the cited case in a certain way. You may also limit the display to those cases that refer to a specific paragraph of a syllabus or a headnote of the cited

---

[14] On custom terminals, you can also press the SHEP key.

case. By pressing the SEGMTS key, you will be instructed how to limit the display. The screen that would be displayed is shown in Figure 8-EE.

```
You may restrict the display to those citations that Shepard's has designated
(by editorial analysis) as dealing with the history or treatment of the cited
case, or to those which refer to a specific paragraph of a syllabus or a
headnote of the cited case.

                      EDITORIAL ANALYSIS ABBREVIATIONS
   HISTORY OF CASE             TREATMENT OF CASE         TREATMENT OF CASE

   (  parallel citation     c  criticised           o  overruled
   a  affirmed              d  distinguished         p  parallel
   cc connected case        e  explained             q  questioned
   Dm dismissed             Ex examiner's decision   Va valid
   m  modified              f  followed              Vo void
   r  reversed              ha harmonized            Vp void in part
   s  same case             j  dissenting opinion
   Su superseded            L  limited
   v  vacated               Lp limited in part

Please transmit, separated by commas, the specific history or treatment
ABBREVIATIONS (or the word ANY for citations with any editorial analysis
abbreviation -- history or treatment) and the NUMBERS of the paragraphs for the
citations you want to display.
Press <ESC> for Local Help                                            CD
```

FIGURE 8-EE
LEXIS PRINTOUT

PROBLEM 8.12   (a) Based on the information presented in Figure 8-EE, how would you limit the display to those cases that have followed the *Montana* case?   (b) How would you limit the display to those cases that have cited headnote (para.) 2 of the *Montana* case?

DISCUSSION OF PROBLEM 8.12   (a) By typing the letter **f** and then pressing the TRANSMIT key, you would limit the display to those cases that have followed the *Montana* case. The first page of that display is shown in Figure 8-FF.   (b) Similarly, by typing **2** and then pressing the TRANSMIT key, you would limit the display to those cases that have cited headnote 2 of the *Montana* case. Note that you could combine these two requests by typing **f,2** and then pressing the TRANSMIT key.

```
                    (c) 1992 McGraw-Hill, Inc. - DOCUMENT 1 (OF 1)

        CITATIONS TO: 99 S.Ct. 970
        SERIES: SHEPARD'S UNITED STATES CITATIONS
        DIVISION: SUPREME COURT REPORTER
        COVERAGE: Shepard's 1943-1986 Supplements Through 01/92 Supplement.

        RESTRICTIONS: F

        NUMBER  ANALYSIS              CITING REFERENCE              PARA   NOTES
        ------  ----------------     -----------------------------  ----   ----------
          1     parallel citation    (440 U.S. 147)
         18     followed              104 S.Ct. 577                   1
                                     Cir. D.C.
         28     followed              677 F.2d 120                    2
         66     followed              747 F.Supp. 766
                                     Cir. 1
         75     followed              817 F.2d 172                    2
         79     followed              836 F.2d 37                     2
        -----------------------------------------------------------------------------
        To see the text of a citing case, press the citing reference NUMBER and then
        the TRANSMIT key.
        For further explanation, press the H key (for HELP) and then the TRANSMIT key.

        Press <ESC> for Local Help                                                 CD
```

FIGURE 8-FF
LEXIS PRINTOUT

3. USING LEXIS AS A CITATOR

You can also use LEXIS as a citator. To do so, you would conduct a LEXIS search designed to retrieve documents that cite a given authority. For example, the following request would retrieve documents in which *Montana v. United States* had been cited: **Montana and 99 pre/5 970** .

Section 8E. Searching for Legislative and Administrative Sources

Research involving legislative and administrative sources on LEXIS follows the same basic pattern as described in preceding sections. You can use the LEXSTAT service to retrieve legislative and administrative sources, such as code provisions or administrative regulations. You can also use segment searches for legislative and administrative materials.

Figure 8-GG shows the segments available for searching the *United States Code*.

```
The following names may be used as a segment name in your search request:

HEADING          CITE            STATUS          SECTION
TEXT             HISTORY         NOTES           SYNOPSIS
DATE

The following name may be used with the arithmetic operators:

DATE


Please type your search request then press the TRANSMIT key.
What you transmit will be Search Level 1.

For further explanation, press the H key (for HELP) and then the TRANSMIT key.
  Press <ESC> for Local Help                                            CD
```

FIGURE 8-GG
LEXIS PRINTOUT

Figure 8-HH shows the segments available for searching state codes.

```
The following names may be used as a segment name in your search request:

CITE             HEADING         STATUS          SECTION
TEXT             HISTORY         NOTES           SYNOPSIS
REFERENCES       RULE            DATE            DIGEST
MESSAGE          EFF-DATE        STATUS-1

The following name may be used with the arithmetic operators:

DATE


Please type your search request then press the TRANSMIT key.
What you transmit will be Search Level 1.

For further explanation, press the H key (for HELP) and then the TRANSMIT key.
  Press <ESC> for Local Help                                            CD
```

FIGURE 8-HH
LEXIS PRINTOUT

Figure 8-II shows the segments available for searching the *Code of Federal Regulations*.

```
The following names may be used as a segment name in your search request:

TITLE               PART               CITE               SOURCE
CHAPTER             SECTION            TEXT               AUTHORITY


Please type your search request then press the TRANSMIT key.
What you transmit will be Search Level 1.

For further explanation, press the H key (for HELP) and then the TRANSMIT key.
  Press <ESC> for Local Help
                                                                    CD
```

FIGURE 8-II
LEXIS PRINTOUT

Section 8F. Other Sources Accessible Through LEXIS

Reexamine the LIBRARIES screens shown in Figures 8-A and 8-B. Note particularly the wide range of materials listed and discussion of those materials in section A(3) of this chapter. The extent to which you will have access to these and other materials depends on your account agreement.

*

Appendix A
CIVIL, CRIMINAL, AND APPELLATE
PROCEDURE IN THE UNITED STATES

Every jurisdiction has procedural and evidentiary rules that govern the form and mode of litigation in its courts. In some jurisdictions, these rules are statutory. In other jurisdictions, courts promulgate them—based either on a court's inherent authority to issue them or a statute authorizing the court to promulgate them. Separate sets of rules govern civil and criminal litigation.[1]

1. CIVIL PROCEDURE

Depending on the jurisdiction, one of two basic sets of procedural rules in civil suits are used in the United States today. One set is the Federal Rules of Civil Procedure. These rules were promulgated by the United States Supreme Court in 1938 pursuant to the Rules Enabling Act of 1934.[2] These rules are used in all federal district courts. Over half of the states have also adopted rules modeled on the Federal Rules of Civil Procedure for use in state trial courts. The Federal Rules of Civil Procedure allow each federal district court to adopt local practice rules, provided that these rules are not inconsistent with the Federal Rules.[3] The other basic set of procedure rules is "code pleading," which originated with the New York Field Code in 1848.[4] Code pleading (and variants thereof) are used in states that have not adopted the Federal Rules.

Both the Field Code and the Federal Rules of Civil Procedure are reforms of the old English system of litigation. English courts were divided into law courts and equity (chancery) courts. Litigation in the

---

[1]The summary in this Appendix is necessarily general in nature. For a more detailed overview of civil and appellate procedure, see Larry L. Teply & Ralph U. Whitten, Civil Procedure 1-60 (1991).

[2]See Rules Enabling Act of 1934, ch. 651, 48 Stat. 1064 (codified as amended at 28 U.S.C. § 2072).

[3]See Fed. R. Civ. P. 83 (district court rules).

[4]See Act of Apr. 12, 1848, ch. 379, 1848 N.Y. Laws 497.

common-law courts was based on "forms of actions" and "writs." Each form of action covered a specific type of substantive right and factual situation. The action was commenced by purchasing a particular writ—for example, a writ of trespass, trespass on the case, general assumpsit, and so forth. Each form of action had its own rules for stating the claim, defenses, and mode of trial.

The common-law courts principally provided monetary relief and were relatively inflexible in dealing with new situations that arose during the development of the common-law system. To deal with the inadequacies of that system, litigants turned to the king's chancellor. The chancellor's power to grant relief ultimately resulted in the development of a separate set of "equity" courts (with an entirely different set of procedural rules).

The principal distinguishing feature of the equity courts was their ability to grant equitable relief (personal orders such as injunctions, subpoenas, specific performance, and reformations), which was unavailable in the common-law courts. These personal orders were effectively backed by the court's contempt powers. One of the principal reforms of both the codes and the Federal Rules was to merge law and equity into one form of action known as a civil action.

Modern civil procedure can be roughly divided into the following stages:

(a) *pleading* (the plaintiff states a claim in the complaint and the defendant states defenses in the answer);

(b) *provisional remedies* (the plaintiff can secure temporary relief to preserve the status quo or assets to satisfy a final judgment);

(c) *discovery* (the parties use various methods of discovery to find out information prior to trial);

(d) *pretrial conferences* (the court can organize discovery and trial through conferences with counsel);

(e) *summary judgment* (one of the parties can obtain a judgment without a trial when (1) no genuine issue of fact exists and (2) that party is otherwise entitled to judgment as a matter of law);

(f) *trial* (the parties present their respective evidence to the trier of fact);

(g) *judgment* (the judge enters an order (judgment) based on the outcome of the trial);

(h) *post-trial motions* (the parties may move for a new trial or judgment notwithstanding the verdict in an attempt to nullify the result of the trial); and

(i) *appeal* (the parties may present errors to an appellate court in an attempt to modify the result of the trial).

(a) Pleading

At the outset of the lawsuit, the parties set out their contentions in pleadings. In early English practice, the pleadings were central to the procedural system. They were relied upon to identify the legal or factual issues in the case. Modern pleading has reduced the importance of the pleading process by relying on discovery, summary judgment, and pretrial conferences (discussed below) to perform many of the functions formerly performed by the pleadings.

The first pleading is called a complaint (or sometimes a petition). In early English practice, it was called a declaration in common-law pleading and a petition or bill in equity. Under the Federal Rules of Civil Procedure, the plaintiff is required, *inter alia*, to set forth a short and plain statement of the claim showing that the pleader is entitled to relief. The purpose of pleading under the Federal Rules of Civil Procedure is to inform the opposing party of the nature of the claim ("notice pleading"). Under the codes, the plaintiff is required to allege a statement of facts setting forth a "cause of action" in ordinary and concise language.

In general, the defendant must respond to the complaint with an answer. In this pleading, the defendant must admit or deny the plaintiff's allegations and set forth any "affirmative defenses" (new facts that constitute a defense). In code pleading states (but not under the Federal Rules), the plaintiff must then reply in a pleading to any affirmative defense. In the reply, the plaintiff may admit or deny the new facts alleged by the defendant. The plaintiff may allege new facts to avoid the affirmative defense raised by the defendant.

A defendant's answer may also contain a counterclaim, cross-claim, or a third-party claim. A counterclaim is simply a claim for relief that a defending party has against an opposing party. When a counterclaim has been asserted, the opposing party must reply. In this context, a cross-claim is one litigated by co-defendants against each other—for example, one defendant may assert a cross-claim for indemnity against a co-defendant (if the defendant is found liable to the plaintiff, the co-defendant is legally obligated to pay that liability). A third-party claim (also known as impleader) allows a defending party to assert a claim against a nonparty who is or may be contingently liable for all or part of a claim already made against the defending party.

A defendant may also attack the "substantive sufficiency" of the complaint. Such an attack asserts that even if the plaintiff proves everything that has been alleged in the complaint, the applicable law does not give the plaintiff any right to relief. Under the Federal Rules of Civil Procedure, this kind of attack may be made in a pre-answer motion to

dismiss the action (Rule 12(b)(6)), the defendant's answer, or other ways. Under the codes, an attack on the substantive sufficiency of the complaint is generally made by filing a "demurrer" (it is also used to attack other defects that appear on the face of the complaint).

Under both the Federal Rules and the codes, this kind of objection must be raised before or during trial or it is waived. The defendant may also attack other defects. Such defects include improper form, improper joinder of parties, the lack of subject-matter jurisdiction (the constitution or the legislature has not authorized the court to hear this type of case), and the lack of personal jurisdiction (the defendant lacks sufficient contacts with the forum and thus the defendant cannot be constitutionally compelled to defend the claim in this court).

(b) Provisional Remedies

Provisional remedies provide temporary relief to the claimant (1) to preserve the status quo until the final remedies, if any, are ordered or (2) to protect the claimant from irreparable loss or injury while the action is pending.

One principal type of provisional remedy is the "preliminary injunction" derived from relief traditionally granted by equity courts. Sometimes, a preliminary injunction is preceded by a "temporary restraining order" (which, unlike a preliminary injunction, may be granted without a hearing or notice upon a proper showing). The other principal type of provisional remedy involves seizure of property. Under some circumstances, courts allow claimants to attach or garnish property to ensure that assets will be available to satisfy any eventual judgment in the case.

(c) Discovery

Discovery encompasses several pretrial procedures that allow the parties to obtain information concerning the case. The principal devices for conducting discovery in modern litigation are as follows:

(1) oral deposition (oral testimony taken similar to trial but a judge is not present;

(2) written depositions (it is like an oral deposition but the questions are submitted in writing to a presiding officer who asks the witness the questions;

(3) interrogatories (sets of relevant questions sent by one party to another party);

(4) production of documents and other tangible things (a party may inspect copy, or photograph relevant documents or other tangible items in the possession of another party;

(5) physical and mental examinations (compulsory medical examinations of parties whose physical or mental condition is in controversy); and

(6) requests for admission (formal requests between parties to secure the admission of facts or of the genuineness of documents in order to facilitate their introduction into evidence at trial.

The discovery stage of a civil lawsuit is meant to work almost entirely without the intervention of the court. Judges will intervene, however, to prevent abuses of the discovery process and to issue protective orders.

(d) Pretrial Conferences

Modern procedure provides for various pretrial conferences. These conferences are designed to allow the court and the litigants to confer about the case. Topics at such conferences include discovery,[5] formulation and simplification of the issues, the possibility of settlement, the disposition of pending motions, and other matters that may aid in the disposition of the action.[6] The pretrial conference ordinarily results in a "pretrial order" that controls the subsequent course of the litigation.

(e) Summary Judgment

Summary judgment allows a party to avoid trial on all or part of any claim, despite denials in the pleadings, if (1) the moving party is entitled to a judgment as a matter of law and (2) no genuine issue of material fact exists.[7]

(f) Trial

At trial, factual issues are resolved by the trier of fact—either a judge alone or a jury. The right to a jury trial is granted by the constitution and sometimes by statute. In general, history plays a dominant role in determining when a litigant is entitled to demand a jury trial. For example, the seventh amendment, which governs jury trials in federal courts, provides that "[i]n suits at common law, where the value

---

[5] See, e.g., Fed. R. Civ. P. 26(f) (discovery conferences).

[6] See, e.g., Fed. R. Civ. P. 16 (scheduling and management of pretrial conferences).

[7] See Fed. R. Civ. P. 56 (summary judgment).

in controversy shall exceed twenty dollars, the right of trial by jury shall be preserved, and no fact tried by a jury, shall be otherwise re-examined in any Court of the United States, than according to the rules of the common law."[8]   The modern right to a jury trial, however, has been greatly complicated by the merger of law and equity.

Proof at trial in the federal courts is governed by the Federal Rules of Evidence, which were enacted by Congress in 1975.[9]   The Supreme Court has been authorized to amend the Federal Rules of Evidence (within certain limits).[10]   Like the Federal Rules of Civil Procedure, the Federal Rules of Evidence have been adopted, in whole or in part, by a large number of states.

Although variations occur, a trial ordinarily proceeds in the following manner:

(1) the jury is selected (if there is going to be one);

(2) the plaintiff and then the defendant make opening statements;

(3) the plaintiff presents evidence on elements of the claim (case-in-chief) on which the plaintiff has the initial burden of production;

(4) when the plaintiff rests (at the close of the plaintiff's case-in-chief), the defendant may move for a "directed verdict" (when there is a jury) or for an "involuntary dismissal" (when the case is being tried to the judge alone); if the judge grants either of these motions (because there has been a failure of sufficient proof), the case is terminated;

(5) assuming that the defendant's motion for directed verdict or involuntary dismissal is denied, the defendant then presents evidence;

(6) when the defendant rests, the plaintiff may move for a directed verdict (when there is a jury);

(7) each side can present further evidence (rebuttal, rejoinder, surrebuttal, and so on); when both sides finally rest, either side may then move for a directed verdict (when there is a jury);

(8) assuming that the judge has not granted a motion for a directed verdict, the parties make closing arguments; either before or after closing arguments (depending on the jurisdiction), the judge orally instructs the jury (if there is one); and

(9) the judge then decides the case or submits the case to the jury (if there is a jury). In most jurisdictions, the jury must be unanimous in its decision.

---

[8]U.S. Const. amend. VII.

[9]Act of Jan. 2, 1975, Pub. L. No. 93-595, 88 Stat. 1926.

[10]See 28 U.S.C.A. §§ 2072-2074 (West Supp. 1991).

(g) Judgment

The result of trial is a judgment—the formal expression of the outcome of the litigation. A successful plaintiff can then enforce the monetary judgment by obtaining a writ of execution. A judgment might also restore property to the plaintiff, enjoin the defendant, order specific performance of a contract, or simply declare the rights of the parties (in an action for a declaratory judgment).

(h) Post-Trial Motions

After a jury has delivered its verdict and judgment has been entered, the losing party may move for a "new trial" or "judgment notwithstanding the verdict." In federal practice, these motions are known as ten-day motions because they must be made no later than ten days after the entry of judgment.[11]

2. PROCEDURE IN CRIMINAL PROSECUTIONS

Pursuant to a Rules Enabling Act, the Supreme Court promulgated the Federal Rules of Criminal Procedure in 1946.[12] These rules, along with the provisions of Title 18 of the *United States Code*, establish the basic procedural steps for a federal criminal prosecution. Prosecutions in state courts generally follow similar steps but also vary in significant ways.

(a) Arrest, Booking, and the Decision
to Charge the Suspect

After a police officer has acquired sufficient information to justify an arrest, the officer arrests the suspect. The suspect will then be taken to a police station or jail and booked (logged-in, photographed, and fingerprinted). Ordinarily, the arrestee will be informed of the charge and allowed to make at least one phone call. Based upon the pre-arrest and post-arrest investigation, the police may decide to release the arrestee. Depending on the jurisdiction, the decision to charge the suspect may be reviewed by a prosecutor.

---

[11]See Fed. R. Civ. P. 50(b), 59(a)(1).

[12]The current provisions governing promulgation of Federal Rules of Criminal Procedure are set out in 18 U.S.C.A. §§ 2072-2074 (West Supp. 1991).

(b) Filing the Complaint

If the initial screening results in a decision to prosecute, charges will be filed in a magistrate's court. Typically, the initial charging document is called a "complaint," which, as defined by the Federal Rules of Criminal Procedure, is a written statement of the essential facts constituting the offense charged. In most jurisdictions, at some point between the filing of the complaint and the defendant's first appearance, the magistrate will conduct an ex parte review of the charges to ensure that there is probable cause to believe the defendant committed the crime.

(c) First Appearance of the Defendant

Rule 5(a) of the Federal Rules of Criminal Procedure provides that a person arrested under a warrant or without a warrant shall be taken without unnecessary delay before the nearest available federal magistrate. If the person was arrested without a warrant, this same rule requires that a complaint be issued "forthwith" showing probable cause for arrest.

For offenses other than those triable before the magistrate (certain misdemeanors), Rule 5(c) requires the magistrate to inform the defendant of the charges, the right to retain counsel (and to have counsel appointed if the defendant is indigent), and the right to remain silent.[13] Rule 5(c) requires the magistrate to inform the defendant that statements made by the defendant may be used against the defendant and that the defendant has a right to a preliminary hearing. The magistrate will also determine that the person in court is the person named in the complaint.

(d) Preliminary Hearing or Grand Jury Review

The next step in processing a felony case in many jurisdictions is a preliminary hearing, which is required in approximately thirty states. In the remaining jurisdictions, the prosecutor can bypass the preliminary hearing by presenting the case to a grand jury for indictment. In the federal system and in several states, a grand jury indictment must be

---

[13] See Fed. R. Crim. P. 5(c); U.S. Const. amend. VI ("In all criminal prosecutions, the accused shall enjoy the right to be informed of the nature and cause of the accusation . . . and to have the Assistance of Counsel for his [or her] defence"); U.S. Const. amend. V ("No person shall . . . be compelled in any criminal case to be a witness against himself [or herself], nor be deprived of life, liberty, or property, without due process of law").

obtained in all felony cases. For this reason, the preliminary hearing is frequently bypassed.[14]

The preliminary hearing, like grand jury review, provides a screening of the decision to charge by a neutral body—the magistrate or the grand jury. The grand jury traditionally is composed of twenty-three persons, but today it often consists of a smaller number. In many jurisdictions, a simple majority is all that is needed for an indictment.

(e) Filing of an Indictment or Information

If the grand jury indicts the defendant, the indictment will be filed with the general trial court—for example, with the federal district court. This indictment replaces the complaint as the charging document.

When grand jury review is not required or the defendant has waived it, the prosecutor will file an "information" with the general trial court. Like the indictment, the information replaces the complaint as the charging document. In jurisdictions that do not require grand jury review, the information must ordinarily be supported by a preliminary hearing "bindover" (unless the preliminary hearing has been waived).

(f) Arraignment and Plea

After the indictment or information has been filed, the defendant will be arraigned. During the "arraignment," the defendant appears in open court. The defendant will be informed of the charges and asked to enter a plea of (1) guilty, (2) not guilty, or (3) nolo contendere (in some circumstances). This plea is often the subject of "plea bargaining."[15]

(g) Pretrial Motions

The defendant can make a variety of pretrial motions, including motions to discover the prosecution's evidence and motions to suppress

---

[14]Cf. U.S. Const. amend. V ("No person shall be held to answer for a capital, or otherwise infamous crime, unless on a presentment or indictment of a Grand Jury, except in cases arising in the land or naval forces, or in the Militia, when in actual service in time of War or public danger . . . .").

[15]See Fed. R. Crim. P. 10, 11 (arraignment and pleas).

illegally obtained evidence.[16]   Notice may also be required of the defendant's intent to use an alibi, the insanity defense, or other defenses.[17]

(h) Trial

The defendant has a right to a jury trial for all felony offenses and for misdemeanors punishable by more than six months imprisonment. Most states also provide a jury trial for lesser misdemeanors. A criminal trial itself resembles the civil trial described in the preceding subsection. The jury must ordinarily be unanimous—whether it be for conviction or acquittal.[18]

(i) Sentencing

When the defendant pleads guilty or is found guilty at trial, the judge will enter a judgment of conviction. The case will then be set for sentencing.

3. APPELLATE PROCEDURE IN THE UNITED STATES

The Federal Rules of Appellate Procedure govern appeals from the federal district courts to the federal courts of appeals in both civil and criminal cases. Procedure in state court appeals usually follows a similar pattern. The United States Supreme Court also has a similar set of rules regulating its appellate procedures.[19]

To appeal a final judgment of a federal district court, a litigant is required to file a notice of an appeal with the clerk of the district court.[20]   In civil cases, a private party has thirty days after the date of

---

[16] See Fed. R. Crim. P. 12, 16 (pleadings and motions; discovery and inspection of evidence and information); U.S. Const. amend. IV ("The right of the people to be secure in their persons, houses, papers, and effects, against unreasonable searches and seizures, shall not be violated, and no Warrants shall issue, but upon probable cause, supported by Oath or affirmation, and particularly describing the place to be searched, and the persons or things to be seized").

[17] See Fed. R. Crim. P. 12.1, 12.2.

[18] See U.S. Const. amend. VI ("In all criminal prosecutions, the accused shall enjoy the right to a speedy and public trial, by an impartial jury of the State and district wherein the crime shall have been committed . . . ; to be confronted with the Witnesses against him; to have compulsory process for obtaining witnesses in his [or her] favor, and to have the Assistance of Counsel for his [or her] defence").

[19] For more information on the methods of obtaining review and the orders and other actions resulting from appellate review, see Larry L. Teply, Legal Writing, Analysis, and Oral Argument 116-20 (1990).

[20] See Fed. R. App. P. 3(a).

the entry of the judgment to file this notice.   In criminal cases, the defendant has ten days after the entry of the judgment to appeal.[21] Upon receipt of the notice of appeal (and the relevant docket entries) transmitted by the clerk of the federal district court, the appeal is docketed in the court of appeals.   After a notice of appeal has been filed, a record on appeal will be prepared and transmitted.[22]

The next step in the appellate process is the preparation and filing of the appellant's and appellee's briefs.   The appellant is also allowed to file a brief replying to the brief of the appellee.[23]   A prehearing conference may be held to consider simplification of the issues and other matters that may aid in the disposition of the action.[24]

The appeal is then ordinarily scheduled for oral argument, but the court may decide to dispense with oral argument.[25]   Finally, judgment is rendered—with or without a written opinion.

---

[21]See Fed. R. App. P. 4 (Appeals of Right—When Taken).

[22]See Fed. R. App. P. 10-12 (record on appeal, transmission of the record, docketing the appeal, and filing the record).

[23]See Fed. R. App. P. 28-32 (regulating the preparation and filing of the briefs).

[24]See Fed. R. App. P. 33 (prehearing conference).

[25]See Fed. R. App. P. 34 (oral argument).

Appendix B
CITING CASE NAMES IN BLUEBOOK FORM

The fifteenth edition of *The Bluebook*[1] establishes detailed citation rules concerning:

    (1) what parts of the case name in the reporter should be included or deleted;

    (2) what words should or should not be abbreviated;

    (3) what spacing should be used; and

    (4) what typeface should be used.

This Appendix is designed to give you practice in applying these rules to case names in twenty practice problems.[2]

1. THE BASIC RULES (BLUEBOOK RULE 10.2.1)

To begin, study carefully *Bluebook* Rule 10.2.1 in a copy of *The Bluebook*. This rule sets out various required inclusions, deletions, and abbreviations for case names cited in *Bluebook* form.

---

[1] Columbia Law Review et al., The Bluebook: A Uniform System of Citation (15th ed. 1991) [hereinafter The Bluebook or Bluebook Rule]. If you are learning Bluebook citation form, purchase of this book is essential. In addition to providing detailed instructions for citing sources, The Bluebook provides useful reference information about United States and foreign court systems as well as the publication of legal sources in those systems. It also prov.'des useful reference information about the availability of periodicals (see T.13: "Periodicals") and services (see "T.16: Services"). The Practitioners' Notes on the blue pages at the beginning of The Bluebook bridge the gap between the law review footnote citation form presented in the main part of The Bluebook and the citation form used by practitioners in court documents and memoranda. You should also note that the "Quick Reference" sections on the inside covers. These sections provide several examples of representative citations in Bluebook form.

[2] In contrast to the rules discussed in this Appendix, The Maroon Book provides the following basic rules for citing case names:

    (1) "Use the case name as reported in the Table of Cases Reported in the first reporter cited, dropping or abbreviating words at the end of each party's name if necessary to keep the case name reasonably short." University of Chicago Law Review & University of Chicago Legal Forum, The University of Chicago Manual of Legal Citation Rule 4.2(a)(i) (1989).

    (2) You may use the running head "if it is sufficiently descriptive of the case name that the reader will be able to locate the case through the Table of Cases Reported, a case name citator, or a law digest in the event of miscitation." Id.

    (3) You should use periods in abbreviations of case names unless you are abbreviating the name of an organization or other entity that is usually referred to by the abbreviation (e.g., NLRB, FTC, etc.) Id. Rule 2.1.

    (4) If a party named in the running head is commonly known by a more familiar name than the one used in the running head, you should use the more familiar one. Id. Rule 4.2(a)(i).

    (5) You may omit the period after the "v" in came names. Id. Rule 2.1.

2. CASE NAMES IN "TEXTUAL SENTENCES"
VERSUS "CITATIONS"

Next read Rule 10.2 (which immediately precedes Rule 10.2.1). Although Rule 10.2.1 is titled "Case Names in Textual Sentences," Rule 10.2 applies the requirements stated in Rule 10.2.1 to all case names, whether they appear as a grammatical part of "textual sentences" or in "citations."[3]

The Bluebook requires "further modifications" when case names are included in "citations."[4] *The Bluebook* uses the term "citations" to mean citations that "stand alone" rather than as a grammatical part of a textual sentence (such as the object of a preposition or a direct object).[5] The following examples illustrate the difference between a *Bluebook* textual sentence and a citation:

In <u>Sorenson v. Gardner</u>, 334 P.2d 471 (Or. 1959), the Oregon Supreme Court held that loss of bargain damages for fraud can be awarded only in suits against contracting parties. (Textual sentence—case used as an object of a preposition).

Loss of bargain damages for fraud can be awarded only in suits against contracting parties; this measure does not apply when the fraud is not that of one who has received consideration as a party to the transaction. <u>Sorenson v. Gardner</u>, 334 P.2d 471, 476 (Or. 1959). <u>Contra</u> <u>Tillis v. Smith Sons Lumber Co.</u>, 65 So. 1015, 1019-20 (Ala. 1915). (Citation—case "stands alone," not a grammatical part of a textual sentence).

Although the decisions on the point are split, <u>Sorenson v. Gardner</u>, 334 P.2d 471, 476-77 (Or. 1959); <u>contra</u> <u>Tillis v. Smith Sons Lumber Co.</u>, 65 So. 1015, 1019-20 (Ala. 1915), the better reasoned view is that loss of bargain damages for fraud can be awarded only in suits against contracting parties. (Citation—case is inserted as a citation clause that can "stand alone" and does not operate as a necessary grammatical part of the textual sentence).

---

[3] <u>Bluebook</u> Rule 10.2 ("Case Names").

[4] <u>See id.</u> Rule 10.2.2 ("Case Names in Citations").

[5] <u>See</u> C. Edward Good, <u>Citing & Typing the Law</u> § 6.3(g) (1987) (coining the term "stand alone").

3. "FURTHER MODIFICATIONS" OF CASE NAMES
IN CITATIONS

Next read Rule 10.2.2. The "further modifications" required by Rule 10.2.2 ("Case Names in Citations") are of two kinds: (a) additional abbreviations—along with a special admonition NOT to abbreviate "United States"[6]—and (b) special treatment for the names of railroads.[7]

(a) Additional Abbreviations

The additional abbreviations are contained in two *Bluebook* tables: Table T.6 ("Case Names") and Table T.10 ("Geographic Terms"). Examine these Tables in *The Bluebook*.

(b) Railroads

With respect to names of railroads in citations, Rule 10.2.2(b) provides that "Co." should always be omitted in citing a railroad or railway company "unless the full party name in the official report is 'Railroad Co.' or 'Railway Co.' "[8]

Union Pacific Railroad v. Railway Co.
(NOT Union Pacific Railroad Co. v. Railway)

Furthermore, according to Rule 10.2.2(b), all *geographic* words in the names of railroads, except for the first word, should be abbreviated "to the initial letter *or* to recognized abbreviations *unless* they complete the name of a state, city, or other entity begun by the first word."[9]

Boston & M.R.R. v. New Castle Elec. St. Ry.
(NOT Boston & Maine Railroad v. New C. Elec. St. Ry. or Boston & M. R. R. v. N.C.E.S. Ry.)

Akron, C. & Y.R.R.
(NOT Akron, Canton & Youngstown Railroad or A.C. & Y. R.R.)

---

[6] See id. Rule 10.2.2(a) ("Abbreviation").

[7] See id. Rule 10.2.2(b) ("Railroads").

[8] See id. Rule 10.2.1(h) ("Business firm designations") and Rule 10.2.2(b) ("Railroads").

[9] Id. Rule 10.2.2(b) ("Railroads") (emphasis added).

4. SPACING OF INITIALS

When the initials of individuals (personal names) are included in a case name—for example, when they form part of a cited business entity, the initials should be typed without spaces between them.[10]

O.J. Jones, Inc.   (NOT O. J. Jones, Inc.)

5. PERIODS IN ABBREVIATIONS

Some entities are commonly referred to in spoken language by their widely recognized initials (e.g., AFL (American Federation of Labor), CAB (Civil Aeronautics Board), CIO (Congress of Industrial Organizations), EPA (Environmental Protection Agency), EEOC (Equal Employment Opportunity Commission), FCC (Federal Communications Commission), FDIC (Federal Deposit Insurance Corporation), FMC (Federal Maritime Commission), FPC (Federal Power Commission), FTC (Federal Trade Commission), HEW (Department of Health, Education and Welfare), HUD (Department of Housing and Urban Development), ICC (Interstate Commerce Commission), NAACP (National Association for the Advancement of Colored People), NLRB (National Labor Relations Board), NRC (Nuclear Regulatory Commission), SEC (Securities and Exchange Commission), and TVA (Tennessee Valley Authority), etc.). These abbreviations may be used without periods in case names (as well as in text and as institutional authors).[11]

6. TYPEFACE CONVENTIONS FOR CASE NAMES IN COURT DOCUMENTS AND LEGAL MEMORANDA

To distinguish citations from the text material in briefs, memoranda, and other court documents, case names (including procedural phrases and the "v.") should be underscored or placed in italics.[12]

State v. Jones
(NOT State v. Jones or State v. Jones)

The court in the Jones case applied the general rule.

---

[10] Id. Rule 6.1(a) ("Spacing").

[11] Id. Rule 6.1(b) ("Periods").

[12] Id. Practitioners' Notes P.1(a) ("Case names (rule 10.2)").

7. PROBLEMS

The following excerpts show the names of cases reported in *United States Reports*, the official reporter for United States Supreme Court decisions.

Using the correct *Bluebook* form, write (in the space provided) the name of the case (1) when that name is going to appear as a grammatical part of a textual sentence in a brief, legal memorandum, or other court document (Text), and (2) when that name is going to appear in a (stand-alone) citation (Cite). Note that sometimes the case name will be cited in the same way in both instances. In that situation, you may simply write "the same" for your answer to (2).

Be sure to refer to relevant parts of *The Bluebook* while you are working on your answers. The answers are set out at the end of this appendix.

PROBLEM B.1

ADAMO WRECKING CO. *v.* UNITED STATES

---

(1) Text:

(2) Cite:

PROBLEM B.2

CITIZENS & SOUTHERN NATIONAL BANK *v.* BOUGAS

---

(1) Text:

(2) Cite:

PROBLEM B.3

EX PARTE CHARLEY WEBB, PETITIONER.

---

(1) Text:

(2) Cite:

PROBLEM B.4

COMMISSIONER OF INTERNAL REVENUE *v.* KOWALSKI ET UX.

---

(1) Text:

(2) Cite:

PROBLEM B.5

CHRISTIANSBURG GARMENT CO. *v.* EQUAL EMPLOYMENT OPPORTUNITY COMMISSION

---

(1) Text:

(2) Cite:

PROBLEM B.6

NEW MOTOR VEHICLE BOARD OF CALIFORNIA *v.* ORRIN W. FOX CO. ᴇᴛ ᴀʟ.

(1) Text:

(2) Cite:

PROBLEM B.7

CALIFANO, SECRETARY OF HEALTH, EDUCATION, AND WELFARE *v.* JOBST

(1) Text:

(2) Cite:

PROBLEM B.8

IDAHO DEPARTMENT OF EMPLOYMENT *v.* SMITH

(1) Text:

(2) Cite:

PROBLEM B.9

THE BREAKWATER.

(1) Text:

(2) Cite:

PROBLEM B.10

LUCAS, COMMISSIONER OF INTERNAL REVE-NUE, *v.* EARL.

(1) Text:

(2) Cite:

PROBLEM B.11

ALEXANDER SPRUNT & SON, INC., ET AL. *v.* UNITED STATES.

(1) Text:

(2) Cite:

PROBLEM B.12

> NEW   ORLEANS   CITY   AND   LAKE   RAILROAD
> COMPANY *v.* LOUISIANA *ex rel.* CITY   OF   NEW
> ORLEANS.

(1) Text:

(2) Cite:

PROBLEM B.13

> STEVENS'S ADMINISTRATOR *v.* NICHOLS.

(1) Text:

(2) Cite:

PROBLEM B.14

> GRUBB *v.* PUBLIC   UTILITIES   COMMISSION   OF
> OHIO ET AL.

(1) Text:

(2) Cite:

PROBLEM B.15

LEM MOON SING *v.* UNITED STATES.

---

(1) Text:

(2) Cite:

PROBLEM B.16

HAZELWOOD SCHOOL DISTRICT ET AL. *v.* KUHLMEIER ET AL.

---

(1) Text:

(2) Cite:

PROBLEM B.17

INTERNATIONAL UNION OF OPERATING ENGINEERS, LOCAL 150, AFL–CIO *v.* FLAIR BUILDERS, INC.

---

(1) Text:

(2) Cite:

PROBLEM B.18

AETNA LIFE INSURANCE CO. *v.* LAVOIE ET AL.

---

(1) Text:

(2) Cite:

PROBLEM B.19

SUMMIT VALLEY INDUSTRIES, INC. *v.* LOCAL 112,
UNITED BROTHERHOOD OF CARPENTERS &
JOINERS OF AMERICA

---

(1) Text:

(2) Cite:

PROBLEM B.20

O'LONE, ADMINISTRATOR, LEESBURG PRISON
COMPLEX, ET AL. *v.* ESTATE OF SHABAZZ ET AL.

---

(1) Text:

(2) Cite:

8. DISCUSSION OF THE PROBLEMS

The correct citations of the case names for the preceding problems are listed below. Brief comments about each citation also are given.

DISCUSSION OF PROBLEM B.1

(1) Text: Adamo Wrecking Co. v. United States
(2) Cite: the same

Case names in briefs and legal memoranda are always italicized or underscored.[13] Note that "United States" is not abbreviated.[14]

DISCUSSION OF PROBLEM B.2

(1) Text: Citizens & Southern National Bank v. Bougas
(2) Cite: Citizens & S. Nat'l Bank v. Bougas

Remember to always check for words that must be abbreviated when citing cases in *Bluebook* citation form. Both "Southern" and "National" are on the *Bluebook* list (see Table T.6).[15]

DISCUSSION OF PROBLEM B.3

(1) Text: Ex parte Webb
(2) Cite: the same

Except in citing certain business entities, given names ("Charley") are omitted from a case citation.[16] Likewise, phrases ("Petitioner") that describe a party that has already been named ("Webb") are omitted.[17]

---

[13] Id. Practitioners' Notes P.1(a) ("Case names (rule 10.2)"). Note that in law review footnotes, only procedural phrases are italicized or underscored. See id. Rule 2.2(a) ("Citations").

[14] Id. Rule 10.2.2(a) ("Abbreviation") ("Do not abbreviate 'United States' ").

[15] See id. Rule 10.2.2(a) ("Abbreviation").

[16] Id. Rule 10.2.1(g) ("Given names and initials").

[17] Id. Rule 10.2.1(e) ("Descriptive terms").

DISCUSSION OF PROBLEM B.4

(1) Text: <u>Commissioner v. Kowalski</u>
(2) Cite: the same

When the "Commissioner of Internal Revenue" is cited, a special rule applies: only the word "Commissioner" is used. Note also that "Commissioner" is not abbreviated if it is the first word in the party's name.[18] Words indicating multiple parties (such as "et al."—"and others," "et ux."—"and wife," and "et vir."—"and husband") should be omitted.[19]

DISCUSSION OF PROBLEM B.5

(1) Text: <u>Christiansburg Garment Co. v. EEOC</u>
(2) Cite: the same

Watch for the names of parties (often governmental entities) that should be abbreviated to widely recognized abbreviations. The "Equal Employment Opportunity Commission" is one of those names. Note that the abbreviation ("EEOC") contains no periods.[20]

DISCUSSION OF PROBLEM B.6

(1) Text: <u>New Motor Vehicle Board v. Orrin W. Fox Co.</u>
(2) Cite: <u>New Motor Vehicle Bd. v. Orrin W. Fox Co.</u>

Given names and initials ("Orrin W.") are retained when they are used in the name of a business entity.[21] "Board" is on the list of *Bluebook*-required abbreviations for case names used in citations.[22] Also, watch for prepositional phrases of location ("of California"). Prepositional phrases of location (other than national and larger geographic designations) are omitted unless it would leave only one word in the name of a party

---

[18] <u>Id.</u> Rule 10.2.1(j) ("Commissioner of Internal Revenue").

[19] <u>See id.</u> Rule 10.2.1(a) ("Actions and parties cited").

[20] <u>See id.</u> Rule 6.1(a) ("Spacing") and (b) ("Periods").

[21] <u>Id.</u> Rule 10.2.1(h) ("Business firm designations").

[22] <u>See id.</u> Rule 10.2.2(a) ("Abbreviation") and Table T.6 ("Case Names").

or entity.[23]   Words indicating multiple parties ("et al.") should be omitted.[24]

DISCUSSION OF PROBLEM B.7

(1) Text: <u>Califano v. Jobst</u>
(2) Cite: the same

Alternative names of a party ("Secretary of Health, Education, and Welfare") should be omitted.[25]

DISCUSSION OF PROBLEM B.8

(1) Text: <u>Idaho Department of Employment v. Smith</u>
(2) Cite: <u>Idaho Dep't of Employment v. Smith</u>

"Idaho" is retained in the citation because it is not introduced by a preposition.[26] "Department" is on the list of *Bluebook*-required abbreviations for case names in citations.[27]

DISCUSSION OF PROBLEM B.9

(1) Text: <u>The Breakwater</u>
(2) Cite: the same

Because "the" is the first word of the object of an in rem action ("The Breakwater" is apparently a ship), "the" should be retained in the citation. Note, however, that in a textual discussion, "the" would not be italicized or underscored ("The Court in the <u>Breakwater</u> case decided that . . . .").[28]

---

[23]<u>Id.</u> Rule 10.2.1(f) ("Geographical terms").

[24]See <u>id.</u> Rule 10.2.1(a) ("Actions and parties cited").

[25]<u>Id.</u> Rule 10.2.1(e) ("Descriptive terms").

[26]See <u>id.</u> Rule 10.2.1(f) ("Geographical terms").

[27]See <u>id.</u> Rule 10.2.2(a) ("Abbreviation") and Table T.6 ("Case Names").

[28]<u>Id.</u> Rule 10.2.1(d) ("The").

DISCUSSION OF PROBLEM B.10

(1) Text: <u>Lucas v. Earl</u>
(2) Cite: the same

      In this instance, "Commissioner of Internal Revenue" is omitted from the citation because it describes a party already named ("Lucas").[29]

DISCUSSION OF PROBLEM B.11

(1) Text: <u>Alexander Sprunt & Son v. United States</u>
(2) Cite: the same

      "Inc." (and similar terms) should be omitted from a citation when another term ("Son") in the party's name clearly indicates that a party is a business firm. Application of this rule involves judgment. In this instance, there is little doubt that the above entity is a business firm because of the presence of "Son" in the cited party's name, and thus "Inc." has been omitted from the citation.[30] Remember that given names ("Alexander") are retained in citations of business firms.[31] Words indicating multiple parties ("et al.") should be omitted.[32]

DISCUSSION OF PROBLEM B.12

(1) Text: <u>New Orleans City & Lake Railroad Co. v. Louisiana ex rel. City of New Orleans</u>
(2) Cite: <u>New Orleans C. & L.R.R. v. Louisiana ex rel. City of New Orleans</u>

      The proper citation of this case involves the application of several rules. In textual sentences, "Company" should be abbreviated to "Co."[33] For citations, remember that special rules apply to citing railroads. All geographic words ("City" and "Lake") are abbreviated unless they complete the name of a state, city, or other entity begun by the first word

---

[29] <u>Compare id.</u> Rule 10.2.1(j) ("Commissioner of Internal Revenue") <u>with</u> Rule 10.2.1(a) ("Actions and parties cited") <u>and</u> Rule 10.2.1(e) ("Descriptive terms").

[30] <u>Id.</u> Rule 10.2.1(h) ("Business firm designations").

[31] <u>Id.</u> Rule 10.2.1(g) ("Given names or initials").

[32] <u>See id.</u> Rule 10.2.1(a) ("Actions and parties cited").

[33] <u>Id.</u> Rule 10.2.1(c) ("Abbreviations").

("Orleans" completes "New"). "Railroad" is abbreviated to "R.R." and no space is left between the adjacent capital letters ("L.R.R."). Furthermore, "Co." should be omitted from the citation (unless the full party name is simply "Railroad Co." in the official report.[34]

In this case, the State of Louisiana brought this action on the information and instigation of ("ex rel.") the City of New Orleans against the Railroad. Thus, the "City of New Orleans" (as the first-listed relator) must be included in the citation.[35] Apparently, the State of Louisiana won below because on appeal to the U.S. Supreme Court, the State is listed on the defendant's side of the "v." In early Supreme Court practice (this case was decided in 1895), the parties' names might be reversed on appeal, depending on who sought review in the Supreme Court. In this instance, the Railroad would be called the "plaintiff in error" and the State would be referred to as the "defendant in error."

At the beginning of these problems, it was stated that these case name excerpts were taken from the official reporter of United States Supreme Court decisions. Because this case is now before the United States Supreme Court, "State of" is omitted. Had this case been before a *Louisiana* state court, this case would have been cited <u>State ex rel. City of New Orleans</u>.[36]

"City of" is not omitted because it *begins* the party's (relator's) name. Note that "of New Orleans" should not be omitted from the citation for either of two reasons—even though it is a prepositional phrase of geographical location. First, its omission would leave only one word ("City") in the party's (relator's) name. Second, there is a specific rule which requires that the geographic term immediately following expressions such as "City of" be retained.[37]

DISCUSSION OF PROBLEM B.13

(1) Text: <u>Stevens's Administrator v. Nichols</u>
(2) Cite: <u>Stevens's Adm'r v. Nichols</u>

"Administrator" is on the list of *Bluebook*-required abbreviations for case names in citations.[38]

---

[34] <u>Id.</u> Rule 10.2.2(b) ("Railroads").

[35] <u>Id.</u> Rule 10.2.1(a) ("Actions and parties cited").

[36] <u>Id.</u> Rule 10.2.1(f) ("Geographical terms").

[37] <u>Id.</u>

[38] <u>See id.</u> Rule 10.2.2(a) ("Abbreviation") and Table T.6 ("Case Names").

DISCUSSION OF PROBLEM B.14

(1) Text: Grubb v. Public Utilities Commission
(2) Cite: Grubb v. Public Utils. Comm'n

Remember to delete words indicating multiple parties ("et al.")[39] and to add an "s" to show plurals of *Bluebook*-required abbreviations ("Utils.") unless otherwise indicated in Table T.6.[40]   "PUC" may be a widely enough recognized abbreviation to be used in this citation and would also be correct.

DISCUSSION OF PROBLEM B.15

(1) Text: Lem Moon Sing v. United States
(2) Cite: the same

Foreign names are covered by special rules.[41]   In this instance, "Lem Moon Sing" is entirely a Chinese name and the given name is retained.   If you did not recognize this name as a Chinese one, you would consult the index to the report to see how it was listed there. Obviously, that possibility was foreclosed in this exercise.

DISCUSSION OF PROBLEM B.16

(1) Text: Hazelwood School District v. Kuhlmeier
(2) Cite: Hazelwood Sch. Dist. v. Kuhlmeier

Words indicating multiple parties ("et al.") should be omitted.[42] "School" and "District" should be abbreviated in citations because they are on the list of *Bluebook*-required abbreviations.[43]

---

[39] Id. Rule 10.2.1(a) ("Actions and parties cited").

[40] Id. Rule 10.2.2(a) ("Abbreviation") and Table T.6 ("Case Names") (T.6 states that "[p]lurals are formed by adding the letter "s" inside the period, unless otherwise stated").

[41] See id. Rule 10.2.1(g) ("Given names or initials").

[42] See id. Rule 10.2.1(a) ("Actions and parties cited").

[43] See id. Rule 10.2.2(a) ("Abbreviation") and Table T.6 ("Case Names").

DISCUSSION OF PROBLEM B.17

(1) Text: <u>IUOE, Local 150 v. Flair Builders</u>   OR   <u>International Union
of Operating Engineers, Local 150 v. Flair Builders</u>
(2) Cite: <u>IUOE, Local 150 v. Flair Builders</u>   OR   <u>International Union
of Operating Eng'rs, Local 150 v. Flair Builders</u>

Special rules apply to union names.[44]   (1) Cite only the smallest
unit ("Local 150"—no other unit is given).   (2) Omit all craft designations
except the first ("International Union of Operating Engineers"—no other
craft designation is given).   (3) Omit all preposition phrases of location
(none are given).   (4) A widely recognized abbreviation of the union
name may be used ("IUOE").

"Inc." was omitted from the citation of "Flair Builders."   It is a
matter of judgment whether "Builders" is sufficient to indicate clearly
that this party is a business firm, but this term is likely to do so.
However, if you included "Inc." in the citation, your answer is correct
because opinions may legitimately differ on this point.[45]

Finally, note that in citations, "Engineer[s]" must be abbreviated
to "Eng'rs" and that "International" is not abbreviated because it is the
first word in the party's name even though "International" is on the list
of *Bluebook*-required abbreviations in case names in citations.[46]

DISCUSSION OF PROBLEM B.18

(1) Text: <u>Aetna Life Insurance Co. v. Lavoie</u>
(2) Cite: <u>Aetna Life Ins. Co. v. Lavoie</u>

"Insurance" is on the list of *Bluebook*-required abbreviations for
case names in citations.[47]   Words indicating multiple parties ("et al.")
should be omitted.[48]

---

[44]<u>Id.</u> Rule 10.2.1(i) ("Union and local union names").

[45]See <u>id.</u> Rule 10.2.1(h) ("Business firm designations").

[46]See <u>id.</u> Rule 10.2.2(a) ("Abbreviation") and Table T.6 ("Case Names").

[47]<u>Id.</u>

[48]See <u>id.</u> Rule 10.2.1(a) ("Actions and parties cited").

DISCUSSION OF PROBLEM B.19

(1) Text: Summit Valley Industries v. Local 112, United Brotherhood
of Carpenters
(2) Cite: Summit Valley Indus. v. Local 112, United Bhd. of Carpenters

    Again, it is a matter of judgment whether "Inc." can be omitted
after "Industries," but in this case it seems clear that "Industries" sufficiently conveys that the party is a business firm.[49] Both "Industries" and
"Brotherhood" are on the *Bluebook* list of required abbreviations for case
names in citations.[50] Note that Table T.6 indicates that the abbreviation
"Indus." includes both the singular and the plural.

    In citing the labor union, follow the steps outlined previously. (1)
Cite only the smallest unit ("Local 112"). (2) Omit all craft designations
("Joiners") except the first full designation ("United Brotherhood of
Carpenters"—note that this situation is different from multiple designations
that modify the same word, such as "Construction & General *Laborers*"
or "Doll & Toy *Workers*," in which the multiple designations are retained). (3) Omit all prepositional phrases of location ("of America").[51]

DISCUSSION OF PROBLEM B.20

(1) Text: O'Lone v. Estate of Shabazz
(2) Cite: the same

    Alternative names of a party ("Administrator, Leesburg Prison
Complex") should be omitted.[52] "Estate of" and "Will of" are not
treated as procedural phrases and thus should be retained.[53] Words
indicating multiple parties ("et al.") should be omitted.[54]

*

---

[49]*Id.* Rule 10.2.1(h) ("Business firm designations").

[50]*See id.* Rule 10.2.2(a) ("Abbreviation") and Table T.6 ("Case Names").

[51]*Id.* Rule 10.2.1(i) ("Union and local union names").

[52]*Id.* Rule 10.2.1(e) ("Descriptive terms").

[53]*Id.* Rule 10.2.1(b) ("Procedural phrases").

[54]*See id.* Rule 10.2.1(a) ("Actions and parties cited").

INDEX

References are to Pages

UNITED STATES PRESIDENT
See Executive Orders; Presidential
   Documents; Presidential Proclamations;
   Treaties and Executive Agreements.

UNITED STATES REPORTS
See Court Reports.

UNITED STATES REVISED STATUTES
See Legislation.

UNITED STATES STATUTES AT LARGE
See Legislation.

UNITED STATES SUPREME COURT
See Court Reports; Courts.

U.S. SUPREME COURT BULLETIN
See Court Reports.

**U.S. SUPREME COURT REPORTS,
   LAWYERS' EDITION**
See Court Reports.

UNITED STATES TAX COURT
See Courts.

**UNITED STATES TREATIES AND
   OTHER INTERNATIONAL AGREE-
   MENTS (U.S.T.)**
See Treaties and Executive Agreements.

UNOFFICIAL REPORTS
See Court Reports.

**WEEKLY COMPILATION OF
   PRESIDENTIAL DOCUMENTS**
See Legislative History.

WESTLAW
   See also Insta-Cite; Shepard's Citations.
Accessing, 325, 326
Black's Law Dictionary, online use, 350
Citator function, 359

WESTLAW (CONTINUED)
Databases and services, 6, 50, 51,
   327-332, 361
Exiting a service, 341
EZ ACCESS, 332-335, 347
FIND
   Cases, 338-340
   Federal regulations, 360
   Statutes, 337, 338
   Types of documents retrieved, 335
MAP command, 359, 360
Printing WESTLAW screens, 340, 341
Search queries, 49, 50
   Conducting new searches, 351
   Connectors, 343-345
   Editing queries, 351
   Executing and viewing results, 347-350
   Field restrictions
      Case law and secondary sources,
         351-354
      Legislative and administrative sources,
         360
   Formulating and executing, 49, 50,
      341-350
   Phrase searching, 345-347
   Root expansion, 345-347
   Search terms, 342, 343
Signing off, 341
Signing on, 326, 327
Star paging, 350, 351
Strengths, 6, 49, 50
Weaknesses, 6, 49, 50

WILSONLINE
See Periodical Indexes.

**WORD OR PHRASE METHOD OF
   SEARCH**
See Legal Research Process.

WORDS AND PHRASES
   See also Dictionaries; Glossaries;
      Thesauri.
West's Words and Phrases set, 69

*